T0341769

Networks of Entertainment:
Early Film Distribution 1895–1915

Networks of Entertainment: Early Film Distribution 1895–1915

Edited by
Frank Kessler and Nanna Verhoeff

British Library Cataloguing in Publication Data

Networks of Entertainment: Early Film Distribution 1895–1915

A catalogue entry for this book is available from the British Library

ISBN: 9780 86196 681 3 (Paperback)

Published by
John Libbey Publishing Ltd, 3 Leicester Road, New Barnet, Herts EN5 5EW,
United Kingdom   e-mail: john.libbey@orange.fr; web site: www.johnlibbey.com

Distributed Worldwide by
Indiana University Press, Herman B Wells Library—350, 1320 E. 10th St., Bloomington,
IN 47405, USA. www.iupress.indiana.edu

© 2007 Copyright John Libbey Publishing Ltd. All rights reserved.
Unauthorised duplication contravenes applicable laws.

Printed and bound in the United States of America..

Contents

Acknowledgements

The editors wish to thank the Research Institute of History and Culture (OGC) and the Institute for Media and Re/Presentation at Utrecht University for providing funding and support to this project.

Eva Baaren, Stephen Bottomore, and Sabine Lenk generously helped us with the editing process. We are particularly grateful to Berber Hagedoorn who, with extraordinary efficiency, formatted the manuscript and made sure we could meet the deadline we were running up against.

Distribution – preliminary notes

Frank Kessler

Utrecht University

What is "distribution"? According to Jean Giraud's invaluable, and indispensable, *Lexique français du cinéma des origines à 1930* there are two meanings of the word, which originally are derived from technical theatre terms, the first one referring to a "detailed listing of the *tableaux* or scenes of a film", the second being the equivalent of the English word "cast". But there is also a third definition – which, of course, is the most relevant one with regard to the problems dealt with in the essays collected here:

> "In the language of cinema economy: intermediate stage between production and exhibition, or the theatre circuit. Providing exhibitors with prints. Synonym of: *renting*".[1]

The corresponding activity, "to distribute", is consequently defined as: "dispatching, placing prints of a film for exhibition purposes".[2] And a distributor is the one who "is in charge of placing the films produced by a firm in a given geographic area".[3]

The different definitions that Giraud proposes for distribution as an aspect of the economy of cinema can be used to map a multi-dimensional field of research raising different sets of questions.

First, distribution has a *relay function*, it serves as an "intermediate stage" making sure that an exhibitor receives a steady supply of prints from the various producers. This may actually also be a reason why, up to now, distribution has been a comparatively neglected area, as historians paid much more attention to the two outer ends of the chain: film production, on the one hand, and exhibition – that is: the ways in which films encountered an audience – on the other. So some of the fundamental questions to ask, are the following: What exactly happens between the two outer ends, between production and exhibition? How did this "intermediate stage" emerge? In what ways did that stage have consequences for production practices, but also for what, finally, audiences will see on the screens of movie theatres? How did this intermediate stage become institutionalised? By which means did producers, distributors, and exhibitors communicate with each other?

Second, distribution is about *placing* the films, or rather the prints for exhibition purposes. What factors do come into play here? How did they influence choices that are being made in this area? How were films distributed physically? Which networks did emerge? What economic, political, legal etc. forces had an influence on the circulation of films? Who controlled what, and at which level?

Third, one of the definitions quoted above mentions the specific *geographic areas* in which distribution takes place. So how did distribution networks function locally, regionally, nationally, and internationally? Were there differences between countries, regions and cities? How were these geographic areas established?

Distribution, in other words, should be understood, in more than one respect, as a key element in the emergence of the institution of cinema. In fact, there isn't really any equivalent for its specific way of functioning in other domains of the cultural industry of that period: in those traditional arts, where one of the defining qualities is the uniqueness of a work, either as an object (a painting, a sculpture) or as a performance (theatre, music, ballet), distribution similar to the way films are distributed is almost per definition excluded. As for works of art that are produced and reproduced in multiple copies (books, etchings, but also gramophone disks), the goal of distribution is to reach a maximum number of buyers. So there are no strategies aiming at the creation of partial monopolies or making choices as to where a copy is to be made available first, as rapidly was the case with regard to film.

Jean Giraud, too, underscores the relative novelty of this phenomenon in the field of the arts. In his entry on "renting" (*location*), which he also gives as a synonym for "distribution", he remarks the following:

> "Fact or action of a producer making films available to exhibitors for rent through specialised agents. In the language of the arts and the performing arts this is a relatively new expression".[4]

Giraud's comment, in fact, applies to "distribution" as well. This, of course, is due to the fact that the term is part of the "language of cinema economy", as stated earlier, and not of the vocabulary of aesthetics. Distribution is first and foremost linked to the institutionalisation of cinema as an industry and a business.

One cannot deny, however, that distribution influences production and exhibition, while also depending on them. Distribution, in other words, cannot be isolated from the formal dimension of film. Formats (shorts, feature films, series, serials), the emergence of the star system, narrative modes: all these aspects are of course firmly rooted in film production, but they also concern, and are determined by, strategies, or practices, of distribution and exhibition. When Ivo Blom, in his important study on the Dutch distributor Jean Desmet, describes distribution as a *missing link* between production and exhibition,[5] one could add that even aspects of film form have to be taken into consideration here. Looking at early cinema from the point of view of this "intermediate stage" of distribution could indeed lead to a reconfiguration of our field of study.

The essays collected in this volume provide many new insights into a number of questions. Thus "geographic areas" – local, regional, national – and their borders appear in a new light when considered from the viewpoint of distribution. And at the same time, the various case studies presented here do also invite us to compare the results and to appreciate the complex differences that are so characteristic for an emerging medium which has to fit into a variety of cultural, political, or social contexts.

Distribution playing a major role in the institutionalisation of cinema, related source materials such as distribution catalogues, ads in the trade press and in newspapers, or company records, become telling documents revealing through which channels films came to audiences, but also how exhibitors were helped in addressing their patrons in a certain way, and how spectators were invited and incited to return to the movies.

Still another question, particularly interesting today, concerns the distribution of early films after their commercial career had definitely come to an end. After all, they continue to be seen: screened by archives, recycled by found-footage artists, re-issued in digital formats, on a DVD or as a downloadable file on the Internet.

Undeniably: there is much more to distribution than meets the eye. A neglected subject, a missing link – yes, but also a force structuring the field in which cinema emerged in the late 19th and early 20th century, a multi-dimensional and multi-faceted phenomenon with an impact on production and exhibition, on offer and demand, on film form and film viewing. Local, regional, and national differences shape the ways that prints circulate internationally, distribution strategies determine when and how products made for an international market are exhibited locally, regionally, nationally. Distribution is, as Giraud put it, "the intermediate stage between production and exhibition [...] in charge of placing the films produced by a firm in a given geographic area" – but it also is so much more.

Notes

1. Giraud, Jean, *Le Lexique français du cinéma des origines à 1930* (Paris: CNRS, 1958): 105. All translations by Frank Kessler. Giraud gives contemporary quotes illustrating each definition. For the first one, the source is from 1909, for the second one from 1923, and for the third one from 1912.

2. Ibid., 104.

3. Ibid., 105.

4. Ibid., 138 (the original text runs as follows: "Fait, ou action, pour un producteur de films, de donner ceux-ci à louage à des exploitants, par l'intermédiaire d'agents spécialisés. Cette acception est assez nouvelle dans la langue des Arts, et dans celle des spectacles."). Interestingly, in the *lemma* "distribution" in Souriau, Etienne, *Vocabulaire d'esthétique* (Paris: PUF, coll. Quadrige, 1999): 599–600, there is no mention of film distribution.

5. Blom, Ivo, *Jean Desmet and the Early Dutch Film Trade* (Amsterdam: Amsterdam University Press, 2003): 25.

PART I

NETWORKS:
Distribution across borders

Rethinking Boundaries. The First moving images between Spain and Portugal

Begoña Soto

Universidad Rey Juan Carlos, Madrid, Spain

Issues pertaining to the map

An initial clarification: although the subject of the first distribution of films in the Iberian Peninsula, along with its mechanisms and networks, is the point of origin for this text, it is not necessarily the only focus of the argument developed here.

Above all, because when I propose to study Spain's first distribution networks, I encounter certain historiographical concepts and stereotypes which deserve at a minimum to be rethought and questioned from a perspective which, if not innovative, is at least different. As such, and according to this approach, there would be two essential focuses of research and discussion for this text: the first distribution networks, and the way they are described by cinema history and historians.

Benedict Anderson[1] establishes, or rather proposes, three institutions of power which mould the manner in which States (in the case discussed by Anderson the postcolonial states) imagine their territories. These institutions are the census, the map and the museum. The immediate and evident question is the relationship between these institutions of the postcolonial states and the topic proposed here.

Let me take these concepts and apply them to the way in which a national cinema is institutionalised by its history. First, the historiography of such a national cinema defines a census, or in other words an anthology or corpus of truly worthwhile films and/or directors, which constitute, according to specific quality criteria or due to particular idiosyncrasies, the 'honours list' that makes up a national filmography.

The complement to such a census is provided by a second element: the museum. We might denominate this element in a variety of ways, but, simply put, I am referring to the various institutions dedicated to the national patrimony, in this case generically speaking the audiovisual and concretely speaking the cinematographic one. Such institutions, once formalised, dedicate themselves to the conservation and inventory of certain objects which, through predetermined criteria, have priority over others. These institutions have the role of spreading a particular view of a given history instead of other possible views.

But it is the third institution, the map, which is of primary concern to me here. The idea of establishing a culturally and geographically defined territory in which to inscribe a given national cinema is one which, despite the fact that it may pass unnoticed and appear obvious, is not any less problematic.

When film historians speak of Spanish cinema, we all seem to have a clear idea regarding what exactly we are referring to. This is despite the fact that the very concept of 'Spanish'-ness is one that today is regularly questioned in the geographical and, especially, the cultural sphere.[2]

Even though this seems to be evident and is repeatedly disputed politically, socially or culturally in daily Spanish life today, when we remove ourselves in time and write cinema history, however, it is as if the geographical sphere, or the map, is not a concept to be questioned. It is almost taken for granted that the geographical and cultural context of what is taken to be Spanish cinema, from the historiographical point of view, is quite clear.[3] However, even in the purely geographical context (without entering into cultural issues) this assumption deserves, at the least, some important qualifications. Some of these qualifications will form the basic theme examined in this article.

Let me take a first example within film history. There is a fact which, although somewhat marginal, does not for that reason deserve to be completely ignored, but which nonetheless generally passes unnoticed.

When the 'invention' of moving images arrived on the Iberian Peninsula,[4] the geographical boundaries of Spain and Portugal (in this case we will focus on those of Spain) were somewhat different from present-day boundaries. What were then generically called Spanish overseas territories (Cuba, Puerto Rico and the Philippines) undisputedly belonged to the map of the Spanish State. But above all, in terms of what interests me here, they were fully integrated into the general circuit of Spanish leisure and culture.[5]

However, I will focus here on a case which is much closer: the relationships between the various locations and/or regions within the same European continent, but belonging to two separate nationalities, those of Portugal and Spain. These relationships were fundamentally characterised by means of communications and transport which were, to say the least, rather precarious. This factor, among others, suggests the inadvisability of assuming as historically evident and unquestionable a view of the nation, in this case the Spanish one, which is as uniform and homogenous as is customarily accepted. It would be useful, as a minimally preventive measure, to maintain a certain distance between what are today considered to be peninsular relationships and what these were at the end of the 19th century.[6]

The map established by the customary circuits of spectacles at the end of the 19th century, whose logical heirs would be the networks later instituted by the first film showings and distribution in Spain and Portugal, has much to do with an issue that is rarely taken into account in cinema histories. This issue, which is a fundamental one from the perspective that I adopt here, is that of the conditions and conveniences associated with the infrastructure of peninsular transportation.

So far, so near: cross-border logics

The first presentations of moving images before an audience on Spanish territory took place in Madrid, and on Portuguese territory in Lisbon. The two sessions occurred within a month of each other and were conducted, according to references in newspapers, with the same machine – an Animatographe that had come straight from London – and by the same businessman, Edwin Rousby.[7] Given this beginning, it is logical to suppose that the cinematographic connections between the two countries, in these initial years, were not only numerous but also very fluid.

Nonetheless, the relationships between the cinema histories of the two countries have yet to be researched. Although in the Portuguese bibliography it is somewhat more usual to cite facts from general and local Spanish history, in Spain facts from the other side of the border are rarely cited.[8] This contrast between the two sides of the border, systematically ignored to date, is essential for the reconstruction of these early years of film.

It is a fact that Lisbon established relationships with Spanish cities and regions which, for reasons of cultural proximity, but above all due to the conveniences derived from geographical accidents and the transportation infrastructure, were better connected with the Portuguese capital than with the two most important Spanish cities, Madrid and Barcelona. This was the case, as demonstrated by cinematographical data, of Seville, in Andalusia in southern Spain, and of La Coruña, in Galicia in the Northwest.[9]

The means of transport were a factor of vital importance in a context where the length of the trip and the ease and convenience of travel were two variables that had to be considered in order not to make things more difficult than they already were. This was in particular crucial for itinerant showmen, who had to travel with the 'tools of the trade' which were not only heavy but in most cases considerably fragile.[10]

If this was the case for show business in general, including for theatre, circuses and operas, with the arrival of the early film equipment the situation was considerably aggravated. The tools that were essential for screening the first movies – the projector and/or camera as well as the film itself – were not only heavy and fragile, but, as if this were not enough, the latter were also inflammable.

This panorama is further complicated if we take into account the fact that early film equipment invariably derived from outside of the Portuguese and Spanish borders, and from places that were not exactly close by or easily accessible. The Peninsula's cinematographic pioneers had neither the tools nor the knowledge required to resolve unforeseen mishaps, let alone repair malfunctioning equipment.[11] And while on tour through Spain and Portugal, they were particularly far from anyone who could assist them directly or at least advise them as to how to solve the problem themselves. Getting to France, the United Kingdom or the United States[12] took in the best case scenario several days, and in the majority of cases several weeks with the transportation available at the turn of the century.

In this situation of obligatory itinerancy and of inevitably complicated transport, it is logical that the early showmen would attempt to minimise their risks and to maximise, to the extent then possible, the ease of their trips. There were two possible options for such trips:

- On the one hand, the railways, which were precarious in both Spain and Portugal at the end of the 19th century. The only direct railway connection with the 'outside' was the one that linked France, via Barcelona, to Madrid (in the centre of the Peninsula), and then extended towards the south up to Lisbon. This trip, which only a few could carry out in relatively comfortable conditions, had a duration that was usually unforeseeable, but of a minimum of a few weeks.

- At the other extreme was travel by sea. Fluid maritime connections were vital to peninsular countries with strategic routes on both the Atlantic and the Mediterranean. The major points of contact with the outside, on the one hand with America and on the other with the rest of Europe, were provided by an important series of ports that extended through the length and breadth of the peninsular coast.

Let us draw a map of peninsular connections, necessarily approximative, without considering the political and administrative boundaries of the two countries. What would first draw our attention, would be the situation of Lisbon which, as an active seaport, was an ideal point of connection between Portuguese and Spanish cities on the Atlantic coast. These were cities which, furthermore, had many and important difficulties in connecting among themselves and with other points nationwide via land transportation. In this sense, Portugal was a point of reference, better connected with a large part of Spanish territory in independence of political or administrative divisions.

In contrast, the Spanish capital of Madrid was the distributing centre and the nexus of connection with the entire Castellan region in the interior. It also had a relatively easy and fluid relationship with Barcelona, the second most important Spanish city in economic and administrative terms. At the same time, this Catalan capital was the most logical link with the Mediterranean coast both in eastern Spain and in south-eastern France, and was therefore an obligatory step for any connections to continental Europe through France.

If we examine a bit more deeply the routes followed by the first films in the two countries, we are led to the conclusion that, most of the time, these routes had little to do with national dynamics.

In the Hispanic/Portuguese case, the logic followed by the expansion and early distribution of film had more to do with commercial routes established prior to the invention of film. And from this perspective it is a fact, and one true not only for the case of film, that some parts of Spain had better and stronger relationships with Lisbon or Oporto than with Madrid or Barcelona.[13] In some cases these relationships focused solely on the commercial, while in others they also had to do with broad cultural affinities.

All of this followed the overriding logic of reducing the length of the trip, minimizing unnecessary effort or risk, and as far as possible increasing the minimal conveniences of trips which by nature were rather uncomfortable. These factors would lead showmen to use the most comfortable and rapid means of transportation in each case, tried and proven by traders and by their own direct predecessors in the leisure business.[14]

A consideration of these economic/cultural relationships shaped by conditions of transport produces a map that has nothing in common with the administratively and politically correct map. A map that, on the other hand, has nothing to do with the intra-peninsular relationships of today.

From where and how

But if this was the interior panorama, the cinematographic consequences and derivations of which have evidently not been thoroughly examined, what turns out to be less evident is how to draw, based on these premises, the panorama of Spain's and Portugal's cinematographic relationships with the 'outside'. In these relationships as well, national or political dynamics do not appear to rule in a clear fashion. In this sense, the presence in Spain of projectors from the United States during the immediate prelude to, as well as during, the Spanish-North American War especially is noteworthy.

The Cuban conflict was widely mentioned and inspired all kinds of patriotic calls in theatrical and musical shows, in an end-of-century Spain for which the loss of Cuba meant a much deeper crisis than that derived merely from the loss of a distant armed conflict. However, surprisingly enough, the development of the war did not seem to affect the projectors and films that came from the 'enemy'.[15]

But leaving aside the special case of the relationship with the United States, let us focus on the other two countries of significance, in terms of film, for both Spain and Portugal: France and the United Kingdom. The argument proposed here is that in the early years, and above all until peninsular transportations were fully stabilised, the distribution of equipment and films followed a logic that had nothing to do with nationalities, but rather with the convenience of travel.[16]

The hypothesis of this text is that these means of transportation resulted in a set of relationships between Spain and Portugal which ignored borders. However, in addition, these networks mediated by communications routes influenced in a decisive manner the way in which cinema was introduced in the different parts of the Peninsula. And, as such, they played a crucial role in the definition of the first film exhibition and distribution networks that were established in the two countries. As a general conclusion, two different lines of influence can be put forward with regard to the emerging spectacle of movies and their trips throughout Portugal and Spain.

One line would take shape on the Atlantic side of the Peninsula, with its centre in Lisbon and encompassing all of Portugal and northwestern and southwestern Spain. This region was much more heavily influenced by Anglo-Saxon early-cinema, both in terms of content and equipment. Meanwhile, the remaining Spanish territory found itself under the influence of French cinema.

Let me look at some clues which form the basis for this hypothesis which, for the moment, remains to be examined more thoroughly. For example, one can establish the generalised use of the term *cinématographe* in most of Spain, while in Portugal and its area of influence the use of the term *kinetoscope* and its variants persisted for a longer period of time. This phenomenon had no linguistic logic with respect to Portuguese or Spanish, beyond the relationships of the terms to their respective French or English origins.[17]

Similarly, we have another indicator, that of the route and places reflected in the first images taken of the Peninsula. The operators associated with Lumière (Jean Busseret – who only did projections but would not take pictures – Alexandre Promio and Francis Doublier) between 1896 and 1898 first made their way to Madrid and Barcelona to take images and later to Seville for the same purpose.[18] Meanwhile, the first images of Lisbon,[19] accompanied by others of the Spanish cities of Cadiz and Seville, were taken by Henry William Short for Robert W. Paul between August and September 1896.

If we look at those who have most studied this topic say regarding the means of transport associated with these two trips for photographing local scenes, we find that Jean-Claude Seguin depicts Promio as travelling by train from Lyon to Marseilles, then by train or boat to Barcelona, and from there to Madrid, undoubtedly by train, and returning in a similar fashion. Amândio Videira Santos describes Short as going from Cadiz and Seville to Lisbon, and from there finally departing for London via Southampton on board the *Danube*.

Such different routes to and from France or England support my hypothesis of the double influence exerted by the means of transport common to the Peninsula. Above all, however, their existence is further vouched for by the already established commercial and touristic routes that preceded all the cinema apparatuses.

Richard Ford, who visited Spain for the first time in 1830, travelling throughout the Peninsula for three years to later write several books to 'guide' British travellers through the "most romantic, exotic and peculiar country in Europe", advises his readers to reach Spain by travelling from Southampton to La Coruña or Gibraltar, and from these cities to enter deeper into the country.[20] Thus the Atlantic coast is the nexus between the United Kingdom and the Spanish interior.[21]

On the other hand, before the imminent journey of his friend Édouard Manet in the summer of 1865 to visit Madrid, Zacharie Astruc, who was already familiar with the country, advised his friend to connect to Madrid from Valencia, which he could reach by boat from Marseilles.[22] Valencia was an alternative to Barcelona given the mutual proximity of the two ports on the same Mediterranean coast.[23]

In sum, the central and Mediterranean connections had, due to geographic and logistical factors, a direct relationship with France, whether by railway to Paris or by sea between south-eastern France (Marseilles) and eastern Spain (Barcelona and Valencia). Meanwhile, the northern Atlantic coast (La Coruña) and the Spanish south (Seville,[24] Cadiz), with the unquestionable assistance of the Portuguese port of Lisbon, had a much easier access to the British Isles (via Gibraltar in the south). All of this must have had direct consequences for the creation and expansion of the first film distribution networks in both Spain and Portugal.

English engineers and French geniuses

Let us move on to the final point that I aim to address, the question of how to tell the cinema history that I have attempted to rethink here in another manner. From my point of view, the problem with respect to the Spanish case is that the relationships with the context of Anglo-Saxon – and, more concretely, British – film via the maritime connections on the Hispanic-Portuguese Atlantic coast have been systematically ignored in film history. Histories of the early years of cinema in Spain are based on, and exclusively describe, the connections and relationships with France.

Of course, this primacy awarded to the French is directly related to factors that are not "historical", such as the type of training received by generations of historians of Spanish film, the translation and publication policies of specialised publishers, etc. But my objective here is not to establish the causes, but rather to put forward some of the consequences of this biased panorama.

In this respect, I can only propose here some points for future research which would allow for the exploration of the effects of this historiographical Francophilia. I will indicate two of the many possible issues.

First, and leaving aside for the moment the complex question of the United States, the stereotypes with respect to France and the United Kingdom in 19th century Spain can be categorised in the following manner: (a) art, spectacles and that which is generically included under the idea of 'culture' come to Spain directly imported from France;[25] (b) technology, science and that which is covered under the idea of 'progress' come from the British Isles.[26]

Since in Spain cinema has been considered almost exclusively a purely French "inheritance" or "importation", histories of Spanish cinema and in Spain have only explored a limited vision of the early expansion of film in the country. We have systematically ignored the 19th century notion of cinema as a technological invention in favour of a vision based on its evolution as a spectacle or cultural form.

Secondly, the relationships with film equipment and content originating in the United States have been simplified in Spanish film history. For example, the arrival of, and advertising regarding, North American equipment and films during the Spanish-North American War have been assumed to be perfectly logical and normal. However, the contradictions in the daily press regarding everything that came from the 'Yankee enemy' suggest a reality that is rather more complex than a simple lack of logic.

Undoubtedly, these two points should be addressed in a manner more complex than the one elaborated here. But what is certain is that the simplistic vision that we have today of geographical and national relationships have not helped at all to clarify our new and old ideas.

My hypothesis primarily proposes something more or less obvious: the distinctions between different national histories, and nationalities in themselves, do not matter much and, as such, are completely disregarded by early cinema in this period. However, above all, what my hypothesis attempts to examine are the historiographical and cinematographical relationships that transcend exclusively national logics. This effort tries to bring to the forefront a conception of national reality in constant evolution, not only culturally and politically, but also dependent and highly changeable in accordance with more prosaic criteria such as, for example, the reality of the means of transport available in each moment and place.

Notes

1. Anderson, Benedict, *Imagined communities. Reflections on the origin and spread of nationalism* (London, New York : Verso, 1983).

2. Minguet, Joan M, 'Lo nuestro y lo ajeno: cine, cultura y nacionalidad' in Alonso, Luis(ed.), *Once miradas sobre la crisis y el cine español* (Madrid : Ocho y Medio/Asociación Española de Historiadores del Cine, 2003).

3. Besides a more or less evident 'regional' battle for dominance in the first national cinema production, in the framework of the centenary of the invention it appears that academic and editorial production integrate, within the concept of Spanish film, the general geographical framework of the Spanish State. On this topic see: Letamendi, Jon, *La cuna fantasma del cine español* (Barcelona: Cims 97, 1999).

4. Madrid, 11 May 1896 and Lisbon, 15 June 1896. For more details see especially, among other possible material: Pérez Perucha, Julio, 'Narración de un aciago destino (1896–1930)' in Gubern, Román; Monterde, José Enrique; Pérez Perucha, Julio, Riambau, Esteve & Torreiro, Casimiro, *Historia del cine español*. (Madrid : Cátedra, 1995); Videira Santos, Amândio, *Para a história do cinema em Portugal I. Do diafanorama aos cinematógrafos de Lumière e Joly-Normandin* (Lisboa: Cinemateca Portuguesa, 1991).

5. Theatrical and opera tours, performances of variety singers, etc. The press referred frequently to such tours of national companies, especially in Cuba.

6. Ringrose, David R, *Spain, Europe and the "Spanish miracle", 1700–1900* (Cambridge : Cambridge University Press, 1996).

7. Madrid: *El Resumen, El País, El Heraldo de Madrid, El Imparcial* : 12 May 1896; *La Gaceta de Madrid*: 16 May 1896. Lisbon: *Correio da Noite*: 15 June 1896; *Diário Ilustrado*: 16 July 1896.

8. We should acknowledge here the exception of historians connected to the Spanish region of Galicia (in the northwest of the Peninsula), whose linguistic and cultural connections with Portugal have been and are characterised by their mutual influence and fluidity. As an example among others, see: Folgar, José María, *Aproximación a la historia del espectáculo cinematográfico en Galicia (1896–1920)* (Santiago de Compostela : Universidad de Santiago, 1987).

9. For more information: Videira Santos, Amândio, *Para a história do cinema em Portugal I. Do diafanorama aos cinematógrafos de Lumière e Joly-Normandin* (Lisboa: Cinemateca Portuguesa, 1991, pp. 107, 239); Folgar, José María, *Aproximación a la historia del espectáculo cinematográfico en Galicia (1896–1920)* (Santiago de Compostela : Universidad de Santiago, 1987, p. 88).

10. Costumes, set elements and props, musical instruments, a variety of machinery, etc.

11. For example, the Portuguese cinema historian Amândio Videira Santos attributes the continuity and success of the shows of the animatographe of Edwin Rousby in Lisbon, in contrast to the short duration and the apparent failure of the Spanish shows of the same machine in Madrid and Seville, to the skill of the Portuguese projectionists: the actor Francisco dos Santos and the electrician and photographer Manuel María de Costa y Veiga.

12. These three countries were the source of the equipment used for shows in both Spain and Portugal in the early years.

13. Cases of Huelva, Seville and Cadiz in southern Spain and La Coruña or Vigo in Galicia, in the northern part of the country.

14. Without forgetting, of course, that in some cases it was the circus or theatrical companies themselves that would carry this early film equipment.

15. Projectors and shows advertised under the name of Wargraph travelled throughout Spain (Madrid, Cadiz, Seville, La Coruña, etc.) without the obvious translation of the prefix 'war' carrying any type of problem for the public in general or the showmen in particular. Edison is interchangeably invoked by the newspapers as the inventor of the 'marvellous' machine which gives life to images and as the creator of arms capable of destroying all of Spain. *"Terrible Edison: The impulse of the war will be enough – says Edison – to launch such a great number of destructive inventions that the world will be overwhelmed with horror". "Edisson (sic) and the war". "... the inventions of Edisson (sic), thanks to which no nation will dare to declare war against the Yankees".* These are translations of excerpts from the press of 1898.

    Let us take the specific case of the city of Cadiz, a strategic Atlantic port in the extreme south of Spain. On 1 April 1898 (barely a month and a half after the explosion of the Maine in La Habana and barely a month before the formal declaration of war between Spain and the United States), the city witnessed the arrival of various demonstrations of the Edison phonographs. On 3 December 1898 (on 10 December, only a week later, the Treaty of Paris would be signed, ending the war with the practically unconditional surrender of Spain and the loss of sovereignty over the colonial territories of Cuba, Puerto Rico and the Philippines), the city witnessed a presentation, according to the local press, of the Wargraph: "such is the name of the latest modern invention of Edison". The inventor was further referred to as "the great Edison".

    Cadiz is taken as a paradigmatic example because in July 1898 emerged a piece of news, apparently spread by the US intelligence service, of an attack on the peninsular coasts. This not only led the fleet of the Admiral Cámara, which had been launched from the Cadiz port in June, to turn back from its route towards the Philippines, but as reflected in the press of the time also caused families on the Cadiz coast to move into the interior to escape the imminent military invasion by the United States.

    All the facts mentioned here have been extracted from the newspaper *Diario de Cádiz,* principal communications medium in the city. For more information consult also: Garófano, Rafael, *El cinematógrafo en Cádiz. Una sociología de la imagen (1896–1930)* (Cádiz: Cátedra Municipal de Cultura, 1986).

16. For treatment of the importation/exportation of cinematographic materials (both films and technology) in later years between Spain and other countries, see: García Fernández, Emilio Carlos, *El cine español entre 1896 y 1939. Historia, Industria, filmografía y documentos* (Barcelona: Ariel, 2002) and Díez Puertas, Emeterio. *Historia social del cine en España* (Madrid: Fundamentos, 2003).

17. Brown, Richard, 'Marketing the cinematographe in Britain' in Williams, Christopher (ed.), *Cinema: the beginnings and the future. Essays marking the centenary of the first film show projected to a paying audience in Britain* (London: University of Westminster Press, 1996).

18. For more on the Spanish images of the *Cinématographe-Lumière* see: Seguin, Jean-Claude. 'La légende Promio' in *1895* (December 1991): 94–100; and Seguin, Jean-Claude, 'Alexadre Promio y las películas españolas Lumière' in *Tras el sueño. Actas del centenario. Cuadernos de la Academia* (January 1998): 11–35.

19. And perhaps Oporto. Images of this city do not appear in the so-called *Tour in Spain and Portugal* (1896) in the brochure edited by Robert W. Paul, October 1896, but it appears that the Lisbon press does mention the exhibition of images of Oporto by the same machine used to show images from the *Tour in Spain and Portugal.* The images of this tour were projected in the Real Colyseu of Lisbon between the end of September and December 1896. Two scenes of Oporto appear to have been shown for the first time between 23 and 28 December of the same year, without the appearance of references as to who took these images. On these topics see: Barnes, John, *The beginnings of the cinema in England 1894–1901. Volume 1 1894–1896* (Exeter : University of Exeter Press, 1998). Videira Santos Amândio, op. cit.

20. Ford, Richard, *Cosas de España* (Barcelona : Ediciones B, 2004) Original: *Gatherings from Spain,* 1846.

21. Supporting what we can suppose to have been a natural route followed by Short in his cinematographic tour: London-Sauthampton-Gibraltar-Cadiz-Seville-Lisbon-Sauthampton-London.

22. Correspondence between Astruc and Manet as reproduced in Melchor, Carlos (ed.), *La España de Manet* (Málaga: Edinexus, 2003).

23. Supporting what Jean-Claude Seguin assumes to be a logical route followed by Promio in his cinematographic trip: Lyon-Marseilles-Barcelona-Madrid.

24. Seville is not a sea port but is the fluvial port directly connected with the Atlantic ports of Cadiz and Gibraltar.

25. Worthy of attention are the numerous 'complaints' in the general press for the excessive 'Frenchification' of the Spanish scene at the beginning of the 20th century.

26. An important number of Spanish cities owe the introduction of electricity and urban water conduits to companies of primarily British origin and capital.

2

What imports may not be able to tell us about the emergence of the last-minute rescue narrative in the American cinema

David Levy

Montréal, Canada

I want to consider, albeit in a tentative way, the role of distribution, which is to say imported film subjects, in a major shift in American film production between 1903 and 1908. In the first phase, producers abandoned the actualities and comedies, the so-called "cinema of attractions" that dominated the vaudeville period dating from 1896 in favor of fictional story films, a trend that appears to have begun in 1903.[1] Initially, much fiction film production in that five-year period took the form of a lecturer-dependent tableaux narrative modeled on the lantern slide show, a form characterized by strong spatial orientation and weak temporality, e.g. Edwin Porter's *Life of an American Fireman* (1903). In the second phase, dating roughly from 1907, we find a trend to the displacement of the tableaux narrative by one possessing a more precise temporal structure, e.g. Vitagraph's *The Mill Girl* (1907). In attempting to explain this type of development there is an inclination, almost without exception, to hunt down a precedent, to identify some prior occurrence, to try in other words to locate the source of the new paradigm not in the circumstance that in fact produced it but in some prior achievement in the cinema or in some other medium.

We achieve a more certain grasp of the sort of shift described above by seeing it as an *overdetermined* displacement, which is to say the consequence of a process of complex causation. The concept of the overdetermination is one I borrow from Louis Althusser who used it to explain, among other things, the fact of the Russian revolution occurring in the most unlikely of European locales.[2] To say that the emergence of the cross-cut last-minute rescue trope was overdetermined is to say that it was neither deliberate nor accidental, that is, neither consciously willed nor the product of coincidence or inadvertence.

Strong claims have, as we know, been made in support of the notion that in its early years the American cinema was highly dependent on inspiration from across the sea. Among the best known example is the notion that Edwin S.Porter, working at the Edison Studio needed to see the work of Georges Méliès or James Williamson in order to complete *Life of an American Fireman* and *The Great Train Robbery* (1903). But this is not a hypothesis that can be sustained by rigorous examination.

16

Distribution & film history

Ivo Blom in his monograph on Jean Desmet called distribution "the missing link", which is to say there may still be less information available on distribution than on production and exhibition.[3] Perhaps for that reason, the role distribution has been assigned in considering questions of film history, especially in our period has been exaggerated by underlying and generally mistaken historical notions.

Richard Abel has shown that if the nickelodeon boom in America, dating from 1906, was inspired by certain film shows those shows were the work of the Pathé studio, the key supplier in 1905 and 1906 of new subjects for the American market.[4] We are nevertheless unable to conclude with any certainty the actual impact of that work on American production, given that, as I will make clear, what happened would likely have happened pretty much independently of the Pathé screenings.

Rescue of the Nickelodeon

If the nickelodeon phenomenon Pathé subjects did much to initiate solved some problems for big city movie entrepreneurs, it created others, and in the solution to those problems we see the true ingenuity of the American cinema.

To begin, we need to look at the relationship between the apparent crisis in film exhibition initiated by the nickelodeon boom dating more or less from 1906 and D.W. Griffith's first last-minute rescue subjects completed at Biograph in 1908, which is to say a mere two years later, subjects that seemed to take a crucial step in managing the formal demands of that crisis. One might be inclined here to recall the dogs-to-sausages trick films of the cinema's early years, which is to say the product that went into the nickelodeon system and may have provided the basis for its great success was not what came out the other end, something the imports do not explain. The simple chases, tour-like sequences, fairy tales, and mini-melodramas that got the boom rolling generally required explanatory help - which they got from the vaudeville house lecturers. With the rapid expansion of the nickel venues, the demand for these explainers began to exceed the supply. Moreover, some nickel managers were inclined to dispense with the cost of the explainers to increase profits. Important story details included in studio catalogue descriptions were now no longer part of the shows. The missing *benshi* brought on an exhibition crisis. Here is a complaint sent to *The Moving Picture World* in February 1908 from a woman in Atlanta, Georgia: "People", she wrote, "grow weary of what they do not understand".[5]

Marked by uneven character development, narrative dependence, an absence of strict shot sequencing and an awkward codification of space-time relations, the lantern show structure of a film like Méliès' *L'Affaire Dreyfus* could not long survive the roughhouse nickelodeon embrace. It had become necessary to abandon the vague temporality of the post-1903 chases and tours for a story structure organized in terms of a more precise and coherent set of temporal relations.

It was at this time that Progressivists and other reformers began to assail the new medium for its pessimism and amorality. As Tom Gunning has shown, this was accompanied by demands in the press for a softer, more puritan, more sentimental mode of screen reality embodied in an autonomous, which is to say narrator-less, independently exhibitable motion picture.[6]

The sub-titleless one reelers Griffith began turning out at Biograph in 1908 appeared to provide a solution to the crisis in the form of coherent, respectable little dramas of rescue suspense, as for example *The Greaser's Gauntlet* (1908), in which a woman arrives at the last minute to save a falsely accused Mexican from a lynching, and *The Fatal Hour*

(1908) with its race to rescue a female detective threatened by a large pistol arranged on the face of a clock.

It is not difficult to note the more or less autonomously exhibitable character of these works. Their core obsession, concealed in melodramatic excess, is less evident: the anxiety of industrial time. Those one-reelers were produced in a period of heavy industrial growth ruled by clock-ordered time - production schedules and delivery dates. A turn of the century government survey found that by 1895, immigrants formed a majority of the adult populations of Manhattan and Brooklyn. Those waves of foreigners worried Progressivists who perceived them as boozers and womanizers lacking in Protestant restraint, men bred, to quote one social historian, "in traditions where work went according to the task or season — not the regulation of the assembly line or clock".[7]

D.W. Griffith's one-reel cross-cut melodramas of the clock with their time devices, some obvious some less so, articulated a type of temporal urgency in terms of a formal structure that responded to certain pressures on the film industry in the period. The components out of which that structure was constructed are familiar enough: the temporal overlap employed by Méliès in his moon-landing, the cut-in seen in the work of early British and American studios, and the quasi-erotic images of women.Those filmic devices were re-constituted in a genre of factory-worker etiquette in a period of burgeoning industrial growth amounting to an equation of chivalrous action with punctuality.

In Biograph's *The Elopement* (1907) an automobile transporting the runaway lovers, pursued in an another automobile by the girl's parents, develops motor trouble. At the now immobile vehicle the girl looks back in the direction from which they have come suggesting not merely a world beyond the frame edge but the pressure of time. Cutbacks follow to orient the story in time as well as space. In the studio's *Old Isaacs, the Pawnbroker* (1908) based on a Griffith scenario, a gravely ill woman threatened with eviction sends her little girl to a charity agency for help. The film cuts back to the ailing mother, the edit focusing story emotion on the urgency of the daughter's mission.

Some of the initial efforts of American producers to depict the dread of tardiness took a more conventional tableaux format. In two Biograph shorts, *Mr. Hurry-Up* and *The Tird Taylor's Dream*, both released in 1907, clock-based exhaustion was rendered in tableaux images of violence and nightmarish mental states. Punctuality is the theme of Edwin Porter's *The Suburbanite's Ingenious Alarm* (1907) in which a Mr. Early is punished for his habitual tardiness by being yanked from his bed and dragged all over town, finally arriving at the office a battered wreck.

Sergei Eisenstein pointed out that before and possibly anticipating Griffith's last minute rescues there were the sensational salvations of stage melodrama.[8] The crucial difference, one Eisenstein ignored, was that in those staged scenes the victim and rescuer appeared in *contiguous* spaces. The scenes thus provided no need nor opportunity for the protagonist to *go to work*, which is to say to cross a space within a time limit as Griffith's heroes were required to do. But then Eisenstein, attempting to see the Griffith films as a stage in the elaboration of montage dialectics, was unable and perhaps uninterested in relating the Griffith *oeuvre* to the predicament of the factory workers of America or anywhere else.

We may note as well that there was no abrupt transition in the displacement of the tableaux rescue by the cross-cut version, no sudden industry-wide formal abandonment of the one-scene rescues featured, say, in Biograph's *The Paymaster* (1906) and

Edison's *The Train Wreckers* (1905). Filmgoers in the period first saw Edison studio cross-cut rescue action in *The Trainer's Daughter* (1907).

Now the question: Did Pathé provide the formula for the rescue of the American film industry?

Among the earliest examples of cross-cutting was Pathé's *I Fetch the Bread* (1905), in which a fellow leaves his dinner guests but instead of a trip to the baker stops off at a number bars. In *Le cheval emballé* (1907) there is cutting between the clock device of a diminishing bag of oats and the rounds of a laundry delivery man; *Chiens policier* (1907) cuts between some policemen and their dogs and a street mugging. In *Tricking His Wife* (1907), a woman attempts to curb the drinking antics of a husband by timing his absences from home.

What the Pathé subjects had in common with their American cousins was little more than the visual representation of clock-like devices, in the case of *Tricking His Wife*, an actual clock. There is no Griffithian damsel in distress in need of some fast rescue action, or the threat of deadly consequences if that action is less than timely. The Pathé films represent a type of rural or suburban comedy and seem without a thematic link to industrial conditions. All of which to say that the pattern we have observed in the American industry is not readily explained or explained at all by a handful of French novelty imports on view in American nickel venues. While we don't know for certain whether American filmmakers at the Edison, Biograph and Vitagraph studios in fact ever saw those Pathé films, it is unlikely they needed to.

Curiously, one or two American studio executives and some reviewers wondered whether audiences would be puzzled by the wordless rescue switchbacks and require an explanation. This is only to say that the problem of the flawed coherence of increasingly lecturer-less shows was a problem they were not unaware of. In an otherwise favorable account of Edwin Porter's civil war drama, *The Blue and the Grey* (1908), a nameless *New York Dramatic Mirror* reviewer on 20 June 1908 hastened to warn period filmgoers of a shortcoming:

> "… when the young officer has been stood up to be shot and the command of 'fire' is about to be given, the scene is shifted to Washington where the girl pleads with President Lincoln. The spectator is thus asked to imagine the firing squad suspending the fatal discharge while the girl rides from Washington to the Union camp. It would have been better if the Washington scene had been inserted somewhat earlier."[9]

A comparable apprehension accompanied Biograph's release of *The Fatal Hour* later that summer. Fearing the consequences of failed semiosis in an increasingly competitive industry and not fully trusting the plot outline in the studio's *Bulletin*, or the method's stage provenance, or audience familiarity with its editing procedures, the studio provided an explanation:

> "This incident is shown in alternate scenes. There is the helpless girl with the clock ticking its way to her destruction, and out on the road is the carriage, tearing along at breakneck speed to her rescue, arriving just in time to get her safely out of range of the pistol as it goes off."[10]

The writer perhaps believed there was much to be gained by adjusting film form to the nickel clientele without it occurring to him that he may have been doing the reverse.

Needless to say, it is important for us to understand the realities of the film trade in as much detail as we can gather without feeling an obligation to make excessive claims about the impact of that trade on production trends.

I do realize that I leave some questions unanswered. No single work, certainly not an academic paper, can or should attempt to answer them all.

Notes

1. Charles Musser, "Moving Towards Fictional Narratives: Story Films Become the Dominant Product, 1903–1904", in Lee Grieveson and Peter Kramer (eds.) *The Silent Film Reader* (Routledge, 2004), 87–102.

2. Louis Althusser, "Contradiction and Overdermination" in *Notes for an Investigation* (Penguin Press, 1962), translated by Ben Brewster.

3. Ivo Blom, *Jean Desmet and the Early Dutch Film Trade* (Amsterdam University Press, 2003).

4. Richard Abel, "Pathé Goes to Town: French Films Create a Market for the Nickelodeon," in Lee Grieveson and Peter Kramer(eds.), *The Silent Cinema Reader* (Routeledge, 2004).

5. See David Levy, "Edwin S.Porter and the Origins of the American Narrative Film, 1894–1907", doctoral dissertation, unpublished, Chapter 5, "Melodramas of the Clock", 285-359.

6. Tom Gunning, "From the Opium Den to the Theatre of Morality: Moral Discourse and the Film Process in Early American Cinema" in Grieveson and Kramer, 145–154.

7. Lary May, *Screening Out the Past* (OUP, 1980).

8. Sergei Eisenstein, "Dickens, Griffith and the Film Today", in *Film Form: Essays in Film Theory* (edited and translated by Jay Leyda) (Harcourt, Brace & World. Inc., 1949), 195–255. The essay was written in 1944.

9. "The Blue and the Grey", *The New York Dramatic Mirror*, 20 June 1908, in Stanley Kauffman (ed.) *American Film Criticism* (Liveright, 1972), 6–7.

10. *Biograph Bulletin*, No. 162 (18 August 1908).

3

'Avoid giving wine to children': George Kleine's correspondence with Cines and the discourse of uplift

John P. Welle

University of Notre Dame, Notre Dame, IN 46556, USA

'George Kleine in the old days', Louella Parsons writes in the *Morning Telegraph*, August 12, 1923, 'was to the motion picture industry what John D. Rockefeller is to Standard Oil. He was [...] one of the pioneers who had joined hands with Thomas Edison to help make the motion picture recognized as a universal form of entertainment. As long ago as the 50-foot film, the time when the funeral of the late President McKinley was shown on the screen, Mr. Kleine was experimenting with film and with projection machine inventions.'[1] Not surprisingly, Kleine's activities find a place in all of the historical accounts of the emergence of cinema in the United States. The most important aspects of his dealings with Italy – (1) his importation of Italian spectacle films, and (2), the story of his attempt to establish a production company outside of Turin in 1913/1914, the Photodrama Production Company of Grugliasco, Italy – have both received the attention of film scholars. William Uricchio and Roberta A. Pearson, for example, have analysed Kleine's handling of Italian spectacle films in the United States[2] and Paolo Cherchi Usai has authored a study of the Photodrama Production Company of Grugliasco, Italy.[3] Kleine's role as a distributor of imported films is also discussed by Charles Mussser in his work on the emergence of the American cinema,[4] in Eileen Bowser's account of the transformation of American cinema between 1907 and 1915[5] and in Richard Abel's dissection of the role of imported films, notably those of Pathé, in the early American film market.[6]

In Italy, Kleine is mentioned in all of the histories of Italian silent cinema beginning with Adriana Prolo in the early 1950s and continuing in the work of Gian Piero Brunetta and Aldo Bernardini in the late 1970s and early 1980s, respectively.[7] Kleine's name can be found in the narrative syntheses for 'gli anni dell'oro' that Vittorio Martinelli provides in his multi-volume filmography of Italian silent cinema.[8] Finally, Kleine is the subject of a short article by Harriet Harrison and Nicola Mazzanti in an anthology of essays on early Italian cinema, *Sperduto nel buio*, edited by Renzo Renzi in 1991.[9]

Despite international scholarly interest in Kleine, and despite a seeming familiarity with his activities and a widespread recognition of his importance, there remain many areas of his career as a distributor and producer in patent need of further study. This paper examines a rather limited area of his voluminous correspondence: following an examination of his comments on Italy in a report he wrote for the Motion Picture

Patents Company in November of 1909 concerning the film industry in Europe, I propose to revisit briefly his letters to the Italian Cines Company in the years preceding the importation of *Quo Vadis?* in the spring of 1913. I will conclude with some suggestions for future research.

As is well known, the formation of the Motion Picture Patents Company in 1908 was instrumental in the beginning stages of limiting the access of imported films to the US market. Kristin Thompson observes: 'Pathé had a license and could import and make films without limitation. Only one importer, George Kleine, had a license and the firm could bring in only 3,000 feet of film per week [...]. It could deal in two brands: Gaumont and Urban-Eclipse. Before the agreement, Kleine had represented nine or ten foreign firms.'[10] 'In November 1911, Gaumont left Kleine Optical [...]. Kleine replaced this brand in January 1912, by becoming the agent for Cines.'[11]

In their cogent analysis of Kleine's distribution of Cines' films, William Uricchio and Roberta Pearson note that 'Kleine's demand for Italian spectacle put him in the position of a cultural negotiator who articulated the desirable qualities of Italian films for American consumption'.[12] While Uricchio and Pearson have analysed Kleine's interest in spectacle, which constituted, in their words, an 'ever-narrowing focus on the potentially most profitable aspect of Italian films in the American market',[13] I focus here on matters preceding although not peripheral to Kleine's commitment to spectacle. The discourse of uplift figures prominently in his correspondence with the Italians and forms a prism through which he views the Italian film industry. Problems of a technical nature, the exigencies of censorship, the divergence of acting styles, the relative merits of various Italian actors and actresses, the success and lack thereof of particular genres in the American market, and the advertising strategies he chooses to employ are all matters that emerge in the course of his correspondence with Cines. In what follows, however, I shall focus primarily on Kleine's rhetoric in his correspondence as it pertains to uplift.[14]

On behalf of the MPPC, George Kleine made a business trip to Europe in the summer of 1909. Upon his return, he filed a report labeled simply 'Motion Picture Patents Company Selig Report;' it is dated 4 November 1909, and provides a useful illustration of Kleine's adoption of the rhetoric of uplift.[15] Describing the conditions for producing and exhibiting films in England, France, Russia, Holland, Austria, Hungary, Germany, Spain and Portugal, he devotes considerable attention to Italy. This country in particular becomes the focus of Kleine's remarks illustrating the moral concerns surrounding the cinema in its transformative years beginning around 1907.

In the first part of the report Kleine describes the film industry in England. With regard to France, he discusses Pathé's dispute with Eastman over film stock and visits the plants of Pathé, Gaumont, and Lux. In Germany, he becomes familiar with the Agfa Company and mentions their film stock. When he visits Italy, he turns his attention to the content of films.

> After leaving these last places I went to Italy and at Torino I visited the Italia Film Company of which Mr. Schemengo is the proprietor. I found him to be a very bright and pleasant man and practically speaking and in fact conceded by Pathé to be the only competitor they have in Europe [...]. Most of the film he makes would be sensational in America, but he is getting away from them. He told me the quality of his film is his best advertisement. He has a very well equipped plant and is doing a business of about 125, 000 feet of film per week.[16]

After describing the Ambrosio Plant in Turin, Kleine moves on to Rome where he visits Cines.

> Cines in Rome have a very large studio but do nothing. Their work is not up to
> the standard quality even in Europe, but once in a while they put out a good film.
> [...] I think they are hardly able to proceed without more capital. The class of film
> they are putting out embraces murder, rape and robbery.[17]

The Italian film industry experienced a crisis between 1908 and 1909. According to
Aldo Bernardini, 'All aspects of production, distribution, and exhibition in the early
Italian cinema are shown to have been affected by the general economic recession of
1907–1908'.[18] Kleine's remarks concerning Cines can be read in light of this downturn.
Moreover, his lack of enthusiasm for the Cines brand in 1909 is interesting given his
later intense involvement with their fortunes in the United States beginning in January
of 1912. The phrase 'murder, rape and robbery', it should be noted, reoccurs in this
report. Kleine adopts it repeatedly as a generic description for films that he considers
'sensational'. In this respect, Kleine's rhetoric illustrates what Uricchio and Pearson,
following Hayden White, have termed the 'period's ubiquitous melodramatic mode of
emplotment': 'reporting [...] perceptions of audiences in melodramatic terms [...]
representations pitting good against evil and featuring hyperbolic language'.[19]

In depicting the film theatres in the various European countries he visits, Kleine once
again singles out Italy, describing it through the prism of the need for uplift.

> In Italy they seem to have more moving picture theatres than in any other place
> on the continent. They also cater to a very sensational order of pictures. There
> you can see flashy bills posted in front of the moving picture shows which depict
> murder, riot, and robbery. This country needs awakening as they are now on the
> downward path, and unless this class of pictures is eliminated, the better class of
> people will remain set against them. The opinion which they now have is that they
> should be closed as immoral and not fit for any decent person and especially
> children to see. This class of pictures I have no doubt is what caused the Pope to
> publish an edict against moving picture shows. At the same time Rome has some
> very fine theatres devoted to moving pictures which are trying to lift to a higher
> class, but are powerless until the manufacturers discontinue making such sensa-
> tional films. This better class of theatres hope[s] that this will occur soon. France
> and Italy and in fact the Latin speaking countries are the only market that permit
> these pictures to run.[20]

Kleine's observations here illustrate the discourse of uplift in reference to the content
of films as well as to exhibition venues. His castigation of 'sensational films' while
voicing support for the 'better class of theaters' reveals class-based elements in the
discourse of uplift.

Shedding light on the broader discursive parameters of the period, Uricchio and
Pearson note

> In the few short years between 1907 and 1913, changes in signifying practices,
> economic organization, exhibition venues, and audience composition gained the
> new medium the approval of many who had formerly castigated moving pictures
> for fomenting disorder among the 'lower orders'.[21]

In terms of film style, these are the years in which alternate editing came into use. As
Eileen Bowser argues, 'it is a particularly apt narrative system for making moral
statements, and the years from 1907 to 1915 were precisely the time when moral uplift
was in demand'.[22] Part of the cinema's transformation during these years involved 'the
industry's drive for respectability: its desire to attract new audiences and to placate its
most powerful critics'.[23]

In its drive for respectability, the cinema found a champion in George Kleine. Like other figures who established the film industry in the United States, Kleine saw his work as consonant with Reformist attempts to ennoble, improve and uplift moving pictures. Kleine's defense of the nickelodeon in 1907, his reports to his business associates concerning the European film industry in the summer of 1909, and his correspondence with various Italian producers in the years of the so-called 'golden age of Italian silent film', i.e. 1911 to 1914, are replete with the rhetoric and vocabulary of uplift.

Further on in his 1909 report to his colleagues in the Motion Picture Patents Company, and warming up to his subject, Kleine observes

> Motion picture manufacturers [...] must expect to be in a bad odium in some countries as long as certain manufacturers make blood-curdling films as they do. In the Lux office the walls are hung with lithographs of films made or in process of making, every one of which depict murder, rape or burglary. This is equally true of Éclair and to some extent of Italia. They all claim those are the films the people want and as long as they demand it, it will be furnished but speaking of the better class of people and the general public these statements are not true. The walls of Cines office are literally covered with this class of lithographs with the exception of a little spot over the manager's desk where there was a dozen photographs of the 'Biograph Company', the Pope which the Biograph Company took some years ago with Cines name under them. Above these little photographs was a lithograph of a man with a gun in his hand, pillaging the place of a couple of Sisters of Charity and with this lithograph being shown during my visit to Rome in all the moving picture theatres, it is no wonder that the Pope does not want Catholics to visit moving picture shows.[24]

Although Pierre Leprohon has argued that the Italian cinema did not experience an early period of disapproval and moral condemnation similar to that of the nickelodeon age in the United States,[25] Italian public officials and the ecclesiastical authorities were not unconcerned about the rapid growth of the cinemas. 'The need for specific regulations began to make itself felt beginning in 1907, with the first large flowering of cinematic exhibition.'[26] On 15 May 1907, for example, Giovanni Giolitti, as the Minister of the Interior, issued a circular enjoining local government prefects to begin to patrol the cinemas. Two more circulars were issued in March of 1908 and in August of 1910. These circulars laid the groundwork for the system of censorship that was established in 1913. Giolitti's circulars were concerned not as much with the safety of the spectators as they were with the content of the films.[27]

While a comparison of the relative degrees of moral criticism surrounding the cinema in Italy and the United States would be of interest, such questions cannot be entertained here. It should be noted in passing, however, that throughout his long career, Kleine would remain interested in the European film industry. As Rita Horwitz observes,

> In the 1920s Kleine made an attempt to realize an idea he had conceived to form an alliance with several European businessmen that would provide a common market for American and European films. Kleine sent his representative Alfred Bourget to France in 1926 to discuss the matter of entering into an agreement looking toward the acquisition of the best foreign products from international sources and the construction of large and important theatres.[28]

Let us now turn briefly to some examples of Kleine's advice to Cines regarding the American market. In a letter of 12 February 1912, for example, Kleine writes

> When we first projected 'The Sheik's Jealousy' upon our curtain, we feared that there might be objections made by the Censors to the opening scenes. We

submitted it to the Chicago board this morning, who passed it *in toto*, with compliments as to its quality, and are now shipping it to New York to be passed upon by the National Board of Censors. In the meantime, we are placing an order, and in case any changes have to be made we will cable.[29]

Kleine is very forthright in his suggestions to the Italian producers. In the following remarks, he combines a concern with censorship with genre considerations:

Such subjects as 'Fatima', 'The Moorish Bride', and 'The Sheik's Jealousy' cannot be used often, no matter how good they may be. We would like strong modern society plays, three hundred (300) metre lengths, clean dramas without violence, that is to say, without the use of pistols, knives, poisons, etc.[30]

With regard to censorship, Kleine instructs Cines as follows pertaining to melodramas involving poverty:

There is one class of pictures which our customers constantly criticise, that is, pictures that show abject poverty. Taking for instance 'Little Charlie's Three Pennies'; we ourselves have had films during the past five (5) years again and again built along those lines: a family with father out of work, no bread in the house, and the utmost anxiety and suffering because of father's idleness; not finding work he attempts suicide and is saved in the nick of time by some philanthropic man or woman who gives father a job. Suicides, either attempted or accomplished, must be avoided, as the Censors will not pass them.[31]

Having been involved in the film business from its beginnings, Kleine was attentive to the fine points of filmmaking. A number of his comments can be grouped under the heading of what he calls 'a lack of attention to detail [...] which can easily be corrected'.[32] Frequently, moralism and Victorian prudishness sit side by side with his attempts to correct various kinds of technical and aesthetic imperfections. The following four examples focus respectively on improperly disarrayed garments, a lack of realism in letter writing, an implausible costume change, and the necessity of avoiding 'giving wine to children'.

Referring again to Miss Leah, it is necessary that care be used in tumbling, that her garments be not improperly disarranged, as for instance, in the film, 'Tooth-ache', and we refer also along these lines to one of the scenes in 'The Carpet Peddler'.[33]

There sometimes occurs a lack of attention to detail in your films, which can easily be corrected. Reference has previously been made to the writing of letters which is sometimes done by the actor with a dash of his pen across the paper, and audiences know that it is impossible to write a letter which appears, in the short time taken by the performer.[34]

Referring again to the question of men becoming too sympathetic with each other, note the two convicts kissing in the penitentiary scene. As an error in detail note also the convict who is clean shaven when he leaves the penitentiary appears with a mustache shortly after.[35]

We presume that our official photographic critic will sooner or later call attention to poor photography in some of our films. For instance, in the film 'Toothache' it frequently happens that Mr. Stout's face shows no detail. It is well to *avoid giving wine to children*, as this is apt to be offensive to American audiences.[36]

The divergence of acting styles between the United States and Europe is a frequent source of complaint from Kleine. The following letter, therefore, is somewhat atypical in this respect. Note, however, the convergence of assumptions about American tastes with a concern for scientific accuracy in the portrayal of hypnotism. The film referenced is entitled 'A Daughter of the Regiment',

> We admire the acting in this film exceedingly, but take the liberty of criticising the emotions of the doctor. We have previously referred to the fact that American audiences are inclined to be critical of men who weep. Otherwise the acting of the two principles is exceptionally clever, and the act of hypnotism seems to be scientifically correct.[37]

In the same letter of February 14, 1912, Kleine writes:

> Referring to the sample 'Innocent' which we received last week the censorship will not permit us to put out films showing robbery scenes blindfolded with criminal intent, etc. As we have previously stated foreign films lose strength in America when in costume of the peasantry.[38]

> 'The Bogus Giant.' In one scene there are three women on the stage in tights. The censorship objects to the exposure of shapes.[39]

Uplift is a response to the moral criticisms leveled at the cinema during its phase of expansion beginning around 1907. Adopting the language of the critics of the nickelodeon, Kleine's rhetoric is consonant with Uricchio and Pearson's observation that 'the film industry often cast its own utterances in melodramatic terms, conforming to the opposition's mode of emplotment'.[40]

As we have seen in Kleine's correspondence with Cines, Italian films in a moment preceding the successful development of the historical spectacle are expected to conform to the norms of censorship and sensibility developed by the American film industry in response to moral criticism. Italian cultural differences, such as 'giving wine to children', for example, or men greeting each other affectionately, need to be expunged from the offending reels. With regard to the conditions governing the American film industry in 1909, Bowser observes:

> With confidence and sincerity, the Motion Picture Patents Company's licensed producers assumed their mission to improve the motion-picture industry and its customers at the same time. To uplift, ennoble, and purify was good business too. Progressive idealism did not conflict with their ideas of how to expand the market. To broaden the base of the audience, to bring in the middle class, to make the movies a respectable place of entertainment for women and children, [...] it would be useful to educate and uplift the immigrant masses and urban poor, who had made movies successful in the first place.[41]

Kleine's correspondence with Cines can be read as a micro-chronicle illustrative of a larger story. Although our focus has drawn attention to the intersection between his dealings with Cines and the discourse of uplift, it should be emphasized that George Kleine certainly merits further study. Given that the 2004 Domitor conference seeks to place distribution more securely on the agenda of early cinema studies, the time is ripe to open up new lines of inquiry into this major figure in order to lay the foundation for a full-scale biography to be realized in the future.

By way of conclusion, therefore, I would simply like to suggest some areas of possible research. Kleine's activities as a distributor intersect with a number of significant historical currents. For example, he was an important leader in developing educational film in the United States. In 1909, he published a distribution catalogue 'suitable for school, church, college and lecture work'.[42] The catalogue brought together actualities, scenic and industrial films as well as films based on literary classics and historical events. Kleine was active in what was known as the "high brow" or "better films movement"[43] and re-cycled Italian historical spectacle films in the 1920s distributing them for exhibition by American schools and universities. Kleine describes the "movement" in a letter to exhibitors:

> Our massive film production *Julius Caesar*, described in the enclosed circular, is now available at $25.00 per day. [...] This Classic is being distributed this season by twenty-two University and other institutional film exchanges throughout thirty states. [...] Many schools, colleges, churches and civic associations which have no auditorium equipped for film projection, are strongly in favor of the 'better films' movement, and would like to exhibit outstanding subjects that have both educational and entertainment values, and which are at the same time beyond criticism. Such institutions are advised to approach the manager of the local moving picture theatre, who is usually very willing to accept suggestions in selecting films for his program, if he has the assurance of endorsement and assistance from local schools, churches and societies. Sometimes the schools arrange to rent the theatre and sell their own tickets for the benefit of a school fund. May we expect your kind order?[44]

In addition to his efforts in the area of educational films, and in establishing links with schools and universities, Kleine had significant dealings with the federal government. For example, he distributed films during WWI to the American troops in their stateside camps as they prepared for deployment to Europe. Together with Thomas Edison, he distributed a film promoting the war effort, *The Unbeliever* (1918), which was highly successful in recruiting Marines. He was active in the Chicago area in raising money for war bonds, testified before Congress on various occasions and was invited to join a number of government committees dealing with the film industry.

In sum, Kleine's prominence as a distributor makes him an attractive subject for further study. Although I have only suggested here a few topics worthy of consideration, the extensive collection of his papers housed at the Library of Congress beckons as a rich source for understanding the role that distribution plays in the establishment of the film industry in the United States in the first three decades of the twentieth century.

Notes

1. Louella O. Parsons, 'In and Out of Focus', *The Morning Telegraph*, 12 August 1923, 4.
2. William Uricchio and Roberta E. Pearson, 'Italian Spectacle and the US Market', *Cinéma sans frontiers 1896–1918. Images Across Borders. Aspects de l'internationalité dans le cinéma mondial: représentations, marchés, influences et réception. Internationality in World Cinema: Representations, Markets, Influences and Reception* (Quebec: Nuit Blanche Editeur, 1995), 95–105.
3. Paolo Cherchi Usai, 'Un americain à la conquete de l'Italie: George Kleine à Grugliasco, 1913–1914, (Première Partie: histoire), *Archives*. vol. IV, nn.22–23 (avril-mai 1989): 1–20; 'Un americain à la conquete de l'Italie: George Kleine à Grugliasco, 1913–1914 (Deuxième Partie: Documents), *Archives*. vol. IV, no. 26–27 (novembre–décembre 1989): 1–20. See also John P. Welle, 'The Last Days of Italian Silent Film: George Kleine's Correspondence with Henrietta Delforno and the Crisis of the 1920s', in Antonio Vitti (ed.) *Incontri con il cinema italiano* (Caltanisetta: Sciascia Editore, 2003), 45–68.
4. Charles Musser, *The Emergence of Cinema: The American Screen to 1907* (Berkeley and London: University of California Press, 1990).
5. Eileen, Bowser, *The Transformation of Cinema, 1907–1915* (Berkeley and London: University of California Press, 1990).
6. Richard Abel, *The Red Rooster Scare: Making Cinema American, 1900–1910* (Berkeley and London: University of California Press, 2000).
7. Maria Adriana Prolo, *Storia del cinema muto italiano* (Milan: Poligono Società Editrice, 1951); Gian Piero Brunetta, *Storia del cinema italiano: Il Cinema muto 1895–1929* (Rome: Editori Riuniti, 1979); Aldo Bernardini, *Cinema muto italiano*, 3 vols. (Bari: Laterza, 1980).

8. Vittorio Martinelli and Aldo Bernardini, (eds), *Il cinema muto italiano 1911. I film degli anni d'oro* (Turin: Nuova ERI, 1996), *Il cinema muto italiano1912. I film degli anni d'oro* (Turin: Nuova ERI, 1995), *Il cinema muto italiano1913. I film degli anni d'oro* (Turin: Nuova ERI, 1994), *Il cinema muto italiano1914. I film degli anni d'oro* (Turin: Nuova ERI, 1993).

9. Harriet Harrison and Nicola Mazzanti, 'La collezione George Kleine alla Library of Congress', in Renzo Renzi (ed.), *Sperduto nel buio: il cinema muto italiano e il suo tempo (1905–1930)* (Bologna: Cappelli editore, 1991), 159–169.

10. Kristin Thompson, *Exporting Entertainment: America in the World Film Market 1907–34* (London: BFI, 1985), 17.

11. Ibid, 25.

12. Uricchio and Pearson, 'Italian Spectacle', 101.

13. Ibid., 101.

14. For a thorough and detailed analysis of the discourses and practices surrounding the social function of cinema as it emerges in the United States see Lee Grieveson, *Policing Cinema: Movies and Censorship in Early-Twentieth-Century America* (Berkeley, Los Angeles, London: University of California Press, 2004).

15. George Kleine, 'Selig Report', 1–10, Container 26, Historical File, George Kleine Collection, Manuscripts Division, Library of Congress, Washington, DC.

16. Ibid., 6.

17. Ibid., 6.

18. Aldo Bernardini, 'An Industry in Recession: The Italian Film Industry 1908–1909', *Film History* 3.4 (1989): 341.

19. William Uricchio and Roberta E. Pearson, 'Constructing the Audience: Competing Discourses of Morality and Rationality During the Nickelodeon Period', *Iris*, n. 17 (Autumn 1994): 44–45.

20. George Kleine, 'Selig Report', 7–8.

21. William Uricchio and Roberta A. Pearson, *Reframing Culture: The Case of the Vitagraph Quality Films* (Princeton: Princeton UP, 1993), 5.

22. Bowser, *Transformation of Cinema*, 71.

23. Uricchio and Pearson, *Reframing Culture*, 6.

24. Kleine, 'Selig Report', 9–10.

25. 'The discredit attached to the early cinema in other countries was non-existent in Italy, where the cinema attracted attention from the elite at a much earlier stage.' Pierre Leprohon, *The Italian Cinema*, trans. Roger Greaves and Oliver Stallybrass (New York and Washington: Praeger Publishers, 1972), 15.

26. Bernardini, *Cinema muto* II, 206. My translation. Unless otherwise noted, all translations in this article are my own.

27. Ibid., 206–207.

28. Rita Horwitz, 'George Kleine and the Early Motion Picture Industry', in *The George Kleine Collection of Early Motion Pictures in the Library of Congress: A Catalog*, (eds) Rita Horwitz and Harriet Harrison with the Assistance of Wendy White (Washington: Library of Congress, 1980), xxii.

29. Kleine to Cines, 12 February 1912, Container 7, Cines, George Kleine Collection, Manuscripts Division, Library of Congress, Washington, DC.

30. Ibid.

31. Ibid.

32. Ibid.

33. Ibid.

34. Ibid.

35. George Kleine to Cines, 14 February 1912. Container 7, Cines, George Kleine Collection, Manuscripts Division, Library of Congress, Washington, DC.

36. Kleine to Cines, 12 February 1912, emphasis added.

37. Kleine to Cines, 14 February 1912.

38. Ibid.

39. Ibid.

40. Uricchio and Pearson, 'Constructing the Audience', 47.

41. Bowser, 38.

42. George Kleine, *Moving Picture World*, 6 November 1909, 641, as cited by Grieveson, 272, no. 160.

43. See Richard Koszarski, 'The Better Films Movement', *An Evening's Entertainment: the Age of the Silent Feature Picture 1915–1928* (Berkeley, Los Angeles, London: University of California Press, 1990), 208–210.

44. George Kleine, undated letter, Container 4, Better and Highbrow Film Movements, 1914–23, George Kleine Collection, Manuscripts Division, Library of Congress, Washington, DC.

Film colour and national cinema before WWI: Pathécolor in the United States and Great Britain

Charles O'Brien

Carleton University, Ottawa, Canada

This brief paper situates film-colour practice during the years prior to WWI in the context of the distribution of Pathé's stencil-colour films in the United States. The examination centers on the following questions: What, from a distribution and marketing perspective, were the key distinctions among the period's various colour processes? Given that film-colour techniques at the time were more advanced and more widely used in Europe than in the United States, how did such techniques differentiate European films on the US film market for promotional purposes? What circumstances, industrial and aesthetic, allowed US film manufacturers during the early 1910s, in response to the American film audience's evident preference for colour films, especially Pathécolor, to promote orthochromatic black-and-white as a viable alternative?

The examination centers on references to film colour in articles, film reviews, and advertisements in the American and British film-trade press between 1910 and 1914. The focus is on forces and conditions specific to the US film market that allowed film colour to evolve during the early 1910s from an attribute of quality filmmaking associated largely with the Pathé company to a distinguishing feature of European as opposed to American cinema. The focus evolves through a comparative analysis that juxtaposes film-colour discussion in the American publication *Moving Picture World* with analogous discussion in *The Bioscope*, the important London-based film-trade weekly. The comparative inquiry is intended to illuminate the distinctiveness of the film-colour situation in the United States during the early 1910s, when aesthetic differences between the stencil colour employed by Pathé and the orthochromatic black and white adopted recently by American film manufacturers came to serve as alternative norms for film-image quality.

National film style circa 1910

The notion that film style might be understood in terms of national categories appears to have taken form as early as 1907, when critics in the new film-trade press began distinguishing American from European films.[1] As Richard Abel shows in his book *The Red Rooster Scare*, film-industry discussions of film colour provided a forum of sorts for articulating the American film industry's nationalization during the late aughts, its formation as a self-consciously national entertainment, whose narratives and visual style could be taken to reflect distinctly American concerns.[2] The preliminary research presented in this paper into national-cinema discussion in the American film-trade press of the early 1910s situates the aesthetics of film colour relative to the international film trade. At that time, American producers – aided by American lawmakers, civic reformers, and foreign policy-makers – were engaging in distribution practices whose effect was to reduce significantly Pathé's share of the American film market. For instance, the General Film Company, the important distributor licensed by the Motion Picture Patents Company, implemented a policy of releasing in the US only a limited number of Pathé's European-made films, thus forcing Pathé in 1911 to open distribution outlets in the United States for the purpose of distributing its popular Pathécolor productions.[3] Moreover, as discussed below, Pathé advertised these colour films in a way that amounted to a reversal of its marketing strategy in the United States during the preceding decade: whereas Pathé had worked since 1903 to associate its name with its achievements in film colour, by 1912 it began marketing its colour films in the United States surreptitiously, omitting references to the Pathé name in its trade-press advertisements for its colour films. The project of reconstructing the history of film colour thus entails a significant archeological component, whereby attention is directed as much to gaps and silences in the historical record as to the record itself.

Pathé as world leader in film colour

Accounts of film colour in the film-trade press of the early 1910s were conditioned by the high-stakes struggle between American and European producers and distributors over the valuable American film market, which in 1910 reportedly encompassed some one-fourth of the world's total number of movie theatres. A consequential development in that struggle occurred in 1910, when editorialists for *The Moving Picture World* began promoting a photographic norm for motion-picture image quality as an alternative to Pathécolor. The campaign in favour of the photographic alternative presupposed that American film manufacturers lacked the patented stencil technology and other colour-related industrial resources needed to meet the Pathécolor standard. Thus, instead of countering Pathécolor with an analogous American stencil process, editorialists for *The Moving Picture World* worked to alter the frame of comparison altogether. Opting to make an aesthetic virtue out of economic necessity, *The Moving Picture World* pushed for an alternative, photographic approach to the film image, founded on the use of new, orthochromatic motion-picture film stock. Major American film companies such as Biograph adopted orthochromatic film relatively quickly, to the point that within a few years the new stock came to define the look of the American cinema.

In altering the field of film-image aesthetics, the American cinema's upgraded, orthochromatic image affected Pathé's established central position in the North American film market – a position linked to Pathé's achievement in film colour. This position first took form as early as 1903, when the titles of all Pathé films – including comedies and other genres typically released in black and white – came tinted a saturated red, thus establishing the company's 'red rooster' logo as the first and most prominent of film trademarks, as Richard Abel has shown.[4] By 1907, Pathé's films were estimated to dominate the American film market, comprising some 60 to 70 percent of the film footage screened in the United States. In establishing the Pathé company's strong market profile in the US, colour techniques appear to have played a key role, with Pathé's large volume of bright polychrome films defining the company's high-quality status. 'Pathé, of course, leads the world in artificial coloring', *The Moving Picture World* acknowledged in 1911.[5]

Essential to this leading position was Pathé's patented stencil-colour process – the world's only industrialized motion-picture colour technology capable of producing a brilliant multi-colour image comparable to hand-coloured magic lantern slides of the finest quality. For American film audiences of the time, Pathé's stencil-coloured films offered viewing pleasure unavailable from the majority of American-made films, which featured straight, photographic black-and-white, bolstered, at best, by familiar mono-chromatic methods of tinting and toning. In contrast, Pathé's stencil-coloured films – made with three separate stencils, thus enabling colour combinations producing the full range of primary and complementary hues – yielded an image whose brilliant polychromaticity was akin to that of the most spectacular of the multi-coloured illustrated song slides, which enjoyed a new vogue in American film exhibition during the early 1910s.[6] Other companies' films may come tinted and toned, but Pathé's were polychromatic in the artisanal tradition of Méliès and the magic lantern.

Used for the company's most expensive productions – including showcase stencil-colour spectacles such as *The Golden Beetle* (1907) – stencil-colouring set an aesthetic standard out of reach for other film manufacturers, who lacked Pathé's patented technology, the extraordinary economy of scale of its production operation, and its colour-related expertise.[7] By 1910 Pathé's stencil-colour films had raised the stakes within the field of image aesthetics so that a marketing distinction was made not only between colour and black-and-white but between the multi-coloured image unique to Pathécolor and the monochromatic methods of tinting and toning relied on by American film manufacturers.[8] A formidable challenge faced the Americans, who lacked the technology for large-scale polychrome motion-picture production, not to mention the industrial know-how. Unable to produce comparable stencil-colour films, American film companies, with the support of film-industry journalists, opted to change the rules of the game by promoting a competing norm of film-image quality – an alternative aesthetic, as it were – grounded on the realism of an improved photo-graphic monochrome.[9] Exemplary here was the American cinema's central genre of the 1910s, the western, made on location in the American Southwest, and, in the celebrated cases, in a manner evocative of fine contemporary still photography.[10]

The orthochromatic alternative

The colour/black-and-white difference as manifest in the film press of the early 1910s must be seen as an ideological by-product of the early film industry's dog-eat-dog capitalism, fueled by the feature-film boom of the early 1910s. But it was also more than that, in that it referred to a genuine phenomenological distinction between artificial and photographic colour. A defining impression of applied colour – including not only stenciled films but also those that were tinted or hand-coloured – was colour's evident role in mediating the viewer's perception of the film image. Shimmering on the image's photographic surface rather than appearing organic to the representation, applied colour seemed supplemental and decorative, as if brushed onto the movie image's photographic surface like a layer of paint. In some cases, the brush-like texture of applied colour seemed phenomenologically continuous with much of Western art history, as Pathé's colour-related promotional material had been keen to stress. In Pathé's ads in Great Britain, for instance, the stenciled image's painterly character was routinely invoked from 1910 through 1913. For instance, according to an ad in *The Bioscope* for the Pathé production *The Smuggler's Wife*: 'The settings and colouring are exquisitely beautiful, and might have come from the brush of a master painter'.[11] Likewise, according to a 1913 London edition of *Pathé Cinema Journal*: 'The Pathécolor is to the moving picture what modern hand-coloured engravings are to photogravures of the best-known works of modern artists'.[12]

During this same period, the situation regarding Pathé's advertising differed significantly in the United States, where producers and film journalists extolled the 'realism' of American film 'photography', and Pathé evidently came to regard Pathécolor's association with the hand-painted tradition as problematic. From the standpoint of the stress in the American film culture of the 1910s on film's possibilities for realist representation à la photography, the familiar virtue of high-quality applied colour – its hand-made character – showed up as a representational defect. In some cases, applied colour seemed to subvert the photographic basis of the motion-picture image, as if it were somehow at odds with the essential properties of film form. As one survey of artificial film-colour processes explained, 'The lack of correct imitation of nature is mainly owing to the fact that an object in such a picture shows as black or grey overlaid with tint and not as colour more or less deep in tone'.[13] This sense that applied colour amounted to a coating added onto a photographic image informed the occasional denigration in *Moving Picture World* during the early 1910s of tinting – the preferred colour technique of the American motion picture manufacturers – as when tinting's inevitable reduction of photographic contrast was said to conceal cinematographic defects rather than to serve properly artistic purposes.[14] In this context, early photographic colour processes – such as, most notably, Kinemacolor, which drew much interest in the English-language film press of the early 1910s – offered the promise of a naturalism unavailable to applied colour of any sort, including Pathécolor.

The promotion in *The Moving Picture World* of a singularly photographic norm of cinema-image quality did not refer to motion-picture 'photography' in the customary, American sense, but rather to the vastly improved tonal range of the new orthochromatic film stock. Sensitive to yellow, green, and ultramarine portions of the light spectrum rather than to blue alone, orthochromatic stock yielded a detailed, sculpted image noticeably superior to ordinary black and white.[15] Orthochromatic stock made blond heroines looked light-haired rather than dark – and open skies showed the shadings of clouds rather than appearing uniformly bleached and empty. Beginning in late 1910, prior to the commercial availability of orthochromatic stock for motion pictures, *The Moving Picture World* editorialized in favour of the universal adaptation of orthochromatic film within the American film industry, and published articles detailing how to chemically alter – how to 'colour sensitize' – ordinary black-and-white motion-picture stock so as to render it orthochromatic.[16]

What had looked like a defect of the American motion picture – what one British reviewer referred to as 'the chalky coldness of black and white photography'– now, with the benefit of orthochromatic treatment, provided the aesthetic benefit of unprecedented realism.[17] According to an editorial in *The Moving Picture World* of December 1910: 'Orthochromaticism, that is, correct tone rendering, [...] should be the basis of the picture of the future – the pictorial moving picture, not the merely photographic moving picture – the black and white or soot and whitewash, that every American manufacturer, almost without exception, is content to put on the market'.[18] In the face of the evident gain in realism, one trade-press editorialist predicted that once the film industry adopted orthochromatic film, 'the black and white picture will be relegated to obscurity'.[19]

The contrast drawn between orthochromatic film and black-and-white puzzles an observer today, when it is difficult for the orthochromatic films of the early 1910s to show up as anything but straight black-and-white. Nonetheless, during the 1910s, orthochromatic film was touted as what might be called a quasi-colour process.[20] Although technically monochromatic, the dramatic increase in spectral sensitivity, evident in the expanded gray range, made the orthochromatic image *seem* polychromatic.[21] Orthochromatic motion-picture film also invited comparison to experimental cinematographic colour processes such as Kinemacolor, based also upon the chemical alteration of the silver compounds in the film emulsion. This shared history of photochemical experimentation and discovery between orthochromatic film and natural-colour processes such as Kinemacolor opened the way during the years prior to WWI for seeing orthochromatic film as a quasi-natural-colour technique, and hence as ontologically distinct from established black-and-white cinematography.[22]

Film colour and the practice of "branding"

The large volume and uniform quality of Pathé's colour films conditioned Pathé's pre-eminence in the film-colour field, to the point that in the United States circa 1910 film colour of the highest grade had become associated largely with the Pathé brand. In contrast to the many companies using colour in an ad hoc fashion, for a limited number of copies of a few exceptional films, as budgets and contracts allowed, Pathé's stencil-coloured films were produced at their own factory and distributed regularly in large batches of hundreds of copies.[23] At the Pathé plant in Vincennes, some 400 employees were estimated to be involved exclusively in stenciling and in other sorts of film-colour work.[24] Given stencil colour's high labour costs, the large operation was an economic requirement: Pathé's coloured films rented for more than their black-and-white versions, but only slightly more; thus, colour prints in big numbers were needed to recoup the production costs. According to a 1913 survey of film-colour practice in the London *Times*, Pathé would make stencils for a film only if it expected to release at least 200 colour copies.[25] With thousands of stencil-coloured Pathé films in circulation worldwide during the late aughts, the stencil-coloured image became the company's colour trademark, as was evident in Pathé's routine stress on colour in its advertisements, and also in attractive promotional brochures, which included 'coloured insets reproduced in the correct colours of the film pictures'.[26]

In the context of this history of brand promotion Pathé's advertisements in the trade press during 1912 signal a radical change in Pathé's approach to marketing its films in the United States. In short, after nearly a decade during which Pathé continually drew critical acclaim for its achievements in film colour, the company deliberately reversed its longstanding practice of using colour to 'brand' its products, and now promoted its stencil-coloured films without ever mentioning the Pathé name. Advertisements appearing in *The Moving Picture World* suggest the extent of the change. While highlighting the topic of film colour, and proclaiming the superiority of European-made coloured films, the advertisements include no reference either to the Pathé name or to the company's trademark rooster logo.[27] The only clue to the company's identity appeared in the journal's index, which, in fine print, 'out-ed' C.G.P.C. as Pathé-Frères.[28] Pathé's colour films continued to appeal to North-American film audiences, but as the company's new, surreptitious marketing suggests, rather than enhance Pathé's effectiveness in the United States, as it had during the previous decade, the Red Rooster label had become a marketing burden.[29]

Indicative of the increased importance to film-image aesthetics of national categories, the C.G.P.C. ads of 1912 invoke the same style difference recently formulated in the American film-trade press, associating layered artificial colour with European cinema and direct orthochromatic photography with American. The C.G.P.C. ads thus implicitly acknowledge that stencil colour no longer represented the one-and-only norm of technical-aesthetic quality but rather a uniquely European conception of film art. In this regard, the text of a C.G.P.C. advertisement of November 1912 is explicit: 'C.G.P.C. films are made up of ideas conceived in Europe, played in Europe, Asia, and

Australia and embody all the scenic wonders of the old world. They are a welcome relief to the monotony of an all American program.'[30] As a sign of the new relevance of national categories to film marketing, the text is worth quoting further:

'There is a peculiar similarity in all American productions which cannot be helped. American players *think* the same way and as a consequence *act* the same way. America cannot lend to the manufacturers of films the scenic beauties of the ancient castles and ruins for settings which abound in Europe. American players cannot play the same scene in the same way European actors would play it.'

Texts such as this suggest the company's embattled position in the wake of American film culture's recent nationalization. After dominating American motion-picture programs just a few years before, Pathé now promoted its coloured films by encouraging exhibitors to infuse 'variety' into film programs that otherwise would be entirely American-made and hence monochromatic.[31]

By 1913, in the wake of the proliferation of orthochromatic motion pictures, circumstances regarding film aesthetics had evolved to the point that it had become possible not just to praise certain black-and-white films but to prefer them over applied-colour alternatives. For instance, in a review of *Ivanhoe* (1913), produced by Herbert Brennon for the Imperial Film Company, the critic commented as follows on 'the perfection of the photography': 'In a picture of this kind, one is apt to regret the absence of colour, but Mr. Palmer, who took the pictures, possesses […] the eye of an artist, and, as a result, the lack of colour is almost rendered unnoticeable by the very beautiful effects of light and shade'.[32] Commentary regarding orthochromatic film's artistic potential often centered on night scenes. In May 1913, for example, *The Bioscope* noted 'a growing tendency amongst producers to rely less upon toning for night scenes, and more upon natural arrangements of light and shade'.[33] Likewise, the five-reel Danish film *Sealed Orders* (Dansk Biograf, 1913) was praised in the same journal for 'its wonderful night effects produced in an entirely natural manner'.[34]

Conclusion

The new enthusiasm in *The Bioscope* for the photographic aesthetic would seem to point to a significant shift within the film-aesthetic field, whereby the polychromatic painterly norm exemplified by Pathécolor became forever displaced by the new norm of orthochromatic monochrome. The project here has been to begin to bring this film-aesthetic shift into focus as an object of film-historical study. Still, it is necessary to stress that much additional research remains to be done, particularly in the face of the historiographical consequences of stencil colour's near disappearance upon France's entry into the war, which ended Pathé's mass-production of stencil-coloured films. In light of the teleological and retrospective tendency of the established historiography of film, stencil colouring's rapid decline as a viable national-film technique helps explain film colour's marginal status within silent-film historiography today, just as it underscores the enduring need to examine the cinema prior to World War One in terms of period-specific forces and conditions, i.e. in its own terms rather than in those of later times.

Notes

1. See Tom Gunning, 'Notes and Queries about the Year 1913 and Film Style: National Style and Deep Staging', *1895* (October 1993): 194–204.

2. See R. Abel, *The Red Rooster Scare: Making American Cinema American, 1900–1910* (Berkeley and Los Angeles: University of California Press, 1999).

3. See Eileen Bowser, *The Transformation of Cinema, 1907–1915* (Berkeley and Los Angeles: University of California, 1990), 218.

4. In R. Abel, *The Red Rooster Scare*.

5. In 'Toning and Tinting as an Adjunct to the Picture', *The Moving Picture World*, v. 8, n. 11 (18 March 1911): 574.

6. See 'The Rehabilitation of the Lantern Slide', *The Moving Picture World*, v. 6, n. 3 (22 January 1910): 83.

7. American companies were rumored to be developing stencil-colour methods, but none were successfully commercialized until the Handschiegel Process of 1914. See 'Tinting and Toning as an Adjunct to the Picture': '[W]e expect soon to see stencil coloured films from an American manufacturer'.

8. See the piece on the studio facilities of the Powers Film Company, in *The Moving Picture World*, v. 6, n. 16 (23 April 1910): 637. 'The Powers Company have a very great command over the tinting, toning and developing of their positives, which are clear, strong, and vigorous pictures, whether they be in monochrome or in color.'

9. In 'Black and White Pictures: Do the Public Prefer Them?' *The Moving Picture World*, v. 7, n. 6 (19 February 1910). This editorial hopefully asserts the American public's 'preference for the black and white picture – the black and white picture, let us say, of the Biograph kind', without, however, providing evidence in support of the assertion.

10. See, for instance, the discussion of location shooting in Biograph westerns in 'Realism in Moving Pictures', *The Moving Picture World*, v. 6, n. 19 (14 May 1910): 775.

11. In *Pathé Cine Journal* [London] (4 October 1913): 36.

12. In 'About Coloured Pictures and Others', *Pathé Cinema Journal* [London], v. 1, n. 13 (27 December 1913): 50

13. In 'Colour Cinematography: Recent Advances', *The Times*, v. 8, n. 37 (3 April 1912): 23.

14. Pertinent here is Giovanna Fossati's discussion of the relevance of photographic norms to film aesthetics prior to WWI: '[T]oning was based on a principle inherent to the medium and therefore did not call for the over-imposing of an external element. This has undoubtedly influenced aesthetic judgment, both as regards cinema and photography, which often led to consider this colouring system [i.e. toning] as better suited for the artistic quality of a product.' In G. Fossati, 'When Cinema was Coloured', in *All the Colours of the World: Colours in Early Mass Media, 1900–1930* (Reggio Emilia, Italy: Ed. Diabasis, 1998), 125.

15. Ordinary, pre-orthochromatic motion-picture stock was mainly blue sensitive. For a brief history of the development of orthochromatic film, see William Broecker (ed.), *Encyclopedia of Photography* (New York: Crown, 1984), 158, 370.

16. See Thomas Bedding, 'Moving Pictures or Moving Photographs', *The Moving Picture World*, v. 6, n. 15 (23 April 1910): 592; 'Orthochromatic Film for Moving Pictures', *The Moving Picture World*, v. 8, n. 1 (7 January 1911): 16; and 'Clouds in the Picture', *The Moving Picture World*, v. 8, n. 8 (25 February 1911): 401. Certain of these accounts suggest that orthochromatic film amounted to a variant of toning, or vice versa.

17. The quotation appears in a review of a two-reel film released in Pathé's Artistic Series: 'The God of the Sun', *The Bioscope*, v. 16, n. 4 (25 July 1912): 291.

18. See, for instance, 'The Picture of the Future: Orthochromaticism and What It Means', *The Moving Picture World*, v. 7, n. 25 (17 December 1910): 1397–1398.

19. In 'Black and White Pictures: Do the Public Prefer Them?'

20. Just as orthochromatic black-and-white captured formerly elusive yellow, green, and blue sections of the colour spectrum, Kinemacolor required the invention of a film stock 'which in ordinary sunlight is sensitive to colour waves from the brightest of violets to the darkest of reds'. In a Kinemacolor promotional brochure reproduced in Roderick T. Ryan, *A History of Motion Picture Colour Technology* (London and New York: Focal Press, 1977), 242. Panchromatic film, sensitive to the entire colour spectrum, with no colour "blindness", was introduced for still photography circa 1906 but would not be adopted for motion-picture use until the mid-1920s.

21. See William P. Herbst, 'Quantity Versus Quality', *The Moving Picture World*, v. 6, n. 16 (23 April

1910): 652; and also J.M.B., 'Éclair Photography', *The Moving Picture World*, v. 8, n. 2 (14 January 1911): 71. 'The light is so good that practically every branch, not to say every leaf, is seen in relief.' Éclair attributed 'the delicate detail and realistic tone qualities of our domestic and imported films' to its superior laboratory work. See also the Éclair ad in *The Moving Picture World*, v. 12, n. 1 (6 April 1911): 7. 'No chalky faces! No glaring highlights! No harsh blacks!' As these references suggest, orthochromatic film was also employed by European companies, and may have amounted to a variant of toning.

22. On the photo-chemical discoveries that since the 1970s opened the way for the development of colour photography, see W. Broecker, ed., *Encyclopedia of Photography*, 540.

23. Other companies besides Pathé used stencil colour during this period – notably Gaumont, Cines, and Ambrosio – but their work 'never reached the level of sophistication of Pathé'. In Giovanna Fossati, 'When Cinema was Coloured', 124.

24. On stencil-colour work at Pathé's Vincennes plant, see Gert Koshofer, *Color: Die Farben des Films* (West Berlin: Spiess, 1988); and the interview with cinematographer Arthur Kingston in Kevin Brownlow, *The Parade's Gone By* (New York: Knopf, 1968).

25. In 'Colour Cinematography: Recent Advances', *The Times*, v. 8, n. 37 (3 April 1912): 23. 'Except when the edition is a large one, say 200 copies of the film, stenciling is not resorted to, as the extra price charged over the ordinary black and white film is only one penny per foot.'

26. In 'Pathé's Latest Coloured Booklet', *The Bioscope* (25 January 1912): 221.

27. An explanation may lie in pressures imposed on American exhibitors. According to one source, referring specifically to the years 1910–1913, 'a great many exhibitors [in the United States] who had wished to show colour films had been deterred by threats that, if they did, their supplies of black-and-white films would be discontinued'. In David B. Thomas, *The First Color Motion Pictures* (London: Her Majesty's Stationary Office, 1983): 26.

28. According to Eileen Bowser, the mandate of C.G.P.C., which stood for 'Compagnie Générale Pathé Cinématographique', was to handle distribution of the company's European films in North America. See E. Bowser, *The Transformation of Cinema*, 287n.

29. On the popularity of Pathécolor, see, for instance, Louis Reeves Harrison, 'Studio Saunterings', *The Motion Picture World*, v. 11, n. 11 (23 March 1912): 944. '[O]ne of the greatest things the Pathé brothers have done is that of presenting colored scenes and plays so that millions may delight in the gratification of what seems to be a universal love of beauty.' The surreptitious approach of C.G.P.C. anticipates that of the Eclectic company, an independent importing firm set up by Pathé in April 1913, after Pathé had 'ran into difficulty distributing its European features in the important American market because the General Film system limited the number of features it could issue and the profits it could make'; moreover, 'Pathé's ownership of this company was not openly acknowledged in the American trade journals until the following year, when Eclectic began domestic production at the Pathé plant and with the Pathé staff'. In E. Bowser, *The Transformation of Cinema*: 218.

30. In *The Moving Picture World*, v. 14, n. 8 (23 November 1912): 744. Other ads for C.G.P.C. appear in the following issues of *The Moving Picture World*: v. 13, n. 12 (21 September 1912): 1147; v. 13, n. 10 (7 September 1912): 947; v. 15, n. 1 (4 January 1913): 17; and v. 14, n. 12 (21 December 1912): 1157.

31. Film reviews in *The Bioscope* during 1912 routinely commented on the quality of film colouring, regardless of whether the films were made by Pathé or by another company; in contrast, reviews in *The Moving Picture World* rarely, if ever, mentioned a film's colour. Did the omission reflect a lack of colour films in circulation in North America? Or did it derive from an editorial policy prohibiting commentary on colour quality altogether, so as to avoid disadvantaging American manufacturers relative to their European competitors?

32. In 'Ivanhoe', *The Bioscope*, v. 20, n. 355 (24 July 1913): 293.

33. In 'The Art of the Camera', *The Bioscope*, v. 19, n. 343 (8 May 1913): 431.

34. In 'Sealed Orders', *The Bioscope*, v. 22, n. 381 (29 January 1914): 491.

PART II

NETWORKS:
Regional distribution and
the problem of the national

La distribution dans la région Lyonnaise: entre spécificités locales et stratégies nationales (1908–1914)

Renaud Chaplain

France

L'analyse de la circulation des films bute sur deux problèmes. Le premier tient à la rareté des sources: la programmation des salles de cinéma est, dans la presse locale, parcellaire et incomplète, ce qui en interdit toute analyse systématique. Le second problème, plus gênant encore, est celui de l'identification des films et des éditeurs. Nous avons, en France, la chance de disposer d'un catalogue qui recense tous les films de fiction produits en France de 1908 à 1918. Cet outil de travail incomparable, établi par Raymond Chirat,[1] donne pour la plupart des films le nom du distributeur ainsi que la date de sortie parisienne.

Cet exposé est le fruit de la comparaison de ces données avec la programmation des salles de Lyon et de sa région ; il sera donc essentiellement consacré – faute de mieux – à la distribution des films français, ce qui limite évidemment la portée de ses conclusions.[2] Néanmoins, la situation des maisons de distribution françaises permet déjà de questionner les notions de diffusion nationale et de pluralité des publics, en dégageant deux temps forts de l'histoire de la circulation des films. Déterminée dans un premier temps par les exploitants locaux, elle est progressivement canalisée par les distributeurs eux-mêmes, qui imposent alors une certaine image du cinéma.

Une distribution balbutiante: la prédominance des exploitants locaux (1908–1911)

Lorsque Charles Pathé décide en octobre 1907 de substituer à la vente de ses films un système de location, Lyon compte cinq salles exclusivement consacrées aux projections cinématographiques dont les programmes, déjà, sont renouvelés chaque semaine. Les propriétaires de ces salles se procurent leurs films par leurs propres moyens, en piochant ici et là dans les catalogues des grandes maisons d'édition, sans être dépendants de l'une ou l'autre. Implantés dans le centre-ville et s'adressant à un public averti, leurs choix dénotent un souci constant de la nouveauté: les films qu'ils programment n'ont en général pas plus de 2 mois de retard sur leur sortie parisienne. Les nouvelles règles de la location, qui imposent le renouvellement de la programmation, ne marquent donc pas, pour ces pionniers de l'exploitation, une rupture profonde. Bien au contraire, ce sont eux qui vont s'imposer comme les principaux acteurs de la circulation des films dans la région.

En effet, les maisons d'édition (à l'exception notable de la société Pathé, sur laquelle je reviendrais) n'ont pas sur Lyon de succursale ni de représentant local, et cela jusqu'en 1912. Or, à partir de 1910, le nombre de salles se multiplie dans la ville, notamment dans les quartiers excentrés. Les nouveaux exploitants, issus des classes populaires ou pratiquant une deuxième activité,[3] n'ont ni le temps ni les moyens de faire de fréquents aller-retours à Paris pour sélectionner leur programmation. En l'absence de maisons d'édition sur place, ils se tournent alors probablement vers les exploitants des salles du centre-ville, qui, forts de leur expérience, s'improvisent eux-mêmes distributeurs. Ils s'appuient pour cela sur les stocks de films qu'ils ont pu se constituer tant que la vente des programmes était encore possible. Stocks qui peuvent être conséquents: lorsque l'un de ces exploitants fait faillite en 1917, il vend son fonds de commerce et pas moins de 100.000 mètres de films,[4] ce qui correspond à plus de soixante heures de projection, soit six mois d'exploitation complète. La circulation de ces films achetés, qui n'obéit à aucun calendrier, souligne le caractère contingent de la distribution.

Les grands exploitants lyonnais, désormais distributeurs, continuent bien sûr de faire venir de Paris les dernières nouveautés. Mais les distribuent-ils, et si oui, selon quelles règles ? La recherche à l'échelon régional ne peut seule parvenir à déchiffrer les rapports entre les maisons d'édition nationales et les exploitants locaux. De nombreuses questions restent donc sans réponse.[5] On peut tout de même les poser: les exploitants ne sont-ils pas amenés à tisser des relations privilégiées avec un distributeur en particulier, devenant de fait un représentant local ? S'ils sont indépendants, ce que la programmation de leurs salles semble démontrer, quelle latitude leur est-elle concédée par les maisons d'édition ? Quel est leur rayon d'action ? Quelles stratégies mettent-ils en place ? Entre la circulation des films accumulés depuis des années et celle des nouveaux programmes se pose évidemment la question de la programmation des petites salles, et de la qualité et de la fraîcheur des films qui y passent. Question qui reste ouverte.

Quoiqu'il en soit, l'absence des distributeurs dans la région ménage un espace aux initiatives individuelles, perceptibles dans l'existence de circuits de distribution locaux. Le plus significatif est à Lyon celui de la diffusion des films italiens, institué par l'un des pionniers de l'exploitation lyonnaise, Alexandre Rota, lui-même italien et distributeur indépendant. De nombreux films des compagnies turinoises Itala ou Ambrosio passent en effet dans son cinéma, parfois une semaine à peine après leur sortie à Turin.[6] C'est le cas du film *Le nozze di oro* (Les noces d'or, 1911) sorti à Turin le 27 octobre 1911 et projeté à Lyon dés le 3 novembre. En l'absence d'accords internationaux de distribution, Alexandre Rota importe sans doute lui-même les films d'Italie – de Lyon à Turin, le trajet est rapide – et c'est par lui, vraisemblablement, que le cinéma italien occupe une place aussi prépondérante dans les autres salles de la ville. Près du tiers des films documentaires tournés à l'étranger qui passent à Lyon est italien ou concerne l'Italie. Les Lyonnais peuvent ainsi assister aux exercices de la cavalerie italienne et rire aux gags de Tontolini ou de Zanetto. Il est remarquable d'ailleurs que tous ces films – documentaires ou fictions – en provenance de la péninsule ne soient jamais projetés à Saint-Etienne,[7] accréditant l'image d'une circulation particulièrement atomisée.

Les spécificités locales engendrées par la liberté d'initiative des exploitants locaux semble donc interdire toute idée de circulation nationale des films. Une maison de distribution, toutefois, fait exception à la règle: la société Pathé.

A la différence de ses concurrentes, la maison Pathé a très tôt mesuré le rôle essentiel de l'exploitation dans la diffusion des films. Elle s'est en effet constitué dans la région lyonnaise (comme, je suppose, dans les autres régions françaises) un vaste réseau de salles de cinéma qui couvre d'abord les grandes agglomérations – Lyon en 1906, Saint-Etienne, Grenoble en 1907 – puis s'étend aux villes plus modestes.[8] Ces salles ne projettent que des films édités par Pathé, ce qui confère à la société, outre l'assurance de voir ses programmes diffusés, une position de monopole. A Villefanche s/Saône, petite ville de 10.000 habitants, la salle Pathé ouverte à la fin de l'année 1908 est ainsi la seule à fonctionner jusqu'en 1913.[9] Pendant près de cinq ans, les habitants de Villefranche ne verront donc que des films Pathé.

Grâce à son réseau d'exploitation, la société peut développer à l'échelle nationale une politique de distribution cohérente et maîtrisée. Pour comprendre celle-ci, il faut revenir sur la signification profonde de la mise en place de la location des programmes, indissociable à mon avis de la production de films artistiques, destinés à un public proche de celui du théâtre. La Société du Film d'Art en 1908, puis la Société Cinématographique des Artistes et Gens de Lettres (S.C.AG.L.) en 1909, fournissent chaque semaine des œuvres cinématographiques tirées du grand répertoire classique du théâtre et de la littérature. C'est sans doute pour promouvoir ces films, qu'elle édite, que la maison Pathé va élaborer un circuit de distribution analogue aux tournées théâtrales, inauguré à Lyon avec la projection le 6 novembre 1908 de *L'assassinat du duc de Guise*.[10] Dés lors, les grands films distribués par Pathé sortent en province avec une régularité de métronome. Jusqu'en 1913, les oeuvres projetées à Lyon ont systématiquement une à deux semaines de retard sur la sortie parisienne, et restent à l'écran une à deux semaines avant de partir vers une autre ville de la région, suivant ce qui semble être un calendrier très précis. A Béziers par exemple, les films qui passent ont invariablement quatorze à quinze semaines de retard sur Lyon en 1909, huit à neuf semaines en 1910.[11] La copie n'est certainement pas la même entre les deux villes, mais cette régularité révèle une stratégie de la diffusion des films Pathé dans les grandes villes françaises.

Cette distribution planifiée ne concerne toutefois que les centres urbains importants. Si l'on observe la programmation de la salle de Villefranche sur Saône, on constate que les films sortent indifféremment avec quatre, six ou douze mois de retard sur Lyon, pourtant située à moins de 40 kilomètres. A Saint-Etienne, la circulation est plus rapide, deux à quatre mois en moyenne en 1908–1909, mais guère plus régulière. La mise en circulation d'une seule copie pour une vaste région, qui semble être la norme, produit de fait un système d'exclusivité qui privilégie le public des grandes villes. Pour prendre un exemple symptomatique de l'inégalité géographique, un court sujet sur le carnaval de Nice de 1909, projeté à Lyon moins d'une semaine après son déroulement, passe à Saint-Etienne avec un retard de quatre mois, et à Villefranche sur Saône avec un retard de près de neuf mois.

Au sein même de l'agglomération lyonnaise, le principe d'exclusivité s'impose. Les films Pathé sont en effet très rarement diffusés dans les autres salles de la ville, et lorsqu'ils le sont, c'est avec un retard de plus d'un an. La multiplication des établissements cinématographiques à partir de 1910 ne change pas la donne. La société Pathé conserve son indépendance en ouvrant elle-même des salles dans les quartiers excentrés, trois à Lyon entre 1910 et 1913. Elle continue ainsi de maîtriser de bout en bout la diffusion de ses programmes, affichant l'image d'une distribution circonscrite à l'exploitation. Mais la multiplication des établissements n'entraîne pas celle des copies: les nouvelles salles Pathé n'obtiennent les films que plusieurs mois après leur sortie dans le centre de la ville.

En comparaison de la politique mise au point par Pathé, la situation de la société Gaumont illustre toutes les difficultés pour les éditeurs de films de se démarquer de la prédominance des exploitants. Jusqu'en 1910, les programmes Gaumont passent indifféremment dans l'une ou l'autre des salles lyonnaises, avec un retard sur la sortie parisienne qui va de deux à six mois. En 1910, le théâtre de la Scala, vaste salle de mille places, se transforme en cinéma. Gaumont va s'accorder avec son propriétaire pour diffuser ses films, qui sortent désormais à Lyon avec systématiquement quatre à six semaines de retard sur Paris. Dans le sillage de Pathé, Gaumont adopte alors à son tour un système d'exclusivité: dans les autres salles de la ville, les films passent deux à trois mois après leur sortie à la Scala.

Il n'est pas anodin que les programmes de la Scala soient alors rigoureusement les mêmes dans leur composition que les programmes qui sortent à Paris, tandis que les salles plus modestes, qui n'ont les films qu'avec quelques mois de retard, proposent une programmation bien plus éclatée. Les prémices d'une circulation nationale des films annoncent déjà une hiérarchie des exploitations. Toutefois, ce premier système d'exclusivité fonctionne ici car la maison Gaumont a à sa disponibilité une vitrine prestigieuse pour la diffusion de ses programmes. Lorsque la Scala arrête la projection des films Gaumont pendant les premiers mois de 1912, ceux-ci sortent à nouveau avec plusieurs mois de retard dans les salles plus modestes de la ville.

On le voit, les éditeurs de films sont entièrement dépendants des exploitants locaux, ce qui leur interdit de leur imposer une promotion spécifique: les films Gaumont, quelle que soit leur renommée, ne sont jamais projetés plus d'une semaine consécutive sur les écrans lyonnais, contrairement aux films Pathé qui bénéficient d'une exploitation spécifique. Jusqu'en 1912, la distribution est, dans la région lyonnaise, subordonnée à l'exploitation.

L'émergence d'une distribution contrôlée (1912–1914)

Dans le courant de l'année 1912, tout bascule. Peut-être attirées par la multiplication des salles, les grandes maisons de distribution – Gaumont, puis Aubert et l'A.G.C. (Agence Générale Cinématographique) – ouvrent des succursales à Lyon, et sont bientôt rejointes par quelques petits distributeurs locaux. Leur installation dans la région change complètement la donne et marque la véritable naissance d'une distribution indépendante, capable désormais d'influer les exploitants sur la promotion des films. Tournant capital dans la perception du cinéma en France, le renversement de situation entre exploitants et distributeurs correspond peut-être à celui du film sur le spectacle.

La première conséquence de ce bouleversement est de mettre fin à la prédominance des exploitants sur la diffusion des films. Les distributeurs, en étant sur place ou représentés (l'A.G.C. représente par exemple quatorze maisons d'édition nationales ou internationales) contrôlent eux-mêmes la distribution de leurs programmes, et n'ont plus besoin d'intermédiaires. Les grands exploitants locaux perdent donc leurs prérogatives et leur liberté d'initiative, ce qui met fin à l'existence des circuits locaux ; s'ils restent distributeurs, c'est en tant que représentant local d'une société nationale. Alexandre Rota, cantonné à la gestion de sa salle, fait quant à lui rapidement faillite.[12] Car le cinéma italien est diffusé par les maisons Aubert et A.G.C., qui ont signé des conventions avec les maisons italiennes pour la distribution de leurs programmes en France. Si l'on constate toujours à Lyon une forte proportion de films italiens, cette spécificité s'exprime désormais dans le cadre d'une distribution maîtrisée à l'échelle nationale.

La deuxième conséquence de l'arrivée des distributeurs est la libéralisation de la circulation des films. L'arrivée des maisons de distribution à Lyon s'est au départ inscrite dans le rapport distributeur/exploitant existant, où chaque distributeur est rattaché à une salle de la ville en particulier. Mais ce système cloisonné va progressivement s'ouvrir. Pathé sépare ses activités exploitation et distribution en ouvrant un nouveau local en 1913, indépendant de sa salle. A la fin de l'année, des programmes

Pathé sortent sur les écrans des salles indépendantes du centre-ville avec deux à quatre mois de retard sur Paris, quelquefois moins. La salle de la Scala, qui ne programmait que du Gaumont, accueille des films édités par Aubert ou l'A.G.C. pour la première fois en septembre 1913. Et les films Gaumont, qui ne sortaient en exclusivité qu'à la Scala, sont désormais projetés dans différentes salles de la ville. Cette libéralisation est facilitée par la normalisation des échanges. En 1912 encore, les exploitants lyonnais renouvelaient leur programme n'importe quel jour de la semaine. En 1913, le vendredi s'impose à tous.[13]

Désormais indépendants, les distributeurs peuvent faire jouer la concurrence entre les salles de la ville, et promouvoir au mieux leurs programmes. Il s'agit d'abord d'imposer à des exploitants réticents la location des grands films sur plusieurs semaines. Le premier, le célèbre *Quo vadis* (1913), reste cinq semaines à l'affiche du Royal en mai 1912. Le procédé va se généraliser dans les années 1913 et 1914 avec la présence de plus en plus forte des longs-métrages. Les distributeurs commencent aussi à mettre en place des stratégies commerciales dans la ville. En mars 1914, Gaumont réussit à programmer les trois premiers épisodes de *Fantômas* (1913–1914), pourtant déjà projetés à Lyon, dans une grande salle de spectacles une semaine avant la sortie du quatrième épisode à la Scala. Un circuit maîtrisé des films s'impose donc progressivement.

Ces nouvelles règles de la distribution n'entraîne paradoxalement pas une multiplication du nombre de copies dans la région. Les maisons d'édition ont toutes, à la suite de Pathé, privilégié une diffusion en exclusivité dans les centres des grandes agglomérations, laissant de côté quartiers et petites villes. A Lyon même, les films sont plus lents à venir de Paris, huit semaines pour la production Pathé, au lieu de deux en 1912. A Villefranche sur Saône, les habitants patientent au minimum trois mois avant de voir les grands films Gaumont qui ont été projetés à Lyon. Mais les inégalités les plus fortes concernent les salles des quartiers populaires de l'agglomération lyonnaise. En 1914, les films qui y passent datent de 1912 ou 1913 et sont en général des productions de second ordre. Les grands films, aux tarifs désormais inaccessibles aux petites salles, sont monopolisés par les grandes exploitations, qui sont les seules à pouvoir les reprendre. A la veille de la guerre, le système d'exclusivité, qui fera flores dans les années 1920, est déjà en place et génère un éclatement des publics.

Notes

1. Chirat, Raymond, *Catalogue des films français de fiction de 1908 à 1918* (Paris: Cinémathèque française, 1995).

2. Pour retrouver la programmation des salles de cinéma, je me suis servi, pour Lyon, du courrier des spectacles du journal *Lyon-Républicain* de 1908 à 1914; à Villefranche/Saône, du *Journal de Villefranche* de 1908 à 1914. J'ai pu comparer les sorties lyonnaises avec celles de Saint-Etienne par l'entremise de l'impressionnant travail de recension de Frédéric Zarch: Zarch, Fréderic, *Catalogue des films projetés à Saint-Etienne avant la première guerre mondiale* (St Etienne: Publications de l'université de St Etienne, 2000).

3. Je renvoie à mon article sur les exploitants lyonnais: Chaplain, Renaud, "Les exploitants des salles de cinéma lyonnaises, des origines à la seconde guerre mondiale", in *XXème siècle, revue d'Histoire* (juillet–septembre 2003); 19–35.

4. *Cinéjournal*, no. 477, daté du 9 mars 1918.

5. La circulation des films sur le territoire français reste en effet *terra incognita*. Un travail, comme celui réalisé à Saint-Etienne par Frédéric Zarch, cité plus haut, montre qu'une comparaison des sources locales pourrait permettre un suivi des films à l'échelon national.

6. Selon les dates de sortie indiquées dans l'ouvrage de Gili, Jean A. et Bernardini, Aldo, *Le cinéma italien de La prise de Rome à Rome ville ouverte 1905–1945* (Paris: Cinéma/Pluriel, 1986).

7. Et cela contrairement à la production Pathé ou Gaumont, dont la plupart des titres projetés à Lyon le sont à Saint-Etienne.

8. Par souci de clarté, j'ai volontairement simplifié les faits. En vérité, les salles ouvertes dans la région lyonnaise le sont par une société indépendante: la société Cinéma-Monopole, créée en juillet 1907 pour assurer la diffusion et l'exploitation de la production Pathé dans le quart sud-est de la France. Quatre autres sociétés fondées à la même époque couvrent le reste du territoire national. Voir sur le sujet l'article de Jean-Jacques Meusy dans Marie, Michel et Le Forestier, Laurent, *La firme Pathé Frères 1896–1914* (Paris: AFRHC, 2004): 21–48.

9. Archives municipales de Villefranche sur Saône, carton I 177.

10. Il est à noter que le film, qui sort à Paris le 17 novembre 1908 est projeté à Lyon deux semaines plus tôt. Point de détail, certes, mais qui pose question: la firme Pathé avait-elle besoin de tester le film avant sa "sortie mondiale"?

11. D'après la presse locale, dépouillée par la Société de Musicologie du Languedoc, et que l'on peut retrouver sur le site: http://perso.wanadoo.fr/st.musicologiedelanguedoc/c_presse.htm

12. Archives départementales du Rhône, carton P 156.

13. A l'exception notable de la Scala, dont le programme est renouvelé le lundi. Spécificité qui la place au dessus des autres salles: de par sa réputation, elle est courtisée par les distributeurs plus qu'elle ne courtise.

6

Une diffusion "nationale" ?
De la circulation d'images locales ou
nationales à Lausanne 1896–1914

Pierre-Emmanuel Jaques[1]

Lausanne, Switzerland

Si, en Suisse, la production cinématographique indigène est restée sporadique et s'est limitée à des actualités ou des vues locales avant la Première Guerre mondiale,[2] il paraît particulièrement opportun d'examiner la circulation de ces images et la place qu'on leur accorde dans l'annonce des projections ou la presse. La question est de savoir si ces images ont suscité un type de promotion particulière et si on leur a accordé une attention renforcée. Un tel examen s'appuie sur le contexte qui voit naître d'importants débats esthétiques autour de la question de l'art national. Ainsi l'historien Hans Ulrich Jost insiste sur leurs enjeux idéologiques en effectuant le lien avec l'affirmation nationale.[3] Si l'historien François Walter peut affirmer que « l'esthétisation du pays en paysage est étroitement associée à la construction de la nation »,[4] on peut alors se demander si la présence de certaines représentations cinématographiques paysagères n'a pas servi une visée nationale. L'historien de l'art Dario Gamboni parle justement d'une iconographie du « sentiment national » pour traiter des nombreuses représentations historiques illustrant des bâtiments officiels, où abondent les figures de Tell, et Christoph von Tavel intègre les images cinématographiques dans ce qu'il nomme « l'iconographie nationale » en insistant sur leur importance, particulièrement dans la période précédant la Deuxième Guerre mondiale.[5] D'autre part, la littérature voit se développer des courants régionalistes, dans l'affirmation desquels les écrivains s'opposent sur la définition d'un art local.[6] C'est aussi la période où fleurissent ces spectacles appelés *Festspiele* qui évoquent des faits et des lieux mythiques.[7] Il s'agit de poser ici les bases d'une analyse concernant la présence de telles images et d'envisager dans quelle mesure leur circulation a pu affecter une construction identitaire.[8] Il est donc assumé ici que la circulation des films ou, autrement dit, la distribution, a joué un rôle socioculturel d'importance. Cette recherche devrait être étendue à tout le pays pour être affinée et approfondie, de manière à corroborer ce qui est entrevu ici, voire, au contraire, à le démentir ou, du moins, à l'affiner.

Les premières projections lausannoises

Pour examiner la question de la présence d'images locales ou nationales pouvant contribuer à façonner un imaginaire commun, il a paru opportun de se pencher sur la diffusion des films dans une ville suisse de moyenne importance, Lausanne, représentative des évolutions affectant plus globalement le pays. Ce chef-lieu du canton de

Vaud, encore largement rural, est en pleine transformation, comme l'indique, entre autres, l'accroissement de la population.[9]

En l'absence de fonds d'archives et de documents concernant l'histoire de la distribution en Suisse, l'examen des programmes constitue une solution appropriée. La distribution est ainsi entendue comme ce qui détermine la circulation des films. Une attention toute particulière a été accordée aux images locales ou nationales dans les annonces et recensions des films à l'affiche. Il s'avérait important d'examiner si une place particulière était réservée aux productions entendues comme « suisses » et si elles avaient suscité des commentaires particuliers.

Les premières projections attestées en Suisse se sont déroulées à Genève, au moment de l'Exposition nationale de 1896 dès le 7 mai.[10] Peu après, du 3 au 19 octobre 1896 se tiennent à Lausanne les premières séances cinématographiques – annoncées comme Lumière.[11] Le premier encart paru dans la presse le 2 octobre 1896 annonce : « Plus de 500 sujets dont le voyage du Tsar. Vues lausannoises. Changement de programme tous les 3 jours. »[12]

Il paraît judicieux de prendre en considération les premières séances organisées à Lausanne en examinant la question des vues locales, en se demandant si les annonces et commentaires publiés alors n'inaugurent pas un mode que l'on retrouvera par la suite. Traitant des projections autour de 1896–97, Georges Sadoul affirme : « Un des éléments d'attraction étaient des films locaux, réalisés dans les rues de la ville où le spectacle devait avoir lieu. » L'historien français donne deux interprétations de l'effet exercé par ces tournages locaux. Il écrit : « Le public n'en venait pas moins le lendemain au spectacle dans l'espoir de se reconnaître, de se voir sur l'écran. » À cette première explication que l'on peut qualifier de plaisir de reconnaissance, Sadoul en apporte une deuxième : « Ce genre de vues avait aussi l'avantage, en montrant des paysages familiers à tous, de convaincre le grand public qu'il ne s'agissait pas d'un nouveau genre d'illusionnisme, mais de véritables photographies animées ».[13] Tout en soulignant le caractère promotionnel de cette pratique, Sadoul propose ainsi une interprétation du succès de ces séances. Il pose l'hypothèse de ce que l'on pourrait qualifier une identification symbolique des spectateurs avec des images familières, permettant de développer le sentiment d'une appartenance à une communauté locale. La reconnaissance directe d'éléments connus favoriserait aussi la croyance dans la fidélité de la reproduction et le caractère authentique des images cinématographiques.

L'examen des annonces parues à l'occasion de ces premières projections est symptomatique des stratégies publicitaires qui insistent d'une part sur la profusion de vues proposées et s'appuient sur des événements déjà largement médiatisés, comme les voyages du tsar, dont la venue en Allemagne et en France fait alors la une des journaux. Au-delà de la masse – on donne le chiffre assurément exagéré de cinq cents vues – la variété des vues proposées, corroborée par le renouvellement fréquent des programmes, est utilisée comme un argument pour attirer le public. D'autre part, dès les premières annonces sont notifiées des « Vues lausannoises », sans qu'elles soient montrées dès le début des projections. On lit dans la Gazette de Lausanne du 5 octobre 1896 : « On nous promet des choses lausannoises : le passage du bataillon de Landwehr n° 8 sur la place St-François, le marché du samedi, etc. » La Feuille d'avis de Lausanne du 8 octobre 1896 renchérit : « Vendredi soir nous aurons une surprise : des vues lausannoises. Qui donc ne voudra pas assister au curieux et amusant spectacle qu'on nous promet ? Rappelons en passant que le cinématographe est ouvert chaque jour de deux à onze heures du soir. » Ce texte est suivi, le jour d'après, par une publicité indiquant : « Aujourd'hui vendredi : Nouvelle série de sujets. Inauguration des vues lausannoises ».

Bien plus que manifester une hypothétique attente de la part d'un public, ces notices servent d'attraction, pour reprendre les termes mêmes de Sadoul. Il s'agit par la répétition de ces annonces et en fournissant des titres suffisamment précis d'attirer le public. La mention d'une *inauguration* de ces vues locales, la tournure interrogative de la phrase, destinée à interpeller lectrices et lecteurs, construisent le caractère exceptionnel de ces images. En plus de signaler la présence d'un cinématographe, ces brefs textes donnent une indication de lecture : certaines parties du spectacle et notamment celles « locales » se voient conférer un relief particulier. Dans notre perspective, on ne s'étonnera pas que figure un défilé militaire parmi ces premières vues, surtout si l'on pense au rôle fondamental accordé à l'Armée dans la construction nationale.[14] Si l'importance de ces vues doit cependant être relativisée, au vu de leur nombre limité et parce que nous ignorons la réaction du public, il convient de relever le souci de saisir des éléments familiers et pittoresques, comme une scène de marché, moment important d'échange entre la ville et la campagne, ou un défilé militaire ayant réuni de fort nombreux spectateurs.

La période foraine

À partir de 1897, la présence régulière de cinématographes est attestée à Lausanne lors des principales fêtes, notamment celles de fin d'année, à Pâques ou en juillet (Fêtes de la Navigation). Cette situation perdure jusqu'en 1912, date à laquelle la municipalité refuse d'accorder les autorisations nécessaires, la Ville arguant d'un nombre élevé de cinémas.

À défaut des programmes exacts, seules quelques lignes directrices ont pu être dégagées pour la période foraine. Deux éléments apparaissent particulièrement significatifs : l'appellation des entreprises et les annonces des projections.[15]

Un élément particulièrement révélateur concerne les dénominations des différentes installations. Dans un premier temps, elles portent quasi toutes des appellations chargées d'une consonance anglo-saxonne ou aristocratique – les appellations de Royal et Imperial figurent en grand nombre : L. Praiss est ainsi muni en 1899 d'un « American Bioscope, der echte und wirkliche Riesen-Cinématographe » qui devient en 1900 dans sa traduction française : le « Bioscope, le seul véritable cinématographe géant américain »[16] avec lequel il tourne jusqu'en Italie, comme plusieurs de ses collègues.[17] Dahlmann-Fasold dirige le *Kinematograph Royal*, Ph. Wallenda *The Imperial Vio*. On trouve encore une entreprise du nom de *The Royal Bio* en 1911, ainsi qu'un *Coliseum of England* et *The American Sun*.

Certaines entreprises adoptent au cours des années des dénominations indiquant d'emblée le caractère "national" de leur firme.[18] En 1903, J. Weber-Clément tourne avec « Le Bioscope. Cinématographe géant », qui devient trois ans plus tard : « Ciné national suisse ». Les papillons publicitaires en soulignent les dimensions (33 m. sur 12) et le nombre particulièrement élevé de places (1200). Le souci de caractériser cette société comme nationale est encore attesté par un dessin à la gouache conservé par la Cinémathèque suisse en vue d'un projet de tente, non réalisé sauf erreur, sur laquelle figure un fronton avec comme enseigne : « Cinématographe Suisse, Famille Weber ». Juste au-dessous est inscrite la devise de la Suisse « Un pour tous, tous pour un », alors que des fresques rappelant des batailles célèbres où s'illustrèrent les premiers confédérés (Laupen, Sempach, Morat) décorent les pans de la tente. Le drapeau suisse y figure en plusieurs endroits. Pour sa part, G. Hipleh-Walt jr. de Bienne parcourt le pays avec « Le Biographe Suisse » dès 1907 au moins. Les en-têtes de ses lettres insistent sur le fait qu'il réalise ses propres bandes : « Spécialités : reproductions inédites faites par l'entreprise ».[19] G. Hipleh-Walt et J. Weber-Clément privilégient donc la référence nationale aussi bien par leur dénomination, le décor de leur installation que leur programme.

La plupart des annonces insérées dans les journaux et les affichettes préservées insistent sur un aspect technique de la projection, que ce soit son absence de tremblement, sa grande taille, la présence de coloris ou de scènes à transformations. Les sujets en rapport avec l'actualité reviennent de manière récurrente et souvent avec insistance. Par ailleurs, plusieurs programmes précisent que seront présentées des vues locales, comme *Le Pont du Rhin à Bâle* ou *Place Bel-Air à Genève*, sans qu'il soit possible de déterminer leur origine. En 1905, L. Praiss annonce au terme de ses projections, fin avril : « La Suisse en Hiver » avec un contenu particulièrement détaillé qui comporte les vues suivantes : « De Coire à St-Maurice.- Gare de Davos.- Coupeurs de glace.- Patineurs à Davos.- Jeu de Banty.- Grindelwald.- Jeu de Curling.- Skis.- Toboggan.- Bobsleighs, etc, etc. » Cette insistance sur des éléments locaux se retrouve dans de nombreux autres programmes. Au dos d'une demande effectuée le 20 novembre 1907 par Dahlmann-Fasold à la ville de Lausanne figure une sélection de comptes rendus publiés dans des journaux lors de ses tournées alémaniques. Tous louent les *Natur-aufnahmen*, intégrant sous ce terme aussi bien des documentaires paysagers que des présentations d'activités industrielles. Des films comme celui relatant « eine Rettungsexpedition von Kandersteg zur Blümlisalp » (un journal de Bregenz) ou « das grosse Defilee in Bern am 13. September 1905, das Winzerfest in Vevey » (*Werdenberger Anzeiger*) suscitent l'admiration.[20]

La présence récurrente de ces sujets locaux correspond à une spécialisation de certaines tourneurs, soucieux de se distinguer de leurs concurrents par leur programmation. Ces vues réalisent une sorte de catalogue des lieux fameux et touristiques de Suisse et présentent des activités s'y déroulant, comme les escalades ou des sports d'hiver. Nombreux sont aussi les films qui se concentrent sur des aspects typiques et folkloriques. On se trouve, loin d'une assertion nationaliste, face à des images animées par un souci de pittoresque et de ravissement. Les éléments nationalistes, ressortent à nos yeux bien plus du contexte de présentation. Les dénominations des entreprises, ainsi que le décor de ces tentes, soulignaient leur caractère national de façon très manifeste. Par ailleurs, L. Praiss conclut son programme par des « groupes patriotiques ».[21] Il faut entendre par là que le spectacle se clôt par un air musical comme l'hymne national ou le Cantique suisse, ce qui renforce ce souci d'ancrer le spectacle dans un contexte patriotique. On peut se demander toutefois si la récurrence de sujets collectifs, puisant à un fonds traditionnel comme les défilés, les fêtes de gymnastique généralement mentionnées comme fédérales et les parades militaires n'ont pas joué le rôle d'amorce pour un imaginaire national.

L'installation des salles cinématographiques et la présence de vues locales

Entre 1908 et 1913, quatre salles ouvrent à Lausanne : le Modern rebaptisé Lux (1908), puis Palace (1913) ; le Lumen (1908) ; le Royal Biograph (1911) ; l'Apollo (1913),[22] auxquelles il convient d'ajouter le Kursaal, où alternent, dès 1913, spectacles scéniques et cinéma ainsi que d'autres lieux de projections plus sporadiques.[23] La plus grande des salles après sa transformation en 1911, le Lumen, abrite fréquemment des concerts et autres représentations scéniques.[24]

La disparition des programmes des cinémas, ainsi que l'imprécision des annonces dans la presse empêche la détermination exacte de la composition des séances, particulièrement au moment de l'ouverture des salles. L'examen de deux publications consacrées aux spectacles, *La Semaine à Lausanne*, qui paraît dès 1908, et de *Lausanne-Plaisirs*, publié dès 1911, ne permet de reconstituer de façon relativement précise que les programmes de la période précédant immédiatement la déclaration de la Première Guerre mondiale.[25]

L'approvisionnement en films

En l'état des recherches, la situation de la location en Suisse avant la Première Guerre s'avère encore mal connue. Outre l'achat, encore possible auprès de certaines sociétés, notamment en Allemagne, on trouve principalement quatre types de fournisseurs. Les exploitants pouvaient trouver des arrangements avec les agences de location ouvertes en Suisse par des sociétés de production elles-mêmes. Une succursale de l'Omnia est ouverte à Genève en 1907.[26] Elle déclare avoir l'exclusivité des films Pathé pour la Suisse, comme nous l'apprend la publication française *Ciné-Journal*.[27]

Les directeurs de salle pouvaient s'adresser à des agences locales de grandes sociétés situées près de la Suisse. En 1912, s'ouvre à Lyon une agence de la Compagnie Générale Cinématographique qui est dite servir aussi les exploitants de Suisse.[28] Sur le même modèle, l'agence munichoise de la Nordisk propose ses services aux exploitants de Suisse.[29]

Des agences de location locales sont aussi fondées qui rassemblent les films de nombreux producteurs. L'Agence Générale Suisse Cinématographique propose une liste de nombreux films comprenant aussi bien des titres Gaumont, Pathé, Harry, Cosmograph, Éclair, Milano, Savoia. Certains films, proposés dans un premier temps par l'AGSC, sont repris par d'autres agences en Suisse, indiquant un régime de sous-location.

Hervé Dumont indique qu'une des premières sociétés de location aurait été ouverte en 1912 : la Monopol Film, suivie par d'autres en 1913.[30] Ce qu'il mentionne renvoie à un type de location particulier, celui du film avec exclusivité pour toute la Suisse, inaugurant le régime de la distribution que l'on connaît encore actuellement. Attestant de ce profond changement, la *Feuille officielle suisse du commerce* inscrit dès 1913 des films dans la section « Propriété littéraire et artistique » du « Bureau fédéral de la propriété intellectuelle », indiquant une protection pour des œuvres cinématographiques.[31]

Mais ces films ont peut-être circulé par d'autres canaux. : G. Hipleh-Walt quand il ouvre une salle à Lausanne est dit pratiquer la vente et la location de films. En 1911, il dirige une « Film-Börse » à Zurich qui est cependant radiée en 1912 suite à une faillite.[32]

L'approvisionnement local

Plusieurs cas de figure se présentent concernant la constitution des programmes lausannois.[33] Dès ses débuts, le Lumen est déclaré être une salle Pathé, situation qui perdure plusieurs années, dans la mesure où l'on trouve à l'affiche en 1914 une majorité de productions Pathé, ou du moins de sociétés dont la diffusion est assurée par Pathé, comme les films de la SCAGL.[34] Le Lux est dit être une salle Gaumont en 1913.[35]

Pour les autres salles, il convient de se concentrer sur les programmes pour percevoir des constantes qui laissent supposer des liens privilégiés avec certaines compagnies. Pour la période de juillet 1913 à août 1914, c'est-à-dire du moment où apparaissent des programmes plus détaillés jusqu'à la déclaration de la Première Guerre qui provoque la suspension des représentations cinématographiques sur ordre de police, certaines constantes apparaissent : le Royal Biograph passe une majorité de films Gaumont, le Palace plutôt des films italiens (Cinès, Itala, Ambrosio). On ne trouve pas une même régularité pour des salles comme l'Apollo et le Kursaal, ce dernier présentant souvent des films un peu plus anciens.[36]

Un point mérite cependant d'être mentionné : Georges Korb, qui dirige le Royal

Biograph, s'avère occuper aussi un rôle important dans la diffusion de films. *Ciné-Journal* annonce qu'il aurait obtenu le monopole pour la Suisse du Film d'art.[37] Il assure, d'autre part, disposer du monopole de *Quo vadis ?* pour la Suisse.[38] En collaboration avec une société regroupant plusieurs salles, il s'assure le concours de M. de Daué à Paris pour l'achat de films.[39] Enfin, en 1914, il reprend la direction d'une autre salle lausannoise, l'Apollo, pour quelques mois.

En regard d'une telle programmation, il va de soi que la part des images de provenance locale est restée maigre. Une difficulté supplémentaire s'élève : le détail des séances est rarement fourni dans leur intégralité. Ainsi, il y a fort à parier qu'une salle passant des actualités Gaumont ou Éclair a certainement accueilli des sujets suisses. De même, les parties documentaires ont dû comporter des images tournées dans le pays : de nombreuses sociétés proposent alors des « pleins airs » tournés en Suisse.[40] Un autre phénomène important apparaît. Une salle insiste régulièrement sur la présence d'actualités locales : le Royal Biograph, de G. Korb. Une première occurrence apparaît en 1912 :

> Mais le numéro sensationnel, celui qui remplira chaque soir la salle, ce sont les films de la fête fédérale de gymnastique. Ils sont de toute beauté, comme les exercices qu'ils reproduisent. Ces exercices étonnent, par leur difficulté et leur perfection ; on les voit de tout près au Biograph, la lutte en particulier. Les exercices d'ensemble sont d'un effet merveilleux. Une scène impressionnante est celle où M. Camille Decoppet [conseiller fédéral vaudois élu en 1912] remet la bannière fédérale à nos confédérés de Bâle, l'orchestre joue l'Hymne national et la salle applaudit.[41]

Ce texte euphorique s'apparente à de la promotion. Comme dans les annonces des forains, il souligne le contexte de présentation, l'accompagnement musical, qui joue un rôle central en donnant un caractère national à certaines images. La présence de ces vues locales s'apparente, comme dans la période foraine, à une forme de spécialisation. Si plusieurs salles annoncent des films locaux, c'est de façon sporadique. Seul le Royal Biograph intègre régulièrement de telles bandes à son programme. Outre la fête de gymnastique de Bâle, les événements ayant mobilisé un opérateur sont des meetings d'aviation,[42] les manœuvres militaires auxquelles assiste Guillaume II en septembre 1912, une scène de marché à Lausanne en novembre 1912, les éléments naturels déchaînés à Vallorbe en janvier 1913, une assermentation du Grand Conseil en mars 1913, qui est dite être diffusée dans toute l'Europe par les actualités Éclair ; un défilé militaire filmé par un opérateur spécialement dépêché par la société Éclipse en septembre 1913 ; les fêtes du Centenaire genevois, où seraient dépêchés trois opérateurs expérimentés.[43] La récurrence de cette pratique mène à l'annonce de la constitution de la marque de « Biograph suisse » avec des « vues de plein air suisse » sous la direction de Korb lui-même, représentée à Paris par M. de Daué.[44]

Cette spécialisation qui prend appui sur l'élément local dresse un catalogue de scènes qui dépasse cependant le simple pittoresque. Les images donnent à voir les représentants de l'autorité et insistent à nouveau sur l'Armée. On remarquera que, par rapport à la période foraine, le caractère local sert à fonder un sentiment patriotique. Le fait qu'on caractérise de « scène impressionnante » la remise de la bannière fédérale aux confédérés de Bâle tient plus au fait que ce soit un conseiller fédéral vaudois qui effectue ce geste qu'à la scène elle-même. De même certaines manœuvres militaires concernent des troupes de la région même. La présence de ces figures locales, que soulignent immanquablement les annonces, constitue l'élément sur lequel on a fondé le sentiment d'une appartenance à une communauté nationale, elle-même constituée de plusieurs entités locales. On se serait donc appuyé sur l'attachement au local pour susciter un tel sentiment patriotique, cherchant ainsi à se conformer à la structure fédéraliste du pays. C'est en fait avec *Guillaume-Tell* à l'affiche au Royal Biograph pour une semaine en avril 1914 qu'apparaît un discours nationaliste qui délaisse cet encrage local :

> Le Royal Biograph a pensé qu'il n'était pas besoin d'aller chercher bien loin les héros créateurs d'une épopée et, pour employer l'expression consacrée, il a fait « filmer » Guillaume-Tell. Et quel plus beau sujet pouvait-il trouver que celui qui inspira à Schiller le sujet de son chef d'œuvre dramatique et fit éclore la plus géniale composition sous la plume de Rossini. Les opérateurs sont allés sur les lieux mêmes de l'action ; le décor où évoluèrent les acteurs qui revécurent devant l'objectif l'Iliade suisse, fut le berceau même qui vit naître nos libertés. Guillaume-Tell a été mis à la scène sous la direction et d'après la documentation de deux écrivains suisses. C'est un spectacle que l'on peut recommander.[45]

Le 25 avril 1914, le même journal, la *Feuille d'avis de Lausanne*, comporte, fait exceptionnel, une publicité d'une page entière avec un petit dessin schématique de la statue d'Altdorf et le titre en un immense lettrage. Cette production est qualifiée de « premier grand film de l'histoire nationale ». On loue aussi *Guillaume-Tell* pour son caractère d'authenticité, dans la mesure où il a été tourné à Uri et Schwyz. L'émotion que générerait cette « reconstitution des principales scènes de notre vie primitive » devrait reposer des « niaiseries habituelles » et constituer un enseignement intuitif particulièrement bienvenu pour les enfants. La sortie de ce film est accompagnée d'un discours qui s'appuie sur la mythologie nationale et cherche à intégrer les spectatrices et les spectateurs dans une communauté qui se reconnaîtrait dans de telles images (comme l'indique ces termes de « nos libertés »). Ce « vivant symbole de l'effort héroïque d'un peuple pour la conquête de la liberté » sert au déclenchement d'une promotion fortement teintée de patriotisme. Plutôt que les vues locales, c'est donc un genre fictionnel qui sert à lancer un tel discours. On soulignera finalement la caractéristique paradoxale que ce film a pour origine une firme allemande, marquant explicitement le fait que la promotion et la reconnaissance nationale n'ont pas pour fondement l'appartenance de la firme productrice au pays. Bien plutôt, la possibilité de s'identifier imaginairement à une production cinématographique prend appui sur un intertexte culturel déjà largement investi d'une portée nationale, comme la légende de Guillaume Tell, et ses multiples adaptations dont celle de Schiller et Rossini. Car il s'agit en fait de *Die Befreiung der Schweiz und die Sage von Wilhelm Tell* (1914).[46] En effet, une publicité parue dans *Ciné-Journal* nous apprend que le film *Guillaume Tell (ou la légende de la libération de la Suisse)* (Prod. : DB) a été « Concédé en monopole (…) à M. G. Korb, Lausanne »,[47] le directeur du Royal Biograph. La publicité et les textes accompagnant la sortie du film à Lausanne se gardent bien de mentionner que ce film annoncé comme « premier chef d'œuvre cinématographique national »[48] est l'œuvre d'une société allemande. Dans les années 1920, la nationalité de l'équipe de production prendra un tout autre poids dans les nombreux débats que suscite la définition du « véritable » film suisse.[49]

Notes

1. Le présent texte a été réalisé dans le cadre d'une recherche menée au Seminar für Filmwissenschaft de l'Université de Zurich, soutenue par le Fonds national suisse de la recherche scientifique, intitulée : « Vues et points de vue : vers une histoire du film documentaire en Suisse, 1896–1964 ».

2. Cosandey, Roland, « Switzerland » in Abel, Richard (éd.), *Encyclopedia of Early Cinema* (London & New York: Routledge, 2005): 619–620.

3. « La nation, la politique et les arts », *Revue suisse d'histoire* 39 (1989): 293–303 ; « Politiques culturelles

de la Confédération et valeurs nationales », in Crettaz, Bernard, Jost, Hans Ulrich, Pithon, Rémy (éds.), *Peuples inanimés, avez-vous donc une âme?* *Images et identités suisses au XXe siècle* (Études et mémoires de la section d'histoire de l'Université de Lausanne, 1987): 19–38. Voir aussi : Omlin, Sibylle, *L'art en Suisse au XIXe et au XXe siècle. La création et son contexte* (Zurich: Pro Helvetia, 2004).

4.   Walter, François, « Lieux, paysages, espaces. Les perceptions de la montagne alpine du XVIIIe siècle à nos jours », *Itinera* 12 (1992): 14–34 ; Walter, François, *Les figures paysagères de la nation* (Paris: Éditions de l'École des Hautes Études en Sciences Sociales, 2004).

5.   *La géographie artistique* (Dissentis: Pro Helvetia, 1987): 167 ; *L'iconographie nationale* (Disentis: Pro Helvetia, 1992).

6.   Clavien, Alain, *Les Helvétistes. Intellectuels et politique en Suisse romande au début du siècle* (Lausanne: Éditions d'en bas, 1993); Maggetti, Daniel, *L'invention de la littérature romande 1830–1910* (Lausanne: Payot, 1995).

7.   Aguet, Joël, « Le théâtre et ses auteurs de 1848 à la Belle Époque », in Francillon, Roger (éd.), *Histoire de la littérature en Suisse romande*, vol. 2 (De Töpffer à Ramuz) (Lausanne: Payot, 1997): 159–175.

8.   Suivant en cela l'analyse de Eric Hobsbawn dans *Nations et nationalisme depuis 1780* (Paris : Gallimard, 1992 [1990]), qui voit la période précédant la Première Guerre mondiale comme un moment prégnant dans l'avènement des nationalismes en Europe.

9.   La population qui compte 39 300 habitants en 1895, en dénombre 47 500 en 1900, 53 000 en 1905, 66 263 en 1910, 70 561 en 1912, selon les décomptes publiés dans *La Semaine à Lausanne*.

10.   Voir Cosandey, Roland et Pastor, Jean-Marie, « Lavanchy-Clarke : Sunlight & Lumière, ou les débuts du cinématographe en Suisse », *Équinoxe* 7 (Histoire(s) de cinéma(s)) (1992): 9–27. On consultera aussi : Cosandey, Roland, « Le Catalogue Lumière et la Suisse, éléments pour une filmographie nationale », *1895* 15 (décembre 1993): 3–30 ; « Les premières images animées en Suisse. Une chronologie remaniée et augmentée (1895–1896) », *Intervalles. Revue culturelle du Jura bernois et de Bienne* 55 (1999) : 23–34.

11.   Il subsiste un doute quant à l'identité de l'organisateur lausannois. Il a par contre été établi qu'une série de vues ont été prises par F. Lavanchy-Clarke. Voir Langer, François, *Per artem probam ad Lumen. Les débuts de l'exploitation cinématographique à Lausanne 1896–1930* (Mémoire de licence de l'Université de Lausanne, 1989) ; Cosandey, Roland, « Clio et les bobines d'Ariane. Le Cinématographe Lumière à Lausanne, 1896–1898 : d'un répertoire à une filmographie », *Mémoire vive* 2 (1993): 9–25. Sur ces séances lausannoises, on consultera aussi l'étude pionnière de Buache, Freddy et Rial, Jacques, *Les débuts du cinématographe à Genève et Lausanne 1895–1914* (Lausanne: Cinémathèque suisse, 1964).

12.   Cette annonce est parue de façon identique dans cinq journaux de la ville : *Gazette de Lausanne, Feuille d'avis de Lausanne, Tribune de Lausanne, Nouvelliste Vaudois, La Revue*.

13.   Sadoul, Georges, *Histoire générale du cinéma. Tome I : L'invention du cinéma 1832–1897* (Paris: Denoël, 1946): 265.

14.   Cette insistance est d'autant plus remarquable qu'un autre appareil de prises de vue (de marque Joly-Normandin) a convergé sur cette même troupe, mais dans une autre partie de la ville, à proximité de la caserne. Voir Cosandey, Roland, *Cinéma 1900 : trente films dans une boîte à chaussure* (Lausanne : Payot, 1996): 60–62.

15.   Les rares affichettes et demandes d'autorisation qui nous sont parvenues sont conservées par la Cinémathèque suisse et les Archives de la Ville de Lausanne.

16.   Louis Preiss, né le 16 juillet 1851 à Gleiwitz, [demande d'autorisation de séjour pour ses employés. Archives d'État, Genève]. Son nom est généralement orthographié Praiss.

17.   Voir Bernardini, Aldo, *Cinema italiano delle origini. Gli ambulanti* (Gemona: La Cineteca del Friuli, 2001). Outre Praiss, A. Bernardini indique le passage de G. Hipleh-Walt, des Leilich, toutes entreprises dont le siège social est situé en Suisse.

18.   Un document conservé par la Cinémathèque suisse, sans date, dresse la « Liste des membres actifs » du « Syndicat suisse des industriels forains et des industries similaires ». Sont donnés comme munis d'un cinématographe : Alex. Dahlmann (Yverdon), Georg Hipleh-Walt (Biel), Hrch. Leilich (Zürich), Wilh. Rosenburg (Bern), Charles Sperl (Genève), Heinr. Weidauer-Wal-

lenda (Bern), J. Weber-Clément (Yverdon). Il s'agit de 7 membres sur une liste totale qui en dénombre 30.

19. Il affirme avoir fondé son entreprise en 1897 et ne craint pas d'annoncer : « La plus grandiose entreprise transportable, la plus perfectionnée, la plus confortable du monde entier ».

20. Demande, conservée à la Cinémathèque suisse, pour le « Kinematograph Royal », qui annonce 600 places et un établissement de 22 m. de façade sur 8 m. de profondeur.

21. Lettre du 26 avril 1898, Archives de la Ville de Lausanne, Corps de police, cote 430, années 1895–1920, cartable 1.

22. Sur l'histoire des salles en Suisse, voir : *Art + architecture en Suisse* 3 (1996) ; sur Lausanne, voir Langer, F., *op. cit.* et Haver, Gianni, *Les lueurs de la guerre. Écrans vaudois 1939–1945* (Lausanne : Payot, 2003), 74–94.

23. Le Kursaal abritait déjà des projections auparavant, mais de façon plus sporadique. Des projections se tiennent aussi, plus exceptionnellement, dans les divers lieux de spectacle de la ville : la salle de Tivoli ; le Casino-Théâtre, appelé aussi Casino de Montbenon, et son jardin ; le Casino Lausanne-Ouchy.

24. Sa capacité de 900 places en fait une des plus grandes salles de Suisse, après l'édification d'un nouveau bâtiment, inauguré en avril 1911, après plusieurs mois de travaux.

25. On ne trouve souvent que la mention de « cinématographe » accompagnée des horaires. Parfois une marque (Pathé). La présence de films plus longs s'accompagna de la mention de leur titre. Seul le Lumen donne de plus amples précisions après sa transformation en 1911.

26. *Feuille officielle suisse du commerce* 124 (15 mai 1908) : 883.

27. E.B.L., « La protection des films en Suisse » 112 (15 octobre 1910) : 9. Cette situation ne doit cependant pas avoir été toujours appliquée avec rigueur.

28. *Ciné-Journal* 178 (20 janvier 1912): 4.

29. *Der Kinematograph* 362 (3 décembre 1913). En 1915, *Kinema* annonce que s'ouvre à Zurich une agence de la Nordisk, la Nordische Film Comp. Gmbh, émanation de la filiale de Berlin (39 (2 octobre 1915): 5).

30. *Histoire du cinéma suisse. Films de fiction 1896–1965* (Lausanne: Cinémathèque suisse, 1987): 24–25.

31. 14 (19 janvier 1914) : 91. *Die Verlobten* (*I promessi sposi* [réal : Ubaldo Maria Del Colle / Ernesto Maria Pasquali]), une production Pasquali & Cie (Turin), est pris en distribution par la Filmgesellschaft « Express » Dederscheck & Cie (Luzern). Joseph Lang (Zürich) s'assure les droits de *Die Herrin des Nils* / *La reine du Nil*, [*Marcantonio e Cleopatra* de Enrico Guazzoni] de la « Cines » (Rome), etc.

32. *Feuille officielle suisse du commerce* 311 (16 décembre 1908) : 2136 ; 249 (2 octobre 1912) : 1725 ; 255 (9 octobre 1912) : 1775.

33. Les remarques suivantes se fondent sur les films annoncés à l'affiche, ce qui occulte les autres titres projetés.

34. *La Revue* (19 avril 1909): 3 : « Le théâtre Lumen s'est assuré la concession des films Pathé dont on connaît la célébrité. »

35. Cf. *Lausanne-Plaisirs* 69 (11 janvier 1913). Cette situation n'a cependant pas dû durer très longtemps, la salle devenant le Palace en juillet 1913, après quelques semaines de fermeture. Elle appartient à la société « The Royal Vio », avant d'être reprise par Paul Siegfried en mai 1914, qui dit avoir l'exclusivité des films Aubert.

36. De façon générale, on remarque que les films passent à Lausanne peu de temps après leur sortie originale en France ou en Italie.

37. *Ciné-Journal* 239 (22 mars 1913) : 14. Mais, il est fort probable que ces accords aient été dénoncés dans un laps de temps fort bref… Il se trouve aussi en relation d'affaires avec la Compagnie Générale Cinématographique de L. Aubert, comme l'atteste une protestation qu'il adresse à *Ciné-Journal* 275 (29 novembre 1913) : 5.

38. 85 (3 mai 1913).

39. *Le Courrier cinématographique* 21 (24 mai 1913): 39.

40. Corroborant cette supposition, on lit dans *La Semaine à Lausanne* 78 (5–12 mars 1910) : 25 : « Mais

ce qui constitue un attrait important des programmes du Lumen, c'est que toute monotonie est exclue par le fait que les paysages ou les scènes présentées sont pris ou posés dans les pays les plus divers. C'est ainsi que, dans la même soirée, on passe de la Suisse à l'Amérique, aux Indes, à la Hollande ou la France, et même les personnes qui ont beaucoup voyagé, apprennent encore des choses souvent inaperçues ou oubliées. » Le Lux passe ainsi *De Viège à Zermatt* selon *Lausanne-Plaisirs* 26 (16 mars 1912). Il pourrait s'agir du film Éclipse daté de 1911. Sur ces films, voir : Cosandey, Roland, « Tourismus und der frühe Film in der Schweiz (1896–1918) », *Cinema* 47 (*Landschaften*) (2002): 50–61. Aldo Bernadini, dans *Archivio del cinema italiano, vol. 1 : Il cinema muto* (Roma: ANICA, 1991), recense ainsi plus de 50 films tournés en Suisse par des sociétés italiennes entre 1906 et 1914. Herbert Birett en a dénombré plus de 120 sur le marché allemand : *Das Filmangebot in Deutschland 1895–1911* (München : Filmbuchverlag Winterberg, 1991). Pour 1912–1920, voir son site http://www.UniBw-Muenchen.de/campus/Film/wwwf ilmbi.html. En France, les sociétés Pathé, Éclair, Éclipse, Gaumont, Radios, Raleigh & Robert, Th. Pathé ont toutes proposé des films tournés en Suisse.

41. *Lausanne-Plaisirs* 44 (20 juillet 1912). La publicité indique : « *La Fête fédérale de gymnastique à Bâle*, Grande vue prise avec autorisation spéciale. »

42. Le meeting d'Ouchy en septembre 1912 et le vol de Grandjean à Ouchy en septembre 1913.

43. *La Semaine à Lausanne* 158 (8 juillet 1914). Une autre salle, le Palace, affirme avoir aussi filmé l'événement.

44. *Le Courrier cinématographique* 7 (14 janvier 1914) : 29. On écrit : « La première [production, i.e. *Chemin de fer électrique de Montreux au Berner Oberland*, selon une annonce publicitaire] fut projetée à Tivoli cette semaine-ci et se fit remarquer par sa belle perspective et sa jolie photo. »

45. *Feuille d'avis de Lausanne* (24 avril 1914). Un texte quasi identique figure dans la *Tribune de Lausanne* (25 avril 1914).

46. *Der Kinematograph* 368 (14 janvier 1914), indique que le film est une production « Deutsche Mutoscope und Biograph » (généralement indiquée comme : Deutsche Mutoskop und Biograph).

47. 287 (21 février 1914).

48. *Lausanne Artistique* 136 (25 avril 1914).

49. Voir : Guido, Laurent, « Controverse sur l'authenticité : *Le pauvre Village*, « premier film suisse », in Pithon, Rémy (éd.), *Cinéma suisse muet. Lumières et ombres* (Lausanne : Antipodes & Cinémathèque suisse, 2002): 111–120.

7

De l'indépendance à l'absorption : le cas québécois

Pierre Véronneau

Montréal, Canada

À cause de sa situation géographique et de la taille de sa population, le Canada a longtemps eu tendance à subordonner son statut d'éventuel producteur culturel à celui de consommateur. Cela se vérifie dans plusieurs domaines et notamment dans celui du cinéma. Le but du présent texte[1] est de s'interroger sur la façon dont la production d'œuvres « nationales », entendues dans le sens de tournées sur le territoire national, s'articule à la distribution sur ce même territoire. Si on le compare à plusieurs autres pays, le Canada possède des infrastructures et un marché limité et se retrouve régulièrement confronté au dilemme d'être soit à la merci des contrôles étrangers, soit d'être obligé de soutenir le développement indépendant de son industrie nationale. L'étude de la distribution des vues animées au Québec (et au Canada) permet d'affirmer que celle-ci connaît un début qui s'apparente à la situation de plusieurs pays, mais une évolution qui le singularise probablement. En nous appuyant sur la nature des films tournés au Québec et l'évolution de leur distribution, nous diviserons l'époque couverte en trois périodes : (1) 1897–1906, les années de l'implantation étrangère ; (2) 1906–1910, les années du développement local et de l'appropriation québécoise ; (3) 1911 jusqu'à la fin du muet, les années de la reprise en main de la situation par les intérêts étrangers.

1897–1906: Les années d'implantation américaine ou étrangère

Pour comprendre notre sujet, il faut rappeler brièvement des éléments contextuels qui touchent aux relations entre le Canada et les États-Unis. L'absence de frontière géographique entre les deux pays encourage au XIXe siècle les échanges Nord-Sud et la pénétration américaine. Au Québec même, le développement du réseau ferroviaire entre New York et Montréal, l'influence de la communauté anglophone et un bassin de clientèle important favorisent la circulation des biens culturels dans l'axe Nord-Sud. Il existe d'ailleurs entre les deux pays un traité de réciprocité qui est dénoncé par les États-Unis en 1866. Dans les mois qui suivent la Confédération de 1867, l'événement qui marque la naissance officielle du Canada,[2] afin d'éviter de se voir imposer des tarifs douaniers, plusieurs compagnies états-uniennes qui font commerce avec le Canada décident d'y établir des succursales. De leur point de vue, le Québec et le Canada constituent un même marché, le prolongement de leur marché domestique. Extrêmement rares sont les Canadiens qui veulent se placer dans une position stratégique pour rester maîtres chez eux. Le début du XXe siècle est plutôt un moment d'intense américanisation économique. Minoritaires par rapport aux Canadiens anglais, les Québécois vont se retrouver à la merci des Américains.

Pourtant, l'élite canadienne-française semble assez peu préoccupée d'une quelconque menace américaine, comme si le danger était passé. Mais celui-ci n'a pas disparu et il revient à l'avant de la scène en 1911 lors du débat sur une éventuelle réciprocité entre le Canada et les États-Unis. Quelques individus influents s'y opposent, comme Henri Bourassa[3] qui publie un pamphlet sur le sujet, *Le spectre de l'annexion* (1912). Il y dénonce la menace états-unienne qui pèse sur l'économie du Québec. Ces nationalistes voudraient s'assurer du développement matériel du Québec, mais sans donner dans le matérialisme états-unien qui serait contraire à la véritable mission spirituelle et civilisatrice du Canada français. Mais leur discours est minoritaire. Au contraire, le premier ministre québécois Lomer Gouin favorise plutôt les investissements étrangers et le développement industriel de la province. Il fait partie de ceux qui se prononcent pour un continentalisme économique et social entre les deux pays.

Caractérisant cette période de transition vers la modernité, l'historien Yvan Lamonde écrit : « La déstabilisation et les 'déracinements' causés par l'industrialisation, l'urbanisation, l'immigration et les ramifications sociales et culturelles du capitalisme à son apogée obligent à la recherche d'une nouvelle façon d'être, de vivre, de penser individuellement et collectivement. Le moderne bouleverse l'ancien ; l'innovation est tout autant dans l'habitat, le vêtement, le travail que dans les loisirs, le transport et les façons de produire, de distribuer et de consommer une variété de biens. Cela signifie, sur le plan de l'histoire des idées, que les contemporains doivent penser ou repenser leur situation, intégrer l'électricité, le tramway, l'automobile, le parc d'attractions, les journaux à cinq sous ; s'adapter aux immigrants établis à Montréal, aux grèves aux 'vues animées' et aux sports professionnels le dimanche. Le discours des élites ne peut plus être le même, ni les perceptions de soi dans le présent et dans l'avenir immédiat ».[4]

Minime en politique et majeure au plan économique, la pénétration états-unienne s'avère particulièrement significative dans le domaine social et culturel. Ce sont ces aspects qui suscitent les plus vives inquiétudes. Dès la fin du XIXe siècle, on parle d'invasion par l'esprit américain, de pénétration de notre civilisation par une autre. Il est vrai qu'avec la présence dans la vie quotidienne québécoise de mass média, de sports, de spectacles en provenance des États-Unis, ou d'organisations syndicales « internationales », etc., le verdict d'américanisation du Québec semble facile à établir. Plus on est nationaliste, plus on dénonce cette contagion et cette infiltration. D'autant plus que la pénétration peut prendre des formes assez dictatoriales.

Ainsi, dans le théâtre lyrique, à la fin du XIXe siècle, les entrepreneurs locaux se voient obligés de passer par des agences américaines pour établir leurs programmes, ce qui entrave le développement d'un univers théâtral typiquement national.[5] Soumise à l'acculturation anglo-américaine, la société montréalaise francophone s'avère incapable de s'approprier ce modèle étranger pour en constituer un mode d'expression original, comme elle y réussit avec ces formes plus populaires que sont le burlesque, le vaudeville ou la revue où elle adapte à son public une tradition et une forme d'art américaines. Comme le résume Mireille Barrière : « Le comportement de l'amateur de théâtre montréalais ne reflète en somme que la conduite ambivalente que l'histoire impose à la population de souche française : une oscillation perpétuelle entre la soumission et la révolte, l'assujettissement et l'indépendance, la conformité et l'originalité ».[6]

Cette situation présente plusieurs analogies avec le cinéma, un médium que l'on ne peut approcher sans prendre plus largement en compte la scène culturelle. Là aussi, la circulation des films et des personnes s'effectue dans l'axe nord-sud. En 1897, plusieurs opérateurs étrangers se rendent à Montréal de manière régulière et cherchent les meilleurs moyens de présenter leurs films. Certains préfèrent les théâtres réguliers où on les accueille à l'entracte. D'autres optent pour des parcs d'attractions, le plus populaire à Montréal étant le parc Sohmer, créé en 1889. En mai 1897, on y érige le Radioscope, un petit pavillon aménagé spécialement pour la présentation des « merveilles animées ». La première phase de pénétration des vues animées en est donc une *implantation* où les projectionnistes de passage et les intermittents de l'exploitation s'insèrent dans un tissu de loisir urbain existant.

Au tournant du siècle, les vues animées s'institutionnalisent petit à petit. Les théâtres de variétés établissent des partenariats permanents avec des acteurs de la distribution américains. Certains choisissent la Lubin Cineagraph, d'autres l'American Vitagraph. Le Kalatechnoscope, dont l'opérateur est William Paley, un *licensee* d'Edison, conclut une entente avec F.F. Proctor.[7] Edison lui-même doit s'adapter à une industrie changeante en créant en 1900 la Kinetograph Co., dont il confie la direction à Percival Waters, un de ses employés new-yorkais.

En janvier 1902, le parc Sohmer inaugure une tradition qui va durer jusqu'en 1910 en projetant des vues dans son pavillon de la musique qui est chauffé durant l'hiver. C'est la Kinetograph qui en a la responsabilité. À cet effet, en 1903, Waters décide d'envoyer à Montréal son demi-frère, Bert Fenton. Celui-ci descend de New York chaque semaine avec son projecteur et ses bobines. Il engage bientôt pour l'aider Léo-Ernest Ouimet, un jeune électricien du parc reconnu pour son habileté en éclairage et effets lumineux. En moins de 10 ans, le parc Sohmer aura ainsi présenté la moitié de la production Edison.

Si cette circulation amène des films états-uniens sur les premiers écrans québécois, elle amène aussi la réalité québécoise à l'écran. En effet, toute cette activité cinématographique a des répercussions du côté de la production. Les premiers films tournés au Québec sont ceux de l'American Motorgraph, qui furent projetés au Théâtre Royal en mai-juin 1897. En février 1898, un opérateur vient tourner des scènes d'hiver « exotiques » à Montréal (du patinage), à Québec (une tempête de neige) et à Ottawa (de la glissade). En novembre 1899, c'est l'embarquement pour l'Afrique du Sud au port de Québec du 2nd Special Service Battalion qui intéresse le caméraman Edison.

En février et mars 1901, Paley arrive avec son Kalatechnoscope. Il consacre beaucoup d'énergie à alimenter Proctor avec des vues locales. Il est alors le plus important projectionniste itinérant à filmer des vues locales. Ses premières vues servent à l'inauguration du Proctor de Montréal en mars 1901. Seuls *Hockey Match on the Ice at Montreal, Canada* et *Montreal Fire Department on Runners* se retrouvent au catalogue Edison de juillet 1901. Les autres titres mentionnés par les journaux en 1901 (*Crowd at the Bonsecours Market, Crowd on Ste. Catherine Street* ou *Boat Trip in Lachine Rapids*) n'y figurent pas.

L'automne de cette même année, Paley est de retour à l'occasion de la visite du duc et de la duchesse de York au Canada. Plusieurs films captent leur voyage, certains tournés par Paley, d'autres, plus nombreux, par le caméraman d'Edison James White. À la mi-février 1902, *Tobogganing in Montreal* est présenté au parc Sohmer. Il s'agit d'un des films Edison qui seront regroupés sous le titre « Quebec Winter Carnival » bien que certains furent filmés à Montréal. Plusieurs films de la série – le catalogue de l'American Film Institute (AFI) en recense officiellement 13 titres – sont présentés au cours des semaines qui suivent au même parc qui se vante d'en avoir la primeur. On peut penser que Paley fut responsable de tout leur tournage.[8]

On retrouve Paley à Montréal en septembre 1902 pour tourner la Fête du travail. Toutes ces vues mettent l'accent sur le pittoresque, autant pour intéresser le public américain que pour conforter l'image stéréotypée qu'ils ont du Canada. Toutefois, puisqu'elles sont présentées au Canada, on peut les qualifier de vues locales destinées au public canadien. Par son importance, leur nombre étonne. C'est la première fois que Montréal et Québec constituent un tel arrière-plan cinématographique.

À la fin de la saison estivale 1903 du parc Sohmer, Ouimet et Fenton aménagent au théâtre National dont le propriétaire, Georges Gauvreau, trouve bientôt que le fait de payer pour le transport et l'hébergement hebdomadaire de Fenton lui coûte trop cher. En 1904, Fenton suggère à Ouimet de rencontrer Waters afin de se porter acquéreur de la franchise de la Kinetograph de Montréal. C'est ainsi que Ouimet devient le représentant d'Edison pour l'Est du Canada. Il fonde la Ouimet Film Exchange. Par voie de conséquence, Fenton cesse bientôt de venir au Canada.[9] Entre temps la Kinetograph connaît un tel succès aux États-Unis qu'Edison et Waters négligent le marché canadien. Ouimet informe ce dernier qu'il devra se tourner vers les Miles Brothers s'approvisionner. Il étend progressivement son réseau de contacts et s'embarque pour la France sur les conseils de Miles qui lui fait valoir qu'Edison ne pourrait intervenir dans des ventes faites au Canada.

En mai 1905, à la fin de la saison hivernale, la Kinetograph refuse de renouveler son contrat avec le parc. Ouimet est libre d'explorer de nouveaux territoires. Il retourne en France avec l'intention de rencontrer Pathé.[10] Il en revient en juillet avec, sous le bras, une caméra Pathé, des pièces de projecteurs, des films et un appareil photo pour fabriquer des plaques. Sur le paquebot, il fait la connaissance de Francis Doublier, un opérateur Lumière qui lui apprend le maniement de la caméra. En janvier 1906, Ouimet ouvre sa propre salle, le Ouimetoscope. Il y présente des vues animées et des chansons illustrées et en quelques semaines, son nom ne se trouve plus associé au parc Sohmer, ni même à la Kinetograph. S'approvisionnant auprès de plusieurs fournisseurs, il a aussi plus de latitude pour établir ses programmes. Il améliore enfin son projecteur dont la brillance et la stabilité deviennent bientôt renommées. Il a tellement de succès qu'il entreprend une première rénovation de sa salle durant la pause estivale. Les journaux le disent le client préféré d'Edison (dont il distribue en trois ans environ 80 titres) et de Pathé.[11] Il s'approvisionne même auprès des indépendants grâce à la Miles Brothers.

Après avoir présenté les réseaux de distribution et de projection des films, il convient maintenant de se demander quelle place y occupe le cinéma local. Pour la période que nous couvrons, de 1897 à 1906 exclusivement, on retrouve 65 titres auxquels sont rattachés un lieu de diffusion et 59 vues tournées mais dont nous avons pas encore repéré le lieu de diffusion. Le public est-il sensible à l'existence d'une telle catégorie de films locaux ? Si on étudie la présentation des vues locales, on peut dire qu'avant 1906 on peut les voir surtout dans trois salles implantées dans la partie anglophone (ouest) de Montréal (Proctor, Windsor Hall, Her Majesty's), dans deux salles francophones situées autour du boulevard qui divise Montréal en Est et Ouest, (Monument national et Théâtre Royal), et évidemment au parc Sohmer situé dans l'Est de la ville. Ces films tournés au Québec proposent, à l'instar de la majorité de ceux qui sont tournés à l'étranger par des Français ou des Américains, une vision stéréotypée et quasi coloniale de la province en ne s'intéressant qu'à ses activités ou ses paysages exotiques, et ses parades ou visites historico-politiques. L'espace public spécifique que constituent les vues locales ne participe pas encore à la construction d'une identité collective.

1906–1910: Les années d'appropriation québécoise

Durant la saison 1906–1907 plusieurs *nickelodeons* ouvrent leurs portes et plusieurs théâtres effectuent des rénovations.[12] Ouimet fait face à la concurrence. La plus importante provient de son ancien patron, Georges Gauvreau, qui annonce l'ouverture d'un grand théâtre de 1100 places, le Nationoscope, inauguré en mai 1907, avec un opérateur de grand talent, Frank Cannock.[13] Leur rivalité se transpose également au plan de l'approvisionnement alors qu'au même moment, aux États-Unis, Edison forme un trust et s'oppose aux distributeurs indépendants. Cela explique pourquoi, à cette époque, Ouimet est devenu, pour une courte période, agent de Kleine Optical.[14] George Kleine était en effet venu à Montréal en août 1907 pour embaucher Ouimet, ce qui ne l'empêchera pas d'ouvrir son propre bureau en novembre de la même année.

La véritable riposte de Ouimet à Gauvreau sera l'ouverture en août 1907 du grand Ouimetoscope, réputé faire 1200 places, pour lequel il engage en décembre un bonimenteur, longtemps après ses concurrents. Malgré les pressions de deux « chaînes » canadiennes, Bennett et Allen, afin qu'Edison mette fin à la licence accordée à Ouimet, celui-ci réussit à conserver sa position au Québec. Le meilleur signe de son importance est qu'il est le seul Canadien à assister en décembre 1907 à la convention de Chicago au cours de laquelle se prend la décision de créer un trust, la United Film Services Protective Association, à laquelle n'adhèrent ni la Biograph, ni Kleine.[15] En janvier 1908, Ouimet est le seul Canadien à faire partie de l'Association dont l'annonce dans le *Moving Picture World* (MPW) mentionne aussi la Dominion Film Service (Toronto) et la Cinematograph (Montréal), identifiées comme des loueurs qui ne font pas partie de l'Association. Mais cette situation va évoluer rapidement car deux mois plus tard, Ouimet rejoint les indépendants et le *MPW* ne mentionne plus aucun membre canadien. Au même moment, le *MPW* divise les fabricants de films entre « Edison Licensees » et « Biograph Licensees » (dont Gaumont et Kleine Optical). À cause de ses relations d'affaires avec Pathé, Ouimet est aussi au premier rang pour présenter les vues Pathé tournées au pays, comme la série *Canada pittoresque* (1906) dont la presse vante la beauté.

La position avantageuse de Ouimet ne dure pas longtemps car Waters ouvre à Montréal en juillet 1908 la Kinetograph Co. of Canada pour prendre le contrôle de la distribution et de la location des films Edison. De facto on veut mettre Ouimet hors jeu. Celui-ci est forcé de restituer au Trust tous ses films, projecteurs et accessoires. Il doit donc se battre et, pour survivre, il renforce son alliance avec Miles. Il réplique aussi en achetant à Pathé une caméra et de la pellicule et en engageant un opérateur. Il tournera beaucoup de vues locales sur lesquelles nous reviendrons.

En janvier 1909, on crée aux États-Unis la Motion Pictures Patents Co. qui s'assure le contrôle de toute la production de films et de fabrication d'appareils. Elle incite tous les loueurs à faire affaire avec elle, et les exploitants à ne projeter de films que sur des appareils brevetés. Laemmle et l'International Projecting and Producing Company s'opposent aussitôt à l'ultimatum du Trust. Leur opposition se porte en territoire québécois. Laemmle inaugure un *exchange* à Montréal en août 1909. Un autre *exchange* montréalais, la North American Film Co, s'affilie à l'Independent Film Service. Si certaines compagnies choisissent plutôt le parti du Trust (la General Film par exemple), la démarcation entre *licensees* et indépendants ne semble pas trop étanche dans la mesure où plusieurs *exchanges* offrent des films des deux catégories pour accommoder leurs clients. De plus des compagnies non américaines ont pignon sur rue dès 1909, comme la Gaumont qui distribuera également quelques années plus tard des vues des indépendants, comme Universal ou Warner, avant que ceux-ci n'ouvrent leurs propres succursales.

C'est dans ce contexte que Ouimet cherche à explorer de nouveaux sentiers pour rejoindre sa clientèle. À cause de la popularité des chansons illustrées, il édite *Les chansons du Ouimetoscope*. En janvier 1908, il lance aussi un feuillet hebdomadaire, *Le Ouimetoscope*, et y publie notamment des résumés des films qu'il présente. Mais sa réponse la plus créatrice et la plus innovatrice à ses problèmes d'approvisionnement sera le tournage des vues locales dès novembre 1906. Son opérateur fournit le Ouimetoscope, ainsi que plusieurs autres *nickelodeons* au Québec. On compte une douzaine de titres en 1907, presque trois fois plus en 1908 et sa production s'arrête début 1909, à l'époque où il se bat devant les tribunaux contre ceux qui veulent freiner ses affaires.

Mais même s'il domine le marché des vues tournées au Québec, Ouimet n'en a pas le monopole. Certains scopes montréalais, comme le Cinématographe, qui fait affaire avec le même opérateur que Ouimet, Lactance Giroux, ajoutent dès février 1907 des vues locales à leur programme. Le Trust prétendant qu'une telle activité violait ses brevets, Ouimet sera menacé. Mais il ne cède pas. En outre il subit une double pression additionnelle : d'une part les menaces de l'Église catholique qui militait en faveur de la prohibition des vues le dimanche. D'autre part celle de la concurrence des exploitants montréalais qui n'hésitent pas à faire venir de New York les primeurs que Ouimet annonce dans les publications locales, au point qu'il va devoir suspendre cette pratique, ou même des exploitants canadiens comme l'Ontarien Bennett et l'Albertain Allen qui veulent prendre de l'expansion au Québec à ses dépens.[16]

Par ailleurs, Edison se pointe à nouveau au Québec après une longue absence. Le *MPW* du 13 mars 1909 présente la série *A Canadian Winter Carnival*. Il s'agit de films d'une bobine, tournés par James White, qui portent sur des sujets comme le ski, la promenade en traîneau ou le patin. On reconnaît encore là les mêmes clichés hivernaux canadiens et les mêmes activités qu'on retrouvait au tout début. White est probablement l'opérateur de *A Cry From the Wilderness*, que le *MPW* du 20 mars 1909 caractérise comme un film dramatique sur fond documentaire se passant chez les Esquimaux de la Baie d'Hudson. Il s'agit d'une des rares fictions tournées au Québec, trois ans avant l'impressionnante vague qui frappera la ville de Québec en 1912.[17] À noter qu'il n'y aura plus d'opérateurs Edison qui se présenteront au Québec après cette série, sauf ceux qui, en juin 1910, doivent passer par Montréal pour prendre le train en direction de Vancouver afin de réaliser pour le Canadien Pacifique treize films se déroulant dans l'Ouest canadien et censés attirer des milliers d'immigrants européens.[18]

Dans la filmographie du Grafics, on dénombre, pour les années 1906–1910, 84 vues locales pour lesquelles fut identifié un lieu de présentation et 60 auxquelles n'est pas encore rattaché aucun lieu. Pour les premières, l'immense majorité est l'oeuvre de Ouimet et est présentée au Ouimetoscope, sauf quelques-unes au Cinématographe et au Parigraphe. Presque rien, à peine 5 pour cent, n'aboutit dans les théâtres anglophones, comme si les 95 pour cent des vues tournées au Québec par les francophones ne s'adressaient qu'aux francophones ou comme si les salles anglophones les boycottaient. Ce qui est plausible car on peut imaginer que dans le domaine de la production, surtout lorsqu'ils s'opposent à des diffuseurs locaux qui se développent également du côté de la production, les Américains essaient d'imposer leur mode de fonctionnement, n'acceptent pas l'émergence d'une production locale et en bloquent la diffusion. On dénote encore, soit dit en passant, une similitude très grande entre la situation de l'industrie lyrique évoquée au début du texte et celle des vues animées.

Par contre, parmi les titres répertoriés mais sans identification de salle, la proportion anglophone s'avère plus importante. Quoi qu'il en soit, on se retrouve de facto face à une ségrégation linguistique, sinon de classe, et les efforts de production locale et d'appropriation du médium se trouvent entravés par ceux qui possèdent des moyens de diffusion dans certains quartiers de Montréal. Toutefois il n'est pas évident que tous les spectateurs recherchent à tout prix des images d'eux-mêmes. On peut d'ailleurs se demander si le public anglo-québécois porte une attention particulière aux vues locales alors que le public francophone retrouve de manière régulière, sur les écrans qu'il fréquente assidûment, des lieux, des événements et des gens dans lesquels il se reconnaît.

1911–1924: Les années de reprise en main américaine ou étrangère

En juin 1910, Gaumont et Kinetograph vendent à Montréal les films de l'Independent Moving Pictures Company.[19] Ils s'annoncent aussi sous le chapeau de Motion Picture Distributing and Sales Co. qui met fin aux querelles internes parmi les indépendants. Les films Universal sont distribués en 1912 par les *exchanges* affiliés aux indépendants. Durant les années 1910, la présence d'Edison s'estompe progressivement et plusieurs compagnies indépendantes ouvrent des bureaux à Montréal.[20] Ces indépendants veulent cependant prendre de plus en plus leurs distances d'avec les rares indépendants québécois, à l'exemple de Ouimet qui se retrouve bientôt presque sans films à distribuer. On comprend pourquoi durant les années 1910, les Américains veulent reprendre en main le marché québécois. Un journaliste estimait en 1912 qu'environ 30 000 personnes fréquentaient chaque jour les salles de cinéma montréalaises[21] et que cela plaçait Montréal en tête de liste en la matière. Il s'agit donc d'un marché assez lucratif.

Ces années-là, on trouve beaucoup d'activité sur le front de la distribution. En 1911, on apprend par un article du *MPW* sur les salles montréalaises que le Gaiety[22] vient d'abandonner le circuit *licensed* et que le Moulin rouge ne présente que des films indépendants. On pourrait penser que les autres sont plutôt du côté des *licensed*. Mais une lettre de juillet 1913 dans la même revue affirme que la majorité des salles présente des films des deux associations. En fait, à partir de 1912, le déclin du Trust s'amorce et la configuration des deux conglomérats – Trust et indépendants – se modifie. Sur le front de la distribution au Québec, les salles indépendantes ferment ou sont vendues à de plus grosses chaînes en attendant d'être avalées par les Américains.[23] Ceux-ci privilégient d'ailleurs l'achat de droits territoriaux pour tout le Dominion, ou par zones géographiques, plutôt que par provinces distinctes, ce qui équivaut aux *State Rights* aux États-Unis.[24]

Ouimet avait été forcé en 1908 de se mettre sur la touche en vendant ses activités de distribution à la Kinetograph. En 1914, lorsque Pathé ouvre une succursale aux États-Unis et propose à Ouimet de devenir son agent pour le Canada, celui-ci accepte et fonde la Pathé's Famous Feature Syndicate of Quebec. Son grand succès est, en janvier 1915, le feuilleton *Les périls de Pauline* dont le roman paraît en parallèle dans le journal *La Presse*. Cette même année, Ouimet prend de l'expansion et incorpore une nouvelle compagnie sous le nom de Specialty Film Import avec des bureaux dans six grandes villes. En 1917, on compte au moins 15 distributeurs à Montréal. Les plus petits ne sortent qu'un film par semaine tandis que les plus importants (Famous Players, General Film, Mutual, Regal, Specialty Film Import, Universal, Vitagraph V.L.S.E.) peuvent en avoir de quatre à huit.[25] Les mêmes firmes possèdent aussi des bureaux à Toronto et parfois dans d'autres villes canadiennes. Mais la situation n'est pas toujours facile. Un journal corporatif écrit : « There is certainly too much film in Canada for the demand, and the expenses of maintaining offices all over Canada is too great for a company to make a profit unless they have anough products to do a large volume of business ».[26] Ainsi Globe Films est absorbé par Regal Films. Il y a aussi des rumeurs qui courent au sujet de Specialty Film Import.

Une des solutions imaginées par les Canadiens pour résister à la main mise états-unienne est encore de jouer la carte de la production nationale. La tendance est pancanadienne. Dans les Maritimes, on tourne *Evangeline*[27] qui fait partie des succès de l'été 1914 à Montréal. En Ontario des compagnies surgissent comme, en 1914, la

Conness-Till Film Co, qui s'établit à Swansea et se présente comme une « Canadian firm established in Canada for the purpose of producing Canadian plays with distinctive Canadian settings and written by Canadians.[28] » Au Québec, cette problématique se pose depuis plusieurs années. Le mouvement contre la présence des films états-uniens sur nos écrans met en évidence l'absence de films canadiens qui proposeraient une autre image et une autre réalité que les films étrangers. Jusqu'à présent, pratiquement seul Ouimet avait tourné des vues locales qui n'étaient d'ailleurs que des actualités.[29] En plein cœur de la tourmente de 1912, les journaux nous apprennent qu'un dénommé Albert J. Gariépy vient de créer l'International Moving Picture avec des capitaux canadiens.[30] Gariépy veut combler une lacune : l'absence de producteurs de vues animées canadiennes. À la différence des vues étrangères qui portent forcément l'empreinte des pays qui les manufacturent, les vues canadiennes seraient distinctes. En plus elles permettraient aux recettes de rester au pays alors que les Américains rapatrient chez eux les bénéfices énormes générés par les scopes.

Gariépy n'est pas le seul à parler de production. De nombreuses compagnies voient le jour, toutes aussi improductives. En fait seule la British-American Film Company finit par produire un film, *The Battle of the Long Sault* (2000 pieds). Le 29 décembre 1912, ce film est présenté au Ouimetoscope. « C'est la première fois que des films confectionnés au Canada représentant un sujet purement canadien, seront vus dans un théâtre canadien par un public canadien ».[31] Ce film met pourtant en vedette des comédiens américains et c'est un Américain qui le réalise. Quelques mois plus tard, la compagnie annonce de nouveaux projets.[32] Aucun ne se matérialisera.

La presse commente la situation locale : « In Canada, at the moment, the production of moving pictures is insignificant. With a mise en scene, unequalled in variety, beauty and magnificence, with a population including every attribute of the picturesque, and with no lack of wit and intelligence on the part of its sons and daughters, Canada has not yet been able to make a commercial success of film production. There are one or two organizations in the field, but so far, they have not yet somehow gained an appreciable footing in a business in which they should be pre-eminent. Our cousins from over the border, even our phlegmatic brothers in old England, can produce films of every degree of excellence, but with every natural advantage, we lag behind. The chief reason for this state of affaires appears to be a certain apathy on the part of Canadian public, to the commercial possibilities of the business ».[33] L'auteur mentionne alors qu'il a devant lui un prospectus d'une compagnie montréalaise dirigée par des notables dont le but était de produire des films authentiquement canadiens et qui n'a pas réussi à amasser les quelque milliers de dollars nécessaires pour lancer l'entreprise.

Inversement, à ceux qui lui écrivent pour demander la mise en place d'une production cinématographique canadienne, Merrick R. Nutting, éditeur du corporatif *The Canadian Moving Picture Digest*,[34] répond que cela est impossible pour au moins cinq raisons : (1) Le marché canadien est trop exigu et le producteur devrait vendre ses films hors du pays pour recouvrir ses frais de production. (2) Il est irréaliste de penser concurrencer les Américains sur leur terrain et il en est de même pour l'Europe. (3) Le Canada doit importer tout le matériel et toute la pellicule, ce qui entraîne des coûts supérieurs en transport et en frais de douane. (4) Le Canada ne pourrait mettre sur pied des centres de production comme il en existe dans l'Est et dans l'Ouest des États-Unis. Les vedettes et les techniciens ne viendraient pas s'établir ici. Tout cela sans compter nos mauvaises conditions climatiques. (5) Le distributeur canadien devrait payer plus cher pour des films canadiens que pour des films étrangers.

À cette époque, retournant à sa pratique antérieure, Ouimet se remet à produire, de janvier 1919 à mars 1921, une série d'actualités, les *British Canadian Pathé News*, qui s'alimentent aux actualités de British Pathé et les complètent. Ces actualités sont en anglais. Dans les années vingt, la production québécoise s'accroît. Les actualités et les courts métrages anglophones trouvent le chemin des écrans. Malheureusement c'est l'inverse qui se passe pour la fiction. Ainsi un réalisateur québécois, Joseph-Arthur Homier, va à nouveau s'essayer à produire localement de tels films. Ses deux longs métrages, *Madeleine de Verchères* (1922) et *La drogue fatale* (1924), sont bien accueillis lors de leur sortie dans la seule salle qui présente du cinéma indépendant, le Saint-Denis. Mais cela constitue un canal fort restreint.

En fait, les rares films produits par des Québécois ne sont pas diffusés par les Américains qui dominent le marché et ne veulent d'aucune manière encourager leurs concurrents. Conséquemment, parce qu'ils ne contrôlent pas la distribution, les Canadiens ont peu de possibilité de se voir à l'écran, ou même de désirer se voir. Si le développement d'une production nationale comme manière de résister à l'envahissement américain constituera jusqu'à nos jours une constante de la vie cinématographique canadienne, on voit bien qu'il est quasiment impossible de développer de manière satisfaisante ladite production et que de toute manière elle a de la difficulté à rejoindre le public auquel elle est destinée. Les Américains font en sorte que le cinéma vu par les Québécois soit et demeure américain.

D'ailleurs si on examine la centaine de vues locales que nous avons repérées pour la période allant de 1910 à 1915, celles qui ont le plus d'envergure sont anglaises. La plupart des vues anglophones passent dans des salles de qualité tandis que les vues francophones héritent des salles secondaires. Dans l'état de nos recherches, on ne sait pas si leur diffusion se fait à la grandeur de la province. La distribution est toujours un handicap pour les vues locales.

Conclusion

Ce texte a permis d'identifier brièvement les principaux acteurs qui s'aventurent sur le terrain de la diffusion des vues animées au Québec : les itinérants ou les intermittents de l'exploitation étrangers qui font du Québec leur destination, les exploitants locaux qui s'adonnent à l'importation et à la distributions des films, les firmes étrangères qui ouvrent des succursales locales, les salles qui s'y approvisionnent. Il a précisé leur mode d'opération en fonction des marchés visés. La fragmentation et la diversification des pratiques de distribution qui marquent les années avant la Première Guerre mondiale font progressivement place à une consolidation autour de pôles locaux et étrangers, puis à une absorption ou une évacuation de ceux-ci au profit de quelques monopoles états-uniens qui remplacent les distributeurs locaux. Nous avons examiné les forces à l'œuvre dans cette évolution, les intérêts en cause et les pratiques de chacun. Nous avons essayé de mettre en lumière les premiers impacts de la monopolisation de la distribution sur la production canadienne. On ne peut corréler, dans l'état de nos recherches, la production de films, les agents qui assurent leur distribution et les salles où ils ont été diffusés à Montréal ou ailleurs.

La situation québécoise au début du XXe siècle ressemble à une situation coloniale où une bonne partie des échanges repose sur une économie de succursales. Ce système a freiné, puis entravé la prise en charge de nos moyens d'expression et fortement balisé nos moyens de diffusion. Notre passage à la modernité s'est effectué, sur le terrain du cinéma, par l'entremise d'œuvres étrangères et plus spécifiquement d'œuvres tournées localement par des étrangers. Les seuls agents de réalisation locaux qui auraient pu participer à l'élaboration d'une telle culture moderne ont vu plutôt les pouvoirs religieux et politiques leur mettre des bâtons dans les roues, et en fin de compte, ce sont eux, et tous les petits exploitants, qui en ont subi les conséquences, les plus gros ayant pu résister et même absorber les faibles indépendants. En définitive, sur une période qui dépasse à peine vingt ans, on aura assisté à une prise de contrôle serrée, sous domination étrangère, d'un secteur clé de l'institution cinématographique, la distribution, et à ses effets néfastes sur la production locale, dont le modèle sera reconduit dans les années subséquentes et dont les conséquences se font encore sentir de nos jours.

Notes

1. La recherche pour ce texte fut rendue possible grâce à une subvention du Conseil de recherches en sciences humaines du Canada. Je tiens à remercier mes auxiliaires, Louis Pelletier et Sylvie Bissonnette, ainsi que le Groupe de recherche sur l'avènement et la formation des institutions cinématographique et scénique (Grafics), Université de Montréal, pour leur précieux appui.

2. Il s'agit de l'établissement du Dominion du Canada, ce terme désignant l'union du Haut-Canada (Ontario) et du Bas-Canada (Québec) datant de 1841.

3. Politicien et journaliste (1868–1952), fondateur en 1910 du quotidien *Le Devoir*.

4. Lamonde, Yvan, *Histoire sociale des idées au Québec. 1896–1929* (Montréal: Fides, 2004): 9–10.

5. C'est vers 1875 que l'American Amusement Industry, prend le contrôle des principaux théâtres nord-américains.

6. Barrière, Mireille, « Montréal, microcosme du théâtre lyrique nord-américain » in Bouchard, Gérard et Yvan Lamonde, *Québécois et Américains. La culture québécoise au XIXe et XXe siècle* (Montréal: Fides, 1995): 374–385.

7. Cette chaîne possède une salle à Montréal.

8. La série comprend d'autres titres comme *The arrival of the Governor General, Lord Minto, at Quebec* que *A dog team*. Selon l'historien Peter Morris – *Embattled Shadows. A History of Canadian Cinema 1895–1939* (Montréal: McGill-Queen's University Press, 1978) –, l'opérateur était probablement Robert Bonine, le même qui avait tourné en février 1902 trois films sur la ville de Québec pour la Biograph. On peut se demander si le même opérateur pouvait vendre des films à la fois à Edison et Biograph. Cela nous semble hautement improbable car Biograph filmait en 68mm et n'a pas transféré ses films en 35mm avant 1902 lorsque son conflit avec Edison fut tranché en cour.

9. En février 1905, Fenton revient au National pour trois mois. Trop occupé, Ouimet ne pouvait en être le seul projectionniste et il caressait d'autres projets.

10. Jusqu'à la moitié de 1904, Pathé fonctionne avec un agent aux États-Unis. En août, il ouvre une vraie succursale. La compagnie a tellement de difficulté à satisfaire les demandes américaines qu'Edison et Lubin achètent les films Pathé les plus populaires pour en faire des copies et les vendre. Ouimet envisageait un tel arrangement pour l'Est du Canada.

11. Ils font référence à Ouimet en utilisant son nom propre, bien que celui-ci ait alors créé sa compagnie, la Ouimet Film Exchange.

12. Certains scopes choisissaient leur nom en référence aux maisons de production, comme le Kinetoscope ou le National Biograph.

13. On lui doit le développement du projecteur Simplex avec Edwin Porter en 1910.

14. Kleine Optical était un agent d'Edison depuis juin 1899. En 1904, il commence à vendre à ses clients des films Pathé et Biograph. En 1906, il est le principal agent des producteurs européens, incluant Théophile Pathé, Gaumont, Urban et Rossi.

15. À la suite de cela, Pathé, Edison et Biograph entreprennent des négociations qui conduisent à la création en décembre 1908 de la Motion Picture Producers Company qui scelle l'alliance entre Edison et Biograph.

16. En fait, en janvier 1909, il y a deux théâtres Bennett à Montréal, l'un qui présente des vues animées après les numéros de vaudeville, l'autre qui se consacre aux vues de première classe.

17. C'est à cette époque que Lubin (*A Gay Time in Old Quebec*), Biograph (*A Sailor's Heart, Pirate's Gold*) et Vitagraph (*The Old Guard*) utilisent la ville comme le cadre enchanteur de certaines fictions. En 1913 Kalem emprunte le même trajet avec *Wolfe, or The Conquest of Quebec*.

18. Voir le *MPW* du 9 juillet 1910.

19. Ailleurs au Canada ce sera Allen Amusement dans l'Ouest (Allen, propriétaire du Canadian Film Exchange), Great Western Film Exchange à Winnipeg et L.J. Applegath & Sons à Toronto.

20. Par exemple Laemmle dont les bureaux sont situés au théâtre Casino. Il sera victime d'un incendie le 26 janvier 1910.

21. « How Montreal pioneered moving picture business », *Montreal Daily Star* (6–04–1912): 22. En 1910, on considère qu'avec une population active de 2 500 habitants, une ville peut supporter un cinéma.

22. Le Gaiety devient le New London à l'hiver 1914.

23. On peut se reporter au rapport de White, Peter, *Investigation into an Alleged Combine in the Motion Picture Industry in Canada*, (Ottawa: Department of Labor, 1931) et à la recherche de Pelletier, Louis, *George Ganetakos et la United Amusement Corporation, Limited, 1910–1930 : formation d'une chaîne de cinémas montréalaise* (mémoire de maîtrise en études cinématographiques, Université Concordia, mars 2004), non publié.

24. La même opposition prévaut aux États-Unis entre ceux qui privilégient la distribution par état et ceux qui préfèrent la distribution par région (par exemple, la Nouvelle-Angleterre).

25. *The Canadian Moving Picture Digest* 2.13 (24–11–1917): 22.

26. Nutting, Merrick R., « Rumor of amalgamation of several Canadian distribution companies », *The Canadian Moving Picture Digest* 3.3 (22–12–1917): 4.

27. Annoncé dans le *MPW* du 31–01–1914.

28. *Beck's Weekly* 25 (5–09–1914): 23.

29. Louis Pelletier a documenté une partie de la question pour une communication intitulée *Montreal Movie Palaces and the Birth of the Newsreel* et faite au colloque de la Society for Cinema and Media Studies, London, mai 2005.

30. Leurs bureaux se trouvent dans l'édifice de Birks au centre ville. Voir *La Presse* (20–07–1912) ; « Million Dollar Picture Company » (*The Montreal Daily Star*): 23–08–1912 ; « Elle s'impose au Canada », *La Patrie* (5–09–1912) ; « Le cinématographe au Canada », *La Patrie* (23–09–1912).

31. *La Patrie* (28–12–1912).

32. À noter que ces années-la, les Américains vont venir tourner plusieurs films au Québec dont l'action est censée se dérouler ailleurs. Mais quelques-uns se passent au Québec, comme *Wolfe, or the Conquest of Quebec* et *The Man of Shame* qui sortent respectivement en 1914 et 1915. Voir Gaudreault, André, Germain Lacasse et Jean-Pierre Sirois-Trahan (éds.), *Au pays des ennemis du cinéma* (Montréal: Nuit Blanche éditeur, 1996).

33. « Bits about the motion picture houses », *Beck's Weekly* 25 (4–07–1914): 24.

34. « Why the production of pictures in Canada is impractical », *The Canadian Moving Picture Digest* 3.5 (5–01–1918): 4.

8

Araignées et mouches : la formation du « système cinéma » et les débuts de la distribution cinématographique en Espagne, 1906–1921

Luis Alonso García[1]

Université Rey Juan Carlos de Madrid, Espagne

Un travelogue du va-et-vient de la formation du « système cinéma »

C'est en 1895 que le cinématographe Lumière, base historique et origine mythique de notre notion de « cinéma » en tant qu'institution socioculturelle, fait son apparition. Sa place, encore de nos jours, dans l'étude des mythes et l'historiographie du cinéma relève d'une synthèse particulière entre la définition esthétique d'une nouvelle forme d'expression : la *photographie vivante* («living pictures»), et la définition économique d'une nouvelle façon de communiquer : l'album de vues domestiques et exotiques comme étant un autre genre parmi les nouveaux moyens photographiques et phonographiques de l'époque.

Cependant, le projet esthétique et économique des Lumière a été détourné par son premier développement historique : « los cines primitivos » (le cinéma des premiers temps, « the early cinema »). Dès 1896 se développe un ensemble hétérogène de formes d'expression réalisées avec ce nouvel appareil polyvalent, mais basées sur toutes sortes de pratiques socioculturelles préalables. Or, en ce début du XXème siècle, la culture est redéfinie sous l'influence de la *Vie Moderne* et de la *Société de Masses*. Entre 1906 et 1921, le cinéma est défini comme un certain objet spécifique, unitaire et fermé ; par ailleurs, il en est de même pour la radio entre le *broadcast* de Lee de Forest (1907) et la *radio music box* de Sarnoff (1916). Le « système cinéma » a été ainsi défini universellement entre deux idéaux contradictoires – le « *septième art* » de Canudo et l' « *énième industrie* » de Malraux – et une réalité sémiotechnique concrète : l'intégration narrative de la chaîne d'images cinémaphotographiques.

Ce changement d'orientation du phénomène cinématographique évoque le projet intellectuel et commercial des Frères Lumière : d'une part, quant à la *puissance bioscopique* de la « nouvelle image », *perdue* avec le caractère pictural et théâtral du cinéma des premiers temps et *récupérée* par le cinéma classique ; d'autre part, par rapport à la *dimension internationale* que les Lumière ont voulue donner au commerce d'appareils et de vues. Cette *internationalisation* à double sens – envoi d'opérateurs, retour de vues – va avoir des répercussions aussi bien sur la définition sémiotechnique et textuelle des styles et des modes que sur la définition politico-économique et sociale des contenus et des formats. Dès les premiers instants, quoi que le cinéma devienne, il sera un « fait universel » de par la diffusion de ses réussites et de par la distribution de ses produits. Dès lors, les réalités multiples des *cinémas nationaux* devront faire face à ce mythe du *cinéma universel*.[2]

Par conséquent, c'est le rôle essentiel que la diffusion et la distribution jouent dans la formation du système cinéma, aussi bien dans la création et la réception textuelles que dans la production et l'exploitation sociale, qui est la base commune reliant et unifiant les différentes périodes ou les différents tournants de l'histoire du cinéma. Or, l'idée selon laquelle le *pouvoir du cinéma* résidait dans la *taille des studios*, la *qualité des films* et les *quotas de films nationaux et/ou européens* a été privilégiée dans tous les esprits à tous les niveaux (courant, corporatif, politique et médiatique) lors de la compréhension du système institutionnel du cinéma – et de son corollaire, l' « *impérialisme américain* » sur les écrans et les consciences du monde entier. C'est le poids insuffisant donné à l'époque par la culture espagnole d'entreprise aux subtils mais fermes réseaux de distribution – par rapport aux attrayants studios de production et aux encore plus fascinantes salles d'exploitation – qui sera le point faible conduisant à l'incapacité à construire un sous-système national lors de la formation du système international et institutionnel du cinéma. C'est ce « déni » (« verleugnung ») du *rôle de la distribution* dans le cinéma espagnol de 1906 à 1923 que nous essayons d'analyser dans ce travail.

Les loueurs de films, les entrepreneurs de spectacles et leurs mauvaises pratiques[3]

Les « alquiladoras » (maisons de location de films) espagnoles sont d'origines diverses : (a) du personnel de sociétés étrangères ; (b) des laboratoires de films et des ateliers fournisseurs et réparateurs d'appareils ; (c) des propriétaires de salles, « espectaculistas » (entrepreneurs de spectacles), de grandes villes et (d) des « manufacturas » (manufactures de films) qui cherchent à écouler leur production. En 1911, les « *vendeurs et loueurs de films cinématographiques* » figurent ainsi pour la première fois dans le barème de la Taxe Professionnelle.[4]

Nous avons recensé pour cette période de 120 à 150 *maisons de location* de films : ce chiffre élevé comprenant aussi bien les « alquiladoras » (loueurs) des maisons nationales que les « representantes » (représentants) des maisons étrangères. Il s'agit, pour la plupart d'entre elles, de petites firmes à caractère régional ou avec l'exclusivité d'une maison étrangère mineure. Nous pourrions établir une liste par ordre chronologique de treize maisons de location espagnoles les plus représentatives, un dixième du total, comme suit : 1906, Diorama (Barcelone) ; 1907, Juan Fuster (Barcelone, Madrid) ; 1907, José Verdaguer (Barcelone) ; 1908, Trust Film (Barcelone, Madrid) ; 1910, José Gurgui (Barcelone) ; 1910, Cabot et Piñot (Barcelone) ; 1912, Román Solá (Barcelone) ; 1913, Miguel de Miguel (Barcelone, Madrid) ; 1914, Ernesto González (Madrid, Barcelone, Bilbao, Valence, Gijón) ; 1915, Enrique de Castro (Madrid) ; 1916, Vilaseca et Ledesma ; 1917, Julián Ajuria (Barcelone, Madrid) ; 1919, Julio César (Bilbao, Barcelone, Madrid).

S'agissant d'une étude des périodiques, il est impossible de préciser leur chiffre d'affaires et leur part de marché. Au début de la période, entre 1906 et 1910, le secteur est entre les mains des représentants des maisons étrangères, même si les premières maisons de location nationales font leur apparition. Barcelone, qui dispose de meilleurs réseaux de communication et de transport et d'un nombre plus élevé de salles stables, prédomine sur Madrid, la capitale, et sur Valence, l'autre grand centre de production de la période. À partir de 1911, les maisons de location nationales vont détenir le plus gros chiffre d'affaires, s'agissant toujours, bien évidemment, de films étrangers. Certaines d'entre elles ont désormais leur siège à Madrid. Même si les maisons de location affirment avoir l' « exclusivité » de leurs produits et garantissent leur « nouveauté », elles partagent toute sorte de matériel, des premières et des reprises, généralement organisé autour des « programmes » (« le programme allemand », « le programme italien » …) et, à partir de 1918, autour de certaines « stars » et certains « studios » ; cependant, au moins jusqu'en 1921, les « series » (films à épisodes) vont prédominer sur les longs-métrages.

Malgré les plaintes continuelles, les années 1910 représentent un âge d'or pour la distribution, qui jouit d'une économie plus prospère et plus aisée que celle de la production et de l'exploitation. Sans aucun doute, les maisons de location nationales prédominent sur les représentants des maisons étrangères grâce à leur connaissance du terrain et des coutumes autochtones. Leur déclin, sans autre réaction que des plaintes, va commencer lors de l'établissement des maisons américaines après la Première Guerre Mondiale entre 1918 et 1923 – plus particulièrement, à partir de 1921, lorsqu'elles s'installent sous leurs marques d'origine – et l'envahissement total des écrans espagnols au milieu des années 1920.

Si dans les années 1910 les douze sociétés mentionnées ci-dessus se partagent une bonne partie de l'affaire, l'apparition de nouvelles firmes a dû être un élément déstabilisateur. Le nombre de salles d'exploitation s'élève à 300–900 entre 1906–1914 et à 1000–1500 entre 1915–1923. Une maison de location pour dix salles semble une proportion excessive. Contrairement au secteur de la production – où de nouvelles manufactures de films ouvrent constamment puis ferment parfois même avant d'avoir réalisé le film pour lequel elles ont été créées … ou toute de suite après l'avoir achevé –, la croissance au niveau des *loueurs de films* et des *entrepreneurs de spectacles* est constante et soutenue, ce qu'un chroniqueur appelle « *la coqueluche cinématographique* » en parlant du nombre excessif de nouvelles salles à Barcelone.[5] D'ailleurs, les maisons de location de films sont très souvent créées par scission et non pas par concentration – hormis le cas extrême de la maison Verdaguer, véritable *école de loueurs de films*. Cette apparition constante de nouvelles firmes résulte premièrement du profond morcellement du territoire espagnol : nous retrouvons aisément les régions géographiques établies pour l'économie du XVIIIème et du XIXème siècles[6] – Barcelone et le littoral méditerranéen, Bilbao et la côte nord, Madrid et les plateaux de l'intérieur, Séville et la vallée du Guadalquivir – dans la propriété des affaires de distribution et d'exploitation cinématographiques ici étudiées. À cette segmentation territoriale il faut ajouter l'atomisation commerciale. En effet, dans l'économie espagnole le caractère familial est privilégié dans la configuration des entreprises.[7] Toute entreprise est basée sur le nom et les actifs d'un ou deux professionnels également propriétaires de la firme.

Enrique de Castro (Madrid, 1915) pourrait être une de ces *grandes maisons de location de films* consacrée à ce commerce régional, loin de grandes villes et des chroniques des revues. Entre 1918 et 1923, elle ne paraît jamais dans les pages d'information de la revue *Cinema Variedades*, mais son message publicitaire est toujours le même dans tous les numéros : « plus d'un million de mètres de films comiques et dramatiques d'une à cinq parties ». À l'opposé, ces mêmes années, Miguel de Miguel (Barcelone, 1915), une maison de location au centre de l'information et de l'exploitation, annonce ses dernières acquisitions sous le titre « l'aristocratie du film ». Face à la croissance constante des affaires du cinéma, les maisons de location ont dû comprendre qu'il était approprié d'augmenter leurs actifs et d'élargir leur clientèle en s'intégrant. Cependant, cette concentration n'a lieu qu'à la fin de la période, lorsque l'expansion des distributeurs américains est déjà amorcée. Une de premières tentatives de concentration d'entreprises et d'assimilation intellectuelle de nouvelles modalités internationales de diffusion et de distribution est certainement le Repertorio Dulcinea. Cette société a été créée le 21 juin 1920 par une demi-douzaine des loueurs de films de l'époque (Miguel de Miguel, Eduardo et Adolfo Vilaseca, José Casanovas et Enrique Piñol ...) et a été dissoute à la fin de la même année.[8] L'hiver 1919–1920 des pages entières sont consacrées à annoncer la première du Repertorio Dulcinea pour la saison 1920–1921, avec des films tels qu'*Intolerance* (David W. Griffith, 1916) ou *Madame Du Barry* (Ernst Lubitsch, 1919). Or, malgré le « succès » des premières, le projet échoue en quelques mois. En effet, il est surnommé « Repertorio M. de Miguel » et est l'objet des plaisanteries d'un commentateur qui fait allusion à « un loueur de films qui a impressionné son visage au début des films qu'il loue ».[9]

La segmentation et l'atomisation du marché de la distribution ainsi que le refus de nouvelles formes s'imposant dans la configuration du système international et institutionnel du cinéma sont les clés de la désintégration du secteur des maisons de location de films nationales. Premièrement, suite aux *excès* des exploitants nationaux à partir de 1914. Ensuite, suite aux *excès* des distributeurs américains lorsqu'ils vont entamer la phase finale de leur expansion mondiale à partir de 1921. Le seul secteur qui – de par son chiffre d'affaires – aurait pu imprimer un caractère national au système international du cinéma sera littéralement désarticulé et mis hors jeu en deux ans. Et presque personne ne s'en apercevra, entre les regrets face à la *blessante absence espagnole* de production et les plaintes face à la *blessante présence américaine* dans l'exploitation. Il convient donc de décrire plus en détail comment cette ruine s'est forgée au sein de la prospérité.

Malgré les mises en garde contre les limites des affaires dans le domaine du cinéma au début des années 1910,[10] rien ne peut dissuader les loueurs de films et les entrepreneurs de spectacles de croire qu'il s'agit d'une *affaire facile* : « Tout le monde sait qu'avoir un cinématographe est un grand pas sur le chemin de la richesse ... mais loin de là ».[11] Mais l'*affaire facile* n'est que le revers de l'*affaire rapide*. Les *bonnes pratiques* économiques qui doivent exister entre les différents acteurs d'une industrie disparaissent face à la prépondérance de la « concurrence négative ».[12] Le marché international étant intouchable de par son propre caractère extérieur, les *mauvaises pratiques* seront toujours accomplies par les différents agents autochtones entre eux. Trois phénomènes illustrent ces mauvaises pratiques : (a) la « reventada » (la projection d'une première dont l'*exclusivité* a été annoncée par et appartient à un autre exploitant) ;[13] (b) le « pase » (l'utilisation d'une bande par plusieurs exploitants dont un seul l'a louée) ;[14] (c) le « refrito » (la reprise de vieux films avec de nouveaux titres pour les faire passer pour des premières).[15]

Les plaintes vont être constantes. La « fragilité du commerce des films »[16] et les « problèmes persistants entre les distributeurs et les exploitants »[17] vont amener à envisager la demande d'une assemblée générale entre les parties;[18] bien évidemment, sans trop de résultats : « Depuis longtemps, ils s'y parlent tous mais, comme dit-on familièrement, on en encaisse peu, très peu d'entre eux ».[19] Précisément, au moment où le secteur cinématographique commence à se consolider à Madrid, l'économie cinématographique espagnole se trouvait de façon endémique dans un point intermédiaire de l' « économie duale », là où les normes de *confiance personnelle* du petit commerce se dissolvent, mais les règles des *rapports professionnels* du grand marché ne sont pas instaurées.

À l'aube de la Grande Guerre, le monde du cinéma caresse l'« espoir » aussi honteux qu'illusoire d'« énormes chances » que la neutralité espagnole entraînera dans un contexte européen hypothétique de « studios paralysés » et d'« écrans désapprovisionnés ». Or, la réalité a été bien différente, car le désapprovisionnement concernait aussi bien la pellicule vierge que les nouveautés. Malgré les rappels à la modération[20] et les mesures mises en œuvre par la Direction Générale des Douanes pour favoriser la circulation du matériel,[21] la chute de l'offre entraîne une augmentation de mauvaises pratiques entre les distributeurs et les exploitants avec la hausse des prix du matériel fourni et la suite des subterfuges autour des films projetés: « reventadas », « pases », « refritos ».[22] Or, la bulle ne se dégonfle pas, même malgré le retour à la normale des pays en guerre et les nouvelles menaces : la hausse du prix des films à cause de la réévaluation du dollar et l'augmentation de l'offre par le matériel en stock mais aussi par le nouveau matériel américain qui arrive en force.[23] C'est le début de la *concurrence sauvage*. D'une part, les exploitants, de plus en plus nombreux, ont toujours tendance – depuis avant la guerre[24] – à diminuer le prix d'entrée et à augmenter la taille et la fréquence des programmes : séances de trois ou quatre heures, voire jusqu'à huit heures par programme et entrée, à renouveler tous les trois jours.[25] D'autre part, face à la surabondance de films étrangers, les distributeurs, de plus en plus nombreux, baissent les prix de location pour pouvoir rester dans les affaires, parfois même en-dessous du prix d'achat du matériel.[26] Cette baisse des prix de location va avoir un effet dévastateur sur la production nationale, ses produits n'étant pas compétitifs.

Le « chaos » est évident,[27] et le secteur de la distribution semble être au bord de « la ruine imminente, du désastre et de la mort des affaires cinématographiques » ;[28] et ceci, non pas par manque de bénéfices, mais par l'absence de perspectives d'avenir et de critères d'action. Ce petit détail marque un changement d'attitude dans la culture d'entreprise : le cinéma est enfin envisagé comme étant plus qu'une poule aux œufs d'or dont on tire profit sauvagement avant de la tuer. La seule preuve, détournée, de ce *changement d'attitude* est le fait que les distributeurs et les exploitants admettent être incapables de s'entendre selon les bonnes pratiques des rapports professionnels.

La formation excentrique du système national du cinéma espagnol

À partir de 1909, la présence du cinéma en Espagne se concrétise. On avait déjà écrit sur le cinéma auparavant : sur ses dangers moraux, ses vertus éducatives, ses affinités artistiques …, mais, au début des années 1910, un esprit corporatif se manifeste par des débats divers sur l'arbitraire de la censure, la perception excessive des impôts, l'absence de soutien institutionnel ou les importations excessives de films étrangers. La solution de tous ces problèmes imposait une réglementation administrative et une autorégulation corporative de l'économie cinématographique. Or, malgré les critiques faites aux excès ou aux retards législatifs, c'est l'échec total de l'autorégulation corporative qui a été la cause du désastre final de la décennie suite à l'incapacité non seulement de régulariser des organisations intersectorielles mais aussi d'obliger à respecter les normes établies.[29]

Pendant toute la décennie, seules seront constantes les demandes concernant l'établissement d' « une Chambre Syndicale qui réunisse les secteurs de l'industrie (producteurs), du commerce (distributeurs) – et de ses trois branches: vente, achat et location – et des entreprises (exploitants) pour défendre l'économie nationale ».[30] Finalement, on évoquera « le besoin d'une institution de sauvegarde ».[31] Malheureusement, il s'agit là d'un trait caractéristique du discours politique national de toute la première moitié du XXème siècle. Or, bien évidemment, l'autorégulation ne peut pas être exigée ni imposée de l'extérieur.

D'ailleurs, dans la citation même se dessine le trou noir qui absorbera les rares énergies restant pour constituer une économie cinématographique nationale. En effet, l'*Industrie,* identifiée à l'*Art* cinématographique – dont personne ne doute plus devant les preuves venant de l'étranger –, est réduite au secteur de la production et à ses manufactures. Tout le *reste* n'est que *Commerce* entre les loueurs et les entrepreneurs, un simple échange de ce qui est créé ailleurs sous les Grands Idéaux de l'Art et de l'Industrie du Cinéma. Les yeux fermés sur la réalité socioculturelle, on adopte une version pervertie du mythe en identifiant et en sublimant les deux termes du couple « art et industrie ». Si cette interprétation semble trop excessive, il suffit de jeter un coup d'œil au même numéro de la revue, où sont détaillées « les raisons esthétiques de la prédominance américaine dans le commerce cinématographique ».[32] À la fin de 1919, un ultimatum est lancé concernant « *la crise du spectacle cinématographique* », c'est-à-dire des secteurs nationaux de ce spectacle.[33] Dans ce même numéro, une première est largement annoncée : *The Birth of a Nation* (David W. Griffith, 1915).

C'est ainsi qu'a cristallisé la plainte qui caractérisera pour toujours le discours espagnol sur le cinéma national : celui-ci semblant traverser de façon intermittente de « bons moments » et de « crises perpétuelles » dans un va-et-vient maniaco-dépressive.[34] Tout est réduit à une défense de notre cinéma envisagé comme étant un « *problème national* » face à l'envahissement américain des salles.[35] C'est là où le discours devient complètement insensé. L'établissement de « quelques manufactures de taille pour de belles raisons de patriotisme et d'intérêt moral »[36] leur semblait donc apporter une réponse suffisante dans la lutte contre les « españoladas » (des films montrant des clichés sur le caractère espagnol) et les « extranjerismos » (des films faits d'emprunts venant de l'étranger): « Rien de mieux pour qu'une fois pour toutes nous soyons connus à l'étranger tel que nous sommes réellement oubliant à tout jamais les mensonges sur nos coutumes, notre manière d'être et nos lois qui circulent au-delà des Pyrénées comme étant parole d'évangile ».[37] Même si ce rôle éducatif de la production avait peu à voir avec la santé financière d'un secteur économique basé sur la distribution et l'exploitation. Tout semblait être réduit à la nécessité d'un « cinéma national » traduisant l' « essence espagnole » sous toutes ses formes : un climat tempéré, des paysages divers et grandioses, des traits psychologiques profonds, des scénarios centenaires, des chefs-d'œuvre ... tout ce qui ferait que « notre pays » devienne une de « premières puissances cinématographiques en Occident ». Cette approche réductrice du cinéma espagnol qui le ramène à un bilan économique donné et à certaines valeurs esthétiques de la production – « Agir pour notre industrie est agir pour notre pays » – aura pour corollaire, selon une logique perverse mais accablante, l'identification et l'accusation du coupable : le secteur de la distribution, « qui n'a pas su donner son avis sur notre oeuvre réalisée ou à réaliser ».[38]

À partir de l'appropriation du cinématographe primordial, l'origine des cinémas des premiers temps a été un « complexe » de formes sémiotechniques et de pratiques de communication sans centre ni clôture. Il ne s'agit pas pour autant d'un objet aléatoire et incontrôlable, mais son devenir dépend de forces politico-économiques et socioculturelles qui dépassent les possibilités d'intervention des domaines épars dont il est l'origine : les vues naturelles, les tableaux-vivants, les fantasmagories, les actualités, les dramatisations morales, les récits visuels ... ou les « visions musicales et les projections parlantes » d'Adrià Gual à la Salle Mercé de Barcelone en 1904.[39] Néanmoins, on a tendance à attribuer un centre, un sens et une fermeture aux praxis socioculturelles diverses. C'est ce que l'on peut appeler, en termes généraux, un « système ». Définir rigoureusement une pratique socioculturelle permet de rentabiliser, par la spécialisation, les coûts de création et les dépenses de production. C'est ce qui est arrivé lors du passage du *Cinématographe* au *Cinéma* selon deux choix : l'*intégration narrative* de la chaîne d'images photographiques et l'*intégration économique* du film dans les réseaux de distribution mondiale. Une telle restriction, l'existence même d'un *système*, donne autonomie et indépendance à son fonctionnement sur le terrain et, par conséquent, attribue le contrôle interne à ses membres. Bien évidemment, ceci n'annule pas les influences venant de l'extérieur, mais les dilue ou les dilate. Tout compte fait, tous les systèmes appartiennent en définitive au complexe socioculturel des idées et des œuvres de l'homme dans son devenir, au hasard de l'humain au sein de l'histoire. Cependant, le système fonctionne comme si ces influences extérieures étaient minimes.

Dans ce travail nous décrivons le fonctionnement du « système cinéma » du point de vue du rôle attribué à la distribution. Notre objectif était d'expliquer la confusion dans laquelle, pendant cette période et quant à ce système, le *discours publique* a plongé la *pratique filmique*. Le problème n'était pas la *toute-puissance matérielle étrangère* mais l'*impuissance mentale* de la culture nationale à comprendre les bases esthétiques et économiques du système cinéma naissant. Toutes les plaintes se résumaient désormais à demander *plus de studios et plus d'écrans* pour le cinéma national : ceci étant la seule et unique façon envisageable de lutter contre l'*envahissement* de produits et de coutumes venus d'ailleurs et la *distorsion* de notre essence dans les « españoladas ». L'idée selon laquelle la puissance de la *diffusion des idées* dépendait plus du contrôle de la *distribution de produits* que de l'existence de studios et d'écrans nationaux a été – et nous semble aujourd'hui – évidente et incontestable.

Cependant, dans cette période de crise, il s'est avéré inconcevable axer la praxis d'un éventuel cinéma national sur les réseaux de distribution – aussi réels qu'invisibles -. Dans un article intitulé « el Capital Español y la Cinematografía », publié par un quotidien de la presse générale,[40] le cinéaste italien Rino Lupo, installé dans la péninsule ibérique, recueille plusieurs dizaines de clichés répétés pendant les deux décennies précédentes. Dans une période où la distribution américaine achève l'envahissement total des écrans espagnols, il est à souligner son *double principe de philosophie économique* : (a) le décalage et la hiérarchie existant entre l'« Industrie » valorisée (la production de films) et le « Commerce » dévalorisé (tous les autres « processus dérivés : l'achat-vente, la location, l'exploitation des salles ») ; et (b) la soumission de l'« esprit industriel » à la « partie artistique », certainement le meilleur moyen de réussite économique car « un bon film n'a pas de concurrents et est toujours vendu à des prix élevés ». Tout se résumait donc en une double soumission : du *Commerce* à l'*Industrie* et de l'*Industrie* à l'*Art*. La réitération maintes fois de ces fausses vérités pendant la période où un système complètement opposé prenait forme – la création soumise à la production, la production soumise à la distribution – a fini par greffer un mythe réconfortant – « oui, je sais … mais quand même … » – qui restera dans le cinéma espagnol longtemps, très longtemps.

Notes

1. Ce travail est basé sur les études lancées pour le projet de recherche « la configuration des notions de "cinéma national" et de "cinéma universel" pendant la période 1906–1921 de la cinématographie espagnole », financé par la Direction Générale de la Recherche de la Communauté de Madrid (DGI/CAM: 06/0137/2000). Il a été rédigé suite aux suggestions et aux remarques de Julio Pérez Perucha, Emilio Carlos García Fernández et Rafael Utrera Macías.

2. Certains de nos derniers travaux sont axés sur ce rapport entre l'*universel* et *le national* : les rapports entre les historiens du cinéma espagnols et leur objet naturel, le cinéma espagnol (García Alonso, Luis, "Anomalías Históricas y Perversiones Historiográficas: de la malquerida a la niña de tus ojos" in *Las Heridas de las Sombras, el Cine Español en los Años 40* [Madrid, Academia de las Artes y las Ciencias Cinematográficas y Asociación Española de Historiadores del Cine, Junio de 2001]: 575–604) ; la transmission courante et académique du mythe de l'*histoire universelle du cinéma* par les manuels (id., *El Extraño Caso de la Historia Universal del Cine* [Valencia, Episteme, 2000]) ou l'indétermination de la notion de cinéma espagnol par rapport au sentiment de crise perpétuelle de sa pratique (id. ([ed.], *Once Miradas sobre la Crisis y el Cine Español* [Madrid, Ocho y Medio, 2003]).

3. Les informations recueillies sont parfois le résultat d'estimations que l'on espère tout au moins fiables faites à partir de l'étude des périodiques de l'époque. Tout particulièrement: AyC: *Arte y Cinematografía* (Barcelone, 1910–1936), *El Cine* (Barcelone, 1912–1927) et *Cinema – Cinema Variedades* (Madrid, 1918–1936). Quoiqu'il en soit, cette étude n'aurait pas été possible sans les idées et les informations apportées par certains ouvrages : le bref et dense panorama général du cinéma muet réalisé par Pérez Perucha, Julio, "Narración de un aciago destino, 1896–1930" in Gubern, Román et alii, *Historia del Cine Español* (Madrid, Cátedra, 1997 [1989]): 19–122 ; les analyses correspondantes dans Pérez Perucha, Julio (ed.), *Antología Crítica del Cine Español* (Madrid, Cátedra, 1997) ; l'étude spécifique du cinéma catalan entre 1906 et 1923 de Palmira González López, *Els Anys Daurats del Cinema Clàssic a Barcelona, 1906–1923* (Barcelone, Institut del Teatre de la Diputació de Barcelona, 1987) ; les travaux très documentés et analytiques sur les années 20 de Joaquín Cánovas "Consideraciones Generales sobre la Industria Cinematográfica Madrileña en los Años Veinte", *Archivos de la Filmoteca* 6 (Junio-Agosto 1990): 14–25 ainsi que "El Cine Mudo Madrileño" in Gubern, Román (ed.) *un Siglo de Cine Español* (Madrid, Academia de las Artes y Ciencias Cinematográficas, 1997): 53–63 ; Cerdán, Josetxo, *La Renovación Industrial que Convirtió a España en un País Apto para el Cine Sonoro, Temporadas 1926–1927/1932–1933* (Barcelone, Universidad Autónoma de Barcelona, Marzo de 1996) ; Fernández Colorado, Luis, *Repercusiones Socio-Industriales y Creativas de la Implantación del Cine Sonoro en España, 1927–1934* (Madrid, Universidad Complutense de Madrid, 1996) ; et, notamment, par son analyse des données industrielles de la période, l'étude générale d'Emilio Carlos García Fernández, *El Cine Español entre 1896 y 1939: historia, industria, filmografía y documentos* (Barcelone, Ariel, 2002).

4. Vallés Copeiro del Villar, Antonio, *Historia de la Política de Fomento del Cine Español* (Valencia, Filmoteca de la Generalitat Valenciana, 1992): 18.

5. *El Cine* (20–07–1912).

6. Ringrose, David R., *España, 1700–1900: el mito del fracaso* (Madrid, Alianza, 1996): 66–89.

7. Cf. Tortella, Gabriel, *el Desarrollo de la España Contemporánea* (Madrid, Alianza, 1995) ainsi que Comín, Francisco / Martín Aceña, Pablo, "Rasgos Históricos de las Empresas en España, un Panorama", *Revista de Economía Aplicada* 4.12 (1996): 75–123.

8. *Cinema* (janvier 1921).

9. *Cinema* (mai-juin 1921).

10. *El Cine* (20–07–1912).

11. *El Cine* (3–01–1914).

12. *AyC* (15–09–1912).

13. *AyC* (15–09–1912).

14. *El Cine* (12–04–1913, 10–05–1913, 20–09–1913, 12–09–1914, 31–12–1917).

15. *El Cine* (18–07–1914).

16. *AyC* (15–03–1913).

17. *AyC* (15–04–1913).

18. « Calma », *AyC* (15–07–1913); « Expectación », *AyC* (30–07–1913); « Desorientados », *AyC* (15–09–1913).

19. *El Cine* (14–07–1914).

20. *AyC* (15–08–1914).

21. *El Cine* (24–07–1915).

22. *AyC* (31–07–1916).

23. « La Invasión Americana », *AyC* (5–10–1917).

24. *El Cine* (31–05–1913).

25. *AyC* (15–01–1919).

26. *AyC* (31–01/31–03–1919).

27. *AyC* (15/20–04–1919).

28. *AyC* (30–09–1919).

29. *El Cine* (14–07–1914); *AyC* (5–10–1917, 31–01/31–03–1919, 15–07–1919).

30. *AyC* (15–10–1919).

31. *AyC* (31–10–1919).

32. « Las Películas Americanas », *AyC* (15–10–1919).

33. « Cinematografía o Dejarlo », *AyC* (11/12–1919).

34. Alonso (2003) op. cit.

35. Sola Mestres, Juan / Fontanals Alfredo, « Al Público Español, Por Nuestro Decoro y Dignidad Cívica », *AyC* (31–10–1919).

36. *El Cine* (16–08–1913).

37. *El Cine* (11–04–1914).

38. Requena, F. P., « De Re Cinematográfica », *AyC*, n° spécial (juin 1920).

39. Minguet Batllori, Joan, "Early Spanish Cinema and the Problem of Modernity", *Film History* 16.1 (2004): 92–107.

40. *El Imparcial* (6–06–1925 et 13–06–1925).

9

Censorship and Film distribution in Russia: 1908–1914

Rashit M. Yangirov

My report is the next part of the subject discussed on the 3rd DOMITOR congress in 1994 and is based on the same sources, but of a later period.[1] As the first historian of the Russian censorship, Nikolai Drizen, remarked in 1916,

> history of the Russian censorship to a certain extent is the history of Russian society. Development of the civil idea and its general experiences, grieves and pleasures always depended on a vigilant eye of a censor permanently guiding its evolution.[2]

In the sphere of entertainment its practice was based on four major priorities: protection of the public from bad influences, such as pornography, protection of religious feelings of believers, non-admission in the dramatic writings of ultra-nationalist ideas, which might cause controversy among various parts of population and last, but not least – protection of the reputation of prominent state and public personalities. Long-term practice of Russian censorship had developed general obligatory limitations: "The state protects not only the royal family, but also their servants, because their behavior could blacken their masters". Even overthrown monarchs, such as Napoleon, were not excluded from the list.[3] Censors kept an eye even at heads of hostile nations, who were protected from any form of criticism. The inner life of the Russian state and its subjects was also protected. No negative reflection could touch social strata like military, nobility, merchants, writers, and even actors. And finally censors shielded the privacy of people "with more or less loud surnames".[4] The Orthodox confession was also protected. Special rules banned images of churches and crosses, religious services and ceremonies, as well as the clergy from on the stage.

Obviously, from the very beginning cinema had been recognized as an organic part of this practice, although serious censorship control was undertaken only from the autumn of 1908 – after regular film theatres were established in the two major Russian cities. In the following decade film censorship had developed some special forms of control, although it hardly differed from the dramatic stage.

Authorities were mainly concentrated on the visualisation of members of the Imperial family who were ranked as the state regalia. Public distribution of their images, including the "Tsar's film chronicle", was regulated by the Imperial Court Ministry, whose officers were charged to see to it "nothing reprehensible from the point of view of censorship or ugly for an eye in relation to the Highest Persons could be observed in moving pictures".[5]

Generally 1908 had introduced some serious innovations in the evolution of film practice in Russia and first of all, in the "Tsar's film chronicle". One of them was the introduction of music in its public screenings. In the first years, as we know, moving images of the Tsar were separated from other parts of the programme and were screened in total silence because music accompanying sacral images was totally forbidden. The archaism of this interdiction had been felt sharply enough and in order to raise its attractiveness, the Court cameraman Aleksandr Yagelsky in November 1908 suggested accompanying films showing the Emperor receiving army parades with military marches as well as films of funerals with church anthems or the mourning march by Chopin. His idea was accepted by the ministry officers, but restricted to Yagelsky personally.[6]

Another important innovation was the editing of the Tsar films, that is the cutting out of various inconvenient persons and situations. In February 1908, the owner of "The Royal Bio" film theatre in Saint Petersburg applied for permission to screen the recent newsreels of a church holiday and army parade in the Emperor's residence in Tsarskoe Selo. After a preliminary viewing of it the court censor considered inconvenient pictures of clergy crossing themselves and bowing to Imperial Persons. Another flaw in the film were pictures of the Sovereign, who repeatedly corrected his moustaches. The final verdict on the film was that it could be publicly screened only after cutting the Tsar's crossings.[7] It was the first case of a new practice, whereas in previous years in such cases the entire film was not recommended for screening.

Another case took place in February 1909 in the film of the funeral of the Grand Duke Vladimir Aleksandrovic. The censor ordered to exclude inconvenient pictures with the Grand Duke Nikolai Nikolayevich who "turns before the audience in different parts with a cigarette between his teeth".[8]

Sometimes censors noticed technical mistakes of cameramen like in December 1914. Then the owner of the "Parisiana" film theatre located on Nevsky Prospekt, applied for permission to screen a newsreel of the celebrations of the Romanov dynasty, which had taken place a year before. One of its sequences fixed the imperial cortege passing through City Street. The censor found that the film represented the Sovereign in a wrong way – surrounded with the enforced military convoy while the cameraman "has deliberately reduced the distance between Sovereign and the escort of honour".[9]

The privacy of the Royal family was also toughly controlled. The Royal couple, for example, personally censored all the pictures of their children and didn't admit any pictures of their informal behaviour in public occasionally included in films.[10] One of the curious cases took place in November 1908 when Yagelsky filmed the Emperor on the board of the Royal yacht "Shtandart" where he informally mingled with the boat crew and tested their meals and vodka. The censor's verdict was that those pictures could have a bad impact on the public image of the Monarch and could be used in a negative way by political opponents.[11]

Looking at more film appearances of Nicholas II it should be added that only from the beginning of 1911 the Royal censor admitted his image in civil clothes – in coat and kettle hat – during a visit to Germany, while before the Emperor was to be seen only in military uniform.[12]

Starting from 1908 the Russian monarch had been regularly filmed not only by Yagelsky, but other Russian and foreign cameramen as well – especially during important foreign trips. Various companies had released documentaries and screened them all over Europe and even applied for new filming in Russia itself. After thorough considerations the Royal Court censors permitted this practice, but only on a limited

Fig. 1. Theatre 'Moulin-Rouge' (S.-Petersburg). Film programme for 26 September –
3 October 1909.

scale. Among those cameramen the Russians Aleksandr Drankov and Vladimir Bulla
should be mentioned in the first place, as well as unnamed cameramen of the Deutsche
Bioscop, Felix Mesguich, Ferdinand Friedrich Guillaume Kemmeler from Pathé and
some others. In March 1909 it was finally decided that "more filming could add
popularity to the image of the Emperor", although Yagelsky kept a privileged position.[13]

The main obligation of the Court cameraman was to film the Royal family and to
arrange private screenings for its members. This practice provided his main income.
By the autumn of 1911 Yagelsky in total had been paid more than 100 thousand rubles
for shooting, film printing, screenings and its preservation etc.[14] This sum was
considered fair enough to compensate his production costs and that's why the same
year the Imperial Court Ministry suggested that Yagelsky could transfer all negative
and positive films of the "Tsar's film chronicle" to the Court depository for free. The
cameraman refused and this long-term dispute about the possession of the film state

regalia continued up to the end of 1916, when Yagelsky died, and with the February revolution of 1917 the material was no longer used.[15]

Papers of the Imperial Court represent Yagelsky as a successful film demonstrator. Throughout the 1910s he had arranged many commercial screenings of the "Tsar's film chronicle", although his enterprise was not able to produce film copies in industrial quantities. Usually he printed not more than two positive copies of the film using one of them in the capital and regions nearest to it. This means that all of the Russian audiences, especially in the far distant provinces, and despite of great demand, could not watch films by Yagelsky, which were replaced by foreign newsreels, produced by Pathé, Gaumont and other companies.[16]

Feature films were also under supervision of the Imperial Court Ministry, but only those, which were related to the person of the Emperor or other members of the Romanov Dynasty. Archival papers refer to only four cases. In this context film manufacturers were anxious to receive positive answers to two questions: whether it was possible to show in it the Royal ancestors of the current Monarch and secondly, whether they would be able to add a note saying that it was made with the authorization of the Sovereign? Obviously, if the last question had a positive answer, it could bring them commercial success. But normally the Emperor and the officers of the Imperial Court Ministry were very careful about this matter and there were only few cases in the history of Russian film production with the direct highest approval or other signs, which could be considered as indicators of their importance from an official point of view.

The first one among them was *Defense of Sebastopol* shot and released in 1911 by Aleksandr Khanzonkov.[17] The film was positively received by Nicholas II, although he noticed some faults in the historical scenery.[18] Public success of the film provoked the film manufacturer to start a new project – jointly with Pathé – the film *1812*, especially arranged for the centennial celebrations of the Patriotic war in 1912. In June 1911 all preparatory materials related to its production (script, sketches of scenery, suits, etc.) were sent for the highest approval to the Imperial Court Ministry. Its officers carefully studied those materials and gave their conclusion. In their mind some battle scenes in the script represented "Russian heroes" incorrectly and in a "non-patriotic" way. Another objection was made by the Church censor, who noticed that the receding French military were wearing service dresses of the Orthodox clergy. This was considered a serious violation of religious feelings, although this detail came from the famous painting by Vasily Vereschagin exhibited in the Tretyakov gallery.[19]

Only after the elimination of those "faults" and "mistakes" Khanzhonkov and Pathé were permitted to film in the Kremlin, and the Military ministry provided them with troops and ammunition for the battle scenes, etc. In July 1912, when the film was ready for public screenings Nicholas II himself and the Court censors viewed a copy and put forward their corrections. First of all the Sovereign demanded to exclude the very first scene of the film where Emperor Alexander I appealed to the Russian people to defend their Fatherland, and after that he was blessed by Orthodox clergy. Nicholas II demanded to exclude this sequence from the film referring to the unwritten rule that his Royal ancestors could not be pictured as dramatic characters. Besides he asked to show the film to the officers of the Joint Staff for historical comments and corrections of the battle sequences. Only afterwards the film could be released and it was specially mentioned as a film approved by the Emperor. This increased considerably the number of prints and helped with its successful distribution abroad.

This case provoked a sharp rivalry between Aleksandr Khanzhonkov and Aleksandr Drankov, who competed in the production of "Tsar subjects" in feature films. The first

LIVADIA.

Dimanche, le 3 Novembre 1902.

Programme des tableaux cinématographiques, presentés par le

photographe de la Cour Impériale

K. E. von Hahn et Cᵉ.

PARTIE 1-re.

Collection de tableaux «Courses des taureaux en Espagne», photographiés et préparés par Lumière, frères à Lyon. (12 tableaux).

PARTIE 2-me.

Collection de tableaux «Courses des taureaux en Espague», préparés d'après le système américain et photographiés par L Gaumont à Paris.

PARTIE 3-me.

1) Koursk. Arrivée de sa Majesté l'Empereur à la porte de Kherson.
2) Crimée. Livadia. Départ de Leurs Majestés Imperiales et de la suite pour la promenade par la porte d'Oreanda.

Fig. 2. Film programme of the Royal Court screening by Aleksandr Yagelsky (Livadia, Crimea, 3 November 1902).

case concerned the jubilee films *The Accession of the House of Romanov* produced by Khanzonkov and *The Tercentenary of the Rule of the House of Romanov* produced by Drankov. Under a special agreement, both films were released simultaneously the same day – 16 February 1913.[20] Drankov's turned out to be more successful and was printed in 107 copies, while Khanzhonkov's film ran only in 86 copies. This competition was continued by films with the same title – *Conquest of Caucasus* which had been released by Drankov and Khanzhonkov in October the same year. This production started after a meeting of Nicholas II with Drankov in April 1913, where the Monarch expressed his desire for a film on the history of the Caucasian war. Even though it was produced by Drankov in competition with Khanzhonkov, the Royal Court ministry missed any reference to the Emperor's desire.[21]

The final episode of this practice of official control occurred in January 1917 when Gregory Liebkin produced the film *The Ice House*, based on the historical novel by Ivan Lazhechnikov. Officers of the Royal Court ministry banned it from screening because the Emperor's ancestor Anna Ioannovna appeared as a character in the film and that's why it had to be put on the shelf.[22] But in couple of months the film's owner rejoiced when after the February revolution he could freely release it and specially mentioned that it had been censored for its truthful depiction of the tsarist regime.

As we know, there was no centralized film censorship in Imperial Russia and in this context the distribution of any film could provoke special precedents in the provinces. Today it is very difficult to establish the motivation for the banning of various films by local police officers, who were in charge of controlling the film repertoire. According to the local press, which regularly marked censorship activities, key reasons of such decisions were the plots, which could provoke public indignation or were offending religious feelings. Presumably, the most scandalous case of this sort had happened in Odessa, where censor Sergey Plaksin in May 1915 banned more than a hundred films –new ones as well as titles from previous years. The major part of the titles belonged to so-called "Jewish" films, but for some reasons this also concerned such innocent titles as *Princess Tarakanova*, *In the Days of Hetmans* and others. The last part of the list named filmed considered as frivolous, like *Husband, wife and her lover*, *The Duel*, *Voluptuousness*.[23] One can presume that the main reason of the censor's decision was the war and his fear that it could provoke troubles in a multi-Ethnic region such as Odessa.

As I mentioned, pornography or the so-called 'Paris genre' on the screen was one of the main subjects of censorship. Up to a certain time it was totally out of any control. According to a memoir,

> the first film theatre in Saint-Petersburg named "As in Paris" was located in a cosy mansion in a court yard of Nevsky Prospekt. Its facade was decorated with huge Parisian colourful posters, input flowers in the summer and in winter – with fur-trees. Its main visitors were well-doing city residents but after midnight its owner screened "the Paris genre" (i.e. purely pornographic pictures) films. Those screenings were arranged free-of-charge and were mostly visited by police officers and wealthy city residents accompanied by smart and decent ladies. Another film theatre named "As in Nice" was located oppositely to the first one. It was also luxuriously designed with silkworm breeding, paintings, gilded furniture, huge mirrors in gold frames etc. But it was well-known in close circles that "As in Nice" in fact was a fashionable brothel arranged under sign of film theatre.[24]

For sure nearly all films of the 'Paris genre' were of French, Italian and partly of German production and they were smuggled into Russia through various channels, mainly through sea ports, like Odessa or Riga. The domestic Russian production is unknown, except for one case with Khanzhonkov. He himself told a story that

> around 1906–1907 he was not successful in the film business and nearly came to bankruptcy. Once he decided to use an opportunity. While his wife was absent from the house, he invited to the summer residence a group of cabaret singers and filmed them in a juicy movie, which did pretty well at the box office. Since that time he started to do well himself, and his enterprise became one of the most solid in Russia. Certainly, once he flourished, Khanzhonkov completely withdrew the film from the screen. But privately he was very fond of telling this story.[25]

The Interior Ministry was very anxious about distribution of various forms of pornography in the country and eagerly joined international efforts against its spread. Its officers attended the first International Anti-Pornography congress in Paris which took place on 21–22 May 1908 as well as the second one from 18 April – 4 May 1910. Then Russia joined the international convention, already signed by 14 European countries and the USA and known as "Arrangement relatif a la répression de la circulation des publications obscènes", which included "dessins, images et objets obscènes".[26] The committee concerned with the press permanently collected related foreign materials[27] and used them in its legislative practice.

In June 1910 the Minister of Interior, Petr Stolypin, issued a special instruction to local governors, explaining what had to be considered as a propagation of pornography in the press. This included advertising of means against pregnancy, medicines for sexual impotence, etc. Films were also on this list.[28] By the end of 1912 the general opinion was that pornography could be subdivided into a rough and a refined form, and film was considered to belong to the second one. The police rigidly watched any signs of pornography and ruthlessly punished owners of cinemas which showed so-called "juicy" films.

In this way both Russian and Western film manufacturers started the curious practice of making hints on pornography. First of all, they used cabaret and farce plays of ambiguous contents and secondly used risky titles in order to attract audience. 1912 also was the year of enormous popularity of Italian and French films on "White female slaves", which were released in series and were nearly the first feature-length ones. Very soon ambiguous film titles also attracted censors who banned their intrusion on public screens or demanded to change them for more convenient ones. For example, in February 1914 the Saint-Petersburg governor reprimanded "for frivolous negligence of duties" one of the censors who permitted to release a film titled *The Criminal Passion of a Father* which had been produced by Drankov.[29] As the governor pointed out the censor has missed this criminal case while, "even its title specifies the necessity to look with special attention to its immoral contents and for that reason a public showing of the film is totally impossible". In fact, this film pictured the life of high society and there was no element of pornography in it.[30]

Sometimes censors used various tricks to stop film manufacturers to reproduce risky subjects. In January 1914, the company of Paul Thiemann applied for permission to set up a screen version of the novel "Sanin" by Mikhail Artsybashev. Although this book was already published, i.e. it had passed censorship, public opinion considered it completely indecent writing. So the Committee on Press replied evasively that it was not competent enough to decide whether it could be screened or not.[31] But it was well known that this institution was responsible for those decisions and in this case it evaded from responsibility in this original manner.

Acknowledgements: I am greatly indebted to the archival officers Svetlana Kazakova and Valentina Loupanova (St.-Petersburg), who has actively assisted in my research.

Notes

1. See: Yangirov, Rashit, *The 'Tsar's Pastime': The Russian Royal Family and Cinema. The Yearly Years (1896–1908) / Le cinema au tournant du siecle/Cinema at the Turn of the Century* (Lausanne-Quebec, 1999).

2. Drizen, Nikolai, *Dramaticheskaia tsenzura dvukh epoch [The Censorship of Drama in Two Epochs]. 1825–1881* (Petrograd, 1916), I.

3. State Archive of the Russian Federation [GARF] (Moscow). 645/1/159/3.

4. Drizen, op. cit., 4–6.

5. Russian State Historical Archive of St.-Petersburg [RGIA]. 776/48/800/13.

6. Ibid., 472/48/800/169–170.

7. Ibid., 472/48/800/109–107.

8. Ibid., 472/48/800/214.

9. Ibid., 472/49/998/262.

10. Ibid.

11. Ibid., 472/48/800/141.

12. Ibid., 472/48/800/351 354.

13. Ibid., 472/48/800/109–111.

14. Ibid., 472/48/787, 794, 1062; 468/14/1103; 468/17/170.

15. Ibid., 472/49/1062/62–66.

16. In May 1917 officers of the former Ministry of the Imperial Court had compiled the general list of manufacturers, who were involved in the production of the Royal documentaries. It included Aleksandr Drankov, "Pathé Frères", Carl Bulla, Aleksandr Khanzhonkov, "Eclipse", "Apollo" (St.-Petersburg), Ian Gutzman (Riga), "Prodafilm" (St.-Petersburg), "Bureau of Cinematographic Equipment" [?], "Gaumont", "Vita" (St.-Petersburg), "Russian Cinematographic Society" (St.-Petersburg), Dmitry Kharitonov (Kharkov-Moscow), "Parisiana Ltd" (St.-Petersburg) and engineer Etlander (Helsingfors). – Ibid. 472/48/1441/139.

17. Tsivian, Yuri and Cherchi Usai, Paolo, Testimoni silenziosi. Film russi 1908–1919 / Silent Witnesses. Russian Films 1908–1919, (Pordenone, London, 1989), 136–138; RGIA. 472/49/1252.

18. See report of Aleksandr Drankov to the Head of the Chancellery of the Imperial Court Ministry of 10 April 1913 on his screening of the film The Tercentenary of the Rule of the House of Romanov to Nickolas II, – RGIA. 472/49/1252/401–442.

19. Ibid., 472/49/969.

20. Tsivian, Yuri and Cherchi Usai, Paolo, Testimoni silenziosi. Film russi 1908–1919 / Silent Witnesses. Russian Films 1908–1919 (Pordenone, London, 1989), 172–174; 206–209.

21. Ibid., 472/49/1252/46–48.

22. Ibid., 776/25/1242.

23. Ibid. 776/22/2/437–440.

24. Orlov, Nikolai, Pervye kinosyemki v Rossii [First Film Shootings in Russia] / Kinovedcheskie zapiski [Film Scholar's Annals] (Moscow, 1999), no. 42, 204.

25. Astromov, Boris. Souvenirs of Khanzhonkov / Art-Ekran [Art-Screen] (Leningrad, 1923). no. 1, 4–5.

26. Printed copy in: RGIA, 776/22/1/79–81.

27. See, for example, "Report from the Joint Select Committee on lotteries and Indecent Advertisements (1908) / House of Commons. London. 1908 (reprinted in 1913)". – Ibid.

28. Ibid.

29. Film directed by Yevgeny Bauer was released on 2 January 1914.

30. [Anon.] Tsenzura kinematograficheskikh kartin [Censorship of the Cinematographic Pictures] / Peterburgskaya Gazeta [Petersburg Gazette], 2 February 1914; RGIA. 472/49/988/190.

31. Ibid., 776/25/1118/10–13.

10

The "backbone" of the business: Scanning signs of US film distribution in the newspapers, 1911–1914

Richard Abel

University of Michigan. USA

US film distribution during the transition era of the early 1910s still is a bit of a mystery – a "missing link", as Ivo Blom calls it, in histories of early cinema.[1] To be sure, previous studies – by Janet Staiger, Robert Anderson, Eileen Bowser, and Michael Quinn[2] – provide invaluable research and analyses of these turbulent years. They have drawn on the trade press, industry documents, and government records to focus on economic and legal practices that created conditions for an industrial structure of distribution (Staiger), on the rise of the Motion Picture Patents Company [MPPC] and its distribution arm, General Film (Anderson), or on attempts to create a viable model of distributing feature films (Bowser, Quinn). While this essay obviously builds on that research, it argues that newspaper ads in selected cities from the Northeast to the Upper Midwest, in conjunction with trade press ads and articles, offer a more finely contoured map of how these distribution models worked at the local or regional level and reveal how the major companies involved in distributing variety programs (General Film, Universal, Mutual) and those distributing multiple-reel or feature films on a regular basis (Warner's, Famous Players) represented themselves to the general public.

Let me begin with an assumption: by the spring of 1911, General Film (which coordinated the rental of MPPC films) and Sales (which had a near monopoly on renting Independent films) had established something like a "closed market" for film distribution in the USA. Using an industrial logic of standardized commodities (distinguishable only in brand name), General Film had moved first to rationalize the industry by guaranteeing licensed exhibitors a "complete service": a variety package of single-reel and split-reel films that could be "freshened" each day. It also instituted a system of standing orders for weekly programs and another of run-clearance zoning that classified theaters so that a limited number had exclusive rights to "first-run" pictures in their area.[3] To secure its own market share, Sales quickly adopted many policies and practices advanced by its competitor, especially the variety package of films that could be changed daily, yet still give priority to "first-run" films.[4] The seeming dominance of these two combined is strikingly evident in the unusual ads that General Film, Victor, and Lake Shore all placed on the first Sunday moving picture pages of the *Cleveland Leader*, in December 1911.[5]

That Sales broke up into at least three factions in the spring of 1912 hardly posed a threat to the burgeoning Independent film production and distribution. Instead, the two strongest rivals that emerged, Universal and Mutual, once again, along with General Film, soon reinstated a closed market for distributing variety programs of constantly changing films.[6] One sign of the stability that the three companies achieved, at least for US manufacturers, was the even more prominent ads for General Film, Victor, and Lake Shore that appeared in the *Cleveland Leader* in December 1912.[7] Another, in the same newspaper, was a weekly report on upcoming films in early February 1913: they would be appearing in first-run theaters already "branded" as Universal, Mutual, and General Film houses.[8] Evidence of the Independents' strength, however, can be found far beyond Cleveland. In late January, Mutual took out a joint half-page ad with the Unique Theatre in the *Des Moines News*, celebrating not only their reciprocally profitable alliance but also the company's status as a "synonym for progressiveness" in the industry.[9] That month, the Venice Theater in Rochester (New York) promoted a similar alliance; in May, both Mutual and Universal ran special ads on a new weekly moving picture page in the *Minneapolis Journal*.[10] At the same time, and continuing for the next three months each Sunday in the *Des Moines Register and Leader*, the two companies began running strip ads that simply circulated the brand names of their regular programs.[11] Although General Film itself did not run such ads, one of its MPPC members, Essanay, did, promoting its "five-a-week" programs of "pure photoplays".[12] Finally, beginning in June, Universal alone promoted its films through the Toledo Film Exchange on the weekly moving picture page of the *Toledo Blade*.[13]

In September 1913, *Motography* claimed that "the single-reel subject" remained "the backbone of the business", and, arguably, the variety program of daily or frequently changed films continued to serve as a major attraction for audiences well into 1914.[14] After all, the variety package that any exchange sent its customers was not unlike a daily newspaper or a constantly updated popular magazine that movie-goers could browse at will in the continuous programs that many theaters still offered.[15] Interestingly, at least two companies circulated graphic images of what they imagined their audience of movie-goers to be. In the summer of 1913, General Film launched a series of ads in the *New York Morning Telegraph*, all linked by its trademark cartoon figure of a uniformed major domo.[16] Most depicted a half dozen people posed at a particular moment of attending a picture theater: lined up to purchase a ticket at the box office, showing the ticket to a male usher, seated (and seen from behind) watching the screen (in this case, a western) or (seen from the front) smiling and laughing in their seats. While all were obviously "clean", well-dressed whites, from little children to elderly grandparents, most were young adults, sometimes grouped in a family (with only one child) but more often as couples, same-sex friends, or single figures absorbed into a happy crowd. And their clothing was suggestive of white-collar workers or either working-class or rural people "out on the town". Several months later, Mutual placed several large ads in newspapers like the *St. Paul Daily News*.[17] One of these also depicted numerous people lined up at the box office (in a far more opulent lobby), including a pair of young women, an elderly couple, several young children, and at least one single man. That the children may not have been chaperoned was indicated by a second ad that showed a mother sending her excited children off to see "Mutual Movies" because "you can safely let the children go *alone*".[18] Mutual's imagined audience also was "clean", well-dressed, and white, the clothing suggestive of middle-class patrons as well as white-collar workers and rural people, as the list of Mutual theaters in Minnesota and the surrounding region attested.[19]

Alternatives to this closed market of the constantly renewed variety package had begun to appear as early as 1911. One strategy, roadshowing, came from the legitimate theater: a distributor took a film "on the road", renting a theater on a percentage-of-the-gross basis. Monopol pioneered this strategy with the five-reel Italian epic, *Dante's Inferno*, advertising the film as "the successor to the Passion Play" and booking it for at least full-week runs in August and September on the prestigious Shubert theater circuit (with ticket prices of 15¢ to 75¢).[20] Another strategy was a "state rights" system of distribution in which a person or firm purchased the right to license a film's exhibition in a particular territory – at legitimate, vaudeville, and/or picture theaters. Although used irregularly for previous "specials", *Dante's Inferno* also showed the system off to real advantage.[21] The earliest state rights bookings (also for a full week) took place in mid-September, from Lawrence (Massachusetts) to Cleveland (at the regular price of 10¢).[22] During the next three months, the film ran from three days to a week or even two weeks (sometimes with an increase in price), in vaudeville houses and major picture theaters throughout the Northeast and Upper Midwest.[23] Thereafter, a host of new or established companies followed one or both of these strategies to distribute nearly every feature-length film (of four or more reels) released on the US market. They included American "specials", from Thomas Ince's *The Battle of Gettysburg* to Universal's *Traffic in Souls*, as well as foreign imports, from Famous Players' *Queen Elizabeth* or George Kleine's *Quo Vadis?* to Eclectic's *Les Miserables*.

Although the trade press consistently promoted the production and distribution of such "special" films, beginning in late 1911, it recognized the difficulty of countering the industry's dependence on the "popular cry" for "first-runs" in variety programs.[24] Rather than a few scattered "special event" films that took six months or a year to circulate widely, argued the *New York Dramatic Mirror*, there had to be "a reasonably dependable supply of new and appealing productions of sufficient strength" and number for the state rights system to demonstrate, as Epes Winthrop Sargent put it, that "a photoplay" not only could be much more than "a daily newspaper" but also be profitable more quickly and assuredly.[25] Sargent was well aware that features required more time, energy, and money to market and demanded of both distributors and exhibitors "a radical departure in [the] usual styles of advertising", promoting each title's unique attraction and targeting its most likely audience, especially through local newspapers.[26] As longer films indeed became more attractive and profitable by 1912, Universal, Mutual, and even General Film found that they could integrate one or more two- or three-reel "special features" into their weekly release schedules. However, the difficulties in distributing longer features persisted, as Helen Gardner's ambitious five-reel *Cleopatra* demonstrates. Much like a theatrical show, *Cleopatra* was "given a try-out ... at a large picture house a few miles outside New York City" in mid-November 1912 and then heavily promoted, not only in the *New York Dramatic Mirror* but also in a full page of publicity stills in the *Cleveland Leader*, of Gardner as that "Sorceress of the Nile".[27] At first, its bookings seemed propitious: two weeks at the Duchess in Cleveland during the Christmas-New Years holidays, an engagement at the prestigious new Gordon Theater in Rochester in late March 1913.[26] Thereafter, it worked its way around the country through the state rights system, ever so slowly and usually for short runs: three days at the Crystal in Minneapolis in May, two days at the Alhambra in Toledo in August, two days at the Palace in Cedar Rapids (Iowa) in September, and a full week at the Star in Des Moines, promoted by an unusual half-page ad in the *Register and Leader*, but not until late May 1914.[29] Only in the summer of 1913 would two US firms finally seek to avoid the problems faced by a film like *Cleopatra* and set out to standardize feature film distribution.[30]

Until now, one of these firms largely has been ignored: Warner's Features.[31] A year earlier, Warner's had begun distributing multiple-reel films, initially sensational melodramas of one kind or another, through nine offices located in the Northeast and Midwest.[32] In late 1912, the company gained a measure of respectability by contracting to release the films of Gene Gauntier Feature Players.[33] The following spring, after the first Gauntier picture, *Daughter of the Confederacy* opened, along with more offices from Los Angeles to Washington, D. C., Abe Warner issued this claim – "American features, made in America by American actors and actresses, now have the call over those made abroad" – and exhorted manufacturers to respond to "the future demand for features".[34] In August 1913, the company was reorganized, as Pat Powers became president, and geared up to offer "an exclusive and permanent weekly service of three incomparable three- and four-reel features", all made by some eighteen independent and foreign producers (among them, besides Gauntier, Helen Gardner Picture Players and Marion Leonard Features) and distributed through some two dozen offices.[35] The Warner brothers' familiarity with northeastern Ohio may have led the company to use its Cleveland office to inaugurate this service, and in September the downtown Princess became one of the first picture theaters to feature Warner's films exclusively.[36] Others soon followed. In New England, the Boston office stressed the company's "variety of features" in its *Boston Journal* ads – in language ("Boys, We've Got the Goods") reminiscent of "straight-talking" Carl Laemmle several years earlier – and signed up exhibitors like the Bijou in Pawtucket (Rhode Island) and the Opera House in Lowell (Massachusetts). In Minneapolis, the company's regional office placed singular ads in the *Minneapolis Tribune*, and in Des Moines, the Colonial abandoned its mixed schedule of American and foreign features for Warner's service.[37] By November, one of Rochester's more "progressive exhibitors", Fitzbaugh Hall, also was showing Warner's Features.[38] The company apparently was successful enough to run full-page bulletins in *Moving Picture World* through March 1914 and supply one of Toledo's principal downtown theaters, the Alhambra, well into the summer.[39] Yet there were signs that its films (perhaps stigmatized as sensational melodramas, more suitable for working-class audiences) eventually could not compete with longer, more "respectable" features: the Des Moines Colonial dropped Warner's Features in December 1913, and the Lowell Opera House and Pawtucket Bijou switched to Famous Players' service in early 1914.[40]

Although it took more than a year for Famous Players to put its ambitious 1912 plans into full operation, the company probably was more responsible than Warner's for regulating and standardizing feature film distribution. In the summer of 1913, Quinn argues, Famous Players concluded that the current state rights system was proving unworkable and moved quickly to establish five affiliated companies that would not only distribute but also participate in financing the company's films.[41] In addition, distribution contracts were issued to a half dozen other established exchanges to handle what ads proclaimed would come to "30 Famous Features A Year".[42] The initial films released in early September exemplified the company's policy, in contrast to Warner's, of headlining major stage actors in film adaptations of major authors and playwrights: Minnie Maddern Fiske in *Tess of the D'Urbervilles* and Mary Pickford in *In the Bishop's Carriage*.[43] Distributed widely around the country, these two films served as a lure to entice major exhibitors, as a large ad in the *Boston Journal* shows, to sign up for the regular schedule instituted later that month.[44] The tactic seems to have worked, as flagship cinemas from the Olympia in Boston, Gordon's in Rochester, and Saxe's Lyric in Minneapolis to Tally's Broadway in Los Angeles and Grauman's Imperial in San Francisco elected to become exclusive venues for Famous Players films.[45] Bolstered by a contractual arrangement to also distribute All-Star features, along with selected foreign features such as the Italian *Last Days of Pompeii* in certain regions, by November Famous Players increased its schedule of releases from three features per month to three or four per week.[46] Although certain titles did not measure up to the high quality promised by the company and did poorly at the box office, overall the Famous Players features proved successful, due in no small part to stars like Pickford in *Caprice* (1913), *A Good Little Devil* (1914), or *Tess of the Storm Country* (1914) and Dustin Farnum in *Soldiers of Fortune* (1914). Here again is a local sign of the company's success: when the first palace cinema, the Garden Theatre, opened in Des Moines in early May 1914, a special newspaper supplement promoted it as the city's exclusive venue for the Daniel Frohman, Jesse L. Lasky, and All Star features that Famous Players sent "direct from New York".[47]

In September 1913, a *New York Morning Telegraph* writer – using a phrase previously reserved for the legitimate theater – described what to look for in the "coming season" of motion pictures.[48] So profound was the impact of "big films" or features that, in the year-end reports on the industry, the trade press almost unanimously agreed that, yes, 1913 "was peculiarly the year of the feature".[49] The term included specials of five reels or more, typically foreign features, irregularly distributed either through a system of roadshowing or state rights licensing. By the spring of 1914, it also included the regular weekly program of up to a half dozen releases of four reels or more, nearly all of them American, a standardized program whose viability Warner's and Famous Players supposedly had now demonstrated.[50] Yet the two companies' contractual arrangements with exhibitors were such that the market for features remained relatively "open" and rather unstable during the 1913–1914 season: what looked like standardization in distribution did not simply translate into standardization in exhibition, as the case of the Colonial, a major downtown picture theater in Des Moines, attests. In the spring and summer of 1913, the theater had been in the forefront of introducing features, most of them Italian and French imports, in three- to four-day or week-long runs. For two months that fall, the Colonial claimed that it was the exclusive "home of Famous Players", yet Warner's Features actually made up half of its programs, with an occasional special thrown in like *The Battle of Gettysburg*.[51] In late October, as mentioned earlier, the Colonial then became an exclusive venue for Warner's, and stayed so through December; when that contract abruptly ended, however, the theater returned (for another four months or so) to an eclectic schedule of American and foreign features (sometimes for week-long runs), from *The Princess of Bagdad* and *Arizona* to *The Fall of Constantinople*, with an occasional nonfiction feature mixed in like *Paul Rainey's African Hunt*.[52] Whereas Warner's films still could be seen in Des Moines at a new theater, the Black Cat, which risked experimenting with daily-changed programs of feature films (not surprisingly, this was unsuccessful),[53] Famous Players was generally absent for nearly six months until its films returned in early May 1914, with the grand opening of the Garden.[54]

If "the motion picture business [was] no longer in its infancy", according to that *Morning Telegraph* writer, and its "backbone" seemed strong enough to support the mutation of a rapidly developing twin, the latter's joints linking distribution and exhibition still were undergoing difficult "growing pains" and bearing the "scars" of repeatedly broken connecting tissue. Would those pains ease when Paramount, for instance, at the beginning of the 1914–1915 season, promised to institutionalize the standardized feature program ever more securely by introducing a form of block booking, and for even more features?[55] Ah, for that, there's another sign: To be continued ... .[56]

Notes

1. Ivo Blom, *Jean Desmet and the Early Dutch Film Trade* (Amsterdam: Amsterdam University Press, 2003), 25.

2. Janet Staiger, "Combination and Litigation: Structures of US Film Distribution, 1891–1917", *Cinema Journal* 23.2 (Winter 1984), 41–72; Robert Anderson, "The Motion Picture Patents Company: A Re-evaluation", in Tino Balio, ed., *The American Film Industry*, 2nd edition (Madison: University of Wisconsin Press, 1985), 133–152; Eileen Bowser, *The Transformation of Cinema, 1907–1915* (New York: Scribner's, 1991), 80–84, 191–233; and Michael Quinn, "Distribution, the Transient Audience, and the Transition to the Feature Film", *Cinema Journal* 40.2 (Winter 2001), 35–56.

3. According to Frederic J. Haskins, licensed films were leased to exhibitors on a scale of highest to lowest prices: a "first run" film had never been exhibited before; a "second run" film was supplied from two to seven days after its original release; a "third run" film was from one week to four weeks old; a "thirty day" film was a month old; and a "commercial" film was more than a month old. Exhibitors, he claimed, tended to arrange their weekly schedule so as to lease "one first run, one second run, and two commercials" for each daily change of program. Quoted by the Goat Man in "On the Outside Looking In", *Motography* (November 1911), 237–238.

4. For information on the Sales company, conceived as early as December 1909, see "The Motion Picture Distributing and Sales Company", *Moving Picture World* (7 May 1910), 724; "The Sales Company", *Moving Picture World* (21 May 1910), 822–823; "The Sales Company To-Day", *Moving Picture World* (4 June 1910), 929; and "Motion Picture Distributing and Sales Company", *Moving Picture News* (15 April 1911), 23–24. The Sales Company apparently did not recall and retire the film prints it leased – The Goat Man, "On the Outside Looking In", *Motography* (November 1911), 237.

5. See the General Film, Lake Shore, and Victor ads, *Cleveland Leader* (10 December 1911), S.5.

6. See, for instance, the Universal ad in *New York Morning Telegraph* (30 June 1912), 4.2: 5, and the Mutual ad in *Moving Picture World* (17 August 1912), 611.

7. See, for instance, the General Film and Victor ads, *Cleveland Leader* (8 December 1912), S.7; and the Lake Shore ad, *Cleveland Leader* (15 December 1912), S.5.

8. "Some Good Things Coming; Week's Gossip in Filmland", *Cleveland Leader* (2 February 1913), B4. Another sign of stability was the extensive listing of licensed and independent film exchanges (in which Mutual and Film Supply overlapped significantly) in the "Classified Trade Directory", *Moving Picture Annual and Yearbook for 1912* (New York: Moving Picture World, 1912), 124–126.

9. See the Unique Theatre ad, *Des Moines News* (26 January 1913), 6.

10. See the Venice Theater ad, *Rochester Herald* (12 January 1913), 19, and the Mutual and Laemmle Film ads, *Minneapolis Journal* (4 May 1913), Dramatic and Social Section, 10.

11. See, for instance, the Universal and Mutual ads, *Des Moines Register and Leader* (4 May 1913), 7. This also was the moment when New York Motion Picture signed a two-year distribution contract with Mutual and agreed to increase its production from six to twelve reels per week – see "N. Y. Motion Picture Co. Signs with the Mutual", *New York Morning Telegraph* (13 April 1913), 4.2: 1; and the Mutual ad, *New York Morning Telegraph* (13 April 1913), 4.2: 5.

12. See the Essanay and Reliance ads, *Des Moines Register and Leader* (20 April 1913), 8. Universal, Mutual, Essanay, and Reliance all ran their final ads in the *Des Moines Register and Leader* (20 July 1913), 12.

13. See the Toledo Film Exchange ad, *Toledo Blade* (18 June 1913), 3.

14. "The Backbone of the Business", *Motography* (20 September 1913), 191. See also the General Film, Universal, and Mutual ads, *Cleveland Leader* (28 January 1914), S.11.

15. The analogy actually had been made as early as "Periodical Topicals", *Motography* (August 1911), 56.

16. See the General Film ads, *New York Morning Telegraph* (20 July 1913), 4.2: 3, (27 July 1913), 4.2: 3, (3 August 1913), 4.2: 4, and (5 October 1913), 4.2: 3. One of the first General Film ads to use this graphic style appeared in *Moving Picture News* (26 April 1913), 5.

17. See the Mutual ad, *St. Paul Daily News* (15 November 1913), 12. Mutual also began to run a series

of ads with its new logo, "the sign of the winged-clock", in the *New York Morning Telegraph* (23 November 1913), 5: 3.

18. See the Mutual ad, *St. Paul News* (29 November 1913), 8.

19. Mutual also placed similar ads in other newspapers as well as the *Saturday Evening Post*, according to a large ad in the Christmas issue of the *New York Morning Telegraph* (14 December 1913), 4.2: 8.

20. See the Monopol Film ads, *New York Dramatic Mirror* (19 July 1911), 24, and (23 August 1911), 22, and *Billboard* (26 August 1911), 51.

21. The film also was favored with excellent reviews and articles – e.g. W. Stephen Bush, "Dante's Inferno", *Moving Picture World* (29 July 1911), 188–189; Rev. Elias Boudinet Stockton, "Impressions of 'Dante's Inferno'", *Moving Picture World* (16 September 1911), 780; and W. Stephen Bush, "Music and Sound Effects for Dante's Inferno", *Moving Picture World* (27 January 1912), 283–284. Pliny P. Craft later was heralded as the originator of the state rights idea in "The Father of the Feature", *Moving Picture World* (11 July 1914), 272–273.

22. See "Dante's Inferno", *Lawrence Evening Tribune* (9 September 1911), 4; and the Mall ad, *Cleveland Leader* (17 September 1911), N.4. The Jake Wells Amusement Company, headquartered in Norfolk (Virginia), also seems to have distributed the film throughout the South – see the Monopol Film ad, *New York Dramatic Mirror* (23 August 1911), 22; and "Dante's Inferno Dates", *Cleveland Leader* (1 October 1911), B.6. For further information on Jake and Otto Wells, see Terry Lindvall, "Cinema Virtue, Cinema Vice: Race, Religion, and Film Exhibition in Norfolk, Virginia, 1908–1922", Commonwealth Conference on American Cinema and Everyday Life, University College London, London, 27 June 2003.

23. William Gane seems to have been licensed to rent the film in Greater New York – see the William J. Gane ad, *New York Morning Telegraph* (7 January 1912), 4.2, 4.

24. See, for instance, W. Stephen Bush, "Do Longer Films Make Better Show?" *Moving Picture World* (28 October 1911), 275; and "The Year 1912", in *Moving Picture Annual and Yearbook for 1912* (New York: Moving Picture World, 1912), 15.

25. "'Spectator's' Comments", *New York Dramatic Mirror* (9 August 1911), 20; and Epes Winthrop Sargent, "Will Specials Lead to Runs", *Moving Picture World* (2 September 1911), 606–607. Sargent also argued that special releases would not harm cheaper theaters – see Sargent, "The Special Release and the Small Exhibitor", *Moving Picture World* (30 September 1911), 965.

26. Epes Winthrop Sargent, "Advertising for Exhibitors", *Moving Picture World* (24 February 1912), 666, and (2 March 1912), 763.

27. "'Cleopatra' Is Given a Try-Out", *New York Dramatic Mirror* (20 November 1912), 31. See the United States Film ads, *New York Morning Telegraph* (15 December 1912), 4: 2; and *New York Dramatic Mirror* (4 December 1912) back cover, and (26 February 1913), back cover. Reviews ranged from the lackluster to the exceptional – see, for instance, Louis Reeves Harrison, "Helen Gardner's Idealization of Cleopatra", *Moving Picture World* (30 November 1912), 859–860; and "'Cleopatra' Is Exceptional Five-Part Feature Release", *New York Morning Telegraph* (15 December 1912), 7: 4. Previously, Gardner had received excellent notices for the lead role in Vitagraph's *Vanity Fair*.

28. See the Duchess ad, *Cleveland Leader* (22 December 1912), M5; and the Gordon ad, *Rochester Herald* (30 March 1913), 22.

29. See the Star Theater ad, *Des Moines Register and Leader* (24 May 1914), 7.

30. One of the first signs of Warner's and Famous Players' moves came in George D. Proctor, "What the Coming Season Means to Motion Pictures", *New York Morning Telegraph* (7 September 1913), 5: 1.

31. Warner's is briefly mentioned, along with three other "big feature combinations" – "Box Office, Paramount, World Film" – in "Kinematography in the United States", *Moving Picture World* (11 July 1914), 179.

32. See, for instance, the Warner's Features ads, *Moving Picture World* (27 July 1912), 364–365, and (19 October 1912), 212. Warner's Features also were included in the column, "Feature Film Company Release Dates", *Moving Picture News* (16 November 1912), 31.

33. See, for instance, the Warner's Features ads in *New York Morning Telegraph* (15 December 1912),

4: 10, and *New York Dramatic Mirror* (18 December 1912), back cover; and "Gauntier Feature Players", *Moving Picture World* (21 December 1912), 1169.

34. See Warner's Features ad and "Gauntier Film Here", *Cleveland Leader* (2 March 1913), M.11; Warner's Features ad and "Gene Gauntier as Girl Spy in New Warner Feature Film", *Cleveland Leader* (9 March 1913), M.5; "Demand for Features", *New York Dramatic Mirror* (23 April 1913), 29; "Warner Back From Long Trip", *Moving Picture World* (26 April 1913), 359; and the Warner's Features ad, *New York Dramatic Mirror* (1 October 1913), 31.

35. "P. A Powers to Head New Warner's Features, Inc.", *New York Morning Telegraph* (3 August 1913), 4.2: 1; "P. A. Powers to Provide Exclusive Films", *Moving Picture News* (9 August 1913), 15; "Pat Powers New Head Warner's Feature Co.", *Cleveland Leader* (10 August 1913), C.4. See also "Helen Gardner Goes on Warner's Programme", *New York Morning Telegraph* (2 November 1913), 5:2; and the Warner's Features ads, *New York Morning Telegraph* (9 November 1913), 5: 3, and *Boston Journal* (15 November 1913), 5. For a summary of the company's history, see "Warner's Features, Inc.", *Moving Picture World* (11 July 1914), 262.

36. See "Warner Service Soon", *Cleveland Leader* (21 September 1913), N.6; and the Warner's Features ads that begin in the *Cleveland Leader* (28 September 1913), N.6. Abe Warner's article on features was reprinted in a condensed form as "Increasing Demand for Good Features", *Cleveland Leader* (3 August 1913), C.4.

37. See the Bijou ad, *Pawtucket Evening Times* (20 September 1913), in the Bijou Theatre and Star Theatre, Pawtucket, Clippings Book, Series IV, Keith-Albee Collection, Special Collections, University of Iowa Library; the Lowell Opera House ad, *Lowell Sunday Telegram* (28 September 1913), 5; "Correspondence: New England and Canada", *Moving Picture World* (4 October 1913), 54; the Colonial ad, *Des Moines News* (25 October 1913), 2; and the Warner's ad, *Minneapolis Tribune* (26 October 1913), Society Section: 13. See also the Warner's Features ads that begin in the *New York Morning Telegraph* (21 September 1913), 5: 3; and the *Boston Journal* (18 October 1913), 5.

38. See the Fitzbaugh Hall ad, *Rochester Herald* (30 November 1913), 19. The term, "progressive exhibitor", comes from a Warner's Feature ad, *Motion Picture News* (25 October 1913), 10.

39. See, for instance, the Warner's Features bulletins in *Moving Picture World* (28 February 1914), 1161, (14 March 1914), 1423; and the Alhambra ad, *Toledo Blade* (4 April 1914), 11.

40. See, for instance, "Davis Will Manage the Bijou Theatre", *Pawtucket Evening Times*, in the Bijou Theatre and Star Theatre, Pawtucket, Clippings Book, Series IV, Keith-Albee Collection, Special Collections, University of Iowa Library; and the ad for the Lowell Opera House, "The Home of Famous Players", *Lowell Sunday Telegram* (22 February 1914), 5.

41. Quinn, "Distribution, the Transient Audience, and the Transition to the Feature Film", 50. See also "Famous Players' Regular Releases", *Moving Picture News* (2 August 1913), 31; "Famous Players to Put Out Regular Releases", *New York Morning Telegraph* (3 August 1913), 4.2: 1; the Famous Players ad, *Moving Picture World* (26 August 1913), 854–855; and Adolph Zukor, "Famous Players in Famous Plays", *Moving Picture World* (11 July 1914), 186. Much like Universal and Mutual, Famous Players also ran strip ads in Sunday newspapers such as the *Des Moines Register and Leader*, from late April through late July 1913.

42. See the Famous Players ad, *Moving Picture World* (6 September 1913), 1030–1031.

43. See, for instance, "Feature Films on the Market", *New York Dramatic Mirror* (10 September 1913), 28, and (17 September 1913), 28; George Blaisdell, "Mrs. Fiske Triumphs as 'Tess'", *Moving Picture World* (13 September 1913), 1155; and George Blaisell, "In the Bishop's Carriage", *Moving Picture World* (20 September 1913), 1266.

44. See the Famous Players ad, *Boston Journal* (13 September 1913), 5.

45. See, for instance, the Gordon Photoplay House ad, *Rochester Herald* (12 October 1913), 23.

46. See, for instance, the Famous Players ads, *Boston Journal* (1 November 1913), 5, (8 November 1913), 5, (15 November 1913), 5, (22 November 1913), 5, and (27 December 1913), 5.

47. See the Garden Theatre ad, *Des Moines Register and Leader* supplement (2 May 1914), n.p.

48. Proctor, "What the Coming Season Means to Motion Pictures", 5: 1.

49. "The New Year", *Motography* (10 January 1914), 17. See also Robert Grau, "New Era for Motion Pictures", *New York Dramatic Mirror* (4 March 1914), 4.

50. See Adolph Zukor's own assessment in "Famous Players in Famous Plays", *Moving Picture World* (11 July 1914), 186.

51. "Namur Signs Up Famous Players", *Des Moines News* (31 August 1913), 6; "Mary Pickford Is at Colonial", *Des Moines News* (21 September 1913), 6; and the Colonial ad for *Theodora*, distributed by Warner's, which also advertises Famous Players at the top – *Des Moines News* (13 October 1913), 6.

52. See the Colonial ads, *Des Moines News* (11 January 1914), 6, (22 January 1914), 10, (8 February 1914), 7, and (22 February 1914), 6.

53. Black Cat Theatre ad, *Des Moines News* (28 February 1914), 2.

54. See, for instance, the Garden Theatre ad, *Des Moines Register and Leader* (5 May 1914), 6. As if offering a preview of coming attractions at the Garden, the Star (whose owner also built the Garden) did present several Famous Player films in March 1914.

55. See, for instance, the large Paramount ad, *Des Moines Register and Leader* (6 September 1914), 7.

56. For a longer, fuller discussion of film distribution in the USA in the early 1910s, see Richard Abel, *Americanizing the Movies and 'Movie-Mad' Audiences, 1910–1914* (Berkeley: University of California Press 2006), 13–42.

Mapping the moving picture world: distribution in the United States circa 1915

Gregory A. Waller

Department of Communication and Culture, Indiana University, Bloomington, USA

What sort of an enterprise was film distribution in the United States during the 1910s? What services did distributors provide? Where were they located? How did they interact with exhibitors, municipal authorities, and censorship advocates? Or, framed in more discursive terms, how was the apparently burgeoning business of film distribution chronicled, imagined, and promoted as the motion picture industry came to take its classical configuration? I propose to explore these questions from what might seem to be an unusual angle, using as my primary source material that appeared under the heading, 'Trade News of the Week', in the pre-eminent American exhibitor trade magazine, the *Moving Picture World*. To give due attention to the wealth of information contained each week in this section of the *Moving Picture World*, I have limited this study to 1915, a key year in the development of the American film industry, marked by, for example, the release of *The Birth of a Nation* and the increasing prominence of venues specifically designed as moving picture theaters.[1]

'Trade News of the Week' consists of a series of columns with titles like the 'Buffalo News Letter', 'California Briefs', or 'Kansas State Items'. The *Moving Picture World* ran an average of 14 pages filled with this type of material per issue. Set in very small font with virtually no illustrations, each page squeezes in about 1750 words, which allows for quite extensive coverage of local and regional trade news. 'News' it surely is – but the information in these columns is also anecdotal, fragmentary, usually unverifiable, self-selected, and often self-promoting.

The *Moving Picture World*'s trade news columns gather a wealth of information from individual theaters, exchanges, regional production companies, sales representatives, newspapers, legislative deliberations, municipal proceedings, concerned citizens, and traveling showmen, all filtered through this trade magazine's own 'special correspondents' in the field. These correspondents apparently both gathered news and also served as conduits for information that the *Moving Picture World* regularly solicited from all its readers. 'Any items of interest that come up may be sent to the nearest correspondent', ran one such solicitation.[2] Utilizing a smaller font size for these columns than for most of the rest of the magazine, the *Moving Picture World* clearly sought to accommodate as much information as possible, thereby enabling a host of readers and potential readers to see their own names in print, to find allies in the struggle against censorship, to pick up business tips, and to feel that they were participating in an ever-expanding, innovative, North American web of motion picture activity – call it a veritable *moving picture world*.

Given these goals, the trade news columns do not rigorously or regularly distinguish among the quite different types of material they disseminate, which range from announcements, gossip, and news to reprinted documents. A 9 January 1915 column from the Boston area, for instance, quotes verbatim a lengthy judicial opinion on theater safety codes and also lists in no particular order more than thirty briefer 'items' about individual theaters and exchange offices, employees and managers, promotional efforts, non-theatrical venues, benefit shows, and local production activity in and around Massachusetts (*MPW*, 9 January 1915, pp. 229–230). While this information can be quite extensive and detailed, it is rarely quantitative, and it is never comprehensive or consistent. That is, the trade news columns do not typically cover all activity in any given locality, state, or region; they do not report on the same activity week-by-week or afford all places the same measure of attention. In effect, the *Moving Picture World*'s columns constitute a primary source that is systematic as well as random, wide-ranging as well as incomplete, in part because the correspondents' filters do not seem to have been very fine: big schemes, mundane plans, personal information, public debate – there's room for all of these in the weekly trade news columns. Indeed, this roominess is one reason why the columns are so interesting as a discursive site and historical resource.

The mass of material found in 'Trade News of the Week' was presumably gathered and made print-ready by the *Moving Picture World*'s 'Correspondents', under whose bylines the weekly columns appear. The location of these correspondents and the areas they reported on constitute a map of the moving picture world by the *Moving Picture World*. Much of the United States came under the purview of one of the regular columns. And this American moving picture world also stretched beyond national borders, since there were also correspondents in Montréal, Toronto, Vancouver, and Ottawa, Canada, as well as Chihuahua, Mexico. Most of the correspondents in the United States were located in major cities, including Atlanta, San Francisco, and Pittsburgh. Others, however, came from less likely places, such as Jacksonville, Florida and Bangor, Maine.

Overall, the information was decidedly weighted toward urban sites outside the West and the South. Moreover, not all columns appeared each week and the ones that did could vary widely in the extent of their coverage: there is much more information about St. Louis and Pittsburgh, for instance, than New Orleans and Cleveland. Still, the *Moving Picture World* was able to spread the word about motion picture activity occurring at innumerable places, big and small, urban and rural, from coast to coast. The columns are, in effect, a notable instance of transcontinental (even trans-national) commercial nation building, demonstrating for their readers how the circulation of the movies and the dynamism of the motion picture business linked localities, territories, entrepreneurs, consumers, and corporations in a networked America.

Not surprisingly, anything that thwarted or threatened the circulation of moving pictures became prime news for the *Moving Picture World*. Hence there is extended coverage of censorship activity and sabbatarian struggles at the local or state level, which far overshadow other newsworthy concerns, like labor disputes, safety regulations, or uplift campaigns endorsing 'better' films for children.[3] At the same time, these columns testify to certain historically specific flashpoints having to do with the exhibition of controversial texts, such as Jack Johnson-Jess Willard fight films, footage concerning the Leo Frank case, 'official' German war films, and, especially, *The Birth of a Nation*, which was then in the midst of its first national release. No more than the many acts of African American protest could prevent the exhibition of *The Birth of a Nation*, extensive lobbying for state censorship would not halt the progress of the motion picture industry – that is the reassuring message of the *Moving Picture World*, a message implicit in the flow of information through 'Trade News of the Week'.

Reading page after page of trade news, the primary impression is of an industry in motion, ever growing, attracting human and financial capital, welcoming technological improvement, and developing ingenious strategies to market its product. As would be expected, most of the 'news' dutifully recorded in these columns concerns commercial exhibition, meaning the constructing, outfitting, operating, buying and selling, and opening and closing of movie theaters; the career moves of individual showmen; and the business of promoting, programming, and screening nationally distributed motion pictures in theaters.

Another important sector of the business that figures significantly in 'Trade News of the Week' are the various activities that linked production and exhibition. 'Distribution' eventually became the preferred term, though the *Moving Picture World* referred to these activities simply as the selling, booking, storing, and transporting of motion pictures. The trade news columns offer a picture of distribution in 1915 from the bottom up, place by place, company by company, salesman by salesman. While this account of film distribution is not comprehensive, fully representative, or even verifiably accurate, it is of considerable historical value as a discursive construct and a starting point for subsequent research into the history of distribution in the 1910s. In particular, these columns point toward the expansion of distribution facilities and the labor of film salesmen, the problem of storing and transporting film, the relations between exchanges and exhibitors, and the early efforts at serving the non-theatrical market.

Exchanges and exchangemen

From the perspective of the larger metropolitan-based distribution companies, the industry was moving swiftly toward what the representative of a new exchange in San Francisco called a 'model of efficiency' (*MPW*, 12 June 1915, p. 1808). For example, the Mutual exchange in Denver was praised for being 'logically arranged' 'in every detail to prevent loss of time' (*MPW*, 16 October 1915, p. 488), and the Famous Players exchange in Pittsburgh 'systematized' its operations via a 'private telephone exchange' linking all its departments (*MPW*, 1 May 1915, p. 758). The goal, couched in language common to rationalist business rhetoric of the day, was to save time and money by centralizing at state-of-the-art urban locations the storage, processing, and shipping of film and promotional material. Thus the Casino Feature Film Company, then servicing 135 theaters in Michigan, boasted of its Detroit facility: 'there are special racks for photos, slides, heralds, advertising matter, etc. as well as a fireproof asbestos film vault, specially constructed with a capacity of 3,500 films. The fourth floor is for stock, advertising matter, and projection. Everything is conveniently arranged, and so systematic that no time is lost doing any part of the work' (*MPW*, 13 February 1915, p. 1020).

Equipped for efficiency, the metropolitan exchange served as a distribution hub for what the *Moving Picture World* suggested was a continually proliferating network of branch offices, bases of operation for traveling salesmen who were on the front lines in the rush to bring the latest motion picture product to even the smallest theater in the most remote hamlet.[4] For instance, the manager of the Fox Film office in Washington, D.C. set the goal of 'having our pictures exhibited in every town of 1,000 or more' in Maryland, Virginia, and North Carolina (*MPW*, 30 October 1915, p. 824).

Thanks to salesmen who ventured far off the beaten path, companies boasted of selling their product to 'little motion picture theaters in mining towns and little desert settlements' in Utah (*MPW*, 17 April 1915, p. 428) and to venues in Midwestern 'towns not on the map or connected with railroads' (*MPW*, 30 October 1915, p. 832). Thus distributors had a major role to play in the capitalist dream at the heart of 'Trade News of the Week' – the dream of an expandable, upgradeable, efficiently serviced market, a nation of screens all with ready access to the latest motion picture product.

Such a dream is concretized in the activities of F.L. Kiltz, manager of Mutual's Kansas City exchange, whose useful method of 'mapping' his territory is praised at some length in a column from December 1915. Using an elaborate system of colored pins affixed to a wall-mounted map of eastern Kansas and western Missouri, Kiltz identified and classified all towns containing picture shows by population, number of theaters, and current service. Pieces of thread connected the pins, showing the routing of films through this territory – all with an eye toward achieving 'the greatest efficiency' in the circulation of Mutual product (*MPW*, 11 December 1915, p. 2046).

Most notices related to distribution in the trade news columns concern the exploits and career moves of individual 'exchangemen' like Mr. Kiltz. The *Moving Picture World* was thereby able to personalize the business of film distribution even as this branch of the industry was depicted as becoming increasingly systematized. Snippets of biographical information work to embody the exchangemen, who were frequently described as veterans of the entertainment or newspaper business. The manager of Metro's Kansas City office, for example, had served in the same capacity for Mutual and before that had worked for Universal, and had been a film exhibitor with various carnivals from 1901–1907 after launching his show-biz career as an acrobat on the vaudeville circuit (*MPW*, 4 December 1915, p. 1872). Such off-handed acknowledgements of intermedia relations help both to mark the motion picture business as the cutting edge of public amusement and also to frame the field of commercial entertainment (and mass communications) as continuous and inextricably interwoven: stage to screen, press to film, traveling outdoor amusement to permanent indoor site.

As Mr. Kiltz's map begins to suggest, motion picture distribution was also understood in geographical terms, with the market spatially divided into regions and localities, serviced by main and branch offices. To cite only a few examples: the Kleine salesmen based in Kansas City were responsible for 'all of Missouri, except for St. Louis, Kansas, Nebraska, Northern Oklahoma and Arkansas' (*MPW*, 20 November 1915, p. 1526); the new V-L-S-E exchange in San Francisco covered the entire West, from Arizona to Idaho (*MPW*, 29 May 1915, p. 1456); and the United Film office in Boston had branches in Buffalo, Syracuse, and Albany, New York, as well as Springfield, Massachusetts (*MPW*, 30 October 1915, p. 822.) In addition to Boston, San Francisco, and Kansas City, the main offices for distributors were – according to the *Moving Picture World* – concentrated on 'film rows' in downtown Atlanta, Chicago, Cincinnati, Cleveland, Dallas, Denver, Detroit, New Orleans, Pittsburgh, St. Louis, Toronto, and Washington, D.C. Urban 'film rows' were no doubt less prominently in the public eye than actual movie theaters, street-level and billboard advertising, and newspaper coverage of the industry, but they were notable nonetheless as one more testament to the presence of the movies in everyday American life.

Metropolitan offices served as hubs responsible for distributing motion pictures through the various regions of the United States and Canada. For example, Dallas, with 12 exchanges clustered within a few blocks, claimed responsibility for the South (*MPW*, 12 June 1915, p. 1818), though Atlanta was also heralded as 'the distributing station for all film companies in the Southern states' (*MPW*, 20 March 1915, p. 1790), as was Cincinnati (*MPW*, 20 February 1915, p. 1161) and New Orleans (*MPW*, 22 May 1915, p. 1301). Clearly, the 'South' as surveyed from Atlanta or New Orleans was not the same as the 'South' that began in Cincinnati or Dallas. Not only those moving pictures overtly concerned with race, but also the practices of film distribution and exhibition have a significant connection to the sometimes contradictory and shifting mappings of American regionalism in the 1910s.

That the information in the trade news columns was self-submitted and very often self-promoting helps to explain the marked emphasis on particular places and individual companies. There is, for instance, considerable information in the *Moving Picture World* on Pathé-Frères' aggressively expanding distribution activities in 1915, particularly related to its serials and weekly newsreel. 'Pathé's new selling plan', declared a notice in March 1915, involved 'the establishment of agents in local centers, with about 100 theaters to each center. Pathé now has fifteen local agencies in the Middle West', with headquarters for the region in Chicago (*MPW*, 6 March 1915, p. 1428). Other items herald the opening of new Pathé branch offices in Indianapolis, Indiana (*MPW*, 4 September 1915, p. 1677), Charlotte, North Carolina (*MPW*, 23 October 1915, p. 646), and Spokane, Washington (*MPW*, 2 October 1915, p. 115) – each office employing several traveling representatives. The four salesmen based in Pathé's Portland, Oregon office, for example, covered Oregon, southern Washington, western Idaho, and a county in northern California (*MPW*, 21 August 1915, p. 1356). Precise information about the distribution of individual films is rarely found in the exhibitor columns, but in March 1915, Pathé's St. Louis exchange boasted of having five prints of the 14-episode serial, *The Exploits of Elaine*, in circulation at 50 theaters in Kansas and Oklahoma (*MPW*, 27 March 1915, p. 1954).

Ben Singer notes that 'beginning around mid-1914, the feature distribution business underwent a major transformation from a haphazard regional enterprise fragmented among hundreds of states rights firms to a national enterprise dominated by about ten big companies'.[5] While the trade news columns underscore the exploits of major companies (some of which specialized in shorts rather than features), they also provide a glimpse of the broader range of distributors, including well-established regional operations like Sol Lesser's Golden Gate Film Exchange in San Francisco. Claiming to have been in the exchange business for seven years, Lesser by 1915 owned 8–9,000 reels (*MPW*, 5 June 1915, p. 1580) and offered his customers a regular twice-weekly series of new 'scenic, educational and comedy subjects' (*MPW*, 11 December 1915, p. 2050). At the other end of the spectrum, a small-scale enterprise like the Pacific Comedy Film Service, also based in San Francisco, might specialize only in comedies (*MPW*, 7 August 1915, p. 1034), while an entrepreneur from Louisville, Kentucky declared his intention to 'work the entire South' with a handful of copies of his sole property, 'four short reels hooked together into a Chaplin program' called *The Mix Up* (*MPW*, 23 October 1915, p. 645). Once again, the weekly trade news columns conjure up a thriving industry that is open to both quick-thinking entrepreneurs and also to ambitious corporations with national business strategies.

The materiality of distribution

One of the most striking things about the discourse concerning distribution in the *Moving Picture World* is the emphasis on the materiality of film as a commodity to be stored, shipped, and rented and on the exchange itself – part storage facility, part modern office, part wholesaler's showroom. Given safety concerns, especially as codified through municipal regulations, the storage of hundreds of reels of nitrate film posed a major challenge and a considerable expense. A new city ordinance in Minneapolis, Minnesota, for instance, required that reels be housed in metal boxes inside a fireproof brick or concrete vault located on the top floor of the building that was equipped with an automatic sprinkler system (*MPW*, 1 May 1915, p. 761). Boston's ordinance added the proviso that only 10 reels of film could be removed from their metal boxes at one time (*MPW*, 17 April 1915, p. 429). In Dallas, city officials further demanded that all heating and electrical work in exchanges be subject to strict inspection, and limited exchanges to occupying buildings of no more than two floors (*MPW*, 5 June 1915, p. 1650). We can only guess about the short and long term effects of such potentially costly requirements. Did municipal regulations discourage exchanges from retaining 'older' film? Did they encourage the consolidation of distributors or indirectly promote illegal alternatives?

Major exchanges, in the public eye and with brand names to worry about, paid due heed to civic concerns and boasted of their fireproof vaults. At the same time they challenged new policies concerning the shipping of films. On the one hand, freight companies like Wells Fargo petitioned the Interstate Commerce Commission to increase the rates charged for shipping films, eventually leading to a ruling that allowed a three-cent increase on a 40 pound package (*MPW*, 4 September 1915, p. 1680). (Reels weighed approximately 10 pounds each.) On the other hand, distributors felt similar pressure from state legislatures and railroad companies. When New York and New Jersey, citing public safety concerns, prohibited films from being carried as baggage on passenger trains, the effect was to boost distributors transportation costs significantly: in New York, for instance, there was a minimum 25 cent charge for motion pictures shipped in baggage cars (*MPW*, 25 September 1915, p. 2214). A Boston ordinance went further by prohibiting films from being carried not only on passenger trains, but also on streetcars and ferryboats (*MPW*, 25 December 1915, p. 2399).

Exchangemen mounted protests against local, state, and federal rulings, and looked for ways to circumvent new regulations. A so-called film 'runner' for Pathé in Newark, New Jersey was arrested for carrying film on a passenger train (*MPW*, 11 September 1915, p. 1870). Perhaps most interesting, these actions by railroad companies prompted some distributors to purchase automobiles. The branch office of United Film in Salt Lake City, Utah, began using a 'seven-passenger automobile labeled with the well known device of the United. This car is used for suburban film deliveries and occasionally has been pressed into service to carry representatives of the United on visiting jaunts into the outlying districts' (*MPW*, 29 May 1915, p. 1455). Similarly, Pathé's Newark branch purchased an 'automobile truck' (*MPW*, 11 September 1915, p. 1870). Plans were announced for a 'film express' that used automobiles to transport films daily between Baltimore, Maryland and Washington, D.C. (*MPW*, 10 July 1915, p. 339), while another auto service offered to deliver films throughout the greater Boston area (*MPW*, 6 November 1915, p. 1165). Such novel experiments might well have had notable consequences: the use of automobiles and trucks to transport film likely opened up greater opportunities for small-scale distributors as well as itinerant exhibitors.

Exchanges in the public sphere

Automobile express schemes, like the elaborate requirements for storage facilities, remind us that the circulation of moving pictures was in a very literal sense a matter of storing and transporting weighty, potentially hazardous reels of film, which, if they were to be profitable, had to be in almost perpetual, if intermittent, motion, both through the sprockets of a projector and also through the world from site to site. Facing the potential economic ramifications of municipal safety codes and Interstate Commerce Commission rulings, it is not surprising that distributors publicly voiced their misgivings and promoted their own interests, sometimes even organizing into 'associations' like the San Francisco Film Exchange Board of Trade and the Exchange Men's Association of Kansas City (*MPW*, 17 July 1915, p. 525). For example, in Portland, Oregon, exchangemen took their concerns about unnecessarily excessive safety requirements to the city commissioners, who then dropped a proposed ordinance (*MPW*, 11 September 1915, p, 1860); while in Atlanta, the Motion Picture Trades Club drafted an alternative to a proposed bill to regulate exchanges (*MPW*, 25 December 1915, p. 2407). Other collective public actions by distributors included arguing against licensing fee increases in St. Louis (*MPW*, 10 July 1915, p. 354) and trying to convince the Louisiana state legislature to pass a bill outlawing the 'sub-renting of films' by exhibitors to other exhibitors (*MPW*, 15 May 1915, p. 1127).

Given the social and cultural history of the movies in the United States during the Progressive Era and theater owners' vested interest in building good community relations, the most intriguing public gesture by exchangemen was the role they occasionally took in challenging local censorship campaigns in Dallas and Portland, Oregon (*MPW*, 7 August 1915, p. 1040; *MPW*, 28 August 1915, p. 1505). In Kansas City, where a proposed censorship law would have charged exchanges $2.00 per reel to cover the costs of local censors (*MPW*, 1 May 1915, p. 756), the exchanges produced a set of 20 anti-censorship slides, which were intended to rotate through area theaters one slide per week (*MPW*, 16 October 1915, p. 487).

The public presence of the distributor was also evident in another, albeit indirect, way. In addition to storing and shipping film, the larger distributors also provided exhibitors with a range of advertising material. For example, the 'paper room' of the Washington D.C. office for the World Film Corporation contained 'slides, photographs, mats, cuts, heralds, window cards and other advertising matter' (*MPW*, 15 May 1915, p. 1123). Not only did distributors make this array of 'advertising matter' readily available, they could also train the exhibitor in what the V-L-S-E branch office in Cleveland called 'advertising methods' (*MPW*, 14 August 1915, p. 1193).[6] Thus the Universal exchange in Kansas City established a 'bureau of publicity to assist exhibitors in the advertising of their attractions and the building up of their business' (*MPW*, 27 November 1915, p. 1692), while the World office in Boston appointed W.H. Fulwood as a 'business stimulator' whose job it was to teach exhibitors 'how to conduct advertising campaigns' (*MPW*, 2 October 1915, p. 108). In certain cases, the exchange itself ran the campaign: Pathé boasted that its new office in Spokane, Washington had access to 10 billboards in the city for 24-sheet posters, as well as plans for smaller three and six-sheet displays (*MPW*, 2 October 1915, p. 115).

Exchanges and exhibitors

Since the *Moving Picture World* was a trade magazine intended particularly for theater operators it placed much emphasis on the relation between distributors and exhibitors, who were both seen as members of a burgeoning industry in a highly competitive marketplace where any edge and any added 'stimulation' mattered. For the *Moving Picture World*, the distributor was most often figured as a salesperson and the exhibitor as a client, though the relation was sometimes conceptualized as being between the distributor as supplier or wholesaler and the exhibitor as user or retailer. In all cases, however, the distributor was understood to be responsible for more than the storage and shipping of films. In addition to supplying promotional material, exchanges offered preview screenings, and the trade news columns suggest that it became standard practice for new or newly refurbished urban exchanges to incorporate 100–200-seat projection facilities (sometimes even with an appropriately pitched floor), allowing for regularly scheduled screenings for exhibitors, who thereby presumably could make more informed booking decisions. The Kriterion exchange in Boston, for instance, included a 150-seat venue with advance screening of new releases every Wednesday (*MPW*, 16 October 1915, p. 476), while the V-L-S-E office in Oakland promised that 'films will be displayed regularly twice a week and older releases will be shown whenever exhibitors desire to inspect them' (*MPW*, 9 October 1915, p. 304). New screening rooms often went hand-in-hand with more refined office décor, like the polished oak fixtures, 'white figured art metal' ceiling, and 'oil paintings of the various stars' that graced World's new Washington, D.C. facility (*MPW*, 15 May 1915, p. 1123).

Fully equipped screening rooms in the larger exchanges, like the opening of new branch offices in small cities and the dispatching of additional salesmen to the provinces, at least implied that the expansion of the distribution business meant increased competition and, hence, what a Detroit exchangeman called a 'better and larger selection' of films for the exhibitor (*MPW*, 6 November 1915, p. 1173). In fact, this is something of a common refrain in the *Moving Picture World*, perhaps best illustrated by a description of Bangor, Maine where 'road men [that is, traveling film salesmen] are so numerous that it is not at all uncommon to meet five or six in Bangor on walking down the street – and Bangor is a city of only 25,000 population. The exhibitors are offered the choice of all sorts of attractions, and, as a result of this keen competition, the exchange men and the road men find that the hardest kind of hard work is essential to success' (*MPW*, 16 October 1915, p. 476). Here, from a small city point of view, is a highly desirable buyer's market, with theater owners (and, it is assumed, audiences) profiting from the 'keen competition' among distributors. Exhibitor/distributor relations, however, could also be figured as much more antagonistic, with exchanges being criticized for foisting beat-up prints on rural theaters (*MPW*, 27 March 1915, p. 1953), and exhibitors serviced by wary exchanges in San Francisco and Washington, D.C. being asked to pay C.O.D. or in advance so as to address 'the matter of poor collections' (*MPW*, 14 August 1915, p. 1189). Such complaints are rare in the trade news columns, suggesting that the saturation of the market with salesman, all in 'keen competition' for the exhibitor's dollar, only benefited the moviegoer and the industry at large.

Distributing the non-theatrical

Finally, while the exhibitor columns offer many instances of films being screened non-theatrically in churches, schools, public parks, hotels, and state institutions, there are also a few references in 1915 to distributors specializing in the non-theatrical market. For example, in San Francisco the Atlas Film Corporation announced its intention to 'handle film used in churches, schools, lodges and other places outside of regular theaters' (*MPW*, 10 July 1915, p. 345) and the Theograph Film Company was organized 'for the purpose of manufacturing and distributing educational films for use in secular schools' (*MPW*, 18 September 1915, p. 2040). 'Specializing in industrial, religious and similar appropriate pictures for churches, schools and Y.M.C.A.'s', the Navajo Film Company, based in Kansas City, was another apparently multi-purpose firm producing as well as 'renting' films (*MPW*, 27 November 1915, p. 1692). In 1915, at least, the *Moving Picture World* saw opportunities in the non-theatrical side of the business, which had its niche within the expanding moving picture world.

The scattered references in 'Trade News of the Week' to distributors specializing in the non-theatrical market are well worth pursuing. In fact, one prime potential use of the *Moving Picture World*'s weekly columns is as a source of leads to be followed in investigating local histories of film exhibition, distribution, and even production. At the same time, I have tried to suggest in this essay other ways of utilizing the wealth of information in columns from across the United States and Canada. Reading this trade magazine (beyond the editorial pages, the film synopses, and the advertisements) as a text with an implicit ideological agenda and an underlying narrative logic helps get at the significant discursive work of the *Moving Picture World*. Its discourse of distribution points both to the significant place of exchanges, 'film rows', and traveling salesmen in the moving picture world and also to a quite material history of how film was sold, stored, and circulated in and through everyday life.

Notes

1. See Keil, Charlie and Shelley Stamp (eds) *American Cinema's Transitional Era: Audiences, Institutions, Practices* (Berkeley: University of California Press, 2004) for a sense of current research on the 1910s.

2. *Moving Picture World*, 3 July 1915, p. 109. All references to material from the trade news columns will be included parenthetically in the text, with *Moving Picture World* abbreviated as *MPW*.

3. In July, 1915, alone, the *Moving Picture World* reported on state censorship activities in Illinois and Ohio; more localized campaigns in Portland, Oregon, Spokane, Washington, and Duluth, Minnesota, and ongoing skirmishes over Blue Laws, which in many localities like Chattanooga, Tennessee kept theaters closed on Sundays.

4. Several of the practices that Walter A. Friedman describes in *Birth of a Salesman: The Transformation of Selling in America* (Cambridge, Massachusetts: Harvard University Press, 2004), including sales contests, incentive awards, and clear marking of territories are also mentioned in the *Moving Picture World*'s accounts of exchangemen. Friedman cites census data that shows the number of traveling salesmen in the United States almost tripled from 1890 to 1910, when the total reached more than 163,000 (*Birth of a Salesman*, p. 92).

5. Singer, Ben, 'Feature Films, Variety Programs, and the Crisis of the Small Exhibitor', in *American Cinema's Transitional Era*, p. 87.

6. Other services offered by exchanges could include the sale of projectors and theater equipment (*MPW*, 24 July 1915, p. 681). Going even further, the Pathé office in Montréal announced that it had installed equipment to develop film, thus allowing for the production of a 'topical weekly of mostly Canadian news' (*MPW*, 29 May 1915, p. 1461).

PART III

NETWORKS:
Local actors

12

'Mr. Elliot Books Chaplins Direct': Essanay's Exclusive's Strategy in Southampton 1915

Michael Hammond[1]

University of Southampton, UK

In the summer of 1915 the film business in Britain had recovered from the disruption of the outbreak of war in the previous year but that recovery was primarily based in the exhibition sector. After an initial scare that the war effort would cause cinemas to close or at the least restrict their opening hours, the year between August 1914 and August 1915 saw increases in cinema attendances, particularly in areas with large military concentrations. On the other hand production figures had by and large remained fairly consistent with pre-war levels of growth. The changes here were largely reflected in the decreasing importation of European product and the fact that British film production had increased 5 per cent to make up 25 per cent of the number of films screened that year. More significant for its implications for the future was that fact that in the same year US imports had continued to grow from 52 per cent to 61 per cent of films available to British exhibitors.[2]

Distribution in Britain had undergone some important changes during the first year of the war. Since 1909 a number of US firms such as Selig and Essanay had established London offices for distribution to Britain, while others such as Keystone and Bison had films released through distribution agents such as London Cinematograph Company and the US based Western Import Company. In both cases these offices often acted as the platform for their wider European distribution. On the British mainland these producers and/or their representatives sold their product to renters who then passed the films through to exhibitors in what was termed the 'open market system'. By the end of the war the open market system had been replaced by an early version of block booking, but the process of this transformation, as with most historical shifts, was neither particularly smooth nor straightforward. The major shift in distribution practices that marked a move away from the 'open market' saw its most highly publicised manifestation in the August 5 edition of *The Bioscope* where the Essanay Film Mfg. Co. announced a change in policy. They were going to release the whole of their output direct to the exhibitor. As is fairly well known this was prompted by the phenomenal success of the Chaplin films which had begun to be released by Essanay in February of 1915 and had been a significant draw for British exhibitors throughout the summer of 1915. This prompted a debate in the trade press running until 1918, the point of which was fairly simple: renters were being by-passed. Essanay offered exhibitors a contract which gave them a maximum of three reels per week from a choice of twelve reels. Chaplin films may, they stated, make up a part of these twelve. This programme included three three reel features, and three single reel films. In addition to this they offered a two reel Chaplin every three weeks and from time to time a six reel Chaplin. Evidence in the trade press shows that exhibitors were particularly unhappy about this and the trade press to some extent supports this. However I would like to look closely at one local area, Southampton, to explore how one exhibitor, Mr. George Elliot of the Carlton, a cinema located near the centre of the town, responded to this phenomenon.

Most British towns the size of Southampton had a high concentration of cinemas per capita. Southampton was typical of this in having 16 cinemas located in or around the Southampton area which had at the time a population of about 119,000. Exhibitors were not only in competition with each other for audiences but also with the two music halls or variety theatres, the Hippodrome and The Palace. These theatres also had cinema exhibition as part of their weekly programme, particularly the Palace which held screenings every Sunday and advertised them as 'first time screened', and offered ticket prices competitive with the high street cinemas. Their ability to secure films as first time screened may have been the result of their being a part of the MacNaughten music hall circuit and therefore enjoying a privileged position with the renters. The Palace was the first place to show the Keystone comedies which featured Charles Chaplin as well as the Selig serial *The Adventures of Kathlyn* (1914) in the spring and summer of 1914. Interestingly it seems that the Sundays only screenings were not conducive to building the kind of customer loyalty even with Chaplin and the serials as was the continuous programme or two-programmes daily practices of the cinemas. In fact the Selig serial, begun 8 August 1914 was discontinued after two weeks, partly due to disruption in the delivery of the films by rail. It is likely that The Palace utilised the screenings on Sunday as a means of cutting back on expenses for musicians by using a smaller orchestra than was required for the live programme which ran from Monday to Saturday. The desire to develop a more loyal clientele for Sunday evenings was not the main objective with these programmes.

By contrast cinema exhibitors' attempts to develop a regular clientele, was paramount in establishing a profitable business. These attempts were partly reflected in the type of programming for films, however other factors also differentiated the approach different managers took. Cinemas in the suburban areas tended to appeal to the local neighbourhood seeking to build up a regular clientele while high street cinemas, those located on or near the main street of the town, depended more on 'passing trade' and sought to attract audiences through innovative front of house activities. Since these cinemas were virtually all products of the first 'picture palace' boom in cinema construction that began in earnest in Britain in 1910, they had a considerable stake in highlighting the 'experience' of their theatre as a differentiating factor. The Carlton, cinema, managed by Mr. Elliot, was located in the retail shopping district just above the high street in Southampton and was a mid-sized cinema (300 seats) in relation to the 600 – 1000 seat halls of his high street competitors. His strategy of highlighting the comforts of his house and the programme helps to illustrate the impact that the encroaching exclusives booking system had on local cinema culture.

Mr. Elliot and the Carlton

George Elliot along with Wilfred Brimble his projectionist were professional showmen who had, since early 1914, been running the nearby neighbourhood cinema, the Northam Picturedrome, in the working class district which served the Southampton docks. The Picturedrome was part of a small circuit of four cinemas owned and operated by local councillor Percy V. Bowyer. Bowyer and his board of investors had been impressed with Elliot's abilities in the successful running of the Picturedrome. Elliot had been the first to secure the Selig serial *The Adventures of Kathlyn* (1914) and had built a regular audience through programming serials and comedies. Perhaps more importantly he had shown initiative in countering the objections to Sunday opening by the local clergy from nearby St. Mary's church by offering the cinema's space as a place for special religious programmes which included live music on Sunday evenings. In June 1915 Bowyer moved Elliot to the Carlton cinema, which was the most prestigious cinema in his circuit. The Carlton on London Road was in reach of the passing trade experienced by the high street houses and at the same time drew upon a primarily lower middle class local clientele. *What's On*, the local entertainment weekly, indicated in its announcement that the interim manager Charles Brown had not been successful in making the cinema profitable.[3]

Elliot's strategy to raise the profile of the cinema began with an event, much like a benefit, which accompanied his taking over of the hall. In the issue of *What's On* the week ending June 26 devoted a column to Elliot's arrival:

> Monday June 14, will be long remembered as a red letter day, when the Carlton Picture House opened under the management of Messrs. Elliot and Brimble. Destiny evidently does not mean that the above house should be a failure; and judging from the representative and appreciative audience the tide has turned and the traditions of The Carlton altered from failure to success.[4]

The ability of Elliot to provide his patrons with their most desired product was based in his assumption of audience preference. In similar fashion to his approach to publicity at the Picturedrome he sought to expand his constituency by advertising the advantages of his cinema to the city at large. *What's On* reported on the 10 of July that he gave sweets to children at Saturday Matinees and compared his inspirational management to the story where Robert the Bruce noticed a spider's web, a fable of perseverance and tenacity. He made changes to the front of house that were lauded by *What's On* as they reported that the "smart attendants see to the patrons as they arrive and conduct them into the comfortable seats".[5] He soon secured a week long run of the Moss Empire's Ltd. London production of *The Midnight Wedding* and advertised it as "stirring and romantic military, teeming with thrilling scenes and incidents". The performance was hampered by the breakdown of the cooling fans which prompted Elliot and *What's On* to announce that the fans "will be completely fixed and in working order for the coming week (and) will make The Carlton one of the coolest halls in the country".[6]

The summer of 1915 was, in one respect, a good one for business as it was the months in which the Chaplin craze in Britain was fully established. If the serial was a form that helped Elliot build his clientele at the Picturedrome, Chaplin was the centrepiece in his bid to attract audiences to the Carlton. His ability to move quickly in this direction is exemplified in the coverage in *What's On* of the 24 July where he announced that "Lovers of Charlie Chaplin will also find their favourite comedian appearing in humorous scenes".[7] For the rest of the summer "Chaplin comedies" featured on the programme without mentioning specific titles of the films. (His front of house featured two life-size Chaplin cut-outs.) Elliot also continued to attempt to attract child audiences by charging 1d and 2d at Saturday matinees.

In a clever combination of attempting to attract children and raising the profile of the cinema as an educational venue Elliot and Brimble took advantage of an opportunity to further integrate their cinema into the community. The children of the Gladstone Club were rained out of their sports day so Messrs. Elliot and Brimble showed three hours of pictures. "The scholars marched to the Carlton just before two o'clock and many of the adult members accompanied the children. The Carlton was crowded [and] the audience voted it [...] the best entertainment they had ever had."[8]

By September Elliot was clearly attempting to expand his audience base by emphasising his commitment to exclusive pictures that "ensure one of originality, freshness of subjects and something far ahead of the old system of cheap films and clap trap style, which will not do for high class audiences". Chaplin films were a standing feature at this point, which indicates that his films were advertised as a cut above the run of the mill comedy. The emphasis on Elliot and Brimble as a manager and technician who would spare no expense continued in the press through their announcement that Elliot was now 'personally' booking his films direct from the film production companies. This reiterates with Essanay policy announcement in August 1915 that they would only deal directly with exhibitors.[9] Elliot's publicised commitment to the exclusive system was probably driven by the desire to publicise the theatre as 'exclusive' in terms of its own taste status thereby incorporating the high class environment of the hall with 'high class' product (he opened, in October, a separate entrance to the luxuriant reserved seats in the balcony). Further coinciding as it does with Essanay's announcement, he was able to present himself as a forward thinking manager, by guaranteeing a steady flow of new Chaplin films.

Elliot and Brimble are an example of the way that cinema managers, with backgrounds as showmen, actively courted particular clientele and this was based on 'producing' their audiences through advertising strategy, cinema decor, house management, special events. The desired effect was to give the impression of a hall that is within the predominant taste parameters of the local area. The choice here of making the house distinct in relation to other houses was to pitch the advertising towards the exclusive, 'high class' audience, which in reality was both an appeal and a guarantee of 'safety' in terms of environment and film content. The entertainment of troops and returning wounded, as well as charity benefits for particular causes were also ways in which cinema exhibitors such as Elliot were able to position their houses as respectable places for friends and families to attend. The war conditions were incorporated into the creation of house identities and cinema owners utilised the connection with the war as an endorsement of their legitimacy. This utilisation of the image of the house prompted, productively for Elliot and Brimble, their quick response to production trends such as serials, Chaplin comedies and exclusive features. Exhibitors with such a close relationship to their audiences looked to distribution and production companies for guidance and advice but maintained an ability to at least partially shape their reception through their assumptions and negotiations with the taste preferences of their audience.

Elliot and Brimble's success with the Carlton did hinge considerably on the Chaplin phenomenon which manifested itself in the summer months of 1915 but continued throughout the rest of the war. Elliot and Brimble did not last as long. Although records are patchy, the partnership was dissolved in 1917 and Elliot ran the cinema on his own until the last year of the war. The Carlton closed in 1922, the victim of competition from the larger, more elaborate 1200 seat Picture House which was only a few hundred yards away and on the main street in Southampton. So in one regard it is possible to isolate Elliot's fortunes as being tied to both the Chaplin phenomena and to the practices of exclusive booking instigated by Essanay.

As we have seen, by early 1915 Chaplins were indispensable products for cinema managers such as Elliott in establishing and maintaining an audience base for cinema at a time when the advent of the war could hardly have seemed more inconvenient. Chaplin's popularity in Britain, as in the US, seemed to arise overnight. As early as

November 1914, his appearance on the Sunday evening film programme of the Palace music hall warranted a mention of his name: "Keystone's latest comic *A Busy Day* presenting Charles Chaplin is sure of a big reception".[10] The trade press began to mention him by name in September 1914 and by the summer of 1915 the Chaplin craze had reached British audiences. In the middle of that summer Langford Reed wrote an article in *The Bioscope* estimating the number of daily performances of Chaplin films throughout 'the world'. His calculations were that "every day he gladdens the heart of no fewer that 12,750,000 people!".[11] He was inspired to write this article while on a visit to Brighton where he noticed that of the twelve cinemas there one third of them were showing Chaplin films. His estimate for Britain was 4,500 appearances per night. The evidence of the number of Chaplin films shown in Southampton during this period supports this. But it also raises the question of how his films were distributed during this period. It is clear that even as early as November 1914 the first of the Keystone Chaplins had made a significant enough impression that the proportion of cinemas showing them, cited by Langford Reed, had already been reached. By the late spring of 1915 there were increasing numbers of Chaplin films featuring in almost every film theatre in the city.

A close look at the titles of Chaplin films shown in Southampton shows that by the summer of 1915 there were still a number of Keystone Chaplins. These continued to be shown throughout the rest of the years of the war as Keystone continued to make them available for renters on the open market. This also allowed cinemas to advertise a Chaplin every week. These overlapped with the newer films he had begun making for Essanay, so that 19 out of the 30 programmes between July and September 1915 showed Essanay films. After September the number of Essanay films declined in proportion to five out of the thirty programmes listed between September to November. This was due to the new exclusives policy that Essanay introduced in September 30 where they rented their film to theatres direct.[12]

In the summer the newer films were shown by most of the cinemas in Southampton. The Palace on Sundays, The Palladium in Portswood, the Carlton, The Alexandra and the Atherley in Shirley all showed the Essanay Chaplins prior to September 30. Following that, the only two theatres to advertise the Essanay films were the Carlton and the Northam Picturedrome. The fact that these two cinemas were part of Bowyer's four cinema circuit suggests that this system of booking was advantageous to the extent that the Bowyer could spread the risk of taking the other less popular Essanay films in order to secure up-to-date Chaplins. It also shows that Chaplin films were able to appeal across class boundaries. Chaplin was as secure a draw at the more upmarket Carlton as he was to the working class audiences at the Northam Picturedrome. Nevertheless, the larger seat prestigious cinemas such as The Palladium and the Alexandra reverted to showing the Keystones, which they could still obtain from the Western Import Company on the open market. They continued to do this until the following summer.

This snapshot of the release/screening patterns and the advertising strategies for Chaplin films at the Carlton in Southampton opens up certain avenues of investigation. One of those has to do with the success of the exclusives policy, another to do with Chaplin's unique appeal for Southampton audiences. In the first instance it is clear that the advantage of the exclusives policy for a smaller cinema operator like Elliot was to secure first time screened and guaranteed popular films. Essanay's policy worked for exhibitors like Elliot who were willing to take on the restrictions to the rest of their programme by securing the new Chaplins. As Essanay had stated, it was possible to book Chaplins as the majority of the package of the films which Elliot did. As new

Chaplin films were not coming out every week, and in fact as he moved into the new year 1916 their frequency was closer to one every month, this did not necessarily tie exhibitors in to a lot of films they didn't want.[13] Elliot seems to have pretty much established his cinema as a place which showed Chaplins weekly and he played Keystones from the open market as well as Essanay.

It is clear that the prevalence of Chaplin films on cinema theatre programmes generally is significant enough to claim that cinema managers considered Chaplin films essential to an attractive and successful programme. However, the overlapping texture of the local distribution and exhibition of Chaplin films provides both an indication of the workings of local distribution practices as they worked in tandem with marketing strategies, and an anomalous instance where Chaplin films, possibly because of their resilient appeal, were consistently replayed by virtually all of the cinemas in the area. From September 1914 to the end of the war Chaplin films, on average, appear on one programme in the town per week. Between April 1915 and April 1916 these appearances were at times on every screen in the city. The Keystone one and two reelers played alongside Chaplin's Mutuals and First National features such as *Shoulder Arms* (1918), screened in Southampton in December 1918, throughout the war and beyond. The Chaplin phenomenon played out its initial stages across the war years and exhibitors such as George Elliot drew significant benefits from this. These benefits from the Essanays were not however considerable enough to prevent the Carlton from running into difficult times after Chaplin left Essanay. A close look at the release pattern of the Mutuals in 1916/17 shows that the more upmarket cinemas such as the Palladium in the well-to-do suburb of Portswood and the largest high street cinema The Alexandra capitalised on exclusive runs of the Mutuals and then later the First National films, known as the 'Million Dollar' Chaplins. Elliot's partnership with his projectionist ended in 1917 and shortly after the war as mentioned he left the cinema as well.

Essanay with its policy of exclusives were not able to hold exhibitors like Elliot following Chaplin's departure, although it is clear that Broncho Billy had been a popular attraction in Southampton prior to the war that popularity was not sustained in the war years. Elliot, with his appeal to a 'better class', was typical of managers across Britain in his attempt to upgrade the social 'respectability' of his cinema. They were constantly facing pressure from local church groups and at times local councils concerning not only the content of the films but also the 'propriety' their establishments. Elliot was one of the first in the town to recognise that the war offered a means by which to incorporate the cinema into the social fabric as an acceptable leisure space through his special programmes for the war effort. However, the size and location of his hall proved ultimately to be a disadvantage. The fact that the larger cinemas were able to pay a better percentage of the house for the Mutuals was a main factor in their ability to gain access to those films exclusively. It is also the case that the content of the Chaplin films began to become more suited to the desired audience at more prestigious cinemas like the Palladium. From fast moving and 'vulgar' slapstick shorts with Mack Sennett at Keystone to the refinement of his comedy and the incorporation of pathos at Essanay and Mutual and finally the move to features at First National, Chaplin's development matched the move toward 'respectability' that the larger cinemas came to represent. Bowyer's circuit began to break up in 1916 as he sold off his interests in two of the four cinemas on the circuit. This left the Picturedrome and the Carlton and by late 1916 Bowyer had sold his interests completely. Although records are not clear on this it appears that Elliot bought the controlling interest in The Carlton when Bowyer bowed out. The fact that Elliot was only able to rent for one cinema as opposed to four meant that he was a lesser attraction for renters and for companies which worked on an exclusives basis. This was not necessarily a problem as a number of local exhibitors often worked together and rented from specific exchanges. However, it appears that Elliot did not take up this option. Elliot was less able to compete in this environment and left to pick up his films on the ever decreasing quality and range offered on the open market where possible and to try to continue to advertise his cinema as a respectable 'cosy' place.

Elliot's example qualifies Rachel Low's characterisation of the small showman as 'ignorant'. In her account of British distribution developments during the war the small exhibitor is the main impediment to the effective organisation of exhibitors generally and therefore the main reason for the capitulation to US industry practices.[14] Following Low's account of the impact of the feature length film on the industry she points to the future where the feature became the standard. Citing the hostility of the exhibitors to films over an hour Low states:

> Knowing what happened later it is impossible not to feel, firstly, that fairly long films were in reality very popular with the public: secondly, that intelligent exhibitors were well aware of this: and thirdly, that the real reason for all this opposition was competitive one. Most of the resistance came from the small showmen. The open market system of many short and relatively undistinguished films, with their process kept down to a minimum by merciless competition, suited them better than the long ambitious super film.[15]

Elliot's example demonstrates that while he may have been resistant to the feature there is every indication that it was the imperatives of local competition for audiences that account for his return to using the open market. His acumen in the early part of the war years at both the Northam Picturedrome and at The Carlton demonstrate that he understood his audiences preferences and was as likely to embrace the feature as he did the serial and Chaplin. In fact Chaplin's move to Mutual and First National which resulted in the feature length *Shoulder Arms* would almost certainly have been Elliot's choice had he been able to maintain an exclusives relationship with those companies in the way he did with Essanay. It seems to be clear from Elliot's example that there were factors at play which were out of his control. His practices of developing a patriotic and 'educational' image for the Carlton and his success with the Essanay Chaplins were picked up on by his larger competitors, most of whom by the end of the war were part of larger national circuits. In this respect his story offers some detail to the impact of Essanay's exclusives strategy of 1915 in Britain.

Notes

1. This article is based on research carried out for my forthcoming book *The Big Show: British Cinema Culture in the Great War* (Exeter University Press, 2005).

2. Kristin Thompson, *Exporting Entertainment* (London: BFI, 1985), 215. These figures were drawn from the British trade weekly *The Bioscope*.

3. *What's On in Southampton*, week ending 26 June 1915. The announcement of Elliot's arrival read: "... there is no doubt that the destiny of the comfortable, cool and nicely furnished 'Carlton' is now on the turn of the tide and success looms ahead ..." .

4. *What's On in Southampton*, week ending 26 June 1915.

5. *What's On in Southampton*, week ending 3 July 1915.

6. *What's On in Southampton*, week ending 17 July 1915.

7. 'The Carlton', *What's On in Southampton*, week ending 24 July 1915.

8. 'The Carlton', *What's On in Southampton*, week ending 7 August 1915.

9. Rachel Low, *The History of the British Film 1914–1918* (London: Allen and Unwin, 1950), 41.

10. 'Sunday Evening At the Palace', *What's On*, week ending 14 November 1914.

11. Langford Reed, 'Chaplin's Wonderful "Feat"', *The Bioscope* (29 July 1915): 524.

12. Kristin Thompson, *Exporting Entertainment: America in the World Film Market, 1909–1934*, pp. 82–83. Thompson has shown that this was a turning point in the history of US film distribution in Britain where the open market system began to be replaced by this exclusive system: "Over the next five years, that system (the open market) turned completely around, so that theatres contracted sometimes for one or two years in advance, for films which had not been previewed, or even made. Britain went from being one of the most flexible, open markets in the world to one of the most rigid, closed ones. The system perpetuated the American firm's advantage, since it kept the theatres tied to their larger outputs, eliminating open playdates into which other countries' films might slip."

13. David Robinson, *Chaplin his Life and Art* (London: Penguin, first published by Da Capo Press, 1985, 2001), pp. 788–794. Chaplin made 14 films for Essanay the first, *His New Job* released 1 February 1915, and the last *Charlie Chaplin's Burlesque on Carmen* released 10 April 1916 after he had moved to Mutual.

14. Rachel Low, *The History of The British Film, 1914–1918* (London: George Unwin and Allen, 1950), 44–45.

15. Ibid., 27.

13

"Zeppelin über Berlin" – on the distribution of an early media event

Pelle Snickars

On a Saturday noon in late October 1904 the first issue of the newspaper *BZ am Mittag* appeared in Berlin. The front page was filled with articles reporting on the Russian-Japanese War and the subsequent storming of Port Arthur. The *BZ* was a true novelty on the Berlin newspaper market. The publisher Ullstein Verlag believed there was a market share to be gained by launching a "Mittagszeitung" keeping the public updated with the latest news during lunch hours. Consequently the *BZ* had to be edited and printed rapidly. Soon the paper advertised itself as the quickest newspaper in the world completely relying on news provided by modern technologies as telephones and telegraphs. Yet in terms of distribution the launching of the *BZ* was also remarkable since the newspaper depended on sales of individual copies only. As Peter de Mendelssohn put it in his seminal book *Zeitungsstadt Berlin*, distribution itself became a trademark of the *BZ*.[1] One could not subscribe to the *BZ*, the idea was instead to deliver it *en masse* onto the streets of Berlin. Each issue was to be individually sold to whoever wanted to obtain a copy. Hence, the distributional strategy of the Ullstein Verlag was to use hordes of young men and boys taking off into different city directions shouting: "Bezett am Mittag", "Bezett", "Bezett". The paper was, thus, literally brought on the market. The typical roll call for the *BZ* soon became an auditative trademark of modern Berlin accentuating the rapid pace and the urban tempo of the *Reichshauptstadt*.

As Peter Fritzsche argued in his *Reading Berlin 1900*, the launching of the *BZ* is best considered a modern mass media event.[2] The newspaper's special distributional strategy is, hence, illustrative of one of many media historical transitions occurring around previous turn-of-the-century. In a German context this particular historical phase of modernity is sometimes referred to as the, "Massenmedialisierung des zweiten Strukturwandels der Öffentlichkeit", a kind of second mass mediated transformation of the public sphere. Even Jürgen Habermas has hinted in an introduction from 1990 to his classic study *Strukturwandel der Öffentlichkeit*, that too little emphasis was put on other media than press in his decisive book. The decline of the "bürgerliche Öffentlichkeit" which Habermas lamented was caused by the expansion of a new broader "massenmediale Öffentlichkeit", a public sphere defined by, but also saturated with mass distributed media to which modern types of daily press as the *BZ* belonged.[3] Early cinema, modern newspapers and other contemporary media can today be considered important historical factors determining a by 1900 decisively established "Medienmoderne" – an epoch certainly stretching back in time, perhaps to the beginning of the 19th century, yet by around 1900 a characteristic German term hinting at the way media

Fig. 1. 'Zeitungsverkäuferin am Potsdamer Platz, 1906, Berlin'.
[Photograph by Philipp Kester. Fotomuseum im Münchner Stadtmuseum.].

had begun to influence and affect, penetrate and regulate experiences in everyday life. Moving pictures and the gradual establishment of a metropolitan film culture did play an important role in this transformation. Yet, in terms of impact on society, early cinema was but one public media sphere, "eine mediale Teilöffentlichkeit" within the greater "Medienmoderne".[4]

A productive way of historically situating and understanding the different public media spheres in previous turn-of-the-century Berlin is to analyse how a major event was mediated and distributed at the time. One such event was the so called "Zeppelin-Sonntag", the "Zeppelin Sunday" on the 29th of August 1909. This article will focus on the dissemination and distribution of this event, in particular through imagistic distribution in various media. But the topic is also linked to key questions on the establishment, differentiation and transformation of the public media sphere around 1900. In the following, daily press as the *BZ* is used as the primary empirical source for detecting various distributional media strategies. As is evident from a photograph taken by Philipp Kester in 1906 – one of Germany's first photo journalists working for a number of German illustrated weeklies – there were numerous publications distributed within Berlin at the time (Fig. 1). Within film and media history, journalism is still an underused, albeit productive resource to add to the repertoire of documents bearing on, for example, film and media culture, the public sphere and historical spectatorship, exhibition and regulation, as well as distribution. In addition, the newspapers examined in this article, *Berliner Lokal-Anzeiger, Berliner Tageblatt* and *BZ am Mittag*, were mass oriented media at the time – in contrast to the fairly limited editions of national German film trade papers as *Der Kinematograph* and *Lichtbildbühne*. The total circulation of the major dailies in Berlin around 1910 adds up to almost a

Fig. 2. 'BZ am Mittag 1909'. Newspaper advertisement with superimposed photograph of the Potzdamer Platz. [Ullstein Verlag.]

million copies on a daily basis. Moreover, the major illustrated weeklies – full of reports on Graf Zeppelin's air travels during the summer of 1909 – had an even higher circulation with the *Berliner Illustrirte Zeitung* and the Berlin based *Die Woche* dominating the market. Thus, the city's mass printed press firmly established Berlin as the "Medienhauptstadt" of Wilhelmine Germany, a city "still in the stages of rapid growth, [where] newspapers established themselves as metropolitan institutions, fashioning new, more assertive journalistic practices".[5]

Yet, as Detlef Briesen has shown in his book *Berlin – die überschätzte Metropole*, "Medienrealität und die empirisch festgestellten Fakten stimmen bei der Stadt Berlin ... nicht [immer]".[6] What a city really is – in comparison to what the public opinion mediated through the press thinks it is or imagines it to be – does not always correspond. The Berlin daily press was a frequent producer of staged urban imagery.[7] Thus, the empirical evidence on media distribution gleaned from the Berlin daily press does not automatically lead to historical assumptions suitable for the whole of Germany. Moreover, even if the analysed newspapers belonged to the most important contemporary German mass media at the time, as modern consumer items their popular appeal was far from the Anglo-American "yellow press". The *Berliner Tageblatt* for instance, never featured any images whatsoever. In an international perspective Berlin dailies were traditional and text oriented nationalistic newspapers, with the *BZ* being slightly more liberal. Still they formed the basis of the city's public sphere shaping notions and ideas of society, culture and economics.

The purpose of the daily press is, of course, news and actualities; the press distributes information to the public on what is happening. The Berlin press around 1910, however, also distributed and mediated information about other mass media, especially in terms of reports on other media depicting current events. This lay in accordance with a German cultural reformist agenda that, in short, tried to avoid reporting on media – and especially film – as popular entertainment and instead wanted to associate media with instructive education, art and the mediation of knowledge. The *Berliner Lokal-Anzeiger* in 1909 for example devoted more articles to mediated sound, gramophones and phonographs than to the medium of film. Mediated sound had an apparent artistic potential and phonographs and gramophones were promoted as private rather than public media.[8] Still, in terms of imagistic distribution there did exist a vital

Fig. 3. 'Zeppelinstag'. Frontpage of the newspaper *Berliner Tageblatt*, 29 August 1909.

appropriation of mediations of actualities. A striking advertisement for the *BZ* in 1909 makes a case in point (Fig. 2). The *BZ* advertisement with a superimposed photograph of the Potzdamer Platz, produced by the Ullstein Verlag, gives a clear indication as to how the press promoted and perceived itself as the primary distributor of current events. As the medium of modernity *par excellence* the press naturally incorporated other media as, for example, photography.

There can be no doubt that the printed press certainly was the primary mediator of events in Berlin around the previous turn-of-the-century. Nevertheless, what is intriguing is how other media rapidly followed in the mediation and distribution process, not the least by catering to a public and commercially profitable demand by visualising events already known. Joseph Garncarz has dealt extensively with the issue within the earliest phase of German film history. Though variety programs around 1900 did present fictional films, Garncarz has argued that visual reports, "optische Berichterstattung", became the staple of the variety and vaudeville show at the time. According to Garncarz, visual reports, "did not provide new information, but visualised events that were already known".[9] By 1910 this was still the case, thus, when reports on media were published or advertised in the press the inserts were often linked to events that newspapers had mediated before. Illustrated lectures on up to date actualities for instance got a fair amount of coverage, and since the Berlin daily press had few illustrations it was common with media tie-ins where the press featured repeated ads for illustrated weeklies – often because they were owned by the same publisher. Indeed, the "Zeppelin Sunday" triggered press advertisement for illustrated lectures on airships, and the *Berliner Lokal-Anzeiger* used Zeppelin's arrival to promote another flying event – "Wrights Flug-Vorführungen auf dem Tempelhofer Felde zu Berlin", the same place where Graf Zeppelin landed his airship. In addition, the "Zeppelin-Sunday" prompted a special illustrated aviation publication, the *Aviatik*, a survey of the history of flying machines published by the *Berliner Lokal-Anzeiger* (who financed Wrights flying attempts) to be promoted in a typical media tie in. The *Aviatik* was distributed as part of the illustrated weekly *Die Woche* – and it hardly comes as a surprise that both *Die Woche* and the *Berliner Lokal-Anzeiger* were owned by the same Scherl Verlag.

On "Zeppelin Sunday" in late August 1909 all of the front pages of Berlin's newspapers were filled with reports, maps and illustrations of the event. The morning edition of the *Berliner Tageblatt* for example featured the headline, "Zeppelinstag" – the airship "ZIII is today expected in Berlin" (Fig. 3). The "Zeppelin Sunday" was without a doubt an early media event distributed in numerous ways within the public sphere of Berlin. Even if the concept of "media events", as described by Daniel Dayan and Elihu Katz in their *Media Events. The Live Broadcasting of History* has predominantly been used in relation to television, there did exist similar patterns of mediation prior to television.[10] Media events are in fact an appropriate way of describing how major occurrences as the "Zeppelin Sunday" was mediated on a mass scale already by 1910. Indeed, Dayan and Katz concept of media events should be historicized. Their book is interesting but as often with communication studies, completely ignorant of the history of visual media prior to television. The visual, then televisial and nowadays digitised way of mediating events and distributing actualities, naturally has a history preceding television and newsreels. This is a media history where early cinema and the visual media practises surrounding it are vital, yet neglected in terms of scholarly research. The history of imagistic distribution of news within the various media networks of modernity is still unwritten.

The Zeppelin flight over Berlin during late August 1909, however, was not only mediated and distributed through the daily press. On the first of September 1909 Messters Projektion advertised in the trade paper *Der Kinematograph* for their yet undistributed nonfiction film, *Zeppelin in Berlin* (Fig. 4). The half page ad stated: "We have made the most meticulous preparations as to Graf Zeppelin's upcoming visit to

Fig. 4. 'Mesters Projektion Zeppelin in Berlin", advertisement in *Der Kinematograph*, 1 September 1909.

Berlin to be able to shoot a highly interesting film. Because of the great public interest devoted to the Graf's air travels, one can assume that our film will become extremely popular among audiences [ein Kassenmagnet ersten Ranges]."[11] Besides a small insert there were no other editorials, articles or advertisements devoted to this major media event in *Der Kinematograph*. In short, film historical facts in the leading German film trade paper are somewhat numb. One reason is that *Der Kinematograph* was published in Düsseldorf, still the point to be made is that film historical research limiting itself to information in trade papers only, sometimes runs the risk of missing intriguing media historical distribution patterns that an event as the Zeppelin flight incorporated. As a matter of fact, Messter's film *Zeppelin in Berlin* was but one of a numerous visual mediations of Zeppelin's arrival in Berlin on "Zeppelin Sunday". Plenty of photographs and filmed actualities – although not mentioned in *Der Kinematograph* – were shot during the day. The *Berliner Tageblatt* later featured a review of a Zeppelin film by Eclipse for example, screened at the scientific lecture theatre Treptow-Sternwarte.[12] Thus, Messter's film was just one depiction within a major distribution media network disseminating this event to the public in various ways.

Still only on an infrequent basis did the major Berlin newspapers publish anything explicit on moving pictures – not even advertisements. But one of the few exceptions was inserts and notifications on nonfiction films of current events as the Zeppelin event indicates.[13] The distribution and mediation of nonfiction film was to a large extent dependent on a press discourse on actualities. By and large this is self-evident, still two particular aspects of visual film reports are worth mentioning. Firstly, the rapidity of filmic reports was sometimes stunning. Half a year after the "Zeppelin Sunday", during spring 1910, Edward VII died in London. The next day the cinema chain Union-Theater boasted in the *Berliner Tageblatt*: "in terms of rapid visual reports [schnelle optische Berichterstattung] the Union-Theater stands in a class of its own. Our cinematogra-

Fig. 5. 'Zeppelin über Berlin 1909'. Stereoscopic photograph from the Kaiserpanorama series *Zeppelin in Berlin*.

phers are already on their way to London to shoot to upcoming funeral, which only 24 hours thereafter will be shown to our audiences."[14] Secondly, the German word "anschaulich" was often used in relation to visual reports on film or in other visual media as lantern slides. A filmed aviation event in early 1909 was for example referred to in the *Berliner Lokal-Anzeiger* as depicting the event in an exact way – "der Biograph [führte] ... [die] Flugmanöver anschaulich vor".[15] The word "anschaulich" – used already to describe the first German illustrated weekly in 1843 – is difficult to translate suggesting a kind of vivid descriptiveness and graphic quality of images. The term is, however, significant since it implies the way photographic media was understood to portray and represent reality, not only in an indexical and documentary way, but also as a representative form of mimetic depiction with media technologies perceived as superior to the human eye.

The discourse around visual reports, "optische Berichterstattung", suggests that newspapers and film, cinemas and mass cultural venues, illustrated weeklies and mass distributed photographs, slides and stereoscopic views, formed an early media network on actualities. This network was primarily content driven rather than media specific and a range of informational and imagistic interaction took place both at the production and distribution level, as well as among recipient audiences. To understand for example the production and distribution of nonfiction film during the period of early cinema, the printed press, and in particular illustrated weeklies, in fact serve as a kind of blueprint to what was considered important and newsworthy to shoot, produce and distribute on film. This is not surprising but the point is that a broader media historical context surrounding such filmed actualities as Messter's film *Zeppelin in Berlin*, reframes and recontextualises them, thus, providing the films with new meaning – not the least in terms of how they were perceived and understood by audiences. Clearly, moving pictures were by 1910 not (yet) a contemporary "Leitmedium", at least not in terms of distribution of events. Other sources hint at a similar interpretation. If one, for example examines the historical directory *Berliner Adreßbuch*, it becomes evident that one has to situate early Berlin cinema within a larger media historical framework. Even by 1910 phonographic companies, not to mention photographic ones, outnumbered film companies. In 1909 only fifty companies dealing with moving pictures were listed in the *Berliner Adreßbuch* – yet four years earlier there had only been ten. Although likely

Fig. 6. 'Internationales Porträt-Institut'. Advertisement in the *Berliner Lokal-Anzeiger*, 28 March 1909.

financed by small fees, the *Berliner Adreßbuch* is a fascinating historical source hinting at the gradual development of an urban public media sphere.

Still there are historical exceptions where, in fact, the medium of film distributed and depicted events even before the daily press. Sticking to the year of 1909 the mediation of the great earthquake in southern Italy around the city of Messina is such an example. The Messina earthquake was a paradigmatic example of a typical catastrophe determining the graphic output in newspapers with numerous illustrations. Yet, moving pictures from the Messina catastrophe appeared in Berlin even before illustrations were printed in the daily press. Already on the first of January 1909 only three days after the catastrophe, the *Berliner Lokal-Anzeiger* reported the next day that a cinema at the current "Kintematographen-Austellung" were to visually report on the earthquake: "die Kino-Austellung am Zoo wird schon morgen (Sonnabend) über die entsezliche Erdbebenkatastrophe in Calabrien kinematographisch berichten".[16] Two days later the same newspaper featured an advertisement for the film exhibition informing the public it had been prolonged and that telegraphically ordered films from Messina were projected as soon as they arrived: "die telegraphisch bestellten Films über die Erdbebenkatastrophe werden stets nach Eintreffen sofort vorgeführt".[17]

Hence, to conclude one might argue that if moving images today in digitised or televised form set the overall news agenda, this is the result of a media historical process that can be traced back to the previous turn-of-the-century. Indeed, the concept of media event is appropriate for describing how a major current event as the "Zeppelin Sunday" was mediated on a mass scale already in 1909. The distribution of this early media event was not only a concern for the daily press or the medium of film. The illustrated press were during the summer of 1909 filled with images of airships. The high-circulation illustrated weeklies *Die Woche* and *Berliner Illustrirte Zeitung* featured numerous visual reports. They were, perhaps, the most important mass media in Germany at the time to visually influence people's views of actualities and events. Beside the illustrated press, post cards with Zeppelin motifs from Berlin were mass produced and distributed. In addition, Zeppelin toys were sold on the streets of Berlin, the vaudeville Berliner Wintergarten included a Zeppelin film in their September program, and August Fuhrmann naturally filled his three Kaiser-Panorama's in Berlin with hundreds of stereoscopic images of the Zeppelin event as for example the series "Eroberung der Luft" or "Zeppelin in Berlin" (Fig. 5).[18]

Various media had in fact constructed the awareness and the attention around the "Zeppelin Sunday" all during spring and summer 1909. Articles and updated reports, illustrations and maps, as well as a lot of graphic advertisement using the public's interest for Zeppelin had filled the pages of Berlin's newspapers. The Internationales Porträt-Institut for example, had a returning and quite intriguing ad in a number of the dailies featuring an airship with the portrait of the Graf, as well as a long poem and a quiz (Fig. 6). Graf Zeppelin was well known, he had conducted flying attempts with his airship for nearly ten years. In 1908 there had occurred a major catastrophe: an explosion destroyed the ship "LZ 4", yet a national fund-raiser provided Zeppelin with new money, and his speech of gratitude to the German people was even recorded on phonograph to be sold.

Hence, already a hundred years ago the public sphere was saturated by mass media forming a variety of "Medienöffentlichkeiten" produced, distributed and received in various ways. A cinematic concept as that on visual reports, "optische Berichterstattung", clearly has to include other forms of media besides moving pictures. If one examines early nonfiction film of current events, a range of other media has to be taken into consideration. Thus, to fully understand early distribution of mediated news a broad media historical perspective has to be applied.

Notes

1. Mendelsohn, Peter de, *Zeitungsstadt Berlin* (Berlin: Ullstein Verlag, 1959).

2. Fritzsche, Peter, *Reading Berlin 1900* (Cambridge, Mass: Harvard University Press, 1996).

3. Habermas, Jürgen, *Strukturwandel der Öffentlichkeit* (Frankfurt am Main: Suhrkamp, 1990), 48. Thus, one of the questions facing media historians today is to analyse not so much the rise of the public sphere but the prolongation and continuance of it in and through other media than the printed press. Research attempts in this direction have been undertaken focusing especially the late 20th century and the medium of television. Yet, between 1850 and 1950 there still exists a substantial historical gap essentially unanalysed in terms of understanding the rise of a mass mediated public sphere outside or in relation to the domain of the press. John B. Thompson in his *The Media and Modernity. A Social Theory of the Media* for example, devotes a number of pages to Habermas and the printed press' importance for establishing a historically situated public sphere. But as he moves on to discuss other forms of mediated public spheres he completely

ignores all the various established mass media around 1900, including film, and quickly moves on to television. Thompson, John B., *The Media and Modernity. A Social Theory of the Media* (Stanford: Stanford University Press, 1995).

4. The public sphere, "Öffentlichkeit", is a notorious difficult concept to translate into English. In the following the public sphere is understood as a forum of public discourses. Indeed, the concept is better used in plural, "Öffentlichkeiten", especially in terms of different public spheres of media. In a German context the concept has been further disseminated, postulating various "Teilöffentlichkeiten" with a difference between "Veranstaltungsöffentlichkkeiten" and "Massenmedienöffentlichkeiten". For a discussion on the concept and its history, see Führer, Karl, Knut Hicketier and Axel Schildt "Öffentlichkeit – Medien – Geschichte. Konzepte der modernen Öffentlichkeit und Zugänge zu ihrer Erforschung", *Archiv für Sozialgeschichte* 41. Jg, 2001, 2.

5. Fritzsche, 2.

6. Briesen, Detlef, *Berlin – die überschätzte Metropole* (Köln: Köln universität, 1990), 148.

7. For a discussion on the early 20th century "image" of Berlin, see Kiecol, Daniel, *Selbstbild und Image zweier europäischer Metropolen. Paris und Berlin zwischen 1900 und 1930* (Frankfurt am Main: Peter Lang, 2001).

8. For a discussion, see Snickars, Pelle, "Reading Berlin 1909. 'Medienöffentlichkeit', Daily Press and Mediated Events", *Kinoöffentlichkeit 1895–1920* (ed. Corinna Müller) (München: Fink Verlag, forthcoming).

9. Garncarz, Joseph, "The Origins of Film Exhibition in Germany", *The German Cinema Book* (eds Tim Bergfelder, Erica Carter and Deniz Göktürk) (London: Routledge, 2002). See also, Garncarz, Joseph, "Die Enstehung des Kino aus dem Varieté: ein Plädoyer für ein erweiteres Konzept der intermedialität" *Intermedialität: Theorie und Praxis eines interdisziplinären Forschungsgebiets* (ed. Jörg Helbig) (Berlin: Erich Schmidt Verlag, 1998).

10. Dayan, Daniel and Katz, Elihu, *Media Events. The Live Broadcasting of History* (Cambridge, Mass: Harvard University Press, 1992).

11. "Mesters Projektion", advertisement in *Der Kinematograph*, 1 September 1909.

12. Advertisement for the Treptow-Sternwarte, *Berliner Tageblatt*, 7 September 1909.

13. Regular film advertisement does not seems to have been published in the major Berlin newspapers on a daily basis until late 1910 or early 1911. On the 15 January 1911, for example, the *Berliner Tageblatt* featured large ads – similar to the ones that had been published by vaudeville venues as Wintergarten and Apollo-Theater for years – for the five U.T Uniontheater cinemas as well as the Mozart-Saal Lichtspiele. The latter, perhaps the most prestigious cinema of Berlin at the time had opened in September 1910. It seemed to have had enough cultural and medial prestige as to be accepted among the "Vergnügungs-Anzeigen", thus, functioning as a pioneer in terms of film advertisement. For a discussion, see Hanisch, Michael *Auf den Spuren der Filmgeschichte. Berliner Schauplätze* (Berlin: Henschel Verlag, 1991), 217–226.

14. Advertisement for the Union-Theater, *Berliner Tageblatt*, 7 May 1910.

15. "Wintergarten", unsigned, *Berliner Lokal-Anzeiger*, 4 February 1909.

16. "Kino-Austellung am Zoo", unsigned, *Berliner Lokal-Anzeiger*, 1 January 1909.

17. Advertisement for the "Kinematographen-Austellung", *Berliner Lokal-Anzeiger*, 3 January 1909.

18. See returning advertisement for the Kaiser-Panorama during September 1909 in the *Berliner Lokal-Anzeiger*.

14

"The Audience Feels rather at Home ...": Peter Marzen's 'Localisation' of Film Exhibition in Trier

Martin Loiperdinger

Professor of Media Studies, Trier University, Germany

The overwhelming majority of film titles which were screened within commercial exhibition in Germany before the First World War were produced by French, British, Italian and other foreign companies. Apart from relatively few topicals and travelogues which were shot by operators of these companies in the German Reich,[1] all these films had to be imported and distributed from abroad. The dissemination of this foreign commodity to German film theaters was organised on a national level. The bulk of the German produced films – far less in number – usually were also distributed in all regions of the German Reich. But there was an exception to the rule which played an important role in short film programmes before the First World War: local films did not go into distribution at all. According to recent publications by Vanessa Toulmin, Stephen Bottomore, Uli Jung, Brigitte Braun and myself, local films were made to be shown to local people.[2] In the words of Stephen Bottomore, local films show a "considerable overlap between the people appearing in the film and those who watch it or are intended to watch it".[3] Their dominant impact on local audiences was recognition.[4]

Local films have been widely neglected, by film archives and film festivals as well as by film historians. Whereas local films had prominent positions within short film programmes at least before the First World War, they represent the most evanescent part of commercial cinema history:

> They were not advertised in the trade journals and, although they were probably shot in large quantities, they were available only in very small numbers of prints. The producers of local films were either local theater owners – as was the case in Trier – or professional production companies that were commissioned by local people or organisations (including theater owners). Probably the bulk of these films were printed only once (which at the same time may explain why most of the local films must be considered lost), since they were playing only at one cinema and probably not for a long period of time.[5]

As an exception to the rule, the case of the city of Trier offers a unique opportunity to study the use of local films in the context of local exhibition. Nearly a dozen local films from 1903 to 1914 have survived which were produced by the Marzen family who ran a travelling kinematograph show in the south-west of Germany, until they took over the Central-Theater, a permanent cinema in the center of Trier, from Anton Burbach, a photographer, and re-opened it on 24 March 1909.

This article tries to give an idea how these local films were used in the competition between Marzen and other cinema enterprises, and what impact they were having on local audiences. Screenings of local films in the Central-Theater did not just offer an additional attraction to the usual show. They were embedded within a broader 'localisation' concept which served to make programmes of foreign films more familiar to local audiences. Observations and considerations on audience address in Marzen's local films from Trier will lead us to more general questions on the relationship between commercial exhibition and amateur film in early cinema before the First World War.

Lecturing in Trier dialect

Three and a half months after the re-opening of the Central-Theater by the Marzen family the local newspaper *Trierische Zeitung* published a long contribution with the title: "In einem 'trierischen' Kinematographen" (In a 'Trierish' kinematograph show).[6] This article portrays the Central-Theater screenings as an outstanding example of moving picture entertainment. Already the headline indicates that the entertaining potentials of the show lie in its somehow local character. This sounds a little bit confusing as clients of kinematograph screenings of the time knew very well that the bulk of the films presented there were of foreign origin. Why, then, could such a show not take place, let us say, in nearby Koblenz or in Cologne? What was it that made it so specifically "Trierish"? After a few general paragraphs on the emergence of kinematograph shows and on the production of moving pictures the author describes the specific local qualities of the Central-Theater screenings. They do not derive from the screen, in the first place, but are produced by the voice of the lecturer:

> It is only the proprietor – in explaining the moving pictures – who makes the cinema 'truly Trierish'. The voice is sobbing, weeping, howling, wailing, laughing, cursing, whispering, rumbling – and this often within five minutes, depending on the situation. Best standard German alternates with the most beautiful Trier dialect. In between, canons are thundering, lightning is zigzagging, steampipes are screeching, a round of a rifle is rattling.[7]

One month later, this article was reprinted in the trade journal *Der Kinematograph*. In an answer to readers' questions in the following issue, the editors revealed Peter Marzen as the lecturer to whom the author of the article had given so much praise.[8] Peter Marzen was a showman. Apparently he commanded over remarkable abilities in performing an impressive 'soundtrack' to silent moving pictures on the screen. He had already served as lecturer for the Marzen family's travelling kinematograph show which had been managed by his father, Wendel Marzen. In the Central-Theater enterprise, Peter Marzen obviously was the key figure from the beginning. He was the person who incorporated the 'local' aspects of the show by standing next to the screen and commenting the short features of the programme in the popular vernacular of the Trier region. Thanks to his performance many foreign characters on the screen spoke in the same dialect as the audience did:

> As much as we enjoyed to find our vernacular treated this way in our home town, we had much to wonder sometimes when one or the other performer on the screen addressed us in a straight Trier idiom, although he was standing on the beach of the Mediterranean, in happy Nizza, in the arena of proud Spain or on the boulevards of Paris.[9]

In order to give some amusing examples, the author of the article quotes Peter Marzen's evocation of a young 'apache's' desperation and of a betrayed Parisian husband's fury. It seems that, during projection, fiction features from abroad received some local 'colour' through Peter Marzen's lecturing performance in the Trier dialect. By adding his local vernacular extras to the moving pictures on the screen, Peter Marzen adapted foreign screen characters to local attitudes of articulating personal emotions such as fury, anger, love, and joy.

Thus, while deriving from the film market which had been 'global' from the beginning, French, Italian, or British moving pictures were 'localised' through oral performances accompanying the film screenings. Lecturing in Trier dialect was Marzen's personal achievement which gave the Central-Theater screenings a certain exclusiveness, since none of his competitors in town could match him. According to his autobiography, Peter Marzen was very proud of the impact of his lecturing on the audience and of its effectiveness in the competition with two other cinema enterprises in Trier.[10] It is not known to what extent his local style of lecturing helped Peter Marzen to win audiences from his rivals to the Central-Theater, but auditive performance obviously was an important field of struggle[11] – apart from the fact that Peter Gitsels actually closed down his Parade-Theater in June 1910, and Otto Waldenburger closed down his Reichshallen-Lichtspiele in July 1912.[12]

Even if Peter Marzen is over-estimating the real effects of his achievements, 'localisation' was certainly the most remarkable effort in his individual style of film exhibition performance. On the basis of his everyday practice of auditive 'localisation', the implementation of local views into Central-Theater screenings was an extra and very special highlight which could only be included in some of the programmes. However, the sheer number of local films which were commissioned and programmed in Central-Theater in the first months upon its re-opening under Marzen's management on 24 March 1909, is a strong evidence of 'localisation' as focus of Marzen's business strategies.

Local views of Trier and recognition

Apart from 'localisation' via lecturing in the Trier dialect, incorporating local views was another means of securing product differentiation in the first years of film exhibition in permanent cinemas. Local films were unique and exclusive 'numbers' at a time when hardly a difference could be made between the short film programmes which were screened, let us say, in two cinemas located in the same street or the same quarter of town.

The film show enterprise of the Marzen family sought entry into the local cinema market of Trier by implementing a remarkable number of local views in the Central-Theater short film programmes. In spring and summer 1909 the only competitor was Peter Gitsels' Parade-Theater. Gitsels also ran another cinema in Koblenz. He had his business in Trier already well established. But also Marzens' programmes were already well known to many inhabitants of Trier. The travelling show "Marzen's Edison's Elektrisches Theater – Kinematograph" had visited Trier with its performances regularly more than once every year since 1902. In order to win local audiences' attention to the Central-Theater premises, it seems that Peter Marzen based the commercial future of the enterprise strongly on local films. Marzen's short film programmes from April to July 1909 included no less than seven local views of Trier: *Domausgang am Ostersonntag* (*Exit from the Cathedral on Easter Sunday*); *Promenadenkonzert an der Porta Nigra* (*A Prom Concert at the Porta Nigra*); *Die alte Römerstadt Trier und ihre Sehenswürdigkeiten* (*Trier, The Old Roman City and Its Sites*); *Frühjahrsspritzenprobe unserer*

Fig. 1. Leben und Treiben auf dem Viehmarkt am 5. Mai. Bekannte Handels-Typen im Wirken (Life and Trade in Viehmarkt on 5 May – Well-known Trafficking Types in Action), 1909: living portraits.

Freiwilligen Feuerwehr am 3. Mai am Stadttheater (The Spring Season Test of the Fire Hose on May 3 at the Municipal Theater); Leben und Treiben auf dem Viehmarkt am 5. Mai. Bekannte Handels-Typen im Wirken (Life and Trade in Viehmarkt on 5 May – Well-known Trafficking Types in Action) which showed scenes from the cattle market; *Fronleichnamsprozession in Trier 1909 (The 1909 Corpus Christi Procession in Trier); Festlichkeiten aus Anlass des 35jährigen Stiftungsfestes des Männergesangvereins «Eintracht» am Pfingstsonntag (Festivities Commemorating the 35th Anniversary of the Foundation of the Men's Choir 'Eintracht' on Whitsun).*[13]

Since the first screening of *Arrivée des congressistes à Neuville-sur-Saône* which Louis Lumière shot on 11 June 1895, and presented to his 'cinematographed' collegues the following day at the Congrès des sociétés françaises de la photographie in Lyons,[14] recognition of 'living portraits' has been the main attraction of local views. By attending the Central-Theater programmes the inhabitants of Trier had many chances to view not only local events, but to recognise themselves and their friends and relatives "in natural size and movement" on Marzen's screen. The local view for instance which covered the prom concert at the Porta Nigra was advertised by the slogan: "Tausende von Trierern in lebender Bewegung" (Thousands of Trierers in living movement).[15] In July 1909, the already quoted article from *Trierische Zeitung* described local films as the most attractive element of Marzens' short film programmes in the Central-Theater:

It is by far most interesting, however, when pictures of Trier are shown to the jubilant audience. In these cases we can see notorious faces of Trierers leaving church, participating in fire drills, witnessing the marching in of a men's choir, or peddling in the Viehmarkt place. The children loudly shout with joy: [in local vernacular] 'hello, this is John, and there is Kathy', while adult viewers call the names of their friends in a lower voice. Everybody is happy to see on the screen the face of somebody they know; they are even more happy, if their own faces are

Fig. 2. Domausgang am Ostersonntag (Exit from the Cathedral on Easter Sunday): Peter Marzen with the waving little girl; next to them to the left, wearing a cylinder: Wendel Marzen.

laughing at them from the screen. Yet, they are annoyed if their own faces look sullen, unfriendly, unfavorable.[16]

Indeed, self-recognition and recognition of friends and relatives actually seems to have been an entertaining and enthusing attraction for viewers. The appearances of local people in Marzen's programmes provoked vivid responses from his local audiences which sometimes were directly addressed from the crowd or from individuals on the screen. Thus, in some local Trier films, viewers' reactions were already inscribed into the moving pictures themselves: Viewers were spontaneously addressed when a laughing and waving crowd of bystanders gathered around the camera during shooting and then, during projection, just laughed and waved to the audience as it happens at the end of the first shot of *Internationaler Marianischer Kongress zu Trier vom 3.–6. August 1912* (*International Marian Congress in Trier, 3–6 August 1912*).

"The audience feels rather at home ..."

According to the 1909 article, local views were well-suited to create a quite intimate atmosphere of private gossip in Marzen's projection room:

> It is then that the Kinematograph loses its character as a virtual theater. The audience feels rather at home and then feels free to frankly criticize friends and foes. The Kinematograph has become a mirror for Trier, not in the sense of the 'official gazette' that covers the magisterial events in Trier, but rather in the sense of the inexpensive fashion magazine for the ladies.[17]

Moreover, the author clearly indicates that the gossiping audience who "feels rather at home" in the Central-Theater is just practising some kind of social control, maybe of surveillance even:

> The cinematographical apparatus does not lie. It shows everyone and everything as it is, as it seems to be and as it ought to be. It tells us who attended Sunday mess

at the Cathedral, who was strolling around during the prom, and it finally 'controls' who attended the religious processions.[18]

The creation of an audience who "feels rather at home" in Marzen's public and commercial venue can be confirmed by a close look at *Domausgang am Ostersonntag*: during the shooting of churchgoers before the cathedral on Easter Sunday 1909, father Wendel Marzen and son Peter Marzen appear before the camera. Peter Marzen has a little girl on his arm. He lifts the girl and makes her wave to the camera – and thus she greets the audience whenever this local view is projected on screen. The girl's gesture (and Marzen's incentive to make her produce that gesture before the apparatus) is a typical gesture of amateur films which cover events of family life and usually are presented to family members, relatives and neighbours in the privacy of people's homes. But Peter Marzen, through the waving gesture of the little girl, does not aim to address his own family: Instead, he directly addresses audiences in his commercial venue, the Central-Theater. Thus the projection room of his cinema becomes a public sphere which is nevertheless orchestrated by patterns of behaviour among the audience which usually take place in private spaces among good friends or family members. This kind of 'localising' foreign film programmes through the implementation of typical elements of family films might have reinforced an intimate atmosphere which had already been created by Marzen's lecturing in local dialect and by audiences trying to recognise or identify themselves or friends and relatives in the moving images of churchgoers on the screen.

The appearance of Peter Marzen in *Domausgang am Ostersonntag* leads to another observation which demonstrates once more that local exhibition performance is inherent to local films already in the making of them: close viewings of extant local films from Trier reveal that Peter Marzen can be recognised in all of them. His appearance happens at least like a cameo right in the beginning when he walks through the frame before the start of a parade or procession as he does in *Internationaler Marianischer Kongress*, or in *Blumenkorso 1914, Veranstaltet vom Radfahrerverein Trier, Gegr. 1885* (Corso of Flowers 1914, arranged by the Cyclists' Club Trier, Founded in 1885). In some local films Peter Marzen can be seen while he is directing the shooting – so during projection the lecturer Peter Marzen could comment his own appearance on screen:

> There were not only masses of Trier's citizens to be seen in the films, but also Marzen himself. More than once he stepped into the frame, directed bystanders, gave little signs to the camera operator, 'organized' the picture, so to speak; he was actor and director at the same time. And when the films were being screened he stood next to the screen explaining himself to the audience. The audience, in turn, was watching Marzen watching himself. It is not very demanding to imagine the effect this had on spectators, even more so if the narrator spoke in the popular vernacular of the region. It is likely that Marzen's comments were humorous and ironic.[19]

Peter Marzen's appearances in person in his films were probably perceived like a trademark. It is now comprehensible that *Trierische Zeitung* could praise his perform-ance of local views as a climax of his Central-Theater programmes. Even apart from such highlights, it has to be underlined that also his unique everyday practice of 'localisation' via lecturing in Trier dialect had exclusive aspects of local stardom which no other competing cinema enterprise in town was able to challenge.

Local films and the *portrait vivant*

The sale of film cameras and raw film stock to amateur photographers was a key concept in the earliest days of cinematography: In 1894, Georges Demenÿ's Chronophotographe was advertised as a camera for taking *portraits vivants* of the beloved ones which were to be animated through his Phonoscope.[20] Also the Cinématographe Lumière had been designed as an apparatus for amateur photographers:

> The Cinématographe is a light machine with an ease of operation which makes it particularly suitable for filming in exterior locations. Let us not forget that Louis Lumière headed an enterprise whose fortune was founded on amateur photographers. When he conceived of the Cinématographe, his first intention was to make it available to informed amateurs. As a simple photographic apparatus, the Cinématographe would record family scenes with the additional element of motion.[21]

Louis Lumière filmed around 100 views in 1895 and 1896. Many of them he shot in order to demonstrate amateur photographers that they could achieve *portraits vivants* of their families with the new apparatus.[22] This initial idea was not realised: Due to the successful introduction to paying audiences the Cinématographe Lumière became a device of making money through the exhibition of film in public spaces.

The work of film pioneers such as Georges Demenÿ and Louis Lumière reveals a close relationship between amateur photography and early cinema. From the advent of cinematography to the 1920s those amateurs who used a film camera to take family films were only very few. Shooting of portraits remained within the field of still photography. These portraits were usually viewed and recognised in privacy. Self-recognition of living portraits was only possible in commercial cinemas and kinematograph shows whenever local films were screened for local people. Audiences paid for an entertainment which was not available at home: recognition of one's own and of relatives and friends from moving pictures which were projected onto a screen. Even if audiences "felt rather at home" in film theaters as they did in Peter Marzen's Central-Theater, the experience of recognition and self-recognition was taking place in public space, and thus made a remarkable difference to private viewings of amateur films which was going on from the 1920s onward. The experience of recognition and self-recognition in local films was bound to local audiences, but it was still a public affair which only later became a private one through screenings of amateur films for small and intimate audiences at one's own home.

Notes

1.   Cf. for an overview on non-fiction films which were shot by foreign companies in the German Reich between 1907 and 1912: Loiperdinger, Martin, 'Das nicht-fiktionale Filmangebot für die Nummernprogramme'. In: Jung, Uli and Martin Loiperdinger (eds): *Geschichte des dokumentarischen Films in Deutschland. Bd. 1: Kaiserreich (1895–1918)* (Stuttgart: Reclam, 2005), 179–190.

2.   Toulmin, Vanessa and Martin Loiperdinger. 'Is it You? Recognition, Representation and Response in Relation to the Local Film', *Film History* 17 (1) (2005): 7–18; Braun, Brigitte and Uli Jung. 'Local Films from Trier, Luxembourg and Metz: A Successful Business Venture of the Marzen Family, Cinema Owners', *Film History* 17 (1) (2005): 19–28; Bottomore, Stephen. 'From the Factory Gate to the 'Home Talent' Drama: An International Overview of Local Films in the Silent Era'. In: Toulmin, Vanessa, Patrick Russell and Simon Popple (eds). *The Lost World of Mitchell and Kenyon. Edwardian Britain on Film* (London: BFI Publishing, 2004), 33–48; Jung, Uli. 'Local Views: a blind spot in the historiography of Early German Cinema', *Historical Journal of Film, Radio and Television* 22 (3) (2002): 253–273; Toulmin, Vanessa. 'Local Films for Local People: Travelling showmen and the commissioning of local films in Great Britain, 1900 to 1902', *Film*

History 13 (2) (2001): 118–138; Hoppe, Karsten, Martin Loiperdinger and Jörg Wollscheid. 'Trierer Lokalaufnahmen der Filmpioniere Marzen', *KINtop 9: Lokale Kinogeschichten* (2000): 15–37.

3. Bottomore, Stephen. 'From the Factory Gate to the 'Home Talent' Drama: An International Overview of Local Films in the Silent Era'. In: Toulmin, Vanessa, Patrick Russell and Simon Popple (eds). *The Lost World of Mitchell and Kenyon. Edwardian Britain on Film*, (London: BFI Publishing, 2004), 33.

4. Cf. Toulmin, Vanessa and Martin Loiperdinger. 'Is it You? Recognition, Representation and Response in Relation to the Local Film', *Film History* 17 (1) (2005): 7–18.

5. Jung, Uli. 'Local Views: a blind spot in the historiography of Early German Cinema', *Historical Journal of Film, Radio and Television* 22 (3) (2002): 255.

6. 'In einem "trierischen" Kinematographen. Plauderei von K. Sch', *Trierische Zeitung*, Nr. 326 (evening issue) (14 July 1909). One month later, this article was reprinted in the trade journal *Der Kinematograph*, no. 137 (11 August 1909). It is also reprinted in: *KINtop 9: Lokale Kinogeschichten* (2000): 11–13.

7. 'In einem "trierischen" Kinematographen', *Trierische Zeitung*, Nr. 326 (evening issue) (14 July 1909).

8. Cf. *Der Kinematograph*, no. 138 (18 August 1909), column 'Aus der Praxis'.

9. 'In einem "trierischen" Kinematographen', *Trierische Zeitung* Nr. 326 (evening issue) (14 July 1909).

10. Cf. Marzen, Peter. *Aus dem Leben eines rheinischen Filmpioniers. Eine Erinnerungsgabe zum fünfzigsten Geburtstag und seiner 35jährigen Zugehörigkeit zur Filmindustrie.* (Saarbrücken n.d. [1933]), 9–11.

11. Cf. Herzig, Michaela and Martin Loiperdinger. '"Vom Guten das Beste" – Kinematographen-konkurrenz in Trier', *KINtop 9: Lokale Kinogeschichten* (2000): 48–50. Gitsels sued Marzen, albeit in vain, on claims related to sound equipment, cf. Braun, Brigitte and Uli Jung. 'Local Films from Trier, Luxembourg and Metz: A Successful Business Venture of the Marzen Family, Cinema Owners', *Film History*, 17 (1) (2005): 22.

12. Cf. Braun, Brigitte. '"Wir Trierer lieben den ,Kintop' über alles" – Die Kinostadt Trier vor dem Ersten Weltkrieg', *Kurtrierisches Jahrbuch*, 42 (2002): 239–273.

13. Cf. *Trierischer Volksfreund* (17 April 1909, 15 May 1909, 16 June 1909, 2 July 1909).

14. *Arrivée des congressistes à Neuville-sur-Saône* is not listed in the Catalogue Lumière, cf. Pinel, Vincent. *Louis Lumière. Inventeur et cinéaste* (Nathan: Paris, 1994), 114.

15. Cf. *Trierischer Volksfreund* (17 April 1909).

16. 'In einem "trierischen" Kinematographen', *Trierische Zeitung* Nr. 326 (evening issue) (14 July 1909).

17. Ibid.

18. Ibid.

19. Jung, Uli. 'Local Views: a blind spot in the historiography of Early German Cinema', *Historical Journal of Film, Radio and Television* 22 (3) (2002): 269.

20. Cf. 'Appareil chronophotographique pour les amateurs', *Photo-Gazette* (25 September 1894).

21. Pinel, Vincent. *Louis Lumière. Inventeur et cinéaste* (Nathan: Paris, 1994), 37–38, quoted from: Gunning, Tom, 'A Mischievous and Knowing Gaze: The Lumière Cinématographe and the Culture of Amateur Photography'. In: Dujardin, Philippe, André Gardies, Jacques Gerstenkorn and Jean-Claude Seguin (eds). *L'aventure du Cinématographe. Actes du Congrès mondial Lumière* (Lyon: Aléas, 1999), 314.

22. See: Rossell, Deac. 'Die soziale Konstruktion früher technischer Systeme der Filmprojektion', *KINtop 8: Film- und Projektionskunst* (1999): 53–81, and Gunning, op. cit.

15

Local distribution: The case of Jens Christian Gundersen in Norway

Gunnar Iversen

Department of Art and Media Studies, NTNU, Trondheim, Norway

In recent years, research on early film distribution has improved somewhat, although it is still a mere fraction compared to literature on production and reception. There still is little interest in distribution, and only a handful of books has been published dealing specifically with early distribution, most notable books by Kristin Thompson (1985) and Ivo Blom (2003). The history of film distribution remains to be written. There are several reasons why the distribution sector has been neglected in film studies; the lack of glamour, creativity and cultural capital in this business side of film, and the lack of primary sources.

Few records of the earliest years of the distribution sector survive, but sources certainly exist, on all levels: local, national and international. The recent example of Ivo Blom, in his excellent study *Jean Desmet and the Early Dutch Film Trade* (2003), shows us how a micro-history based on primary sources not only enriches the knowledge of early Dutch distribution, but gives us new perspectives on international distribution in the early 1910s.

In this article, I will present a small sample from an ongoing project resembling the work done by Ivo Blom. Recently, the business archive of the Norwegian cinema owner, producer and distributor Jens Christian Gundersen was rediscovered in the vaults of the Norwegian Film Institute. This archive, 73 large books containing carbon copies of the outgoing correspondence of Gundersen, is a 'treasure chest' and a unique source, tracing the day to day business of film distribution in Scandinavia from 1907 to 1926. This archive enables us to get a richer picture of the business history which has been so lacking in scholarship on early film to date.

At the moment, I am working my way through these large books, and I have not read and analysed more than one third of the material, so in this essay I will present Jens Christian Gundersen and his work as a distributor in Scandinavia, and then, as a case study, outline his work as the representative or agent of Éclair in Norway and Scandinavia.

Gundersen and film distribution in Norway

A solicitor and amateur dramatist, Jens Christian Gundersen (1868–1945), became the most influential cinema owner and film distributor in Norway from 1907 to 1919. Setting up business in Kristiania, Norway's capital, in 1907, he acquired cinemas in several cities and established several film distribution companies, building a small cinema empire. He was an agent with exclusive rights for the Scandinavian or the Norwegian market for companies like Vitagraph, Nordisk, Ambrosio, Luna, Edison and Éclair.

In 1911, he directed the feature film *The Demon* (*Dæmonen*), a sensationalist melodrama photographed by Alfred Lind in Denmark, one of the very first Norwegian fiction films. *The Demon* was a modest success, and was also shown in Sweden and Denmark, but remained Gundersen's only directorial work. Most of all, he was a businessman who saw opportunities in the new film trade.

The first permanent cinema in Norway opened late in 1904, and the years 1905 and 1906 saw a "cinema fever" in Norway; most cities and towns got several permanent cinemas in these years. Gundersen entered the world of film in 1907, when he set up three separate companies. These companies either owned cinemas, or was companies that distributed films. The combination of cinema ownership and distribution proved to be important, as well as an international network; in 1911 Gundersen also became a part-owner of a large cinema in Denmark, and his stocks in the Danish company Det Skandinavisk-Russiske Handelshus earned him the place on the board of directors.

Apart from the modest production of actualities, and feature productions of Gundersen and another cinema owner, Halfdan Nobel Roede, there was almost no film production in Norway until the late 1910s, so the nation's dependence on foreign sources was total. The Norwegian market was largely dominated by French and Danish film until the First World War, but even before the war American films became steadily more popular and important in the business.

In 1907, Gundersen, and other cinema owners in Norway, bought films directly from production companies and international distributors. Even in this early phase, films were seldom offered bundled together as a whole evening's programme, but bought and re-sold separately, according to the specific taste in a city or a smaller town. The same film could be shown in neighbouring theaters, but most often as part of quite different programmes.

Until the early 1910s, Norway had an open-market system, where international producers sold their films directly to a Norwegian cinema owner or through a distributor or agent, to as many theaters as possible.[1] Exclusive contracts were rare, and even after a system of agents with exclusive contracts first emerged around 1910 or 1911, a film might still be sold or rented to a number of theatres in the same city or district.

Gundersen became an important agent, buying films from other agents, especially in Copenhagen, for his own cinemas, or selling films to other Norwegian cinema owners on a market in Kristiania. By 1910, Gundersen arranged special previews of films for potential buyers and customers. Twice a week, on Tuesdays and Fridays, Gundersen's buyers saw films from different production companies, and on Wednesdays and Saturdays Gundersen returned some of the unsold films to the agents or production companies in Europe.

The films that Gundersen received were very seldom films that were pre-sold unseen to him, and that he was obliged either to use in his own theatres or sell to other cinema owners. Most of the films that he received were samples; so-called "échantillons". The samples Gundersen received were always complete films, but the prints were usually used, either as un-sold samples presented elsewhere or second-hand copies, and Gundersen frequently complained that he could not sell the samples he had received because they were too worn, and that showing old samples made a bad impression on his potential buyers.

Production companies often tried to get Gundersen to sell their films blindly, but no cinema owner in Norway accepted blind booking. In a telegram to an assistant in Paris in 1919, Gundersen remarked that even in selling well-known, so called "special" films, he needed samples and viewings: "Nul acheteur içi achéter *Judex* sans voir un échantillon".

Important in this business were descriptions of the stories, because Gundersen sometimes received film copies with only French or German titles, and posters and photographs. In his business correspondence there are numerous letters complaining to different production companies about the lack of PR-material; especially Vitagraph in Paris was notoriously slow to send him the material he needed to sell their films. Again and again he pointed out that the cinema owners' choices were made not only by seeing the film, but also after having seen the publicity material they could buy and use, and the slowness of Vitagraph in sending him the material, was one reason why he gave up his role as agent for Vitagraph in 1922. The distributor John Olsen in Copenhagen, one of the most important agents in Scandinavia, whom Gundersen had collaborated with for years, became the new general agent for Scandinavia.

The system of agents was ill designed to provide producers with direct information about conditions in specific foreign markets, and the complaints from agents in small countries like Norway were often ignored. The case of dealing, or not dealing, with the emergence of different censorship practices in Europe in the early 1910s, can illustrate this point.

The distribution business in Norway changed drastically in 1913, when Parliament passed The Film Theatres' Act, stipulating that the municipal councils were to license all public showings of films within the area of their jurisdiction, resulting in a municipal cinema system, and establishing a Central Board of Film Censors.[2] Norway was among the nations which imposed particularly stringent censorship standards, and were inclined to ban movies on the basis of their treatment of sexual and criminal subjects. After 1913, many of the samples Gundersen received from different production companies were unfit for distribution in Norway, but his complaints to some of the firms he represented were ignored. American films became harder to sell, and especially films from Vitagraph. In his correspondence to the Paris office of Vitagraph, Gundersen frequently complained about being ruined by the costs of returning films which were not even worth showing to cinema owners, because they would be banned by the Censorship Board. In a letter to Vitagraph in Paris in 1916, he stated that he was being ruined by returning "tous les films, que la censure interdit".

Censorship in Norway changed in 1921, becoming less stringent, but at that time distributors faced competition from a new and large distribution company that was established in 1919, Kommunernes Filmscentral, owned by the many new municipally owned cinemas, as well as by American companies, that established their own offices in Norway: United Artists in 1922, First National in 1923, MGM in 1925 and Paramount in 1928.[3]

In 1926, even Kristiania's cinemas were taken over by the municipality, concluding a "municipalisation" of the cinemas in Norway, and Gundersen gave up his cinemas and distribution companies, becoming the first director of the municipal cinemas in Norway's capital Kristiania.

Éclair in Norway and Scandinavia

Jens Christian Gundersen acted as an agent for many production companies in different countries. Here, however, I would like to outline his work as the representative or agent for Éclair in Norway and Scandinavia from 1909 to 1912, as a case study.

Gundersen became the general agent of Éclair for Scandinavia in 1909, but lost this position in 1911, when Danish agent Ove Davidsen became general agent for Scandinavia. Gundersen remained Éclair's agent for Norway, until Éclair in 1912 decided not to use a general agent or several agents for Scandinavia, but dealt directly with cinema owners or distributors in the different Scandinavian countries. Gundersen kept buying Éclair-films directly from France for his cinemas in Norway during the 1910s.

Even before Gundersen lost the position as general agent, Copenhagen was an important centre for the distribution of copies as well as samples within the Nordic countries. In 1909 and 1910, Gundersen's letters to Éclair in Paris gives us an interesting picture of the distribution of samples or copies to cinema owners and distributors in Sweden and Denmark, and many of the samples shown in Sweden and Norway had Danish titles.

As agent for Éclair, Gundersen was supposed to sell as many copies of the films as possible. He always received samples, and these samples were either sold, returned or re-routed to another agent, who tried to sell them in his territory. Sometimes Gundersen sold the samples, sometimes he ordered new copies from France. Agents often swapped films, and Gundersen made frequent deals with other agents. If Gundersen managed to sell an Éclair-film in Sweden and Denmark that Ove Davidsen was unable to sell through his connections, Gundersen would get an additional 3 percent of the usual 15 percent on the transaction. The connections between the agents were numerous, Gundersen sold films from Vitagraph or Svea to Davidsen, while Davidsen not only sold Éclair-films to Gundersen, but also films from Lubin, Itala or Deutsche Bioscop.

Indeed, the transactions could become quite complicated, especially in the years of the open-market system, and before the emergence of clear-cut exclusive contracts. The case of Éclair's *Zigomar* (Jasset, 1911) illustrates this. *Zigomar* was distributed just after Ove Davidsen in Copenhagen had become the general agent for Scandinavia, and Gundersen mostly dealt with Davidsen.

In the case of *Zigomar*, news of the film reached Gundersen long before Davidsen could supply him with copies or PR-material, and cinema owners in Norway started to complain to Gundersen about the delay. Normally films from Éclair were shown at the same time in Norway, Sweden and Denmark, but in this case, *Zigomar* became a hit in Denmark three weeks before Gundersen was able to get a sample copy for the Norwegian market. His clients threatened to buy copies directly from Germany, because they were informed of the film's popularity in the neighbouring countries, and in several letters and telegrams Gundersen tried to find out whether *Zigomar* had exclusive copyrights, or not.

Obviously, Davidsen had sent all the first copies that he was able to get of *Zigomar* to the more lucrative markets of Denmark and Sweden, leaving Gundersen with his angry clients. This undermined to a certain degree Gundersen's position as a distributor and agent for Norway, and Davidsen made matters even worse by allowing a competitor of Gundersen in Norway to rent a copy from Denmark, so that even one of his competitors as cinema owner in Kristiania got a copy of *Zigomar* before Gundersen himself. By the time Gundersen could show *Zigomar* in his cinemas, the film had been screened already in several Norwegian cities.

The case of *Zigomar* seems to be an exception, but it shows that in the case of very popular and sought-after films, agents or distributors could break all written or un-written agreements. Mostly, however, things did run quite smoothly, at least in the case of films from Éclair.

Conclusion

The period between 1907 and 1916 was a transitional period in the history of film distribution. In these years, many fundamental changes took place in film history; the transition from the world of pioneers to an institutionalised world, the rise of the feature film and the star system, and the new hegemony of American film in the world market.[4] The study of distribution is a very fruitful way of looking at this important period in new ways.

Once the analysis of the 73 books of carbon copies of Gundersen's day to day business is completed, the next step will be to compare Gundersen's development as a film distributor in Norway and Scandinavia with others, like Jean Desmet in the Netherlands, to see if Gundersen's business as distributor was different from or comparable to that of distributors abroad.

At this stage in my research, some patterns emerge. Unlike Desmet, Gundersen never offered complete programmes to Norwegian cinema owners, and the emphasis on PR-material is very interesting. It seems that at least as early as 1910 it was impossible to sell a film in Norway without a full "package" of PR-materials: programs, posters and photographs. In Norway, the transition from short films to feature films was smooth, and distributors just switched to selling more and more longer features.

Many of Gundersen's letters offer examples of changes in the taste of the audience as well as changes in distribution practices. Censorship and the rise of the star system changed spectatorship as well as distribution. From the mid-1910s, Gundersen would put more emphasis on the stars in the films than the films themselves. In 1910, Gundersen could report back to Éclair in Paris, that it was "plus facile de pouvoir vendre des series comiques et panoramiques", but six years later the sample of the Dutch feature *Das Wrack in der Nordsee* (*Het Wrak in de Noordzee*, 1915) was returned to Amsterdam Film Compagnie, because "die Hauptschauspielerin nicht genug interessiert". In this way, the study of distribution, and the work of a distributor, could also throw light on the production and reception history of early film.

References and literature

Abel, Richard, *The Ciné Goes to Town – French Cinema 1896–1914* (Berkeley: University of California Press, 1994).

Blom, Ivo, *Jean Desmet and the Early Dutch Film Trade* (Amsterdam: Amsterdam University Press, 2003).

Disen, Ole H.P., *Den Store Illusjon – Filmbyråenes Historie* (Oslo: Norske Filmbyråers Forening, 1997).

Evensmo, Sigurd, *Det Store Tivoli* (Oslo: Gyldendal, 1967).

Griffithiana 47 (May 1993).

Iversen, Gunnar, Norway, in Tytti Soila, Astrid Söderbergh Widding and Gunnar Iversen, *Nordic National Cinemas*, ondon: Routledge, 1998), 102–141.

Iversen, Gunnar, "Den hemmelighetsfulle demon – Jens Christian Gundersens *Dæmonen* og norsk filmhistorieforskning", in Bastiansen, Henrik G., og Øystein Meland (eds.), *Fra Eidsvoll til Marienlyst – Studier i Norske Mediers Historie fra Grunnloven til Tv-alderen* (Kristiansand: Høyskoleforlaget, 2001), 102–114.

Thompson, Kristin, *Exporting Entertainment – America in the World Film Market 1907–1934* (London: British Film Institute, 1985).

Vasey, Ruth, *The World According to Hollywood, 1918–1939* (Exeter: University of Exeter Press, 1997).

Notes

1. Blom, Ivo, *Jean Desmet and the Early Dutch Film Trade* (Amsterdam: Amsterdam University Press, 2003), 30.

2. Iversen, Gunnar, Norway, in Soila, Tytti; Söderbergh Widding, Astrid and Iversen, Gunnar: *Nordic National Cinemas* (London: Routledge, 1998), 106–107.

3. Evensmo, Sigurd, *Det Store Tivoli* (Oslo: Gyldendal, 1967): 109ff; Disen, Ole H.P., *Den Store Illusjon – Filmbyråenes Historie* (Oslo: Norske Filmbyråers Forening, 1997), 68ff.

4. Blom, Ivo, *Jean Desmet and the Early Dutch Film Trade* (Amsterdam: Amsterdam University Press, 2003), 26–27.

16

Infrastructure, open system and the take-off phase. Jean Desmet as a case for early distribution in the Netherlands

Ivo Blom

Department of Comparative Arts Studies of the Vrije Universiteit, Amsterdam

At the 2004 Domitor conference on distribution, my book *Jean Desmet and the Early Dutch Film Trade* came up in several papers.[1] The idea of film distribution as a missing link, proposed in my introduction, was taken up by several researchers, sometimes even in order to prove the contrary. The book popped up again and again, sometimes seeming an obligatory mentioning (Delendam Carthaginem...), sometimes misquoted. The lack of large competitive business archives and the lack of inventory of the existing ones proved to be two reasons for neglect in the field, but were in themselves not sufficient enough. It is clear that distribution seems to lack the glamour or adventure associated with production or the social studies approach connected with reception, though I tried to indicate in my book that both are there in film distribution. It forces researchers to acknowledge that the money factor is simply an inherent aspect of the film world, whether you like it or not. In any case, it proved that a great need for research on early film distribution exists and that it is a shame that we had to wait until the Summer of 2004 to have such an intense conference on the very subject. Within the following pages, it is impossible to resume the extensive work that went into my book, which was based on a PhD, on years of academic research thus, and I therefore cannot but refer to my publication on Jean Desmet for further reading.

The last machine

One aspect that felt absent in the first days of the conference was the very concrete, material image of the film distribution world which Jean Desmet and the Desmet business archive can give us. Not only a concrete, vivid image of Desmet's own activities, but also of the world in which he was operating. The Desmet archive permits you to observe the European network of 1910 through the eyes of a film distributor.

In Richard Curson Smith's and Ian Christie's fascinating Anglo-Dutch television documentary *The Last Machine* (1995), the train is considered the first machine of the 19th century and cinema the last machine. In my exposé, the link of trains with films is laid out again, through the concept of *infrastructure*. Thanks to a quickly expanding railway network, a new branch in film business could expand quickly: film distribution. One network enabled another, infrastructure in the literal sense brought about a cultural infrastructure, which was to last until well after the Second World War. Film

Fig. 1. Poster for Desmet's Rotterdam-based Cinema Parisien, designed by Julien Felt.

culture acquired a form and shape in the first two decades of the twentieth century. New categories such as film distribution and film exhibition entered the language. These sectors expanded and became highly professional. They bargained or engaged in power struggles with each other, as well as with other groups such as the authorities, the general public and the production companies.

Around 1910, Europe knew a very detailed and well-functioning network of railway lines, connecting the various countries and their main cities. On the eve of the First World War, it was very easy to transport films from one country to another, especially in the Northern and Western part of the European continent. Around 1910, cities such as Berlin, Brussels and London developed into centres of film trading where films from all countries, companies and genres could be acquired. The film trade blossomed into an efficient business sector by anticipating the weekly program changes at permanent cinemas. The offices of the various companies tended to be clustered together in the same city districts and were never far from a railway terminal or from the printing business. One of these distribution centres was for instance the Friedrichstrasse in Berlin, near the Bahnhof Friedrichstrasse. Business was transacted in the three business languages of English, French and German, and full advantage was taken of the modern technologies of telephone, telegraph and typewriter.

A small country with little national production such as the Netherlands benefited much from this situation. Most films had to come from other countries such as France, Italy, Denmark, Germany and Britain. When film distribution really started to take shape, that is around 1908–1914 when cinema openings boomed in the Netherlands, many became cinema owners, but just a handful of entrepreneurs stepped into the proverbial niche in the market. One of them was Jean Desmet, who was active as one of the first Dutch distributors around 1910–1914. Desmet had started out as a travelling cinema owner, had opened his first cinema in Rotterdam in 1909, soon to be followed by others, but in contrast to many of his fellow exhibitors he also stepped into the field of importing and renting films (Fig. 1).

Thanks to Desmet's vast business archive, but also thanks to his enormous remaining film stock of about 900 films and his great collection of publicity materials, we nowadays get a very close insight into the early years of Dutch film distribution, and indirectly also into European film distribution. On the details of his distribution, that is: both the international purchase and the (mostly) national rental side of it, I have written extensively over the last years in journals such as *KINtop*, and the outcome of it all was first my dissertation in 2000 and subsequently my book *Jean Desmet and the Early Dutch Film Trade* in 2003.

Desmet's story illustrates the international character of cinema around 1910 and the way in which the speed and scale of international forms of communication were laying the foundations of what can be seen as an early form of 'global culture'. Films from all nations could be sent all over the world with few problems. All you needed to do was adapt the dialogue titles to the language of the particular country concerned. It is a development that fits Roland Robertson's description of globalization.[2] Robertson identifies five phases of increasing global concentration and complexity. The third of these phases, which he calls the *take-off phase*, occupies the period between the 1870s and the mid-1920s. These are years during which globalization begins to accelerate. The word 'accelerate' fits very well to our train metaphor here and indeed many films from Desmet's holdings display fast trains, cars, airplanes or even zeppelins. Desmet himself by the way was fascinated by fast deluxe cars and planes. Some of the most typical signs of the take-off phase are a rapid increase in the number of international companies and agencies, the growth of global forms of communication, the adoption of uniform international time zones, the development of worldwide competition and international prizes, and the development of universal norms of citizenship, law and human identity.

Thanks to this take-off phase, the infrastructure for film distribution was available and distribution could develop at rapid speed, though not without obstacles. As a matter of fact, there are several examples in my book which indicate exceptions to this general pattern. In 1909, Holland accepted a uniform clock-time (Fig. 2). The railways had exerted great pressure to get a similarly uniform time, although the end product still differed both from the rest of Europe and from the time they used in their own system. The railway had already opted for Greenwich Mean Time in 1892, but at the last minute in 1909, the Dutch authorities settled for local Amsterdam time as the measure. This differed by half an hour from Greenwich Mean Time (which applied in Belgium) and from Central European Time (which applied in Germany). This system remained in operation until the Second World War when the German occupiers made an end to this absurd exceptional clock and henceforth we have Central European Time.

In 1910, the Netherlands too, along with the countries surrounding it, possessed a ramified and smoothly running railway network, with good and fast connections to other countries. Films could either be sent by post or put into the special luggage vans of international trains. There were five trains a day between Amsterdam and Berlin and back, and at least four (or more, if you changed trains) between Brussels and Amsterdam. The trip from Berlin to Amsterdam took eleven hours, and from Brussels-North to Amsterdam, three and a half hours; the latter is not so much longer

Fig. 2. Trilingual poster for *Strength of Men* (Vitagraph, 1913).

nowadays. Thousands of film cans were sent by train, but also posters, often preceding them one week.

As Figure 2 shows, companies such as Cines and Vitagraph used two or three different languages, clearly destined for the European market, for their posters, as in this case for the Vitagraph film *The strength of Men* (Vitagraph, 1913). And let's not forget the vast paper correspondence of letters, invoices, intertitle lists etc. sent by railway or, if the films came from London, by boat and by mail. Next to the railway network, the shipping lines network enabled film distribution considerably.

Holland as open system

Comparing the early Dutch film distribution with other European nations, one concludes that Holland knew an *open system*, in contrast to, for instance, France and the United States, indicated as *close systems* by Kristin Thompson in her pioneering study on distribution, *Exporting Entertainment*.[3] In the early stages, the production companies in the two countries mentioned formed a closed front with sweeping powers of control over film trading and cinema exhibition. During the heyday of travelling cinema, the Netherlands had been heavily dependent on Pathé, but this situation changed dramatically after 1909. The offer became much more multiform: competing French companies as Gaumont and Éclair, but also competing producing nations such as Italy, Germany and Denmark manifested themselves. Thus, a niche for competition in the distribution field arose, thanks to this growing variety of films on offer. Independent distribution started to boom as a new and prosperous section within film culture. Schemes like the creation of the Belge-Cinéma subsidiary, through which Pathé sought to incorporate both Belgium and the Netherlands, proved unsuccessful in Holland. Like Britain and Germany in the years before 1914, the Netherlands was a country where it was possible for anyone to import, distribute or hire movies.

From 1910 to 1912, Jean Desmet started his distribution on a sort of second-hand basis. He bought complete programs of one-reelers that had had a run for a few weeks in Western-Germany. When Desmet was busy importing these programs, however, the feature-length film appeared on the European market and quickly urged film distributors to change policies, as soon as it was clear the long film was there to stay. Desmet switched from one German seller to another to obtain henceforth programs with one longer film in it. When in early 1912 his Dutch clients became more demanding, he even dropped his second supplier and switched over to direct purchase. That is, buying from production companies such as the German companies Messter, Eiko and Luna, but also buying from international distributors and resellers such as Louis Aubert in Paris, who sold films by the Italian Cines, the Anglo-American distributor M.P. Sales Agency which sold films by American companies such as Kalem and Lubin, or Nordische films, the German distribution branch of the Danish Nordisk.

All in all, the international film industry had become one huge mechanism parts of which all had to function synchronously to keep it moving. Desmet realized this in good time and made sure that his organization was up to scratch. His position in the film world had improved. By taking his films directly from production companies, and ordering his films by the title – instead of by the meter – he had acquired greater influence on the composition of cinema performances. From now on, he compiled his own programs. Sometimes Desmet went off to view and purchase movies himself, for instance in Berlin, but mostly German and Belgian agents would travel to show the film to local renters This was common practice in neighbouring countries such as Germany, as Thompson has indicated in *Exporting Entertainment*.[4]

Müller

Thompson's study, dating from 1985, marked out the terrain of an investigation of film distribution in Europe, but there was no extensive and detailed treatment of the subject for several years afterwards. The tide turned in 1994, – happily for me, I might say, as that was the year I started my PhD on Desmet – with the publication of Corinna Müller's *Frühe deutsche Kinematographie. Formale wirtschaftliche und kulturelle Entwicklungen 1907–1912* (Early German Cinematography. Formal, Economic and Cultural Developments 1907–12).[5] The striking feature of this book is Müller's thesis of an alternative periodisation of film history, which abandons the idea of a stylistic transition from a 'cinema of attractions' to a 'cinema of narrative integration' favoured by American film historians, and proposes the more prosaic scenario of a socio-economically determined passage from short to long films. 'It may be helpful', she says, 'to characterize the historical phases of film as determined simply by certain dominant film lengths, and to analyse representational and narrative changes on this basis'.[6] Where the advent of the long feature was for e.g. Janet Staiger just one important force of change in the film world, Müller sees it as the principal agent of transformation.[7] Staiger views the long film as an essentially technological issue, albeit one with economic consequences. For Müller, on the other hand, it is in the first instance an economic 'given' with socio-cultural implications.

Müller points out that cinema chains appeared at an early stage in Germany – there was talk of a 'cinema boom' in 1907 – and were accompanied by industrial concentration. Price wars, ever more frequent changes of program (sometimes thrice weekly) and the second-hand trade were beginning to ruin the whole business. This spiralling devaluation of the market reached a crisis point in 1907–09. The solution turned out to be the long film. The need arose for a specialized business sector capable of guaranteeing weekly or twice-weekly changes of program. The distribution industry mushroomed into being, and a shift took place from selling to renting. It was only with the coming of these distributors that the renting of individual films got underway in Germany, bringing to an end the era of the autonomous short film.

To make the renting of individual films attractive, a system of sole rights for distributors was devised, under which a distributor could acquire exclusive rights in a given geographical area –a country or a province– for a stated period of time, which might be one or several years. The distributor could then assign part of his rights on a film to a cinema operator, conferring upon him the exclusive right of exhibition within a defined area – usually his own city – for a specified exhibition date, which might be that of a film's very first screening. This is the origin of the film premiere. Rapidly rising prices enabled producers to work with bigger budgets. The growing popularity of these 'sole-rights' or 'monopoly' films owed much to their image of exclusiveness, which the publicity surrounding them carefully cultivated by foregrounding and mythologizing the main actors. The star system was making advances. Names were becoming symbols. The new system justified increased admission prices. It called for luxurious surroundings. Motion-picture theatres were modelled on large dramatic theatres and opera houses. Film began to compete with established culture, seeking to legitimize itself by adapting its visual narrative forms to traditional dramatic structures, by accepting and applying censorship, by opening sumptuous theatres with fashionably dressed front-of-house staff and by getting itself talked about in the quality newspapers.

Comparing Holland with Germany and Belgium

The main outlines of the developments in the Netherlands coincide with those sketched for neighbouring Germany by Corinna Müller. However, there are also noticeable differences between the Dutch and German situations. All the important structural changes that Müller observes in Germany also took place in the Netherlands, although generally at a later date. This applies to the rise of permanent cinemas, the breakthrough of the long film and the introduction of the exclusives. The Netherlands was spared the crisis experienced by the German film world preceding the introduction of long films and exclusives, as the boom in permanent cinemas started later.

In 1910, Germany and the Netherlands were film-exhibiting rather than film-producing countries, which distinguished them from countries such as France and Italy. In Germany, however, there was talk of a rapidly growing film-production industry just before the outbreak of the First World War. In the Netherlands the proportion of Dutch films to the total number of films on offer in cinemas was negligible and would remain so, despite the presence of film companies such as Hollandia. From 1913 onwards, many German films found a ready market in the Netherlands and began to acquire a reputation as films of quality. This was particularly true of the exclusive films, which were often prestigious literary dramas with well-known actors such as Albert Bassermann, or melodramas featuring early European stars such as Asta Nielsen and Henny Porten (Fig. 3). As Müller shows in her book, a great change took place in Germany in 1911–12 with the exclusives, but apart from the Asta Nielsen craze, this development only began to work its way through to the Netherlands in 1913. Before that, the main attraction had been the Danish thrillers, which were sold outright to any buyer. During the First World War, foreign films slowly disappeared from the German 'Kinos', whereas international films remained on offer in the Netherlands. Another big difference was pre-war Berlin's position as a major junction of the international film trade. Amsterdam has never enjoyed this position. It became just a national centre of film trade, largely after the establishment of the film exchange in 1916. The war actually stimulated film production in both countries, although Dutch output was on a much

Fig. 3. Poster for the Asta Nielsen-film *Heisses Blut* (Deutsche Bioscop, 1911).

more modest scale. The permanent presence of films from abroad undoubtedly had a part in this. In this respect, my own research does not so much challenge Müller's work as indicate the very important changes that took place in cinema after 1912, the point at which her study breaks off.

A comparison with Belgium, the country's other neighbour, also reveals similarities. Belgian production was even more negligible than Dutch production in the second decade of the century and, like the Netherlands, Belgium was a net exhibitor of films with a strongly international orientation. But here too there were differences. To begin with, Belgium had a far more extensive film culture than the Netherlands. The Belgian lead was due partly to the Belgian economic boom. As Guido Convents stated in 1994:

'This country in the heart of Europe was one of the richest and most densely populated industrial areas on the continent'.[8] The volume of imports required by the abundant Belgian cinemas was probably higher than that needed in the Netherlands. Brussels was situated closer to Paris, so that films could be brought in more quickly from the French market. But the Belgians also undoubtedly enjoyed better contacts with the London and Berlin trade, for in the Brussels of around 1912 it was possible to buy or rent the films of from all the most important international production companies. Agencies jointly catering to Belgium and the Netherlands could also be found there sometimes.

In the Summer of 1914, both the railway network and the film distribution network were abruptly ruptured, and for more than four years the Dutch had to obtain their films with great difficulty. The few French films that arrived – though they did – had to come through London which wasn't easy because of the war at sea and other obstacles. The war probably caused Dutch distributors to shift their focus permanently from Brussels to London and Berlin.[9] Subsequent developments, however, go beyond the scope of this article and of *early* film distribution.

The above mentioned indicates how useful and essential a transnational comparative approach is to research in early film distribution, in particular concerning cultural and transportional infrastructure, open and closed systems, and setting up an entire new sector of the cinema world.

Notes

1. Ivo Blom, *Jean Desmet and the Early Dutch Film Trade* (Amsterdam: Amsterdam University Press, 2003).

2. Roland Robertson, 'Mapping the Global Condition: Globalization as the Central Concept'. In: Mike Featherstone, *Global Culture: Nationalism, Globalization and Modernity* (London: Sage, 1990), 15–30.

3. Kristin Thompson, *Exporting Entertainment: America in the World Film Market, 1907–1934* (London: BFI, 1985). Strangely enough the book didn't come up very often in the Domitor conference.

4. Thompson, 36–37.

5. Corinna Müller, *Frühe deutsche Kinematographie. Formale, wirtschaftliche und kulturelle Entwicklungen 1907–1912* (Stuttgart, Weimar: J.B. Metzler, 1994). See also Peter Lähn, 'Afgrunden und die deutsche Filmindustrie. Zur Entstehung des Monopolfilms', in Manfred Behn (ed.), *Schwarzer Traum und weisse Sklavin. Deutsch-dänische Filmbeziehungen 1910–1930* (München: edition text + kritik, 1994), 15–21; Evelyne Hampicke, 'Vom Aufbau eines vertikalen Konzerns. Zu David Olivers Geschäften in der deutschen Filmbranche', Ibid., 22–29.

6. Corinna Müller, 'Filmform und Filmgeschichte', in Corinna Müller/Harro Segeberg, *Die Modellierung des Kinoprogramms zwischen Kurzfilm und Langfilm 1905/06–1918* (München: Fink, 1998), 55. 'Cinema of attractions' is a term used to describe the early years of cinema, when 'display' (colour, sensation and visual tricks) was more important than narrative structure. Tom Gunning, 'The Cinema of Attraction: Early Film, Its Spectator and the Avant-Garde', in *Wide Angle* 8, 3/4 (1986): 63–70, reprinted in Thomas Elsaesser, Adam Barker (eds), *Early Cinema: space – frame – narrative* (London: BFI, 1990), 56–62.

7. Janet Staiger, 'Combination and Litigation: Structures of US Film Distribution, 1896–1917', *Cinema Journal*, vol. 23, 2 (Winter 1983): 41–71.

8. Guido Convents, 'Motion Picture Exhibitors on Belgian Fairgrounds', *Film History* 6 (1994): 239.

9. An in-depth analysis of the system of Desmet's earliest distribution was done by my student Rixt Jonkman. Through her research as an intern at the Filmmuseum, she managed to raise interesting questions about systematic research into – and databases on – early cinema, in her case on early film distribution. See her contribution elsewhere in this volume.

PART IV

PRACTICES:
Distribution strategies

17

Politics, steam and scopes; marketing the Biograph

Paul C. Spehr

Former Assistant Chief of the Motion Picture, Broadcasting and Recorded Sound Division, Library of Congress, Washington, DC, USA

It can be argued – and I am about to do just that – that at the very end of the nineteenth century, in 1898 and 1899, the most effective motion picture enterprise in the world was the New York based American Mutoscope Company. The company expanded to England in 1897 and by 1898 had opened branches in Paris, Berlin, Amsterdam, Brussels, Milan and Vienna as well as offices for South Africa and India. Its films were featured on variety programs at Keith Albee's theaters in New York, Boston, Philadelphia and Providence as well as three of the most prestigious houses in Europe: The Palace Theatre of Varieties in London; Folies Bergère in Paris and the Wintergarten in Berlin. In all of these locations the company's "Biograph" was proclaimed the finest projection system extant and their films were favorably received by both critics and audiences. The Biograph continued to be a feature at these theaters for the next several years and it was also touring to theaters in other cities in the US, England and the Continent. In fact, the company was hard pressed to meet the demand for its projection service.

In addition to its Biograph projector, the company was aggressively marketing their flip-card viewing device, the Mutoscope, which was promoted as a useful advertising tool as well as a means of entertainment and diversion in a variety of public places.

The company's founders, the now well known KMCD group: Elias B. Koopman, Harry Marvin, Herman Casler and William Kennedy Laurie Dickson, must have been pleasantly surprised at their rapid success because it came about by happenstance – despite appearing to be a carefully plotted capitalist venture.

When the company's Biograph projector made its debut in October, 1896 at Oscar Hammerstein's Olympia Theater in what is now Times Square, New Yorkers had been offered such a variety of motion picture devices that cynics were already complaining about the confusion caused by the flood of "scopes" and "graphs" that kept appearing.[1] But in spite of its late arrival, within three months the Biograph had moved to the front rank, becoming the show of shows in the movie field.

The Biograph was a phenomenon and this paper examines the opening presentation of the Biograph and the way that the company's unique business practice was influenced by the very favorable response it received.

Although it had been "on the road" for several weeks, the official premier of the Biograph projector took place before an invited audience on the night of October 11th,

Fig. 1. Oscar Hammerstein's Olympia Theater where the Biograph was premiered October 11, 1896. [National Museum of American History, Smithsonian, Gordon Hendricks Collection.]

1896. Hammerstein's Olympia was filled with officers of the New York Central Railroad Company, officials of the Republican party and groups supporting William McKinley, the party's candidate for President. The highlights of the show were pictures of Niagara Falls, the New York Central's Empire State Express which carried visitors to the falls, a campaign parade for McKinley in his home town, Canton, Ohio and a view of the candidate purportedly receiving the news of his nomination on the lawn of his home. It was a highly partisan audience. Railroad companies, the New York Central among them, were primary sponsors of McKinley's campaign and had subsidized travel for about 40,000 McKinley supporters to Canton on the day that W. K. L. Dickson and his youthful assistant Gottlob Wilhelm Bitzer (better known as Billy) filmed the candidate. The films opened the program and they were presented with orchestral accompaniment and sound effects. The noise of rushing water complemented the views of Niagara, and whistles, bells and sounds of steam enhanced the Empire State's charge toward the audience. The parade and view on McKinley's lawn were apparently accompanied by familiar campaign songs but few in the audience heard them for the zealots began cheering during the parade scenes and rose to their feet when the candidate appeared on screen. Some began shouting "speech! speech!" Nervous laughter followed as the partisans realized how paradoxical it was to shout at an image on a screen. But their laughter was quickly drowned out by cheers and applause which continued for five minutes while the film was rewound and run for a second time – prolonging the pandemonium.[2]

This was duly reported in the papers and there was so much attention paid to the political enthusiasm that it was a day or two before the press began reporting the impact that the film of the Empire State Express had on the audiences. Dickson positioned the camera as close to the tracks as possible and the train, which was a dot in the

Fig. 2. The New York Journal's coverage of the 1896 Presidential election.

background at the opening of the shot, filled the screen as it roared past the camera at the record speed of sixty miles per hour. It was the most sensational of the early railroad films and it genuinely started fledgling viewers, particularly those seated close to the left corner of the screen where the locomotive suddenly vanished just as it reached the greatest magnitude. Reports of people scrambling out of their seats and ladies fainting soon began to appear.[3] The enthusiasm stirred at the invitational showing continued the rest of the two week run at Hammerstein's. McKinley supporters and groups of railroad executives bought blocks of seats and this continued when the program moved to Koster & Bails Music Hall at the beginning of November. Newspapers reported cheering crowds and even yells of "Speech! Speech!" – an interesting indication that readers of the reviews of the opening were impressed and amused by the over-reaction of the first audiences? On the day of the election the images of McKinley, the Empire State Express and Niagara Falls were projected on a large outdoor screen mounted on the side of the office building housing William Pulitzer's *New York World* as part of the paper's coverage of the election returns.[4] In December the Mutoscope company signed a contract with B.F. Keith and the Biograph opened at Keith's Union Square where it remained for the better part of the next decade.

The Biograph's rapid success can be attributed to several factors. The quality of the image was a primary factor. It was much better than any competing projection system. The images were recorded on film that was 3 inches wide and 2½ inches high, more than five times larger than the so-called "Edison standard" of 1 inch by ¾ inches which most competitors used: roughly the difference between IMAX or 70 mm and today's 35 mm formats. The images were exposed at a rate of from 30 to 40 frames per second, about double the speed used by most European producers. The large image improved clarity and sharpness and the more rapid exposure rate improved steadiness and reduced flicker. The images were particularly impressive on a large screen. The one at Hammerstein's filled the proscenium and the huge image greatly enhanced the startling impact these films had, particularly on those near the screen.

Audiences were also impressed because the films were well made. W. K. L. Dickson was in charge of production and he was one of the most experienced – and talented – film producers extant. By the fall of 1896 he had produced some 180 or 190 films, including many that are icons of the screen's first days: Fred Ott's famous sneeze, Eugene Sandow flexing his muscles, Annabelle's several dances, Annie Oakley, etc. Although he has usually been called a cameraman, an assistant almost always operated the camera while Dickson arranged the shot, rehearsed and timed the action and directed the "take". In other words, he acted as producer-director. Although both *Empire State Express* and *McKinley at Home* ... have a candid quality, a close examination shows the care and planning that produced them. Dickson spent about a week and made at least seven shots before getting the exact shot he wanted for *Empire State Express*. For the film of McKinley, he used the candidate's home, a background of leafy trees and a well manicured lawn to create the image of a home body. McKinley was dressed in lawyer-ly fashion emphasizing his status as a former congressman and governor. The action was controlled by the assistant accompanying McKinley, supposedly giving him the announcement of his nomination as Republican candidate. Dickson apparently rehearsed and timed the shot with the assistant, then briefed the candidate before the take. The resulting scene completely belied the chaotic day on which it was filmed. It was the busiest day of McKinley's campaign. Just off camera there was a platform where McKinley greeted those 40,000 visiting supporters who had begun arriving by train early in the morning and continued to stream past his house all day long.

A subtler, but equally important factor in the company's success was its financial structure. It was established with a well subscribed initial offering of $2,000,000 and their backers allowed them to create a library of more than sixty subjects before any were shown to the public. This reserve gave them great flexibility in programming. Furthermore the company's shares were owned by investors with strong connections in banks, railroads and publishing houses; people with connections useful to facilitate productions. Dickson had full cooperation of the staff of the New York Central when filming *Empire State Express* and another of the company's stockholders was Abner McKinley, the brother of William McKinley, and even though he had only a few shares he was a useful channel to the presidential candidate as well as his political supporters.

Ironically, although it was an instant success, the Biograph projector was an after-thought. As the company's name indicates, the American Mutoscope Company was established to manufacture and market the flip card viewing machine and at the time of its incorporation the KMCD group had designed and built the Mutoscope viewer and a camera to take pictures, but there was no projector and no apparent plans to project films. Although entertainment was an element in the business plan, many of the investors were attracted to the Mutoscope by the expectation that it would be a useful tool for advertising and other business related purposes. Commerce was, after all, a more reliable and substantial investment than an ephemeral field like entertainment. The company was incorporated at the end of December 1895, almost exactly the same time that the Lumière Cinematograph made its debut at the Grande Café. The enthusiastic response to the Cinematograph and the debut of the Edison-Armat Vitascope forced them to reconsider and the Biograph was hastily designed during the spring of 1896. Since it used the same size film as the Mutoscope, the results were impressive.

While we usually think of advertising as a secondary aspect of the motion picture industry, it was an important part of the business plan of American Mutoscope company and it remained important through the 1890's. The premiere program at Hammerstein's was an effective demonstration of the propaganda powers of moving

Fig. 3. *The Empire State Express.* [Library of Congress.]

images. The films of Niagara Falls and the New York Central Railroad promoted travel, and the parade in Canton and film of McKinley at home were political advertising. It was a very soft sell, of course – a precursor of the product placement and subliminal advertising so common today. There were no slogans, trade marks or insistent voice-overs, but the visual impact impressed the railroad men and politicians who made up the audience. Although created to promote travel and votes, the films had enough

Fig. 4. *McKinley at Home, Canton, Ohio.* [Library of Congress.]

Fig. 5. Biograph projector showing *Empire State Express*, as shown in an article about the American Mutoscope Co. ("The Art of Moving Photography" about the American Mutoscope Co. camera & rooftop studio, *Scientific American*, Vol. LXXVI, No. 16 (17 April 1897): 248–249.)

appeal to please and entertain the public and both *Empire State Express* and *McKinley at Home* remained on the company's programs for months afterward. The railroads were impressed with the results and they continued to sponsor film production by Biograph and other companies.

The enthusiasm for the films of McKinley lasted through the election in November and his inauguration the following March. This opened another, unanticipated market – visual news. The timely publication of photos illustrating current events was relatively new and images that moved were particularly appealing to a public that was just beginning to relish the prospect of having candid pictures of current events and famous people available within days rather than weeks or months later. The first audiences came to movies out of curiosity, but they returned to enjoy the novelty of experiencing a reality, or what seemed a reality, they had never known before. In fact, filming famous people and current events became a dominant activity for the company during the next few years. More than a few times audiences at theaters in New York and London were shown events that occurred earlier that day, a practice that thrilled audiences and generated favorable publicity for the company. The company's crews also took still photos which were used for publicity and supplied to newspapers, magazines and other publications. In 1901, Harry N. Marvin, the Vice President of the American company and the M of KMCD, compared the company to a news bureau.[5] Interestingly, this was apparently not viewed as competition by the press as the British company had financial backing from the heads of two of England's leading publishing houses, Sir Cyril Arthur Pearson and Sir George Newnes.[6]

But however up to date the pictures were, they were projected for a relatively small audience, mostly middle class patrons in family oriented variety theaters. In 1901 there were only twenty Biograph projectors in use in North America.[7]

The Biograph was large, awkward and very difficult to operate. It could only function

Fig. 6. The popular actress Anna Held looking at a movie in a Mutascope. In 1901 the company hired Anna Held to publicize the Mutoscope. [LC]

effectively in the hands of a trained operator so the company chose not to offer it for sale, instead they contracted with theatrical organizations to provide an entertainment package consisting of a projector, operator and a changing variety of films which usually lasted ten to twenty minutes. Because of their demonstrated superiority, they were able to command a higher fee for this service than any competing company. Long-term contracts with prestige venues like Keith's; the Palace, Folie Bergère and the Wintergarten were supplemented by shorter contracts with theaters and touring showmen operating outside the major population centers. This provided a stable, predictable foundation for their business and the American and British companies made little effort to expand projection to smaller venues. Instead, they relied on the Mutoscope to make their films available to the mass audience with the expectation that the pennies and nickels dropped into the slots would build profits.

But the Mutoscopes only served one viewer at a time so to make this plan work, machines had to be produced – a lot of machines! Several thousand for North America and an equal number for Europe. Mutoscopes were originally produced at Harry Marvin's machine works in Canastota, New York where Herman Casler supervised operations. The machine works also built Biograph projectors and few modified versions of their Mutograph camera. Casler could not produce enough for the European market so the British company contracted with Leon Gaumont and Marshall & Co. of Salford, England to produce elements for several thousand Mutoscopes.[8] The machines for European use were assembled at the British company's headquarters in London. Both companies had ambitious plans. Like the Biograph, Mutoscopes were not for sale, nor were the rolls of picture cards. Instead they were available for lease on a territorial basis and a number of regionally financed subsidiary companies were formed in the U. S. and England. These companies then sub-contracted with third parties to place the machines in hotels, railroad stations, shops, bars and other places of public access. Although the companies' publicity did not stress it, the regular production of saucy films with subtle and not-so-subtle erotic themes shows that stag bars and amusement parlors were also on their agenda. A steady supply of new subjects was available and the American company established an "exchange" operation in New York where licensees could swap titles they had shown for ones that they had not shown. Mutoscopes were also available to merchants and manufacturers for sales and demonstration of products and a number of films were made to fill such orders.

In retrospect it is clear that the Mutoscope was a detour from the path that commercial cinema was following and that it was a mistake to invest so strongly in peep show machines. But this was not apparent at the time, and the impressive number of prosperous business men willing to invest in the Mutoscope illustrates this rather clearly. Machines offering the public candy, gum or the opportunity to weigh themselves were commonplace and the notion that you could collect money day and night without having a paid employee on site was attractive – the Mutoscope companies pointed to an additional bonus: you did not have to restock their machines on a daily basis. Although the business never achieved the ambitious goals that the British and American companies announced, quite a few machines were produced. Harry Marvin reported that there were about 4000 Mutoscopes in use in the U. S. in 1901.[9]

But the Mutoscope and Biograph business began to sour soon after the new century began. In fact, the early success of the Biograph was very short lived, peaking about 1898 or 1899. Variety theaters in Europe and North America began to object to paying the premium price asked for Biograph programs and this, combined with disappointing returns in the Mutoscope market, created a sudden decline in profitability. By 1901 the large format was no longer a novelty and there was increasing competition from rivals who also specialized in filming current events. This occurred at a time when the public was increasingly attracted to longer story films produced by Méliès and others. It was difficult for the Mutoscope companies to adjust to the changing market. The sprocket-less film they used made it hard to emulate the tricks that made Méliès films so popular and, though the capacity of the camera had been enlarged, they could not match the larger loads that 35 mm cameras began using. If they increased the length of their films the large format and rapid rate of exposure they used consumed so much film that production costs skyrocketed. The only way that they could cope with declining bookings was to drop their price which ate into their operating capital. At the end of 1902 the Palace Theater cancelled the Biograph, ending a continuous run of nearly five years and this virtually ended the British branch's theatrical operation. The company limped on another five years before closing operations. Although the German company remained in business for several years, the other international branches were closed, or effectively shut-down early in the twentieth century.

The American company fared better, though it took several years for them to adjust to the new market conditions. The Keith Albee theater circuit continued to feature the Biograph on its programs, though they negotiated a lower fee for the weekly program. In the Spring of 1902, after a favorable decision in their protracted legal battle with Edison, the American company began offering their films for sale in "standard" format: sprocketed 35 mm film running at 15 frames per second. They also began selling Méliès and Warwick productions and by the Spring of 1903 their advertising claimed that they were the largest dealer in the world.[10] In other words, although they continued to produce large format films for several more years, they joined the mainstream film market and continued as Edison's most successful American rival. And, of course, during the period when D. W. Griffith was the company's most active director, they were clearly America's leading film company.

The brief success of the international Mutoscope companies illustrates the rapidly changing market that characterized the first years of film commerce. So what conclusions can be drawn?

First, the brief, but profitable life of the Biograph predated and anticipated the experiences of other film companies who introduced proprietary formats – systems that required special equipment and were incompatible with commonly used equipment. Among these would be early sound systems such as Gaumont's Chronophone, Edison's Kinetophone and DeForrest's Phonofilm; color systems like Kinemacolor; stereoptic images and other large screen formats such as those devised by Gaumont, the Lumières and Edison as well as later systems like Magnascope, Grandeur and Cinerama. Like the Biograph, the appealing innovations they introduced were off-set by the high cost of equipment, complicated technology and, very often, an inability to supply a steady supply of fresh films that appealed to the mass market – though this was never a fault of the Mutoscope companies.

The growing strength of competition is an indication that by the early 1900s the quality of both cameras and projectors using "Edison standard", i.e. 35 mm film, had improved enough to offset the Biograph's advantage. Film became more reliable, emulsions more rapid and Eastman, the dominant film manufacturer, was producing longer rolls of film. Cameras had been modified to use the longer loads and projectors redesigned to reduce flicker. More importantly, except for the restrictions in the States that resulted from Edison's lawsuits, the use of 35 mm was so widespread that there were very few obstacles to the movement of film from city to city; country to country and continent to continent. And, in those days when films were usually made without titles, there were no serious obstacles to the presentation of images produce in one country in a country with different languages and customs. The route to this ever-expanding international market was the "Edison standard", 35 mm film.

The almost universal acceptance of a standard format forced the American Mutoscope Company to modify their market strategy and it represented a reversal of the assumption on which the company had been founded. When the business was launched in 1896, the KMCD group, and their financial backers, shared Thomas Edison's belief that control of machines, i.e. cameras, projectors and Mutoscopes, was the key to profitability, but by 1902 it was evident that producing and selling film was more lucrative. And it remains so today.

The experience of the Mutoscope companies should not be regarded as purely negative. They had developed a pattern of production that served them well for the first dozen years of the twentieth century – and foreshadowed present day practice. Whenever possible films were carefully planned and produced by a team: a director assisted by a camera operator. This laid the groundwork for Griffith's later accomplishments and provided a model for future production. There was a two pronged approach to their potential audience. They found a niche for their films among the family oriented, middle-class audiences in the variety houses and they continued to produce films designed to appeal to the more prosperous middle class as well as the growing working class audience. The premier at Hammerstein's Olympia showed that it was possible to stimulate intense reactions that went beyond satisfying the curiosity of an audience or creating a brief sensation. While it was not possible to make every film an emotional experience, producers continued to strive for creativity that went beyond mere exhibition. The company's crews had learned from W.K. L. Dickson that movement and action were essential to film production and these continued to be characteristics of Biograph productions. If there is an American style, action and audience involvement are certainly crucial elements. The elements of an "American style" can be traced to the premier of the Biograph at Hammerstein's in October, 1896 and even though the sensation that the Biograph created has long since faded, the company's impact is still felt.

Notes

1. In 1897 what we know as Times Square was still Long Acre Square. It became Times Square early in the twentieth century.

2. National Museum of American History, Smithsonian, Gordon Hendricks Collection, *New York*

Daily Advertiser, 13 October 1896. It was also reported in *New York Clipper, New York Press* and other papers.

3. Stephen Bottomore is the author of a thoughtful article about the phenomenon of "women fainting" and people ducking under their seats during early film showings, "The Panicking Audience?: early cinema and the 'train effect'" in *Historical Journal of Film, Radio and Television* 9 (2) (1999): 177–216. The reports of the first screenings of "The Empire State Express" support his observation that audiences were as startled by the sudden disappearance of the image as by the threat posed by the onrushing locomotive.

4. NMAH, Hendricks, *The World*, Sunday, 1 November 1896, p. 10.

5. Edison Historic Site. Testimony of Harry N. Marvin, July 23, 1901, in Equity, No. 6928, Thomas A. Edison, Complainant, vs. American Mutoscope Co., Defendant. "[...] we soon found that the public demanded of us the prompt and reliable service of the daily newspaper rather than the artistic or aesthetic finish of the weekly or monthly magazine. That is to say, the public has expected us to gather the news in a pictorial way and disseminate it at once."

6. Richard Brown and Barry Anthony, *A Victorian Film Enterprise* (Trowbridge, England, Flicks Books, 1999), 122–126.

7. Ibid.

8. Ibid., 78–79.

9. Ibid. and Harry Marvin, op. cit.

10. Kemp R. Niver (ed.), *Biograph Bulletins, 1896–1908* (Los Angeles, Locare Research Group, 1971), 59–73. Later in 1903 they added Warwick Trading Company, Urban Trading Co., Hepworth & Co., Robert W. Paul and Leon Gaumont & Co. By this time Méliès had opened a branch in New York but AM&B was still selling Méliès films.

18

The price of independence: The Rolin Film Company's quest for distribution

Richard Ward

Associate Professor, Communication Department, University of South Alabama, USA

In 1914, the Rolin Film Company joined the mushrooming roster of start-up film production firms in the Los Angeles area. Like many similar concerns, Rolin was the product of youthful enthusiasm and hubris, founded by a man whose belief in his filmmaking abilities and the unlimited financial rewards of the young motion picture industry somewhat outstripped the reality of the situation. That Rolin survived its formative years and actually thrived, being renamed the Hal Roach Studios in the early 1920s and remaining in business until 1960, was due largely to the unflagging determination of its founder and a stroke or two of phenomenally good fortune.

When 22-year-old Hal Roach founded the production company that would ultimately bear his name, he had only a single year of motion picture industry experience behind him. He had arrived in the Los Angles area in 1913 as a construction worker, but soon found a new line of employment as a movie extra. Enthralled by filmmaking and possessing boundless drive and ambition, Roach attained the position of assistant director by the end of 1913. By mid-1914, and with the help of a small inheritance, Roach founded Rolin.

The name Rolin was derived by a combination of the first letters of the last names of Roach and his principal partner, Dan Linthicum, an acquaintance from Roach's acting experience. Linthicum would soon withdraw from the business, but a third partner, Dwight Whiting, would be a major influence over the company's formative years, providing a solid background in business experience that Roach lacked.[1]

The Rolin articles of incorporation, dated 23 July 1914, outline an ambitious and far-ranging entertainment conglomerate. The stated purpose of the firm was to

> […] carry on the business of furnishing amusement to the public: to purchase, acquire, lease, own, buy, sell and manage theaters, play-houses, gardens, roof gardens, opera houses, parks, concessions, motion picture houses and other places of amusement […] to carry on the business of managers, proprietors of theaters, opera houses and other places of amusement; to employ vaudeville performers, actors, singers, musicians […] to acquire, own, purchase of dispose of plays, copyrights and dramatic and musical productions […] to conduct public and private amusements, consisting of literary and musical performances, parks and picnic grounds [sic] containing dance pavilions, roller coasters and similar amusements […] to carry on the business of restaurant keepers and vendors of wine, spirits and tobaccos, mineral waters and provisions […] to print and publish […]

any play, poem, song or words of this the company may have copyright [...] to buy, sell, lease and generally deal in motion picture films [...].[2]

Whether or not any of the aforementioned activities, aside from the very last, were actually intended by the young firm is doubtful: the Rolin Film Company seems to have been established for the sole purpose of becoming a film producer. The other endeavors mentioned in the corporate charter more than likely were simply included to cover any foreseeable eventuality for a company in an industry in which it was common to have various entertainment interests.

By mid-September of 1914, the Rolin company had produced four one-reel comedies, all directed by Roach and highly improvisational in nature. The cast and crews for these films were acquaintances from Roach's stint as a movie extra and assistant director, and included Harold Lloyd. Lloyd's aim at this point in his career was simply to become a screen actor. He had no particular interest in comedy and, unlike most other players in film comedy of the 1910s, he did not come to film from a vaudeville/music hall comic career. It was to the great fortune of Roach, Lloyd and Rolin that Roach seized upon Lloyd's athletic ability and pushed him into slapstick comedy. Despite the fact that comedy had not been his focus, Lloyd would become one of the screen's most popular comedians by the 1920s, and would be the sole reason for the early survival of Rolin.

However, Rolin quickly discovered that it had a major problem. In a scenario which has been repeated ad-infinitum throughout film history, Rolin's youthful management blithely assumed that once produced, their films would automatically find their way into theaters full of appreciative audiences. Producing films without a distribution commitment was as big a mistake in 1914 as it is today. Distribution firms are the gatekeepers for the industry, the one and only key to access theaters and their paying audiences. Producing a film without an advance distribution contract usually places the producer the desperate situation of having to accept unfavorable distribution terms just to get the film shown. The Rolin Film Company's adventure in securing distribution during its formative era is the focus of this paper.

Distributor #1: Sawyer, Inc.

In September 1914, Hal Roach journeyed to New York City with his company's four completed one-reel comedies seeking distribution. He believed he had found a good fit in Sawyer, Inc., the self-proclaimed "World's Largest Film Mart" which had opened for business just two months prior to Rolin.

Sawyer had been incorporated with much fanfare in the trade press in May 1914 by Arthur H. Sawyer, former general manager of the Kinemacolor Company of America. *The Moving Picture World* was greatly impressed by the elegance of the new company's office suite, particularly the "Pompeiian Projection Room", with artificial flowers and vines hanging from its arbored ceiling and kept at a constant cool temperature by electric fans circulating air over a spraying, perfumed, multi-colored water fountain at the base of the screen. Sawyer's stated goals were summed up by its General Manager, W.H. Rudolph:

> Our aim is to provide expert service in the matter of marketing features – that is, in getting the pictures which producers make before the public in a way which will make them most profitable to those who own or control them. To the makers of pictures we offer the argument that all they have to do is provide the negatives. After we have accepted the negatives, we take care of the remaining details [...].
>
> We have the positives and prints made, provide all printing and advertising matter,

advertise the pictures to the trade and general public, and make returns to the producers on the basis of whatever contracts we make with them.[3]

Sawyer both dealt in states rights and in direct rental to exhibitors. Under the states rights system, a producer (in this case, Sawyer) divided the country into regions and contracted with local firms for the distribution of films within each region. This practice amounted to farming distribution responsibilities out to subcontractors, diminishing Sawyer's share of the box office receipts and virtually eliminating any hope for adequate financial return to the original producer. Sawyer anticipated that its use of states rights distribution was just a transitory phase and planned to open actual distribution offices of its own around the country as its financial returns permitted such expansion. Sawyer's business plan included its own in-house production of "short-length features:" 2000 foot films with strong stories and players that would make them viable competition to standard features. In fact, at the time it opened in May 1914, it announced that it was already involved actively producing films at a rented facility at Asbury Park and that it further planned to open a studio at Saratoga Springs, NY.

In a wonderfully contradictory advertisement in *Moving Picture World* in May 1914, Sawyer attempted to position itself as a straight-talking, honest-dealing purveyor of films:

> The "Old Bull" seems to be the ONE GREAT FEATURE of the Feature Film Business these days […]. THERE IS NO BULL IN THE SAWYER ORGANI-ZATION […]. We don't claim our Features to be the Best Features in the World – That's Bull. We don't tell you our Features are Smashing all Box Office Records – That's more Bull. We don't tell you every foot of our film has a punch and a couple of kicks, and that you must have our Features to do business – That's a whole herd of Bulls.
>
> When we talk to you, Mr. State Rights Man, we talk to you straight from the shoulder – man fashion – and we don't plaster our statements with a myriad of brainless adjectives. While "Magnificent", "Wonderful", "Lavish", "Finest", "Marvelous", etc., would no doubt legitimately express the quality of our output, we are satisfied to tell you, and back it up with facts, that SAWYER FEATURES ARE GOOD FEATURES, AND THE PRICE IS LESS THAN EVER BEFORE OFFERED ANYWHERE. For the first time in *your* life.[4]

The ad then closes with "WATCH! IN A FEW DAYS!! A SAWYER SENSATION!!!"

By August 1914 Sawyer's distribution organization seemed to be taking shape. Sawyer announced that it was in the process of opening a system of offices that would divide the country into thirty zones, with each zone receiving a single print of each Sawyer release. Yet an evaluation of these offices reveals that most were pre-existing local distributors who were acting as distribution subcontractors for Sawyer. By the beginning of 1915, Sawyer listed 21 zone offices, but 15 of those went by names other than "Sawyer". Furthermore, five of the six "Sawyer" named branches did not list a physical street address, leading one to wonder if they actually even existed outside of the Sawyer advertising copy.[5]

Beyond physical expansion, the Sawyer organization to which Rolin was about to entrust its pilot comedies planned an expansion of its release schedule. As of 1 August 1914, Sawyer had 18 films in circulation, ranging from three to six reels. Sawyer announced that this would soon be supplemented by the distribution of one-reel comedies produced by four different companies, resulting in a weekly output of 3 features each week and 3 one-reel comedies. After 1 October, the number would increase to 6 of each per week.[6] Rolin's product was to number among the 12 weekly releases, along with films produced by other start-up hopefuls as The Santa Barbara Motion Picture Company, The Phoenix Film Company of San Rafael, California, and The Japanese American Film Company ("Operated and Controlled by Japanese" according to Sawyer's ad copy).[7] As with all of Sawyer's producers, Rolin would get a 50/50 split of Sawyer's returns after Sawyer's distribution expenses were deducted.[8]

In late October and presumably still in expansion mode, the Sawyer organization announced the formation of an affiliated concern, The Flamingo Film Company. Flamingo would produce two and three-reel "feature" comedies and would have offices adjacent to those of Sawyer. The noteworthy aspect of Flamingo is that it seems to have been created as a reaction to the perceived violence and vulgarity of Mack Sennett's highly popular Keystone comedies, comedies which greatly influenced the early Rolin style. Upon Flamingo's formation, Arthur Sawyer asserted "there is an insistent demand for a higher standard of motion picture comedies than single-reel farces and burlesque productions, the Flamingo Film Company will seek to satisfy it to the utmost". Admitting the popularity of "slap stick farce", Sawyer explained that he believed that "there is a very high place not yet attained for comedies of two, three and even five reels. […]. It is an admitted fact that the drama for the screen has advanced to a higher artistic plane than has the film comedy." The Flamingo Films would aspire to reach that plane.[9] In seeming contradiction to Sawyer's stated goals, one of the first Flamingo releases was a 4-reel comedy/drama called *Without Hope* produced by Fred Mace, a comic thoroughly schooled in Keystone roughhouse. Mace had enjoyed a certain level of success as one of the first members of Mack Sennett's Keystone stock company, but he left Sennett for what was ultimately an unsuccessful attempt at independently producing and directing his own comedies. *Without Hope* was one of these efforts. He was shortly back working for Sennett, but his star had faded and he died in 1917.

By this point, things were not going well for Sawyer, Inc., either. As with many of the producers it represented, Sawyer was apparently fueled more by high hopes and ambition than a sound grasp of the motion picture business. Beyond its own organizational problems (the fact that it was a distributor without an actual distribution network), most of Sawyer's product was made by neophyte producers with little filmmaking skill. Sawyer was a weak distributor with inferior product, and it distributed its last films in January 1915, a mere eight months after its incorporation.

Whether or not Sawyer actually distributed any of the early Rolin product is difficult to establish. An absolute lack of any mention of Rolin product in Sawyer's release schedules tends to indicate that it did not, although that apparently wasn't for want of trying. When Rolin approached Pathé about distribution of its product in March 1915, it learned that Pathé had already seen (and been unimpressed by) much of it during an earlier visit by Sawyer representatives. At the end of 1914, Rolin sued Sawyer and collected $1500, but it is unclear whether that was for back film rentals owed by Sawyer or (more likely) for breach of contract.[10] In any case, if any of the early Rolin films did receive theatrical exposure, given the disorganized and deteriorating state of the Sawyer firm, their release was probably not very widespread.

Distributor #2: United Film Service

By the end of 1914 Rolin was actively seeking a new distributor. It began a promising set of negotiations with United Film Service, an organization with close ties to the Warner brothers, for new one-reel comedies and two-reel dramas. As with Sawyer before (and Pathé later), United and Warners' were located in New York City. Making a sales call to promote the Rolin product necessitated a cross-country train trip for Hal Roach (or, occasionally, Rolin's junior partner, Dwight Whiting).

Warner's Features, Inc. had been formed from Warner's Feature Film Company in August 1913. While Abe Warner had been president and Harry Warner had been secretary-treasurer of the earlier firm, the new configuration had P.A. "Pat" Powers as president, Abe Warner as Vice President and Harry Warner as sales manager. Similar to Sawyer (in more ways than at first apparent) Warner's Features seemed perfectly suited to Rolin's distribution needs. As explained in an article in *Moving Picture World*,

> The Warner idea was to buy films in the open market, to avoid all contract entanglements which might result in the company's exploitation of something not up to standard because of obligations previously incurred, and to pay the highest prices to film manufacturers in order that the house of Warner might be the first place visited by the producer with something particularly meritorious to sell. Important also was the company's plan to protect the exhibitor by granting him exclusive rights to Warner features in his territory.[11]

Warner's Features operated twenty-six branch distribution offices to cover the US and Canada. Its release schedule was made up almost exclusively of three reelers, released at a rate of three per week. When they did release a longer film (up to six reels) they regulated their output so as not to exceed nine reels per week. Producers routinely doing business with Warner's, included Sid Olcott International Players, Colorado Motion Picture Company, Albuquerque Film Manufacturing Company, Miller Bros. 101 Ranch Features, and Paris Éclair.

By late 1914, Warner's Features had a sibling to distribute short (two reels and less) as opposed to feature (three reels and more) films. United Film Service, also headed by Pat Powers, released comedies produced by United Motion Picture Producers, Inc., Gaumont, the Sunshine Film Corporation and dramas produced by Sam Warner's Regent Film Company.[12]

By every indication at the end of 1914, Rolin was poised to become the newest United Film Service producer. Both parties were interested, and the only point still open to negotiation appeared to be how many reels of Rolin product United would accept per week.[13] Dwight Whiting urged caution in dealing with the Warners' in light of rumors concerning their financial stability, but Rolin's sea of red ink and growing stack of unsold films ultimately overwhelmed his business intuition, and he gave Roach the green light in early January 1915 to "close with Warner".[14]

By mid-February, the Crystal Film Company, one of United's New York City-based producers, was in possession of several of the early Rolin comedies and at least one two-reel drama entitled *Into the Light*. Crystal was to hold the negatives until United retrieved them to begin making positive prints for theatrical release.[15]

Unfortunately, the United Film Service would turn out to be another disappointment for Rolin. By mid-March Whiting was in New York City. He wired Roach that:

> UNITED LIKED DRAMA TWO IMMENSELY BUT REJECTED ALL NINE COMEDIES. SAID CENSOR SAW "WILLIE RUNS PARK" AND WOULD TURN IT DOWN AND [any] LIKE IT. WILL SHOW DRAMA THREE TOMORROW [...] UNITED AT BEST IS RISKY AND UNSTABLE PROPOSITION AND WILL TRY EVERYTHING ELSE BEFORE CLOSING [a deal with] THEM.[16]

Whiting's assessment of United, which had come under new management, worsened when he reported to Roach one week later.

> SHOWED UNITED DRAMA TWO AND THREE. GRAHAM, NEW PRESI-

DENT, WAS SCORNFUL AND SAID DIDN'T SEE HOW THEY COULD PASS CENSORS. WITH YOUR PERMISSION AM GOING TO TELL UNITED TO GO SOMEWHERE. FROM GENERAL OPINION HERE THEY ARE ABOUT GONE AND BY GIVING THEM PICTURES WE ARE PROBABLY THROWING THEM AWAY.[17]

However, all of the news from the East Coast wasn't grim. By this point Whiting was negotiating with Pathé, which had just agreed to buy a single Rolin comedy.

Distributor #3: Pathé

As has been well documented in Richard Abel's *The Red Rooster Scare*, Pathé Frères was one of the most prolific of the early film companies, with a volume and quality of product that far outstripped its American competitors. At the height of its success and largely because of it, Pathé found itself vilified in the American press as a purveyor of violent, immoral "foreign" film fare which posed a real danger to the values of the American audience. On the other hand, the American public was depicted as safe with the more robust and wholesome film product from American studios.

In an effort to remove the stigma of "foreignness", Pathé, during the period of 1908 to 1910, both joined the Motion Picture Patents Company, rather than fighting Edison and his Trust, and opened its own film production facility (to make "American" films) and laboratory in New Jersey. Still, the odds were daunting. The amount of Pathé product reaching the screen through the MPPC's General Film distribution was less than Pathé had released before the Trust, causing Pathé to look for alternate distribution channels. Additionally, Pathé had overextended somewhat in its global operation, forcing a period of retrenchment. Finally, after 1914 much of the global market was in shambles.

Starting in early 1913, Pathé circumvented General Film by distributing some of its excess product through Eclectic Films. Eclectic had started life as Cosmopolitan Films, but in January 1913 changed its name (largely because "Cosmopolitan" had already been taken by another film firm). Eclectic's stated policy was to release "the best from a chain of European studios with particular regard to fitness of subject for American audiences", an effort, no doubt, to shield itself and its product from the charges of cultural annexation that had been heaped upon foreign films.[18]

In 1914, General Film began substituting the new "Hearst-Selig News Weekly" newsreel in the place of the established "Pathé Weekly". Pathé's response, removing its newsreel completely from General Film and setting up sixteen film exchanges to sell it directly to exhibitors, was softened somewhat by a diplomatic statement by Pathé that these actions "should not be considered in any manner as a fight against the General Film Company [...]. At the same time, we believe that it has committed a breach of contract in forcing the substitution of another weekly for Pathé's Weekly [...]."[19] In the prcoess, the Pathé Weekly was cut from two to one reel per week, "eliminating many trivial subjects and giving the cream of the world's events only".

By the summer of 1914, the Pathé newsreel underwent another change. Pathé announced a news *daily* that would be issued in 200 foot (approximately 3 minutes) installments five days per week. Exhibitors would be encouraged at week's end to splice the installments together for a standard one-reel review of the week's events. Perhaps the greatest innovation of the news daily was that it would both be shot and printed on Pathé's non-flammable safety stock, which would permit the raw footage to be sent in from cameramen in the field *and* the finished theatrical release prints to be shipped though the United States mail, allowing faster and cheaper delivery than that customary through the private courier services required for the transportation of the highly flammable nitrate film stock that was in standard use in the United States until 1950.[20]

Another innovation of 1914 saw Pathé distributing its most famous serial, *The Perils of Pauline*, on an unusually large number of release prints. As Pathé's announcement reasoned, traditionally distributors made as few prints as possible.

> These prints have been worked from house to house as long as they would hold together and as long as the projection on the screen resembled in any way a decent picture. This often resulted in a very poor projection on the screen of the theater showing the film after it had become a few weeks old. In spite of the fact that the natural result was a black eye for the firm producing the picture, the extra returns from the poor print were considered to be of more value than the good name of the manufacturer, and the old prints were kept working long after they should have been in the scrap heap.[21]

Before *Perils*, normal number of prints produced was 25 to 30, one print for each exchange. Eclectic and Pathé produced 147 prints of the first episode of *Perils*, and claimed greater profits as a result. More exhibitors could now show the film when it was new, and they benefited from a concurrent publication of the plot of *Perils* in newspapers nationwide – thus being able to show the film at approximately the same time as the press coverage, rather than weeks later. Exhibitors in some locals were experiencing such success with *Perils* that they began issuing reserved seat tickets, in some instances covering the entire run of the series. "It is the same old story. A quick turnover, better service, more first runs [at higher rental prices], pleased exhibitors and interested patrons – a combination that cannot be beaten."[22] Ironically, of course, neither the original negative nor any of this record number of prints is known to have survived, and *Perils* is only available in the United States today in a re-edited French release, with French title cards crudely translated back into English.

Despite the innovations, Pathé's initial efforts at independence were counterproductive, resulting in fewer theatrical bookings than it had managed to get through General Film.[23] At this point, however, fate and global conflict intervened. Having seen his film empire in Europe all but cease operations due to the outbreak of the First World War, Charles Pathé decided to turn his considerable personal energies toward the revitalization of his American subsidiary. Arriving in the United States in October 1914, he announced that

> the present upset in France has seemed to me to afford a splendid opportunity [...] to study American conditions, to get acquainted with the American market [...]. To attain the most desirable end I shall devote much time to watching [...] in the theaters what kinds of subjects most thoroughly meet with the public approbation and also to completing my own organization here that I may the better meet the requirements of the time [...]. My intention is to become a picture publisher or editor – to publish films as others publish books. I accept negatives where they accept manuscripts.[24]

Pathé continued that he did not believe that it was possible for a single studio to produce everything – that a better system would have a distributor choosing from the best of multiple producers.

Part of Pathé's stated objective was to take a greater interest in distribution. His intent became clear in January 1915, when Pathé formalized control over Eclectic and its national distribution network of twenty-two branch exchanges. Eclectic was renamed Pathé Exchange, Inc.[25] While Pathé Exchange shared a corporate office suite with the American branch of Pathé Frères, the two maintained a certain degree of separation.

The former was incorporated under and subject to American law while the latter was a French concern. This led to interesting operational quirks such as operating two separate cashier windows – one for each firm.

Charles Pathé sailed for Europe in January 1915, leaving management of his American operations in the hands of Felix Malitz. Pathé left saying he hoped the American concern could "obtain very quickly the result we are aiming at, namely to obtain on the American market what we have obtained on the world market [...]. [B]e well aware that in the motion picture industry, which embraces the universe, the firm you are connected with is the first in the whole world and that it only depends upon you, owing to our particularly advantageous position, to occupy unquestionably the first place in America."[26]

In March, in a *Moving Picture World* article entitled "Felix Malitz – Pathé Guiding Spirit", Malitz announced that he intended to put the business on "a scientific basis of commercial efficiency". The article claimed that his efforts had already borne financial fruit.[27] Yet a mere two weeks later, in an article entitled "Charles Pathé the Guiding Spirit", *Moving Picture World* carried the Pathé announcement that "the guiding spirit of the House of Pathé always has been, at present is, and always will be Charles Pathé himself". Felix Malitz "no longer has any connection whatsoever with either Pathé Frères or Pathé Exchange, Inc. The offices formerly held by him are now held by Charles Dupuis and L. Gasnier." Louis Gasnier, an early director of France's premier film comic, Max Linder, is perhaps best remembered today as the director of 1938's *Reefer Madness*. The Pathé announcement concluded, "Charles Pathé will continue to live in New York, and will devote his energies to the American branch of his great business".[28]

So it happened that Felix Malitz in the midst of his brief tenure as guiding spirit when Dwight Whiting, frustrated at the pace of negotiations with United Film Service, paid a visit to Pathé's screening room in March 1915. His initial report to Roach was a rather gloomy assessment.

> GOT POSITIVES ALL COMEDIES BUT PARK PICTURE FROM UNITED. SHOWED TO PATHÉ WHO SAID HAD BEEN SHOWN THEM BEFORE BY SAWYER. THEY WILL TAKE TWO OF THEM AT MOST. WILL DISPOSE OF EVERYTHING FOR AS MUCH AS I CAN AND WE WILL START A-FRESH. IT IS NO USE TRYING TO PUT BUM STUFF AND UNLESS WE CAN DO THE WORK IT IS HOPELESS. PATHÉ WILL TAKE GOOD COMEDIES ONLY AND THAT MEANS EXCELLENT. THEY LIKED LLOYD'S WORK [...][29]

Pathé wound up accepting a single comedy, *Just Nuts* featuring Harold Lloyd as a Charlie Chaplin derivative character named "Willie Work". The bulk of the early Rolin product that was not accepted by Pathé was turned over to Motion Picture Specialties Corporation with Rolin's instructions to sell the pictures under any terms possible. Under this arrangement, two of the dramas and at least one of the comedies received limited exposure under the auspices of a variety of distribution firms.

During the summer of 1915, Rolin continued to produce films on speculation, some of which were accepted by Pathé and some not. Finally, in October 1915, Pathé committed to a long-term distribution contract with Rolin for a series of one-reel comedies featuring Lloyd as a new Chaplin knock-off named Lonesome Luke. As part of the contractual agreement, all Rolin films would continue to be judged on their individual merits by Pathé's six-member screening committee, which would still reject any films deemed substandard. This remained a major point of contention between

Rolin and Pathé for several years, particularly since Pathé was not obligated to pay for any films its committee rejected.[30] That aside, after an extremely rough inaugural year, Rolin embarked on what was to be a successful if occasionally acrimonious association with a major distributor, cranking out a new Lonesome Luke "Phunphilm" one-reeler every week for release through Pathé Exchange.

Notes

1. Randy Skretvedt, *Laurel and Hardy: The Magic Behind the Movies* (Beverly Hills: Moonstone Press, 1987), 36.
    Bernard Rosenberg and Harry Silverstein, *The Real Tinsel* (London: Collier-Macmillan, Ltd., 1970), 15–16.
    Mike Steen, *Hollywood Speaks!* (New York: G.P. Putnam's Sons, 1974), 363.
    Rolin Board of Directors Minutes, 17 August 1914. University of Southern California, Hollywood Museum Collection, Hal Roach Studios, Business Ledger 1914–1921

2. Rolin Articles of Incorporation, 23 July 1914. University of Southern California, Hollywood Museum Collection, Hal Roach Studios, Business Ledger 1914–1921.

3. "Sawyer, Inc. Quarters Superb", *Moving Picture World* (11 July 1914): 258–259.

4. Sawyer Advertisement, *Moving Picture World* (16 May 1914): 917.

5. Sawyer advertisements, *Moving Picture World* (1 August 1914 and 23 January 1915). The exchange location listed by Sawyer were: New York City (Colossus Film Company), Atlanta (Hybar Film Corp.), Albany (Terwilleger and Shackett), Boston (Phoenix), Buffalo (Terwilleger and Shackett), Chicago (Union), Detroit (Casino Film Company), Dallas (Dallas Film Company), Kansas City (Interstate Feature Film Company), Montréal (Allied Features), Los Angeles (Nat A. Magner, Inc.), Denver (Sawyer), Minneapolis (Sherman Feature Film Service), Philadelphia (Interstate Film Company AND Fairmont Feature Film Exchange), Omaha (Sawyer), San Francisco (Nat A. Magner, Inc.), Salt Lake City (Sawyer), Nashville (Anderson Film Exchange), St. Louis (Sawyer), Pittsburgh (Pittsburg-Sawyer Company) and Seattle (Sawyer).

6. *Moving Picture World* (1 August 1914): 717.

7. Sawyer Advertisement, *Moving Picture World* (10 October 1914): 138–139.

8. Rolin Board of Directors Minutes, 15 September 1914. University of Southern California, Hollywood Museum Collection, Hal Roach Studios, Business Ledger 1914–1921.

9. "Flamingo Company Organizes", *Moving Picture World* (31 October 1914): 618.

10. Rolin letter, 1 February 1918, File 1918. Bill to Rolin from David Powell, Counselor at Law, New York City, 20 February 1915, File 1915. Both University of Southern California, Hollywood Museum Collection, Hal Roach Studios.

11. "Warner's Features, Inc"., *Moving Picture World* (11 July 1914): 262.

12. "United Film Service Outlook", *Moving Picture World* (16 January 1915), 354.

13. Telegram from Rolin (Los Angeles) to Hal Roach (New York City), 30 December 1914. University of Southern California, Hollywood Museum Collection, Hal Roach Studios, 1914–1915 Business Correspondence File.

14. Series of telegrams from Dwight Whiting (Los Angeles) to Hal Roach (New York City), 31 December 1914, 3 January 1915, 8 January 1915. University of Southern California, Hollywood Museum Collection, Hal Roach Studios, 1914–1915 Business Correspondence File.

15. Letter from Roach to Crystal Film Company, 430 Claremont Ave., NYC, 15 February 1915, and reply form Crystal, 26 February 1915. University of Southern California, Hollywood Museum Collection, Hal Roach Studios, Rolin File 1915–1920.

16. Telegram from Whiting (NYC) to Roach (Los Angeles), 15 March 1915. University of Southern California, Hollywood Museum Collection, Hal Roach Studios, Business Correspondence File.

17. Telegram from Whiting (NYC) to Roach (Los Angeles), 20 March 1915. University of Southern California, Hollywood Museum Collection, Hal Roach Studios, 1914–1915 Business Correspondence File.

18. *Moving Picture World* (11 January 1913): 181.

19. "Pathé Opens Exchanges", *Moving Picture World* (16 May 1914): 975.

20. "Pathé Putting Out News Daily", *Moving Picture World* (13 June 1914): 1524.

21. "Expediting Service", *Moving Picture World* (11 July 1914): 284.

22. "Expediting Service", *Moving Picture World* (11 July 1914): 284.

23. "Pathé in Mutual", *Variety* (31 October 1914): 25.

24. George Blaisdell, "Charles Pathé, Film Publisher", *Moving Picture World* (14 November 1914): 904–905.

25. *Moving Picture World* (2 January 1915): 30, and (16 January 1915): 314–317.

26. "Pathé Sails for Europe", *Moving Picture World* (16 January 1915): 342.

27. "Felix Malitz – Pathé Guiding Spirit", *Moving Picture World* (13 March 1915): 1583.

28. "Charles Pathé the Guiding Spirit", *Moving Picture World* (27 March 1915): 1914h.

29. Telegram from Whiting (NYC) to Roach (Los Angeles), 20 March 1915. University of Southern California, Hollywood Museum Collection, Hal Roach Studios, 1914–1915 Business Correspondence File.

30. Telegram from Hal Roach in NYC to Rolin, 14 October 1915. University of Southern California, Hollywood Museum Collection, Hal Roach Studios, 1914–1915 Business Correspondence File.

19

Distribution sérielle et synchronisation du spectateur aux premiers temps du cinéma

Nicolas Dulac

Université de Paris III and Université de Montréal

L e cinéma est, à de multiples égards, un art sériel. Non seulement l'est-il dans son fondement même – la pellicule est constituée d'une série de photogrammes – mais les films sont également appelés, au sein de l'industrie dominante du moins, à être produits, distribués et consommés *en série*. Derrière ce truisme se cache en effet tout un pan de réflexion riche de sens pour l'étude du cinéma en tant que divertissement de large consommation, pour ne pas dire en tant qu'art de masse, expression lourde d'équivoque s'il en est. Depuis l'avènement des serials au tournant des années 1910 jusqu'aux franchises hollywoodiennes actuelles, tout porte à croire que l'industrie du cinéma s'appuie largement sur un certain « modèle sériel », dont la pérennité témoigne à elle-seule de son efficacité et de son impact considérable au niveau de la production et de la consommation des films.

S'il est possible d'envisager la sérialité comme un principe structurant d'envergure, un modèle qui, moyennant quelques modifications, a su perdurer au sein de l'industrie cinématographique tout en contribuant à la façonner et en assurer le succès, cette étude se voudra, en revanche, beaucoup plus modeste. Il s'agira ici de se tourner vers les tout premiers temps du cinéma et d'y voir comment un certain modèle sériel s'est progressivement imposé, avant même l'instauration de réseaux de distribution indépendants, comme une véritable stratégie « distributionnelle », semblable à celle employée par la presse à grand tirage et l'industrie paralittéraire qui fleurissent à la même époque. Cela n'a pas de quoi surprendre, si l'on considère que ces différents médias participent conjointement à cette mouvance d'envergure, à la fin du 19e siècle, vers une véritable culture de masse et se partagent une clientèle somme toute similaire. Bien évidemment, l'industrie cinématographique naissante présente des particularités étrangères au médium littéraire, tant dans la nature même du produit offert que dans son espace de consommation. Toutefois, les deux institutions n'en présentent pas moins une ressemblance fondamentale : elles fabriquent rapidement et régulièrement du « divertissement » bon marché, qu'il leur faut ensuite distribuer à grande échelle sous forme de produits morcelés ou, à tout le moins, « morcelables ». C'est précisément là, au niveau de la distribution donc, que les industries cinématographique et paralittéraire se recoupent, dans la mesure où chacune cherche à tirer profit de la nature fragmentaire ou épisodique de leur produit, à convertir la dimension sérielle du médium en un avantage commercial.

Seulement, réduire la sérialité à sa seule fonction commerciale serait négliger sa portée et son importance dans le développement du médium. S'il se présente avant tout comme une stratégie visant à maximiser les profits, à rentabiliser au maximum chaque copie d'un même film, le modèle sériel aura également un impact déterminant sur la façon de concevoir les vues et de les consommer. Bien sûr, proposer un « modèle sériel » qui présiderait, de façon générale, à l'élaboration et la distribution des vues, suppose d'emblée une approche conceptuelle, approche qui, du reste, demandera à être éprouvée au contact d'analyses historiques plus détaillées.[1] Cela dit, aborder la sérialité comme une stratégie d'ensemble qui traverse, à différents degrés, l'industrie cinématographique, permet de dégager les modalités fondamentales de ce qui apparaît comme un universel de la culture de masse, un principe constitutif qui trouve sa pertinence et son efficacité à tous les niveaux de la production.

Distribution sérielle et synchronisation du spectateur

De toutes les étapes qui, du tournage jusqu'à la réception des vues, sous-tendent la production cinématographique, la distribution est sans doute celle qui a suscité le moins d'attention théorique de la part des chercheurs. La distribution, puisqu'elle est avant tout synonyme de « commercialisation », est intimement liée à la vente d'un produit, elle suppose ententes commerciales, rendement, efficacité, etc. Ainsi, contrairement à la production ou à la réception des films, elle semble offrir peu de potentiel théorique, dans la mesure où elle ne débouche pas, à première vue, sur quelque polysémie interprétative, de nature esthétique, cognitive ou autre. De sorte qu'on a tendance à limiter l'étude de la distribution à une approche « économico-industrielle », qui caractérise la plupart des écrits portant sur le sujet. Cette approche, tout à fait légitime au demeurant, risque toutefois d'enfermer la distribution dans ce que Rick Altman appelle une « histoire de filières », pendant de l'histoire traditionnelle au sein duquel la perspective historique adoptée se suffit à elle-même et fonctionne, pour ainsi dire, de manière autarcique. Cette filière, ici l'histoire économique, consisterait à appréhender la distribution comme une pratique industrielle autonome ou, comme le dit Altman, à « chercher les effets industriels d'une cause industrielle »,[2] négligeant du même coup l'impact que la distribution pourrait avoir sur la conception des vues ou sur leur réception. Or, la position intermédiaire qu'elle occupe dans le processus global de production exige, en quelque sorte, que l'on aborde la distribution non pas comme une pratique isolée, mais relativement aux différents aspects de la pratique cinématographique qu'elle est à même d'influencer.

Cette entreprise est d'autant plus hasardeuse qu'il est difficile de cerner, dans le cinéma des premiers temps, une entité pleinement autonome que l'on appellerait *distributeur*.[3] En effet, comment cerner le « champ d'action » de la distribution alors que la structure économique de l'industrie ne cesse de changer dans les premières années suivant l'émergence des vues animées? C'est pourquoi, plutôt que d'aborder la distribution comme étant le fruit d'une entité particulière, il s'avère plus pertinent de l'appréhender comme une fonction, une « fonction-distribution » donc, qui peut, selon les cas, relever de diverses instances. Cette fonction, d'un point de vue pragmatique, est double : d'une part, via la vente ou la location de bandes aux exploitants, elle assure la diffusion des vues sur un territoire circonscrit et selon une certaine fréquence. D'autre part, elle emploie un ensemble de procédés visant à stimuler les ventes et augmenter la demande pour de nouveaux titres, afin, bien évidemment, de rentabiliser au maximum chacune des copies manufacturées. Cela se fait principalement grâce à un contrôle direct de l'offre, dont elle est garante, et par l'entremise d'un discours institutionnel, essentiellement publicitaire.

Cette fonction première doit donc être comprise en envisageant la position intermédiaire qu'occupe la distribution dans le processus générale de production des vues. C'est dans cette fonction « médiatrice », semble-t-il, que réside l'essence même de la distribution, son véritable objectif. En effet, le rôle fondamental qui incombe à la distribution est avant tout de *synchroniser* la production et la consommation des vues. Dans une logique de rentabilité maximale, propre aux différents produits culturels de masse, la clé du succès est non seulement de faire en sorte que le consommateur consomme, mais, à plus forte raison, de s'assurer qu'il consomme *régulièrement*, à un rythme qui coïncide avec la cadence de fabrication des nouveaux produits. Après tout, quelle que soit la stratégie commerciale déployée par une entreprise, le succès d'un produit dépendra toujours du consommateur, de celui qui tirera un nickel de sa poche pour aller voir le dernier programme de vues animées. Assujettir la consommation des vues aux modes de production de ces dernières consiste ni plus ni moins à façonner le spectateur, créer en lui des besoins, en faire une entité prévisible. Or, contrôler le spectateur, c'est contrôler l'industrie. Voilà pourquoi la distribution peut être perçue comme un pont entre la production et la réception des vues, elle agit, en quelque sorte, comme un « poste d'aiguillage », par l'intermédiaire duquel l'industrie tente d'orienter les habitudes de consommation du spectateur, le « diriger » toujours davantage vers les salles obscures. Sous cet angle, la distribution ne se résume plus uniquement aux processus de diffusion ou aux enjeux commerciaux qui en découlent directement, mais elle devient une étape charnière dont l'impact se fait sentir à la fois en amont, dans le processus même de fabrication des vues, et en aval, dans les habitudes de consommation du spectateur.

Conséquemment, on comprend mieux ce qui fait de la distribution le principal enjeu au sein d'un système de production sériel. Faut-il rappeler que, d'un point de vue commercial, on ne « distribue » que des marchandises qui sont, précisément, fabriquées en série, ou alors en très grand nombre. On dira que l'on distribue des tracts, des journaux, des rations, mais pas des Vermeer, des antiques ou toute autre production artisanale. C'est donc avant tout par le truchement d'une stratégie distributionnelle adéquate qu'un bien produit en série se verra, éventuellement, consommé en série, c'est-à-dire de façon répétitive et régulière. La production sérielle de masse, comme le disait Marc Le Bot, est « un système essentiellement distributionnel », un « art combinatoire » :

> [...] parce que les éléments n'y sont définissables, en dernier ressort, que par leur commutabilité dans la structure du système, effaçant ainsi leur sens propre, devant celui de leurs manipulations; parce que la rationalité du système, en conséquence, tient à sa capacité de combinaison et parce que la fascination qu'elle exerce tient au rythme même – rapide, en accélération constante – qui règle l'ordre de ses successions.[4]

Voilà, précisément, ce qui se cache sous l'appellation « sérialité », c'est-à-dire un ensemble de stratégies qui fait de la série un système signifiant, à la fois pour l'industrie et pour le spectateur : commutation, combinaison, succession, rythme de diffusion, etc. L'historiographie classique a largement ignoré cette dimension distributionnelle et a surtout préconisé une approche « singularisante » des vues animées. Il est toutefois nécessaire que l'on examine les films au regard de leur concaténation potentielle dans les catalogues de vente et dans les sites d'exhibition. Comme le suggère Le Bot, ce n'est plus tant le sens de la vue en elle-même qui importe dans un tel système distributionnel, mais plutôt la signification qu'elle acquiert au sein d'une série de plus grande envergure, au contact d'autres vues faisant partie d'un même ensemble.

À cet égard, les fabricants de vues (qui tournent et produisent des vues en série) et les exhibiteurs (qui présentent des vues en série) chercheront respectivement à faire de la sérialisation un procédé efficace et rentable. S'il est difficile de déterminer, avant l'émergence de bureaux de distribution indépendants, la « part distributionnelle » qui incombe au producteur ou à l'exhibiteur, on peut tout de même dire, de façon générale, que ces deux instances cherchent à synchroniser leur pratiques respectives, à faire coïncider la « fréquence de production » avec la « fréquence de projection ». Le but étant, bien évidemment, de synchroniser à son tour le spectateur avec le mode de diffusion des vues, en faire un spectateur sériel. De sorte que l'on tend toujours vers une symétrie idéale entre production et consommation : la sérialisation qui s'opère du côté de l'industrie, synonyme d'augmentation de l'offre, de diminution du coût de revient et de maximisation des profits, doit correspondre à une sérialisation du côté du spectateur, synonyme, cette fois, d'une recherche de plaisir sans cesse renouvelée, d'une jouissance sans cesse différée.[5]

Les prémisses du modèle sériel

Cette tentative visant à faire concorder production et consommation est un critère essentiel à l'essor commercial de tout produit culturel de masse. L'intégration verticale des grands studios américains, qui s'opère progressivement tout au long des années 20, et la stratégie du *block booking*, qui s'avérera décisive au sein du système hollywoodien, répondaient directement de cette nécessité commerciale. Déjà, au tournant des années 10, le serial s'imposait d'ailleurs comme un format hautement efficace, voire le format par excellence, afin de synchroniser le spectateur avec la cadence de diffusion. En effet, le potentiel commercial du serial réside essentiellement dans une symétrie quasi totale entre le mode de production et de consommation des vues, rendue possible grâce à une diffusion périodique soutenue, un système de vente jumelée sciemment orchestré et des récits résolument sensationnalistes et potentiellement infinis. La grande popularité que connaîtront les serials dans les années 10 et 20 ne fait que confirmer le succès de la formule,[6] similaire à celle mise de l'avant par le roman-feuilleton. Seulement, ce modèle sériel fait état d'une stratégie distributionnelle qui, pour l'industries cinématographique, a mis plusieurs années à s'instaurer, stratégie qui découle de nombreuses expérimentations sur le format des programmes et de modifications notables dans la structure de l'industrie cinématographique. Peu de temps après l'avènement des vues animées, on peut déjà relever certains procédés de sérialisation au niveau de la production, de la promotion et de l'exhibition des vues, qui tendent également vers une synchronisation production / consommation.

Il semble, en effet, que le cinéma ait misé très rapidement sur des stratégies similaires à celles utilisées par l'industrie paralittéraire, qui apparaît véritablement dans la première moitié du 19e siècle suivant l'émergence du feuilleton dans les journaux et autres revues populaires.[7] Or, s'il est un aspect essentiel qui a permis non seulement de distinguer la paralittérature des Belles-Lettres, mais également d'en assurer le succès auprès des lecteurs, il s'agit assurément de sa diffusion et des stratégies qu'elle sous-tend. Paul Bleton, dans un essai pénétrant sur la paralittérature, s'est penché sur les différentes caractéristiques commerciales qui distinguent ce qu'il appelle « l'Industrie du Récit en tant que livre, saisi par le Loisir » de la tradition élitiste de l'édition littéraire.[8] Afin de mass-médiatiser ses nouveaux produits sériels, l'industrie naissante du roman-feuilleton devait, toujours selon Bleton, opérer des changements d'envergure dans la façon de penser la production des écrits :

1. Augmenter le nombre de titres publiés par rapport à celui de ces collègues spécialisés dans l'édition belles-lettres.

2. Régulariser son approvisionnement en manuscrits.

3. Expérimenter sur les supports, les formats, les techniques de reproduction, afin de trouver la formule la plus compétitive.

4. Créer une demande dans le lectorat cible, fidéliser ce dernier – pour lui faire absorber les grands tirages –, programmer la rapide obsolescence de ses produits et la facile substitution de l'ancien par le neuf – pour mieux pouvoir offrir ses nouveaux titres.[9]

Ces stratégies générales trouvent également écho dans l'industrie cinématographique des débuts, qui, elle aussi, misera sur un spectateur-sériel afin de garantir son succès. Bien avant l'avènement du long-métrage ou du serial, diverses stratégies vont se manifester dans la façon de tourner, de vendre et de présenter des *blocs* de vues, des séries donc, qui gagneront progressivement en efficacité commerciale et en pouvoir de séduction. S'il n'existe pas encore de compétition entre « belles-vues » et vues populaires, on peut opposer l'industrie naissante du cinéma aux formes de divertissement « socialement estimées », comme le théâtre ou l'opéra. Or l'enjeu soulevé par la sérialisation, dans le cas des « vues saisies par le Loisir », est le même : fournir une attraction abordable, continue et diversifiée, dont l'accessibilité surpasse grandement celle des formes plus « nobles » de divertissement. La production rapide des vues deviendra rapidement l'une des exigences principales afin de permettre à l'industrie de se démarquer en tant que nouvelle attraction populaire.

Dans un premier temps, cependant, la production cinématographique ne peut guère prétendre à une véritable stratégie sérielle. La cinématographie des débuts est foncièrement artisanale, voire expérimentale, et s'avère une entreprise encore trop précaire et trop risquée pour qu'on puisse la qualifier d'industrie. On produit des vues *en* chaîne, mais pas *à la* chaîne. Les films sont souvent « fabriqués sur mesure pour une situation particulière » et il n'existe pas encore de véritable distinction entre les nombreux intervenants.[10] La distribution, quant à elle, se résume généralement à la vente directe, par le fabricant, de bandes à l'exhibiteur. Compte tenu que les vues animées s'implanteront d'abord au sein de différentes institutions de divertissement déjà établies, les fabricants chercheront peu à contrôler la diffusion et l'exhibition des vues.

Pourtant, à défaut d'une stratégie commerciale scrupuleusement élaborée, on peut déjà repérer une certaine forme de synchronisme entre les méthodes de fabrication et d'exhibition des vues. Au moment de l'émergence des vues animées, on n'envisage pas encore ces dernières comme des unités potentiellement liables, mais plutôt comme éléments totalement commutables, substituables. Suivant une logique qui répond aux exigences du format du spectacle de variétés, l'heure n'est pas à la possible concaténation des vues, mais à l'accumulation d'effets attractionnels ponctuels et immédiats.[11] En fait, la stratégie initiale sera toute axée sur la différentiation du produit, ce qui se comprend aisément si l'on considère la nouveauté du dispositif et son pouvoir de fascination. En vampirisant diverses institutions culturelles, en réactualisant certains tropes appartenant au domaine de la prestidigitation ou de la lanterne magique par exemple, le cinéma insiste sur l'aspect *novelty* du dispositif, son caractère insolite et surprenant qui le distingue, précisément, des autres divertissements populaires. Conséquemment, les premiers programmes de vues animées, insérés la plupart du temps dans des spectacles de nature très diversifiée, miseront sur la surprise, la différenciation, essayant par là-même d'exacerber le pouvoir de fascination des vues.

Durant cette ère de la *novelty*, le potentiel attractionnel du cinéma devait être sans cesse réaffirmé en insistant sur la diversité des sujets et sur la capacité du nouveau dispositif à produire rapidement de nouveaux titres. En effet, la vertu de ce nouveau dispositif réside non seulement dans son aptitude à restituer des images en mouvement, mais également dans le fait qu'il s'agit d'une nouvelle technologie qui effectue le travail, un appareil capable de produire du divertissement *rapidement, inlassablement*. Par ailleurs, en multipliant à foison les titres, les fabricants de vues s'assuraient de toujours pouvoir offrir quelque chose de nouveau aux spectateurs, même si les sujets en eux-même n'étaient guère renouvelés. Prolificité et rapidité d'exécution sont ici les mots d'ordre. Pas un catalogue de vente n'oublie de mentionner la vitesse à laquelle il produit de nouvelles vues, pas plus qu'un exhibiteur n'oublie de mentionner la fréquence à laquelle il modifie son programme.[12] Comme le disait Bleton pour la paralittérature, les fabricants de vues vont rapidement régulariser leur approvisionnement en vues et augmenter le nombre de titres par rapport aux différentes formes de divertissement plus mondain. On produit rapidement et régulièrement, question de combler continuellement l'appétit du spectateur, appétit d'autant plus grand, d'ailleurs, que le prix d'entrée demeure à la portée de tous. La *novelty* stimule à elle seule la production répétitive des vues et chaque nouveau titre est en soi un prétexte suffisant pour attirer le spectateur. Avec un système de distribution élémentaire, la principale tâche des fabricants était donc de fournir régulièrement et en grand nombre de nouveaux titres, afin de profiter au maximum de cet engouement soudain pour les vues animées, engouement qui, du reste, ne saurait tarder à s'essouffler. Cependant, cette relative autonomie dont jouissent fabricants et exhibiteurs ne saurait perdurer dans un mode de production sériel. Si l'aspect *novelty* du dispositif permet, au départ, de garantir à lui-seul une certaine symétrie entre la production et la consommation, c'est-à-dire d'attirer régulièrement le spectateur par une diversité croissante de titres, une stratégie distributionnelle plus conséquente sera de mise une fois cette fascination initiale envolée.

En fait, une totale autonomie de l'exhibiteur permettait d'intensifier encore davantage la différenciation du produit, ce dernier pouvant sélectionner, adapter, modifier les vues à sa guise. C'est lui qui agissait comme l'instance finale de production de sens, comme l'a judicieusement souligné Miriam Hansen : « It is a mark of early cinema's specificity that its effects on the viewer were determined less by the film itself than by the particular act of exhibition, the situation of reception. ».[13] Cela est d'autant plus vrai que les fabricants n'exercent pas de réel contrôle sur le choix des vues par l'exhibiteur. Les catalogues de vente de l'époque témoignent bien, dans un premier temps, de cette « division des tâches ». On y trouve peu de suggestions quant au contenu éventuel des programmes et peu de stratégies quant à une éventuelle vente en bloc. On veut avant tout écouler des bandes et quoique tournées en séries de trois ou quatre vues, on ne cherche pas particulièrement à les vendre en lots. Dans un catalogue distribué par F.Z. Maguire & Co., par exemple, on annonce cinq vues Edison tournées au parc d'attractions de Coney Island en 1896. Bien que les vues y soient listées les unes à la suite des autres, il n'y a aucune mention de l'achat potentiel de la série entière et chaque résumé est indépendant des quatre autres.[14] Dans les catalogues Gaumont, on indique même à l'aide d'un astérisque « les vues de premier choix » plutôt que d'utiliser une stratégie de vente « en bloc ».[15] De plus, dans un de ces catalogues Gaumont, on précise sous les listes de vues thématiques (comme celle du *Défilé de chars de la Mi-Carême 1897, à Paris*, en trois vues) qu'il s'agit bel et bien de « bandes séparées », au lieu d'insister, comme on le fera bientôt, sur le fait qu'il est possible de les abouter en une seule bande.[16] D'ailleurs, l'emploi du mot « série », dans les catalogues comme dans la presse,[17] désigne généralement la vue en tant que telle, c'est-à-dire en tant que « série photographique »[18] ou série de photogrammes, et non pas en tant qu'éventuel regroupement thématique de vues.

Cette relative autonomie des intervenants s'avère cependant un obstacle lorsque les pressions du marché exigent une certaine standardisation, lorsque le fabricant se doit de manufacturer des produits en série, selon certaines modalités éprouvées et efficaces. D'ailleurs, on constate que cette pression commerciale se fera sentir chez les producteurs et, de part et d'autre de l'Atlantique, on remarque des changements notables dans la façon de concevoir, de tourner et de promouvoir les vues. Ainsi, cette période de *novelty*, généralement caractérisée par la fascination exaltée du spectateur et par la présentation désarticulée des vues animées selon le modèle du spectacle de variétés, s'avère probablement beaucoup plus courte, ou beaucoup moins répandue, que ne l'ont prétendu les historiens du passé.[19] La *novelty* des vues animées s'effritant rapidement, ce sera, en partie, du ressort de la distribution d'en prolonger le pouvoir de fascination. C'est donc, comme le disait Bleton, par une expérimentation sur le format de diffusion, que l'on sera à même de trouver la formule la plus compétitive.

Séries thématiques ou de l'infinie réitération

L'une des premières stratégies sérielles utilisées sera probablement le tournage, puis la vente (ou la location) de séries de vues thématiques aux exploitants. Dans deux articles portant sur la programmation de l'American Mutoscope and Biograph Company, Nico de Klerk a pertinemment démontré que dès 1897, les programmes de vues animées proposés par cette compagnie, bien qu'insérés dans des spectacles de variétés, ne répondaient pas de la même structure éclatée que le reste de la représentation.[20] Contrairement à ce que voudrait la « thèse moderniste » d'inspiration benjaminienne, les programmes de la Biograph ne misaient pas tant sur la surprise, le choc, la désarticulation, les sensations fortes, mais fonctionnaient plutôt de manière à créer différents liens – narratifs, symboliques, thématiques, etc. – entre les vues. Ainsi, la série exhibitionnelle prend ici un tout autre sens. Chaque vue n'est pas uniquement assemblée en fonction de sa teneur attractionnelle, mais également en fonction de son contenu, dans le but de créer un certain discours, voire un certain récit. Bien sûr, les programmes de vues animées du London Palace Theater de Londres, sur lesquels s'appuient l'argumentation de de Klerk, ont cette particularité d'être entièrement conçus par la Biograph et non pas par l'exploitant de la salle. C'est donc le fabricant qui décidait du programme et qui fournissait l'équipement et le personnel nécessaires à la projection des vues, s'assurant du même coup d'une symétrie idéale entre production et exhibition. À cet égard, de Klerk ajoute que cette stratégie avait tout pour satisfaire les deux partis impliqués : « In fact, it's more likely that the film company's programming strategies and the theatre management's policies were increasingly geared to one another ».[21] Même si la plupart des fabricants n'avaient aucun contrôle direct sur la programmation éventuelle de leurs bandes, leur objectif reste bel et bien le même que celui évoqué par de Klerk, c'est-à-dire de proposer à l'exhibiteur un choix de vues qui répondent le mieux possible aux besoins de ce dernier. En un mot, de synchroniser leurs pratiques respectives.

Dès 1898, mais surtout à partir de 1900, les programmes de vues animées vont progressivement s'organiser autour de certains thèmes généraux ou motifs narratifs, selon une structure beaucoup plus cohésive que le format de variétés. En fait, cette organisation sérielle prend d'abord naissance au moment du tournage, alors que les opérateurs photographient plusieurs films ayant pour sujet un même événement ou un même lieu. Bien évidemment, tourner successivement plusieurs vues, en des endroits rapprochés et en un court laps de temps, présente d'évidents avantages commerciaux pour une compagnie : en plus d'emballer rapidement un bon nombre de vues, elle s'évite de dépenser inutilement pour le déplacement d'une équipe de tournage. Un simple coup d'œil aux catalogues de production Edison et Lumière, par exemple, nous montre que la pratique des « tournages multiples » s'est rapidement généralisée. En effet, il est difficile de trouver des vues qui, en 1900, ne s'insèrent pas dans un ensemble thématique de plus grande ampleur.[22]

Bien que le tournage de séries de vues était pratique courante dès les tout premiers temps du cinéma, on ne faisait pas nécessairement la promotion d'une possible vente en lot dans les catalogues. Cependant, cette situation va changer rapidement et on constate bientôt une adhésion mutuelle des éditeurs et des exhibiteurs à un certain modèle sériel. Ainsi, vers 1897, les séries thématiques vont commencer à apparaître dans les catalogues de vente, agissant comme programmes « préconçus » pour l'exhibiteur. En effet, les éditeurs vont progressivement tenter d'avoir un plus grand contrôle sur la distribution et l'exhibition des vues, de synchroniser l'achat des bandes en fonction de leur production en série. Plusieurs indices montrent que, du côté du fabricant comme de l'exhibiteur, on commence de plus en plus à concevoir les vues comme des unités pouvant former un tout cohérent.

Les différentes compagnies de production développeront ainsi des stratégies de vente pour tenter de capitaliser sur les séries thématiques, ce qui les amènera à repenser la distribution des vues. L'intérêt économique d'une vente en blocs ne fait pas de doute : vendre des groupes de vues est nécessairement plus rentable que de vendre des vues à l'unité. C'est pourquoi on voit apparaître dans les catalogues de plus en plus de mentions concernant l'agencement possible des vues.[23] Les techniques diffèrent pour suggérer un tel assemblage, certaines étant plus explicites que d'autres. Dans le cas de courtes séries de deux vues, on utilisera parfois la mention *bis* pour suggérer leur agencement potentiel. Dans un catalogue Pathé de 1900, par exemple, deux vues intitulées *Courses de Taureaux de Roubaix* sont identifiées par les numéros 322 et 322 *bis* respectivement.[24] S'il s'agit ici d'un seuil minimum d'assemblage, la plupart du temps les regroupements se présentent de manière moins équivoque. Parfois les vues sont numérotées, parfois elles sont suivies d'une mention du genre de celle qu'on retrouve dans le catalogue Lumière de 1901 pour la série *Panorama sur la ligne de Beaulieu à Monaco* : « Ces trois dernières vues peuvent être ajoutées l'une l'autre ».[25] De façon plus explicite, un catalogue de la Warwick Trading Company dit ceci concernant une série de onze vues de corrida : « When joined and shown consecutively as here arranged, [they] constitute a thrilling exhibition of 10 minutes duration ».[26] Parfois, c'est l'éditeur qui se propose d'abouter lui-même les vues en une seule bande. D'ailleurs, il est intéressant de constater que l'utilisation dans les catalogues et dans la presse du terme « série » est, surtout après 1900, attribuée à un ensemble de vues et non plus à la vue en tant que telle, suggérant ainsi une certaine forme d'unité inter-vues.[27] Le terme « série », par ailleurs, ne désignait pas uniquement un groupe de vues couvrant un même lieu ou un même événement. Les éditeurs regroupaient parfois des vues ayant une thématique commune, mais qui ne se développaient pas nécessairement autour d'espaces adjacents (comme cette série macabre produite par Pathé qui dépeint six « modes d'exécution capitale » dans différentes villes du monde).[28] On utilise aussi le terme « série », de façon plus générale, pour désigner un « genre » (vues comiques, vues historiques, etc.). Ainsi, la sérialité se manifeste comme un véritable vecteur de standardisation, tant dans la façon de concevoir que de vendre les vues, selon un modèle sériel qui s'éloigne résolument du format vaudevillesque.

Il est difficile de déterminer avec précision l'impact de ces stratégies de vente en blocs sur la programmation des exhibiteurs. En effet, des études extensives sur la programmation d'un grand nombre de salles seraient nécessaires pour décrire les changements qui s'opèrent dans la façon d'appréhender la présentation des vues. Toutefois, il ne fait aucun doute qu'une grande majorité d'exhibiteurs ont progressivement adopté une programmation thématiquement plus cohésive. Pour la simple et bonne raison, d'ailleurs, que les fabricants produisaient de plus en plus de séries thématiques. Le succès d'un exploitant de salle reposant essentiellement sur sa capacité à modifier régulièrement son programme, il était contraint de se procurer ce que les différentes compagnies de vues animées avaient à lui offrir. Tout porte à croire, au demeurant, qu'une fois l'aspect *novelty* du dispositif envolé, les spectateurs se réjouissaient des programmes thématiques et que l'exhibiteur avait tout avantage à « faire le saut » dans ce sens. Charles Musser mentionne que dès 1897, aux États-Unis, l'arrangement efficace des vues et la création de « mondes temporels ou spatiaux », étaient devenus consubstantiels à la réussite d'une séance.[29] Cela permettait en quelque sorte de réintégrer la *novelty* à l'intérieur des programmes de vues en exploitant de nouvelles particularités du médium. La situation était sensiblement la même en France, où les programmes à saveur touristique connaissaient un immense succès.[30] L'insertion de vues thématiques dans les salles d'exhibition ne se faisait pas nécessairement à raison d'une série entière par séance, mais plutôt par addition de plusieurs séries plus courtes. Habituellement, seuls les événements publics de grande importance (couronnement, cortège funèbre, parade militaire) et les « programmes touristiques » se voyaient décerner une séance entière.

Suivant cette logique sérielle, les fabricants vont, presque spontanément, miser sur l'actualité et la situation politique pour construire leurs séries. À cet égard, la guerre hispano-américaine et la guerre des Boers vont donner lieu à des séries d'envergure, exploitant plusieurs stratégies que l'on retrouve dans la presse à sensation. Ces séries, produites entre autres par Edison et Biograph,[31] tiraient non seulement profit de la fibre patriotique des spectateurs, mais bénéficiaient en plus d'un paratexte journalistique important, assurant un certain savoir préalable du spectateur eu égard aux événements représentés. Ces séries témoignent, en premier lieu, d'une véritable prise de conscience quant au potentiel narratif de ces regroupements de vues et à la nécessité d'offrir un ensemble cohésif. La série Edison qui retrace l'arrivée triomphale de l'amiral Dewey à New York après sa victoire sur la flotte espagnole est un exemple particulièrement évocateur. Tournée en 1899 et composée de 24 titres, cette série débute avec une vue, vraisemblablement falsifiée, montrant le départ de l'amiral Dewey vers l'Amérique depuis le port de Gibraltar. Bien qu'il est fort peu probable que cette vue soit originale (une seule vue ne justifierait certainement pas le coût d'un voyage de l'autre côté de l'Atlantique),[32] cet exemple reflète bien le désir de poser un « début », nécessaire à l'élaboration d'un récit cohérent. Chez Biograph, on retrouve, dans le même ordre d'idées, plusieurs vues truquées du navire USS Maine. Le prétendu sabordage de ce navire par les Espagnols a été un événement crucial dans le déclenchement des hostilités et s'avérait donc un sujet de choix pour les éditeurs. Or, personne n'avait filmé ce navire avant le naufrage, problème auquel plusieurs compagnies, dont Biograph, ont remédié en baptisant différemment une autre vue montrant un navire. Le USS Massachusetts devenait ainsi le USS Maine. Dans d'autres cas, on tournait simplement de fausses vues du Maine se faisant attaquer.[33] Encore une fois, on s'assure d'élaborer un programme à teneur plus ou moins narrative, à même d'offrir au public un ensemble relativement cohérent et d'autant plus apte à réactualiser des faits déjà connus du spectateur.

Ce type de séries démontre, en second lieu, le caractère extensif d'une telle stratégie distributionnelle. En tablant ainsi sur des événements de l'actualité, les exhibiteurs étaient en mesure de susciter une consommation répétitive de la part du spectateur. En effet, comme c'est le cas pour le roman-feuilleton, la nature fragmentaire et épisodique du produit devient une occasion de prolonger l'intérêt du public, de lui faire consommer du « semblable » ayant l'apparence du « nouveau ». Comme le montre

Nico de Klerk au sujet des nombreuses vues Biograph portant sur la guerre des Boers, le tournage d'un nombre restreint de nouvelles vues était un prétexte suffisant pour façonner un « nouveau » programme. En ajoutant quelques nouveaux titres et en les entremêlant avec des vues programmées par le passé, ou alors simplement en modifiant la répartition des vues au sein du programme, l'exhibiteur créait de légères variations de sens, suggérait de nouvelles interprétations, tout en utilisant une formule déjà éprouvée. Les séries thématiques se présentaient ainsi comme un « cocktail de répétition et d'innovation », qui, selon Bleton, est « ce à quoi s'attend tout lecteur sériel ».[34]

Ainsi, les différentes stratégies des fabricants pour vendre en bloc des séries de vues aux exploitants (selon une méthode qui s'apparente à un système de production discontinue ou *batch production*), témoignent encore une fois d'un désir de symétrie entre la production et la consommation. Cela devient profitable pour les deux partis uniquement si la chose se montre efficace auprès du public. C'est pourquoi l'on tente de solliciter un nouveau type d'appréhension de la part du spectateur, qui s'appuie non pas sur la seule griserie passagère, mais davantage sur le caractère informatif ou narratif du programme. La standardisation qu'opère la sérialité permet ainsi d'établir des marques de permanence que le spectateur est à même de connaître et d'anticiper, à l'aide desquelles il façonne ses propres attentes et peut ensuite juger de la représentation. Dès lors, la stratégie sérielle ne se résume plus seulement à l'agencement des vues au sein d'un même programme, mais préside également à la production et à l'exhibition des vues à plus long terme, de jour en jour, de semaines en semaine.

En fait, cette stratégie est sensiblement la même que celle déployée, à la même époque, par la presse à grand tirage. Les fabricants de vues devaient, comme les rédacteurs de journaux populaires, s'approvisionner régulièrement en sujets dignes d'intérêt (parades, inaugurations, désastres naturels, sites touristiques, etc.) afin de maintenir l'engouement du spectateur, le fidéliser en lui donnant sa dose d'« informations » et de « nouveautés ». La presse populaire et le cinéma procédaient par là-même à une certaine « spectacularisation » du réel,[35] d'autant plus attrayante qu'elle est potentiellement inépuisable, c'est-à-dire capable de surseoir indéfiniment aux attentes du spectateur. Cette accumulation de faits divers, de paysages exotiques, de rassemblements festifs qui, de semaine en semaine, se renouvelle sans cesse, se présente, selon les mots de Merleau-Ponty, comme un monde inépuisable, « ouvert », capable de « nous renvoyer au-delà des ses manifestations déterminées, de nous promettre toujours "autre chose à voir" ».[36]

Les stratégies sérielles discutées ci-dessus font état de certaines caractéristiques inhérentes au mode de diffusion de nombreux produits culturels de masse. En fait, pour qu'une tradition artisanale se développe en véritable industrie, celle-ci doit nécessairement introduire dans son fonctionnement une certaine logique sérielle, afin, comme le disait France Gascon, de créer de la stabilité et de développer une méthode qui « voudrait éviter le désordre et l'irrégularité ».[37] La production de séries thématiques s'est vite présentée comme une stratégie efficace et économique, qui devait cependant recevoir l'aval du spectateur. En stimulant la vente de séries thématiques les fabricants s'assuraient une productivité maximale, proposant un format exhibitionnel qui répondait de façon symétrique au mode de production des vues. Ces séries, une fois transposées en programmes dans les sites d'exhibition, venaient modifier substantiellement l'expérience du spectateur, auquel on proposait désormais des spectacles davantage cohésifs, à teneur plus informative ou narrative.

Mais pour attirer le spectateur à la prochaine séance, pour faire de lui un véritable spectateur sériel, les intervenants devaient s'assurer de fournir rapidement et régulièrement de nouveaux produits. Une telle prolifération des vues pourrait sembler aberrante, surtout si l'on considère la récurrence des sujets et des « trames narratives » ainsi que les innombrables formes de *remakes*, parfois plus ou moins avoués. Pourtant, cette accumulation répétitive de vues est particulièrement appropriée au sein de la dynamique mise en place par l'industrie. D'un côté, cette distribution sérielle intempestive fait sens pour le spectateur, elle agit comme une garantie quant à la nature et à la qualité de la vue. Autrement dit, le spectateur est à même de retrouver dans la vue ce qu'il y cherche, c'est-à-dire ce qu'il y a déjà trouvé précédemment. Comme pour le lecteur de feuilleton, le retour, la répétition, la régularité de certains aspects au sein des vues assurent la fidélité du spectateur. Cependant, et c'est peut-être là un paradoxe propre à tout produit culturel de masse, les vues doivent être renouvelées fréquemment, puisque si le spectateur cherche à retrouver un plaisir similaire, il n'en cherche pas un qui soit tout à fait identique, il veut du nouveau tout autant que du semblable. Cette dimension contradictoire est, en grande partie, prise en charge par la distribution et c'est en cela, précisément, qu'elle parvient à façonner le spectateur.

En effet, il semble que les méthodes de distribution employées avant même l'émergence massive de bureaux de distribution indépendants, autour de 1907, soient à même de créer un sentiment de nouveauté chez le spectateur et ce, malgré une fréquence de distribution effrénée qui empêche un véritable renouvellement. En fait, la distribution massive et régulière des vues animées a pour effet, comme le disait Bleton, de programmer leur rapide obsolescence et ainsi, d'assurer leur facile remplacement par de nouvelles vues. En stimulant de cette façon la demande, les procédés distributionnels créaient eux-mêmes ce besoin de nouveauté, proposant continuellement un nouveau leurre pour attirer le spectateur. Ce qui s'opère, via cette distribution sérielle, c'est ni plus ni moins que la formation du spectateur, dans les deux sens du terme. D'une part l'industrie essaie de le modeler, d'en faire un consommateur fidèle, pour ne pas dire un consommateur sériel, et, d'autre part, il acquiert une connaissance, il apprend à maîtriser certains aspects des vues, il en comprend davantage les rouages, il se crée des attentes.

Bien sûr, il s'agit ici avant tout d'un modèle, une tendance générale, qui aura de multiples façons de se manifester au sein de l'industrie. La synchronisation de la production et de la consommation se fera souvent par l'entremise de politiques économiques draconiennes, comme on en retrouve durant le Trust Edison ou tout au long de l'ère des studios. Seulement, on aura constaté que dès les toutes premières années du cinéma, certaines stratégies de distribution sérielle vont, à l'instar de la presse à sensation ou du roman-feuilleton, pousser le spectateur à une consommation répétée, en offrant sans relâche de nouveaux produits, en le confortant sans cesse dans son désir de toujours voir « autre chose ».

Notes

1. Ce texte s'inscrit dans le cadre d'une recherche de doctorat qui s'interroge sur la notion de sérialité dans le cinéma de grande consommation, afin d'en évaluer la pertinence commerciale pour l'industrie cinématographique ainsi que son impact sur le spectateur.

2. Altman, Rick, « Naissance de la réception classique. La campagne pour standardiser le son », *Cinémathèque* 6 (automne 1994): 99.

3. On peut difficilement, dans le cinéma des premiers temps, associer une *action* précise à un *acteur* précis, comme ce sera le cas au sein du système « tayloriste » mis de l'avant par les grands studios, à la fin des années 10. André Gaudreault, dans un article consacré aux différentes opérations de montage dans le corpus Lumière, parle d'ailleurs d'« instances » et non pas d'individus pour désigner les différents intervenants « virtuels » qui se chargent d'abouter et de commercialiser les vues. Voir Gaudreault, André « Fragmentation et assemblage dans les vues Lumière », *Visio* 7.1–2 (printemps-été 2002): 59–73.

4. Le Bot, Marc, « Séries et sérialité », *Revue d'Esthétique*. « L'art de masse n'existe pas » 3–4, (Paris: Union générale d'éditions, 1974), 40.

5. Cette réciprocité du modèle sériel correspond à ce que Paul Bleton appelle la « dyade du marché » dans l'industrie paralittéraire. Voir Bleton, Paul, *Ça se lit comme un roman policier... Comprendre la lecture sérielle* (Québec: Nota Bene, 1999), 230.

6. Sur l'ampleur du phénomène aux États-Unis, voir Stamp, Shelley, *Movie-Struck Girls. Women and Motion Picture Culture After the Nickelodeon* (Princeton: Princeton University Press, 2000), 102–153.

7. Pour un survol concis de l'émergence du roman-feuilleton en France, voir Queffélec, Lise, *Le roman-feuilleton français au XIXᵉ siècle* (Paris, PUF: 1989).

8. Paul Bleton, op. cit., 26.

9. Ibid., 31.

10. Rick Altman, op. cit., 99.

11. À ce propos, Charles Musser écrit ceci : « Generally, no thematic, narrative, spatial, or temporal relationships existed between scenes. [...] Rather, exhibitions were initially organized along variety principles that emphasized diversity and contrast even while the selections often built to a climax and ended with a flourish ». L'exemple qu'il mentionne d'une représentation new-yorkaise du Cinématographe Lumière en mars 1897, est pour le moins révélateur d'un tel penchant pour la diversité, l'exhibiteur ayant, semble-t-il, éloigné volontairement les vues entretenant un lien thématique entre elles (les vues tournées en France, celle tournées à New York, les vues à caractère ludique) : 1. *Lumière Factory* 2. *Columbus Statue, Entrance Central Park* 3. *A Battle with Snowballs* 4. *Niagara Falls* 5. *Children Playing* 6. *Dragoons of Austrian Army* 7. *Brooklyn Bridge* 8. *French Cuirassiers* 9. *Union Square* 10. *The Frolics of Negroes While Bathing* 11. *Card Players* 12. *Shooting the Chutes*. Voir Musser, Charles, *Emergence of Cinema*, op. cit., 179.

12. Les exemples sont légion dans les programmes publiés dans la presse : « Entire change of program for second evening », « This list is constantly being added to and brought up-to-date », « Tous les soirs, changement de spectacle », etc.

13. Hansen, Miriam, *Babel and Babylon: Spectatorship in America Silent Film* (Cambridge, Harvard University Press, 1991), 93–94.

14. Musser, Charles, et al., *Motion Pictures Catalogs by American Producers and Distributors, 1894–1908: A Microfilm Edition* (Frederick: University Publications of America, 1985, rouleau 1).

15. Catalogue Gaumont, no. 137 (mai 1899): 3.

16. Ibid.

17. Au sujet du vocabulaire utilisée dans la presse pour décrire les vues animées, voir Karine Martinez et Jean-Pierre Sirois-Trahan, « La vue animée dans le discours journalistique (1896–1908) », in Albera, François, Marta Braun et André Gaudreault (éds), *Arrêt sur image, fragmentation du temps / Stop Motion, Fragmentation of Time* (Payot Lausanne: Lausanne, 2002), 309–320.

18. Catalogue Gaumont, no. 137 (mai 1899): 3.

19. Voir, par exemple, le célèbre ouvrage de Allen, Robert C., *Vaudeville and Film, 1895–1915: A Study in Media Interaction* (New York: Arno Press, 1980).

20. Klerk, Nico de, « Pictures to be shewn: programming the American Biograph », in Popple, Simon et Vanessa Toulmin (éds), *Visual delights: essays on the popular and projected image in the 19th century* (Flicks Books: Trowbridge, 2000), 204- 224 et « Programme of programmes: the London Palace Theatre of Varieties », *Griffithiana* 66–70 (2000): 241–247.

21. Klerk, Nico de, « Programme of programme », op. cit., 247.

22. C'est le cas, principalement, pour les vues d'actualité : de tous les films d'actualité produits par Edison entre 1896 et 1900, soit environ 600 vues, on en dénombre à peine 20 qui soient « solitaires », c'est-à-dire qui ne fassent pas partie d'un ensemble de vues liées thématiquement ou géographiquement. La pratique des tournages multiples est tout aussi omniprésente dans la production Lumière. Comme chez Edison, on ne compte qu'environ 3 pour cent de vues de « plein air » qui, dans le catalogue Lumière, n'ont pas de lien direct avec la vue précédente ou celle qui suit. Pour un relevé exhaustif de la production Edison et Lumière, voir respectivement Musser, Charles, *Edison Motion Pictures, 1890–1900: An Annotated Filmography* (Gemona et Washington: Le Giornate del cinema muto et Smithsonian Institution Press, 1997) et Aubert, Michelle et Jean-Claude

Séguin (éd.), *La Production cinématographique des Frères Lumière* (Paris: Éditions Mémoires de cinéma et Bibliothèque du Film, 1996).

23. André Gaudreault nomme cette opération « assemblage *in texto* sur titres dans catalogues ». Voir Gaudreault, André, « Fragmentation et assemblage dans les vues Lumière », op. cit., 66–67.

24. Catalogue Pathé Frères, (1900): 23.

25. Cité dans Gaudreault, André « Fragmentation et assemblage dans les vues Lumière », op. cit., 68.

26. Cité dans Bottomore, Stephen, « Shots in the Dark : The Real Origins of Film Editing », in Elsaesser, Thomas, (ed.), *Early Cinema. Space, Frame, Narrative* (London: BFI, 1990), 106.

27. Martinez, Karine et Jean-Pierre Sirois-Trahan, « La vue animée dans le discours journalistique (1896–1908) », op. cit., 312–316.

28. Catalogue Pathé Frères (août 1904): 117.

29. Musser, Charles, *Before the Nickelodeon. Edwins S. Porter and the Edison Manufacturing Compagny* (Berkley/Los Angeles: University of California Press, 1991), 100.

30. Abel, Richard, *The Ciné Goes to Town* (Berkley/Los Angeles, University of California Press, 1998), 17.

31. À titre d'exemple, Edison a produit, en 1898 et 1899, plus de 110 vues ayant pour sujet la guerre hispano-américaine et les festivités qui suivirent la défaite espagnole. Voir Musser, Charles, *Edison Motion Pictures, 1890–1900*, op. cit.

32. Musser, Charles, *Edison Motion Picture, 1890–1900*, op. cit., 535.

33. Musser, Charles, *The Emergence of Cinema*, op. cit., 240–241.

34. Paul Bleton, *Ça se lit comme un roman policier*, op. cit., 30.

35. Au ce sujet de l'effritement des frontières entre réalité et représentation dans la presse à grand tirage, voir Schwartz, Vanessa R., « Setting the Stage : The Boulevard, the Press and the Framing of Everyday Life », *Spectacular Realities : Early Mass Culture in Fin-de-siècle Paris* (Berkeley/Los Angeles/London, University of California Press, 1998), 13–44.

36. Merleau-Ponty, Maurice, *Phénoménologie de la perception* (Paris: Gallimard, 2002), 384.

37. Gascon, France, « La notion de série et son rôle dans le développement d'une tradition artisanale », in Ayot, Pierre, et al., op. cit., 82–83.

Monopolizing episodic adventures: series and seriality in Germany, 1914–20

Rudmer Canjels[1]

Research Institute for History and Culture, Utrecht University, The Netherlands

In German film journals of August 1914, advertisements appeared claiming a new world record had been set: an 8000 meter film that had cost one million mark to produce. The film would be released soon and in it audiences could see elephants, tigers and buffalos, all creating much excitement and danger for the main actress. The German film journal *Lichtbild-Bühne* announced it was the latest interesting innovation in cinema and welcomed the film with the words 'Willkommen, schöne Kathlyn'.[2] It was the American serial *The Adventures of Kathlyn* (1914), released in Germany as *Die Abenteuer der schönen Kathlyn*.

With *Kathlyn* a new film structure arrived on the German film market. However, the serial structure with its continuous storyline did not fare well in Germany. Chapters of this American serial had to be seen in order, they often ended with an exciting cliffhanger and were released in a strict pre-planned schedule of one episode per week. This rhythm could not immediately be translated into the German system of distribution and exhibition. While in America the serial could at first function as an alternative film form between the short and the long feature, in Germany there was less need for this: the feature model of the Monopol-film was already in place. It was nevertheless through the use of Monopol-series that in Germany the serial structure with the corresponding block-booking practices as well as its distinctive rhythm was introduced. At the same time various forms and uses of seriality were tried out, forms that better fitted the specific national situation.[3] Though control of the market through block booking would subside somewhat after the war, its utilization during the war shows an important shift in power relations, from production to distribution. Just like seriality, this was a process that continued and did not end with the peace treaty of the First World War.

Exclusive Monopol-films

At the time of *Kathlyn*'s release, the Monopol distribution system was already firmly in place. "Monopol" is a term that has nothing to do with the subject matter of a film, but refers to a release format. It was a trading practice within the distribution system designed for films that were to be handled by exclusive regional contracts and to be rented instead of bought (much like the American zoning distribution system). A distributor obtained exclusive rights from the producer in order to exploit a film in a specific region. Exhibitors of that region then had to acquire from the distributor the right to exhibit the film. The transference of the screening rights to a theatre is in a way the essence of the Monopol agreement. The transfer of the film copy itself is merely secondary, however important the copy for showing might be.[4]

The Monopol-film system focused on expensive, multiple-reel feature films featuring well-known stars. As Corinna Müller has shown, it was especially because of the introduction of films that were focused around a star, such as Asta Nielsen, that Monopol-films were used more often from 1911 onward.[5] With a Monopol-film, the appearance of a star, the length and scope of the film, all could be marketed as something special, something worthwhile for audiences, exhibitor and distributor alike. *Lichtbild-Bühne*'s editor in chief Arthur Mellini complained however in 1914 that with the new system one almost needed to have a manager or an impresario and the separation between producer, distributor and exhibitor was lost.[6]

Alongside the Monopol-film, also Monopol-series were used. Asta Nielsen films could be booked separately or as a package. This was called a series and consisted of a whole seasonal output, usually of around six films that still had to be produced, for instance the *Asta Nielsen series 1912/1913*. The term series has nothing to do with a continuing storyline: it is a framework of production and distribution, at first usually centered around an actor or actress. It was still possible to book films from a series separately. This would change within a couple of years, then the exhibitor was obliged to rent all the titles of a series, even the lesser ones.

Vanishing adventures

Selig's *The Adventures of Kathlyn* was one of the first American serials to be released in Germany, and possibly one of the first in Europe. According to the *Lichtbild-Bühne* article, *Die Abenteuer der schönen Kathlyn* had thirteen episodes and was on its way from England to Germany.[7] The first episode was about 900 meters long, the other parts around 600 meters, which meant approximately the same length as when it was shown in America.

The Adventures of Kathlyn, because of its use of a cliffhanger ending, is often considered the first true American serial. Perhaps more important is the related fact that the chapters could not be seen in random order, while episodes were released in a strict pre-planned schedule. This new cinematic structure was noted by *Lichtbild-Bühne*. It was announced as a self-contained organic unity, which, like an exciting novel, captured the audience and which created a forceful necessity to see the next episode. 'Ein Roman, der verfilmt wurde, den man lesen muß, ohne mitten drin aufhören zu können; ein Film, den man sehen muß, um nächste Woche wieder ins Kino zu gehen, da die Spannung dazu zwingt. Dem Publikum ruft der Verfasser ein "Muß" zu, und in diesem Zwingen liegt der Erfolg der Sache.'[8]

With the arrival of the serial in Germany it was also noted that instead of having only a limited time, interest in the theatre was held now for a quarter of a year. 'Die schöne Kathlyn wird nicht nur auf der Straße und im Salon das Tagesgespräch sein, sondern den Gesprächsstoff liefern für ein Vierteljahr'.[9] Promotional materials were therefore even more important and they were announced as such in advertisements. Unlike serial advertisements in American film journals, no graphic images of action and danger accompanied the film campaign (Fig. 1).

Kathlyn never seems to have made it from England in its original form. When the Eclipse Company, Selig's representative in Berlin, advertised the serial again three months after the first promotions, it had eight episodes of a 1000 meters.[10] Perhaps the thirteen-week release schedule was found too long and it was decided that the episodes should be longer. In the Netherlands such longer versions with fewer episodes were used from

Fig. 1. Advertisement for *Die Abenteuer der schönen Kathlyn*
(*The Adventures of Kathlyn*, 1914). *Lichtbild-Bühne* 34 (1914): 2.

1916 and on. A Dutch journalist once mentioned in a film journal that it was cheaper to fill a program with episodes of a serial than with one feature.[11] However, German feature films of the early teens usually lasted around an hour, therefore the adjustment from 600 to 1000 meters could also have been done to make it similar to the length of a Monopol-film.[12]

Unfortunately not much is known about what happened to *Kathlyn* when it was released in Germany. Eclipse had sold the distribution-rights to two companies, as a result of which *Kathlyn* popped up at the end of 1915 as part of the Philantropische Lichtbilder Gesellschaft's output. It was now advertised as a film of three 'Akte', not as an episode, serial, series or multipart film.[13] The scheme of releasing it in a distinct rhythm clearly had evaporated. From the other distribution company, the Dekage Film Gesellschaft from Cologne, no announcements have been found.

Irregular monopolizations

In these war years American serials were popular all over the world. However, apart from *Kathlyn*, no other foreign serial production seems to have been released in Germany during the war, even though American films could be imported until 1917. *Kathlyn* was in Germany confronted with a different environment than in America. The total length and scope of the serial made it attractive as a Monopol-film, but the distribution model of the Monopol-film made it difficult for an episodic production to fit in.

Distributors had advertised *Kathlyn* as a Monopol-film, not specifically as a Monopol-series.[14] Around 1914, only the very well-known stars were distributed and packaged as a series. Kathlyn Williams, who played Kathlyn, was no star in Germany. If *Kathlyn* had been released as a Monopol-series, there would have been some snags as well. The Monopol-series were not designed to be released like serials and were not shown in regularized time slots of for instance one episode per week. Monopol-series were released in a rather jumbled and irregular way. Before signing on to a series, it was not known exactly at what time the pictures would be released. The release would occur as soon as the film was finished. Advertisements of exhibitors made the audience aware of the fact it was part of a series, for instance the third film from the Mia May series. The effect of a series may have stimulated the audience to see every film from a series. However, a viewer could not form the habit of going every week or month to a particular theatre in order to see the next release.

It was from 1915 on that more and more Monopol-Series were put on the market. By that time there was a Suzanne Grandais series, a Maria Carmi series, a Mia May series, a Psilander series, a Hedda Vernon series, but series also existed for directors, like the Lubitsch series or the Richard Oswald series, or for fictional characters like the Joe Deebs series. Famous names were exploited as brands in order to secure a whole production line. Several times a year a segment of that brand was released to exhibitors, who often had not known any details about the films before signing on. Separate films could usually not be obtained anymore; it was only possible to rent a whole series. The films in the series did not have a continuing storyline; each film was a different story. With returning characters, like for instance the extremely popular detective sleuths, each time a new murder or mystery had to be solved. In order to create a rhythm with a more addictive impact, a serial needed to be released as a Monopol-series, but with a much stricter production and release form.

The creation of serial life

According to distributor Wilhelm Graf from the Dekage-Film-Gesellschaft, at the beginning of 1916 Monopol-series were getting rather irritating. Film distributors as well as theatre owners were under the obligation to buy a pig in a poke. 'Before it had not mattered that much, because it would only concern audience favorites. A weaker picture of these favorites would still draw enough people.'[15] Now, Graf complained, there were also series-films with unknown artists that were sold through big unjustified advertisements. 'It is already too late when the flop is noticed and it is getting harder to find the good series.' Another problem was censorship, which caused irritations when only three of the six films could be shown. Wilhelm Graf proclaimed that only series with really first-class stars and directors should be made, the rest had to disappear as soon as possible. It was not the producer, but the distributor and the exhibitor that suffered. Graf himself had until that time not ventured much into Monopol-series, apart from the unsuccessful distribution of *Kathlyn* back in 1914. Soon after his statement he would sign up for a few series himself that year: the Emilie Sannom Sensation Serie 1916/17, a Stuart Webbs detective series as well as the *Homunculus*-series (Fig. 2).

Homunculus, directed by Otto Rippert, was the first German Monopol-series that clearly did have a continuing storyline and that did have a production schedule of several episodes. The production company Deutsche Bioscop announced in advertisements that each episode had a self-contained storyline; it was through the character of Homunculus that the episodes would be connected.[16] *Lichtbild-Bühne* praised the fact that director Otto Rippert had succeeded in the hardest part, 'jeden Teil als Film für sich abgeschlossen zu gestalten, ohne an dem Gefüge des ganzen Cyclus zu rütteln und zu gemahnen'.[17] *Homunculus* tells the story of an artificial man created by a scientist, who wants to make a perfect creature of pure reason. Homunculus, however, resents the fact that he is not a real human being, has no soul and cannot feel or give any love, as a result of which he vows to take revenge on humanity itself. The six episodes, around 1500 meters each, had to be seen in order and were part of an overarching and continuing story, beginning with the birth and ending with the death of Homunculus.

The block-booking scheme of the Monopol-series fitted the serial feature quite well.

Fig. 2. Advertisement for *Homunculus* (1916). *Lichtbild-Bühne* 28 (1914): 46.

Rippert only had to adjust the freestanding Monopol-series into a connected storyline. Like other Monopol-series, there was no clear release schedule beforehand. From episode descriptions it seems no cliffhangers were used.[18] There was thus less pressure for the viewer, while enough interest could be created to see the next chapter. *Homunculus* provided a structure that was able to work inside a Monopol system, a system with, apparently, a constantly flexible schedule. When the first two episodes of *Homunculus* had been finished earlier, they were also distributed earlier. This surprised the *Lichtbild-Bühne* who reminded readers that often series contracts had to be rearranged, but usually it meant a later release instead of an earlier one.[19]

In Berlin's prestigious theatre Marmorhous, *Homunculus* was released over almost five months, with two weeks to one month between episodes. When released in Hamburg, there was a different irregular schedule altogether. Interestingly, about half a year later in the Netherlands, instead of a somewhat unclear release schedule, *Homunculus* was screened at one episode per week, just as had been done with two previously released American serials. Because of this strict distribution system, Homunculus' revenge ended in the Netherlands within six weeks.[20] The rhythm of exhibition and possibly the heightened addiction of the audience that was gained, meant however loss of flexibility. When there was a need to hold an episode for a second week, this could be done in Germany, but not in the Netherlands. Almost immediately after the serial had been shown in the Amsterdam theatre Cinema Palace, it was shown again, but this time in a different and cheaper theatre.

Power of distribution

To release a Monopol-series without a strict schedule was not without dangers. The changing release dates already irritated exhibitors. The many series pinned down theatres too much either to still be able to change schedules easily, to take up another series or even be able to show all films that were rented.[21] But not only exhibitors, distributors also complained that it was clotted. 'The market is flooded with film-series and in 1916/17 more than 40 series will appear', wrote distributor A. Czillard in *Der*

Kinematograph. The situation did not look very promising. 'Diejenigen Theaterbesitzer, die unvorsichtigerweise mehr Serien abgeschlossen haben als sie abnehmen können, spüren schon heute, dass es unmöglich ist, alle die Serien abzunehmen, die sie abgeschlossen haben. [...] Es ist meine Ueberzeugung, dass in diesem Seriensystem augenblicklich eine ungesunde Ueberproduktion herrscht und die unangenehmen Serienfilm die ganze Filmindustrie schädigen'.[22] It is easy to see how distributors were getting perhaps too depended on the series. *Lichtbild-Bühne* made an announcement (or perhaps rather an overt advertising) that the distribution company of Frankfurter Filmkompagnie was ready for the new 1916/1917 season:

> 'Wer Detektivfilms will, dem bietet er die Joe Deebs-Serie dar; wer für phantastische Abenteuer schwärmt, findet bei der Frankfurter die Phantomas-Serie. Weitgehenden künstlerischen Anforderungen entspricht die Hedda Vernon-Serie; trotz großer Opfer sicherte sie sich die Henny Porten-Serie, während sie andererseits auch die Treumann-Larsen-Serie nicht außer Acht ließ. Der Erfolg von „Nebel und Sonne" bestimmte die Firma, sich auch die Mia May-Serie zu sichern, daneben als Pendant mit der Maria Carmi-Serie zu paradieren. Für Humor sorgt sie durch die bekannte Müller-Lincke-Serie, den meisten Erfolg erhofft sie aber von den so beliebt gewordenen Alwin Neuß-Films.'[23]

If a exhibitor filled his theatre with only these series, a steady release seemed necessary and advisable. Manager and impresario skills were indeed needed for producer, distributor and exhibitor to keep such an organization on track. Adjustments were not welcome.

On 30 October 1916, not long after *Homunculus* had premiered in Berlin and Czillard had written his letter, the society of theatre owners of Groß-Berlin and Provinz Brandenburg came together to talk among other things about the "Serienfrage".[24] The direct reason for the meeting were the renting restrictions of the Henny Porten series from the Hansa Film Verleih. Hansa would only distribute Henry Porten Films to cinemas if they also rented twenty other films by Messter.[25] So it was not merely a question of block booking a series, but also a question of block booking extra films (thus corresponding to the American model of block and blind booking). *Lichtbild-Bühne* calculated that taking the whole series including the unwanted films would amount to one third of programming space.[26]

Many theatre owners, but also some producers and distributors, were present at the meeting. Chairman Koch protested against the series film deals that producers and distributors were closing. According to him, after the contract had been signed the producer had no interest in creating a quality series and it was in their interest to make it as cheap a possible. 'Der Fabrikant lege keinen Wert auf das Sujet sowie auf die künstlerische Ausgestaltung, und der Theaterbesitzer sei zu seinem Schaden dem Verleiher gegenüber zur Abnahme der Films verpflichtet. Der Kinobesitzer sei alsdann nicht mehr in der Lage, sein Publikum zufriedenzustellen und auf Gnade und Ungnade dem Verleiher ausgeliefert, der seinerseits wieder dem betreffenden Fabrikanten sich verschrieben habe.'[27] The notion that producers purposely cheapened their product was considered absurd by *Lichtbild-Bühne* (that in this Monopol discussion seems to have been more on the side of the producers and distributors than exhibitors).[28] It responded that there always remained the fear of the producer that the following season of a series would not be bought. But perhaps there was more truth in Koch's statement than what *Lichtbild-Bühne* saw as complaints by those who had set themselves the system of Monopol-series in motion by wanting to secure all films of certain stars. Film director Ernst Reicher admitted a year later that the costs of the Stuart Webbs series had doubled, and that he could not keep up the same level of quality as in the first episode of the series. Reicher, having no answer himself, wondered how it would be possible not get into a downward spiral and how to distribute the costs evenly.[29] If one also keeps in mind a remark on "Films außer der Serie", namely that films that turned out to be very good were suddenly taken from the series and rented separately, thereby lessening the series as a whole, it seems a Monopol-series could indeed fizzle out more easily with unpleasant consequences.[30]

The meeting of theatre owners was concluded with the decision that as of 1 April 1917 members were obligated to not make any deals over series. Members even authorized the board of directors to work as fast as possible to get all other associations of theatre owners in Germany to follow this decision. One however has to be careful not to get lost in the many conflicting and overlapping arguments. Sometimes the various interests are not as clear as one would like them to be. For instance, the consequences of the decision remain rather vague. While it was decided to not make any series deals anymore, during the same meeting a deal was also made with Herr Ebner, a representative from the Hansa Film Verleih, that from 5 April 1917 it was possible to just rent the Henny Porten series 1917–18, without any other films. However, there had to be paid a surcharge, the height of which varied according to separate agreements between leaser and renter. The board agreed with the settlement; it was to each exhibitor's discretions how to make the deal.[31] Whatever the consequences were, the meeting shows that exhibitors were pushed into the position of simply presenting the completed features of a production company, which they received in a continuing (though not steady) release form.[32]

Series were a welcome system of block booking and assured income. It provided producers and distributors with an important tool to push block booking even further, though the rising prices and unclear release schedules did present an unwelcome hazard. By mostly offering series, not much room remained for the exhibitor to adjust the film program. Some distributors however tried to capitalise on the irritations of exhibitors and specifically announced in their advertisements that they made no use of Monopol-series.[33]

Mistress of the world

In 1917 the *Lichtbild-Bühne* had mentioned in a reaction to the series protest, that perhaps block booking was not a good or fair system, but it was partly caused by the war-induced situation of having only a small distribution area.[34] Siegmund Jacob, looking back from 1922 as manager of the Ufa distribution, also saw the great need for product during the war as the origin of the Monopol-series. 'Wie in den meisten Branchen war auch bei uns der Hunger nach Ware größer als das Angebot, und aus dem Bestreben heraus, sich Ware für lange Zeit zu sichern, sind die Serienabschlüsse, die Vorausbestellungen von Filmen, die noch nicht einmal angefangen waren, zu erklären'.[35]

Indeed, immediately after the war less Monopol-series films were offered, even though still no trade was possible with other countries. However, according to 'Tb.' who wrote to the speaker's corner of the film journal *Filmwelt*, Ufa was one of the culprits who in February 1919 still acted rather aggressively towards exhibitors. 'Tb.' felt that the fear of foreign import was the reason for some distributors to advance their season 1919–20 (from 1 April to 1 February 1919) in order to clog the cinemas with German films so that later in the year there was no more room left for import of foreign films. He advised not to sign up for a new series including films that were not delivered until autumn anyway.[36] Ufa's ace in this matter was *Die Gräfin von Monte Christo*, soon renamed *Die Herrin der Welt*, which was conspicuously not advertised as a series, but as one big film

Fig. 3. Advertisement for *Die Herrin der Welt* (1919).
[*Erste Internationale Filmzeitung* 40 (11 October 1919).]

of eight episodes by director/producer Joe May, whose previous expensive Großfilm *Veritas Vincit* (1918) had been a huge success.

The titles and length of *Die Herrin der Welt*'s episodes were already printed in advertisements of February 1919 although the film still had to be shot. The release dates were also set and Joe May clearly noted that eight weeks after the premiere the final episode would be shown. As a reassurance, May claimed that the films were also understandable for audiences who had not seen the first episodes and that an advance notice at the end of the films was used to focus on the next chapter.[37] So five years after the failure of *Kathlyn*, in November 1919 there finally was a serial film with a precise rhythm of consumption[38] (Fig. 3). The enormous undertaking of a serial like *Die Herrin der Welt* could however not be done by everybody. Eight features of around 2000 meters had to be lined up and had to wait until they could be released in schedule to make profit. Costs were claimed to be around eight million mark. No serials of this size were made afterwards, it was rather the seriality of the two to four-part feature films that would be used in the years to come; Joe May's next film *Das Indische Grabmal* (1921) consisted of two episodes.

After the blockade had been lifted in 1921, adjusted American serials of around six episodes did also fill the screens. However, in 1920 already one of the first American serials after the war was released, or to be precise, re-released: *Die Abenteuer der schönen Kathlyn*. This time individual episode-titles were announced in many exciting advertisements, featuring explosions, animals and of course Kathlyn. (Fig.4) The further development of the Monopol-series, the success of *Die Herrin der Welt*, as well as the start of the expensive Großfilm had helped to make a "proper" feature serial release possible. Not only a rhythm of distribution was found, but also a striking advertising scheme was taken up. Incidentally, the length of the American serial was adjusted again. *Kathlyn* had this time become a serial of five episodes (with a total of 27 'Akte'), thus again corresponding more closely to the longer feature productions that were available.

Fig. 4. Detail advertisement *Die Abenteuer der schönen Kathlyn* (*The Adventures of Kathlyn*, 1914). *Lichtbild-Bühne* 48 (1920): 69.

Conclusion

For a serial structure to work at its best, a strict production and release form had to be in place, one from it was not easy to deviate. Monopol-series had made distribution of a package of films possible in Germany, but it also stood in the way of slick release schedules. Monopol-series clotted the distribution through block booking (and even block booking other films together with a series). Obviously, during the war there was a shortage and restrictions of raw film stock, which certainly would have obstructed a punctual production. The Monopol distribution pattern had plunged the market into a series frenzy that only with the end of the war was to become less. Monopol-series created at one point an almost endless supply of features that exhibitors just had to take. Shifts in power relations between production company, distributor and exhibitor took place during the isolation of the first World War, but it was a process that continued afterwards as well.[39] In fact it seems the huge number of two and three-part features that were produced as well as the many imported and adjusted American serials in the early twenties almost tried to recreate the Monopol-series effect. Seriality would on a smaller scale also be part of German productions well into twenties, not only with adventure style serials like *Der Flug um den Erdball* (1925) or *Die Frau ohne Namen* (1926–27), but also with artistic productions like *Die Nibelungen* (1924). The seriality that had evolved out of the Monopol-series would continue to change and play an important part in the further developments of the German film industry.

Notes

1. This article has been written with support of the Research Institute for History and Culture (OGC), Utrecht University, the Netherlands. Research for this article has been made possible by a grant from the Netherlands Organization for Scientific Research (NWO).

2. "Ein 8000 Meter-Film", *Lichtbild-Bühne* 34 (1914): 36.

3. On 8 July 1914 an advertisement appeared on the cover of the German film journal *Der Kinematograph*, which announced that the Gaumont film company would release a new sensational detective film in August 1914. On the cover a dark figure resided over a city. It would become a rather horrible but fitting entrance: with the arrival of Fantômas (it was he who loomed on the cover) the First World War started. Fantômas followed however more a series structure (apart from episode two). In Germany the episodes seem to have been distributed separately.

4. See also Dr. Richard Treitel, "Film- und Kino-Recht II", *Der Kinematograph* 500 (1916); and "Film- und Kino-Recht III", *Der Kinematograph* 506 (1916).

5. Corinna Müller, *Frühe deutsche Kinematographie: formale, wirtschaftliche und kulturelle Entwicklungen, 1907–1912* (Stuttgart: Metzler, 1994), 105–157.

6. Arthur Mellini, "Die Bilanz der Winter-Saison", *Lichtbild-Bühne* 32 (1914): 12.

7. "Ein 8000 Meter-Film", *Lichtbild-Bühne* 34 (1914): 36.

8. Ibid., 34.

9. Ibid., 36.

10. Advertisement, *Lichtbild-Bühne* 48 (1914): 38–39.

11. Felix Hageman, "Seriefilm of niet?" *De Film-Wereld* 51 (1919): 2. See also, Rudmer Canjels, "Adapting Film Serials: Multiple Cultural Models for the Cliffhanger in the 1910s and 1920s", *Film and its Multiples: IX International Film Studies Conference*, Anna Antonini (ed.) (University of Udine, Udine: Forum, 2003), vol. 9, 269–282; and "Beyond the Cliffhanger: Distributing Silent Serials. Local Practices, Changing Forms, Cultural Transformation", PhD thesis, Utrecht University, The Netherlands, 2005, 113

12. Corinna Müller, "Variationen des Kinoprogramms. Filmform und Filmgeschichte", *Die Modellierung des Kinofilms: zur Geschichte des Kinoprogramms zwischen Kurzfilm und Langfilm (1905/06–1918)*, vol. 2 (Munich: Wilhelm Fink, 1998), 64.

13. Advertisement, *Lichtbild-Bühne* 53 (1915): 8.

14. Advertisement, *Lichtbild-Bühne* 48 (1914): 38–39.

15. Wilhelm Graf, "Der Monopolfilm-Vertrieb", *Lichtbild-Bühne* 8 (1916): 16.

16. Advertisement, *Lichtbild-Bühne* 42 (1915): 32. The tagline 'self-contained storyline' was used in advertisements of American and European serials (with or without cliffhanger endings) of later date as well, if only to assure the audience it could understand the story without having to have seen the previous parts.

17. "Homunculus, III. Teil.", *Lichtbild-Bühne* 43 (1916): 50.

18. Two episodes of *Homunculus* are preserved in the Berlin and Prague film archives. There also exists a part of the 1920 Decla condensation, shown during the 22nd Pordenone silent film festival (2003). Original transitional breaks between episodes are difficult to pinpoint because of fragmentation and condensation.

19. "Was die "L.B.B." erzählt", *Lichtbild-Bühne* 39 (1916): 32.

20. Rudmer Canjels, "Serials in Nederland: 1915–1925", Master's thesis, Utrecht University, the Netherlands, 1999.

21. Alfred Rosenthal, "Die deutsche Kinematographie im dritten Kriegsjahr", *Der Kinematograph* 521/522 (1916).

22. A. Czillard, "Das Geschäft in Rheinland und Westfalen", *Der Kinematograph* 508 (20 September

1916). This is probably the same person as A. Szilárd from the Rheinische Film-Gesellschaft, see note 30.

23. "Für die neue Saison gerüstet", *Lichtbild-Bühne* 20 (1916): 50.

24. "Zur Serienfrage", *Der Kinematograph* 537 (1916).

25. Messter had set up Hansa in 1914 as distribution company to make him independent of regional distributors and to market the Henny Porten films. A similar integration of production with distribution had already happened earlier with another company. In order to secure exclusive rights to actress Asta Nielsen's films as well as director's Urban Gad's films, PAGU formed in 1911 the International Sales Company. Both companies used the Monopol-film to push their products. Peter Lähn, "Paul Davidson, the Frankfurt Film Scene and Afgrunden in Germany", *A Second Life: German Cinema's First Decades*, Thomas Elsaesser and Michael Wedel (eds) (Amsterdam: Amsterdam University Press, 1996) 85.

26. "Die Serien-Films", *Lichtbild-Bühne* 12 (1917): 12.

27. "Die Serien-Films", *Lichtbild-Bühne* 12 (1917): 12. More on the meeting in "Ein Protest der Theaterbesitzer", *Lichtbild-Bühne* 11 (1917): 36

28. According to *Lichtbild-Bühne* it was also the duty of the exhibitor 'to support the German producers and distributors in any way, in order to not obstruct the future of the German film production'. "Die Serien-Films", *Lichtbild-Bühne* 12 (1917): 46.

29. "Der Verkaufsvertrag für Filmserien", *Lichtbild-Bühne* 49 (1917): 12 and 16.

30. A. Szilárd, "Serienwut-"Kulturfilms"-und Propagandafilms, Cöln", *Lichtbild-Bühne* 52 (1917): 71.

31. Around May 1917, Hansa Film Verleih also had a Viggo Larsen series ('10 Filmen, Dramen, Lustspiele, Detektivfilme') a Bruno Decarli series ('6 grossen Dramen') and an Arnold Rieck series ('4 glänzenden Lustspielen'). Advertisement, *Der Kinematograph* 541 (1917).

32. On 19 March 1919 there was another protest organized by the society of theatre owners of Groß-Berlin and Provinz Brandenburg against the series block-booking practises. This time it was also about the unfair price systems. 'Herr Böhm von der Hansa-Film-Verleih G.m.b.H. forderte bei Abschluß der ganzen Serien 2000 Mark und für Henny Porten allein 4000 Mark pro Woche. ... Dasselbe Spiel wiederholte sich bei Herrn Jacob von der „Ufa".' "Aus den Vereinen", *Lichtbild-Bühne* 12 (1919): 38–39.

33. One of them was the Philantropische Lichtbilder Gesellschaft that earlier had released Kathlyn. Advertisement, *Lichtbild-Bühne* 16 (1917): 8.

34. "Die Serien-Films", *Lichtbild-Bühne* 12 (1917): 52.

35. Siegmund Jacob, "Evolution des Verleihs", *Lichtbild-Bühne* 37 (1922): 12. Jacob was once part of the Frankfurter Filmkompagnie who, as we have seen, in 1916 seemed to have had only Monopol-series on offer; Ufa had bought the distribution company in 1920. Klaus Kreimeier, *The Ufa Story: a History of Germany's Greatest Film Company, 1918–1945* (Berkeley, California: University of California Press, 1999), 30.

36. Filmwelt distanced itself from these opinions. 'Sprechsaal: Diese Rubrik stellen wir unsern Lesern zwecks öffentlicher Aussprache zur Verfügung, ohne uns jedoch mit ihren Ausführungen in jedem Falle zu identifizieren.' Tb, "Sprechsaal, Film-Abschlüsse für die Serien 1919–20", *Filmwelt* 5 (1919): 36 and 38.

37. *Filmwelt* 7 (1919): 62–63. This cannot be seen in the episodes one, four, five and six that are available at the Cinémathèque Royal, Brussels.

38. In the end the first episode was released on 28 November 1919, six weeks later than originally scheduled.

39. In the years to come Ufa would continue to invest in distribution companies, solidifying its vertical expansion. At the end of the 1920s 65 per cent of all films exhibited in Germany were distributed by 16 majors (Ufa, National, Südfilm, Bayerische, among others); Ufa alone being responsible for 19,6 per cent. Kreimeier, *The Ufa Story*, 68. Joseph Garncarz, "Production", *The BFI Companion to German Cinema*, Thomas Elsaesser and Michael Wedel (eds) (London: British Film Institute, 1999), 196.

PART V

PRACTICES:
Distribution paratexts

21

Les consignes de l'« éditeur » pour l'assemblage des vues dans les catalogues de distribution

Pierre Chemartin et André Gaudreault[1]

Département d'histoire de l'art et d'études cinématographiques, Université de Montréal, Canada

Une recherche en cours depuis une douzaine d'années a déjà amené l'un des signataires du présent texte à proposer une « théorie générale des opérations d'assemblage » dans les vues animées.[2] L'hypothèse de départ de cette recherche a permis de dégager trois instances susceptibles de prendre en charge les activités de fragmentation ou d'assemblage des vues, au cours des premières années d'exploitation du cinématographe : l'opérateur (qui œuvre *in vivo*), l'éditeur (qui œuvre *in vitro* et *in texto*) et l'exhibiteur (qui œuvre *in situ*).

Ainsi l'*opérateur* est-il souvent amené, sur les lieux même du tournage, et au moment même où il tourne (= *in vivo*), à opérer ce que l'on a pu désigner comme un « découpage *in vivo* sur négatif non développé », en ayant tout simplement recours à l'arrêt-manivelle, cette procédure consistant en une suspension *momentanée* des opérations de filmage et qui lui permet notamment de sauter certains moments morts, dans un défilé par exemple. Cette première forme de « montage » n'implique, au moment du tournage, *aucune rupture dans le support filmique lui-même*. Il s'agit donc d'un « montage caméra », un montage virtuel en un sens.

De son côté, l'*éditeur* poursuit des actions dites d'assemblage sous deux aspects. Soit par l'activité « éditoriale » qui est sienne dès lors qu'il juxtapose et regroupe les vues, sur le plan de la seule mise en page, dans les catalogues (= *in texto*) qu'il édite ; s'opère alors une activité *implicite* de « montage », que l'on désigne comme « assemblage *in texto* sur titres dans les catalogues ». Soit encore par son intervention, matérielle, sur les bandes elles-mêmes, qu'il coupe et fragmente, et dont il raccorde les segments (pour débarrasser la bande des images défaillantes que produit plus d'un arrêt-manivelle ou, encore, pour juxtaposer un certain nombre de vues, scènes ou tableaux, qu'il colle les uns à la suite des autres). L'opération suppose que, de retour en « laboratoire » (= *in vitro*) une fois le tournage terminé, l'on coupe la bande et qu'on la « re-soude » ou, encore, qu'on assemble des bandes distinctes (ou des fragments d'icelles) et qu'on les colle les unes aux autres. L'on est alors en présence d'une activité *explicite* de montage, considérée comme « assemblage *in vitro* sur négatif développé ». Il ne s'agit plus, ici, d'un « découpage » de la seule *action filmée* : le *support filmique* est en effet lui-même affecté par l'opération, et la pellicule (du moins le négatif) présente un certain nombre de hiatus.

C'est de la première de ces deux catégories, soit l'« assemblage *in texto* sur titres dans les catalogues » dont nous allons rendre compte dans le présent texte. Mais terminons d'abord notre premier tour d'horizon des activités de montage ayant cours à l'ère du cinématographe.

De son côté, l'*exhibiteur* n'est pas en reste en ce qui a trait au montage des bandes. On distingue aussi chez lui deux types d'assemblage, effectués sur le site (= *in situ*) même d'exploitation : d'une part, le « montage *in situ* d'un programme composite », de l'autre le « collage *in situ* sur copie d'exploitation ». Il s'agit de l'opération, pratiquement statutaire pour tout exhibiteur, qui consiste à juxtaposer et à coller, bout à bout, les diverses bandes des programmes de vues, ainsi que des diverses opérations de montage auxquelles l'exhibiteur a recours, de façon assez massive, sur des copies qui, ne l'oublions pas, lui appartiennent. L'amplitude de pareille opération est à peu près équivalente à celle qui prévaut dans le cas de l'éditeur. D'ailleurs, et c'est là un point sur lequel nous reviendrons abondamment, c'est souvent par l'exhibiteur que l'éditeur fait effectuer diverses opérations qui auraient pu lui échoir : la « commande » est justement passée à l'exhibiteur, comme on le verra dans le détail, par les consignes que l'éditeur formule à l'intention de celui-ci dans les catalogues qu'il édite.

Ce qui nous donne le tableau de la Figure 1.

Du côté de l'*opérateur* :

   Découpage *in vivo* sur négatif non développé

Du côté de l'*éditeur* :

   Assemblage *in texto* sur titres dans les catalogues

   Assemblage *in vitro* sur négatif développé

Du côté de l'*exhibiteur* :

   Montage *in situ* d'un programme composite

   Collage *in situ* sur copie d'exploitation

Fig. 1. Typologie des opérations d'assemblage dans les vues animées.

La présente étude viendra donc préciser, en quelque sorte, cette première typologie, du côté de l'éditeur. Nous consacrerons en effet nos efforts à essayer de comprendre comment, *en tant que « marchand de vues »*, c'est-à-dire en tant qu'instance *responsable de la vente* des bandes, et de leur *mise en marché*, l'éditeur est appelé à développer l'idée même du montage des bandes. Un montage qui, on l'a vu, est établi sous sa gouverne (par devers lui, dans l'« espace de la réalisation », pour reprendre l'expression suggérée par Roger Odin[3]), mais qu'il incite souvent à faire pratiquer par celui qui le suit, dans la chaîne des opérations qui vont de l'enregistrement de la vue à sa projection sur une toile : l'*exhibiteur* de vues animées.

Une attention toute particulière sera donc portée, ici, aux pratiques d'assemblage *in texto*, et aux consignes de montage contenues, çà et là, dans les catalogues de vente. Des consignes de la sorte consistent, dans lesdits catalogues, en incitations *implicites* ou *explicites*, encourageant l'exhibiteur à assembler une bande avec une autre. L'éditeur peut aussi user de quelque stratégie, visuelle ou scripturale, pour faire paraître les vues à la faveur de regroupements thématiques ou événementiels, ce qui amènera l'exhibiteur à les *montrer* (et, éventuellement, à les *monter*) les unes à la suite des autres. Les catalogues, faut-il seulement le dire pour s'en convaincre, constituent une source de documentation d'une importance considérable pour l'historien du cinéma, puisqu'ils

	SERIES "D."				
84	The Diamond Jubilee Procession:—Part I. The Queen's carriage preceded by Lord Wolesley, followed by the Duke of Cambridge and Princes, grooms, &c.	75	4	0	0
85 to 95	Parts II. to XII. of the Jubilee Procession showing the Royal carriages, foreign Princes, Artillery, Life Guards, Hussars, Lancers, Colonials, Naval Contingent, &c. ... ... each part	75	4	0	0
96	Boxing match between Toff Wall and Dido Plum, first round	75	3	0	0
97	Second round		3	0	0
	These two can be joined in one length.		5	10	0
98	Arrival of Royalty at Military Tournament and reception by Colonials	75	3	0	0
99	Parade of Grenadier Guards at Military Tournament	75	3	0	0
100	Opening of Victoria Era Exhibition by H.R.H. Duke of Cambridge	75	3	0	0

Fig. 2. Exemple d'une consigne d'assemblage, tiré d'un catalogue de Robert William Paul de 1896–1897.

témoignent indirectement des pratiques d'exhibition ayant cours aux tout premiers temps du cinéma, à l'heure de ce que l'on a, ailleurs, pu appeler la « cinématographie-attraction ». Les mentions dont il est ici question (voir l'exemple des vues nos 96 et 97 dans la Figure 2) visent donc, non pas les consommateurs de vues eux-mêmes (les spectateurs), mais ces « professionnels du spectacle » que sont les exhibiteurs de vues animées. Elles veulent en effet, pour l'essentiel, suggérer un arrangement des vues, *avant leur projection*, en fonction de critères déterminés par l'éditeur.

Les activités d'assemblage au niveau de l'éditeur

Les pratiques qui président, à l'époque de la cinématographie-attraction, à la *fabrication des vues* ne sont bien sûr pas tout à fait les mêmes que celles qui prévaudront pour la *production des films*, une fois que sera mise en branle, autour des années 1910, le processus d'institutionnalisation du cinéma. C'est, bien entendu, une situation similaire en ce qui concerne la mise en marché et l'exploitation des vues et des films. Du côté de l'« exhibition » des vues, par exemple, la donne changera complètement, on l'a souvent répété, dès lors que, vers 1908, les éditeurs cesseront de *vendre* leurs films aux exhibiteurs pour, plutôt, les leur *louer*. Les exhibiteurs seront ainsi dépossédés de leur titre de propriété sur des bandes qu'ils n'oseront désormais plus retoucher. Plutôt : sur des bandes qu'ils n'auront, finalement, plus même le *droit* de retoucher. L'*exhibiteur de vues* de la cinématographie-attraction sera ainsi bientôt mis au rancart, pour faire place à l'*exploitant de salle* de l'institution. Celui qui montre les films sera donc ainsi totalement exclu, par l'institution, de la chaîne de fabrication des films. Ce faisant, l'institutionnalisation du cinéma renforcera une tendance déjà sensible à l'époque même de la cinématographie-attraction : la spécialisation des tâches.

Bien entendu, pareille spécialisation n'est ni utile, ni nécessaire, au cours des toutes premières années d'exploitation du cinématographe, mais il n'est pas long qu'elle commence à se faire sentir. Les premières années du cinématographe, disons avant le tournant du siècle, l'« idéateur » de la vue prise sur le vif, c'est normalement l'opérateur lui-même, et c'est ce même opérateur qui fait, de facto, office de « réalisateur » de la vue (c'est lui qui décide de ce qu'il captera et c'est lui qui donne les consignes éventuelles aux « figurants »). Souvent, en effet, ces tournages sont le fait d'une seule personne, un opérateur, qui est, normalement, au service d'un « fabricant de vues animées » (lorsque ce n'est pas lui, aussi et en même temps, ledit fabricant…). On peut donc dire que, dès le premier bout de la chaîne de fabrication (*ab ovo* et *in vivo*), c'est toujours-déjà le fabricant (le fabricant lui-même, ou une personne à sa solde, peu importe pour nous) qui est, en règle générale, l'instance responsable de la mise en images d'un sujet filmé.

C'est cependant du côté de l'« édition » elle-même des vues animées que la fonction de « fabricant » trouve son terrain de prédilection. Une fois coiffé de sa casquette d'*éditeur*, le fabricant intervient en tant qu'*assembleur* des vues, par le truchement d'une manipulation des bandes filmiques, ou encore, comme on l'a mentionné plus haut, en tant que simple marchand de vues. C'est dans ce dernier cas que l'éditeur transforme, pour les pages de son catalogue, le texte filmique en un texte scriptural et qu'il y juxtapose les vues selon un ordre et une disposition qui aura souvent comme finalité d'inciter l'exhibiteur à des regroupements d'ordre thématique ou narratif.

Enfin, *in situ* et *in fine*, l'exhibiteur de la vue intervient à son tour, comme on l'a déjà mentionné, en tant que monteur de programmes cinématographiques et en tant que montreur de vues. Ce qui implique, de sa part, une participation active à la réalisation du produit fini tel qu'il sera proposé au spectateur (cela, sans même tenir compte des nombreuses autres interventions de l'exhibiteur qui viendront affecter le « rendu écranique » : accompagnement musical, prestation du bonimenteur, etc.).

On peut donc diviser les espaces d'intervention selon trois « sites », trois espaces différents : le site de la captation des images, celui de l'édition des vues et celui de leur exploitation. Une fois ces distinctions faites, il nous est possible de suggérer un nouveau tableau où les diverses instances impliquées dans la cinématographie-attraction trouvent leur place. Il y aurait, du côté de la prise de vues, ces deux instances que sont l'opérateur-en-tant-qu'-*idéateur*-de-la-vue et l'opérateur-en-tant-que-*réalisateur*-de-la-vue ; du côté de la mise ne marché des vues, il y aurait l'éditeur-en-tant-*qu'assembleur*-de-la-vue et l'éditeur-en-tant-que-*marchand*-de-vues. Et, du côté, enfin, de l'exploitation, l'exhibiteur-en-tant-que-*monteur*-de-programmes et l'exhibiteur-en-tant-que-*montreur*-de-vues (voir Figure 3).

	Prise de vues (captation)	
1.	Ab ovo :	L'**opérateur**-en-tant-qu'-**idéateur**-de-la-vue
2.	In vivo :	L'**opérateur**-en-tant-que-**réalisateur**-de-la-vue
	Mise en marché des vues (édition)	
3.	In vitro :	L'**éditeur**-en-tant-qu'**assembleur**-de-la-vue
4.	In texto :	L'**éditeur**-en-tant-que-**marchand**-de-vues
	Exploitation des vues (exhibition)	
5.	In situ :	L'**exhibiteur**-en-tant-que-**monteur**-de-programmes
6.	In fine :	L'**exhibiteur**-en-tant-que-**montreur**-de-vues

Fig. 3. Tableau des instances impliqués dans la fabrication et l'exploitation des vues animées à l'époque de la cinématographie-attraction.

Aux premiers temps du cinéma, l'éventualité de l'amalgame des six instances proposées ici est à son plus fort. Les distinctions que nous faisons entre les fonctions d'idéateur, de réalisateur, d'assembleur, de marchand, de monteur de programmes et de montreur de vues ne sont en effet pas apparues du jour au lendemain. Avant 1900, il arrivait encore souvent que les trois instances fondamentales que sont l'opérateur, l'éditeur et l'exhibiteur s'incarnent dans la même « organisation », si ce n'est dans la même personne. Il est vraisemblablement arrivé à un certain nombre de reprises que Georges Méliès, pour ne prendre que cet exemple, ait *lui-même* montré (en tant qu'*exhibiteur*), dans sa salle à *lui* (celle du Théâtre Robert-Houdin), des vues qu'il aurait non seulement produites (fabriquées en fait) *lui-même* (en tant qu'*éditeur*), mais du tournage desquelles il aurait été *lui-même* responsable, et pour lesquelles il aurait lui-même tourné la manivelle (en tant qu'*opérateur*). Ainsi, des premières vues de plein air qu'il a produites, en 1896, avant de commencer à proposer à sa clientèle des vues magiques et fantastiques.

Les subdivisions que nous proposons ici, pour artificielles qu'elles puissent paraître, veulent exprimer le travail d'instances en interaction, agissant les unes en fonction des autres, sous la supervision d'une « tête pensante », le fabricant. Il s'agit, avant tout, de désigner des opérations qui n'existent pas encore, techniquement du moins, de façon autonome, tout en en soulignant l'impact réel dans la genèse de la vue eu égard, notamment, à la vente et à l'exhibition de la vue. Autrement dit, il s'agit de voir comment l'« amont » pense l'« aval » ou, comment le fabricant est amené à anticiper l'exhibition via des suggestions d'assemblage. D'une certaine façon, cette pratique rentre de plain-pied dans les stratégies de vente des fabricants, ceux-ci cherchant par-dessus tout à fidéliser une clientèle disparate, constituée, pour l'essentiel, de particuliers, forains et conférenciers. Cette clientèle, à bien des égards, était à ce point hétérogène qu'il devait importer, pour les éditeurs, de proposer le plus large panel de vues possible tout en répondant aux besoins particuliers de chaque exhibiteur.

Avant que la distribution n'existe en tant que telle, c'est-à-dire en tant que procédé de contrôle des agents responsables de l'exhibition des vues, les fabricants cherchaient surtout à attirer, puis à fidéliser les professionnels du spectacle, tentative qui devait conduire, plus tard, à une relative homogénéisation des spectacles cinématographiques. Pour les fabricants, le procédé le plus efficace consistait, précisément, à vendre les vues en « paquets » plutôt que « séparément » et donc, par voie de conséquence, à proposer dans les catalogues des regroupements de toutes sortes, méthode qui avait pour but de constituer, avant même l'assemblage final, des programmes *déjà* cohérents, *déjà* homogènes.

Les catalogues comme antichambre de la « pluriponctualité »

L'assemblage *in texto* sur catalogue, dans la mesure où il consiste d'abord et avant tout en une *suggestion* de l'éditeur lui-même, et non en un assemblage *concret* des bandes entre elles, forme une catégorie d'apparence virtuelle. Mais il a très vraisemblablement donné lieu à des assemblages ou des montages effectifs, qu'il s'agisse de programmes composites ou de collages sur copies d'exploitation. Par définition, l'assemblage *in texto* consiste en une juxtaposition qui est toujours-déjà de type « inter-vues », puisqu'elle suppose la réunion de vues différentes mais complètes. Cependant, étant donné l'importance des mentions disponibles dans les catalogues, il convient de distinguer ces suggestions d'assemblage en fonction de leur degré d'« explicité », lequel reflète, d'une certaine façon, l'effort du fabricant à constituer préalablement des *séries* ou des *suites*. L'activité « scripturale» de ce dernier, donc, menait l'éditeur à opérer selon deux types d'intervention : soit selon une forme *implicite* d'assemblage, par le truchement de la mise en page des catalogues ou de marqueurs visuels, soit encore par des instructions *explicites* d'assemblage des vues.

VOYAGE

DE MONSIEUR LE PRÉSIDENT DE LA RÉPUBLIQUE

EN RUSSIE

606	Arrivée de M. le Président à Saint-Pétersbourg.
607	M. le Président passant devant la Compagnie d'honneur.
608	Défilé de la Compagnie d'honneur.
609	Arrivée de M. le Président et du Czar à Peterhof.
610	Suite du cortège passant devant l'amiral Avelan.
611	Officiers russes attachés au Président et Journalistes.
612	Revue de Krasnoë-Selo : Charge des hussards de l'Impératrice.
613	Revue de Krasnoë-Selo : Artillerie.
614	— — Cosaques.
615	— — Artillerie de forteresse.
616	— — Grenadiers.
617	— — Infanterie.
618	— — Pages.
619	Panorama de la ligne de Peterhof.

Fig. 4. « Voyage de Monsieur le Président de la République en Russie ». [Catalogue Lumière, 1901.]

La première forme, parce qu'elle reste relativement implicite, fonctionne à la façon d'une suggestion, et non d'une consigne : l'ordonnancement, la disposition, l'agencement même des titres supposent déjà que les vues se complètent. Les catalogues présentent alors les vues par *séries* ou en *suites*, dont certains éléments peuvent être « cimentés » aux autres par l'inscription de ce que l'on appellera un « sur-titre », à l'image du « Voyage de Monsieur le Président de la République en Russie » (voir Figure 4), qui encourage l'exhibiteur à regrouper les vues par assemblage. Le sur-titre, qui pouvait bien sûr servir dans la publicité destinée aux exhibiteurs, ne correspondait cependant à rien, sur le plan matériel – puisque l'on ne pouvait pas commander ce titre pour l'achat des vues (il n'est pas numéroté, on ne l'a pas affublé d'un nom de code télégraphique, etc.), sinon à une volonté, de la part de l'instance « éditoriale », de pousser l'exhibiteur à réunir plusieurs vues sous un même chapeau. À l'exhibiteur, ensuite, de mettre en évidence, auprès de son public, la cohésion du spectacle : l'exhibiteur en-tant-que-*monteur*-de-programme a la charge d'assembler les vues par collage ou d'ordonnancer un programme composite ; conjointement, l'exhibiteur en-tant-que-*montreur*-de-vues a la charge de commenter les vues et, donc, d'assurer la continuité du programme.

La deuxième forme d'incitation à l'assemblage de la part des instances responsables de la vente (de la « distribution ») des vues est, elle, tout à fait explicite. Il s'agit, littéralement, d'instructions précises adressées à l'exhibiteur pour qu'il se procure un certain nombre de vues d'une même série, pour les assembler lui-même avant de les projeter.

> 1228   NICE : Sa Majesté Carnaval et le char des
>   Limonadiers.
> 1229   —   Le char des Berceuses et de la Chanson.
> 1230   —   Panorama sur la ligne de Beaulieu à
>   Monaco. I.
> 1231   —   Monaco. II.
> 1232   —   Monaco. III.
> *Ces trois dernières vues peuvent être ajoutées l'une à l'autre*

Fig. 5. *Panorama de Beaulieu à Monaco I, II et III.* [Catalogue Lumière, 1901.]

La constitution de courtes séries de vues, par assemblage, était au départ sous l'entière responsabilité de cette instance externe à la fabrication des vues animées qu'est l'exhibiteur, mais elle pouvait déjà être suggérée et encouragée par l'éditeur, l'instance responsable de la mise en marché des vues. Ainsi, chez Lumière (Figure 5), de cette note inscrite dans le catalogue à propos des trois vues intitulées *Panorama de Beaulieu à Monaco I, II et III* : « Ces trois vues qui se suivent et peuvent être *raccordées* ont été prises à l'un des endroits les plus pittoresques de la Côte-d'Azur. » Un autre exemple, issu du catalogue de la Warwick (Figure 6), montre que l'assemblage est motivé par la succession de vues destinées à être montrées d'un bloc. Ici, la catalogue indique que les vues 7061 et 7062 se suivent et complètent la première, la vue 7060 : « This is a continuation of 7060, and includes the best views of this grand Canon » et « This is the shortest section of the most picturesque run and can be joined to 7060 and 7061 ».

En plus des mentions explicites poussant l'exhibiteur à regrouper les vues chronologiquement ou par thèmes, les catalogues contiennent également des remarques concernant les assemblages opérés par lui, sur demande (celle de l'exhibiteur, au moment où il commande les bandes). Il ne s'agit pas, à proprement parler, d'assemblages *in texto*, mais de mentions soulignant explicitement l'intervention *in vitro* de l'éditeur. L'assemblage n'est pas seulement *suggéré* via la juxtaposition de titres dans le catalogue, mais *proposé* en sus par le fabricant lui-même. Ainsi, de cette mention tirée du catalogue Gaumont de 1899 : « Les pellicules de 5 à 10 mètres de sujets différents pourront être

> 7060 ... **THROUGH THE FRASER RIVER CANON OF THE ROCKY MOUNTAINS ON THE CANADIAN PACIFIC RAILWAY**
>   A grand panoramic picture photographed from the " cow-catcher " of the engine. **Length 300 feet.**
>
> 7061 ... **A " PHANTOM RIDE " ON THE CANADIAN PACIFIC RAILWAY OVER THE ROCKIES**
>   This is a continuation of 7060, and includes the best views of this grand Canon. **Length 400 feet.**
>
> 7062 ... **PANORAMA OF THE FRASER RIVER CANON**
>   This is the shortest section of the most picturesque run and can be joined to 7060 and 7061. **Length 200 feet.**

Fig. 6. Vues no 7060, 7061 et 7062. [Catalogue Warwick, 1902.]

Scene XII.

At the Top of the Pole.

CAPTAIN KETTLE is here seen seated on the Top of the Pole smoking a cigar in his usual characteristic attitude, as if he owned the earth, the Union Jack proudly flying beneath him.

N.B. — The British Flag may be replaced, when desired, by the American, French or German, to suit various audiences.

Code word—**Arctic.**   Length **600** feet.   **Price 6d. per foot.**

Fig. 7. *At the Top of the Pole.* [Catalogue R.W. Paul, décembre 1903.]

réunies moyennant un supplément de 1 franc par fraction de bande. » L'éditeur peut également adapter les vues en fonction du public visé et s'offrir d'assembler les bandes dans cette optique, comme c'est le cas, par exemple, pour la vue R.W. Paul intitulée *At the Top of the Pole* (Figure 7), évoquant la conquête du pôle par un explorateur anglais : « N.B. – The British Flag may be replaced, when desired, by the American, French or German, to suit various audiences ». L'éditeur anticipe l'exhibition en adaptant les vues en fonction de sa clientèle.

Plus généralement, on peut aussi considérer comme activité de mise en syntagme de la part des éditeurs de vues la constitution de séries pour fins de classification des films.

VUES COMIQUES

872 Duel au pistolet n° 2 .
873 Un prêté pour un rendu !n° 2 .
874 La nourrice et les deux soldats n° 2 .
875 La nourrice et le soldat amoureux.
876 L'enfant au ballon.
877 Une farce à l'homme endormi (la mouche).
878   —   . la pipe en papier .
879   —   le pot de peinture .
880 Le scieur de bois mélomane.
881 Jean qui pleure et Jean qui rit.
882 Sérénade interrompue.
883 L'amoureux sans perruque.
884 L'ivrogne.
885 L'amoureux dans le sac.
886 Scènes burlesques devant un café. I.
887   —   —   —   II.
888   —   —   —   III.
889 Le remouleur et l'assiette au noir.

Fig. 8. « Vues comiques ». [Catalogue Lumière, 1901.]

Pour l'éditeur, véritable origine du discours tenu dans les catalogues de vente, l'idée de « série » est d'abord et avant tout une idée pratique, en vue de la « distribution » des vues. Il s'agit d'aider l'exhibiteur à s'y retrouver dans cet amoncellement de vues qui, avec le temps, paraissent aussi nombreuses qu'elles sont courtes. Il faut bien ordonner les vues, par catégories, pour aider le client à faire son choix. Les vues ainsi regroupées n'ont souvent rien à voir les unes avec les autres sur le plan du tournage. Tout ce qu'elles ont en commun c'est, en principe, de partager des sujets, des thèmes, de la même famille. La *série du catalogue* n'en reste pas moins l'antichambre de la pluriponctualité. Elle suppose une forme minimale de juxtaposition, même si les vues elles-mêmes restent dans le giron de l'uniponctualité. Il s'agit en fait d'une « uniponctualité à répétition » ou, comme on a pu le proposer ailleurs, d'une *uniponctualité réitérée* (uniponctualité qui consiste en un amalgame de segments donnant lieu à une addition de tableaux plutôt qu'à une concaténation de plan).[4]

Qu'il élabore des *séries* de vues sur des thèmes équivalents ou des *suites* de vues destinées à être présentées les unes après les autres, l'éditeur encourage spontanément le regroupement des vues en « séances » de projection ou, à tout le moins, en « chapitres ». Cette dernière activité consiste pour l'essentiel, dans le catalogue de vente, en brèves consignes ou en suggestions, certaines notules mentionnant ici les assemblages à préparer, là les possibles rapprochements à faire entre les vues. Ces notules et mentions diverses soulignent aussi les regroupements thématiques en opérant par juxtaposition de vues liées entre elles, comme c'est le cas dans la Figure 8, raison pour laquelle il convient d'être doublement attentif pour établir des distinctions entre titres et sur-titres.

Comment l'éditeur entre dans la sphère de l'exhibiteur

Les pratiques relatives à la vente et l'assemblage « virtuel » des vues aux premiers temps du cinéma montrent qu'il est difficile, pour ne pas dire impensable, d'envisager le travail de l'éditeur, c'est-à-dire du fabricant de la vue en tant qu'assembleur, en dehors de la sphère de l'exhibition. Le cinématographe, quoiqu'il constitue au tournant du siècle un dispositif de vision relativement nouveau, emprunte à de nombreuses traditions scéniques et littéraires. À ce titre, les éditeurs se soumettent aux conventions, normes et pratiques auxquelles les exhibiteurs ont recours pour la projection des vues. Conscients de la spécificité médiatique du spectacle cinématographique et de son potentiel commercial, les éditeurs ont très vite cherché à normaliser les pratiques d'exhibition en fonction de leurs besoins, soumettant aux exhibiteurs des vues animées destinées à être imbriquées les unes dans les autres ou, dans d'autres cas, suggérant des assemblages de tableaux pour accentuer, par exemple, certains effets comiques ou compléter des séries documentaires.

Ce phénomène s'est très rapidement accentué, on le sait, avec la mise au pas des exhibiteurs par les fabricants de vues. Les catalogues de vente témoignent, justement, de cet « assujettissement » progressif des exhibiteurs via la « distribution », c'est-à-dire la vente ciblée des vues par l'éditeur et, à terme, le droit de regard du fabricant sur l'« exploitation » proprement dite. De 1905 à 1915, l'on assiste à l'avènement et à l'institutionnalisation d'une industrie cinématographique, laquelle ne peut plus souffrir l'intervention des exhibiteurs dans la « diffusion » des vues. En contrôlant presque complètement l'« exploitation » des vues, en obligeant les exhibiteurs à se contenter de projeter des vues qui ne leur appartiennent plus (et qu'ils louent dorénavant) et en empêchant ces derniers d'intervenir dans l'assemblage desdites vues, les fabricants devaient finalement parvenir à limiter ou à empêcher les instances responsables, *in fine*, de la transformation des vues, à s'inféoder tous les intermédiaires situés en « aval » de leur propre champ d'action.

Avant l'institutionnalisation du cinéma cependant, le fabricant, ou plus précisément l'éditeur, ne se préoccupe que très indirectement de l'exhibition. Nous disions que celui-ci se présente à la fois comme un assembleur et comme un vendeur de vues. Deux instances en une, deux tâches distinctes : l'assemblage de vues et la confection de catalogues. Ces deux tâches concernent deux « départements » distincts : celui de la préparation des copies et celui de la mise en marché. L'opérateur confie au premier des deux départements plusieurs bandes cinématographiques, lesquelles peuvent former une *série* fonctionnant sur la base de rapports thématiques entre les vues, ou une *suite* fonctionnant sur la base de rapports chronologiques linéaires. À ce stade, l'éditeur dispose desdites vues à sa guise, en assemblant les négatifs développés. Au niveau du département de la mise en marché, l'éditeur suggère un assemblage dans les catalogues de vente. Ces deux étapes successives d'intervention, pour artificielles qu'elles puissent paraître, correspondent à deux réalités bien distinctes, même si, nous l'avons dit, il est impossible de penser l'assemblage *in texto* sans l'assemblage *in vitro*.

Le fabricant, donc, *conçoit*, *arrange* et *prépare* les vues en fonction de l'exhibiteur : ainsi, l'idéation et la réalisation de la vue, l'assemblage et la vente de la vue ne peuvent être conçues en dehors de la sphère de l'exhibition. Autrement dit, en anticipant la préparation et la vente de la vue via l'assemblage *in vitro* et les consignes *in texto*, le fabricant s'arroge déjà un droit de regard sur l'aval, c'est-à-dire le spectacle cinématographique lui-même. Bien sûr, là encore, il paraît difficile d'appréhender cette pratique sans envisager certaines réalités économiques du cinéma des premiers temps : les tableaux et les vues sont vendus séparément à l'exhibiteur et ce dernier, qui est à la fois « monteur » de programme et « montreur » de vue, dispose des bandes cinématographiques comme il l'entend. L'activité de l'éditeur en tant marchand de vue ne se limite donc à la fabrication des vues que de façon occasionnelle, celle-ci s'intéressant nécessairement de près, et ce pour des raisons essentiellement pécuniaires, à la préparation des spectacles cinématographiques, via la mise en marché d'unités filmiques destinées à être assemblées les unes aux autres.

Notes

1. Ce texte a été écrit dans le cadre des travaux du GRAFICS (Groupe de recherche sur l'avènement et la formation des institutions cinématographique et scénique) de l'Université de Montréal, subventionné par le Conseil de recherches en sciences humaines du Canada et le Fonds québécois de recherche sur la société et la culture. Le GRAFICS fait partie du Centre de recherche sur l'intermédialité (CRI).

2. Voir notamment Gaudreault, André, « Frammentazione e assemblaggio nelle vedute Lumière », in Quaresima, Leonardo, Alessandra Raengo et Laura Vichi (éds.), *I limiti della rappresentazione. Censura, visibile, modi di rappresentazione nel cinema* (Udine: Forum, 2000): 23–48 – article aussi paru en anglais dans *Film History* (Vol. 13, no 1, 2001): 76–88 et en français dans *Visio, revue de l'Association internationale de sémiotique visuelle* (vol. 7, nos 1–2, printemps-été 2002): 59–73 – et Gaudreault, André (collaboration Jean-Marc Lamotte), « Fragmentation et segmentation dans les "vues animées" : le corpus Lumière », dans Albera, François, Marta Braun et André Gaudreault (éds.), *Arrêt sur image, fragmentation du temps. Aux sources de la culture visuelle moderne / Stop Motion, Fragmentation of Time. Exploring the Roots of Modern Visual Culture* (Lausanne: Payot-Lausanne): 225–45 – article aussi paru en anglais dans *The Moving Image, The Journal of the Moving Image Archivists* (University of Minnesota Press, Spring 2003): 110–131.

3. Voir Odin, Roger, «Pour une sémio-pragmatique du cinéma», *Iris* 1, 1 (1983): 67–81.

4. Voir Gaudreault, André et Frank Kessler, « L'acteur comme opérateur de continuité, ou : les aventures du corps mis en cadre, mis en scène et mis en chaîne », in Vichi, Laura (éd.), *L'Uomo visibile. L'attore dal cinema delle origini alle soglie del cinema moderne / The Visible Man : Film Acting from Early Cinema to the Eve of Modern Cinema* (Udine: Forum, 2002), 23–32.

22

Cataloging contingency

Jonathan Auerbach

University of Maryland, College Park, USA

As part of an ongoing systematic study of early cinema catalogs, I propose here to offer a preliminary stylistic and rhetorical analysis based on over 3,000 British and American descriptions of early films made between 1894 and 1900. On the American side, I will be concentrating on Edison entries conveniently reproduced in Charles Musser's annotated filmography, although I also have looked at American Mutoscope and Biograph, and other American production company catalogs such as Lubin and Selig.[1] For the British films I have relied mostly on the catalog descriptions reprinted in the appendices to each volume of John Barnes' five-volume study of the beginnings of cinema in England.[2] I hope in the future to include French films from this period as well, although Lumière catalogs for one generally offer only titles and little else in the way of description. But for now I have confined myself to early Anglo-American cinema. Treating these catalog descriptions in their entirety as a kind of literary subgenre, I am less interested in reading them as historical documents that confirm certain facts about the films themselves. Instead, I see them as self-reflexive metacommentaries that reveal complex and sometimes contradictory assumptions about cinematic representation and practice.

At the onset let me clarify what I will not be doing. I will not be trying to match or compare these descriptions with films that can be seen in the archives, nor will I be offering a longitudinal study that looks for changes over time between 1894 and 1900, although such an approach is certainly worth pursuing. Nor will I try to tackle the tricky question of tracing authorship, or spend much time attempting to define exactly what differentiates a catalog entry from a description in a bulletin, a printed program, an advertisement, or a contemporaneous trade journal. For the sake of consistency, I have limited myself to the first and generally most extensive description taken from those official catalogs printed by the film production company or its affiliated distributor.

The first and most obvious point to make about these catalogs is that their primary purpose was to induce exhibitors to buy particular films, so that these descriptions essentially function as advertisements at the same time that they purport to offer objective information about the contents of each film. So as we might expect, there's a fair amount of hyperbole saturating the descriptions, particularly the Edison and Warwick Trading Company catalogs, which reiterate that a given film is the "first", "finest", "best", "unique", "most interesting", "different", or simply "splendid" so often that these superlatives quickly lose all meaning. Perhaps more noteworthy is the way that these superlatives are attached both to a nascent sense of implied genres (linked to content matter) and of audiences: how a given film is the "finest marine" picture ever made, or the "best negro subject yet taken" (E, 120), or how another film will be splendid especially for children. In the case of all three of these examples, hyperbolic praise extended beyond any given individual film to delineate and particularize broader categories of early cinema subjects and viewers. Such praise not only encouraged exhibitors to subdivide films according to different genres, but in effect actively helped to create and standardize these very genres.

Often a film's popularity will simply be predicted by assertion as the closing tag line of a description – "sure to be well-received". Or else emphasis will fall on a film's potential to incite particular emotions, as in the claim "promotes laughter" (E, 224). These are classic examples of the ad man's enduring faith in a self-fulfilling prophecy, in other words, that saying it will make it so. But occasionally the description will allude to more empirical data after the fact, such as one entry that remarks in the past tense that "this picture created a furor in New York" (E, 207), or another that notes than audiences of 18,000 flocked to the Eden Musee and Koster and Bial's the day after the film (of Admiral Dewey) was taken (E, 733). Beyond the issue of popularity, a fair number of descriptions include suggestions or instructions to exhibitors about how to show film: which ones would make a "good opening picture", for example, or how to build a sequence of films, or what sort of music might serve as an effective accompaniment. An exhibitor clearly would be more likely to purchase a film or set of films if he knew exactly what to do with it – how to maximize his investment.

Such explicit instructions to exhibitors lead me to my second point: that virtually all of these early descriptions are preoccupied with the materiality of the film medium. By 1898 the catch phrase "sharp and clear" is so pervasive, with very little variation (sometimes "distinct" or "clearly defined"), that to omit the phrase from a description would suggest that the film in question was hardly visible.[3] And yet running counter to this focus on the clarity of the film, that which can be seen with absolute transparency, there's an equal if not greater emphasis on "effects", particularly those effects that veil or obscure translucency: "smoke", "steam", "wave", "water", "fire", and (my favorite) "horse", to name the most common. Derived from eighteenth-century stagecraft as well as the history of optics, "effects" emerges as a crucial shorthand term early on (1894) in these descriptions, cutting across categories of genre.[4] We find the word used most frequently in the Edison catalogs, where the word seems uncannily to anticipate Hollywood's subsequent obsession with flashy "special effects". The British, on the other hand, use the term a bit more sparingly, preferring the qualifier "effective". Such a shift from noun to adjective allows the British catalogs to call attention to the "detail" or contents of a given film, in other words, the wealth of information it presents, or the fact that it contains "human interest" (B, vol. IV, p. 200, 9) or "historical interest".

The contradiction or at least tension between the phrase "sharp and clear" and the word "effect" is often elided or finessed in these descriptions by a loose appeal to mimesis more generally. The adjective "realistic" shows up on occasion, the noun "realism" more infrequently, while the phrases "true to life" or "full of life" are quite pervasive, even though what "life" means here remains a bit obscure. In the British catalogues, particularly Robert Paul's, the term "natural" (B, vol. IV, p. 216, 8) is invoked in quite interesting ways, often paired with a "but" or an "although" in contrast with a film's humor ("comic but natural"), as if the elements of a film that make it natural and those that make it funny were somehow at odds with one another. Paul is also unusual for mentioning the role of acting in his films, often describing them as "well-acted", which I take to signal his acute awareness of the expressive human form and face at the heart of his endeavors. In his earliest catalog entries of story films dating from 1898, for example, we find an intense effort not simply to describe but rather to interpret the inner emotions driving gesture and movement. Actions are called "impudent", "conceited", or "clumsy", or said to be taken "in disgust" (B, vol. III, p. 174, 1). Within a year or two this sort of active attempt to penetrate into the interiority of figures gives way to more externalized accounts in keeping with Edison, Warwick, and others, now letting exhibitors and audiences make such inferences for themselves.

If the mystery of human motive triggers one sort of interpretative self-consciousness in some of these descriptions, another sort of self-consciousness centers on the early cinematic apparatus itself. Cecil Hepworth catalogs are especially interesting in this respect. Many of his earliest descriptions from November 1899 (appearing in a WTC catalog published the same month and year) make explicit reference to the placement of the camera and how such placement affected the picture. Perhaps aiming at aspiring cinematographers in addition to exhibitors, these descriptions rhetorically serve to educate rather than simply sell. Describing a river Thames panorama, one entry reads: "The picture is taken from the front of a steam launch traveling up-stream and passing under the bridge. The stereoscopic effect sometimes associated with these pictures is well shown in this..." (B, vol. IV, p. 200, 9). Another links fixed camera position to matters of composition, concluding a polo match description by noting: "Some interesting bits of play come within the scope of the film" (B, vol. IV, p. 202, 21). A third description raises the issue of duration: "During the period of the picture no less than three Express Trains rush through ..." (B, vol. IV, p. 198, 1).

The question of duration highlighted in this entry leads me to my final point: how a good number of these descriptions foreground the coincidental, the accidental, the unforeseen and unexpected, in other words, the contingent. The theoretical significance of contingency for early cinema has been cogently examined in a recent book by Mary Ann Doane, *The Emergence of Cinematic Time*, but the practical, textual traces of this desire to represent happenstance can be detected in the catalogue descriptions themselves.[5] Looking for patterns in these descriptions, we see that certain subjects would seem to invite the contingent or "entirely unpremeditated', as one entry (B, vol. IV, p. 251, 5279) puts it: water rescues, children at play, uncontrolled animals, storms, fire runs, military battles, and street scenes such as Edison's *Arrest in Chinatown* (E, 397). With fire runs and rescues, as I have previously argued, the concept of practice helps mediate the distinction between a "real" event and a "fake" one.[6] Many of the Edison runs, for example, represent firemen in their training routine planning and preparing for fire by going out on exhibition runs. Often an entry, in a wonderfully ambiguous phrase, will insist that a clip shows the "actual process" of rescue or firefighting. Yet this is a far cry from filming a "pre-arranged" catastrophe or a disaster "made to order" such as the staged spectacle of two trains colliding (E, 162). Edison catalogues for the most part are not forthcoming about whether a particular run or rescue is practice or the real thing (which is quite unlikely). But when something startling is captured on film, such as a horse suddenly slipping during a McKinley parade, the description is sure to foreground the lucky event: "This film is one of much interest as it shows the accident of the day" (E, 293). Another Edison entry makes an even stronger point of emphasizing "the very strange coincidence" (E, 767) that produces an incongruous sudden juxtaposition between traditional and modern modes of transportation, a source of unintended humor, when in the midst of an automobile parade two old ladies drive by in an old buggy drawn by a mule.

Beyond the sheer novelty of shooting something that would allow a film company, from a marketing perspective, to differentiate its products from the predictable ones of its competitors, this emphasis on the fleeting and ephemeral, as Doane suggests, would seem to lie at the heart of early cinema representation. The contingent confers authenticity, with one catalogue entry after another taking pains to stress that its pictures are not "pre-arranged". This is especially true in the case of battles. Edison catalogues would rarely explicitly label a reenactment as such, but to sharpen the contrast between "real" and "fake" a WTC Boer War scene from 1900 insists: "This and the following films are the only subjects yet photographed while the guns were in action (not prearranged for the occasion)" (B, vol. V, p. 224, 5722), while the very next entry (5723) reminds us that "very few of the thousands of people who will see the reproduction of these films 'will think of the poor devil who turned the handle of the camera'." Here the contingent is fused with self-consciousness about the apparatus (and the real risks to its heroic operator) in order to reinforce the authority of the film.

In certain entries the accidental occasion and the vigilance of the cameraman are similarly described as coming together to produce striking results: "Our artist seized the opportune moment to catch this picture…" (E, 503). While "artist" is a relatively uncommon term to refer to the camera operator, it works effectively in this case to enhance the skill and foresight of the human agent over the seeming randomness of the action itself. Although audiences and exhibitors didn't want to believe that these actuality films were simply staged for their benefit, neither did they easily accept that they magically appeared without some controlling human intervention. We find this sort of delicate balance negotiated in an unusually suggestive entry from the International Film Company (winter, 1897–8) for a film entitled *Drowning Scene at Rockaway* that is remarkable enough to quote in full:

> This is one of the most thrilling and realistic scenes ever offered to the public. Showing party of four persons struggling in the water, and their unsuccessful attempts to right one of their boats which has capsized. After repeated efforts, one of the gentlemen finally succeeds in getting the lady and himself on top of the keel, (which is still uppermost), only to fall over backwards at the first wave. By a fortunate coincidence our operator was on the spot at the time of this accident and availed himself of the opportunity to secure this picture for exhibition purposes. An immense hit at the New York beaches. Very sharp and clear.[7]

This single entry contains virtually every kind of catalog convention that I've discussed so far: hyperbolic superlatives about the film's quality, both in terms of affect ("most thrilling") and mimesis ("realistic"); an attention to the materiality of the medium ("Very sharp and clear"); claims about the film's popularity ("an immense hit") localized for a particular audience ("New York beaches"), although it's a bit odd to think that a film about drowning would so appeal to swimmers; and finally, a preoccupation with the contingent ("By a fortunate coincidence"), combined with the cameraman ("on the spot") and the apparatus ('for exhibition purposes"). Unfortunately the actual film in question no longer exists.[8] While it is most probable that this drowning was staged, like Edison's picturing of lifeguards practicing sea rescues, in its depiction of "on the spot" filming the unsettling description does not bother to reveal the ultimate fate of the four drowning persons. A kind of authenticity and suspense are thus purchased at the expense of the credible, but what exhibitor could have resisted buying this film, if only to find out what happened in the end?

Let me conclude by briefly bringing up a few curious anomalies to this code of the authentic, contingent moment – a convention that dominates many of these early cinema catalog descriptions. Such anomalies serve as the exceptions that prove the rule, throwing into sharp relief the kind of assumptions that operate otherwise as the norm. Take this rather strange entry from a Siegmund Lubin catalog for a racist film entitled *Who Said Chicken?* (1901): "All coons like chicken…The subject is that of a darkey of immense proportions talking to the audience. The head occupies the entire screen. Incidentally the subject was that of a southern darkey, said to be 98 years of age. He has about three teeth left and they look like old fashioned tombstones."[9] While there is some effort to make the subject true to life by announcing the elderly biographical figure behind the blackface show, such an attempt is undercut by that abrupt non sequitur "incidentally", as well as references to the massive size of his head on the screen and the weird poetic simile comparing his teeth to tombstones. The entire description (if one can call it that) wobbles wildly between the real and the surreal. Although throughout this essay I've resisted the urge to try to attribute authorship, it's difficult to imagine that this passage's exercise in free association could have been written by anyone but Lubin himself, exuberant, irrepressible, colorful, crude, extravagant. Lubin catalog descriptions in general tend to be over the top in their salesmanship, such as this breathless description of his (probably duped) film *The Trial of Captain Dreyfus At Rennes, France*: "Here is undoubtedly a film that will make a fortune for its owner…The action is so real that your audience will be moved to tears, not to mention the excitement it will create, and many strong men will jump to their feet and show their indignation in both word and action. No film of any subject has ever been produced that is so realistic, and men who are wise will buy this film at once."[10] What's most "real" here is the overpowering urge to say absolutely anything to make "wise men" buy the film. A seemingly innocuous race between children, a rather typical subject for early cinema, presents another sort of anomaly that exposes a different kind of hidden agenda at work in these descriptions: "A very picturesque scene of small waves breaking among the rocks. A number of small boys have been induced – for a consideration – to run a race from a distant point towards the camera, jumping from rock to rock where necessary …" (B, vol. III, p. 198, 51). Here the prearranged status of the shot is not suppressed but rather openly announced, along with the pecuniary motives that inspired the boys' actions – the only mention of payment that I have detected in any of these catalogs. This insider knowledge further implies a witness present during the filming rather than a more neutral observer detailing simply what appears on the screen. Articulating what elsewhere remains only implicit, this brief glimpse into the business of early cinema helps us to see how such catalogs actively worked to shape exhibitors' and audiences' understanding of their films.

Notes

1. Musser, Charles, *Edison Motion Pictures, 1890–1900: An Annotated Filmography* (Washington, DC: Smithsonian Institute Press, 1997). Subsequent references to this edition will be parenthetically listed with an "E" followed by the filmography's control number. I have not bothered to cite very common short phrases that appear repeatedly in many different catalog entries.

2. Barnes, John, *The Beginnings of the Cinema in England, 1894–1901* (Exeter: University of Exeter Press, 1996, 1997, 1998). Individual titles and first publication dates as follows: *The Beginnings of the Cinema in England* (1976), *The Rise of the Cinema in Great Britain: Jubilee Year 1897* (1983), *Pioneers of the British Film 1898: The Rise of the Photoplay* (1988), *Filming the Boer War:1899* (1992), *The Beginnings of the Cinema in England, vol. 5* (1997). Subsequent references to these five volumes will be parenthetically listed with a "B" followed by volume number in Roman numerals, page number, and when available, original catalog control number.

3. See Gerry Turvey, "Panoramas, Parades, and the Picturesque: the Aesthetics of British Actuality Films, 1895–1901", *Film History*, 16 (2004): 9–27 for an excellent discussion of how matters of clarity turn up in early catalog descriptions. Turvey discusses a series of other concepts embedded in these descriptions such as composition, camera placement and movement, duration, and sequencing. Turvey's analysis resembles my own, although I draw on American examples as well as British, and am less interested in examining these catalogs in terms of aesthetics than in terms of their rhetorical appeal, intended as they were to sell films.

4. The OED gives 1736 as first usage for "effects" meaning "the impression produced on a beholder, hearer, or reader, especially by a work of art or literature". I suspect the optical, scientific tradition for the word, and the stage meaning come together during the late eighteenth-century, during the age of the phantasmagoria and other large-scale visual displays, such as in a 1786 handbill promoting "the most striking effects of Nature" produced by a variety of exhibitions and spectacles such as Loutherbourg's Eidophusikon (reprinted in Richard Altick's *The Shows of London*). By the mid 1800s "pictorial effect" was a common term for theatrical mise-en-scène.

5. Doane, Mary Ann, *The Emergence of Cinematic Time* (Cambridge, MA: Harvard UP, 2002).

6. Auerbach, Jonathan, "Caught in the Act: Self-Consciousness and Self-Rehearsal in Early Cinema", Gaudreault, Andre, Russell, Catherine, and Veronneau, Pierre, eds, *The Cinema, A New Technology for the 20th Century* (Lausanne: Editions Payot), 91–104.

7. "International Photographic Films", Musser, Charles, et al. *Motion Picture Catalogs by American Producers and Distributors, 1894–1908: A Microfilm Edition* (Frederick, MD: University Publications of America, 1985), E-002, control number 295.

8. Very few films exist from International, which went out of business by 1898. See Musser, Charles, *The Emergence of Cinema* (Berkeley: University of California Press, 1990), 247. Another entry from the same International Film Company catalog is even more astonishing, purporting to show a "genuine lynching scene" in which the victim is "swung into eternity, as bullet after bullet is fired into his swinging and writhing body". The description adds parenthetically that "(By our contract with the authorities names of party and place cannot be given.)", *Lynching Scene*, control number 301.

9. *American Film Institute Catalog of Motion Pictures Produced in the United States, Beginnings 1893–1910*, vol. A. pt. 1 (Lanham, MD: Scarecrow Press, 1995), 1185.

10. Ibid., 1093.

23

Comparing catalogues

Ian Christie

Birkbeck College, University of London, UK

For scholars of early cinema, the catalogues of the first filmmakers are obviously important, since they give us a more complete view of this period than would be possible from the patchy survival of actual films and other records. Alongside other kinds of evidence such as copyright records, trade press advertisements and company records, they allow us to be more 'properly' historical by providing complete source documents, and so have methodological as well as empirical significance. Above all, they give a more complete view of production, especially in the very early period, when even copyright records in the United States are likely to be misleading.[1] In other countries where no such copyrighting was practised, catalogues provide the only primary source for production, and as such have helped to guide the creation of filmographies and programmes of identification and restoration.[2] Where the rate of film loss has been high, as in Britain, catalogues provide vital underpinning for understanding early production and sales.[3] In the case of Robert Paul, where only some eighty films are known to survive out of an estimated 800 produced between 1895 and 1909, they provide the best available documentation of Paul's activity as a producer and seller of films.

However, catalogues are not neutral or objective documents, but require interpretation like any other historical artefact. They are perhaps best understood as a genre that emerged very shortly after the pioneer producers discovered there was a market for their output during 1896; and one that developed rapidly as a competitive field of discourse, when non-producing sales agents began to appear on the scene. The character of the early market in 1896–7, and its use of what are as yet little more than price lists, can be gauged from Stephen Herbert's published anthology of catalogues from the Slade Collection.[4] But even among these, a contrast emerges between the strictly descriptive titles provided by the Lumière agents Fuerst Bros. and Philipp Wolff and the discreet salesmanship employed by Maguire & Baucus for their Edison subjects and by Paul, both of which use 'fine' and 'especially fine in colours' to promote selected titles.

These early catalogues also advertise projection and other equipment, underlining the fact that the pioneer producers were supplying films as part of a new apparatus, and were all established in other forms of business before film took off – Lumière in photographic materials manufacture, Edison in a range of electrical businesses and phonographs, and Paul in the relatively new profession of electrical instrument making. To some extent their advertising follows the traditions of specialist manufacturers, from optical instruments to mechanical and electrical equipment, couched in the language of quality, craftsmanship and service, much as this had been deployed since

To Old Friends . .

and

New Customers. . .

The Manufacture of all apparatus and film subjects offered in this Catalogue is carried out in my own factories, with the exception of a few special lime-light fittings of other makers included for the sake of completeness.

Fig. 1. A personal introduction to Robert Paul's 1901 catalogue of equipment and films.

the eighteenth century.[5] But if these are essentially price lists for objects, there is another family of catalogues produced by the manufacturers of 'texts', beginning with the publishers of books and sheet music. Here, some degree of aesthetic *evocation* had long been required; and by the latter half of the nineteenth century, with the growth of a mass reading public, served by cheaper printing, publishers were intent on developing strong 'brands' within areas of the market which they sought to dominate. Among the well-known examples of this trend would be Hetzel in France, who promoted Jules Verne's *Voyages extraordinaires*, and in Britain, Blackie and Son, with their 'Reward' and 'Stories for Boys' series.[6] Somewhere between these two kinds of activity and their attendant publicity, there is the most immediate precursor (and companion) to the early film business, namely the 19th century magic lantern trade, soon to be joined by the picture postcard business.[7] David Robinson has suggested that there were roughly three stages of development in the lantern slide sales catalogue, starting with brief lists in pamphlet form in the 1850s, followed by substantial 'reper-toire' catalogues of between 2000–3000 titles by the 1870s.[8] Finally came the 'monu-mental' catalogues of the 1880s and 90s, such as Hughes's with 170 illustrated pages; and Newtons', with 1200 pages detailing between 100,000 and 200,000 slides.[9]

On a more modest and accelerated scale, it would appear that film catalogues – at least in Britain – recapitulated these stages, moving from single-page lists and handbills in 1896–7, to more developed pamphlets between 1898 and 1903, followed by the most encyclopaedic – from Warwick, Paul, Cecil Hepworth and, after he left Warwick in 1903 to trade in his own name, Charles Urban. Urban's 'Urbanora' catalogue listed a massive collection of non-fiction subjects which he continued to distribute even after the new long fiction film began to re-shape the cinema industry from 1910 onwards.[10] By this date, the importance of catalogues had sharply declined, with trade advertising and eventually regional sales representatives playing a more important role. It may be

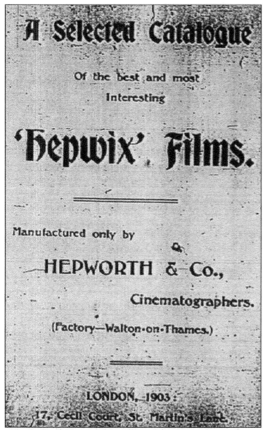

Fig. 2. Cecil Hepworth's substantial 1903 catalogue, from the climax of the 'catalogue' period.

that the climax of the catalogue as the principal form of communication between film suppliers and customers was quite short, from about 1902 to 1906.

The most extensive series of early British catalogues that have been preserved are those of Paul and by reading these in counterpoint to Hepworth, Williamson and others, some kind of industry trajectory can perhaps be deduced.[11] Paul's *Illustrated Catalogue* of August 1898 is a substantial 32 page booklet, identified as 'List no. 15', and while this states that 'supplements are issued at intervals' it is clearly intended to be kept for reference.[12] Apart from the large number of well-reproduced frame-stills (thirteen full pages, with six on each page), which would seem to make this the earliest illustrated film catalogue, the most striking feature is the catalogue's international address: each film has its 'code-word' (Paul's distinctive ordering system) in German and French as well as English. This often involves more than literal translation, as the code-words – the forerunners of the formal titles that Paul was using by 1900 – are intended to summarise the film's theme or most striking feature. Hence *Kitchen*, a variation on the 'servant's courtship' theme, in which the mistress discovers her servant's young man being entertained and sends for the police, is entitled *Küchenglocke* and *Découverte*; while what has become *Come Along, Do!* by 1900 – Paul's famous two-shot film about an elderly visitor to an art exhibition coming across a nude statue, to his wife's annoyance – is here *Exhibition* and *Bildergallerie* in German, but *Choquée* in French. By 1900, however, the translations have disappeared, which may indicate either that Paul's trade with the Continent had diminished, or that it no longer depended on such tokens of internationalism.

If we compare the catalogues of two leading British producers of the second phase, Paul and Hepworth, several interesting trends become apparent. First, in addition to the discourses of 'quality' and 'service' which are also broadly typical of all specialist suppliers of this period, there is also a strong sense of the producer as an individual addressing his emerging clientele. This is particularly marked in Paul's 1901 catalogue, which has eight pages of introduction devoted to a detailed and illustrated account of Paul's new studio and 'film works' at New Southgate. From the heading 'To Old Friends and New Customers ...', accompanied by a photograph of Paul, the tone is

ARTISTIC TITLE SLIDES.

Nothing detracts from the effectiveness of an Animated Photograph Exhibition, more than plain, crude or badly lettered title announcements. I have therefore, made a speciality of supplying exhibitors with good title slides and have designed a special series of announcements for my new films, an example of which is shown above. These are supplied with clear letters on a black back ground, and tinted in suitable colours. They are found to be much appreciated by the public as a relief to the moving pictures.

Plain title slides can also be supplied for any of my films, at a nominal charge, in white letters on black ground.

Special title slides, with any wording, are made to order at the shortest notice.

"Artistic Series" of slides, tinted	each	2/-
Plain title slides, from stock subjects	"	1/-
" " with special wording	"	2/6
Portrait slides, from any non copyright photograph ...	"	2/6

(Additional Copies, each 1/-).

TITLING FILMS.

When it is required to give the title of the film on the screen without the use of lantern slides, I supply short lengths of film containing photographs of any of my title slides, at the rate of 1/- per foot with a minimum charge of 5/-.

SPACING FILM.

Perforated to Edison Gauge, for joining up films.

White (unexposed)	per foot	2d.
Black (exposed and developed)	" "	3d.
Clear, printed with spacing lines	" "	4½d.

Fig. 3. Paul was a leader in offering exhibitors the means to improve their shows. Title slides would soon lead to printed opening titles, pioneered by Paul.

resolutely personal: 'the manufacture of all apparatus and film subjects offered in this catalogue is carried out in my own factories …'; 'every article supplied by me is the best of its kind …'; 'my experience in the manufacture of Animated Photograph machines and films dates from the year 1894 …'. There is also a detailed account of Paul's terms of business, covering preview facilities, methods of despatch, advertising support, account procedures, and information about the buying back of used films and the option to hire rather than buy.[13] Hepworth's large 1903 catalogue has an introductory note on 'Animated Photographs in Colours' which strikes a note of realism. After admitting that 'a great deal of nonsense has been written … in reference to cinematography in colours', Hepworth notes that 'we have never made such promises', before going on to claim that 'nevertheless we have approached nearer to the ideal than anyone else' with a choice of brown, red or blue toned prints. We do not know who wrote the considerable amount of text that makes up these catalogues, but the personalities of Paul and Hepworth are strongly present in their styles of address.[14]

A second striking feature of second phase catalogues is their tutelary concern with the presentation of films, and specifically with the 'shape' of the show. As early as 1899, Hepworth suggests that three films of the Henley Regatta may be connected: one is described as a 'corollary' of a film taken two days earlier from the same viewpoint, while *Henley Regatta – A Crowded Course* 'may with much advantage be joined to the preceding view and shown in connection therewith'.[15] Similar advice is given for a group of railway 'phantom ride' subjects, where *View from Rear of Train passing through a Tunnel* is described as 'of startling effectiveness, especially if joined between two of the engine-front pictures'.[16] By 1900, special attention is being given by producers to the thematic and compositional linkage of sequences within a show. Paul recommends *Flag*, 'a large Union Jack fluttering in the breeze' as 'forming a suitable prelude' to five 'Shipping and Marine Subjects', beginning with the launch of a liner, which has 'the vessel appearing to glide towards the audience'.[17] Here we can see a clear shaping

The British Navy.

181 "Curtain" Picture—Furling Sail on H.M.S. St. Vincent.

In this unique photograph nothing is seen at the commencement except a huge white sail which occupies the entire view! The lower edge of this is gradually hoisted, discovering a whole group of bluejackets pulling the halyards, and a most attractive effect is produced as the sail gradually rises and discloses the sailors behind. This film would form a most excellent opening picture for any series descriptive of England's might, or the lives of her Naval Heroes.

Length 50 ft. Price £1 0 10

Fig. 4. Concern with 'the shape of the show': a recommendation from the Hepworth catalogue.

intention; and this section of the catalogue finishes with *HMS Victory* seen firing a salute on the occasion of the Kaiser's visit to Portsmouth, described as 'a magnificent and stirring scene suitable for the close of an exhibition'. A Cowes Regatta group of six films is similarly presented in recommended order, with an 'introduction' and 'finish'.

A better-known instance of such packaging, for topical and dramatic effect, is the series of films covering President McKinley's funeral after his shooting at the Pan-American Exposition in 1901, taken by James White for Edison. These were offered in the Edison Films catalogue either as separate subjects or as a series of six linked by dissolves, under the title *The Complete Funeral Cortege at Canton, Ohio*.[18] In this case Edison also produced a special memorial subject, *The Martyred Presidents*, described as 'most valuable as an ending to the series of McKinley funeral pictures'.[19] In Britain, both Hepworth and Paul were giving thought to the opening of the show. Hepworth billed his *Furling Sail on HMS Vincent* (1900) a *'Curtain' Picture*, since the effect of the sail that occupies the whole screen being raised to reveal gradually the sailors behind 'would form a most excellent opening picture for any series descriptive of England's might, or the lives of her Naval Heroes'.[20] Paul, meanwhile, was offering 'artistic title slides' which could also be supplied as lengths of film, since 'nothing detracts from the effectiveness of an Animated Photograph Exhibition more than plain, crude or badly lettered title announcements'.[21] The example he illustrates is an elaborate mock-medieval title design for his major Winter 1901 release, the 'sumptuously produced extravagaza', *The Magic Sword*.[22]

In this transitional period, when film exhibition was still strongly rooted in such established patterns as the lantern lecture or musical evening, with many members of the trade still sceptical that moving pictures could constitute a complete entertainment, the catalogues provide important insights into actual practice. Giving the titles of films was clearly expected, and could be either by lantern slide or filmed title – or, presumably, by means of spoken introduction. The issue of lecturers or live narration has been extensively discussed by early cinema historians, and is complicated by the tendency of contemporary documentation to take it for granted. However, we find Paul offering in support of his *Army Life* series, 'explanatory and picture-slides', which he says 'are

(Third Edition.)

PREFACE TO THIRD EDITION.

" Rescued by Rover " has, we believe, already had a larger sale than any other cinematograph film ever produced. However that may be, we have certainly worn out *two* negatives, and have actually found it necessary to *retake the entire picture a third time!* It was universally admitted that the second edition was better than the first, and although we hesitate to say we have beaten that again, we can state that without doubt the third edition is in every way as good as the second. Many who have seen it declare it to be even better. Anyway, the difference is very slight indeed. The popularity of the picture is as great as ever, and repeat orders are constantly coming in to renew the films which have been worn out by continual showing.

Length and price remain as before.

No. 902. Rover takes a call.

Everybody knows now that the film "Rescued by Rover" is dead certain to provoke loud cries of "encore" wherever shown. It is not convenient to you to repeat the picture to satisfy the call, and you have to tell the audience that encores cannot be taken. But if "Rover" himself could come before the curtain and take the call as other great actors do, the demand would at once be satisfied, an excellent effect would be created and everybody pleased. Here is a dainty little fifty foot film which exactly meets the case. Just a portrait of "Rover," head and shoulders, the full size of the screen. The very thing you want!

LENGTH, 50 FEET.   Price, £1 5 0.

(METRES, 15.25.)

Fig. 5. Hepworth's *Rescued by Rover* was already a hit in 1904, and needed re-making as well as offering an opportunity for further promotion of its 'star' Rover.

essential where a lecturer is not employed'. It would appear that the lengthening catalogue descriptions of film provided from around 1901 were intended more to brief lecturers than to advertise the films. The catalogue text for *The Magic Sword*, Paul's longest film to date at 180 feet, runs to over 600 words and would take considerably longer to read aloud than the film's duration, but certainly helps elucidate its elaborately compressed story. In the case of James Williamson, already a successful lantern lecturer before he started making films, there is persuasive evidence that his catalogue text for such novelty films as the split-screen telephone comedy *Are You There?* (1901) and *A Big Swallow* (1901) are effectively dialogue suitable for accompanying the performance of these highly original subjects.[23]

Musical accompaniment is an equally important and much-debated aspect of the transitional period, but also one that surfaces only occasionally in the contemporary literature. It comes to the fore in Paul's and Hepworth's catalogues when both experiment, briefly, with films intended to be synchronised to live performance. Paul makes much of the four 'songs with animated illustrations' offered in his 1901–2 catalogue, noting that one of these, *Britain's Tribute to Her Sons*, has been 'specially composed for me' and that all were successfully premiered at the Agricultural Hall and St George's Hall in London.[24] Another, *Ora Pro Nobis; or, The Poor Orphans Last Prayer*, is a typically sentimental Magic Lantern subject, and was offered with optional slides 'completing the incidents', which hints at the contemporary concern over self-suffi-cient filmic narrative. Four years later, and in similarly patriotic vein, Hepworth would offer *The Death of Nelson*, an 'illustrated song', which is 'intended to be shown during the singing of the very celebrated song of this name, and is so timed in the taking that each scene corresponds [...] with a verse of the song'.[25] *The Death of Nelson* was supplied with a lantern slide of Nelson's tomb, intended to be shown during the introductory recitative, and with sound effects ('the booming of the guns skilfully introduced') 'a most impressive, stirring and impressive effect' was guaranteed. Both of these isolated ventures belong to the intermedial phase of sound-image relations, seeking to anchor the visual narrative in pre-existing conventions. Paul insists that his 'illustrated songs' are 'infinitely superior' to any recorded sound accompaniment, but did not persevere with such experiments. Hepworth, however, would launch his Vivaphone system in 1910 as part of the widespread renewed interest in mechanical synchronisation.

As the pioneers' catalogues mature, carrying only selected earlier films forward, they provide a valuable indication of what had remained popular. In an early example of an explicit remake, Paul's 1896 *A Soldier's Courtship* returns in an 'up-to-date edition' as *Tommy Atkins in the Park* in 1901; and Paul's pioneering 1901 Dickens adaptation *Mr Pickwick at Wardles* reappears without explanation in his 1906 catalogue. In 1905, Hepworth makes the most of the unprecedented success of his *Rescued by Rover* (1904) which had led to the negative being no longer printable, running the original descrip-tion, followed by a 'Preface to the Second Edition' ('owing to the phenomenal demand for copies ...') and a 'Preface to Third Edition', claiming that this last is even better than the acclaimed second version. To capitalise even further on this success, he also offers *Rover Takes a Call* as a 'dainty little fifty foot' curtain call by the canine star. Paul, meanwhile, devoting much of his attention away form the studio to records of exotic places and industries, would insist on the difficulty of filming his latest subjects. For his first series of Norwegian Films in 1903, he was at pains to convey how difficult it had been to persuade Laplanders to 'collect their Reindeer from the hills, and bring them down to be animatographed'; and of a panorama from the top of the Raftsund mountains, he writes, 'after many hours of perilous climbing, my operators were able to get to the top, and secure a magnificent picture'.[26]

A combination of factors brought about the decline of the catalogue after 1906 as the main sales platform for fiction films, although it continued to be important for non-fiction and films intended for amateur use. The growing number of trade journals carried descriptions of new releases, while an expanding network of sales agents and branch offices provided a more active form of promotion. We cannot take the earnest world of the catalogues simply at face value, since we know from other sources that there was piracy, 'passing off', highly variable technical quality, and much else to complicate the idealised picture they offer. But during what I've called the 'second phase' of the business, at least in Britain, the catalogues of Paul, Hepworth, Williamson and Urban give us the most complete first-person narratives of the emerging industry[27] – until the trade papers expand that account into a polyphonic, truly industrial discourse.

Notes

1. Charles Musser makes the point that 'during certain periods, fiction films were copyrighted but news films and other actualities were not', in his introduction, 'How to Use This Filmography – and Why', to the exemplary *Edison Motion Pictures, 1890–1900: An Annotated Filmography* (Pordenone: Le Giornate del Cinema Muto, 1997), 53.

2. The Lumière restoration programme carried out by the French Archives du Film was able to use the Lumière catalogues as a guide in its search to locate hitherto missing or misidentified subjects.

3. Ironically, although the survival rate of early British films has been dramatically altered by the recovery of the Mitchell and Kenyon hoard, these were not the subject of catalogues like those of other British producers, and the impressive analysis that has been performed on them by Vanessa Toulmin and her colleagues has made use of other sources and techniques. See Vanessa Toulmin, Simon Popple and Patrick Russell (eds), *The Lost World of Mitchell and Kenyon* (London: British Film Institute, 2004).

4. *Victorian Film Catalogues*, edited by Stephen Herbert, in association with Colin Harding and Simon Popple, reproducing catalogues by Fuerst Bros, Gaumont, Maguire and Baucus, Robert Paul, Watson & Sons and Philipp Wolff from the W.D. Slade Archive (Hastings: The Projection Box, 1996).

5. See, for example, the optician's trade card from c.1725 showing instruments and prices illustrated in Hermann Hecht, (ed.) Ann Hecht, *Pre-Cinema History: an encyclopedia and annotated bibliography of the moving image before 1896* (London: Bowker Sauer/British Film Institute, 1993).

6. Pierre-Jules Hetzel (1814–1886) was the publisher of Balzac and Hugo before he launched an educational series, *Le Magasin d'éducation et récréation* in 1864, to which Jules Verne began contributing his didactic adventure novels. Under Hetzel's guidance, Verne's *Voyages extraordinaires* became a major publishing phenomenon in serial and book form, continuing after the former's death. The Glasgow printer and subscription publisher Blackie became a major supplier of juvenile fiction in the late 19th and early 20th century when their 'Reward' series capitalised on a demand for school prizes after the implementation of the 1870 Education Act (see Administrative/Bio-graphical History, Records of Blackie and Son Ltd, University of Glasgow Archive Services at http://www.archives.gla.ac.uk/collects/catalog/ugd/051-100/ug d061-pfv.html

7. Changing postal regulations allowed the picture postcard to appear in Britain in 1894 and the earliest lists or catalogues of postcard series were published at almost exactly the same time as early film lists: e.g. James Valentine's Scottish views (Dundee, from 1897) and Raphael Tuck's series of twelve 'Views of London' (London, 1898). Several companies, such as Bamforth, produced lantern slides, postcards and films. See *University of St. Andrews Valentine Collection*, St Andrews University Library [n.d.]; J.H.D. Smith (ed.) *The Picture Postcards of Raphael Tuck & Sons* (Colchester: International Postcard Market, 2000).

8. David Robinson, 'Catalogues', in Robinson et al. (eds), *Encyclopedia of the Magic Lantern* (London: Magic Lantern Society, 2001), 57–58.

9. Slide catalogues did not disappear immediately after the arrival of moving pictures; and many companies traded in both media well into the 20th century. See, for example, the 1908 catalogue of Williams, Brown and Earle of Philadelphia, advertising 'Finest Imported Moving Picture Films' from Hepworth, the Graphic Cinematograph Company, Cricks & Sharp and R. W. Paul, as well as '40, 000 slides' (*The Edison Papers* microfilm, BFI Library).

10. Subtitled 'We Put the World Before You by Means of the Bioscope and Urban Films', Charles Urban's first catalogue appeared in November 1903. His second, the *Revised List of High-class Original Copyrighted Bioscope Films*, was published in 1905, running to 322 pages. See Luke McKernan, *'Something More than a Mere Picture Show': Charles Urban and the Early Non-fiction Film in Great Britain and America, 1897–1925*, Unpublished PhD Thesis, University of London, 2003.

11. Paul lists and catalogues that have been preserved run from 1896 to 1907.

12. Robt. W. Paul, *Illustrated Catalogue of a New and Original Series of Standard Animated Photograph Films*, August 1898. Price sixpence. (Preserved in British Film Institute Special Collections.)

13. On the early rise of rental as a response to the topicality of Anglo-Boer War films, see Richard Brown, 'War on the Home Front: the Anglo-Boer War and the Growth of Film Rental in Britain', *Film History* 16, (1) 2004: 28–36.

14. We do however know who wrote the text of the special catalogue for Paul's *Army Life* series, since the introduction is signed 'Robt. Paul' and written in the impersonal first person: 'it occurred to the writer ...'; the writer has to thank the officers ...', etc. Stylistic continuities suggest that Paul may have had a close involvement with his other catalogues. *Army Life; or, How Soldiers are Made* (1900), BFI Special Collections/Barnes Collection.

15. *'Hepwix' Films: A Selected Catalogue* (London, 1903), p. 12. Since Hepworth began production in 1898 and catalogued films chronologically, these numbers 27, 30 and 31 can be assigned to 1899, although their description appears in a later catalogue, which is the earliest that survives. See John Barnes, *The Beginnings of the Cinema in England, 1894–1900, vol. 5: 1900* (Exeter: University of Exeter Press, 1997), 156.

16. *'Hepwix' Films*, 17. These can also be attributed to 1899.

17. Robt. W. Paul, *The Hundred Best Animated Photograph Films*, Season 1900–1 (London, 1900), 13–14. I am grateful to Vanessa Toulmin of the National Fairground Archive, University of Sheffield, for access to this rare catalogue.

18. For details, see Charles Musser, *Before the Nickelodeon: Edwin S Porter and the Edison Manufacturing Company* (Berkeley and Oxford: University of California Press, 1991), 184–185.

19. Musser, *Before the Nickelodeon*, 186.

20. No. 181, *'Hepwix' Films*, 32. An *Unfurling Sail* was also offered as 'a most effective finish to any series of Naval pictures' (no. 204, 37).

21. Paul, 1901 catalogue, consulted in British Film Institute Special Collections [no page numbers].

22. See my discussion of this film, *'The Magic Sword*: Genealogy of an English Trick Film', *Film History* 16 (2) (2004): 163–171.

23. Martin Sopocy quotes Williamson's son Alan confirming that the catalogue texts were by Williamson, in *James Williamson: Studies and Documents of a Pioneer of the Film Narrative* (Cranbury, NJ: Associated Universities Press, 1998), 36–39.

24. The commissioning of this 'patriotic song', like a number of Paul's films of the period, was clearly prompted by the Anglo-Boer war, which is specifically mentioned in the catalogue entry.

25. No. 837, *'Hepwix' Catalogue*, 119.

26. Robt. W. Paul, *Magnificent New Series of Norwegian Films*, July 1903.

27. Discussion of Urban's catalogues, the most important for non-fiction, has not been possible in this short paper and these require their own comparative analysis, starting from Luke McKernan's invaluable work in his edition of Urban's memoir, *A Yank in Britain: The Lost Memoirs of Charles Urban* (Hastings: The Projection Box, 1999) and his thesis, already cited.

"As pleasing as it is incomprehensible": Film catalogues as paratext

Marta Braun and Charlie Keil

Ryerson University, Toronto, Canada; and University of Toronto, Canada

In his catalogue of 1896, Francis Jenkins characterises the power of cinema in terms typical of many such descriptions of this era: he speaks of the camera enabling the spectator to see "a scene [from life] again" and as an instrument which "is silent and almost mysterious […] like a spectre visitor from a strange world […] marvellous and almost beyond belief".[1] While early film catalogue rhetoric often descends into self-conscious hyperbole, it also expresses the efforts of manufacturers and distributors to put into words the capacity of a new medium based on photographic reproduction. As such, the film descriptions and exhortations directed at potential exhibitors constitute the fledgling industry's attempts to define the ineffable qualities of cinema. In their own way, these catalogue descriptions, often the only traces we have left to us of vanished films, operate as a blueprint for subsequent forms of film criticism, generating genre categories, offering ways of understanding the specificity of the medium and its possible spectatorial effects, and setting out criteria for appreciation.

As the chief aim of the catalogue was to assist the prospective purchaser in choosing films and to advise him in the proper manner of showing them, catalogue copy works at coaching exhibitors while also stressing the merits of the material on offer. For this reason, every film title is a gem, and the economic viability of a career in film exhibition a foregone conclusion. Therefore, we can hardly look upon the film catalogue as a reliable index of how manufacturers viewed the nascent industry and the value of its products, nor can we divorce the sentiments expressed from the traditions of rhetorical excess that salesmanship had already established even at this early stage in the history of marketing. Nonetheless, the persistent promotional strategies that emerge can justifiably lay claim to our attention as indications of those attributes of early cinema which its purveyors assumed would be most appealing. In this instance, attempts at defining the medium cannot be separated from a vision of film as a form fully competitive with established entertainments. Recast in commercial terms, what we encounter is still not so far from Bazin's myth of total cinema.

The catalogue works to reassure its reader of the proven popularity of films, and at the same time it stresses that the medium offers an experience different from any other type of entertainment. In the same way, catalogues sell film exhibition as a sound and time-tested business proposition while soliciting the interest of novice entrepreneurs with promises that no expertise is required. Thomas Armat's catalogue of 1901 favourably compared being a film exhibitor to setting up a legitimate theatrical concern, stressing that for cinema, the "winning combination is *cheapness* and *efficiency*, the qualities which a four years' test has already demonstrated to be the one possessed by the animated picture machine".[2] At the same time, Armat did not neglect those qualities of the medium that rendered it distinctive: "an audience can visit during an evening the remotest corners of the earth and see accurately and inexpensively reproduced the real, moving, actual life of the scenes visited. Such results, constantly renewed, can never go stale".[3]

Through descriptions such as these, the catalogue suggests that the essence of film is both a capacity to make immediately familiar what the viewer has never seen before and, by dint of its being filmed, refashion the prosaically familiar into something entirely new. It is in these descriptions that early film is, as Jenkins suggests, so real as to be almost beyond belief. The catalogue descriptions tell us that familiar material will arouse predictable responses and conform to audience expectation while at the same time they assert that the familiar, once filmed, also becomes completely novel. Here the banal is exciting and the impossible merely ordinary. Identified with life, motion pictures come to define it: only if it is filmed, according to these descriptions, is it a reality worth experiencing.

According to these catalogues what film provided, then, was the possibility of enhanced perception, or, as Raff & Gammon described it in 1896 when promoting the Vitascope, "nature outdone":

> When the machine is started by the operator, the bare canvas before the audience instantly becomes a stage, upon which living beings move about, and go through their respective acts, movements, gestures and changing expressions, surrounded by appropriate settings and accessories – the very counterpart of the stage, the field, the city, the country – yes, more, for these reproductions are in some respects more satisfactory, pleasing and interesting than the originals.[4]

With cinema's potential so defined, the earliest catalogues need go no further than to stress the specificity of the medium. Cinema offers pictures that move. Just as the stereoscope capitalised on the three dimensionality of the image, film mediates visual experience by replicating what is both visible *and* visible in duration. Although this sounds like stating the obvious, the catalogues emphasize the fact that the pictures move as a key aspect of their value, even when the movement represented is not the main focus of the film in question. And while "full of action" and animation are often cited as attributes, it is not just the excitement provided by dancers, cavalry charges and train movements that is being promoted, but the allure of such ordinary events as feeding pigeons or washing horses. And when movement does become the main focus of the film, the descriptions seem at a loss for words:

> In this scene, the camera was placed in the front of an engine going towards a tunnel at… 50 miles an hour. At first the effect on the audience is one of wondrous beauty, but as the train rapidly approaches the dark tunnel and is then plunged into the inky darkness, the effect on the audience is simply marvellous.[5]

Films are championed for their inherent capacity to enliven the ordinary subject by the very fact of its being realistically reproduced. The central irony evident here is that film's capacity to provide an unprecedented degree of realism was also its most obvious claim to novelty. Reality, as defined by the catalogues, has two aspects: the authenticity of the filmed subject and the unmediated nature of its representation. The latter includes the transparency of the image, its sharpness, clarity, size, definition, and the smooth movement of transition from one image to another – rather than, as the 1903 Lubin catalogue notes, "the sharp, jerky motion shown by other film manufacturers". Lubin's description of a film of the warship Columbia emphasizes how the quality of the film allows you "to believe that you are viewing a real ship in real water instead of her photograph".[6] This "quality" in early films refers less to the content of the subjects and more to their photographic clarity (or, by extension, their ability to harness attributes of photographic excellence, such as composition). Clarity guarantees legibility, and legibility affords the viewer the potential for perusal of the image. Accordingly, detail which might otherwise seem unworthy of notice becomes a major selling point of the films: "This is a clear and distinct picture in which the complexion of the bather and the white soapsuds is strongly marked";[7] "The charge retreat and salute make this one of the most animated pictures ever made. The glistening of the sabers is plainly visible".[8] As much as the film is prized for its capacity to replicate the normalcy of vision, it is also particularly valued for its ability to capture what cannot be fixed by the eye, ephemeral phenomena such as the movement of water, the fall of snow, the wake of foam, the swirl of dust or dirt, and the gushing of "Old Faithful".

The catalogue descriptions emphasize another aspect of reality – the authenticity and accuracy of what film reproduces. The figures are "life size", the incidents "true to life", the picture "full of reality": "The views are actual reproductions and are in every instance photographed from life",[9] notes an Edison catalogue from 1900, while another avers that "the scene is produced as it actually occurred. The figures are life size and well in the foreground".[10] As late as 1905, the reliability of the film's reproduction is insisted upon. In the comic *Watermelon Patch,* the description reads, "All of the watermelon thieves are genuine negroes".[11] To underline the authenticity of rendering (which, according to an Edison Films supplement of May 1898, will satisfy "a craving of the general public for absolutely true and accurate details"),[12] the catalogues often describe where the cameraman stood, or the conditions under which the filming took place. Here is a description of the funeral cortege of President McKinley from a 1902 Edison film catalogue:

> With the exception of the portion of the film where the President's body was carried into the City Hall, a pouring rain was falling during the exposure of the pictures. While the President's body was being transferred from the hearse to the City Hall a singular occurrence took place. The rain ceased falling almost simultaneously with the body being lifted from the hearse and the sun burst forth during the brief interval that was necessary to carry the casket to its resting place. Immediately the body had passed into the City Hall the sky became clouded and the rain again began falling [...] the view which we present of the President's body being taken into the City Hall is rendered perfect by the sudden bursting forth of the sun as described above.[13]

Another description of the same cortege in Washington offers a different perspective:

> Our camera having been above the heads of the people, a most novel effect is secured. As the camera rotates, the base and steps of the Capitol are brought into view and the crowd is shown crushing and struggling [...][14]

One encounters a constant reiteration of, and insistence on, authenticity: the correspondence of the images to the pro-filmic defines what is extraordinary about the ordinary subject and ordinary about the extraordinary. The latter includes not just the exotic, but that which is ordinarily inaccessible: the accidental and fortuitous. The catalogue exalts films in which the camera has seized accidentally on random events which are inevitably dire: a drowning at Rockaway is "one of the most thrilling and realistic scenes ever offered to the public" because "[b]y a fortunate coincidence our operator was on the spot at the time of this accident and availed himself of the opportunity to secure this picture".[15] The life saving services of the Pacific Coast life guard combine the fortuitous accidents with the crashing of waves and foam, while a "genuine" lynching, filmed in Texas (though "the names of party and place cannot be given"), is "thrilling and realistic".[16]

Ironically, both aspects of film's claim to total realism come to be an important selling feature of fiction: *The Great Train Robbery* (Edison 1903) "has been posed and acted in faithful duplication of the genuine 'Hold Ups'",[17] *Western Romance of the Days of '49* (Lubin 1908) is "enacted by real Indians and real cowboys",[18] and Méliès' *Monster* (1903) "possesses an extraordinary fascination" because "[i]t gives during the whole time the perfect illusion of reality".[19] Fantasy and puzzle films, on the other hand, are promoted precisely for the manner in which they *sever* the camera's reproduction of reality from the event. Where other descriptions tell the reader where the camera or camera man was positioned, in trick films the apparatus and technology is posited as mysterious. Almost all the Méliès film catalogues emphasize the films' "fascinating effects, disappearing effects, novel effects, and illusions", and the catalogue descriptions entice the exhibitor and viewer with a challenge to discover how the various tricks were accomplished: "here is a film that will keep you guessing".[20]

These aspects of the medium as delineated in the catalogue descriptions, eventually assume another function: by 1907 they marshal films into incipient genres. Motion and animation become the selling points for dance films, comic chases, fights (both between humans and between animals), cavalry charges, and races on foot and in automobiles. Authenticity sells the actuality, the travel film, pictures of other peoples and races as well as the drama; the filmic revelation of that which usually remains unseen sells pornography, while the kind, number and mystery of the illusions in the trick film convince the spectator of their value and excitement.

By this time too, stills from the films have become more commonplace – although the wealthier concerns such as Pathé and Lubin had been using them since 1903 and 1905 respectively – and the struggle of the catalogue writer to describe film's distinctness shifts from the task of addressing the medium's specificity, to recognizing its increasing affinity for narrative. A directive in the 1904 Kleine Optical Company catalogue anticipates the concern for narrative structure that will become central to the single-reel era and points to the way the story film will change the emphasis of catalogue descriptions:

> There should be no lagging in the story [the film] tells; every foot must be an essential part, whose loss would deprive the story of some merit; there should be sequence, each part leading to the next with increasing interest, reaching its most interesting point at the climax, which should end the film. A story which can be well told in 300 feet loses force if stretched to 500 feet, and is correspondingly weakened.[21]

As cinema moves into its transitional period, catalogue descriptions reflect the growing conviction that filmic pleasures are explicable, even calculable; images now supply the details which had eluded mere words, and narrative renders the mysteries Francis Jenkins once remarked upon a remnant of a bygone era of novelty.

Notes

1. C. Francis Jenkins Catalogue, July 1896, n.p.
2. Thomas Armat Catalogue, 1901, p. 8.
3. Thomas Armat Catalogue, 1901, p. 9.
4. Raff & Gammon Catalogue, March 1896, n.p.
5. International Photographic Films Catalogue, Winter 1897–98, p. 16.
6. S. Lubin Company Catalogue, 1903, p. 81.

7. Maguire and Baucus Catalogue, January 1897, p. 4.
8. Maguire and Baucus Catalogue, April 1897, p. 6.
9. Edison Manufacturing Company Catalogue, March 1900, p. 14.
10. Edison Manufacturing Company Catalogue Supplement No. 4, May 1898, p. 4.
11. Edison Manufacturing Company Catalogue, October 1905, n.p.
12. Edison Manufacturing Company Catalogue Supplement No. 4, May 1898, p. 2.
13. Edison Manufacturing Company Catalogue, September 1902, p. 14.
14. Edison Manufacturing Company Catalogue, September 1902, p. 15.
15. International Photographic Films Catalogue, Winter 1897–98, p. 5.
16. International Photographic Films Catalogue, Winter 1897–98, p. 18.
17. Edison Manufacturing Company Catalogue, January 1904, p. 5.
18. S. Lubin Company Catalogue, 1908, n.p.
19. Méliès Catalogue Supplement 1, 2, 3. 1903, n.p.
20. Sears, Roebuck and Company Catalogue, 1900, p. 52.
21. "About Moving Pictures", Kleine Optical Company Catalogue, 1904, p. 31.

"Liste für gebrauchte Films zum Verkauf": Used Films for Sale in Germany and Austro-Hungary (1911–13)

Janelle Blankenship[1]

Department of German, New York University

Selling damaged, junk, or surplus stock films is a distribution practice that is well documented in Victorian film catalogues and price-lists. Robert Paul's 1897 "List of films for the 'Animatographe'" (among the papers of the W.D. Slade archive) offers a surplus stock of films, already exhibited "a few times" in Paul's own shows, at a reduced rate of 20 shillings. There is an even greater rebate on what he labels "damaged films", now offered at 10 shillings.[2] Many distributors of early cinema felt threatened by such price reductions, as they were by emerging pirating practices. For example, the Fuerst Brothers based in London (the "sole agents" of Lumière cinematography for the United States, the United Kingdom, and the Colonies) warn the public of pirate dupe films "offered at reduced rates". Duplicated films, they state, could lead to technical difficulties, such as films being torn by projector sprockets due to shrinkage:

> The genuine films are accurately perforated, consequently in the duplicating process, proper allowances cannot be made for the two shrinkages of the film-stock, in developing, etc. This shrinkage cannot be readily detected in one or two pictures, but will amount to almost an inch in about 20 feet of film. As a result the perforations do not fit the sprockets and the picture when projected jumps on the screen, or is torn by the sprockets. This fact alone makes a duplicated subject worthless, as clearness is most important in a film, so as to allow enlargements to more than life size.[3]

This discussion of sprockets and shrinkage is immediately linked to the discourse on clarity that is so pervasive in the hyperbolic descriptions of early cinema catalogues. Fuerst Brothers warn us that "when duplicated, films become much inferior and almost worthless, as the sharp definition is lost".[4] This is the flip-side to the horror story of shrinkage; in the rhetoric of authenticity taken up by many Victorian catalogue writers, "clarity" is a rhetorical reminder that theirs are not cheap, unscrupulous copies, but authentic, no doubt expensive originals. Paul introduces his list of used films for sale in the same year by stating that his prints are made on transparent film, are "clear and sharp", true to gauge, and made to Edison standard perforation.

Dishonest distribution took on many forms, both real and imagined, in the early period.[5] The Fuerst Brothers' price list points to two types of dishonest distribution, here sensationally scandalized to the point where it becomes distribution deception. In addition to piracy, the brothers call our attention to the deception of circulars and advertisements wherein foreign films are offered at reduced rates under names that are similar to that of Lumière (Lemaire, Lumaire, etc.). To illustrate their call for clarity and authenticity, the list concludes with its own "signature event", an iconic image showing what a genuine film trade mark, stamp, signature, and standard gauge look like, graphically demonstrating the difference between Edison and Lumière perforations.[6]

"Film" is frustratingly unreliable or unstable on another level, as well. It resists classification by genre. The Fuerst Brothers urge their readers to carefully peruse their price list of 625 films, as they have found it "impossible to properly classify the subject". Why this uncertainty or illegitimacy concerning genre? When, if ever, does genre *cease* to be an uncertain category? In what follows I will speculate on the vagaries or openness of genre in the context of the early cinema catalogue and price list, using as my primary point of departure two pre-war inventories of "used films for sale". I want to suggest some ways in which such lists, as historical sources, can enrich our understanding of early cinema. Even while the texts seek to establish rigid signatures – criteria and code for judging the value of film material as object – they also problematize film's "becoming genre", becoming classified or classifiable.

If early cinema is simply a series of views, then why not forgo genre and instead count countries, if not accounting for style then at least geographical specificity or origin? The Fuerst Brothers list operates under this logic. There are "general views", "comic views", and then countries. France is well represented, but there are also foreign views from Germany, Spain, Russia, Switzerland, North America, Turkey-in-Asia, and Turkey-in-Europe, England, Sweden and Australia. Under the national categories the organization is not uniform. At times, there are topical sub-divisions, for example, military views, or geographical sub-divisions, cities. The final pages of national subject classifications dissolve into an eclectic hodge-podge of attractions: "various", "Ashantee negroes", "gymnastics", "clowns", further military views, royal subjects and imperial events and then "special subjects". While "special subjects" is certainly a proto-genre, variety theater categories such as dance, combat (Edison), or gymnastics (Fuerst Brothers) speak to a classificatory logic that all but disappears by 1910. The earliest catalogue attempts to articulate genre are at best, frustrated. Classic examples are Gaumont's 1897 list of 120 "animated views" (no genre designation necessary) or the Fuerst Brothers who throw up their hands in despair and say it is impossible to classify the object.[7] In contrast, Oskar Messter's pre-war inventory, "Liste für gebrauchte Films zum Verkauf", published late 1911 or 1912, is a highly focused presentation that no longer needs sub-categories or terms such as "miscellaneous" and "various". It generates genre categories that allow one to abstract from the specific or individual and move to the level of the universal.

Messter classifies over 450 films in his inventory under the following genres: (1) *Industrielle und Naturaufnahmen* [Industrial and Nature Shots]; (2) *Tierbilder und Naturszenen* [Animal Pictures and Nature Scenes (Expeditions)]; (3) *Dramatische Szenen* [Dramatic Scenes]; (4) *Marine, Militär, und Sport* [Marine, Military, and Sport]; (5) *Humoristische und Trickfilms* [Humor and Trick Films]; (6) *Spezialaufnahmen* [Special Shots]; and (7) *Aktualitäten* [Topical Films]. His catalogue's creative role is to draft a provisional "map" of genres to display and advertise early film. This list also documents the flexibility of genre categories in early cinema. Just as, in traveling cinema and magic lantern shows, one set of local films or landscape slides could be substituted for another or re-titled to meet the expectations of a particular audience, the travel films listed in Messter's inventory work on multiple levels, crossing numerous categories. A walk through a zoo in London is advertised as a "nature scene", a drive through the alps is advertised as "Marine, military and sport", *Corfu through the telescope* (a popular vacation spot for the *Kaiserliche Familie*) is marketed as a "nature shot" or expedition, and *Around the world by car* is marketed as a "special shot".[8] Seven films from a Raleigh & Roberts (Warwick) travelogue series on Africa (1907–08) are also listed under the two separate, but obviously related ethnographic genres,[9] the "industrial and nature shots" and "animal and nature scenes". Unlike Paul, who assures exhibitors that his used prints are "carefully tested before being packed", Messter states that his films are sold as is "without guarantee as to exact length and condition".[10] In his list of over 450 titles there is only one film that he highlights as a recent acquisition, *Willys Zauberstab* [*Willy's Magic Wand*, 1908 Eclipse], now described as "new". To be sure, the used film inventory is a catalogue stripped bare: It consists of skeletal outlines of the films themselves: no synopses, little description, only inventory number, title, "approximate length in meters", and "price per meter". The shortest films advertised, *Lebende Karikaturen* [*Living Caricatures*, 1908 Elge-Gaumont] and a fragment from a 1908 Nordisk film about elephant young, *Junge des Riesentieres*, are 38 and 39 meters, respectively. The longest film advertised, at 336 meters, is *Griechisches Idyll* "z. Teil kol." [*Greek Idyll*, selectively tinted], directed by Louis Feuillade (1909). A quick glance at Herbert Birett's *Film Offered in Germany from 1895–1911* confirms my initial suspicion that close to half of the films Messter advertises are imports.[11] Pathé and Eclipse are the major players, but Warwick travel films play an important role as well, especially in the documentary genre, "Industrials and Nature Shots". Domestic production is also well represented, including that of Messter himself, leading pioneer of the German film industry. Messter's expansive listing of genres is a fascinating meta-commentary on his own film production: it starts with travel and nature shots, with "views", goes through the traditional lists of drama, marine and military pictures, trick and comedy, to end with his recent fascination, actualities. Messter is clearing out his old collection of "cinema of attractions" in order to make mental and physical space for new feature film and newsreel productions.[12] His painstaking inventory is an archival event, an elaborate historical record that tells us of Messter's immense reach as a businessman, showman, producer, and distributor in Wilhelmine Germany.

From 1908 on Messter explored the newsreel possibilities of film, founding a weekly newsreel *Messter-Woche* in 1914. His inventory list includes early examples of his company's coverage of sensational "media events" such as the destruction of the Zeppelin II on 24. April 1910 and the Berlin train catastrophe of 26. July 1908. Messter's full titles to these two films included the month, day and year of the newsworthy event: here, due to space limitations, only the catastrophe is listed. Other disasters are included under different genre headings. Messter includes an earlier media sensation, *Theater-brand in Chicago* (Pathé Frères), as a "dramatic" picture. The film documented a devastating fire in the Iroquois theater in Chicago (1903). The fire took approximately six hundred lives during a Saturday matinee of a new play, "Mr. Blackbeard". It was certainly a dramatic event that incited visual curiosity and gawking. Yet why not classify this media event as actuality or "special shot"? This is not the only vagary or uncertainty of Messter's "price list".[13] Another catastrophe advertised is a flooding of the Elb river, now listed as a "nature scene". Not surprisingly, colonialist pictures on "natives building bridges" and "the cultural work of the whites" are listed as "industrial" and "nature shots", but so are international balloon competitions – and these are certainly not ethnographic. Messter takes news-worthy events and turns them into "natural

Fig. 1. 'No Hands Needed' – Messter's Kinetoscope.

views" or "dramas", more in keeping with a "cinema of attractions" classification than a system based on fiction/non-fiction distinction.

The "view" monopolizes much of his list, just as it monopolized motion picture production during the first decade of film history. Genre itself is striving to contain the view – only the view is larger than genre. Perhaps Messter needs to purge his archive of the earlier attractions before he can move on to embrace the *Wochenschau* news-gathering system and the longer feature film, with more established narrative. Messter was a showman who moved in many circles and a mechanic who patented untold apparatuses, including a coin-operated "Kosmoskop". For this apparatus he shot an early advertising film about a woman getting into a bath.[14] A prospectus that illustrates the kinetoscope demonstrates the primacy of the cinema of attractions to this early moment of the motion picture, as the man eagerly bends over (no hands needed!) to examine the bathing beauty (Fig. 1).[15] The curious view united imperial children at play with titillating nudes, catastrophes with military maneuvers. For Messter, *Aktualitäten* are ephemeral moments of history that call out to be archived, media events that are tied to a specific time and place. Yet in this inventory Messter seeks to distinguish the topical from the "special shot" to make the "view" more nuanced and targeted, anticipating future developments. Whereas *Aktualitäten* refer to historical, monumental events, *Spezialaufnahmen* suggests a broader category that could include events that were sensational but perhaps not singular, like *The Burning of a Petroleum Tank*, *Around the World in a Car*, even *Children of the Crown Prince at Sea*.[16]

As the archival composite film *Der Kaiser macht einen Spaziergang*[17] illustrates, one can string together the titles/intertitles of topical films from this period and shots of Kaiser Wilhelm and the German *Kaiserpaar* to sketch out the precarious pre-war position of Germany and Austria. No doubt these *Aktualitäten* were for a brief, shining moment extremely popular in theaters, but they quickly expired as the public tired of last year's catastrophe or last year's ceremonial pomp. What makes a film "used" or junk here has less to do with the film's shelf life and more to do with the new information demands of a news-hungry genre and audience. In recognizing this, Messter necessitates a career move that will not jettison, but expand the Messter-Film GmbH interest in actuality, alongside the feature film, showcasing Henny Porten as "star attraction".

It is indeed significant that of the many short comedies by Messter found in the inventory,[18] none feature Porten, who was vital to his attempt to push through a new distribution system in Germany, the *Monopolfilm*.[19] Although the Messter finding aid in the federal archives has given this price list a tentative date of 1910, Birett's volume can be used to determine that the films in the list span the years 1902–11. The inventory was compiled late 1911 or slightly thereafter. In 1911, Messter moved into the glass atelier on Blücherstrasse, Berlin. In the same year, he promoted Porten through a poster campaign: acting in approximately twenty of his feature films, she attains star status. Around 1911 Messter's career shifts in another way as well. He decides to withdraw from the microscopy branch of "optics" that he inherited from the business of his father and grandfather. From 1900 until 1910, Messter had worked intensively with Professor Scheffler at Zeiss laboratories on microscopic photography.[20] As Albert Wangemann, apprentice to the company "Ed. Messter, optisches und mechanisches Institut" writes in a memoir, the Messter-Mikroskop was quite popular among physicians at the turn-of-the-century. Wangemann even surmises that Messter-Microscopes could have rivaled medical instruments of German optical firms such as Zeiss[21] and Leitz, if they had hired a better manager for the division on optics.[22] As late as 1914, the Messter optical projection equipment for sale included a "Mikrokino" for microscopic shots, as well as a "Projektionsmikroskop" that could be coupled to a camera. In his 1879 price list, Eduard Messter already differentiated with great care between optical, mechanical and surgical devices. The frontispiece for his catalogue of observing instruments illustrates a gigantic spirometer that was used to test the power of the lungs. The apparatus is a larger-than-life composite image of the "vivifying physiological gaze", "animation" as scientific observation. At least twenty years before Oskar's "Kinetograph" and "Kosmoskop", Messter mechanics explored how magic lanterns and medical instruments could capture movement, both on and off the screen.

C. Francis Jenkins in his 1898 history of cinema defined a scientific vision of "animation" as the "philosopher's dream" that could be realized most fully in cinematographic pictures. He praises the filming of clouds in their "ever-shifting forms", "the flight of the dragonfly", "the movement of the blood in capillary vessels", the growth of plants and "motion in the physical world as well as in the world of animated beings". Cinema is science, "the only exact measurement of observed phenomena", and Jenkins elaborates on its dream geography, writing: "Motion in the physical world as well as in the world of animated beings is an essential attribute of life, and the growth of animals, birds, microscopical germs, bacteria, microbes, etc. could be studied. Possibly there are interesting phenonema of a complex physical nature developing so slowly as to escape our observation under ordinary means of investigation."[23] Like Jenkins, Oskar Messter promotes the cinematograph as a tool for scientific demonstration in his 1897/98 catalogue of "living photography" (only one section of Eduard Messter's larger illustrated catalogue on optics). In his theoretical introduction to the list, he also describes film as a scientific performance of the modern experience of tempo and nature, writing that a projectionist can display the hidden movements of bacteria, the formation of crystals, the life of a plant "at either an accelerated or a decelerated rate".[24] The catalogue differentiates between projectors for "scientific purposes", for "grand stage presentations", for "amateurs", and "for small shows and private demonstrations". His catalogue lists a time-lapse picture of a flower display and he writes that this film has "exclusive scientific interest".[25] Along with Lumière remakes, time-lapse flowers and natural "views", Messter also advertises marches, shown "at a quick rate", a Prussian gallop, and other patriotic pictures (secret views of the imperial family, etc.).[26]

If for Messter around 1913/14 the military actuality has come to replace the scientific film and trick film in terms of its ability to capture the tempo of modernity, the unexpected, catastrophic, ephemeral and contingent life, this is a telling of genre that has its own local history and other local histories contradict it. The "cinema of attractions", a form on the boundaries of scientific and amusement cinema, is by no means dead across Central Europe at this time. Here we come to investigate our second list of used films for sale. While in Berlin in the 1910s, Oskar Messter already turned away from microphotography to embrace the military actuality and ultimately, the machine gun, other provinces in Germany and Austro-Hungary were just starting to delve into the utopia of microcinematography and nature magnification on the screen.[27] In 1911 in Prague, KINOFA "the first Czech company for lending and selling films" was founded by Josef Kejø and A. Rott.[28] For a very short period, the company produced slapsticks and feature films: then it turned primarily to scientific films and documentaries, such as *Farming in Bohemia*.

In the Czech film periodical *Kino* in 1913 we find not one, but two different price lists of used films for sale. The shorter list is entitled an "antique store of used films" ("we will sell well-preserved, good films"),[29] published on 5 December 1913.[30] The "store" lists titles followed by one word telegraph-style designations popular in the cinema of attractions period, "dances", "nature", "fairy tale", "comic", "comedy" (once with exclamation point), "true-to-life", "tinted". The longer list, published on 24. October 1913, was part of KINOFA's response to an accusation by critic Josef Lukavsky that they had not been productive.[31] This catalogue was intended to boost local distribution of documentaries that had already been marketed somewhat successfully outside the province of Bohemia. The introduction to this list of used films for sale laments: "Two thirds of them have not been played in Prague! Everything was bought by those outside and the foreign [countries]! Now it is up to the enterprises of Prague to catch up on what they missed."[32] This odd "double abroad" refers to Austro-Hungary beyond the province, beyond the Kingdom of Bohemia, and to the abroad outside the *Kaiserreich*.

KINOFA's executive director responsible both for production and marketing, Antonin Pech, speaks succinctly of the goals of local Prague cinematography in 1911: "The First Prague Production of Cinematography Pictures A. Pech, Prague II, Rieger Embankment no. 29, produces: cinematographic pictures, timed and staged for specialized theatres, as well as for scientific and advertising purposes [...] new and used film for sale".[33] Promoting cinematography as a tool for scientific demonstration – this was Messter's concern in 1897 and is that of Pech in 1911. Two years later, in 1913, cinema-goers in Prague experience KINOFA's heyday of the scientific film spectacle of the body. Ondøej Schrutz directs a film entitled *The Physiology of a Lymnaea Embryo* (74 m). A Pathé film about the plague and another picture on the "wonders" of x-raying the body[34] were shown frequently. The KINOFA list advertises several physiology films produced around 1911 by primary director Pech, including *The Life of a Killed Frog* and *Life in Sea Aquariums*.[35] KINOFA also advertises two popular science films entitled *The Contents of a Little Pond* and *Vaccine Production*. To the list of descriptive genres found in the "antique store" (comic, comedy, actuality, sport, nature, trick, and fashion), KINOFA adds "scientific", a genre that deals with enhanced perception, nature observed or outdone.[36] Life is here a physiological category and the camera penetrates hidden interior movement, non-indexically, in addition to reproducing movement in the traditional sense, mimetically, on the screen. Science is sensational: in Prague, a pocket of the "cinema of attractions" witnesses production that had long since disappeared from the general catalogue mapping of other countries. And this fascination with an early scientific moment of film exhibition happens at a time when cinema owners are just starting to discover the American "modern", even debating how to best translate the word "hit" into suitable Czech.[37]

Notes

1. I would like to thank Simon Krysl [Duke University] and Dr. Ivan Klimes [National Film Archive, Prague] for providing translation assistance and access to trade publications, KINOFA catalogues, and Czech programming.

2. Robert W. Paul, "List of Films for the 'Animatographe'", *Victorian Film Catalogues: A Facsimile* (London: Projection Box, 1996), 27–30; 27.

3. Fuerst Brothers, "Price List of Lumiere's Cinematograph". *Victorian Film Catalogues: A Facsimile* (London: Projection Box, 1996), 3–14; 4. The editors of this volume write that this is an "unlikely warning about pirate dupe films being torn by the projector sprockets due to shrinkage" (48).

4. Ibid.

5. Film industry leader Oskar Messter loudly accused competitors of "copying" protected material, including the apparatus. As early as 1896, Messter took out a half-page ad in *Der Komet* to reproach Hermann O. Foersterling for pirating his "Kinetograph" and catalogue. He writes: "a Berlin firm, which calls itself a cinematograph 'Factory' [...] not only tried to copy my legally protected apparatus, but also almost exactly reprinted the text and form of my catalogue". *Der Komet*, no. 610 (28 November 1896): 16, as quoted in Deac Rossel, "Beyond Messter: Aspects of Early Cinema in Berlin", *Film History*, 10 (1998): 52–69, 56. The last word on this scandal was had by Foersterling, who ridiculed Messter's charges, writing that Messter's apparatus was nothing other than a highly polished piece of junk – "who's laughing now?" Messter was successful in suing Foersterling on the use of the word "Kinetograph", which he had protected as a trademark. See *Der Komet*, no. 613 (19 December 1896): 24 and Rossel, "Beyond Messter", 65, n. 20.

6. Each film, the brothers state, is sold in a tin box which has a cover stamped "Cinematograph, August and Louis Lumière" in raised lettering. But the bold "signature" on the strip, ever so slightly overshadowing the name Lumière, belongs to the Fuerst Brothers, the "genuine" dealers or distributors (4).

7. Gaumont, "Catalogue", *Victorian Film Catalogues: A Facsimile* (London: Projection Box, 1996), 15–16.

8. According to Birett, *Um die Welt im Automobil* was a five-part travelogue [Warwick, 1908] (Birett, 3, 667).

9. Other ethnography and expedition titles included in the inventory are *Besuch in Hagenbecks Tierpark*, *Wie man in Afrika reist*, *Südpolarexpedition*, and *Bilder aus Westafrika*.

10. Oskar Messter, "Preisliste für gebrauchte Films" (Signatur 263), *Nachlaß Oskar Messter. Bestand N 1275*, ed. Babett Stach (Koblenz: Bundesarchiv, 1994).

11. Herbert Birett, *Das Filmangebot in Deutschland 1895–1911* (München: Filmbuchverlag Winterberg, 1991).

12. The films that Messter is selling post-date the "cinema of attractions" period, if it is seen to strictly end in 1897. I prefer to use Tom Gunning's more elastic conception of the "cinema of attractions", which emphasizes exhibition over narration as a paradigm that dominates cinema until 1906–1907. For Messter's list not only includes select shorts from this earlier period (1903–1906), it also includes films that are remade at a slightly later date, but based on earlier "exhibition" films, like *Jagd nach der Kegelkugel* (Eclipse, 1909), a creative spin on *The Pumpkin Chase*, often attributed to Emile Cohl.

13. The "drama" section also includes the documentary *Bilder aus dem amerikanischen Farmerleben*.

14. The title in the *Kosmoskop* prospectus, *Damenbad*, could also be the film listed in the special catalogue of 1897/1898, No. 14 *Bade zu Hause*, an advertising picture for *Wellenbad-Schakuel*.

15. "'Kosmoskop'. Patent Messter Automat zur Wiedergabe lebender Photographien" (Signatur 264), *Nachlaß Oskar Messter. Bestand N 1275*, ed. Babett Stach (Koblenz: Bundesarchiv, 1994). What is not altogether clear is whether or not it is the "name" or the apparatus itself that Messter has patented.

16. The price of a film in Germany at the time ran somewhere between 60 pfennigs and 1.20 marks per meter; the "used films" of Messter's list are 10–50 pfennigs per meter. The cheapest finds can be found in the *Spezialaufnahmen* and *Aktualitäten* sections. A staged medieval tournament was, however, an expensive "special shot" (50 pfennigs per m).

17. *Der Kaiser macht einen Spaziergang*, Netherlands Film Museum, 2004. Also see Martin Loiperdinger's essay on the imperial family as early film stars: "The Kaiser's Cinema: An Archeology of Attitudes and Audiences". In *A Second Life*: 41–50.

18. Over 20 Messter-Film GmbH productions are listed under "Comic" or "Trickfilms", including *Das Junggesellenhoroscop*, *Die Konkurrenten*, *Der berühmte Tenor*, and *Bundrika die Negerköchin*.

19. In June 1913 Messter proposed to release Porten films to Dutch distributor Jean Desmet as a monthly serial, an early example of the *Monopolfilm*. Under the new distribution system, one purchased exhibition rights for a specific time and place, instead of buying used prints. Apparently there was the fear that second hand films at knock-down prices would "choke the market". See Ivo Bloom, "Filmvertrieb in Europa 1910–1915: Jean Desmet und die Messter-Film GmbH, " *KINtop* 3 (1994): 73–92 and Martin Koerber, "Oskar Messter, Film Pionier", 58.

20. Wilhelm Scheffler, "Über mikroskopische Aufnahmen", *Berliner klinische Wochenschrift* (1910, Jg. XLVII), no. 12: 536–537. Messter writes about his early interest in microphotography and time-lapse in his autobiography *Mein Weg mit dem Film* (Berlin-Schöneberg: Max Hesses Verlag, 1936), 123–124.

21. Zeiss also manufactured an "episcope", a magic lantern projector used by anatomist and pathologist Salomon Stricker in Vienna.

22. Early in his career, as Wangemann recalls, Messter purchased a film from the Warwick Company on the art of magnification, Arthur Melbourne-Cooper's *Grandma's Reading Glass* (1906). He also purchased films from Charles Urban's "Unseen World" series. The Austrian film archive has a canister marked Oskar Messter, Berlin, which contains a nitrate print with the German title: *Unter dem Mikroskop. Larve der Wasserfliege* (Urban, 1903). Albert Wangemann, "Meine Lehrzeit im Hause Messter, 1898–1901", *KINtop* 3 (1994): 33–42. On Melbourne-Cooper's role in film history, see Tjitte de Vries' article in the same volume, "Arthur Melbourne-Cooper, Film Pioneer" *KINtop* 3 (1994): 143–160. "Grandma's Reading Glass" was formerly attributed to pioneer G.A. Smith.

23. C. Francis Jenkins, *Animated Pictures: An Exposition of the Historical Developments of Chronophotography, its Present Scientific Applications and Future Possibilities, and of the Methods and Apparatus Employed in*

the Entertainment of Large Audiences by means of Projecting Lanterns to Give the Appearance of Objects in Motion (Washington DC: H.L. McQueen, 1898), 104.

24. Oskar Messter, "Bilder-Verzeichnis. Lebende Photographie (Kopie) 1897/1898" (Signatur 146). *Nachlaß Oskar Messter* (Bestand N. 1275).

25. According to Messter, the time lapse film of 1897 of a flower bouquet that blossoms and wilts was shot at an acceleration rate of 1500.

26. Messter was always interested in "good military pictures". But in the early catalogue science is held out as another possibility for cinema, or it at least serves as another exquisite model for how the cinematograph could capture mobility, tempo and hidden "views".

27. In Messter's later career, flower physiology and microphotography gradually give way to the shock of series-photography explosions of human heads. Technical plans of machine guns and war-time series-photographs of explosions are available in the German Federal Archives in the file 2.1.3.4 "Ed. Messter Abt. Optik Berlin/Optikon Ag Zuerich/N.V. Techn. Maatschij. Aerofoto Amsterdam" (Signatur 273–294). *Nachlaß Oskar Messter* (Bestand N. 1275).

28. Vjekoslav Majcen; Johann Böhm; Karel Tabery, ed. Nemý film v Rakousko-Uhersku. *Silent films in the Austro-Hungarian Monarchy : 1895–1918.* [Praha] : FITES, 1995. 16–21. This catalogue commemorates an international seminar on early cinema, held on 5 April 1995, supported by the Czech Ministry of Culture. The catalogue also contains important research on Early Croatian Film and the traveling cinema of Central Europe.

29. "Antikvariát Kinocentrála", *Kino* 10 (5.12.1913): 12.

30. Nature, folk, scientific, and sport films dominate the list. The store includes one of the same German comedies that Messter advertises in his inventory (*Schwiegermutter lernt reiten*).

31. Between 1911 and WWI, only 30 feature films were made in Prague, most under 350 m. By comparison, in Vienna between 1908 and 1914, 120 feature films were produced and in Budapest, between 1912 and 1914, approximately 50. Jiøí Havelka, *Kronika našeho filmu, 1898- 1965 [Chronicle of Our Cinema]* (Praha: Ès. Filmový ústav, 1967), 39.

32. The introduction to the list of "used films" was published in *Kino* I/3 (1.3.1913): 6. The list itself was published in *Kino* I/4 (24.10.1913).

33. *Èeský kinematograf* I, no. 1 (1.1 1911), 16.

34. *Blood Circulation in the Living Human Body*, using X-rays to show circulation.

35. Other scientific films were made for Prague Professor of Physiology, Dr. Eduard Babák – *Axalotl, The Production of an Inoculation Substance* or *Vaccine Production and Animals*.

36. The genres/descriptors in the KINOFA list are trick, fashion, women, nature, sport, dance, comic, comedy, actuality, scientific, synchronous with music. Architectural pictures, wedding pictures, christening pictures, advertising pictures, family pictures, and miscellaneous pictures are also enumerated.

37. The first film produced by KINOFA was a production on the craze for the *culotte* (women's trouser), a feature that was marketed as a fashion flick, *modní*.

PART VI

PRACTICES:
Non-theatrical distribution

26

Sunday and Holy Days

Tony Fletcher

Founder member of The Cinema Museum, London, UK

The distribution network for the Animated Photograph began early in Britain. Agencies were already in existence to provide entertainments for fetes, functions and musical events. The Cinematographist/Lanternist took their place with the other entertainments which included: Minstrel Troupes, Banjo Bands, Ventriloquists, Punch and Judy and Conjurers.

A number of Cinematographists advertised themselves in the pages of "The Era" and "The Showman" including Irving Bosco, Charles Connor, Professor Ricardo and Edward Longstaffe.[1] Other agencies existed such as the "Concord Concert Control",[2] the "Wilfred Schreiner Agency"[3] and "Harrods", one of London's largest stores. Although the Harrod's Cinematographist/lecturer is not named, a photograph does appear in one of their annual catalogues which is recognisable as Charles Goodwin Norton and his son.[4] Norton was a business man who supplied his services for a fee, and one of his clients was "The National Sunday League" which only operated on Sundays.[5]

In June 1904, a French visitor to London described it as "A City of the Dead" – "Where are the People!"[6] That summer, however, over fourteen art galleries and museums were open free of charge on Sundays; Henry Wood conducted his orchestra at the Queen's Hall, Langham Place; and the parks had Band concerts to entertain the locals.

The organisation responsible for this activity was "The National Sunday League" which was founded in 1855 by R.M. Morrell. While in Germany, Morrell had observed that German craftsmen were able to improve their technical knowledge and skill by visiting museums and libraries on Sunday, whereas in London due to the influence of the Sunday Observance Societies and other religious based bodies, this was not possible.[7]

Morrell, who considered himself to be "a working man" began his campaign in order to gain some of these advantages for the workers of London. For him the choice was between "the awful dullness of the English Sunday" and the "Public House". He was supported by such influential figures as Charles Darwin and Professor Huxley. The "League" organised seasonal excursions during the summer to the seaside and country and for those that preferred to stay in the city, they organised bands to play in the Public Parks.

During the winter months, "Sunday evenings for the people" were inaugurated at St. Martin's Hall, Long Acre. Several of the lectures were delivered by Professor Huxley, who was President of the "Sunday Lecture Society". Although the "League" had to fight legal disputes in order to continue their struggle for entertainment on Sunday, they received the support of Edward, The Prince Of Wales. Other activities that the "League" organised included a "Shakespeare Society" as well as concerts for the poor children of the workhouses. The composer Sir Joseph Barmby and the Pre-Raphaelite artist William Morris both became active supporters.

London was the centre of the "League's" activities, but branches also opened in other metropolitan cities of England during the 1890's, including Bradford, Bristol, Halifax, Leeds and Tyneside.

The Lecturer (1896–1905)

The Sunday afternoon or evening lectures were considered as "cultural" and not just entertainment events. The venues used by the lecturers in London were mainly Public Halls including the Town Halls of Shoreditch, Holborn, Bermondsey and Battersea. These lecturers gave illustrated talks usually on a topic of the day and were illustrated by Oxy-Hydrogen slides. In December 1896, Charles Goodwin Norton delivered two lectures on "Animated Photography", but used only Oxy-Hydrogen slides as illustration rather than animated photographs. Two other Lanternists, George Offor (January 1897) and W Chard (December 1897) followed Norton's example.[8]

The earliest lecturer to have incorporated animated photography into his presentation seems to have been the War correspondent Frederick Villiers. Between November 1897 and January 1898 he gave three lectures on the subject the "Graeco – Turkish war, illustrating it with scenes from the war which he had filmed himself. In 1902, he gave two further lectures to the "Society" on "Coronations I have seen at Home and Abroad" and used animated photographs provided by "The Egyptian Hall".

During the period 1897 – 1905, eight lecturers gave illustrated talks incorporating animated photographs. They were: Dr. G Marcel Andre (1900–03), Horace Banks (1898–1905), S.P. Coryn (1899), T.C. Hepworth (1898–99), J. Brandon Medland (1898–1904), D.W Noakes (1898), C. Oswald (1898) and F. Villiers (1897–1902). In March 1898, D.W. Noakes lectured on "Marvels of the Victorian Era",[9] while in January1899, Sydney P. Coryn delivered two lectures entitled "Through Canada with a Cinematograph" which featured "living pictures of life on ranch and prairie".[10]

Between October 1898 and October 1899, Thomas Craddock Hepworth gave four lectures all on photographic themes. After October 1899, he continued giving lectures to the "League" but without the use of a Cinematograph.[11] In 1898, C. Oswald lectured on the topic of Animated Photographs using Professor Roland's cinematograph.

Three of these lanternists were regular exponents of the Cinematograph for the Sunday League during this period,[12]: (a) J Brandon Medland gave six lectures at fourteen venues during 1898–99 with his Vit-Autoscope M/C. Like T.C Hepworth, his topic was also "Photography"(including "colour photography"). During 1903–04, he returned to the circuit giving four performances with his "Viagraph" or "Vitascope" M/C. (b) Horace Banks' speciality was "Pictorial Tours". The venues on his letterhead included Opera Houses, Winter Gardens, Town Halls, Music halls, Theatres and seaside Piers. He gave five lectures for the "League" between January 1898 and November 1905.

These were:

   (i)   England and America (including scenes of The Spanish-American War)

   (ii)   Japan and its People.

   (iii)   Picturesque New Zealand – The Britain of the South.

   (iv)   A Visit to the Land of our Allies.

   (v)   Japan in Peace and War.

His entertainments also included a concert party, patriotic songs and recitations.

(c) Dr.G. Marcel Andre delivered three lectures between November 1900 and January 1903:

(i) Old and New Paris and the Exhibition

(ii) America in Two Hours (or alternatively in 60 Minutes)

(iii) A Visit to America

Although Andre is not named in the Journal, he was probably the lecturer for the Ober-Ammergau Passion Plays, which were performed at six venues between October 1900 and October 1902. In one of these lectures thirteen Animated Films were displayed.[13]

List of Public Halls (1897–1905)

Battersea Town Hall	November 1897 – March 1905
Bermondsey Town Hall	January 1898 – December 1905
Croydon Public Hall	January 1899 – October 1900; + November 1903 – February 1904
East Ham Town Hall	October 1903 – December 1903
Holborn Town Hall	October 1898 – November 1898
The Horns Assembly Rooms, Kennington	March 1898 – February 1899
Myddleton Hall	January 1898 – February 1898
Newington Public Baths	March 1899 – October 1899
Prince of Wales, Kentish Town	March 1902
Public Hall – Caledonian Road	January 1899
Rotherhithe Town Hall	October 1902
St Pancras Public Baths	January 1902 – February 1904
Shoreditch Town Hall	November 1897 – March 1904
Stratford Town Hall	January 1899 – March 1905

The yearly attendances for the "League's" lectures increased annually:

1901–02	115,925
1902–03	454, 896
1903–04	600,000
1904–05	800,000[14]

Between August and November 1905, 21 Halls had given entertainments on 21 Sundays with attendances approaching 300,000. Cheap prices were available at most venues – 3d, 6d, and 1/-, whereas at the more up market "Alhambra" and "Queen's Hall" prices were 2/-.

By April 1905, the League claimed to be exhibiting the Cinematograph to 20,000 people each Sunday night during the winter months. They claimed that the pictures often pointed out a moral such as the evil effects of dishonest or immoral conduct.[15]

The attitude of the London County Council (LCC) in the early years was to turn a blind eye to what was happening on Sundays. They did not seem to wish to get embroiled in the argument, but instead wanted to provide the people of London with reasonable recreation facilities on Sundays. In 1898, the regulations relating to the Cinematograph which the LCC had passed, were not being enforced on Sundays, mainly because of the refusal of the Fire Services to inspect on Sundays on grounds of cost. However, in April 1905, the LCC began to challenge Cinematograph Exhibitions and tried to persuade venues to adhere to the 1898 regulations.

They were concerned about fire risk involving celluloid film. At the People's Palace on the 9 April 1905, an audience of 2,000 passed a resolution which opposed the Council's directives to prevent the Cinematograph being shown on Sundays.

The National Sunday League Journal gave very little space to its Cinematograph activities, apart from advertising them. For them, Animated Photographs were part of the Sunday programme which also included vocal and instrumental items. The reviewers of the Journal occasionally gave an indication about the use of the Cinematograph. In a review of Feb 1900 of a programme at Prince's Hall, Kennington on the 21 January 1900, it was stated that some of the Animated photographs gave glimpses of nurses attending the wounded in South Africa.

A review in the February 1904 issue on the "Alhambra" programme shown at the Public Hall, Croydon, in January 1904, stated that "Specially instructive were the pictures relating to the different phases of Bee Life and the Circulation of the blood in the webbed foot of a frog" (a reference to "The Unseen World" Series). The Journal also reported that at the Grand Theatre, Fulham, on March 6th, views of "Port Arthur" and "The Fleet" were shown.

The term "Animated Photography" seems to be a generic one. Programmes with this title and without a named exhibitor had been advertised as early as October 1899. From April 1905 the Islington Empire advertised "Animated Photographs" without naming the exhibitor, suggesting that the display may have been organised "in – house".

Variety Halls (1900–07)

Alexandra Theatre (Palace Theatre)	March 1905; March 1907–
Stoke Newington	December 1907
Borough Theatre, Stratford	April 1905–07
Broadway Theatre, Deptford	March 1902–07
Camden Theatre	October 1904–07
Canterbury Theatre of Varieties	December 1904–05
Chelsea Theatre of Varieties (Chelsea Palace)	October 1903–07
Duchess Theatre Balham	October 1904 – February 1905
East Ham Palace	October 1907 – December 1907
The Empire, Croydon	October 1906–07
Empress Theatre of Varieties, Brixton	March 1907 – December 1907
The Grand, Clapham Junction	October 1905–07
The Grand, Fulham	December 1901 – March 1904
Islington Empire (New Islington Empire)	March 1905–07
Kennington Theatre	January 1906–07
National Palace, North End, Croydon	November 1900 – March 1901
People's Palace, Mile End	November 1903–07
Prince's Theatre, Poplar (New Prince's Theatre)	February 1906 – November 1907
Putney Hippodrome N	January 1907 – November 1907
Walthamstow Palace	February 1904 – March 1907
Woolwich Grand Theatre	February 1902 – October 1907
Woolwich Hippodrome	November 1907 – December 1907

During the winter season of 1906/07, 478 concerts were given at 21 Theatres and Halls in London and suburbs with over 700,000 attending. The decision by the "League" to extend its venues to the use of Variety Theatres brought them into contact with the Cinematograph Agencies which were already involved in this active entertainment circuit.

There was a complex network of distribution agencies at work. during this period, (a "black hole" in our film history!) Several of the major distribution Agencies such as

"Ruffell's" and Walterdaw do not seem to have been used by the "League". David Devant ran the Cinematograph Agency for "The Egyptian Hall" of Maskelyne and Cooke. Following Cooke's death and the move from the "Egyptian Hall" to St. George's Hall, Devant became Maskelyne's new partner and continued the Film Exhibition service.

By the autumn of 1907, the majority of venues had adopted the term "animated photograph" without naming the Exhibitor. Again, very few reviews of Cinematograph performances appeared in the Journal. After he attended the concert on Sunday, 10 March at the "Chelsea Palace", the reviewer stated that "as usual I did not look at the Animated photographs and [...] the custom of getting the pianist to play is a good one".

The Animated Photographs seem to have been mainly shown at the end of these programmes.

On Sunday, 6 November 1907, at the Broadway Theatre, Deptford, Animated photograph illustrations were shown of "The Life of a Fireman in New York" and on 17 November 1907, at the same venue – "the Saving of a Child's Life through the Sagacity of a Dog", which was the film most applauded by the audience.

After 1907, it is uncertain whether these Cinematograph Agencies continued to operate to such a degree. It seems likely that the Variety venues which had taken over from the Public Halls, had installed their own permanent equipment and used the Cinematograph on a daily basis as a major feature of their entertainment which signalled the arrival of "The Electric Cinematograph Theatre".

Cinematograph Agencies (1899–1907)

Title	Period	No of performances
Imperial Bioscope	1901–06	126
The "Matagraph"	1901–07	121
"From the Egyptian Hall"	1899–1905	74
The Edisonograph	1901–05	71
Jury's Imperial Bioscope	1906–07	70
Biograph(American Biograph)	1903–06	64
Beard's Imperial Cinematograph	1905–07	60
Jeape's Animated Photographs	1904–06	31
From "Alhambra"	1903–05	30
Rockett's Bio-Stereoscope	1905–06	23
Animatograph	1905–07	19
Dell's Lifeograph	1900–02	14
The Mutograph	1904	12
Raymond's Bio-Tableaux	1905–06	11
Walterdaw's Bioscope	1906	3
Trewer's Imperial Bioscope	1906	5
Ruffell's Animated Photographs	1905–06	3
Kaleidograph	1904	1
Electric Bio-Tableaux	1903	1
Dudgeon's Bioscope	1901	1
The Bioscope	1905	1

Often at the last showing of the winter season, any profits after expenses, were given to a local charity. One of these charities was run by the President of the "League", Sir William Treloar, who in 1907, became the Lord Mayor of London; his special chosen charity was the Home for Cripples at Alton in Hampshire. Most of the charities to have benefited from the Sunday League profits were local hospitals, e.g. Bolingbroke Hospital, Surrey Dispensary, The Waterloo Road Hospital for Women and Children, The North East Hospital for Children, The West Ham Cottage Hospital, The Woolwich and Plumstead Cottage Hospital and The Royal Jubilee Hospital, West Kensington. After a gap of some years, several lecturers using Animated Photographs re-appeared on the circuit. Between October 1906 and March 1907, W. Stuart Scott gave three lectures on "The Cornish Riviera", "Southern Ireland" and "A Trip to Killarney". In November 1907, Harry De Windt lectured on "Through Savage Europe".

Salvation Army

Unlike their secular counterparts who used the Cinematograph mainly on Sundays during the winter months, some religious societies considered every day to be a "holy day" and used the Cinematograph as a proselytising tool, endeavoring to attract men away from the evils of alcohol.[16] The Salvation Army was at the forefront of this campaign and for approximately 12 years used the Cinematograph to convert the sinner. Their journal, "The War Cry" considered that there were two sensorial paths into the soul – through the ear and through the eye.

In February 1897, Henry Howse, who ran the Salvation Army Limelight Department, had acquired a Lumiere camera. By 1903, together with F.R. Cox (General Booth's Private Secretary) they started to produce their own films which were mainly topical but also included some attempts at fiction. They developed their films themselves, which had been shot at 15 frames per second. One of the their shows featured the following films: "An Open-Air Salvation Meeting in the Whitechapel Road", "A Train Approaching", "Drilling by Juniors of The Salvation Army" and "Their Colony at Hadleigh Farm". The films were accompanied by a string band which played a selection of Salvation Army tunes.[17]

Howse and Cox documented significant Salvation Army Events including accompanying General Booth on several international tours. Howse was responsible for building an extensive distribution network throughout Britain.

In January 1904, the Salvation Army gave shows at the Palace Garden Hall, Nuneaton. Admission prices were 1/-, 6d and 3d (for the back seats) with a special exhibition for children for 2d at 6.00 pm. Cox was the lecturer while Howse operated the Cinematograph. One film entitled "Our Slummers at Work" included an open-air fight.[18]

In 1904, The Salvation Army, which considered itself to be the "Cinema of the Working Classes", opened a Hall in Oxford St. London, where films were exhibited for an entrance fee of 1d. Another permanent Cinematograph Exhibition in London at this period was the Polytechnic in Regent Street, which charged 2½d for admission.

By 1905 there were over thirty Salvation Army Centres throughout England which showed films on a regular basis. In October 1906, the Salvation Army issued a 108 page catalogue which included both their own films and those of commercial companies. Their motto was "They win souls for God (especially on Saturday nights)".[19]

The Salvation Army Department also supplied the Imperial Chrono which they advertised as "King of the Bioscope" and shared premises with the Walterdaw Co. at their showroom at 22, Cecil Court, Charing Cross Road. They used a "Gaumont + Cie" machine which utilised the Demeny System patent, and the hire of the films was limited to the users of the Chrono-Bioscope. In the introduction to the Catalogue, it stated that the Salvation Army appeals to the hearts and minds of all classes and that "we recognise that all reasonable and lawful means may be used to attract the people and to influence them for good". It sought to provide subjects to deal with all kinds and conditions of men:

"We desire to attract them to the Army Hall and to influence them there. In some cases we shall only succeed at the moment in directing them from the Theatre, Music Halls and Pub". […] "Our topics apply to the enforcing of temperance, morality, bravery, purity, nobility of character, defending the weak and helping the poor. In addition, a careful selection has been made of natural subjects; a great variety of "Travel" has also been introduced, and such humorous matter as clean and wholesome."

Each film bore the official crest of the Salvation Army.

The films were divided into 12 Sections:

Section I.	**"Indian Scenes"** (13 films) incl. "Farewell of Commissioner Higgins"
Section II.	**"British Scenes"** (19 films)
	incl. "Scenes in the Slums"
	"On Mile-End Waste, East London",
	"A Thrilling Rescue from the River"
	"Feeding the Poor"
	"Slum Open Air"
Section III.	**"Pictures of General Booth's Great Mother Tour"** (11 films)
	incl. "Evangelism by Motor" – "St. Just to Aberdeen"
Section IV	**"Pictures Illustrating the General's Visit to Palestine and the Holy Land"** (8 films)
Section V	**"Congress Pictures"** (23 films)
	incl. "Salvation Negro"
	"Negro officers"
Section VI	**"Scriptural Subjects"** (4 films)
	incl. "Christ Amongst Men" – a series of 22 scenes lasting 2150 ft. The film could either be loaned as a whole or in two parts.
	Also: "Saved by a Lie" – "The Story of a Crime" and "What the Salvation Army can Do" (4 scenes)
Section VII	**"Special Subjects"** (2 films)
Section VIII	**"Travel – Geography by Cinematograph"** (168 films)
	Arranged in sets as follows:
(a)	Samoa and Fiji Islands (15 films)
(b)	On the Mentone – Nice Route (8 films)
(c)	Saint-Raphael to Hyeres Route (1 film)
(d)	Through the "Gorges Du Var" (4 films)
(e)	Panoramas in the South of France (10 films)
(f)	Electric Railway from Fayet to Chaumoise (4 films)
(g)	Railway ride from Grasse to Nice (2 films)
(h)	Through the "Gorges Du Var" (4 films)
(i)	Railway from La Mure A St George-de-Caumiere (3 films)
(j)	Pierrefitte-Cauterets-Luz Company (9 films)
(k)	China (16 films)
(l)	Sunny Spain (11 films)
(m)	Picturesque Portugal Portrayed (9 films)
(n)	German Pictures (13 films)
(o)	English Pictures (10 films)
(p)	Pictures of the Emerald Isle (14 films) incl. "Roadside snapshots taken from Kenmare and Glengariff of very dirty Irish Peasant children, who are dressed in rags (from old potato sacking) – one of the little girls lifts her skirt to wipe her nose and displays her rags – or rather

her want of them"
(q)   A Trip to the Giant's Causeway, Co. Antrim Ireland (7 films)
(r)   A Day in Burns' Land (2 films)
(s)   American Pictures (2 films)
(t)   In Lovely Switzerland (3 films)
(u)   Russian and Siberian Pictures (Hahn Jagelsky Collection)
(v)   India (5 films) incl. "Bombay" (HQ of the Salvation Army in India and Ceylon)
(w)   Egyptian Pictures (15 films) incl. "a number of little niggers at cricket"

Section IX   **"Pictures of Great Industries"**

(a)   Afloat and Ashore (10 films) incl. "A Day from a Colliers Life (10 scenes) (at Wigan) – "We have thousands of beautiful Salvation Army soldiers who work in coal mines"
(b)   North Sea Fisheries (4 films) (Set of 4 – 320 ft.)
(c)   Toilers of the Deep (22 subjects totalling 1050 ft.)
      Also: "Visit to a Tea Plantation in Ceylon" (series of pictures) – "much of the tea consumed by S A members come from this plantation".

Section X   **Historical and Current Events:**

(a)   Coronation Procession of King Edward VII and Queen Alexandra (14 films)
(b)   The King in Ireland (2 films)
(c)   The King's State Visit to Scotland (3 films)
(d)   President Loubet's Visit to London (4 films)
(e)   The King of Italy in Paris (2 films)
(f)   The King of Italy in England (10 films)
(g)   Nelson Centenary (celebrated 21/10/1905)
(h)   May Day festivities at Knutsford
(i)   San Francisco after the Disaster (2 parts)
(j)   Procession entering State Dhurbar at Delhi 1/1/1903
(k)   The Eruption of Vesuvius
(l)   The King of Spain in London
(m)   The Royal Wedding
(n)   England v Japan (at play)
(o)   Launch of the "Katori" by Princess Arugawa
(p)   The Earthquake in Italy (9 scenes)

Section XI   **Films of General interest:**

(1)   With the Fleet –Series of Naval Pictures (12 Titles)
(2)   Cruise in a Rough Sea
(3)   Black Beauty
(4)   Rescued by Rover
(5)   Salmon Poachers – A Midnight Melee
(6)   The Village Blacksmith
(7)   The Dog Detective
(8)   Desperate Poaching Affray
(9)   A Romance of the Underground Electric Railway
(10) Baby Farming; or The Child Stealers
(11) Gutter Sportsmen
(12) The Druids
(13) The Prodigal's Progress
(14) The Aeroplane Accident
(15) A Water Polo Match
(16) Army Life as it Might Be – A Lesson from France
(17) Absent Without Leave
(18) Down the Chute

(19)   An African Ostrich Farm
(20)   Belle Isle Cave in a Storm
(21)   Military Pushball on Horseback
(22)   The Gypsy Fortune – Teller
(23)   Saved by a Pillar Box
(24)   Cruelty to a Horse
(25)   The Latest Steerable Balloon
(26)   Playmates
(27)   A Message from the Sea
(28)   The Story of a Colliery Disaster
(29)   The Sailor's Wedding
(30)   The Somnambulist
(31)   How the Poor Help the Poor – based on a popular song –

"It's the poor that helps the poor,
When Poverty knock at the door;
Those who live in mansions grand
Often fail to understand
The meaning of that word
"Hunger", I am sure
But the poor, they know the meaning and so
It's the poor that helps the poor."

Briefly, the film may be summarised as follows:

Scene 1.   A London Doorstep
A woman derelict –"Move on" – "I'm starving, Constable" –
"'Ere y'are, missus, get this down yer" – "Gawd bless yer, Constable!"

Scene 2.   A Street in the East End
Grandma takes home the washing – the load is too heavy – collapses –
Young factory girl to the rescue. "That's all right, ma, I ain't so old
as you".
"Thanks, my gal, you're a good sort, you are."

Scene 3.   The Navvy's dinner hour
A frugal meal on a seat in the park – The tramp –
" 'E looks a bit peckish!" – "Say, mate, 'ave a bit o' this, that's right,
now a drink." " 'Ow d'yer feel now?" "Better, eh?" – "Good luck to
yer, mate"

Scene 4.   A Slum in Pennyfields.

No money to pay the rent –furniture turned out into the street –
"Come on, out you go!" – Mother and child homeless – The coster
comes in time – "Shove 'em into my barrow, my missus will put you
up until your troubles are over".

(32)   Pigeons at St. Mark's, Venice.
(33)   Brown's Half Holiday
(34)   The Silver Wedding or Traitorous Guest.
(35)   Fantastic Fishing
(36)   The Pickpocket: A Chase through London
(37)   A Great Temptation – Synopsis detailed
Scene 1. Want –A Woman tempted –The Fall
Scene 2. Elopement by Motor car
Scene 3. Outside the Pawn shop – a friend in need is a friend indeed
Scene 4. Discovery
Scene 5. The Tempter Unmasked
Scene 6. The Wages of Sin
Scene 7. Just Punishment – A Noble Vengeance – Forgiveness –
        Restoration
(38)   The Gentleman Beggar

(39)	Children of the Slums – "A Day in the Country by means of the Fresh-air Fund of the "Daily Express" and Salvation Army. Hundreds of poor children are taken for a day in the country every summer – the Army takes thousands of children out every summer.
(40)	Man The Lifeboat
(41)	Life of a Cowboy – includes a scene entitled "Collection for Salvation Army Lassie
(42)	The Train Wreckers
(43)	The Fire Fiend
(44)	Professor List's Performing Animals
(45)	French Troops Marching
(46)	French Cavalry Drill
(47)	A Maiden's Dream
(48)	Britain's Boys
(49)	Fancy Diving
(50)	Stolen By Gypsies.

Section XII	**Humorous and Trick Films**
(1)	Off for the Holidays
(2)	The Lost Child
(3)	The Tramp's Dinner and Dessert
(4)	The Workhouse Granny, Age 93
(5)	Grandpa and the Butterfly
(6)	A Friend in Need
(7)	Rescued in Mid-Air
(8)	A Day at Brighton
(9)	Fixing the Swing
(10)	The Burglar and the Girls
(11)	The Penalty of Fame
(12)	A Motor Bicycle Misadventure
(13)	The Missing Legacy or The Story of a Brown Hat
(14)	The Baby Show
(15)	Snowballing
(16)	Willie, Tim and the Motor Car
(17)	Santa Claus! Mistake
(18)	Buying a Horse
(19)	What's the Joke?
(20)	Nosey Parker
(21)	Oh! That Hat
(22)	The Bad Halfpenny

In early 1907, with funds from their Cinematograph displays, the Salvation Army purchased their Training College for Officers at Clapton. At the same time, Howse left to become a full time Cinematographer for Walturdaw. However, in 1908, Commissioner Hay took a more Calvinistic moral position to the Cinematograph. He closed down their film exhibition service and production department. Consequently the exhibition of moving pictures were banned until 1961.[20]

Conclusion

By focusing on two bodies, one secular and one religious, both of whom incorporated Animated Photography between the years 1897–1907 it is possible to gain an idea about two of the circuits for film distribution that existed during this period. From around 1907, an expansion took place in the distribution of Animated Photography – the "entrepreneurs" took over from the moral and caring attitudes of the National Sunday League and the Salvation Army (as well as other similar religious and secular groupings). These organisations had maintained a vision of a social and spiritual uplift for the working man, woman and child, which was in opposition to the money making morality that was about to happen.

Notes

1. "The Era" (February 1898); "The Showman" (January 1902 and March 1902).

2. LCC Min 10, 805.

3. LCC Min 10, 832.

4. Year Books are held at Harrod's own Archive.

5. Most of the information relating to the National Sunday League (NSL) has been taken from their monthly publication: "Free Sunday Advocate and National Sunday League".

6. NSL June 1904.

7. NSL Jan 1906.

8. George Offor was managing director of "Bonn's Kinematograph Ltd." – see Volume 2 (page 41) of *The Beginnings of Cinema in England* (John Barnes).

9. Ibid., 64–65.

10. Patrick Loobey in "Cinema and Theatres of Wandsworth and Battersea" (page 26) spells his name as Dr. Coyne.

11. He was the father of Cecil Hepworth.

12. I believe that some of these lectures were on the subject of the cinematograph – i.e. introducing the machine to the public – and not just using it to project pictures.

13. See: Illustration on page 81 of *Living Pictures* Volume 1 No.2 "The London County Council and the Cinematograph" (1896–1900) (by the Author).

14. NSL Jan 1906.

15. LCC Min 10, 929.

16. Other reloigious orientated organisations involved in film during this period included: "Poly-technic Young Men's Christian Institute", "The Wesleyan Movement", "The Leysian Mission", The Church Missionary Society", Spiritualist Groups and "The Church Army" (see Stephen Bottomore, "Projecting for the Lord – The Work of Wilson and Carlile" *Film History* 14 (2) 2002).

17. Sources used for information on the Salvation Army included:
(a) "The War Cry" 12.12.1903 (page 10); (b) "The Field Officer" October 1906, 382–383; (c) "He was There" – Memoirs of F. Hayter Cox., 1949, 70); (d) "New Light in Limelight – The Salvation Army and the Film Industry 1890–1910' – John Cleary, 56

18. "He was There" – F. Hayter Cox. 1949, 70.

19. "Selected list of Films available for Renting Purposes by the Salvation Army Cinematograph Department" – original held at SA Archives.

20. "New Light in Limelight – The Salvation Army and the Film Industry 1890–1910" – John Cleary, 56).

Local entertainment and national patriotism: the distribution of colonial films in Early German cinema

Wolfgang Fuhrmann

University of Kassel, Germany

This essay focuses on the distribution of colonial films in Germany between 1904 and 1908 and deals in particular with non-theatrical distribution at a time when cinema was not yet fully institutionalized in Germany. The article wants to show in what way non-theatrical distribution was an alternative and a strong competitor to the commercial distribution system. At this time colonial films were not produced and distributed by the German government but by private film-amateurs, a few film companies, and colonial lobbyists such as the German Colonial Society: the *Deutsche Kolonialgesellschaft*.[1] They all had very different ideas about how to make colonial films available to the German public.[2] The different distribution contexts reveal local, regional or national distribution strategies that each position colonial films quite differently in German film culture. From this perspective, the study of distribution can be a chance to approach the historical reception of the films.

Traveling the colonies

When the German public learned about a premiere of colonial films with films from the African colonies at the Berlin Colonial Museum in April 1905, the films that were shown were not shot by a member of the colonial administration or commissioned by the Colonial department. The films' producer and operator was the entrepreneur and cinematographic amateur Carl Friedrich Müller (1868–1935). Müller made two extensive "film-trips" to the German African colonies from October 1904 until February 1905 and between January and May 1906.[3] For almost two years Müller was the only one in Germany who had films from *all* the African colonies.[4]

Müller's decision to travel to Africa was not exclusively a patriotic endeavor for the benefit of the fatherland but a combination of private and business interests. Moreover, Müller had several partners within the colonial lobby, who had their own interest in his successful film trip. Especially the exploitation of his films after his return shows in what way the films were carefully launched in Germany so that he and his collaborators could reap the utmost benefits of the films.

In his hometown Altenburg, Müller ran a very popular restaurant and beer garden on a little island in the lake of the city of Altenburg, called the *Insel*. After the purchase of a film projector in April 1904 Müller organized regularly film screenings during the summer season on the *Insel*. The film screenings definitely had their share in making Müller's restaurant the number one spot in the region for a joyful weekend entertainment and for other local entertainment venues it was hard, if not impossible, to compete with it.

With the new exclusive films from the African colonies, shot on 35mm, Müller could rise the popularity of his screenings, which was one more chance to consolidate his position as a successful and creative entrepreneur in the Altenburg region. To keep the local audience interested Müller used his colonial films very economically. He never showed all his films at once but programmed the films in separate screenings and continuously added new films from his journeys to his programs. A little zoo on the *Insel* with exotic animals that Müller had bought on his journeys made the Africa film-programs a real 'exotic experience'. From this perspective it was not colonialism as a political issue that made Müllers film screenings something special in his hometown, but the extraordinary activity of an Altenburg citizen who had traveled the African continent.

This aspect is also emphasized in the advert for Müller's film-premiere in March 1905 in Altenburg. It shows that the public could visit first Müller's African exhibition with all kinds of souvenirs and ethnographic objects before attending in the afternoon his screening and lantern slide show "My African Journey from Naples to Cape Town". (Fig.1) The emphasis on the very personal experience of his 'journey' makes the colonial aspect secondary. One first indication is given by the short summary of his slide show. One series showed Müller's visit of some Altenburg compatriots, *Landsleute*, which gave the local exhibition a very familiar undertone. Second, the film screening did not exclusively show "African living photographs", *Afrikanische lebende Photographien*, but also panorama shots of Rome, the Stephan's square, and Naples. In this respect, Africa and the colonies were 'only' stops on Müller's long and extraordinary journey. The films rather were part of a potpourri of travelogues and, therefore, correspond much more to the reception context of the early travelogue as it is described by Jennifer Peterson, a "… a substitute for actual travel that could be experienced by those without the financial means to tour around the globe".[5]

Even if the local public came to see Müller's films from Africa, the colonial films were not the programs' highlights. As the advert shows, Müller combined his personal travel films with other films such as "Mit dem Automobil nach dem Mont-Blanc" (With the automobile to the Mont-Blanc) and "Krönungsfest in England" (Coronation festivity in England). The observation in the advert that the last film was "the longest existing film ever" underlines once more that the colonial meaning was only secondary in the local context. Müller addressed the Altenburg public not as colonial patriots but as an audience that was interested in new visual spectacles and a high quality program of exclusive films.

But the Altenburg audience did not just benefit from Müller's unique footage from Africa at a time when no other colonial film material was available. A very personal kind of film-exchange between Müller and South Africa also made it possible to see films that no other cinema in Germany could show in this order or quality. On his first journey Müller made a stop in Durban, where he met one of the founding figures of South African cinema, Mr. Wolfram. According to Thelma Gutsche's study of early South African cinema, Wolfram was the most important film owner in South Africa at that time and known for his "quality programs" with British "educational films" and French "fantastic films".[6] Since Müller was not just traveling the colonies for shooting films but also to show films from the German *Heimat* to the local German and African public, I suppose that also the Durban public saw a very unique German film program

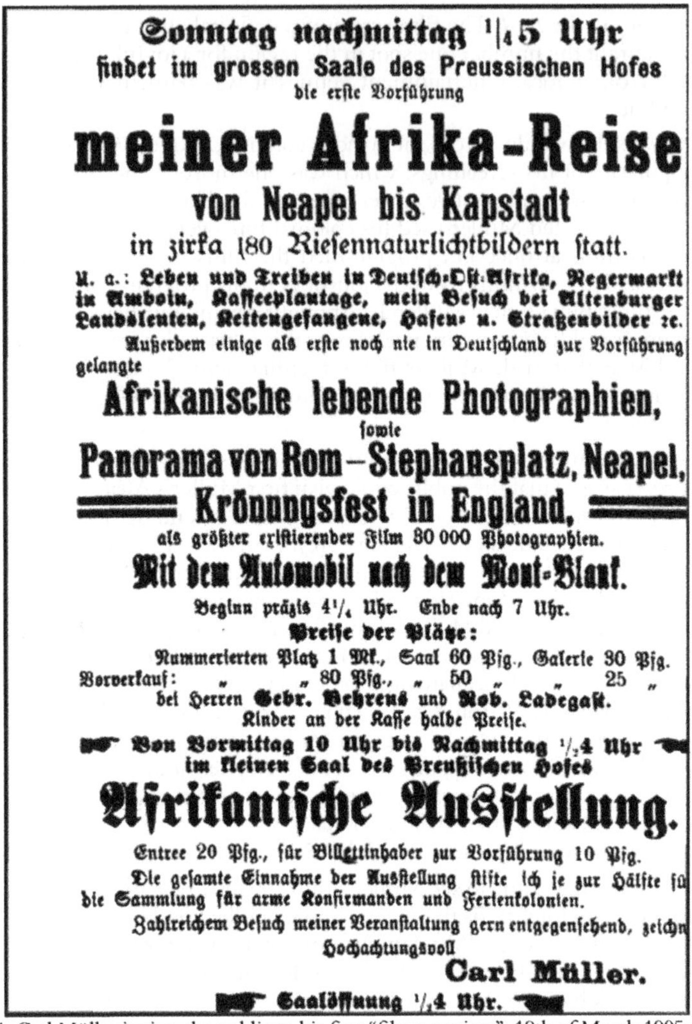

Sonntag nachmittag 1/4 5 Uhr
findet im grossen Saale des Preussischen Hofes
die erste Vorführung
meiner Afrika-Reise
von Neapel bis Kapstadt
in zirka 180 Riesennaturlichtbildern statt.
U. a.: Leben und Treiben in Deutsch-Ost-Afrika, Negermarkt in Amboin, Kaffeeplantage, mein Besuch bei Altenburger Landsleuten, Kettengefangene, Hafen- u. Straßenbilder 2c.
Außerdem einige als erste noch nie in Deutschland zur Vorführung gelangte
Afrikanische lebende Photographien,
sowie
Panorama von Rom – Stephansplatz, Neapel,
Krönungsfest in England,
als größter existierender Film 80 000 Photographien.
Mit dem Automobil nach dem Mont-Blanc.
Beginn präzis 4 1/4 Uhr. Ende nach 7 Uhr.
Preise der Plätze:
Nummerierten Platz 1 Mk., Saal 60 Pfg., Galerie 30 Pfg.
Vorverkauf: " " 80 Pfg., " 50 " " 25 "
bei Herren Gebr. Behrens und Rob. Ladegast.
Kinder an der Kasse halbe Preise.
Von Vormittag 10 Uhr bis Nachmittag 1/2 4 Uhr
im kleinen Saal des Preußischen Hofes
Afrikanische Ausstellung.
Entree 20 Pfg., für Billettinhaber zur Vorführung 10 Pfg.
Die gesamte Einnahme der Ausstellung stifte ich je zur Hälfte fü die Sammlung für arme Konfirmanden und Ferienkolonien.
Zahlreichem Besuch meiner Veranstaltung gern entgegensehend, zeichn
Hochachtungsvoll
Carl Müller.
Saalöffnung 1/4 4 Uhr.

Fig. 1. Carl Müller invites the public to his first "film premiere", 19th of March 1905 at the *Preußischer Hof* in Altenburg. [Source: *Altenburger Landes-Zeitung*, 18.03.1905.]

in December 1904. In turn, the Altenburg public had the chance to see a sample of Wolfram's South African quality film program at the end of July 1905, when Wolfram made a short stop in Altenburg during his trip through Europe. The screening was promoted as a program that had never been shown in Germany before.[7]

Variety and faked films

When Müller remarked that he had all the negatives of his films that were the first and only existing films from the colonies and therefore without competition, he was not quite right. Already in 1905 the Leipzig distributor Adolf Deutsch offered two films from Africa *Afrikanische Kriegsbilder* (African war images) and *Ostafrikanische Truppenschau* (East-African Military Parade). The geographic proximity of Altenburg to Leipzig (ca. 30 km) gives reason to speculate whether the two films were Müller's.

Also before 1905 films from the colonies seemed to have existed. As Corinna Müller has shown German cinema is rooted in the variety theatre and it is in the trade press of this entertainment sector where we probably find the first offers of colonial films.[8] In April 1904 the *Internationale Kinematographen-Gesellschaft G.m.b.H* from Berlin offered two films from German South-West Africa.[9] The company not only promoted "interesting" scenics of 20 meters from the colony, but also announced that more scenics from the colonies with images of the Herero uprise would follow within a very short time.[10] In the following weeks the film company did not mention again new material from the colony, which suggests that either the material never did reach Germany or that the films' quality was too poor to be offered to the variety theatres.[11] However, an important aspect in the company's advert campaign indicates another form of 'colonial' films that were distributed among the variety theatres. In the advert the company underlines that the existing films are no fakes or staged films, which suggests that staged films about the Herero-War in the German South-West colony also existed.[12] Unfortunately we do not have very much detailed information about the production of faked Herero-War films but the following description of the dramatic stage play *Die Schwarze Hölle* (The Black Hell) that premiered in July 1904 at the Belle-Alliance-Theater in Berlin gives an idea what such films were about and looked like.

The stage play tells the story of a young couple that are soon to get married. The man leaves his fiancée for fighting in the South-West colony. At home the woman has nightmares about the fate of her fiancé. The dream sequence is visualized through a film projection and shows the man fighting against a Herero Warrior. The young woman screams in her sleep and wakes up; the door bell rings and her fiancé safely enters the stage.[13]

The film sequence clearly is a colonial example of Tom Gunning's 'cinema of attractions' that, in this case, stages a thrilling and spectacular moment from the battlefields in the colony for the paying audience.[14] In terms of distribution, however, staged colonial films only seem to have been distributed for entertainment purposes in the variety programs and never got access to the venues of the organized colonial public as represented by the German Colonial Society, which I will discuss in the next paragraph.[15] As one review of a colonial film screening in one of the Society's branches suggests, 'real' colonial patriots preferred authentic films to faked staged films.[16] The success story of colonial films, therefore, is not to be found in the annals of the commercial cinemas nor in programs of the variety theatres but in the well-organized network of the German Colonial Society. In contrast to Carl Müller's efforts to use his films in order to consolidate his reputation in his hometown, the Colonial Society had a strong interest to win, with the help of film screenings, the general public for colonial matters.

Colonial films for the masses

The proliferation of voluntary associations was "one of the most remarkable cultural phenomena of the *Wilhelmine* epoch".[17] The biggest and most influential colonial association was the German Colonial Society that considered itself a center for all colonial matters.[18] Hundreds of local branches made the Society present in almost every German city and town. Even if not every town had a local cinema around 1905, the associations' clubhouses and meeting places presented an alternative network of venues for film screenings.[19] In 1905 the Colonial Society realized the effectiveness of the new medium and contracted Müller after his successful premiere in Berlin. From April 1905, Müller's films could be seen in the Colonial Society's branches all over

Germany: in big cities such as Berlin, Leipzig, Hamburg, Frankfurt, Stuttgart, Breslau or Cologne and in smaller cities like Neumünster, Homburg or Pirna.

The screenings in the Society's branches were carefully organized. Days, sometimes weeks, in advance the local public was informed about the upcoming event in the city. Although the Colonial Society's membership was dominated by professionals in business and industry, film screenings were not just organized to address the Society's members in a new-fashioned way. The Colonial Society wanted to reach broader circles that were outside the movement: the Society was clearly aiming at the masses.[20] Exact numbers about the size of the film audiences do not exist but studying the individual reviews shows that most of the screenings were sold out. Hundreds or thousands of viewers a day were not unusual.

However, in contrast to the theme of traveling that characterized the local Altenburg screenings, Müller's films in the Colonial Society's branches were most effective in terms of their colonial ideological meaning. Films with panorama shots of the African colonial cities, scenes on board a German Steamship liner on its way to Africa, the arrival at the colonial harbor, buildings of the colonial administration, sisal and coffee plantations, views of the African jungle, panoramic shots of the coastline, military exercises of Askari soldiers in East Africa and of German military forces, phantom rides into the Usambara mountains in East Africa and the South West African desert, the local transportation systems, the efficiency of the colonial judiciary, dances of African natives, an African market and other images of colonial daily life literally showed the colonies *in motion* and offered the Colonial Society the chance to present a positive image of the colonies.

In contrast to Müller's local strategy to attract the home town public with a program of a 'local globetrotter', the example of the Pirna screenings in December 1906 shows that Müller's colonial films were first of all promoted as a "Great exhibition of Living Pictures and Slides from the German Colonies" that were "highly worth seeing", *höchst sehenswert* (Fig. 2). The emphasis that the films had already been shown in colonial metropolises such as Berlin and Hamburg, was certainly part of the Colonial Society's strategy to turn colonial patriotism into an every German citizen's duty. In this respect the Pirna audience could be given the feeling to be part of the national colonial audience.[21]

Regional strategies: the Woermann Company

As important as Müller's cooperation with the Colonial Society was his acquaintance with Adolph Woermann, the director of the biggest shipping company at that time. Through Woermann Müller got in contact with the German Navy League. Since neither the size of the German ocean-going fleet nor the size of the merchant fleet was sufficient to conduct a colonial policy in grand style, Woermann was a leader among those who voted for the expansion of the German merchant- and sea fleet.[22] Events at which his concept found the strongest support were film screenings for the Navy League. Woermann sponsored Navy Leagues' organized trips for students and teachers (*Schülerfahrten* and *Lehrerfahrten*) to the German harbors during the summer break.[23] To host the students and teachers Woermann offered free board and lodging on his ships that anchored there. In 1905 and 1906 Müller's colonial film shows were part of the daily programs of these visits. At such screenings Müller's films served to demonstrate the need for a strong merchant fleet for colonial trading and a powerful ocean-going fleet to protect trading and the colonies, while the recent events in the South-West colony were an additional argument to emphasize the need for Germany's military presence in the colonies.

Fig. 2. The DKG adresses through Müller's screenings the local colonial public /Pirnaer Anzeiger/, 7.12.1906.

The 'Kinemtographenkampagne': 1907/08 – 1908/09

At the end of 1906 the Colonial Society purchased Müller's films, probably with the intention to start its own film archive, similar to the already existing huge still picture archive. Since 1891 the Colonial Society was running the picture archive that increased year by year through the purchase of new lantern slides and through donations of originals or duplicates from official, commercial, or private collections.[24] The pictures were usually compiled into larger series and covered all aspects of colonial life. The archive was not exclusively for the Society's branches, and series could be borrowed by other patriotic associations, schools, and other public institutions as well.[25]

Müller's films could only be a first step towards a colonial film archive that offered the same broad range of topics like the picture archive, but already in 1907 new films could be added. While the "film archive" received new films from the German New Guineas from the German steamship line *Norddeutscher Lloyd*, the film company *Deutsche Bioscope-Gesellschaft* offered the Society to include their new films from the West African colonies into the Society's colonial film programs. The cooperation between the Bioscope and the Colonial Society is particularly interesting as it underlines the attractiveness of the non-theatrical market. The Bioscope not only became the Society's official exhibitor of colonial film programs for the Society's so called *Kinematographenkampagne*, cinematographic campaign, but it also run a double distribution strategy. Probably the same material that was shown in the Society's branches could also be purchased by the commercial cinemas. This way, around 1907/08 the Colonial Society had more than 10,000 m of colonial film available. Calculating an average projection speed of between 16 and 18 frames per second this made between nine to ten hours of film from the German colonies.

The Colonial Society started the *Kinematographenkampagne* rather successfully. Between October and December 1907, the *Bioscope* was booked for 120 screenings on 45 days in 39 different places.[26] For the screenings the *Bioscope* offered full service and supplied the branches with posters and programs. The risk of empty screening halls was minimized through a cooperation between the Colonial Society and the German Navy League, that had contracted the Deutsche Bioscope as well.

The audience's chance to see film programs not in public cinemas but in one of the Colonial Society or the Navy League's branches gave traveling exhibitors a hard time. Associational screenings were a threat to the commercial business.[27] In an article in the *Kinematograph* in February 1908 exhibitors attacked the Navy League and called for resistance against the Navy League's screenings. Although activities of the Colonial Society were not mentioned in this context, the fact that the Society and the Navy League were cooperating with each other at this time and both had contracts with the Deutsche Bioscope makes this criticism also relevant for the general discussion of the relationship between the commercial film business and non-theatrical/associational film screenings. Cinemas complained that:

> "Where [the Navy League] has done a screening, private cinema owners' chances for business are without any doubt lost, since soldiers are ordered by companies to the screenings, schools and other institutions usually have to line up and in fact everybody else with two pennies left in his pockets is mobilized."[28]

The exhibitors' concern about the 'associational cinema culture' at that particular time becomes even more plausible if we look at the size of the cities and towns in which colonial film screenings took place. The majority of reports of screenings in 1907 and 1908 did not come from big cities but small towns where a local commercial cinema culture was probably not yet established. Associational film screenings therefore may have indeed posed an existential threat to local exhibitors.

The article continues, that the Navy League forced the owners of local lecture halls to cancel contracts with commercial exhibitors, in order to make possible the Navy League's screenings. Exhibitors were therefore emphasizing their own patriotic commitment and promoted their cinemas as institutions of patriotic integrity. They considered their film programs as an important contribution in the formation of the public's patriotic way of thinking:

> "We are at least as good patriots as the Navy League and its members, we are paying no small fees for our cinemas, without covering them up patriotically, and we present programs in which the patriotic feelings of the citizen are continuously strengthened and consolidated."[29]

But cinemas did not have to worry for too long. Already in 1908 screenings in the Colonial Society's branches decreased in number and came to an end by the end of the year. Rather than suggesting that it was the members' lack of interest in the colonial matters, I would suggest that the Colonial Society, and voluntary associations in general, had to face structural improvements and new conditions in the cinema landscape that made associational screenings less popular.

Between 1907 and 1909 the number of colonial film releases increased so that viewers were not longer dependent on the Colonial Society. Parallel to this, the number of cinemas increased continuously. Second, as reviews show, film screenings in the branches seemed to suffer from technical problems with regard to their films' quality.

The more operators traveled the colonies, the more they learned about how to produce good films under extreme climatic conditions: In other words, operators learned how to improve the films' quality. Third, the production of new films was costly and the Society was never a really rich association.

Finally, while traveling film exhibitors considered associational screenings to be unfair competition, the Colonial Society in turn realized that the variety in the programs of commercial cinemas was a strong competitor to their screenings. Although colonial film programs were never exclusively compiled from colonial films but also included slapstick shorts and other 'interesting films', reviews of film screenings in the branches show that these screenings suffered from parallel film screenings of other exhibitors that most likely had also colonial films in their programs.[30]

Efforts to use film to promote the colonies for propaganda purposes were not lacking after cessation of the colonial screenings by the Colonial Society. For the local branches film screenings remained one of the possible propaganda techniques. The organization of film screenings in this case was no longer coordinated with the Society's office in Berlin but most likely with a local exhibitor. The financial resources available to the Colonial Society limited their efforts to buy new films from the colonies and even if the Society could not close any contracts with professional film companies, for the Society it was just a question of the right moment for starting again with film screenings in the branches, whose success was beyond any doubt.[31]

Non-theatrical distribution within a private or associational framework challenged commercial cinemas, even if only for a short period as it was the case with colonial films. However, considering the network of voluntary associations, the limited circulation of the films' within a local context or the entertainment sector such as the variety theatre, the study of the distribution strategies in early cinema seems to be particular productive in the case of early nonfiction films. The broad range of topics that characterize this early film form shows how every aspect could be turned into a new cinematic experience. Early nonfiction cinema, therefore, might be an indication for the existence of very different 'cinemas' that each had their own individual distribution practice.

Notes

1. Fuhrmann, Wolfgang, 'Propaganda, Sciences, and Entertainment. German Colonial Cinematography: A case study in the history of early nonfiction cinema'. Ph.D. Dissertation Utrecht University, 2003.

2. In fact, the German government never produced colonial films for propaganda purposes by itself and only started at a very late stage to support actively the production of such films.

3. On his first journey Müller only visited the East African and the South-West African colony. On his second trip Müller he visited Togo, Cameroon and again German South-West Africa.

4. Other films from the colonies existed as well around 1905 but no other producer/distributor could offer films from all the German colonies.

5. Peterson, Jennifer, "Truth is stranger than fiction': Travelogues from the 1910s in the Nederlands Filmmuseum', in Hertogs, Daan and Nico de Klerk (eds), *Uncharted Territory. Essays on early nonfiction film* (Amsterdam: Stichting Nederlands Filmmuseum, 1997).

6. Gutsche, Thelma, *The History and Social Significance of Motion Pictures in South Africa 1895–1940* (Cape Town: Howard Timmins, 1972).

7. *Altenburger Landes-Zeitung* (22 November 1905).

8. Müller, Corinna, *Frühe deutsche Kinematographie. Formale, wirtschaftliche und kulturelle Entwicklung 1907–1912* (Stuttgart, Weimar: Metzler, 1994).

9. *Der Artist* 1002 (24 April 1904).

10. In January 1904 the Herero-German war broke out. When it ended in 1908 the majority of the Herero people had been killed. Today, the war is considered to be one of the first genocides of the 20th century.

11. A small article from May 1904 supports the last suggestion. Though the article mentions that new material has arrived, the company did not promote these films in the following adverts. *Der Artist* 1006 (22 May 1904).

12. Garncarz, Joseph, 'The Origins of Film Exhibition in Germany', in Bergfelder, T., Erica Carter and Deniz Göktürk (eds), *The German Cinema Book* (London: BFI Publishing, 2002), 112–120.

13. *Der Artist* 1013 (10 July 1904).

14. Gunning, Tom, 'The Cinema of Attractions: Early Film, its Spectator and the Avant-Garde' in Elsaesser, Thomas (ed.) *Space, Frame, Narrative* (London: BFI Publishing, 1990).

15. Another screening of unique footage from Africa that was probably shot in the hinterland of German East Africa supports my thesis. The African explorer, zoologist, and wildlife protectionist Carl Georg Schillings (1865–1921) was probably one of the first German filmmakers to bring back films from Africa, when he returned from his last East African expedition in 1903. Some of his films were shown in April 1905 at the popular variety theatre, the Hansa Theatre in Hamburg. To my knowledge the colonial movement ignored his films that were never mentioned in the context of any of the German Colonial Society's film screenings. *Artistische Nachrichten* (April 1905): 5.

16. *Gränzbote*, Volks-Zeitung von der oberen Donau 97 (26 April 1907).

17. Roger Chickering, *We Men who feel most German. A Cultural Study of the Pan German League, 1886–1914* (Boston: Goerge Allen & Unwin, 1984), 183.

18. For a detailed analysis of the Society's role in Imperial Germany see Pierard, Richard, *The German Colonial Society 1882–1914*. Ph.D. Dissertation State University of Iowa, 1964.

19. Fuhrmann Wolfgang, 'Locating Early Film Audiences: voluntary associations and colonial film', *Historical Journal of Film, Radio and Television* 22.3 (2002): 291–304.

20. Deutsche Kolonialgesellschaft, *Vorstand* (22 May 1907): 32.

21. The non-colonial part of the programs are not unmentioned but it is only after the visual colonial attractions such as Togo, Cameroon, German South-West Africa and German East Africa that the viewer could also watch other shorts.

22. Schinzinger, Francesca, *Die Kolonien und das Deutsche Reich. Die wirtschaftliche Bedeutung der deutschen Besitzungen in Übersee* (Wiesbaden: Franz Steiner Verlag, 1984).

23. *Afrika-Post* 127, 08.09.1905: 269, *Die Flotte* 9 (September 1906): 130.

24. See also: Fuhrmann, Wolfgang, 'Lichtbilder und kinematographische Aufnahmen aus den Kolonien', *KINtop* 8 (1999): 101–116.

25. Deutsche Kolonialgesellschaft, *Jahresbericht* (1905): 51.

26. Deutsche Kolonialgesellschaft, *Jahresbericht* (1907): 47.

27. 'Der Deutsche Flottenverein als Schausteller', *Der Komet* 927 (27 December 1902); 'Flottenverein und Kinematograph', *Der Komet* 1083 (23 December 1905), quoted in: Diederichs, Helmut H., 'Die Anfänge der deutschen Filmpublizisitk 1895–1909', *Publizistik* 1 (1985): 55–71.

28. 'Die Kinematographen-Theater und der Deutsche Flottenverein', *Der Kinematograph* 60 (19 February 1908).

29. Ibid.

30. Fuhrmann, Wolfgang, 'Locating Early Film Audiences'.

31. The example of a film screening at the Lorraine branch in St. Avold in March 1914 shows that some branches did not even hesitate to show foreign film productions such as Paul Rainey's *Reisen Und Grosse Jagden in Innern Afrikas* (Lassoing Wild Animals) to attract the local public to a patriotic endeavor in support of German colonialism. *DKZ* 18 (2 May 1914): 303.

Early forms of film distribution in Germany, 1896–1905

Joseph Garncarz

Theatre, Film and Television Studies, University of Cologne, Germany

In this article I would like to describe the development of film distribution in the early German film industry.[1] My analysis will reveal that the German situation differed from the US situation as we know it. The main difference is that in Germany (and in other European countries) the travelling shows developed as a specific exhibition form that was crucial for the establishment of film as a mass medium. The characteristics of these travelling shows were that they used their own mobile theatres, presented only films, and regularly appeared at festivals, markets and fairs that took place throughout the year.[2] Even before cinemas, namely permanent theatres presenting mainly films, boomed from 1905/06 on, the travelling shows made film accessible to a million spectators per week from every social class and region in Germany. As in the US, variety theatres showed "living pictures" as one of the acts in their lively entertainment programmes. But in contrast to the US, the variety theatre did not play the central role for the diffusion of film nor for the development of a specific cultural identity of the new medium. Both of these early exhibition venues in Germany, i.e. the travelling shows as well as the variety theatres, developed their own distribution form, which was shaped by their specific cultural traditions and was economically best suited for their conditions. Firstly, I will analyse the distribution forms of the German variety theatres and travelling shows in detail; secondly, I will ask whether the innovations in the distribution sector that cinemas brought with them changed the distribution practices of the other venues. The most important source for research on the early German film industry before 1905 are the trade journals of variety artists and travelling showmen, especially *Der Artist* and *Der Komet*. Every piece of information, from articles to advertisements, was systematically examined to answer the questions under discussion.

The film distribution system of variety theatres

Since variety theatres had a fixed location and usually presented shows on a daily basis, they had to draw the same audience over and over again, so they needed a regular supply of new films. Larger variety theatres would have been able to make a profit within two to four weeks with a film programme if they bought it, but this was not possible for smaller houses, and this practice would not have been in accord with the organizational structure of the variety business. Thus a distribution system developed that involved hiring the entire film act, i.e. operators along with projectors and films, just as acrobats or comedians were contracted. Within a few years, due to changing economic condi-

Meinen seit December v. J in den **Berliner Reichshallen** als am Orte bestfunctionirenden

Kinetographen, lebende Photographien,

Bildergrösse: 3 zu 2,15 m, mit gut besetztem, stets wechselndem Repertoir, sowie effectvollem von 70 Glühlampen erleuchteten Rahmen, wünsche ab 1. Mai weiter engagirt zu sehen. Offerten bitte per Adr.: **Arthur Fränkel, Berlin, Friedrichstr. 17a,** oder **Reichshallen** an mich selbst zu adressiren.

Max Körbitz.

Fig. 1. Ad by the variety artist Max Körbitz searching for an engagement with his cinematograph at a variety show *Der Artist*, 633, 28 March 1897.

tions, two different forms of this system developed, which differed according to whether independent variety artists or the film companies themselves were hired. Insofar as access to a supply of films that was large enough existed and could be made available in the variety theatre presenting a film act, both forms allowed adapting programmes to the specific tastes and interests of the audience present.

At first, variety artists bought projectors and films from different companies such as Oskar Messter, H.O. Foersterling or H. Schmidt and offered cinematograph acts to variety theatres. Between 1896 and 1901, variety artists regularly advertised their film acts in trade journals such as *Der Artist* alongside acrobats and dancers (Fig. 1). However, around 1900, due to dropping prices for projectors, film companies established a new form of distribution to eliminate the variety artists as middlemen and secure their own profit. Thus many film companies began renting operators, projectors and films at lower prices to variety theatres directly; before 1901, an engagement such as Messter's

Fig. 2. Ad by the Dutch film company Anton Nöggerath searching for an engagement at a German variety theatre *Der Artist*, 991, 7 February 1904.

at the Apollo-Theater in Berlin was the exception. Around 1900 the first ads by film companies that directly addressed variety theatres appeared in *Der Artist*. Between 1900 and 1902, companies that can be found in this trade journal are Film-Fabrik Nöggerath (Amsterdam), Messters Kosmograph-Compagnie m.b.H. (Berlin), the Internationale Kinematographen-Gesellschaft m.b.H. (Berlin), and Jules Greenbaum's Deutsche Bioscope-Gesellschaft m.b.H. (Berlin) (Fig. 2). German film companies dominated the variety market, because they best met the demand for the so-called *optische Berichterstattung* ('visual reports'), which became the staple of the show in Germany's international variety theatres around 1900. Visual reports, which were the predecessors of cinema newsreels, visualized the current events that were considered culturally relevant by producers and audiences. Not only were these companies located in Germany, where events of national importance took place, but their collaborators were also more attuned to the events in which German audiences were especially interested. As a result of the changing distribution strategy, after 1901 hardly any ads by independent variety artists for cinematograph acts can be found; instead, variety artists placed ads to sell their projectors and films, which had lost their value for them.

The film distribution system of travelling shows

The travelling film shows worked with a distribution system that differed from the variety theatre system and was based in the established tradition of the itinerant entertainment business. Travelling showmen did not rent their equipment, such as carousels and swings, they bought it. Accordingly, showmen wanting to present films bought a mobile theatre, a projector, a screen and a collection of films. Buying films was the most profitable solution under the conditions of a constantly changing audience as well as the logistically optimal one, because renting films would have been difficult to organise in a business that was constantly on the move. When travelling showmen wanted to stay in one place for a longer period, e.g. for a festival that went on for more than two or three days, or when competition was extremely strong in a particular location, they would bring along a collection of films as large as several hundred titles, from which programmes could be put together that would keep audiences entertained. Since showmen had the chance to directly monitor audience reactions to find out which types of films were preferred, they would select their programmes according to demand.

The travelling showmen bought single films, not pre-selected programmes, and they usually bought them directly from film producers. Production companies advertised a selection of their supply in the most important trade journal of the travelling show business *Der Komet* (Fig. 3). Customers could either make a selection directly from these ads or order a catalogue to look at the entire stock. German producers who regularly advertised were Oskar Messter (from 1896 on), the Internationale Kinematographen-Gesellschaft (starting in 1901), and Jules Greenbaum's Deutsche Bioscope-Gesellschaft (as from 1902). A small number of German producers faced a large and annually growing number of foreign producers who advertised with a much greater frequency – these included the US company S. Lubin (starting in 1901), the French companies Pathé (starting in 1901) and Gaumont (as from 1903), as well as the British Warwick Trading Company (as from 1903). Before German branches were opened, as Pathé's for example did in Berlin in late 1903, travelling showmen would order abroad, unless a German supplier existed, such as Gustav Leis for S. Lubin in Pirmasens.

With the growing number of travelling film shows competition intensified around 1904/05. As a consequence, several travelling showmen went out of business. Others bought a large number of new films, because competition increased the likelihood that

Fig. 3. Ad by Pathé's German sales office offering films to the German travelling Showmen *Der Komet*, 977, 12 December 1903.

Fig. 4. Ad by the travelling showman J. Dienstknecht selling several of his films *Der Komet*, 1072, 7 October 1905.

a certain film had already been presented to a particular audience by a rival company. Both groups started to sell their used films, which they advertised in *Der Komet* (Fig. 4). Addressees of such ads were competing travelling show companies as well as cinemas, which appeared around 1905 in the centres of large cities and spread to the smallest provincial towns within a few years.

The influence of cinemas on the film distribution systems of variety theatres and travelling shows

Permanent theatres presenting only films appeared in considerable numbers around 1905/06, because the boom of large department stores had become a threat to small businesses and therefore many salesmen decided to convert their shops into store-front film theatres.[3] One condition for this was a steady supply of films, which was readily available due to the existing large demand by the travelling shows – a market for which Pathé produced with the greatest success. Travelling shows significantly influenced cinemas: They served as a cultural model for the programming and presentation of films.

For cinemas, it made more sense economically to rent films rather than to buy them, because their audiences stayed the same, and the daily presentation of films with a change of programme several times a week necessitated a very large turn-over. The only near functional equivalent was an exchange system among a group of cinemas entering into an agreement that each would buy a relatively small stock of films and trade their films among one another. Thus, in Germany, a rental exchange system developed around 1906/07 as a consequence of the cinema boom – in the US, by contrast, the opposite was the case, i.e. the nickelodeon boom was partly brought about by the development of the rental system.[4] The first film distributors in Germany were not distributors exclusively, but rather cinema owners who also functioned as distributors – with the exception of Pathé, which began to rent films directly to German cinema owners in 1907. Some travelling showmen who gave up their itinerant entertainment business and instead opened cinemas also became distributors, such as, for example, Hermann Josef Fey and Theodor Scherff. Contrary to common assumptions,[5] permanent cinemas did not rent entire film programmes, but put these together in accordance with audiences' preferences.

The development of the new distribution system of cinemas at first had no repercussions on the distribution systems of variety theatres and travelling shows, i.e. these exhibition venues continued the established practices of hiring the complete film act and buying films, respectively. This also clearly shows how well these systems were functionally adapted to their contexts. However, apart from the rapid spreading of cinemas, there was one event in the distribution sector that was partly responsible for the demise of the travelling film show business after 1911. In October 1912, Pathé was the first and until 1914 the only company on the German market that turned to solely renting their own films instead of selling them, and thus the travelling showmen lost their most important supplier. Most travelling showmen turned to other entertainment forms (e.g. carousels), but some opened their own cinemas.

Translation by Annemone Ligensa

Notes

1. A more detailed study of early forms of film distribution in Germany can be found in my book on the emergence of cinema in Germany: *Die Entstehung des Kinos in Deutschland 1896–1914* (Frankfurt am Main: Stroemfeld, 2007, forthcoming). Reference to contemporary sources can be found there.

2. Garncarz, Joseph: 'The Origins of Film Exhibition in Germany', Tim Bergfelder, Erica Carter, Deniz Göktürk (eds): *The German Cinema Book* (London: BFI, 2002), 112–120.

3. Garncarz, Joseph: 'Über die Entstehung der Kinos in Deutschland 1896–1914', *KINtop* (11, 2002): 145–158.

4. Musser, Charles: *The Emergence of Cinema* (Berkeley, Los Angeles, London: University of California Press, 1994), 365–368.

5. Müller, Corinna: *Frühe deutsche Kinematographie* (Stuttgart, Weimar: Metzler, 1994), 47–73.

'Just like a Public Library maintained for public welfare': 28mm as a comprehensive service strategy for non-theatrical clientele, 1912–23

Anke Mebold

Bonn, Germany

Introduction

The knowledge about the 28mm gauge and its world-wide spread is still rather fragmented, and may remain so due to large gaps in the extant documentation.[1] What lies at the core of my intention is to shed some light on the bold and innovative distribution move into the amateur, or 'salon' sector that Pathé Frères initiated in 1911 with the 28mm Pathé KoK system and its highly differentiated international marketing, and how this salon concept, specifically in the US, very quickly carried a large share of its momentum into the educational sector.

The defining attributes of the 28mm system are: simplicity and portability of the equipment, non-flammability of the film material, and absolute incompatibility with theatrical 35mm film and equipment. These attributes appear to define the market niche occupied by 28mm in a different fashion in each country.

An attempt at outlining some of the general amateur and educational market circumstances using Germany as an example

In Germany the professional 35mm standard remains the dominant format even in amateur circles until the advent of 8mm film. Those small gauge formats that acquire a limited presence in Germany before the early 1930s are 17.5mm, 9.5mm and 16mm.

In 1928 Wolfgang Jaensch ponders the film format choices for the amateur.[2] To him the most significant considerations for the amateur are price and compatibility, and regardless of cost he postulates as the ideal amateur format the 35mm 'Normalfilm'. He exhibits certain hostility towards the diversity of small-gauge formats available and provides a list in chronological order of their appearance on the market.

He summarizes:

> "Luckily most of these formats are not wide-spread or they no longer merit serious consideration by the amateur. [...] The 'Halbnormalfilm' [17.5mm] has much, if not everything to recommend it."

Yet, as Jaensch points out, 17.5mm by 1928 has definitely failed to carve out a

Normalfilm	35	mm breit;	Bild 18 ×24 mm
Ernemann-Einlochfilm	17,5	mm breit;	Bild 11,5×15 mm
Pathé-Kok-Film . . .	28	mm breit;	Bild 14,5×19,5 mm
American-Safety-Standard-Film (wie vorstehend, jedoch andere Fortschaltlöcher),	28	mm breit;	Bild 14,5×19,5 mm
Movette-Film	17,5	mm breit;	Bild 9 ×12 mm
Halbnormalfilm . . .	17,5	mm breit;	Bild 8,2×11 mm
Pathé-Baby-Film . .	9,5	mm breit;	Bild 6 × 8,5 mm
Eine-Kodak-Film . .	16	mm breit;	Bild 7,5×10,5 mm
Pathé-Rural-Film . .	17,5	mm breit;	Bild 9,5×13,5 mm

Fig. 1. Film gauges as presented by Jaensch 1928 'in the order of historical development'

permanent niche on the market, and 9.5mm and 16mm are the only options: 9.5mm has the advantage of price and a sizeable selection of equipment, while 16mm is considered to be the future in spite of high cost. Already, Jaensch points out, the available 16mm equipment has exceeded the presence of 9.5mm equipment. He writes:

"The situation in Germany is rather favourable in this regard, as here neither one nor the other format has gained dominance; Germany has up to this point been a country of film amateurs based on 'Normalfilm'."

He closes his chapter on film formats with the statement:

"Further formats are not to be expected; should tendencies to 'enrichen' the world with such become apparent, then the amateurs must form a solid front of determined protest."

Nevertheless, Germany certainly did embrace the 8mm format just a few years later, in 1932, but one could postulate that in Germany the proliferation of amateur and educational use formats – lacking interchangeability and universal validity – must have aroused more suspicion, annoyance, and rejection than in other markets. The amount of extant 28mm films and equipment in Germany appears extremely limited,[3] and there are no signs of German language on surviving 28mm film, equipment, nor in paper documentation. Therefore most items were probably imported from France and Great Britain into the collections of archives and museums after the actual 28mm era was over: So far there is no trace of an attempt at distribution of the Pathé KoK system on the German Market. Given that Pathé removed from the German market in August 1914, just before the outbreak of WWI,[4] the time frame for marketing 28mm in Germany would have been extremely limited, or would have required a distribution entity highly independent from Pathé Frères themselves.

The fire risk from a German perspective

The issue of fire risk posed by the 35mm nitrate material, which lies at the heart of the 28mm safety venture, is briefly discussed by Jaensch in as late as 1929.[5] He mentions a German manufacturers' agreement to produce small-gauge film only of non-flammable materials, and, himself a proponent of the 35mm gauge as standard also for the amateur market, he mentions that 35mm can also be manufactured of non-flammable material, usually marked by edge-code as 'Schwerentflammbar' (hardly inflammable), 'Sicherheitsfilm' (safety film) or 'Non-flam'. Yet, in his 1929 publication he concedes

Name der Stadt¹)	Zahl der Kinematographenbetriebe im Jahre:		Bestehen dort Polizeiverordnungen:			Zahl der Brände in Kinematographenbetrieben im Jahre 1909
	1.1.1900	1.1.1910	sicherheitspolizeilicher Art?	zensurpolizeilicher Art?	Sind jugendl. Personen vom Besuch durch sie ausgeschlossen?	
Übertrag 15	262		5	7	4	10
Frankfurt a. O.		3				
Halle		9	ja			
Hamburg	1	40	ja	.		2
Hannover		14				1
Kiel		12	ja	ja (wie Altona)		
Königsberg		18	ja			
Leipzig		31 (seit 1906)	ja	ja		2
Liegnitz		2				1
Lübeck		5 (seit 1906)	ja			
Magdeburg		10	ja			3
Metz		6				1.
München		28	ja	ja	Schulpflichtige Kinder ohne Begleitung Erwachsener.	
Posen		8	ja			
Remscheid		2		ja	Schulpflichtige Kinder ohne Begleitung Erwachsener.	1
Stettin		11				2
Straßburg		7	ja	ja		
Stuttgart		9	ja (als Ministerialerlaß von 1905)	ja (als Ministerialerlaß von 1908)		1
Würzburg	1	4				
Zusammen: 33 Städte	Insgesamt: 480		Insges.: in 17 Städten	Insges.: in 14 Städten	Insges.: in 6 Städten	Insges.: 24

¹) Die freigelassenen Felder bedeuten eine Verneinung der Frage.

Fig. 2. First part of an overview of the cinema business – including its fires – in Germany, published by Hans Werth in 1910.

that little use is made hereof, due to the mechanical strain in professional operation that the safety materials are less capable of enduring.

In contrast to this, 1911 Liesegang wrote about the fire risk attending Cinematograhic screenings:

"It is easy to understand that the introduction of a non-flammable or at least hardly

Name der Stadt¹)	Zahl der Kinematographenbetriebe im Jahre: 1.1.1900	1.1.1910	Bestehen dort Polizeiverordnungen: sicherheitspolizeilicher Art?	zensurpolizeilicher Art?	Sind jugendl. Personen vom Besuch durch sie ausgeschlossen?	Zahl der Brände in Kinematographenbetrieben im Jahre 1909
Altona		6	ja	ja (für den ganzen Regierungsbezirk Schleswig)	Kinder unter 15 Jahren.	
Berlin	Einige Wanderunternehmen.	139	ja (vom 30 September 1907)	ja (vom 20. Mai 1908)		7
Bochum		10				
Braunschweig		7 (seit 1906)	ja	ja		
Bremen		4	ja	ja		
Breslau		15				2
Kassel		5				
Crefeld		3				
Danzig		8		ja		
Darmstadt		3			Alle schulpflichtigen Kinder ohne Begleitung der Eltern oder Vormünder.	
Dortmund		10	Es sind allgemeine Bestimmungen aufgestellt, die im einzelnen Fall als polizeiliche Verfügung zugestelt werden.			
Düsseldorf		10		ja		
Elberfeld		6				
Essen		21		ja	Alle Personen unter 16 Jahren ohne Begleitung Erwachsener.	1
Frankfurt a. M.		15			Alle Personen unter 16 Jahren ohne Begleitung der Eltern oder Vormünder.	
Zusammen: 15	Summa: 262		Summa: 5 Städte	Summa: 7 Städte	Summa: 4 Städte	Summa: 10

¹) Die freigelassenen Felder bedeuten eine Verneinung der Frage.

Fig. 3. Second part of Werth's overview of the cinema business.

flammable film material would mean an immense advance. The difficulties posed by the manufacture of such a film are extraordinary, many attempts have failed."[6]

That he would be ignorant of the advances which Pathé Frères were making at just that time is surprising. Nevertheless, for two more decades, instead of using safety film which has become available, Germany comes up with a rather intricate system of minimizing the fire risk while continuing use of nitrate film in the amateur and educational film sector: classification of projectors. This system is explained in detail by Wolfgang Jaensch in the context of use of film in the German school system:

"Following suggestions made by the Industry and the 'Deutsche Kinotechnische Gesellschaft' some years ago a classification system was sought. For three years this system has been in effect in a few German states (Saxonia, Prussia, Bavaria) and it is recognized by others. A Reichs-wide legislation based on the experience gained is to be expected shortly."

The three levels of fire safety classification are defined in the following manner:

Class A: "This includes cinema machines, where film stopped in the gate ignites before one minute has passed." Class B: "[...] after 1 minute but within the first 60 minutes". Class C: "[...] after 60 minutes". "Machines of Class B and C may be used with 'Stillstandseinrichtungen' [devices for stopping film in gate]. (B-Machines only if ignition of the film takes place after 10 minutes or later.) Furthermore, machines of these classifications can be placed within the auditorium if certain regulations are adhered to, thus are not tied to a specific machine-room (also named 'Vorführrraum' [Projection Booth]) which in many instances is difficult if not impossible to create. [...] Machines must be identified by type tags, also required is a classification certificate, which serves as a kind of operation-permit".[7]

To maintain safe operation of the projectors within this complex system for safe-guarding spectators, the operators were professionally trained by the 'Lichtbildstellen'.

Great Britain's approach to safe projection circumstances

In contrast, Great Britain, dealt with the problem in a different manner. Requirements for public exhibition had been legislated by the *Cinematograph Act of 1909*, the result thereof was a choice of: permanent booth, portable booth or safety film. In a rather charming chapter titled: *What to do if the Film Fires*,[8] Bernard E. Jones in 1919 (which places this publication at the climax of 28mm presence in the US and certainly at a moment of flourishing 28mm operations in Great Britain) specifies the procedures required of the professional film operator and the circumstances of operation and booths:

"When a portable operating box is used it should be constructed of No. 16 gauge sheet iron, and be not less than 6 ft. 6 in. x 5 ft. x 4 ft. 6 in. in dimensions, on angle-iron frame, well fitted, and lined with sheet asbestos; and there should be a self-closing door opening outwards, with flange inside, leaving the door flush and smoke-tight. There may not be more than two openings for each lantern in front, having reasonably heavy shutters, working in iron guides, dropping freely and smoke-tight, held up by a light cord and released instantly from outside or inside, either or both, when they close automatically; bushed and insulated openings for the electric cables; and the floor shall, if boarded, be covered with asbestos or other fire-resisting material. [...] The portable box is being rapidly replaced by a permanent chamber, built of brick or concrete, or with a lining of fireproof slabs not less than 3 in. thick, having a self-closing door and shutters fitted in a similar manner to those in the portable box.

The fire appliances required are: Two buckets of water, one bucket of sand, and a wet blanket. Except the operator and his assistant, no other person is allowed to be in the box with them while operating, unless the local authority requires the presence of a fireman. [...] Only the spool of film actually being exhibited must be in the operating box. Other spools of film must be kept outside, each one being brought in separately as required, and then placed outside after exhibition."

And if the film does fire:

> "Should the film fire in the gate of the projector, always remember that the first thing to do is to keep cool. Don't be in a hurry. Know exactly what you should do, then do it, deliberately and promptly, entirely without flurry. This is just where the difference comes in between a well-trained operator and a mere 'handle-turner'."[9]

A comparative look at historical and contemporary sources makes it clear that the question "how dangerous is nitrate film" – in the film theatre, as well as in the film exchange or rental library – has never been easy to resolve, and assessment depends on circumstance and the terms of reference chosen.[10] One ought keep in mind clearly the distinction between legislation, relevant insurance regulations, and the less quantifiable factors: economic interests, and fear, in various shapes and guises.

Starting with the availability of safety film in 1909, an effort spearheaded by the French Company Pathé Frères, the question of safety film vs. the professional 35mm standard became a matter of local, regional or national law,[11] while in many instances also a question of complying with – or ignoring – insurance regulations. Yet that which was placed at stake was not just the user's loss of economic compensation in case of fire, instead the choice had ethical dimensions for the distributor as well as the exhibitor: the use of safety material was the sole "fool"-proof and fail-safe method to protect the lives of film spectators – most of these probably unaware of the peril that nitrate film posed to their physical health, while more aware of the heated contemporary debates concerning the moral perils of film, and theatre-attendance.

The fire risk must be considered higher in non-professional but public circumstances, where large audiences gathered in contained spaces, often in the absence of sufficient emergency exits, and at the mercy of non-professional projectionists, with ill-maintained machines and highly flammable film in their midst. Which made these markets the most natural target for the acetate materials, which had just become available in fairly acceptable quality as substitutes for the tried and proven nitro cellulose film stocks.

Marketing of the Cinematographe de Salon "Kok" in France and the consequences of war on the international relations of film business

In June 1908 Charles Pathé communicates to the board of Pathé Frères his plans to develop and market equipment suitable for home use, and already in 1909 he announces that development has been completed. The same year, non-flammable film of satisfactory quality has become available through Pathé Frères. Almost immediately, the French government declares the use of nitro cellulose film illegal, but the law never comes into force due to the resistance of the industry.[12]

By 1911 Pathé has made non-flammable film available in many countries, and the decision is taken to create branch-companies to market the salon equipment. The legal nature of these branch-companies was to be determined according to the particular situation of each country.[13] In August of 1911 the Pathé KoK system is registered internationally, and late that same year it is premiered on the domestic French market. Far from being simply a safe alternative to 35mm nitrate stock, 28mm film forms the basis for a comprehensive service strategy aimed at the new non-theatrical outlets that were emerging simultaneously with the industry's commercial distribution of theatrical motion pictures. The KoK system is comprised of projector, camera, and a "repertoire des films ininflammables" for sale and rental[14] and is offered along with a diversity of accessories. One of the marketing mottoes is "Le Cinema chez soi!" clearly delineating the targetted markets: any gathering of people that might enjoy or make use of film, yet prefers or is bound to a location that is not a theatre equipped for professional projection.

With the beginning of WWI in the summer of 1914, the Pathé KoK system has been on the market for two years, the French government declares nitro cellulose essential for the war effort. Pathé has increasing difficulties to fulfill its national and international clients' demand for raw stock. Vast quantities of film prints are recycled to bridge the shortage, while Pathé rapidly loses its dominant international position, very notably in the US. All Pathé export to the US ceases.

The US government on the other hand takes a different approach to the war-time economic and social situation, which is to the advantage of its domestic film industry as well as its export of films:

"[...] official belief that the national motion picture industry was an essential one was put to a severe test as quickly as December, 1917, when it had to be decided to allow, for the continued manufacture of films, a generous share of the supply of nitric acid which was needed also for high explosives."

As a result, America gains an international advantage of long-lasting effect, by supplying the European market with product they can no longer produce themselves:

"[...] English, French, Italian and German film production, having been shut down to a mere dribble through the exigencies of war beginning in 1914, the European supply of pictures had been coming heaviest from this country"[15] – the US.

The US and 28mm standardized safety

There were two systems of 28mm safety film in distribution in the United States which each require brief comparative summaries. In 1912 Willard B. Cook acquires the exclusive rights to distribute the Pathé KoK system under the name of Pathéscope in the US, the same name that is used in Great Britain. He conceives and gradually establishes an extensive rental library system in the US, and sells the equipment, initially imported from France along with the films (their sources soon diversify) and the raw stocks for the accompanying camera. During the course of WWI he is forced to develop new models for projector and camera which are indigenous to America. At that point, his operation has certainly drawn the attention of the educational market and the industry in general, and he is 'joined' around 1917 by Alexander Victor.[16]

After quite a battle against the interest and fears of the theatrical film industry, Victor, inventor and manufacturer of many things including film stock and film equipment, succeeds in April of 1918 in acquiring the Society of Motion Picture Engineers' label 'Safety Standard Film' for a 28mm film format, which differs from the patented Pathéscope format only in that it has three perforations on both sides of the film frame in contrast to the Pathé 3:1 sprocket configuration. This renders Victor's films compatible with Pathéscope equipment, but Pathéscope films not with his machines. Victor's format is internationally referred to as the American Safety Standard. (Oddly, the negative film supplied for the cameras of both 28mm systems was perforated 3:3, and, incidentally, is nitrate film.)

It is essential to keep in mind, that the SMPE had adopted the 35mm format only less than one year earlier, in July 1917, as the 'Professional Standard Film'. Therefore, the standardization of the 28mm format, being the second undertaken by the SMPE, places the format (which at that point has shaped and held a US market-share for over 3 years), in an official, direct relationship, be it partnership or opposition, with the 35mm gauge.

The leverage that the 28mm format gained by its SMPE promotion to 'Safety Standard', while additionally bearing the approval seal 'enclosing booth not required' of the Underwriters' Laboratories, can not be underestimated, and once in place forestalls the debate and main argument prevalent against the 28mm cellulose acetate format: the vast quantities of film titles available at that time in 35mm nitro cellulose.

Yet the general debate concerning the merits of non-theatrical vs. theatrical distribution remains vivid, and focused around a number of unresolved central issues which considerably hinder the unhesitating development and growth of the non-theatrical resources and libraries throughout the life-span of 28mm:

1. Specifying desirable and undesirable film content for the greatly differing fields of non-theatrical exhibition (the home market, educational field, religious organizations, more specific arenas such as advertising, marketing, selling, training, military uses, governmental uses such as publicity campaigns etc.)

2. Identifying the changing needs and demands of target audiences, and exploring/tapping their willingness to spend money

3. Balancing the advantages and disadvantages of utilizing film product available cheaply or free of charge due to other backing interests, for example governmental or industrial

4. Channeling the motivation of non-theatrical producers (often unusual mixtures of idealism and/or business-acumen) into a steady film output of marketable content, in order to reliably provide quality product exclusive to the growing non-theatrical market

5. Convincing the theatrical field that non-theatrical exploitation is an additional source of income, not a threat to profits – and, furthermore, not a mere dumping ground for extremely outdated or worn-out filmmaterial

The Pathéscope Company of America

Willard B. Cook incorporated the Pathéscope Company of America in 1913 with an authorised capital of one million dollars, and registered the Pathéscope trademark on 12 May 1913.[17] His financial backing for the ambitious enterprise "came from vaudeville entrepreneur Percy G. Williams and from John T. Underwood of the typewriter manufacturing family".[18] According to Krows,[19] Cook's first office space in the planning stages of his distribution operation was in the Browning Building at 36th street, then held by James C. Milligan. "Milligan, later to be known as one of the most popular advertising solicitors in the motion picture trade-paper field, took a strong and sympathetic interest in Cook's project". To raise funds, and ensure nation-wide presence, Cook sold regional sales rights, among others to W.J. Baumer who formed the Pathéscope Company of Chicago.[20] Another regional subsidiary was the Pathéscope Company of New England located in Boston.

In the first serious marketing campaigns leveraged in 1914, Cook employed inventive advertising strategies for launching the Pathéscope system, involving transatlantic travel, dance films for home-entertainment, and competitions for projectors to be given away to various school systems, amongst them the NYC public schools.[21] Most advertisements are not found in the trade press, but in publications not specific to film: common daily newspapers, such as *The Saturday Evening Post* and the *New York Times*, and in pastoral periodicals for the leisure classes, such as *Country Life* and *Home and Garden*. Clearly one of the major targets was the educational sector, advertisements were placed in the *School Board Journal, Better Schools* and *Normal Instructor and Primary Plans*, while the religious sector was covered with ads in *Expositor* and *Don Bosco's Messenger*.[22]

Among the Pathéscope publications[23] is an extensive, 243 page Educational Catalogue edited by the Assistant Superintendent of Schools, Newark, NJ and printed by Rand McNally as a "First Edition".[24] It was intended, obviously, exclusively for educational uses, mostly for "classroom use in every grade, from Kindergarten to High". Earlier, in 1917, one of the marketing brochures of the Pathéscope Company claims:

"The superiority of the Pathéscope for this purpose has been signally recognized by its purchase and adoption by nearly one hundred of the Public Schools in New York City alone. Those interested should send for our booklet 'Education by Visualization'."[25]

The *New York Times*, in its section 'Written on the Screen' writes on March 2, 1919, citing the *Educational Film Magazine*:

"Contracts have been awarded by the New York City Board of Education for rental of motion-picture films for the day and evening high and elementary schools [...] The arrangements cover one year from Feb.1, 1919, are of a blanket character without specifying the number of films or rentals to be paid, and were signed with the Pathéscope Company of America and the Charles Beseler Company [...] out of 600 school buildings in Greater New York 200 are equipped with motion picture projectors [...] most of the projectors were purchased with funds raised by the school children themselves[...] Only a few of the machines were installed by Board of Education funds."

Early in Cook's marketing campaign, a display ad is printed in the *New York Times* from 26 July 1914 with the headers *The Pathéscope "The Companion Entertainer to the Talking Machine". Wonderful New French Invention That Astonishes the Scientific World*, stressing the international scope of the system and its marketing. It is declared "patented in every country in the world",[26] the versatility of its design is emphasized and the triumphant conclusion states:

"The Pathéscope offers the only complete and perfected product and service covering the entire range of Cinematography. We furnish a simple and perfect Camera, develop and print films, supply a safe and simple projector and furnish an ideal and convenient Exchange Service of the World's best subjects; all at the minimum of expense consistent with the quality of the product."

An advertisement found in the *New York Times* Classified Ads on 1 March 1921 provides an impression of the ambience of the Pathéscope film library, its aspirations, pretensions and its service:

"Young lady of refinement and pleasing appearance wanted by Christian firm to qualify as librarian in safety film exchange, [S.] [F.] E. permanent position: must be capable, ambitious and able to serve and satisfy high-class clientele; best surrounding; opportunity for advancement and ultimate high salary. Pathéscope Co.; Aeolian Hall, 35 W. 42nd St., New York."

The prestigious Aeolian building, Cook's carefully chosen site of operations for The Pathéscope Salon, is located on the west side of Fifth Avenue, directly facing the New York Public Library. Cameras were sold not only at The Pathéscope Salon at Aeolian Hall directly, but also by dealers of photographic equipment, as a display ad in the New York Times on 7 Nov 1915 testifies: 3 Manhattan stores are listed: "Herbert and Huesgen, 18 East 42nd St., Paul A. Meyrwit, 389 Fifth Ave., J.L. Lewis, 522 6th Avenue".

Determining the exact nature of interdependence between Pathé in France, Pathé operations in the US, and Cook's Pathéscope Company of America in terms of logistics is difficult. Provision of film stocks as well as equipment and accessories only initially was through France. Anthony Slide reports about Cook that:

"[I]n 1916 he founded his own laboratory in Long Island City, where 35mm films were reduced to 28mm. [...] The raw stock also was first shipped from France, but later Eastman Kodak began to make it available."[27]

The *List of Non-Inflammable Pathéscope Films*, probably dating from ca.1915, states:

"Copying apparatus has recently been imported from Paris, and the Pathéscope Company of America is now reproducing in Pathéscope size under royalty license the best films of the prominent American producers".

Earlier in the *List* the statement can be found that "an average of five new films are issued weekly".[28] According to Alan Kattelle:

"Cook was determined to ensure an ample supply of films for his projectors and expanded the company's production facilities. By 1922 the company owned two factories in New Jersey for developing and printing, one in Bound Brook, the other in Jersey City."[29]

A Pathéscope sales brochure from 1920 lists four US Pathéscope labs in an image-caption: "Laboratory – Long Island City. [...] Other Pathéscope Laboratories in Boston, Buffalo, Philadelphia, Toronto, London and Paris."[30] The same brochure also declares that in March 1916 the entire remaining stock of KoK machines in France was purchased by the Pathéscope Company of America, which would date the cessation of 28mm marketing by Pathé in France.

Cook developed his independence from the French suppliers from the beginning, through continual adaptation and improvement of equipment, according to Alan Lott.[31] It is unlikely that any part of the Pathéscope Company of America operation was still dependent upon import from France by the end of WWI.

Early on the Pathéscope Company of America founds an industrial unit, managed by Pathéscope agent J. Alexander Leggett:

"We have a thoroughly organized and perfectly equipped Industrial Film Department [...] We film anything, anywhere, in the highest style of the art for those who require the best."[32]

After WWI the efforts of the Pathéscope Company in the industrial field intensify. Clinton F. Ivins formerly at Universal, becomes head of a regular production unit.[33] An advertisement of March 20, 1921 in the *New York Times* proudly lists the United Drug Company, the Diamond Match Company and the General Electric Company among the prominent customers, in an article titled 'Selling with Motion Pictures. Business men THINK in pictures'. It remains unclear how many of these commissioned productions would have been shot on 28mm, in contrast to being produced in 35mm and then reduction printed for distribution and exhibition only.

The various editions of Pathéscope Catalogs from 1914 onwards employ a twofold strategy: they increasingly integrate feature films for entertainment purposes to maintain a balanced menu of education, enlightenment and amusement, while also publishing catalogs aimed directly at the educational market. The initial concept, as stated in one of the early promotional brochures, promised that "The Pathéscope Exchanges contain subjects to suit every taste, every mood, any age and all occasions".[34] The same brochure, on the page entitled 'Pathéscope Film Exchanges', explains idea and process behind the film exchange, asserting: "It is just like a Public Library maintained for public welfare. It is maintained to supply a community interest at the minimum individual expense", and proceeds to argue for careful handling by the users, prompt return of films to the exchange and a general participation in keeping the films in circulation: "Every Pathéscope owner is interested in maintaining his Exchange at the highest pitch of efficiency and economy". The pricing scheme elaborated on the following page further pursues this concept by offering significant advantages to high-intensity users.

Pathéscope versus Kodascope

Around 1923 the Pathéscope library concept is directly imported into the 16mm Kodascope libraries installed by Kodak as one essential marketing effort for their new 16mm safety film gauge. This is clearly apparent not only in the mimicry of name, but also in the overall catalog lay-out and graphic design, the initial editions very closely resemble the Pathéscope catalogs. Willard B. Cook, though in theory Kodak's competitor, yet the most proven man in the field of non-theatrical film rental libraries, was without delay hired by Kodak to organize and put into operation the Kodascope library. The central Kodascope office was located adjacent to the Pathéscope Office in Aeolian Hall, 35 West 42nd Street, New York, possibly to facilitate Willard B. Cook's supervision of both film libraries, initially. Cook for a while continued to service the 10.000 Pathéscope projectors he claimed were then in the field.

Three Kodascope branches are listed on the first catalog edition copyrighted 1924:

> *Kodascope Library of Boston, Inc., 80 Boylston Street, Boston, Mass., Kodascope Library of Chicago, Inc., 38 So. Dearborn Street, Chicago, Ill., Kodascope Libraries, Inc. 241 Battery Street, San Francisco, Cal.*[35]

The Boston address also housed the Pathéscope Company of New England, it is probable that the Chicago and San Francisco addresses played a similar double role for the two safety library systems and that the infrastructure built by the Pathéscope and American Safety Standard systems facilitated a smooth transition to the 16mm era.

Willard B. Cook's 1924 Kodascope catalog still contains more or less the same classifications as his third and last edition Pathéscope catalog copyrighted 1922 did.[36] The Pathéscope catalog lists the number of subjects in each class:

1.	Travel, Sports, Manners and Customs	250
2.	Industries, Forestry and Agriculture	132
3.	Popular Science, Natural History	147
4.	Comedies and Juvenile	130
5.	Dramas, Serials	240
6.	Religious	22
7.	Reconstructed and Modern History	19
8.	Animated Cartoon Comedies	51
	Total number subjects	**991**

The first Kodascope catalog offers far less subjects with a total of only 213 films, includes subjects on "Useful Arts" into class 3, lists Dramas – excluding Serials – as Class 8 instead of Class 5, pretends to have a class 5: Religious subjects, but in the index and body of the catalog simply proceeds after class 4 directly to class 7: Animated Cartoon Comedies (48 subjects) and then closes with class 8: Dramas (64 subjects). Class 2 has taken a severe blow, and only features 4 subjects. Hardly any films overlap between the Pathéscope and Kodascope libraries.

Yet, even the Kodascope catalog edition of 1926[37] is still extremely similar in layout and design. In contrast to the 1924 edition, it has an increased listing of seven Kodascope libraries in the US, one of which is, coincidentally, in the Keenan Building, Pittsburgh, PA. This address also housed the United Projector and Film Company, a 28mm distribution enterprise active also in Buffalo NY, and operating with the Victor equipment.[38] International Kodascope libraries are proudly announced in London, Melbourne, Buenos Aires, all of these cities, where the Pathé KoK system appears to have been in active, successful distribution.

William F. Kruse in an article focussing on Willard B. Cook's endeavours, attempts to outline the difference in the concept of the Pathéscope and Kodascope Libraries:

> "Pathéscope's outreach for educational status is entirely absent from the Kodascope listing. The latter very definitely aims at the home market, and any incidentally educational titles seem to have been used merely to fill out a reel of cartoons or comics."

Kruses summarizes the accomplishment of Cook, "under Cook's expert management the Kodascope Libraries became the most successful of all serving the home market".[39]

By 1922, the first clear indicators of the demise of 28mm appear in the New York Times: A display Ad announces as a special offer a complete, though used outfit for only $ 100: used 'Popular' Model Pathéscope, 5 Reels of used film, a 4 1/2 by 6 foot screen (new) and a box and 4 lamps (new), offset against the usual cost of $338 for the same selection of new equipment. Next year's November and December Ads feature the '10th Anniversary Price Reductions Offered only until January 1st', with the New Premier Pathéscope selling at $200 instead of $290, 'Motion Picture Cameras at less than the cost of good still-picture cameras', and 'Fine Period Model Cabinets at Half Price'.[40]

By 1928 the decline of the 28mm Pathéscope system is undeniable: Herbert C. McKay, director of the New York Institute of Photography, writes in his classic *Amateur Movie Making*:

> "24 [sic!] mm. Gauge – Pathéscope, Victor Safety
>
> The last mentioned size has become practically obsolete as it lacks advantages of both 35mm. (standard) and of substandard films."[41]

Kruse's article provides information about the activities of Cook until the eve of WW II: "He continued as head of the Kodascope Libraries until it was closed in 1939 [...]".[42] Willard B. Cook died on February 20, 1952, and both *Variety* as well as *New York Times* published short obituaries. According to *Variety* "He was former prez of Pathéscope Corp of America, g.m. of Kodascope Libraries of N. Y., and ex-head of Society of Motion Picture Engineers". The *New York Times* describes him as an "early promoter of narrow-gauge motion picture films and projectors for use in homes and institutions". Some details are reported: that Cook was born at Erie, Pa., was a 1892 graduate of the University of Virginia, came to New Rochelle near Manhattan in 1917, has surviving family members and for 23 summers lived aboard his yachts.

In a comprehensive history of the non-theatrical field published in installments in *Educational Screen*, Arthur Edwin Krows provides some detailed knowledge of Cook's enterprise. The installment of November 1939 names Cook's endeavour with the Pathéscope Company of America enthusiastically a 'story with a hero'. Unfortunately, Cook's vision for Pathé's 28mm safety film system proved prophetic but premature, and more than a decade later, with his help, Kodak's 16mm system came nearer to the full exploitation of its potential.[43]

Notes

1. This text must be understood as a collection of evidence and information concerning the 28mm film format, that is, one of the earliest uses of safety film material. Along this compilation concept I have chosen to cite my sources in many instances, rather than summarize, paraphrase or interpret their content.

2. Jaensch 1928: 19–23. Translation Anke Mebold.

3. Filmmuseum Berlin – Deutsche Kinemathek and Deutsches Filmmuseum Frankfurt am Main have some 28mm films and also 28mm apparatus in their collection (Frankfurt a KoK projector serial no. 589), the Deutsches Technik Museum Berlin has a Pathé KoK projector (serial no. 5494) and two reels of undeveloped 28mm negative rawstock (nitrate), the Filmmuseum Potsdam has a selection of 28mm projectors (one of which is a KoK Projector with a Pathéscope New York emblem, serial no. 6168) and cameras (one of which is a KoK model camera serial no. 815).

4. Elsaesser 2004, 405.

5. Jaensch 1929, 41–42. Translation Anke Mebold.

6. Liesegang 1911, 233–244. Translation Anke Mebold.

7. Jaensch ca. 1929, 111–112. Translation Anke Mebold.

8. Jones 1919, 170–199.

9. The instructions continue: "As a matter of fact, the careful operator should have neither a film fire nor even a break at any time. Such a contingency ought not, and should not, occur at all. It will not occur, if the operator has properly examined and mended the films, and kept the machine clean, well lubricated, and in good working order – in short, if he has conscientiously done his duty, and cheerfully complied with the regulations, both written and unwritten."

10. Compare the highly informative debate on the AMIA-listserv 28 June through 5 July 2005 regarding the scientific background of extinguishability vs. inextinguishability of nitrate fires; also worthwhile in this context would be a comparative study of the nitrate storage and preservation policies of the larger national film-collecting institutions in various countries.

11. Compare also Lescarboura 1921, 415–416.

12. Cook 1918: 89: the discussion after Cook's presentation touches upon this situation in France.

13. Kermabon 1994, 19–29.

14. Pathé Cinema ca. 1919: front pages, unnumbered: "prix de vente: Film impressioné le mètre 1fr. 25" and "tarif de location 1 bobine (100 à 120 mètres environ): Pour une journée 1 fr. 20".

15. Krows February 1939, 52.

16. For more detailed information, see Mebold and Tepperman 2003.

17. Newnham 2005.

18. Slide 1992, 35.

19. Krows Nov 1939, 349.

20. Krows Nov 1939, 349.

21. See Mebold and Tepperman 2003.

22. Kruse 1964, 576.

23. Numerous publications were printed: announcements, manuals, film lists, bulletins, and catalogues, serving the purpose of advertising the system, sell equipment, incite a variety of heretofore unknown uses, promote the rental library system and its advantages, and keep customers happy and operations smooth by instructing everyone carefully regarding use and maintenance.

24. Balcom 1922, II.

25. Pathéscope 1917, 8

26. The **KoK projector serial no. 589** of the Deutsches Filmmuseum displays the following information, though not entirely legibly:
    Patented 1911
    Patentado en Brazil No. 63[1]
    Mexico 15 de Octubr 1910 No. 11071

Chile No. 248_
Republica Argentina No. 7843
Patent applied for in USA.
Brevets Deposés en Suisse et en Russie

The **Kok no. 5494** of the Deutsches Technik Museum Berlin displays a list of Patents and Brevets concerning the following countries: France, Belgium, Sweden, Norway, Brazil, Chile, Argentina, USA, Suisse and Russia, whereof USA is only applied for.

An English Collector has in his collection **3 KoK projectors**: projector #1 is serial no. 583, #2 is no. 10928, #3 is no. 11920. The countries listed differ greatly between his #1 and #3 projector concerning the patents received and applied for. His projector #3 lists Brazil, Mexico, Chile, Argentina, Cuba, Peru, Uruguay, New Zealand, India, Commonwealth, Canada, Suisse and Russia.

27. Slide 1992: 35–36.

28. Pathéscope Company of America ca. 1915: pages not numbered.

29. Kattelle 2000, 137.

30. Newnham 2005: Scanned image from sales brochure including caption.

31. Lott [not dated], 28.

32. Pathéscope [early, not dated, 'Royal Patrons']: [14] titled: Commercial and Industrial Filming

33. Krows Nov 1939, 362. Krows also provides very interesting background info regarding experience and career of the involved.

34. Pathéscope [early, undated, 'Royal Patrons']: [6] titled: The Pathéscope Film

35. Kodascope Libraries 1924, 3.

36. Pathéscope Company of America 1922, 3.

37. Kodascope Libraries 1926, 1–13.

38. A detailed account of this 28mm operation is forthcoming. Claim of the first known catalog edition (not dated, pre-dating 1921) of the United Projector and Film Company was that 'it unites in one library the best of' the two prior 'serious attempts to organize a library for institutions, schools, churches and private homes', explicitly referring to the Pathéscope Company of America and the Lincoln Parker Company as its predecessors.

39. Kruse 1964, 579.

40. New York Times Display Ads 18 November 1923 and 2 December 1923.

41. McKay 1928, 426.

42. Kruse 1964, 579.

43. Krows November 1939, 332.

Bibliography of works consulted and referred to:

American Museum of Photography [1949]: American Museum of Photography: 'Inauguration of the Motion Picture Section, November 1st, 8:15 p.m.' in *Announcement from American Museum of Photography* (Philadelphia, [1949])

Balcom 1922: Balcom, A.G. (ed.): Descriptive Classified Catalogue of Educational Films for Classroom Use (New York: The Pathéscope Co. of America, 1922)

Cook 1918: Cook, Willard Beach: 'Advantages in the Use of the New Standard, Narrow Width, Slow-Burning Film for Portable Projectors' in *Transactions of the Society of Motion Picture Engineers*, No. 7, 1918

Deutelbaum [not dated]: Deutelbaum, Marshall: 'Rediscovering The Yellow Girl' in *Image* (Rochester: George Eastman House in-house magazine, no date on copy) – Also read as a paper at the symposium 'An American Century of Photograpy, 1840–1940'

Elsaesser 2004: Elsaesser, Thomas: 'The Presence of Pathé in Germany' in *La Firme Pathé Frères 1896–1914* (Paris: AFRHC, 2004)

Jaensch 1928: Jaensch, Wolfgang: *Hallo, Sie filmen noch nicht? Kurzgefasste Anleitung für Amateur Kinematographie* (Berlin: Union Deutsche Verlagsgesellschaft, 1928)

Jaensch 1929: Jaensch, Wolfgang: *Wie man filmt* (Berlin: Union Verlag, 1929)

Jaensch ca. 1929: Jaensch, Wolfgang: *Projektion für alle* (Berlin: Union Deutsche Verlagsgesellschaft, ca. 1929)

Jones 1919: Jones, Bernard E. (ed.): *The Cinematograph Book. A Complete Practical Guide to the Taking and Projecting of Cinematograph Pictures* (London: Cassell and Company, rev. edn., 1919)

Kattelle 2000: Kattelle, Alan: *Home Movies. A History of the American Industry, 1897 – 1979* (Nashua, New Hampshire: Transition Publishing, 2000)

Kermabon 1994: Kermabon, Jacques: *Chronologie*, in *Pathé: Premier Empire du Cinéma* (Paris: Éditions du Centre Pompidou, 1994)

Kodascope Libraries 1924: Kodascope Libraries: *Descriptive Catalogue of Kodascope Library Motion Pictures Classified for Convenient Reference* (New York: Kodascope Libraries, 1924)

Kodascope Libraries 1926: Kodascope Libraries: *Second Edition Descriptive Catalogue of Kodascope Library Motion Pictures Classified for Convenient Reference* (New York: Kodascope Libraries, 1926)

Krows 1938–1944: Krows, Arthur Edwin: 'Motion Pictures – Not For Theaters' in *Educational Screen* (monthly installments September 1938 – June 1944, incomplete)

Kruse 1964: Kruse, William F.: 'Willard Beach Cook – Pioneer Distributor of Narrow-Gage Safety Films and Equipment' in *Journal of the SMPTE* (Vol. 73, July 1964)

Lescarboura 1921: Lescarboura, A.C.: *Cinema Handbook. A Guide to practical motion picture work of the non-theatrical order, particularly as applied to the reporting of news, to industrial and educational purposes, to advertising, selling and general publicity, to the production of amateur photoplays, and to entertainment in the school, church, club, community center and home* (New York: Scientific American Publishing Co. Munn & Company, 1921)

Liesegang 1911: Liesegang, Franz Paul: *Handbuch der praktischen Kinematographie. Die verschiedenen Konstruktions-Formen des Kinematographen, die Darstellung der lebenden Lichtbilder sowie das kinematographische Aufnahme Verfahren* (Leipzig: M. Eger, 1911)

Lott [not dated]: Lott, Alan E.: '28mm The First Safety Gauge, Part I and Part II' in *unknown magazine* (England: copied from unknown magazine, no date)

McKay 1928: McKay, Herbert C.: *Amateur Movie Making* (New York: Falk Publishing Company, 1928)

Mebold and Tepperman 2003: Mebold, Anke and Charles Tepperman: 'Resurrecting the Lost History of 28mm film in North America' in Film History (Vol. 15 No. 3, 2003)

Newnham 2005: Newnham, Grahame L.: *The New Premier Pathéscope 28mm Projector* at www.pathefilm.freeserve.co.uk/28premier.htm (22 August 2005)

Pathé-Cinema ca. 1919: Pathé-Cinéma: *Cinématographe de salon. Répertoire des films ininflammables* (Paris: ca. 1919)

Pathéscope 1917: *An Announcement of the Pathéscope. The First Complete, Safe and Thoroughly Practical Equipment for Taking and Presenting Motion Pictures for the Home, the School, the Institution, or Business* (New York: The Pathéscope Co. of America, 1917)

Pathéscope [early, not dated, 'Royal Patrons']: Cook, Willard Beach: *Pathéscope* (New York: early, not dated) 20 pages

Pathéscope Company of America ca. 1915: The Pathéscope Company of America: *List of Non-Inflammable Pathéscope Films* (New York: ca. 1915) The list features a total of 555 subjects, and chronologically lists 463 reels, the final item being reel No. 463: European War, 1914, (Part 4) ... Class 4.

Pathéscope Company of America 1922: The Pathéscope Company of America: *Descriptive Classified Catalogue of Pathéscope Safety Standard Films*. Third Edition (New York: 1922)

Pathéscope Ltd London [early, not dated]: Pathéscope Ltd London: Pathéscope Films (London: not dated) [A Film List available to me in photocopy only, possibly incomplete, subdivided into two categories: G4 General Subjects and E4 Educational Films, containing 78 reels of the first and 61 reels of the second class.]

Slide 1992: Slide, Anthony: *Before Video: A History of the Non-Theatrical Film* (New York: Greenwood Press, 1992)

30

Bringing movies into the home: distribution strategies for 17.5 mm film (1903–08)

Martina Roepke

Utrecht University, Utrecht, The Netherlands

About 100 years ago, in 1903, Heinrich Ernemann from Dresden introduced the first home cinema system on the German market. It enabled amateurs of the upper class to exhibit films in private homes. Films for home screenings were either purchased from the manufacturer or self-made with a camera for 17,5 mm film. Home cinema in this particular cultural form had a short existence, remaining on the market only for about 10 years.[1]

We don't know much about this early form of home cinema, and only a few films on 17,5 mm can be found in film archives.[2] But the Ernemann distribution catalogues can tell us about the advent of film in the home context. These catalogues – as I want to show – are not just descriptions of the content of the individual films, but can be seen as pragmatic instructions on how to present, contextualize, and actually 'read' the films within this particular exhibition context. In this sense they contribute to the discursive construction of the new medium that had yet to define its place within the emerging mass culture at the beginning of the 20th century.

The 'Kino'

Ernemann's little film camera, the *Kino*, as it was called, was a little wooden box weighing only 800 grams which could be used for shooting, developing, and projection. The films for the *Kino* were 15 or 30 meters long and came in little cassettes that could be adjusted to the camera that cost 150 Marks, a small fortune at the time. Together with the *Kino* Ernemann sold a short manual, informative and instructive but also programmatic in character, that heralds the role that the *Kino* could play within entertainment and education as well as the construction of family memory. The last, it was argued, would become obvious by comparing film to photography: Moving images could capture the expression of the human face more 'realistically' than 'dead' photography.[3]

But Ernemann's *Kino* in the homes of upper-class amateurs was meant to be more than the replacement of an old medium by a 'better' one. It was supposed to be more than 'living photography'. Ernemann did not only sell the hardware but was active in establishing a film distribution network for the home market, enabling Ernemann-

Fig. 1. Manual for the 'Ernemann-Kino', 1903.

amateurs to screen not only their own, self-made films, but a whole range of other films that could be ordered from the manufacturer.

Ernenmann's home cinema often is referred to as the first movie system in Germany targeting the amateur exclusively.[4] However, as we will see, the significance of Ernemann's home cinema system lies in the fact that not only did it encourage amateurs to get at least semi-professionally involved in film production but also led them to bring films produced for different professional contexts into their homes. In the following remarks I want to discuss this early form of home cinema more closely. In doing so I will leave the question of technical novelty and the spirit of invention aside and will first look at the kind of films offered by Ernemann for home screenings. Secondly I will discuss the question how those films were meant to enter the homes and entertain this particular audience of upper-class families. In this context the film catalogues containing detailed film descriptions gain a major relevance. I will offer some ideas concerning the pragmatic function of those texts, propose a reading of selected catalogue passages in order to show how different strategies are at work here, and finally reflect on the status of this new medium, home cinema, within film and media history.

The network

Heinrich Ernemann has been characterized as a 'businessman' par excellence, dynamic and ambitious in developing marketing strategies.[5] Beginning in 1898 he manufactured professional and amateur photo cameras in Dresden, and within a few years the cameras were exported to many different countries in Europe. The main reason Ernemann became involved in the distribution of films was probably – as for many manufacturers in those years – to promote his hardware. With the *Kino* he intended to expand his business and to gain a position within the promising field of cinematography.

However, Ernemann did *not* produce the films himself, but simply copied films made by his clients in a lab that he ran in Dresden. Where did those films come from?

In the manual that came along with the Kino the clients are invited to sell their 'best' films back to manufacturer for public distribution. This can be seen as a strategy to stimulate production that would be honored and recognized by the selection of films for public release.[6] According to the film catalogue from 1904, all films offered were shot with the *Kino* on 17.5 mm film. This indicates that the assumed high quality of the catalogue films was meant to promote the quality of the raw film as well as of course the camera.

What is interesting here is that the films listed in the catalogue obviously come from very different production contexts, of which family scenes form only a small percentage. Among the contributors were probably local producers, small entrepreneurs, and individuals interested in technology. They used the little camera in all different kinds of production contexts for all different purposes. In addition Ernemann maintained contacts with scientists and researchers and institutions which made use of the *Kino* for the purpose of documentation, instruction, or propaganda. This group of clients formed a network that contributed to Ernemann's film programme and included:

- The Technical University in Dresden, where researchers were keen to explore the new medium's possibilities in a scientific context;
- The Zoological Institute of Berlin (Zoololgisches Institut Berlin), where film was used to document animal behavior;
- Institutions of military and sport in Lower-Saxony, which used film to support their public image as well as for training purposes;
- Small entrepreneurs and individuals interested in technology in Dresden who would document events in and around the city;
- Local film producers, producing dramatic, comic, and pornographic films;
- Traveling showmen who used the *Kino* as a fairground attraction but eventually also acted as traveling film producers;
- Amateurs, wealthy aristocrats, and businessmen who used the *Kino* camera in their free time and sent in their films from their favorite vacation spots and idyllic family life.

Looking at this network of contacts, we get the idea that Ernemann took advantage of the success of his *Kino* inside established institutions, among professionals as well as amateurs and within only a couple of years he managed to build a huge network. Since Ernemann accepted apparently everything that was out there on 17.5 mm no matter what it was and where it came from to serve his own commercial interests – this can be described as a 'all-you-can-get'-strategy.

The films

The films available for home screening could be selected from catalogues which came along with the camera equipment. Films of special interest or for specific audiences were offered in extra catalogues. For instance, scientific films were offered to scientists and researchers, and films for a male audience, not recommended for family viewing, were also offered in separate catalogues. Ernemann promised to update the film catalogues regularly and also offered to supply films on special topics on request.

In 1903 only nine films, 3 to 12 meters long, were listed in the manuals that came along with the *Kino*. But the film lists from 1905 already contained 125 films of between 7 to 30 meters with a maximum of 40 meters and the latest film list I have from around

1908 offers about 300 films. These films were listed under different categories. Between 1903 and 1908 the categories were, with slight changes, the following:

- Humorous films
- Historical films
- Military films
- Technical Films
- Sport
- Streets and cities
- Animals and ethnography
- Children's life
- Diverse
- Magic

A special film list announced scientific films and films for *Herrenabende* (not recommended for family viewing). These catalogues reflect not only the diversity of Ernemann's film supply. In addition to the length, title, and topic of the films, the catalogues also included short descriptions of all films, and sometimes suggestions were made on how to exhibit them.

The catalogues

The catalogues contained a wide range of films, all of which had been circulated earlier in different contexts and had addressed different audiences: scientists, family fathers, fairground publics, and members of different societies. In those contexts they had been working to produce different effects, such as amusement and surprise, scientific knowledge or memory. When they entered the Ernemann distribution system for home cinema, they were detached from those contexts in order to function within the new context: a specific form of upper-class entertainment. This means that in order to make home cinema work at that particular moment, films from all those different contexts mentioned above had to reach an audience with particular expectations and experiences.

What has been repeatedly pointed out by scholars of early cinema also applies to home cinema in this formative period: here, films were more or less open texts, mute strips of moving images, and their readings depended on the specific contexts of exhibition, for instance the narration of a presenter or explanatory written material. The analysis of Ernemann's distribution catalogues is a fruitful method to study such processes. The pragmatic function of the film descriptions is to guide the reader through the lists of titles and facilitate selection. Furthermore we can assume that they formed the basis for what the audience was told before or during the projection. Given this pragmatic function, I take the film descriptions to be both selection devices for the operator *and* reading devices for the audience. With the following examples I will briefly illustrate this double function, thereby closely analysing different textual strategies, their rhetoric, and cultural function.

Let us first look at the military films. Many of the films are described as showing marching soldiers and parades. Others depict exercises, like crossing a river with horses. It is likely that those films were shown to high-ranking military officers or political representatives but also to a fairground public to demonstrate the strength and discipline of the soldiers. Furthermore within military institutions themselves those films might have been served instructional purposes.

Looking closely at the descriptions of those films in the catalogue, we can identify different textual strategies to relate them to the experiences and expectations of the home audience. For instance, the strategy of describing the films as very interesting for 'everybody who once was a soldier'.[7] This strategy addresses the spectator as someone having very specific experiences in relation to the event depicted. It opens the film up to at least two possible readings: the first possible reading would involve relevant expert knowledge, enabling the spectator to identify the exercises in the film and eventually judge them by their precision or degree of difficulty; a second possible reading could be described in terms coined by Roger Odin as the mode by which family films are perceived, one which involves personal memories of the spectator leading him back to his experiences of the time passed in the military.[8] Both readings, the expert reading and the home-movie-reading of the military film, rely on a very specific prior experience on the part of the spectator. But they differ fundamentally in the way this experience is activated by the catalogue text.

If we look even closer, we see that the catalogues actually contain quite a wide range of different textual strategies by which the audience's involvement is guided and structured. Staying with the military films for a moment, we find them in some cases described as 'interesting also for laymen who never have been in the military',[9] a strategy pretty much in opposition to what I described earlier. How a spectator lacking the relevant experience could possibly enjoy military films becomes clearer in the case of the film *Kavallerie-Patroullie im Wald* (*The cavalry in the forest*).[10] Here the catalogue promises that the audience would enjoy the film *because* of the beautiful landscape in which the exercise takes place.[11] The reading proposed here shifts the focus of attention onto what is actually only the background in the films' instructional reading, namely the landscape. In foregrounding the medium's capacity to depict the landscape in which the exercise takes place as 'beautiful', the reading suggested puts the film in the pictorialist tradition of landscape painting and photography, one that the home audience is likely to appreciate.

Yet another way of attracting the audience to military films is applied in the case of *Schwimmübungen einer Kavallerie-Abteilung* (*Swim-exercises of the cavalry*).[12] The film apparently shows the exercise of cavalrymen in a boot that maneuvers horses through water. The film is described as 'very exciting because the audience would expect the boat to sink and the horses to escape at any moment'.[13] What is interesting here is that it is neither the perfection of the exercise presented nor the bravery of the soldiers that is evoked in the mind of the spectator, but the worst-case scenario which is actually *not* seen in the film: the sinking of the boat. This textualization of the film dramatizes the events depicted, by stimulating the imagination and creating eager expectations about what *could* happen – an involvement of the spectator which is typical for many fictional genres.

Let us take another example, the film entitled *Im Affen-Theater* (*In the monkey-theatre*).[14] This is a film that was probably made by a traveling showman to be shown on the fairground itself and eventually was taken over by Ernemann later. In the catalogue we can read about this film:

> 'The monkey theatre has always been a popular attraction at fairgrounds and markets. Our film shows the crowd watching with obvious delight the funny monkeys, which perform as ropedancers and jugglers.'[15]

What is interesting here is the way the catalogue description frames this fairground spectacle for the home audience by highlighting certain aspects of the scene. Most importantly: it is not the monkeys, that are placed in the center of the home audience's attention, but the fairground *audience watching the monkeys*, that is highlighted for the film audience. What becomes obvious is that the pure production of a fairground spectacle seemed not to be appropriate to attract the home audience. Instead of inviting the film audience to enjoy the monkeys' dance, the catalogue puts the audience at a distance from the acrobatic performance. Considering the social class in which home cinema took place at that time, the textual strategies at work here can be seen as establishing a mode of reading that allows a manifestation of cultural distinction.[16]

The cultural positioning of the audience is also clear in the following example, the description of a family film, listed under the rubric *Children's life* in the catalogue. While family films can be seen as central building-blocks of a particular family's collective memory, they obviously require a new framing for an audience that bears no relationship to the people in a film that was simply chosen from the catalogue. A film *Die ersten Eßversuche mit dem Löffel* (*First attempts to eat with the spoon*) shows – according to the description – twin babies at the table:

> 'According to the twins spoons belong to the more unpractical things that one could imagine. How much better one could eat without a spoon! This image shows us how the twins are trying their best to adopt to our culture and to become acquainted with the way we use the spoon.'[17]

This catalogue description puts the presumably well-known struggles of family life at an ironic distance from the audience and seeks to initiate reflection on the amusing difficulties of bringing up little children. In this way it reframes the event depicted for the audience and actually turns watching the babies making a mess with their food into watching the process of civilization itself. This is what learning to live in a culture is all about.[18] A similar strategy is at work with the film *Die ersten Schritte* (*First steps*)[19] which offers the spectator the opportunity to see 'see the pure happiness of a mother on the face of the young woman'.[20] The home cinema audience of cause lacks any personal relationship and emotional involvement to the boy on the screen, what is so characteristic for the viewings of family films. For this particular audience watching someone else's family film it is the mother that is put in focus by the distribution catalogue. Her smile is linked to the abstract concept of 'motherhood' as an value accepted within the audience, thereby contributing to the ideological notion of the nuclear family as the basis of happiness.

Conclusion

Above we have identified a couple of textual strategies at work in the Ernemann distribution catalogues, all of which aim to make the films offered 'readable' by an home audience: Reference to prior experience of the spectator (here: military experience) or to familiar forms of visual representations (here: the landscape); dramatization of the events depicted and emotional involvement (here: the sinking of the boot); identification with general values related to the events depicted in the film (here: motherhood); reflection on cultural achievement and the social position of the spectators (here: eating manners). Those strategies, I have argued, were the result of a specific distribution strategy, one that was born from the idea of exploiting the different spheres of production for the home market. The 'all-you-can–get-strategy' by Ernemann brought into the homes almost everything that was 'out there' on 17.5mm – even pornographic films. It was left to the amateur to make an selection out of what he had to offer, and Ernemann carefully guided him in this cultural transfer. In this sense the descriptions are more than descriptions; they are little pedagogical narratives, directed towards the audience that had yet to learn not only to handle the camera, but also how to 'read' films within the home context. My analysis of those texts relied on this character of a 'Gebrauchsanweisung' in this broader sense, devices on how to select, present, and read films in the home context.

Ernemann's *Kino* remained on the market for only a short time. The distribution of 17.5 mm film stopped in 1908, the production of the *Kino* in 1913.[21] While films in the professional circuit increased in length from 1906 on, Ernemann's films had – due to technical problems posed by the center perforation – to remain short. It is very likely that Ernemann was able to survive in the years around 1905 by buying some old copies from film producers that had gone out of business. But soon the films distributed must have looked pretty outdated and uninteresting. Although the manufacturer promised regular updating of offerings we do not really find many change in the last film catalogues of 1907 and 1908. It seems the film supply stagnated at that moment. Home cinema as cinema became less interesting – for the audience and for the manufacturer – because 'cinema' was being transformed from a traveling business into a local institution.

Ernemann's home cinema was launched before 'the institutionalization of cinema' had taken place in Germany, and this is what makes it an interesting case in yet another respect. The cultural form of what later became cinema was still to be defined, and there were different social and institutional contexts where the potential of the new technology was tested. Films were exhibited in many different cultural spheres, like universities, schools, laboratories, royal palaces, variétés, fairgrounds, as well as in the homes of upper-class amateurs. In this context the film descriptions from the Ernemann distribution catalogues can be seen as contributing to a discursive construction of a new medium, home cinema. This construction of home cinema as a new medium relies on two main ideas: the amateur as both *producer and consumer* of films and the *program* as presentational format for the home audience. Those two aspects enabled the home audience to watch themselves right next to the parade of the Kaiser – a sort of media experience which can be seen as the significant contribution to the emerging film culture early home cinema had to offer.

This vision of a new medium, home cinema, reminds us of other new media at other times, most obviously television and the internet, media that emphasize the program, and give the spectator the possibility to fill in this program with his own productions. However, home cinema in this particular cultural form did not survive the competitive struggle among visual technologies at the beginning of the last century. In this sense the discursive construction of early home cinema does not only contribute to the history of cinema but can in a broader sense also contribute to the process of media diversification and cultural change that we have been facing during the last hundred years.

Notes

1. For a history of the Ernemann company, see Göllner, Peter, *Ernemann Cameras. Die Geschichte des Dresdner Photo-Kino-Werks* (Hückelhoven: Wittig Fachbuchverlag 1995), which devotes only a few pages to the *Kino*.

2. For a short discussion of the Ernemann-Kino in Germany see also Kuball, Michael, *Familienkino: Geschichte des Amateurfilms in Deutschland* (Reinbek/Hamburg: Rowohlt 1979). For information about an ongoing research project on 'Ernemanns Kino' initiated by the author and Henk Verheul in cooperation with the Dutch Smallfilmarchive: http://web.inter.nl.net/users/ernemann/

3. *Neuer Kinematograph für Amateure. Ernemann Kino, Modell 1907, Liste No. 120*: 6.

4. Göllner, Peter, *Ernemann Cameras. Die Geschichte des Dresdner Photo-Kino-Werks*. (Hückelhoven: Wittig Fachbuchverlag 1995): 47.

5. Ibid.

6. Amateurs from the mid-1920s on discussed vividly the possibilities of professional involvement by selling their films, for instance to the 'Deutsche Wochenschau', and re-earning at least part of

their production costs. At the basis of this discussion lies a definition of the concept of amateurism, that would, according to some member of the amateur film movement of those years, exclude all forms of commercial activities. See for a detailed discussion of this point Roepke, Martina, *Privat-Vorstellung. Deutsches Heimkino vor 1945* (Hildesheim: Olms-Verlag, 2006).

7. *Films für den Ernemann-Katalog. Kinematograph für Amateure, Film-Liste No. 12*, Film No. 467.

8. Odin, Roger, 'Rhétorique du film de famille', *Rhétorique, Sémiotiques, Révue D'Esthétique* (1979, no. 1–2): 340–373.

9. *Films für den Ernemann-Katalog. Kinematograph für Amateure, Film-Liste No. 12*, Film No. 450.

10. Ibid., Film No. 416.

11. Ibid., Film No. 416.

12. Ibid., Film No. 435.

13. Ibid., Film No. 435: 13 (author's translation).

14. Ibid., Film No. 589.

15. Ibid., Film No. 589:24 (author's translation).

16. For a detailed account on the concept of cultural distinction see Bourdieu, Pierre, *La distinction. Critique social du jugement* (Paris: Les éditions de minuit, 1979).

17. *Films für den Ernemann-Katalog. Kinematograph für Amateure, Film-Liste No. 12*, Film No. 583: 27.

18. For a detailed account on this view see Norbert Elias, *Über den Prozess der Zivilisation I-II* (Frankfurt/Main: Suhrkamp 1969).

19. *Films für den Ernemann-Katalog. Kinematograph für Amateure, Film-Liste No. 12*, Film No. 455.

20. Ibid., Film No. 455: 26.

21. Around that time Pathé in France and Edison in the US had launched small film systems that used safety film. The 17.5 mm *Einlochfilm* from Ernemann was a non-safety format. For a detailed account on Edison's attempt to enter the home market see Singer, Ben, 'Early Home Cinema and the Edison Home Projecting Kinetoscope', *Film history*, 2, 1985: 37–69.

PART VII

PRACTICES:
Distribution into the Future

31

'Avant-guerre' and the international avant-garde. Circulation and programming of early films in the European avant-garde programs in the 1920s and 1930s

Ansje van Beusekom

Department of Media and Culture Studies, Utrecht University, The Netherlands

The Dutch Filmliga was initiated and founded in 1927 by a group of Amsterdam students. As a membership organisation, it distributed a monthly program of avant-garde films in seven Dutch cities and published a magazine: *Filmliga*. The Dutch Filmliga existed until the summer of 1933, *Filmliga* continued until 1936.

The second program that the Dutch Filmliga presented, in October 1927, contained two early films of Pathé: *Pardonne grand-père* (*Vergiffenis van een grootvader*) (1908), a melodrama and *L'obsession d'or* (*Het visioen van de rijkdom*), (1906) a *féerie* or fairy play, both so-called 'avant-guerre' films, in Dutch: vooroorlogsche film. The rest of the program consisted of the *Kipho-film*, *Les Miracles du Cinéma*, Cavalcanti's *Rien que les heures* (1926) and René Clair's *Entr'acte* (1924): a mix of avant-garde film, and experiments with cinematic technology.

In the program notes the 'avant-guerre' films were announced in bombastic phrases, imitating the style of the old days at the fair:

> 'Ladies and Gentlemen, we have the honor to present to you two moving pictures created by Pathé-Frères in 1906 [...]. A tragedy in many interesting parts, like: the fair youthful worker – madame et la dame de compagnie – the beggar as marriage breaker – ostracized – four years later – the killing three – hunger....hardship....o, my child! – love conquers all [...]. As second part [...] a dramatic art film sketch with fairy-like inserts of a higher world, represented in natural Pathé color.'[1]

In *Filmliga*, Menno ter Braak, one of the founders and theorists of the organisation, reviewed the program a month later. He wrote about the 'avant-guerre' films and emphasised the extravagant acting of the poor artist, who transcends in his dream to a hand colored heaven, to conclude:

> 'All consciousness of the power of cinematography is still lacking: there are no close-ups, no independent expressions, only cliché's of reality reproduced in ridiculously enhanced melodramatic style. Not only the ladies' fashion is dated

here, also Film is not born yet from the cinema. "La technique est à la base de la conception", but in these films there is no film technique, so there is no conception!'[2]

However, he continues, the Pathé-films had their function in the program: to ridicule the literary subject as a necessary subject of a film [het onderwerp-om-het-onderwerp te ridiculiseeren]. Cavalcanti and Clair showed in their films what a film liberated from the literary subject could look like. Although not totally convinced about the results, he praised their avant-garde experiments as steps in the right direction to film as an autonomous art.

This attitude towards early cinema can be regarded as emblematic for the writers of *Filmliga* as Tom Gunning has argued.[3] The Amsterdam students, who were about to discover art in the films of the international avant-garde, considered early films as "bad" films. Reading this, one can wonder why they bothered at all to show early film in their programs. In other writings they did not show much appreciation for early cinema either. They categorised the 'avant-guerre' films as boring, ridiculous and outdated, but worst of all: 'avant-film'.

So, why did the Filmliga show the pre-war films in their carefully constructed programs? One answer to this question is rather pragmatic and instrumental. For the films in their programs, the founders of the Filmliga were dependent on their associates in Paris and Berlin, respectively Mannus Franken and Ed. Pelster in Paris and Joris Ivens in Berlin. However, they considered Pelster and Franken ideologically less important for the organisation than their own work of composing programs and publishing film criticism in the magazine. The case of *Feu Matthias Pascal* (1925) obtained with much difficulties by Franken in Paris but 'thumbed down' without much consideration by the Amsterdam program committee, does not leave much room to think that Franken was high in the hierarchy.[4] One wonders if Franken and Pelster even had the power of persuasion to make the others show early films, provided they actually had come up with the idea all by themselves. Fact is, they didn't. The Dutch Filmliga copied the program style from French avant-garde film theatres and adopted their conventions.

While visiting Paris in the previous years, all members of the Filmliga board were impressed by the cinephile film culture they encountered. However, Franken was the only one who really became immersed in it: he knew filmmakers and wrote about the Paris film scene long before the Filmliga existed. He stayed regularly for longer periods in Paris in the years prior to the Filmliga and wrote about the Parisian art cinemas such as Jean Tedesco's Le Vieux Colombier, the Studio des Ursulines, and also about the ideas of Louis Delluc. During the first years of the Filmliga, he was therefore the man with the contacts so much needed by them. He made possible visits to the Netherlands of cinéastes such as René Clair and Germaine Dulac and together with Ed. Pelster he provided the Filmliga with all the French avant-garde films they showed. The two of them formed a good team: Franken had a taste for the new and Pelster had the feel and stamina for business. Pelster had started his career in the movie business as early as in 1911, as Celine Linssen in the most recent history of the Filmliga so lively describes.[5] In Paris he also saw the programs of Le Vieux Colombier and Studio des Ursulines containing 'avant-guerre' and scientific as well as ethnographic documentaries. He introduced their eclectic format to the Filmliga.

Pelster had Cavalcanti's *Rien que les heures* in his possession before the idea of a Dutch Filmliga was born and he searched for an opportunity to show it in a suitable setting. He also owned the rights of Pudovkin's *Mat* (*Mother*, 1926), whose hasty prohibition in the regular cinemas by the four mayors of the big Dutch cities after the big success of *Battleship Potemkin*, brought him together with the film loving students and artists of Amsterdam. The nightly screening on 13 May 1927 of *Mother* in the *Kring*, a club for artists and art lovers requiring a membership, actually triggered the founding of the Filmliga, but that is another history.[6]

Important for my argument, though, is that after this notorious night, in order to give the press an idea of what the Filmliga would be about, Pelster compiled a program that contained the following: one reel of *Rien que les heures*, four documentary films of Polygoon, James Cruze's *Jazz* or *Beggar on horseback* (1925) and an unspecified film 'd'avant-guerre' of 1910. The program was screened at CAPI's screening room, the business of the father of Joris Ivens, who was its managing director at the time. Most likely, the film 'd'avant-guerre' came from Pelsters own stock and he bought it from Jean Desmet in 1927, according to a contract in the Desmet archive.[7] I go into this in such detail, because it not only shows how important Pelster was for the formation of the Filmliga, but it also shows how his supply of films and French ideology found its way into the Filmliga programs. He introduced the French eclectic avant-garde/avant-guerre/documentary program format in the Netherlands. Pelster also showed himself less biased towards early films than Ter Braak and Scholte. In his report on the opening of Studio 28 in Paris he compares the entr'acte of magic lantern slides with the screening of avant-guerre films in favor of the latter and praises the 'surprising effects' of early films.[8]

Although Pelster might have introduced the French format in the Netherlands and obtained the 'Liga'-films, the theorists Henrik Scholte, Menno ter Braak and L.J. Jordaan formed the program committee as soon as the Dutch Filmliga started its screenings in October 1927. In the first issue of *Filmliga*, Ter Braak explained its programming policy in an article entitled: 'De esthetiek van het filmprogramma' (The Aesthetics of the Film Program).[9] Ter Braak praised the good intentions of the Studio des Ursulines, that combined many different styles – '(historical mistakes, document and '"film",) (historische vergissingen, document en "film")' – and argued bluntly that programs in commercial cinemas could unintentionally give a similar variety, but in their case it was purely accidental. One of the tasks he saw in store for the Filmliga was the improvement of the variety of the film program:

> 'The film program, a sequel of different dynamic compositions, has to be organised expertly in order to allow the compositions to complete each other and to differ in a meaningful combination.'

Legitimating the Filmliga therefore consisted in showing the cinematographic 'state of the art' and its history:

> 'It has to show the spectator its own sufferings, the uncountable detours, the 'prehistoric' mistakes, he photographed theatre, the desperate expressive gestures, the mad eye rolling, the barely controlled lens.'[10]

Before Ter Braak could function fully as a theorist and critic, practices he favored and hopefully wished to himself to do in the near future, it was necessary to show films in an intelligently and aesthetically organised program. It will be clear that from his point of view, Pelster with his background in the movie business could not be trusted with this heavy responsibility. Moreover, the article leaves us no doubt about the category Ter Braak had put the 'avant-guerre' in: it was one of the pre-historic sufferings.

However, not all members shared his negative opinion on the early films, correspondence with other departments of the Filmliga, for instance the one in Utrecht, show that sometimes they were also appreciated. According to the concept of the Utrecht manifesto, an 'avant-guerre' film was good for the program in order 'to discover the present in the difference [from the past]'.[11] The Filmliga screened 'avant-guerre' regularly, starting out as a film number in order to distract, but gradually for more educational, historical or aesthetic purposes. In the later seasons, early films were integrated in special lectures for Liga members on the history of film, namely those of Jean Painlevé and Alberto Cavalcanti. In this different context the lecturers used other fragments, which they appreciated more on a film historical level, instead of regarding these fragments as 'avant-film'. Willem Bon followed their example and edited a 'found-footage' film avant-la letter with old newsreels and a compilation *Voici Paris*.[12]

Film theater De Uitkijk

Pelster continued his own programming strategies with 'avant-guerre' films in Theater de Uitkijk. This first art film theatre in Amsterdam, opened its doors on 8 November 1929, following the example of Pelster's ideal art house Studio 28 in Paris. The opening program consisted of a compilation of films of Amsterdam of 30 years ago and the Filmliga 'avant-guerre' classic *Het vizioen van den rijkdom*. Furthermore, they screened *Heien* (Ivens, 1929) before the main feature *La Passion de Jeanne d'Arc* (Carl Dreyer, 1928), and *Le jardin du Luxembourg* (Mannus Franken, 1928) afterwards. In the reviews all attention was reserved for *Jeanne d 'Arc* and in some cases to the new films of Ivens and Franken. Nobody mentioned the early films, but they functioned evidently different than as the usual Filmliga laughing stock. The spectacular 'feerie' of Segundo de Chómon, *L'obsession de l'or* (Pathé, 1905), was screened not as a 'non-filmic mistake', but rather as one extreme of the cinematic spectrum: the fantastic on the one end and the non-fiction documents of the city views on the other.

Although the Filmliga founders had wished for a theater as such from its first days of existence, the collaboration between the two organizations was not satisfactory. Over the years, resentment had grown between the pragmatists and the theorists. The former, especially Franken and Pelster, felt a lack of recognition for their work, while the latter hardly could get used to the competition and the independency of De Uitkijk. The business organization in the Maatschappij voor Cinegrafie heading the sub-organisations Centraal Bureau voor Ligafilms and Theater De Uitkijk complicated the daily practices even more. Ed. Pelster as director of the Centraal Bureau voor Ligafilms was responsible for the distribution, and at the same time he was the director of De Uitkijk. In the first position he obtained films and distributed them to the Uitkijk and the different departments of the Filmliga. Soon the latter blamed him to keep some titles for the Uitkijk exclusively. The magazine *Filmliga* did not spare the Uitkijk programs: as soon as a little common cinema (cartoons, American comedy) appeared among the Liga classics, de Uitkijk was sharply criticised. Ter Braak also scrutinized the act of programming, referring once more to the difficult but highly responsible task of composing a good film program.[13]

One of the first programs was harshly criticized by Henrik Scholte. *Tolstoi intime* (1908), was on the program, together with *Grass* (Shoedsack and Cooper, 1925). Pelster had obtained *Tolstoi intime* from Jean Mauclaire, the director of Studio 28, and the film did not belong to the set avant-guerre films screened by the Filmliga. Scholte reviewed the Tolstoi film in *Filmliga* and in doing so he formulated his criteria for a good 'avant-guerre' film: out-datedness, strangeness and ridicule.[14] This film had nothing of the kind that made avant-guerre films worth showing. '[…] but, why show it if it is not old, strange and therefore not amusing enough to be regarded as 'avant-guerre'?' He considered this bad choice emblematic for the rest of the program and blamed De Uitkijk for putting the cinema ten years back instead of ten years ahead.

De Uitkijk continued its programming despite all criticism and rather looked at Paris than listen to their former companions. Scholte may not have liked *Tolstoi Intime*, but the film can be considered as a film club regular: it popped up several times in Paris and London.

Paris: Le Vieux Colombier, Studio des Ursulines and Studio 28

Tolstoi intime was also shown by Jean Mauclaire in Studio 28 together with Deslaws *La marche des machines* accompanied by the Rumorharmonium of Luigi Russolo in a special program around the exhibition of Prampolini.[15]

Why did the French film clubs and specialised film theatres show films 'd'avant-guerre'? I will try to answer this question with the help of Christophe Gauthier's dissertation *La Passion du Cinéma, Cinéphiles, ciné-clubs et salles spécialisées à Paris de 1920 à 1929.*[16] An amalgam of ideas concerning the preservation, re-releasing of old films merged with a lingering awareness of a history of film that needed to be written, and a more recent complaint about the programming policy of commercial cinemas. Framed in an educational context, these ideas were first formulated in incidental lectures and from 1924 regulated in screenings of alternative film circles.

Gauthier mentions a lecture in June 1920 delivered by André Antoine who had tried to purchase copies of old films at the big studios:

> 'M' étant addressé à quelques-unes des plus grandes maisons d'edition, j'ai eu la désagréable surprise de constater qu'elles n'ont même pas gardé une collection de leurs productions.'[17]

Nevertheless, he managed to show some fragments of pre-war films to illustrate his lecture. The interest in the preservation and showing of pre-World War I films continued in 1921 with an inventory of the film stock in business archives in order to find out how much was left of the Parisian cinematic documents. Victor Perrot, a city official at the time, and Pierre Desclaux, the vice-president of Association des Amis du Cinéma, executed the inquiry with cooperation of Léon Gaumont.[18] Filmmaker and critic Henri Diamant-Berger supported the idea of rescuing old films and wrote about it in *Cinémagazine*. Scientific films and documentary films were their first concerns, not fiction or artistic films. Their interests were educational and historical rather than film historical and can be regarded in a context of loss: loss of a worldwide hegemony in the film industry, and loss of the pre-war amusements.[19]

Others, like Ricciotto Canudo and Louis Delluc developed the idea that film could be a potential art form that grew parallel with the idea that cinema had a history of its own and that certain films had marked its artistic evolution. The idea of a history of film re-emerged soon after World War I and must be seen in the context of an ideology of progress. Modern writers about the cinema, like Louis Delluc, only became interested in the new medium from 1916 on. In contrast to the anti-Americanist Dutch cinephiles, Delluc was converted from theatre to cinema through American films: cowboy films with William Hart (*Rio Jim*), Sennett slapsticks with Charlie Chaplin, soon to be nick-named 'Charlot', and furthermore Griffith's epic *Intolerance*.[20] For Delluc pre-war French fiction films represented non-cinematic, old-fashioned and boring ideas. With Max Linder as a positive exception he regarded French film as filmed theatre or literature, and filmed literature did not count as 'cinema'. Thus, for him the French 'avant-guerre' film heritage was more of a burden than a source of inspiration. He took an opposite position to Diamant-Berger for instance, on the status of French cinema. Where Diamant-Berger must have felt a sense of longing for the great days of Pathé and Gaumont, Delluc embraced the invasion of American films. Despite his early death in 1924, we can hardly underestimate the impact of his writings on the avant-garde film culture and its conventions, also in the Netherlands.

French 'avant-guerre' films did not have the 'photogenetic' qualities Delluc expected from good cinema. Worse even: what could have been good, was ruined by the French mise-en-scène according to his complaint about Max Linder:

'Va-t-on le laisser à son ancient procédé? Il y gaspille des trésors de bonne humeur. Faute d'un impeccable metteur en scène, il perd les trios quarts de sa généreuse verve naturelle. Dommage, dommage!'[21]

For my argument, Delluc's critical interventions mean that the adjective 'avant-guerre' contained a contradiction in appreciation right from the start and one has to reconstruct the screening context carefully to find out if its connotation was positive or negative.

Showing non-fiction pre-war films thus started in an educational context as illustrations in lectures and was taken into the domain of the avant-garde by the policy of the film theatres. They distinguished themselves from the commercial movie theatres with another kind of film program. They tried to offer a well balanced film program grouped around a certain theme instead of offering just entertainment. In the early 1920s many critics complained about the distribution and programming practice in Parisian commercial cinemas. They protested against the *'programmes salades'* that showed everything to please everybody everywhere and pleaded for specialised theatres with *'contre-programmes cinéphilique'*.[22]

Jean Tedesco was the first to open a special film theatre at Le Vieux Colombier dedicated to *reprises* (reruns), avant-garde experiments, ethnographic documentaries and early scientific films. He started in November 1924 and his main purpose was to educate his audience in watching film. One of his hobby horses was the expression of time with cinematic means. He organized several lectures about acceleration and slow motion in film. His selection of pre-war films remained restricted to non-fiction films, later called 'Films du Laboratoire du Vieux Colombier', that contained films as *La vie d'une plante*. According to Gauthier, the press in the early 1920s mentioned collectors of films who found old films at the flea markets around Paris coming from the stock of bankrupt itinerary showmen and he is convinced that Tedesco was among them.[23] Tedesco also calls for smaller regional distribution offices to preserve old 'forgotten' non-fiction films for the sake of film history. Despite its good intentions, Le Vieux Colombier struggled through its first year of existence, but managed to survive due to lectures of cinéastes who presented their own avant-garde work, festival-programs dedicated to Charlie Chaplin, D.W. Griffith films produced at Triangle, Scandinavian films of Sjöström and German Expressionist films, as well as a lecture dedicated to the origins of cinema containing films of the Lumière brothers.

Armand Tallier and Laurence Myrga were the first who systematically showed 'avant-guerre', and they coined the term in January 1926 with the opening of Studio des Ursulines. 'Cinema des premiers temps' opened every program and contained films of Léonce Perret from 1910–1912 and actualities (topical films). The early films seem to have functioned as a running gag: a hilarious and light-hearted start of a program full of surprises. In general the promotion and programming of Studio des Ursulines was much more successful than that of Le Vieux Colombier and they made of 'avant-guerre' a brand category they exported not only to other 'salles spécialisées', but also to film clubs and filmligas abroad. Jean Mauclair's Studio 28 opened in 1928 and followed Studio des Ursulines successful approach in programming 'avant-guerre'. *Tolstoi intime* was among these films.

Also Le Vieux Colombier adopted the term 'avant-guerre' for early fiction films: for the first time in 1928, announcing the film *Le petit modèle de Mont Martre* screened before *En Rade* (1928) of Alberto de Cavalcanti. Thereafter the term was used more often. In 1927, though, the term 'classique' announced *Easy Street* (1917) of Charlie Chaplin, and it will be clear that 'avant-guerre' and 'classique' had different meanings: the former old and curious in order to give a sense of the past and later called 'primitives', the latter old but (still) good, thus ready to recycle anytime and to be canonized. Also the term auteur is attached to 'classic films' of Chaplin, Griffith, Lupu Pick, Wiene, Murnau, Lang and Sjöström. The early films of Leonce Perret and Max Linder, so big in their own pre-war time, had to wait a little longer to be regarded as classics.

Typical in terms of distribution was the fact that the alternative cinemas operated as distributors of the films of the avant-garde in international alternative circles. As *Tolstoi intime* shows, this was also the case for the 'avant-guerre'-films.

London: the Film Society

Tolstoi intime was also screened by the Film Society in London in October 1927 in a program with Eggeling and Richters films, a Mack Sennett comedy, some film technical experiments and as piece de resistance Ermoliev's, *Taras Bulba*.[24] Compared to this list of the first '100 programs of the Film Society', this program is exemplary for the Film Society's way of programming.

The Film Society in London had its first screening in October 1925. Founded by Ivor Montagu and Adrian Brunel after an inspiring encounter with the alternative film culture in Paris, the Film Society was nonetheless modelled after a very British organization, the Stage Society. The Stage Society staged commercially 'unwanted' plays for an audience of members on Sundays. Likewise, the Film Society planned to screen films that no commercial movie-theatre was interested in for several reasons: too strange, too difficult, too old, too foreign or too modern. The Film Society aimed 'to introduce films of artistic, technical and educational interest, and to encourage the study of cinematography, and to assist such experiments as may help the technical advance of film production'.[25] Like the Parisian 'salles spécialisées' and the Dutch Filmliga the Film Society offered different film programs for its membership audience. Different from the ones in commercial movie-theaters. Its most important contacts for film supplies were Le Vieux Colombier in Paris and the Film Arts Guild in New York. They kept up their activities until 1939, a long period. According to the memory of Montagu, the Film Society introduced about 500 films during its existence from which 312 (111 features, 201 shorts) would have had no screening otherwise.[26]

As the programs show, the Film Society tried to find a mixture of experimental or avant-garde films, foreign features, and compilations of extracts to illustrate specific technical aspects. Furthermore, they included early films among which pre-war films as Broncho Billy and Max Linder, scientific films, and documentary shorts like fashion journals. In his 'Extra list for Statisticophiles' Montagu categorized 63 short 'Primitives (before 1920)', by far the largest category in titles but not in meters.[27] Revivals of old favorites among which Chaplin (10 films) definitively takes the lead, are categorized as Comedy. Mutual Chaplin's as *Charlie Champion* and *Charlie at the Show* are to be found on the programs of the Parisian 'salles specialisees' and on those of the Dutch Filmliga as well from November 1929 on. They functioned as classics right from the start and would never have been called 'primitives' as the Film Society labeled other early films in 1937. In retrospect, Montagu called these films 'grotesques' and positioned them against the 'masters': 'A point about the short revivals. These, including two Méliès, three one-real Griffiths, three one-reel Pickfords, ten Chaplins, a Keaton, a Linder, a Bunny and Flora Finch, etc., were shown partly to recall the work and appearance of early famous players and masters, but otherwise – I fear – as grotesques. They dated from 1897 to anywhere in the 20th century teens. It emphasizes the significance in film history of our operating period – so rich for the art in expressive-development – that most films made up to only six years before we began could already appear primitive and grotesque.'[28]

As far as I can see, The Film Society never used the term 'avant-guerre' but called the early films 'revivals' or 'resurrections' later replaced with 'classic' or 'primitive'. In attitude the Film Society programs may have been the less biased – with an exception for the British films – and lightest ones if we compare them with the Film Liga programs and those of the Parisian film theatres. The latter were more pre-occupied with its national avant-garde or heritage, while the Filmliga was more concerned with high-brow aesthetics where in there was no place for American cartoons, slap-stick, scientific experiments or well made features. De Uitkijk programs looked more like those of the Film Society: also revivals of good features, cartoons and comedies.

However, this was not only a matter of choice: thanks to stricter censorship in England, many films that were screened exclusively by the Film Society were programmed by commercial movie-theatres in the Netherlands. The Filmliga could not afford to rent famous Soviet films and compete with commercial cinemas for instance. According to Jen Samson, '[a]s a non-profit making limited company, the Council had to rely on its members travels abroad to borrow prints for the shows'.[29] Looking at the elaborate programs and the quantity of films the Film Society showed and with the experiences of Pelster of the Filmliga in mind, I find this a too romantic view. It is a little hard to believe that '[…]money was only ever spent on the preparation and English titling of borrowed copies, on musical scores, on full orchestra's and on payment of any duty imposed by Customs'.[30]

Counter programs, early film and the process of canonization

In this paper I have tried to investigate the term 'avant-guerre' within the context of avant-garde film programming in Amsterdam, Paris and London. What kind of films were announced with the adjective 'avant-guerre', how and why were the films programmed in different countries? The early films of French origin that circulated in avant-garde programs were distributed by the same theatres that also distributed the avant-garde films: Le Vieux Colombier, Studio des Ursulines and Studio 28. They were not distributed as programs but as single films.

Balanced variety, historical interest and an emerging sense of film history seem to have been important factors for all alternative screenings. Showing 'avant-guerre' or a 'revival' was useful to stake out the contrast between the past state of the art of film. As early as the foundation of the Film Society in London in 1925 and the first Filmliga in the Netherlands in 1927, the French program format of the special film theatres as Le Vieux Colombier (for the Film Society) and Studio des Ursulines (for the Filmliga) had become a norm. The eclectic 'contre-programme cinephilique' functioned as an example to be followed wherever a film club was founded. The new ones that were founded after World War II in Europe, the United States and Canada, adopted the program format as well. By that time they no longer showed 'avant-guerre' because the term 'primitive' had replaced it in order to distinguish the category from 'classic'. Old films were included in the programs with a reason: to enhance the dialectic, to fit the theme of a special event or to be a special event in itself, for instance American Silent Comedy (NFT), and because they were received enthusiastically by their audiences.

Showing films that were out of the regular distribution was a novelty in the 1920s and it continued to be exclusive to alternative film circles ever since. By screening old films the alternative circles distinguished themselves from commercial exhibition, moving away from entertainment to educational purposes. The eclectic program format supported this distinction and made the act of programming a creative one. Since we know now so much more about early film and cinema, we can say that this creative act was not invented by the programmers of the avant-garde, but instead re-introduced at a moment in history when it was no longer customary in commercial cinemas. Indebted to Charles Musser who started the research on the exhibitor as creator, I would say that the 'avant-guerre' program started a second life in the avant-garde cinema infrastructure that lasted much longer than the 'avant-guerre' films in its programs.[31]

Notes

1. Program 'Tweede voorstelling', reprinted in: *Filmliga 1927–1931* (Nijmegen: Sun, 1982), 57. 'Dames en Heeren, hierbij hebben wij de eer U te presenteeren twee aangrijpende levensbeelden, door de heeren Pathé-Frères gecreëerd in het jaar 1906 [...] A tragische roman [van een lichtzinnige vrouw] in vele boeiende tafereelen, als daar zijn: de schoone, jeugdige arbeider –madame et la dame de compagnie – de bedelaar als huwelijksverstoorder – verstooten – vier jaar later – de moordende boom – honger ... ellende ... o, mijn kind! – liefde heelt alles. Als tweede deel [brengen wij U dan een kunstfilm, waarin de laatste ontdekkingen der cinematographie tot uiting zijn gebracht: Het Visioen van den Rijkdom (Hoe een schilder van den hongerdood gered werd).] Dramatische kunstfilmschets met feeërieke inlagen van een hoogere wereld, in natuurgetrouwe Pathé color weergegeven.' Translated by Ansje van Beusekom.

2. Ter Braak, Menno, 'Onze tweede matinée', *Filmliga. Orgaan der Nederlandsche Filmliga* 1: 3 (November 1927): 3. 'Alle bewustzijn van de macht der cinégrafie ontbreekt nog; er zijn geen close-up's (dat typische machtsmiddel van de camera!), er is geen zelfstandige expressie, er zijn slechts werkelijkheidscliché's, die gereproduceerd werden in belachelijk-verhevigde tragiek. Hier is meer dan de damesmode verouderd; hier is de film nog niet geboren uit de bioscoop! "La technique est à la base de la conception"; hier, waar geen filmtechniek is, is ook geen conceptie!' Translated by Ansje van Beusekom.

3. Gunning, Tom, 'Ontmoetingen in verduisterde ruimten. De alternatieve programmering van de Nederlandsche Filmliga' in: Linssen, Céline, Schoots, Hans, Gunning, Tom, *Het gaat om de film! Een nieuwe geschiedenis van de Nederlandsche Filmliga 1927–1933* (Amsterdam: Bas Lubberhuizen/Filmmuseum, 1999), 243.

4. Linssen, Céline, "Unaniem rot- stop-hedenavond vergaderen' De geschiedenis achter de schermen van de Nederlandsche Filmliga' in: Linssen, Céline, Schoots, Hans, Gunning, Tom, *Het gaat om de film! Een nieuwe geschiedenis van de Nederlandsche Filmliga 1927–1933* (Amsterdam: Bas Lubberhuizen/Filmmuseum, 1999), 92–93.

5. Ibid., 100–119.

6. Ibid., 18–35.

7. Ibid., 116 n. 234: Contract Desmet – archief, doos A 20/21, 'Filmhuur 1927/1928'.

8. Pelster, Ed, 'Opening van de Studio 28 te Parijs', *Filmliga* 1:7 (Februari 1928): 8. 'Maar zoo aardig en verrassend het het effect is van een film d'avant guerre, zoo moordend is dit experiment. Geen aanbevelingswaardige herhaling voor de Liga! Wij leven te snel ... dit is té ver, té dood en té begraven.'

9. Ter Braak, Menno, 'De esthetiek van het filmprogramma', *Filmliga* 1:1 (October 1927): 2–4.

10. Idem, 'Het filmprogramma, een opeenvolging van verschillende dynamische beeldvlakcomposities, behoort deskundig te worden geordend, opdat de composities elkaar aanvullen en afwisselen in een waardigen samenhang'. And: 'Het moet den toeschouwer den eigen lijdensweg vertoonen, de tallooze afdwalingen, de "praehistorische" vergissingen, het gefotografeerd tooneel, die wanhopig naar expressiviteit gymnastiseerende gebaren, dat verdwaasd oogengerol, de nauwelijks beheerschte lens'. (p. 3) Translated by Ansje van Beusekom.

11. *Concept Manifest Utrecht*, Filmliga secretariaats archief (NFM): 136.

12. Van Beusekom Ansje, Ivo Chamuleau et al, 'Programmaoverzicht'. In: Linssen, Céline, Schoots, Hans, Gunning, Tom, *Het gaat om de film! Een nieuwe geschiedenis van de Nederlandsche Filmliga 1927–1933* (Amsterdam: Bas Lubberhuizen/Filmmuseum, 1999), May 1930 and December /January 1929/1930.

13. Ter Braak, Menno, 'Filmprogramma's in 'De Uitkijk'', *Filmliga* 3:5 (February 1930): 60. 'De samenhang der programma's is nog niet altijd bepaald door de eischen der harmonie; maar aangezien het geen geheim is , dat juist de verzorging van een behoorlijk bijprogramma tot de moeilijkste organisatorische aangelegenheden behoort, willen wij in dit opzicht onze critiek tot een meer gevorderd stadium sparen.'

14. Scholte, Henrik, 'Programma De Uitkijk: Gras etc.', *Filmliga* 3:2 (December 1930): 25. citaat, 26. 'Uit den aard der zaak kan men van 1908 niet anders verwachten, maar waarom dan 'vertoonen als zij niet oud, niet mal en daardoor niet amusant genoeg is om voor "avant-guerre" te kunnen doorgaan?'Translated by Ansje van Beusekom.

15. Invitation pamphlet Studio 28 for the opening on 15 November 1928.

16. Gauthier, Christophe, *La Passion du Cinéma, Cinéphiles, ciné-clubs et salles spécialisées à Paris de 1920 à 1929* (Paris: AFRHC, 1999).

17. Ibid., 43.

18. Ibid., 90.

19. See for an overview of the illustrated lectures of L'Association des Amis du Cinéma, ibid., 346–352.

20. Lherminier, Pierre (ed.), *Louis Delluc. Ecrits cinématographiques I. Le Cinéma et les Cinéastes* (Paris: Cinémathèque Française, 1985).

21. Ibid., 63.

22. Gauthier, Christophe, *La Passion du Cinéma, Cinéphiles, ciné-clubs et salles spécialisées à Paris de 1920 à 1929* (Paris: AFRHC, 1999): 41.

23. Ibid., 120.

24. Booklet that contains 'a complete list of films shown by The Film Society since its formation in 1925' of 100 programs. Archief Simon Koster (NFM-Amsterdam).

25. 'Constitution and Rules of the Film Society Limited' quoted in Sexton, Jamie, 'The Film Society and the Creation of an Alternative Film Culture in Britain in the 1920s'. In: Higson, Andrew (ed.), *Young and Innocent? The Cinema in Britain 1896–1930* (Exeter: University of Exeter Press, 2002), 292.

26. Montagu, Ivor, 'Old Man's Mumble. Reflections on a Semi-Centenary', *Sight and Sound* 44:4 (Autumn 1975): 220–224, 247.

27. Ibid., 224.

28. Ibid., 223.

29. Samson, Jen','The Film Society, 1925–1939'. In: Barr, Charles (ed.), *All our yesterdays. 90 years of British Cinema* (London: BFI, 1986), 307.

30. The Film Society Collection at the BFI, contains several bills of payment for film rentals or buy's and related correspondence, in: Item 15, Film Society Performances; Item 17, Films from other countries.

31. Musser, Charles, 'The Eden Musee in 1898: The Exhibitor as Creator', *Film and History* (December 1981): 73–83.

32

The imagination of wireless distribution

Wanda Strauven

Film Studies, Department of Media Studies, Universiteit van Amsterdam, The Netherlands

E nell'anno 2000 chi sa se una macchina di proiezione cinematografica non possa ritrarre e proiettare subito la persona interlocutrice, nei suoi atteggiamenti nel proprio gestire durante la conversazione [telefonica], dando modo all'uno di scrutare l'animo dell'altro presente e assente, prossimo e lontano trecento chilometri?[1]
A.G. Bragaglia (1913)

In the 1910s the fascination for long distance transmission systems is recurrent in Futurist writings, manifestos and poetry. One of the central concepts of Marinetti's poetics is the 'wireless imagination' or 'imagination without strings' (*immaginazione senza fili*), which is directly inspired by the telecommunication technique of the wireless telegraph (*telegrafo senza fili* or T.S.F.). In the bellicose poem *Zang Tumb Tumb* (1914), Marinetti visualises the electromagnetic waves of the T.S.F. piercing a 'Turkish captive balloon' (Fig. 1). The words 'pallone frenato turco' are disposed in the form of a circle which is perforated by the vibbrrrrations of radio waves. This auto-illustration 'concerns the interception and disruption of wireless messages, an apt metaphor for free words not shut up in books or bound by traditional syntax or genres, but available, in the air for taking'.[2]

The wireless telegraph, as a two-way system of (coded) word transmission, prepared the ground for the so-called telephotography. Futurist photographer Anton Giulio Bragaglia refers in his article 'In the year 2000' to the invention of the French engineer Edouard Belin who in 1907 experiments the projection (or transmission) of still photographs at a distance. In the same year 1907, in Germany, Arthur Korn transmits a photograph from Berlin to Paris, to the headquarters of the journal *L'Illustration*. Korn, who started already in 1904 with telephotographic experiments within the borders of Germany (Fig. 2), foresees a very useful application of his invention: thanks to the telegraphy of images, the police can disseminate – nationwide and across the borders – portraits of criminals on the run.[3]

Telecinema in vogue

In 1908, Georges Méliès explores the cine(ma)tic possibilities of Belin's apparatus in *La photographie électrique à distance* (US title: *Long Distance Wireless Photography*). That is, he transforms the principle of telephotography into that of telecinematography: the wireless transmission of moving pictures. The issue is actually much more complex, involving – as I will discuss below – different degrees of 'translation' (from immobile to mobile, from outer to inner). For the moment, I want to draw the attention to the emergence of the telecinematographic hypothesis (or science fiction), of which

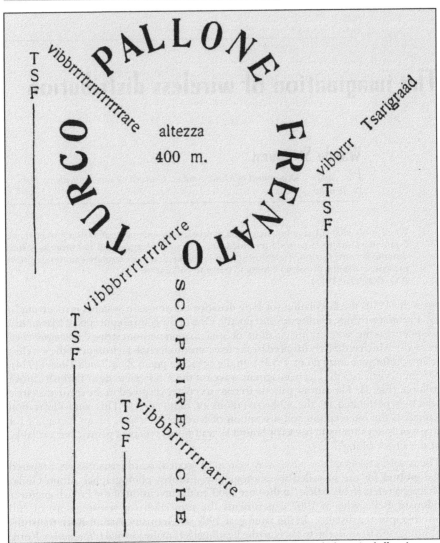

Fig. 1. Filippo Tommaso Marinetti, *Zang Tumb Tumb* (1914): 'Turkish captive balloon'.

Méliès's film is only one example. Jean Giraud in his *Lexique français du cinéma. Des origines à 1930* enters as many as five different expressions connected to the long distance concept: *télécinéma*, *télécinématographe*, *télé(-)cinématographie*, *télé-phono-cinématographie*, *téléphoscope*.[4] The last two entries are the most recent ones, dating respectively from 1930 and 1920. It is worth noticing that Giraud does not enter the word *télectroscope* (or Electric Telescope) that appeared in several scientific writings in the late 1870s.[5] The oldest example Giraud records concerns the entry *télécinématographe*, which made its first appearance in 1898 in *La Nature*: 'En attendant que le cinéma nous dote d'un télécinématographe'. Follow, in time, two quotations relating to *télé(-)cinématographie*: the first reference which dates back to 1909 only announces the apparatus necessary for long distance cinema, while the second gives the first full definition of the concept

Fig. 2. One of the first telephotographic experiments by Arthur Korn, dating from 1904.

and links it to the invention of tele-photography: 'L'heure est peut-être proche où la téléphotographie (c'est-à-dire la transmission au loin de documents photographiques) deviendra la *télécinématographie*, transmission à distance de scènes photographiques animées'. This quote is taken from the *Larousse Mensuel Illustré* of October 1910. Giraud registers another early reference that appeared in April 1912 in *Ciné-Journal*, which mentioned 'un intéressant article sur le *Télécinéma*, c'est-à-dire sur la cinématographie à distance' that was published in the weekly supplement of *La Tribuna*.

It is striking that the concept of telecinematography is in the air precisely in the transitional period when cinema shifts from being a fairground attraction to an institutionalised form of entertainment, with the opening of fixed movie theatres and the organisation of a distribution network. In those years, as G.-Michel Coissac observes: 'C'était un besoin de propager partout l'idée du cinéma, de créer de centres de diffusion, d'aménager de nouvelles salles; pour cela, une vigoureuse campagne fut entreprise; malheureusement, les règlements de police, souvent draconiens et mal inspirés, ne favorisent guère l'ouverture d'établissements sédentaires'.[6] The idea of creating *centres of diffusion* in order to *propagate the cinema* can be seen as a response to the technological fantasy of telecinema which would have allowed filmmakers to send their products directly and simultaneously to the most remote locations on earth (without restrictions from the police!). Even if the intention of this article is not to prove any causality between reality and fantasy, or between the lack of concrete distribution networks and the imaginary solutions which eventually will find concrete applications in the course of the twentieth century, I will however propose to read some imaginary image transmission systems of the 1900s, 1910s and 1920s as possible alternatives to film distribution. More specifically, I will investigate how filmmakers fantasized about the possibility of transmitting moving images by means of the telegraph, the telephone and the radio, in a period when television was not yet operative. With this reading I hope to offer a useful framework to (re)think the distribution of early cinema, i.e. from the perspective of early telecommunication.

Distribution, diffusion

In 1925 Coissac speaks about distribution in terms of 'diffusion'. Centres of diffusion are needed to spread out the idea of cinema, to bring the cinema to the eyes of everyone. To distribute is to propagate, to disseminate. James Monaco in his *Dictionary of New Media* defines distribution as 'the dissemination of media products'.[7] In 1907 Korn proposes to use his telephotographic apparatus to diffuse or circulate head shots of wanted criminals. The revolutionary aspect of Korn's (or Belin's) invention is that the distribution can take place without delay; it is immediate and, at least theoretically, without boundaries. Likewise, Marinetti's free-word diffusion is conceived as a boundless system; the (imaginary) wireless transmission of words makes these words obtainable for everyone, 'in the air for taking'. Since Futurist words often have a strongly iconic dimension, their wireless transmission can be seen as a (imaginary) model for image transmission: should images, still or moving, not be available in the air for everyone?

Most relevant in terms of distribution is the geographical reach of the different wireless telegraph systems: messages can be sent all over the world, and with the advent of the *téléphoscope* any film projection would possibly be 'envoyée simultanément sur plusieurs écrans et à n'importe quelle distance'.[8] Distribution is generally defined as the 'intermediate stage between production and exhibition',[9] the so-called 'missing link'[10] because invisible (or intangible), manifestly underestimated and often forgotten in the study of cinema. For the purpose of my paper, it is critical to understand that this 'intermediate stage' or 'missing link' is not only an abstract (or figurative) concept of economics; on the contrary, it is a very physical step in the life of films which, after their production, are *placed* in different areas in order to be shown or exhibited to different publics.

Significant, in this respect, are the descriptions given by Giraud in his *Lexique* for the entries *distribution* and *distributeur*.[11] Next to the strictly economic meaning of 'stade intermédiaire', Giraud defines *distribution* as 'Placement des copies auprès des exploitants'; and, similarly, *distributeur* is described as 'Celui qui est chargé du placement, sur une certaine étendue géographique, des films produits par une firme'.[12] How the films (or film copies) are actually placed is not specified by Giraud (are they transported in special carriages, packed in special boxes?), but he is clear about the fact that distribution takes place over a 'certain geographical range' (regional, national or international is still to be determined). Distribution is not a local issue; distribution is inter-locus: it's about how to get a film copy from one place (production) to the other (exhibition).

A working telecinematographic device could have been very helpful in the early days of film distribution, not only because its geographical reach would have been (at least theoretically) unlimited, but it would also have made superfluous and obsolete the physical placing (or displacement) of film copies. We know that still today hard copies of moving pictures are circulating and being projected in movie theatres, although it is (theoretically and practically) possible to transmit entire feature films via electronic signals. Wired movies can be downloaded and watched on computer screens; wireless clips can be caught and peeped at on cellular phone screens. The advantage of the wireless, in comparison to the wired, is that the user can move freely (at least within the geographical reach of the signals), and that innumerable places can be connected with each other (e.g. a wireless phone call between two persons who are walking in two different cities means a connection between continuously changing places: place A – place B; place A' – place B'; place A" – place B"; etc.). Wireless seems to mean boundless, but it actually means bounded motion (i.e. freedom of movement within a certain circuit).

Transmission, translation

In the early days of the twentieth century, the freedom of movement for wireless transmission users was very limited, as attested by Méliès's *Long Distance Wireless Photography* where the electronic transmission takes place in one and the same room:

Fig. 3. Georges Méliès, *La photographie électrique à distance* (1908): the laughing old lady.

the laboratory of a telephotographer (Méliès himself). More importantly, the telephotographed subjects have to stand still; and during the transmission some coding/decoding occurs. This is a remarkable theme that will return in other futurological fantasies. It is not unlikely that this kind of 'translation' was inspired by the fact that the wireless telegraph originally consisted in sending coded messages. In 1900 George Iles observes: 'All these [wireless telegraphy] methods, diverse as they are, have one limitation – their messages must take the form of an arbitrary code of signals. "A" must be a short tap and a long one, and so on throughout the alphabet. It remained for the telephone to banish this one restriction, and so marry sound and electricity that a metallic thread carries electrical pulses which are virtually those of every tone and cadence of the human voice.'[13] Méliès is not dealing with the human voice, but with the human body. In *Long Distance Wireless Photography* an old couple visits the atelier of the telephotographer. A group of assistants brings in a huge cabinet containing the belinograph and places it in front of an immense wheel. A black screen drops from the ceiling and is hung in front of the cabinet. The demonstration can begin! First, the telephotographer transmits the image of a still photograph, depicting three scantily (and transparently) dressed Graces, onto the screen. The image becomes a living portrait: at the beginning the projected Graces stand still, imitating the position of their photographic source, but then they start moving their arms and change position. The second experiment consists in transmitting the image of a living person. The apparatus is moved forward in order to give the spectator a better view. A young woman is brought in. She poses next to the cabinet. While the living person remains immobile, her double moves independently: she starts flirting with the old man, blows kisses through the air. Subsequently, the old couple is invited to be telephotographed. When the old lady is subjected to the process, the telephotographed image of her face in close up (Fig. 3) bursts into laughter, which is catching for all the persons present in the laboratory, including the lady herself. The telephotographic experiment of the old man is more revealing, showing us the head of a little monkey with nervous expressions (Fig. 4).

Fig. 4. Georges Méliès, *La photographie électrique à distance* (1908): the alter ego of the old man.

When the old man finds out about his alter ego, he gets furious and knocks over the apparatus.

Thus, not only is Méliès's machinery capable of producing independently moving images (transforming the principle of telephotography in that of telecinematography), but it also enables us to scrutinise or scan the inner soul of the persons who undergo the experiment. It seems as if telecinema can reveal their states of mind, exactly as photographer Bragaglia predicts in 1913 regarding the future applications of the telephone. Bragaglia also foresees some problems concerning the interpretation of these 'translations' of the inner soul, such as the impossibility of physically slapping or kissing the interlocutor, according to the needs (e.g. in case of anger or passion).[14] One could only slap the projected image (or the apparatus, following the example of the old man in *Long Distance Wireless Photography*). In Maurice Elvey's science-fiction or 'near-future'[15] film *High Treason* (1929), in which videophone communication is made fully operative, the same frustration regarding the lack of physical contact returns; two lovers, from two opposite political camps (United Europe vs. Atlantic States), are unable to embrace each other over the line. But seemingly there is the expectation that technology will soon change this situation, since one of the lovers says: 'I can't kiss you by wireless *yet*'.[16]

In the second half of the 1910s, Marinetti wrote a (sci-fi) film script entitled *Speed*, consisting of eleven tableaux. The last scene, 'Futurist Man in One-Hundred Years', depicts the life of a politician who is surrounded by the latest technological devices, among which a telephone system that visually 'translates' the places he (or his voice) runs through: 'Work corner in a train hurtling at top speed. Telegraphic keyboard and countless telephone receivers. The receiver is transformed, under his mouth, by turns, into the interior of a workshop, a board room, an elegant drawing-room, an astronomical observatory, a room of the Stock market, an arsenal, the tent of a five-star general.'[17] Clearly, this flow of images does not 'translate' words of a human voice at the other

Fig. 5. Marcel L'Herbier, *L'Inhumaine* (1924): 'Sur cet écran de télévision tandis que vous chantez vous allez voir paraître ceux qui vous écoutent à travers la Terre'.

end of the line; it does not concern any human conversation, but rather decodes the communication into visual ubiquity, into a continuous moving from one place to another, an incessant 'zapping' through space. So, it seems that the 'translation' does not involve the receiver, but only the transmitter.

An inverse situation is exposed in *L'Inhumaine* (1924) by Marcel L'Herbier, when the opera singer Claire Lescot (= the inhuman woman) is invited by the young Futurist engineer Einar Norsen to travel by means of the T.S.F. ('télégraphie sans fil'). In reality neither she nor her image will be travelling, only her voice (which reflects the basic principle of the radio). In return, the images of her listeners will travel towards her: 'Elle voyage sans bouger à travers l'espace aboli ... / ... à travers les joies et les douleurs des êtres ... / Elle oublie *le temps*'.[18] Claire Lescot sings in front of a microphone and on a (television) screen her audience, spread all over the world, is projected (Fig. 5), in different states of mind. L'Herbier offers us a two-way transmission system (as the radio originally was), with audio input and visual output. The receiver, not the transmitter, is actually travelling through space. As in the futurological fantasy of Marinetti, the principle is that of ubiquity or 'abolished space'.

Futurological modes of distribution

On the basis of the above examples, it is possible to draw different models of alternative film distribution. In the 1900s, telegraphy, and more particularly telephotography, inspired Méliès for the exploration/experimentation of electronic transmission of moving images; in the 1910s, the Futurists were optimistic about both the diffusion of wireless messages (T.S.F.) and the visual potentialities of the telephone; and in the 1920s, the radio (or 'the wireless'[19]) was transformed in the imagination of Marcel L'Herbier in some kind of *radiovision* or *radiocinéma*.[20] These futurological modes of distribution all take into account the issue of spatiality or geographical reach; and, interesting enough, they all entail some form of 'translation' or transformation, as if this were the latest attraction (comparable to the X-rays vogue).

These three distribution modes, based on or inspired by the possibilities of the telegraph, the telephone and the radio, are futurological in the sense that they are both futuro-technological (fantasies about the technological future) and science-fictional (fictionalisations of science). (Real) scientific inventions are fictionalised, that is, appropriated and transformed into new (reel) inventions, which could be read as popular or artistic responses to the problem of distribution as inter-locus: how to get moving images from one place to the other. In the above examples, most of the transmitted moving images have a living source (instead of a film copy or print), hence the 'translation' in the intermediate stage.

The examples used were chosen on purpose from three different decades (1900s, 1920s, 1920s), in order to illustrate different phases or applications of the telecommunication industry. Deliberately, I have not taken into account films such as *Les cartes vivantes* (*The Living Playing Cards*, 1905) and *La lanterne magique* (*The Magic Lantern*, 1903) by Méliès, which also involve a sort of wireless transmission, but which are not inspired by the newest telecommunication technologies. Whereas *The Living Playing Cards* shows us an advanced (and impossible) form of conjuring, *The Magic Lantern* explores the possibilities of film projection (and self-projection) without the use of slides, i.e. without (photo)graphic source. These are two examples of retro-technological fantasies. The apparatus operated in *Long Distance Wireless Photography*, on the contrary, can be considered futurological because based on the latest invention of Belin.

With futurological modes I do not necessarily intend future or near-future modes. If some of the above imaginary modes of distribution can be linked to or compared with recent applications of the telecommunication industry, it was certainly not written in their (imaginary) history to evolve in that manner. We can only try to read the possible futures of these fantasies, i.e. *a* future and not *the* future.

Notes

1. 'And who knows if in the year 2000 a film projector will be able to portray and project the interlocutor in his/her proper attitude of gesticulation during the [telephonic] conversation, allowing one to scrutinise the soul of the other, being present and absent, close and 300 km away?' (my translation). Bragaglia, Anton Giulio, 'Nell'anno 2000', *Patria* (26 January 1913), reprinted in Bragaglia, Anton Giulio, *Fotodinamismo futurista* (Torino: Einaudi, 1980), 240.

2. Webster, Michael, *Reading Visual Poetry after Futurism* (New York: Peter Lang, 1995), 33.

3. 'Peut-être verra-t-on désormais moins d'assassins disparaître sans laisser de traces et rester impunis. Les commissaires des gares frontières de Feignies, d'Avricourt, etc. ceux des ports, recevront des télégrammes de ce genre: "Un crime vient d'être commis ce matin à Paris. On soupçonne le sieur X... qu'on croit en fuite. Surveiller les trains (ou les embarquements) et l'arrêter au passage. Ci-joint le portrait du coupable présumé."' Korn, Arthur, 'La télégraphie des images', *Je sais tout* (18 April 1907). See also Lange, André, 'Arthur Korn (1870–1945), l'inventeur de la téléphotographie', *Histoire de la télévision* (http://histv.free.fr/korn/korn.htm)

4. Giraud, Jean, *Le Lexique français du cinéma. Des origines à 1930* (Paris: CNRS, 1958), 196–197.

5. See Lange, André, 'Les premiers textes scientifiques et littéraires sur la télévision (1877–1900)', *Histoire de la télévision* (http://histv2.free.fr/anthologie.htm)

6. Coissac, G.-Michel, *Histoire du cinématographe. De ses origines à nos jours* (Paris: Editions du "Cinéopse", 1925), 355.

7. Monaco, James, *The Dictionary of New Media* (New York: Harbor Electronic Publishing, 1999), 92.

8. Aladin, *La lampe merveilleuse* (23 January 1920), quoted in Giraud, 197.

9. Monaco, 92.

10. Blom, Ivo, *Jean Desmet and the Early Dutch Film Trade* (Amsterdam: Amsterdam University Press, 2003), 25.

11. I wish to thank Frank Kessler for having suggested me to re-read the wireless transmission issue from the perspective of Giraud's definition of distribution.

12. Giraud, 105.

13. Iles, George, *Flame, electricity and the camera* (New York: Doubleday & McClure, 1900), 227.

14. Bragaglia, 240.

15. See Koeck, Richard and François Penz, 'Screen city legibility', *City*, vol. 7, no. 3 (November 2003), 368.

16. Intertitle of the film.

17. Marinetti, Filippo Tommaso, 'Speed', *Fotogenia*, no. 2 (1995), 147.

18. Intertitles of the film.

19. According to Monaco's *Dictionary of New Media*, the first meaning of wireless is 'British for Radio'; only more recently, it is 'a synonym for cellular telephony or regular telephone service that uses microwave antennas rather than twisted pair, wireline or fiber optic cable' (279).

20. Giraud defines *radiovision* as 'Conjugaison du cinéma et de la radiophonie' and *radiocinéma* as 'Spectacle utilisant les moyens de la radio et ceux du cinéma; transmission de l'image filmique sur le ondes' (170). According to Giraud, both terms, used in 1929 by Moussinac, are unclear and almost indistinguishable from *télévision*.

Les films impossibles ou les possibilités du cinéma

Viva Paci

Université de Montréal, Canada

Dans les pages qui suivent on esquissera d'abord un portrait de quelques « formations discursives »[1] isolées à la lecture de la presse spécialisée, corporative, française du début des années 10. Au-delà du fait que les journaux corporatifs mettent en place des discours multiples, de natures différentes (économique, technologique, politique, esthétique et d'actualité), il est possible de retrouver des régularités qui relient plusieurs de ces discours. Et cela permet, bien sûr, de retracer les aventures d'un marché.

Dans un deuxième temps, je proposerai un cas particulier, celui d'une rubrique intitulée *Les Films impossibles*, que publie *L'Écho du cinéma* en 1912. L'étude du cas de cette rubrique permet de voir entre autre comment, dans la nouvelle configuration du marché de ces années-là, une idée nouvelle se loge dans les discours: la « fidélisation » du public. *Les Films impossibles* c'est un concours ouvert aux lecteurs, et ce public est certainement ciblé en tant que *pars pro toto* du public de cinéma en général.

C'est précisément dans ces années que l'exercice de la distribution va prendre une ampleur tout à fait différente dans l'industrie du film. Les raisons sont multiples, dont le fait que le système de production qui était très centralisé (pensons au cas Pathé) se transforme en un nouveau type de marché, composé de plus petits éditeurs de films (Éclair, SCAGL, etc.), et que, de plus, l'industrie commence à séparer l'un de l'autre ses secteurs: boîtes de production, compagnies de distribution et circuits d'exhibition.[2] Dans cette nouvelle situation, il est plus important qu'avant d'avoir une relation continue avec le public. Bon nombre de nouveaux débats qui font surface dans la presse spécialisée, par exemple sur la *critique*, les *exclusivités*, ou le cas du concours *Les Films impossibles*, ou plus généralement certaines interrogations sur la *qualité artistique* des films (ce qui constitue une *nouveauté* dans les discours de la presse durant ces années), me semblent préoccupés par l'idée de conquérir un public et de le fidéliser.

Nouveaux journaux pour un nouveau marché

Afin de se donner une délimitation temporelle, on pourrait considérer que cette période est inaugurée par un tournant symbolique: le fameux « Congrès International des Fabricants de films » tenu à Paris au mois de février 1909 et présidé par Georges Méliès ([…] ironie du sort, si l'on pense que ses affaires n'allaient pas très bien à cette époque).[3] On y confirme, on le sait, le passage du système de vente de pellicules de l'éditeur à l'exploitant, à un système de location. De toute évidence le passage au système de location des films change tout particulièrement la configuration de la distribution, posant les bases officielles pour une réorganisation du marché.

Bien entendu, s'intéresser à la presse corporative implique déjà une délimitation temporelle: en effet, si *Le Fascinateur*, bulletin catholique,[4] commence ses activités en janvier 1903, ce n'est qu'en août 1908 que le *Ciné-journal*, journal hebdomadaire, considéré comme le premier organe régulier de l'industrie cinématographique, ouvre ses portes.[5] C'est au tournant des années 10 que l'offre de revues augmente sensiblement, atteignant un sommet remarquable de 6 revues (pour le seul territoire parisien) en 1912: *L'Écho du cinéma* (1912), *Le Cinéma* (1912), *Le Cinéma et l'Écho du cinéma réunis* (1912–1923) ; *Pathé Journal* (1912- après 1914) ; *L'Industrie cinématographique* (1912-après 1914) et *Film-revue* (1912 – après 1914).[6] Ce qu'on peut retenir, c'est qu'après que *Le Fascinateur* eût ouvert la voie en 1903, ce sera seulement au tournant des années 10 que la presse commence à orienter son travail vers les travailleurs du cinéma, sans passer par le bon Dieu. Globalement, le nombre important de ces nouveaux journaux illustre bien une volonté de définition d'un discours et aussi une volonté de mise en forme d'un marché.

Cette multiplication des titres, ainsi que la séparation des autres corporations,[7] signalent la naissance d'une presse professionnelle institutionnalisée. Et lors de la naissance d'une institution, on le sait, on retrouve facilement – surtout dans une lecture *a posteriori* – la mise en place et la mise en ordre (par ailleurs toute *institution* discipline, n'est-ce pas ?) assez systématiques des nœuds importants.

Une des batailles qui se met en branle dans la presse spécialisée, durant ces premières années, concerne la naissance de la critique.[8] La question se cristallise autour du choix entre une vraie pratique critique sur le modèle de le critique théâtrale et le simple recopiage des notices sur les films que les catalogues des éditeurs diffusent. Il s'agit donc d'une question qui concerne directement les journaux, à un niveau interne, mais qui en même temps en dit long sur la représentation du cinéma au sein de l'industrie, et sur la recherche des moyens de communication plus efficaces entre l'industrie et le public. Dix ans nous séparent de « l'époque Delluc », et pour le moment plusieurs positions se bornent à exprimer une hostilité aveugle envers la critique. Ainsi *Argus* (Organe professionnel du cinématographe, du phonographe et des industries qui s'y rattachent)[9] qui dessert les intérêts des exploitants, prend ses distances par rapport à la pratique naissante de la critique. La revue *Argus* en 1909 se définit ainsi: « un journal d'utilité, non de luxe. [...] Un journal d'information, non de critique ».[10] Selon eux, l'un des défauts de la critique est d'« *influencer* » (je souligne) les directeurs de salles. Dans la même veine, Jean Durand, réalisateur de films comiques chez Gaumont, écrit le 7 octobre 1911 dans *Le Courrier cinématographique*, fâché par la critique qu'il venait d'y lire:

> « Veuillez noter que je ne [...] tolérerai dorénavant aucune appréciation déplacée touchant mes bandes ou moi-même. La première qualité d'un critique est la courtoisie [sic !] ».[11]

Le critique boudé était sans doute *Le Mauvais Œil* qui signait la rubrique « Les films tels qu'ils sont, *critique impartiale* » [je souligne].[12] Entre « courtoisie » et « impartialité », les *phrases d'armes* étaient ainsi, pour le moins, très divertissantes.

Dans un des articles sur la question de la critique que l'on retrouve dans le *Ciné-Journal* (Organe hebdomadaire de l'industrie cinématographique), la critique sert de bouc émissaire pour un problème de marché. Le 11 novembre 1911 dans l'article « Les idées de M. L. Aubert sur le Marché Cinématographique », suite à une réunion du Syndicat des Exploitants Français du Cinématographe portant sur la question des *exclusivités*,

Louis Aubert, *loueur*, expose ses réflexions personnelles sur l'état de crise du marché. « Le Cinématographe a eu le malheur de ne pas être, jusqu'ici, envisagé comme Industrie normale et durable. Les trois catégories – Éditeurs – Loueurs – Exploitants, qui devaient dès le début, rester bien séparées, se sont mélangées. Le mal est fait, il est trop tard pour y remédier [...] Il ne faudrait pourtant pas l'aggraver encore pour le plus grand profit d'une quatrième: 'La Presse'. La critique des films, inaugurée dernièrement, même si elle était impartiale [il se réfère certainement aux « critiques impartiales » du *Mauvais Œil*, VP], aura à mon avis de très graves inconvénients. En faisant l'éloge de quelques très bons films, environ 1.500 mètres sur une production hebdomadaire de 15.000, vous dirigerez tous les exploitants sur ces 1.500 mètres de 1er choix, d'où programmes semblables et course éperdue aux Nouveautés. Augmentation de frais de programmes et débâcle d'un grand nombre d'exploitation [...] ».[13] Dans *Le Cinéma et l'Écho du cinéma réunis* (journal hebdomadaire, illustré, indépendant)[14] nous assistons à une sorte de suite à l'attaque que le distributeur Aubert avait lancée à la critique, sous la plume de G. Pierre Martin dans « La Critique », un des articles de la longue série « L'Art cinématographique. Études Comparatives ».[15] Dans la perspective qui est propre à cette série d'articles, on cherche à donner ses lettres de noblesse au cinéma, en passant par les enseignements que prodiguent les autres arts. Il en va de même pour ce qui est de la critique cinématographique, dont les armes n'étaient pas aussi affinées que celles de la critique théâtrale. « L'effort des écrivains et le travail des artistes ont le Droit d'exiger une Presse à côté de la Réclame payée et du compte rendu catalogué ». En fait, quand la critique cinématographique aura fait ce saut de qualité dans la pensée et l'expression, elle génèrera: « Une émulation, un désir de succès, une recherche constante [...]. Nous aiderons à la victoire du génie sur la médiocrité. »[16]

Si la critique est considérée comme une arme de diffusion ou d'obstacle à la diversité du cinéma, il y a une autre bataille, à un niveau plus général, dans les colonnes de ces journaux, qui en encadre la question. C'est la bataille pour la légitimation de l'Art cinématographique,[17] qui occupe la place la plus importante durant ces années 10. Évidemment, le discours est trop vaste et déjà parcouru par d'autres chercheurs: l'interrogation sur une correspondance entre art et cinéma qui m'intéresse ici est celle, remarquablement nouvelle, qui s'articule à propos de la *spécificité* du cinéma et de la valorisation ponctuelle du *caractère artistique* des films. Si le *flou discursif* s'empare souvent de la presse sur ce sujet, dans un journal en particulier, *L'Écho du cinéma*, on débat de façon singulière et riche d'avenues pour le futur à propos de la *spécificité* du cinéma et du *caractère artistique* des films. Dans le premier numéro, à la page 1, après l'éditorial de la revue, appelé « Notre Programme »,[18] Fouquet, le rédacteur en chef, débute l'activité de son journal par un article appelé « Les Films Artistiques ».[19] Dans « Les Films Artistiques », de façon inattendue, sans beaucoup de comparaisons possibles avec d'autres positions de l'époque qui cherchent les lettres de noblesse du cinéma toujours ailleurs que dans les composantes du cinéma, Fouquet débute son argumentation comme cela:

> « Les progrès de la photographie, l'habilité des opérateurs, la netteté des images résultant de l'intensité de la lumière et de l'agencement particulier des appareils et des écrans ont permis d'obtenir, en cinématographie, des magnifiques films, dont quelques-uns sont de véritables œuvres d'art ».

Cette remarque, avec les quelques qui suivent à propos des scénarios parfois naïfs, proposent une vraie observation sur le cinéma. C'est la bonne photographie, dans le sens du mot qui nous est contemporain, qui donne son caractère artistique à un film, non pas le geste du grand acteur de théâtre, ni le scénario du grand écrivain, mais la bonne photographie, l'opérateur habile et, en fin du compte, les belles images de cinéma. *L'Écho du cinéma* annonce une attitude nouvelle, vouée à la recherche des propriétés caractéristiques du cinéma. De telles positions, singulières pour l'époque, sont exemplaires d'un besoin de définition du cinéma (ce qui est à la base de la naissance même de ces journaux), et seront maintes fois reprises dans ce journal.

Bien que dans d'autres articles il défendait l'idée selon laquelle l'art du cinéma se découvrirait davantage dans l'exploitation des éléments des autres arts (comme par exemple *le mime* ou *les poètes*), même G. Pierre Martin, dans « Le Cinéma. Outil d'art », avait assumé une position qui valorisait les propriétés du cinéma. Sa position se trouvait à cheval entre les premiers enthousiasmes pour le cinématographe, ceux de *La Poste* ou du *Radical* de décembre 1896, et les positions plus visionnaires, et sensibles à la nouveauté irréductible du cinéma, des années 20. Martin écrit: « Le Cinéma se fera le sculpteur de la vie. Le Cinéma martèlera dans l'immortalité [la] vie multiple d'une œuvre dramatique. Le Cinéma fixera l'insaisissable ».[20]

Le cas singulier et symptomatique d'une nouvelle relation avec le public: *Les Films impossibles*

Dans le même ordre d'idée, la spécificité du cinéma est au centre d'une rubrique, publiée dans *L'Écho*: le concours pour le public appelé « Les Films impossibles ». Ce concours semble s'inscrire parfaitement dans le cadre des réflexions de l'époque qui cherchent une définition pour le cinéma.[21] Dans les discours qui s'interrogent sur le statut du cinéma par rapport aux autres arts, *Les Films impossibles* se situent dans un terrain moins fréquenté de la réflexion. On y ouvre une interrogation sur le propre du cinéma, tout en adressant la question au public, dans la tentative, je dirais, de ménager une planification du marché.

Le libellé du concours dit: « Rien ne semble impossible aujourd'hui en cinématographie. Tous les sujets, même les plus extraordinaires, peuvent être mis en scène. Nous demandons à nos lecteurs d'imaginer de courts scénarios, intéressants ou comiques, qui ne puissent pas être réalisés à la scène. Les concurrents dont les idées seront les plus ingénieuses auront droits à un abonnement d'un an au journal *L'Écho du cinéma*. Les scénarios les plus intéressants seront publiés ».

Le concours sera affiché à partir du premier numéro de la revue, le 19 avril, rendez-vous fixe sur la deuxième page, et il y demeurera jusqu'au quatrième numéro de la revue où l'on publiera le gagnant du premier prix.[22] Il sera suivi, dans le 5ème numéro, par une sélection des autres sujets de films proposés, et dans les numéros 6 et 7, par une série d'articles signés Géo. Méliès, écrits en réaction au concours, où il commence de façon prometteuse: « les articles consacrés aux *films impossibles* [m'ont] particulièrement intéressé, puisque, ainsi que vous le savez, je me suis fait la spécialité de réaliser en cinématographie les impossibilités les plus extravagantes »,[23] mais après l'article de Méliès disperse quelque peu les arguments.

Le film qui gagne, n'est pas impossible, puisque « rien n'est impossible en cinématographie », mais il est difficile à réaliser: il porte le titre de *Un drame dans les airs*.[24] Une histoire d'amour et de jalousie est le prétexte pour une scène spectaculaire dans les airs: un concours d'aéroplanes et un accident sont le clou du spectacle. La mort spectaculaire d'un personnage donnera lieu à une autre catastrophe (le suicide par coup de pistolet d'un autre personnage).[25] Les sentiments et l'émotivité à fleur de peau que de toute évidence on vise, me semblent être une conséquence du déploiement de vues spectaculaires, dans une subordination de la narration à l'attraction. Si la primauté, la qualité, du sujet et donc du scénario sont des nouvelles tendances à suivre à cette époque du cinéma (et de cela on discute massivement dans la presse), dans ce concours nous voyons se dégager littéralement, dans la *recherche de sujets qui ne sont réalisables qu'au cinéma*, une *spécificité* du cinéma.

Les sujets des *Films impossibles* tout en demeurant chronologiquement à l'intérieur du paradigme de l'intégration narrative (1908–1914) dont parle Gunning,[26] s'en éloignent. Dans cette « intégration narrative », pensons par exemple à *Zigomar* qui est l'un des exemples suggérés par Gunning, les trucs par arrêt de caméra et substitution à la Méliès prennent une autre dimension en devenant un élément de l'avancement global du récit. Ici, dans les sujets proposés par les lecteurs de *L'Écho du cinéma* se manifeste au premier degré ce qu'est l'attente du public envers les films et plus généralement envers le cinéma: et cela semble définitivement être de l'ordre de la *situation spectaculaire capable après coup de générer une émotion forte* à la fois chez le personnage et chez le spectateur. Ce que le public demande en ce moment, au cours de ce printemps 1912, n'est pas de l'ordre d'un merveilleux ponctuel à insérer à l'intérieur d'une structure de récit, justement narrative, mais plutôt, des films qui soient carrément tiraillés entre l'attraction pure du dispositif (ici le public propose des sujets qui ne peuvent qu'« être réalisés par le cinéma », que seulement le dispositif cinématographique peut donner à voir), et, éventuellement, une identification au personnage que même une faible structure narrative peut construire. Le concours était après tout, malgré tout, un concours de *sujets* de films, et donc appelait à développer une idée de scénario, et non des propositions de trucages.

J'aimerai éventuellement proposer la formule de « narration spectaculaire », plutôt que d'« intégration narrative », afin d'*attirer* davantage l'attention sur le caractère spectaculaire que le public recherche. Ce caractère spectaculaire incarne encore, bien que différemment, l'*idée de cinéma* qui s'était formée au fil des années, et qui se caractérisait par ses *attractions monstratives*.

Dans le numéro 5, *L'Écho* publie les résumés d'autres *films impossibles* sélectionnés.[27] « *Les Chutes du Niagara*: Tableau émotionnant. Une barque disparaît dans les tourbillons, apparaît ensuite un instant au milieu de la cascade et s'engloutit définitivement [...] ». « *La guerre de demain*: De grands ensembles, des combats acharnés avec les engins de destruction les plus modernes, des explosions [...] ». « *L'effondrement de la Tour Eiffel*: « Le scénario manque d'intérêt, et au moyen de décors on peut donner l'illusion du cataclysme ». Et ça continue comme ça: « un éditeur hésiterait évidemment à se payer la Tour Eiffel pour créer un film sensationnel [sic !]. » « *Un grand criminel*: Scène d'assassinat se terminant par une décapitation [...]. » « *Le repas des tigres*: On a déjà vu des scènes dans lesquelles un homme était la proie des bêtes féroces [...]. » « *Voyage au centre de la terre* [...]. »[28] Grâce à sa capacité, propre, de donner à voir de choses merveilleuses, de rendre possible l'impossible, le cinéma en 1912, aux yeux du public doit assurer son rôle de médiateur entre ce dernier (le public) et le monde, mais à la façon de l'attraction.

En utilisant à quelque reprise le mot « merveilleux », on a pas voulu renvoyer à une classification todorovienne,[29] mais plutôt, à une argumentation typiquement méliès-sienne, où merveilleux est synonyme d'*impossible*, et l'impossible se réalise justement au cinéma. « Je me suis fait la spécialité de réaliser en cinématographie les impossibilités les plus extravagantes », disait Méliès.[30]

Et cette possibilité de montrer l'impossible apparaît pleinement comme une possibilité spécifique du cinéma. Le théâtre, terme de comparaison inévitable pour le cinéma dans ces temps-ci, ne peut pas en faire autant sur la scène, même pas sur la scène du théâtre Robert-Houdin.

Par le biais d'un concours, la presse spécialisée avait essayé, bien avant que les histoires des coulisses du cinéma et les vies de stars ne passionnent des milliers de lecteurs, de fidéliser le public en s'adressant directement à lui. Donner au public l'impression de choisir ses sujets de films assurait une part de succès au marché. Une opération de *marketing* dirait-on aujourd'hui, avec, en prime, un prix final: un an d'abonnement gratuit. D'autre part, cette situation ne pouvait se produire qu'à un moment de changement du marché: un organe issu de l'industrie était en train de chercher en dehors des frontières des professionnels de l'industrie ce qu'était le *propre* du cinéma.

Ce bref parcours et cette étude de cas nous a permis de voir avec plus de netteté certains des enjeux qui animent les débats dans la presse au début des années 10, des tensions très vives et des zones de flou entre un désir de dramaturgie et l'attraction du spectacle, et qui ont assisté à la naissance d'un personnage singulier, qui aura plus que son mot à dire quant au destin de ce nouvel art et de la forme du marché de la distribution: le caprice du public.

Notes

1. Cf. Foucault, Michel, *L'Archéologie du savoir* (Paris: Gallimard, 1969), en particulier le chapitre « Les régularités discursives ».

2. Selon une périodisation proposée par Richard Abel ce changement se situe justement entre 1911 et 1914. Cf. *The Ciné Goes to Town. French Cinema 1896–1914* (Berkley: University of California Press, 1994).

3. En 1909 Méliès cesse sa production cinématographique, mais il est possible que la Star-Film ait cessé son activité dès les derniers mois de 1908. En 1911 Méliès recommence à tourner. Ses films seront désormais distribués par Pathé. En 1913 les productions Star-Film sont définitivement interrompues. En 1914 Gaston Méliès a cessé sa production aux États-Unis. Cf. Deslandes, Jacques, *Le Boulevard du cinéma à l'époque de Georges Méliès* (Paris: Cerf, 1963), 96–97.

4. La revue *Le Fascinateur*, fondée en 1903, était éditée par les Éditions de la Bonne Presse, et dirigée par Georges-Michel Coissac. Coissac disait que la mission du *Fascinateur* était « d'apprendre à tous ses lecteurs l'art de *fasciner* un auditoire par des récréations utiles, spécialement par les projections fixes, le cinématographe, la photographie et le phonographe », cité in Jeanne, René et Charles Ford, *Le Cinéma et la presse 1895–1960* (Paris: Armand Colin, 1961), 76. Les informations détaillées sur les revues corporatives qui suivent ont été rassemblées à la médiathèque de la Cinémathèque québécoise. Je tiens à remercier Pierre Véronneau pour avoir mis à ma disposition des textes difficilement consultables autrement, et Louis Pelletier pour la précision de ses commentaires.

    Une autre source qui m'a fourni quelques informations dont je rapporte le contenu dans les notes qui suivent a été le « répertoire des périodiques spécialisées » disponible à la BiFi, dont le catalogue est consultable aussi en ligne:

    http://www.bifi.fr/doc_site/expert/periodiques/francais/alpha/alpha1.html

5. *Phono-ciné-gazette*, « Revue des machines parlantes et du cinématographe. Phonographes, gramophones, etc. Cinématographe, optique et acoustique », semble être la première revue à aborder les sujets sous un angle professionnel et à se soucier de la corporation dans son ensemble. Son fondateur Edmond Benoit-Levy, avocat de Charles Pathé, est particulièrement attentif aux problèmes juridiques et économiques du cinéma. Fondée en 1905, en 1907 la revue est favorable au remplacement de la vente des films par leur location. La fin de la parution de *Phono-ciné-gazette* est liée à la création d'un nouvel organe, *Ciné-Journal*, qui le désignera en 1909, dans le n. 71, du 21 décembre, comme son successeur à la suite d'une « transmission amicale des pouvoirs », 3–4.

6. Qui se rajoutent à: *Ciné-Journal* (1908–1938), *Argus* (1907–1913), *Phono-Cinéma-Revue* (1908–1910), *Le Courrier cinématographique* (1911–1937), *Cinéma revue* (1911 – après 1914). Les informations sur les périodiques que je n'ai pas pu consulter directement sont tirées de l'article d'Emmanuelle Toulet, « Aux sources de l'histoire du cinéma … Naissance d'une presse sous influence », *Restaurations et tirages de la Cinémathèque française* (vol. IV, 1989), 14–25.

7. À la fin du XIXe et aux premières années du XXe siècle les premiers pas du discours sur le cinéma se faisaient dans des journaux et des revues d'autres corporations technico-spectaculaires. Des

rubriques techniques sur le cinéma étaient hébergées par exemple dans la corporation de la lanterne magique, en milieu anglo-saxon (*The Optical Magic Lantern Journal and Photographic Enlarger*, London), de la phonographie (*Phonoscope*, New York), et de la photographie en milieu français (*Ombres et lumières* et *La Mise au point*).

8. Ce n'est pas sans intérêt de remarquer que Georges Lordier, déjà fondateur de *L'Écho du cinéma* et ensuite directeur de *Le Cinéma et l'Écho du cinéma réunis*, crée en février 1913 le « Syndicat de la presse cinématographique ». Il en fut le premier président, entouré de Georges Dureau (fondateur de *Ciné-Journal*) et de Charles Le Fraper (directeur du *Courrier Cinématographique*) et du directeur de Gaumont-Actualité, Henry Lafargette. Durant cette période d'institutionnalisation deux types de journalisme, la presse imprimée et la presse filmée, avec Gaumont-Actualité, se retrouvent donc dans le même groupement des représentants de la presse cinématographique.

9. *Argus* (1907–1913) se présente comme « un organe périodique de la corporation des exploitants de cinéma », et s'oppose à la politiqué centralisatrice et monopoliste de Pathé. Cf. Toulet, op. cit., 17 et 18.

10. *Argus*, n. 101 (février 1909), cité in Toulet, 18.

11. Dans *Le Courrier cinématographique* (« Organe hebdomadaire indépendant de la cinématographie, des arts, sciences et industries qui s'y rattachent »), n. 13 (7 octobre 1911), cité in Toulet, 20.

12. Cette rubrique avait été inaugurée par *Le Courrier cinématographique*, dans son cinquième numéro, le 11 août 1911.

13. *Ciné-Journal*, n. 168 (11 novembre 1911): 25 et 27.

14. *Le Cinéma et l'Écho du cinéma réunis* commence le 19 juillet 1912 avec le n. 21. Il existera jusqu'en 1923 – interrompu entre 1914 et 1916.

15. La série « L'Art cinématographique. Études Comparatives » avait commencé dans *L'Écho du cinéma*, n. 8, 14 juin 1912. Un autre article, dans le même esprit programmatique, de G.P. Martin avait précédé la série, dans le n. 5 (17 mai 1912), « Le Cinéma. Outil d'art », 2. Martin y faisait l'éloge du cinéma comme moyen de rendre éternelle la vie des œuvres d'art.

16. Dans *Le Cinéma et l'Écho du cinéma réunis*, n. 25 (16 août 1912): 1–2, Martin présente aussi les raisons de l'absence de la critique cinématographique: « La Presse technique n'avait pas, ne pouvait pas avoir l'indépendance nécessaire ; et puis le Cinéma n'était pas encore une manifestation d'Art ». La presse était en fait très souvent liée de très près à des éditeurs.

17. Pour un panorama des positions des « plumes cinématographiques » sur cet aspect, je renvoie à l'article de Jean-Philippe Restoueix, « À l'origine du *septième art*. La constitution du discours sur le cinéma pensé comme art à travers les revues spécialisées avant 1914 », in Jean A. Gili, Michèle Lagny, Michel Marie, Vincent Pinel (éds.), *Les Vingt premières années du cinéma français* (Paris: Presses de la Sorbonne Nouvelle, 1995), 311 et suivantes.

18. Mentionnons au passage que dans « Notre Programme » la rédaction du journal manifeste un intérêt central, et nouveau, pour un public tout genre, des professionnels aux passionnés de cinéma, in *L'Écho du cinéma*, dans le numéro inaugural, à la première page: n. 1 (19 avril 1912): 1. Fouquet sera ensuite aussi rédacteur en chef de *Le Cinéma et l'écho du cinéma réunis*.

19. In *L'Écho du cinéma*, n. 1 (19 avril 1912): 1.

20. In *L'Écho du cinéma*, n. 5 (17 mai 1912): 2.

21. Je ferais remonter ces réflexions à celle de Canudo de 1908 « Trionfo del Cinematografo ». Ici il cherche à identifier le cinéma comme radicalement différent des autres arts (différent par la *vitesse*, et avec le souhait qu'il puisse donc un jour être vraiment le moyen d'expression de la réalité contemporaine). Cf. « Trionfo del Cinematografo », *Il Nuovo Giornale* (25 novembre 1908) Firenze. En italien in: Grignaffini, Giovanna, *Sapere e teorie del cinema. Il periodo del muto* (Bologna: CLUEB, 1989): 105–111. Canudo reprend ce texte dans: « La Naissance d'un Sixième Art. Essai sur le Cinématographe », *Les Entretiens Idéalistes* (25 octobre 1911), repris in *L'Usine aux images*, édition établie par Jean-Paul Morel (Paris: Séguier/Arte Éditions, 1995), 32–40.

22. Dans ce même quatrième numéro *L'Écho du cinéma* affichera un nouveau concours adressé aux lecteurs: « Concours de Caricatures », où l'on « ouvre nous colonnes à nos lecteurs en vue de les provoquer à un nouveau tournoi », pour la création de « courtes légendes, aussi spirituelles que possible, accompagnées de dessins amusants ou de caricatures ».

23. Géo. Méliès, « Le Merveilleux au cinéma », *L'Écho du cinéma*, n. 6 (24 mai 1912): 1, et n. 7 (31 mai 1912): 2.

24. Dix ans auparavant Gaston Velle, à la Pathé, avait déjà réalisé un film du même titre, *Un drame dans les airs*, inspiré de l'homonyme nouvelle de Jules Verne. Mais il ne s'agit pas là d'un inspirateur de notre *film impossible*, puisque l'histoire du film Pathé est tout à fait différente.

25. In *L'Écho du cinéma*, n. 4 (10 mai 1912), 2.

26. Cf. surtout l'article de Tom Gunning, « Attrazioni, inchieste, travestimenti, Zigomar, Jasset e la storia dei generi cinematografici », *Griffithiana*, n. 47 (1993): 110–134 ; et Gaudreault, André et Tom Gunning, « Le cinéma des premiers temps: un défi à l'histoire du cinéma », in Jacques Aumont, André Gaudreault et Michel Marie (éds.), *Histoire du cinéma. Nouvelles approches* (Paris: Publications de la Sorbonne, 1989), 49–63.

Pour la petite histoire « domitorienne », au dernier Congrès DOMITOR, à Montréal en 2002, Richard Grusin, dans sa *Synthèse du colloque*, avait mentionné qu'en « tant qu'étranger, pouvant observer la configuration anthropologique », le peuple de DOMITOR, semblait tenir en grande considération un oracle nommé Gunning, auquel grand nombre de contributions faisaient appel pour s'attirer la faveur des dieux …

27. In *L'Écho du cinéma*, n. 5 (17 mai 1912): 2.

28. Le résumé dit: « Visiblement inspiré par un des plus intéressants romans de Jules Vernes. N'est pas impossible à réaliser. Il suffit pour s'en rendre compte de voir les scènes de *L'Enfer de Dante* [*Inferno*, de F. Bertolini e A. Padovan, 1911] ou celles de Géo. Méliès ». Or ce qui est un peu drôle c'est que le 3 mai 1912 était sorti *À la conquête du Pôle*, qui est un *flop* commercial. Méliès avait engagé ses immeubles de Montreuil avec Pathé qui avait financé les films. Les mauvais résultats commerciaux des derniers films lui coûtèrent ses propriétés, qu'il dû abandonner en 1923. Et, pendant ce temps, il y a des sujets de films qui gagnent des prix en demandant de voir la même chose … il faut croire que c'était du moins mis en scène autrement … pauvre Méliès … L'information concernant l'hypothèque est tirée de Malthête, Jacques et Laurent Mannoni (éds.), *Méliès: magie et cinéma* (Paris: Paris musées), 2002.

29. Todorov, Tzvetan, *Introduction à la littérature fantastique* (Paris: Seuil, 1970) ; les éléments qui définissent la catégorie du merveilleux sont des faits concrets qui se donnent dans un univers régi par des lois étrangères à celles qui règlent le nôtre. Éventuellement le cinéma même pourrait être considéré comme médiateur d'un « merveilleux instrumental », un merveilleux qui serait donc motivé par l'entremise du cinéma comme vecteur du récit. N'est-ce pas parce que nous sommes à l'intérieur de l'univers parallèle que le cinéma crée, que nous pouvons accepter les visions impossibles qu'il nous offre ? Si pour Méliès, en deçà des catégories de Todorov, il s'agissait de toute évidence du fait que le cinéma est une machine à produire du merveilleux (à condition qu'on fasse preuve d'une totale maîtrise artistique à toutes les étapes de la création du film, nous rappelle Méliès), les spectateurs de 1912, les mêmes qui rejettent *Voyage au pôle*, désiraient un merveilleux réaliste: pas de Yeti, mais un bateau qui disparaît et refait ensuite surface dans les flots des chutes du Niagara, la Tour Eiffel qui s'écroule de façon spectaculaire, etc.

30. Géo. Méliès, « Le Merveilleux au cinéma », *L'Écho du cinéma*, n. 6 (24 mai 1912): 1.

Any ID? Building a database out of the Jean Desmet archive

Rixt Jonkman

Universiteit van Amsterdam, The Netherlands

Introduction

Both in his book *Jean Desmet and the early film trade* (2003) and in his article in this volume, Ivo Blom gives an overview of Jean Desmet and early film distribution in the Netherlands. The archive Desmet left the Netherlands Filmmuseum not only contains lots of films and publicity materials, but also his vast business correspondence. Ivo Blom has extensively studied Desmet's business archive to learn more about distribution in the Netherlands, but the archive still contains numerous interesting materials that are worth taking an even closer look at. Using materials from Desmet's archive, I have carried out a survey on his distribution practises during the period 1910–12.[1] For this survey, I used a database as a tool to structure the data. The project had two stages. The first one was to make a detailed overview of all the films Desmet had purchased between 1910 and 1912. The second was to make a database for the data about the distribution or renting of these films from 1910–12. The goal of my project was to take a closer look into a specific period, enabling us to learn more about distribution and programming. The years 1910–12 were, for instance, the period in which longer films were introduced, quickly gaining popularity. By putting Desmet's practises under a microscope, we gain insight about what generally happened within Dutch film culture in this period. The structure of my article is as follows. I will first explain how I constructed the overview of Desmet's purchases; subsequently how I made the database and what it looks like; then the application of the database and some research examples; and in the end I will discuss some issues that arose during the making of the database.

Overview of Desmet's purchases

From October 1910 until March 1912, Jean Desmet bought his films in packages on the second hand market in Germany. He had two suppliers in these years. From October 1910 on, he bought his films from the Westdeutsche Film Börse in Krefeld, and in July 1911 he changed to the Deutsche Film Gesellschaft in Cologne. Every week he got a package of about 14 films (2500 metres), sufficient for two complete film programmes. Mostly these were short films. Every week all the genres were present: drama, comedy, and non-fiction (mostly travel films). With the film package he received a bill, still existing in the Desmet business archive, kept at the Filmmuseum. Figure 1 shows a bill for the films Desmet received on 9 September 1911 from the Deutsche Film Gesellschaft. This bill contains the German title, the length of the film,

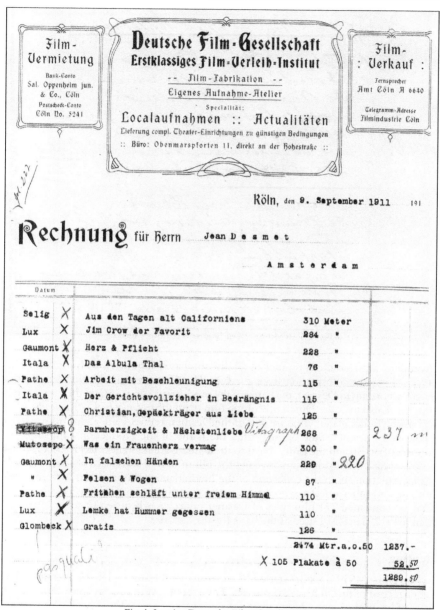

Fig. 1. Invoice Deutsche Film-Gesellschaft.

the price per metre, the total price, the name of the production company and the film length according to Desmet. Desmet always re-measured the films he received and if the film was shorter than the length on the bill, he would claim the price difference from the company. The name of the production company is mentioned only on the bills from the Deutsche Filmgesellschaft, not on the bills from the Westdeutsche Film Börse, unfortunately.

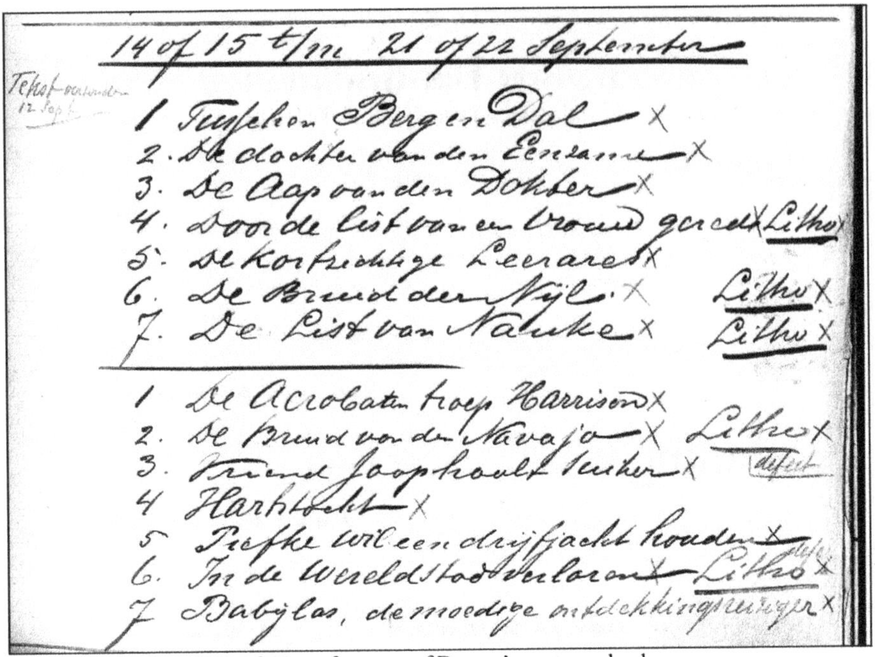
14 of 15 t/m 21 of 22 September

Tekst verzonden 12 Sept.

1 Tusschen Berg en Dal X
2. De dochter van den Eenzame X
3. De Aap van den Dokter X
4. Door de list van een vrouw gered X Litho
5. De kortzichtige Leeraresse X
6. De Bruid den Nijl. X Litho X
7. De List van Natuke X Litho X

1 De Acrobatentroep Harrison X
2. De Bruid van den Navajo X Litho X
3. Vriend Jaap houdt lekker X defect
4 Hartstocht X
5 Piefke wil een drijfjacht houden X
6. In de Wereldstad verloren X Litho X
7 Babylas, de moedige ontdekkingsreiziger X

Fig. 2. Entry from one of Desmet's customer books.

I compiled a list on the computer of all the purchased film titles, with the following entries. First the information from the bill: The German title, the film length, the length according to Desmet, the name of the production company and the name of the supplier. I also took the Dutch title of the film from the *customer books ('Klantenboek')* – about which more later – that are part of the Desmet archive. I also added information I collected elsewhere: the original title, the name of the production company, the country of origin and the genre. Next to these, there are references to Herbert Birett's books on early cinema in Germany[2] and the Filmmuseum Database (FMDB), with all the information about the collection of the Netherlands Filmmuseum. With the help of these and other reference books, I tried to identify as many titles as possible. The final list contained 771 film titles of Desmet's purchases between October 1910 and March 1912. This list I used as the basis for the database.

Renting

In November 1910, Desmet started his regular distribution in The Netherlands. He kept a record of this in his *customer books*. These books were also my source for Dutch titles of his films. Figure 2 is an image of one entry in one of those books. Shown are the films Desmet rented on 14 or 15 until 21 or 22 September 1911 to P. Silvius, owner of the Dordtsch Bioscope Theater, a cinema in Dordrecht, a medium-sized town in the southwest of Holland. Desmet (or a member of his staff) has written down the Dutch titles of the films sent to this customer. He divided the 14 films in two packages of seven films. In the example of Fig. 2, Desmet also made a note of the first and last day of the screening, the type of publicity material (Lithos) he had sent, and when he had sent this– mostly a week in advance of the films. In other entries he sometimes adds the price, the exact dates when the films were shown and when he received them

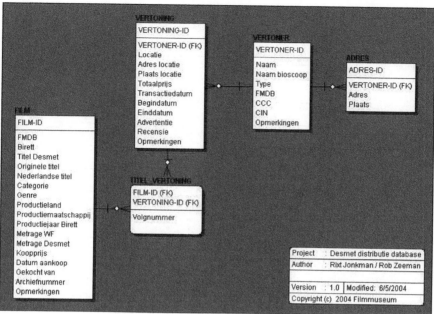

Fig. 3. Structure of the database.

back. As one can see from this example, not all the information was always included. From these entries, I compiled a list of exhibitions. This contains information about where and when a programme of films was shown. The films are not directly inserted in the exhibition table, but connected to the exhibitions via a separate list. I made a third list, that of the exhibitors. This list contains information about Desmet's customers. It has a link to the *Netherlands Cinema History Database*, which is Karel Dibbets' database on all the cinemas in the Netherlands and which also contains information on people involved in the Dutch film business.[3] I thus collected the data and established three lists: one of film titles, one of the exhibitions and one of the exhibitors.

Distribution database

This distribution database is a relational database and was built in MS Access. Figure 3 shows a schema of the database. It consists of different tables that can be combined or linked together, hence it is called a relational database. These tables are from left to right, the table of film titles, the table of the exhibitions and a connection table that links a title to an exhibition and the table of exhibitors connected with a table of their addresses. The information in the tables is interconnected through identification numbers, the so-called *ID-numbers*. Every film has its own number, every exhibition has its own number and all the exhibitors have their own number. The table *exhibitions*, contains the titles Desmet had sent on one day to one person. The films are inserted by making a connection between the list of the film titles and an exhibition. This connection between an exhibition and a film is made through these ID – numbers via this separate connection table. The titles were inserted in the same order as Desmet wrote them down in his customer books. Each film has links that connect it to other databases, such as the Filmmuseum Database, which contains additional information about the film.

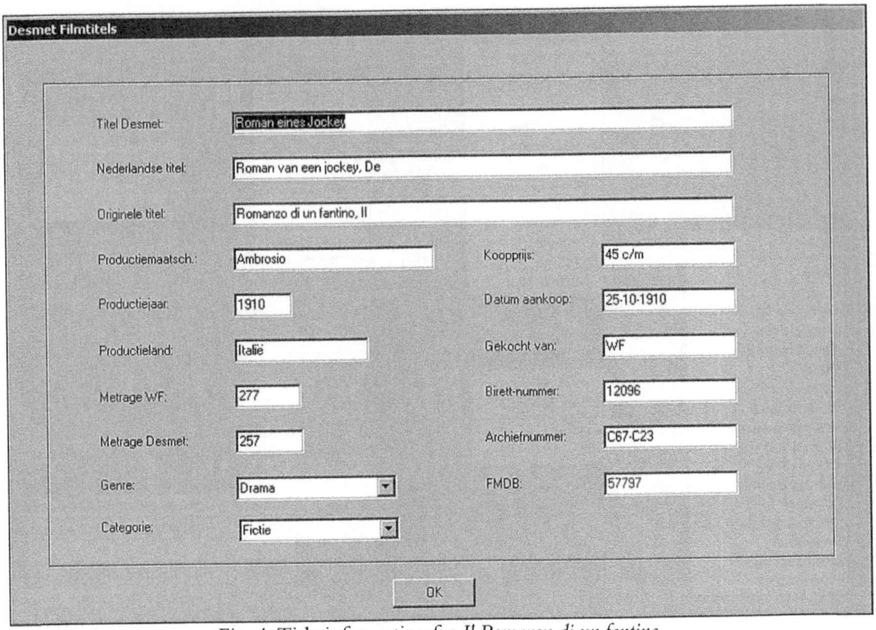

Fig. 4. Title information for *Il Romanzo di un fantino*.

The database application

When all the exhibitions and films from the customer books have been entered, the database will present a complete overview of all the exhibitions with all films shown and all exhibitors involved. In this pilot stage only the raw database and a simple interface are available, but a web interface for the database with some possibilities for asking research questions is under construction and will be available online through the Filmmuseum website when ready.[4] The illustrations that accompany the examples below are taken from the raw database and the search interface.

The database can be used for different kinds of questions. For instance for research on what film programmes looked like and how they developed through time. The database can answer questions such as: How long was an average programme? How many films did it contain? How many different genres were present and exactly which genres did it contain? In which order were the films placed? Does this change over time? What happened for instance when the longer films (800–1000 metres) were introduced? We can also pose questions about customers in the distribution field. What kind of customers did Desmet have? Where did they live? How often did they rent a programme and for how long? In this way the database can be a tool to learn more about the film situation in the Netherlands during this period.

The programme in which we built the database, MS Access, can be used to ask these systematic research questions to the database, *queries*, which will generate lists we can use for empirical research with statistics. I will now give two examples of queries we have performed with the database.

Search example 1

With the database we can research the 'life' of a film print. When did Desmet buy the print? To whom did he rent it? How often did he rent it and how long did he continue

naam	locatie	plaats_loc	begindatum	einddatum	orginele_titel
Lier, WJ van	bioscoop	maastricht	17-11-1910		Romanzo di un fantino, Il
Sips, PHJ	Hof van Holland	Breda	2-12-1910		Romanzo di un fantino, Il
Cremer, J	Bioscoop	Enschede	7-12-1910		Romanzo di un fantino, Il
Brasse, Fritz	Kermis	Nijmegen	10-12-1910		Romanzo di un fantino, Il
Brasse, Fritz	Kermis	Kampen	16-12-1910		Romanzo di un fantino, Il
Alten	Bioscoop	Middelburg	18-12-1910		Romanzo di un fantino, Il
Vet Wegkamp, H.	Kermis	Zaandam	24-12-1910		Romanzo di un fantino, Il
Bolkestein	p/a scouwburg Varrenhorst	Steenwijk	16-2-1911		Romanzo di un fantino, Il
Uges, R	bioscoop	Groningen	13-3-1911	20-3-1911	Romanzo di un fantino, Il
Silvius	bioscoop	Dordrecht	22-3-1911	1-4-1911	Romanzo di un fantino, Il
Röhr & Laidan	bioscoop	Tilburg	11-5-1911		Romanzo di un fantino, Il
Haan, J de	Cinema Parisien	Utrecht	2-6-1911	8-6-1911	Romanzo di un fantino, Il
	bioscoop	Rotterdam	22-6-1911		Romanzo di un fantino, Il
Gennes, W	bioscoop	Hoorn	14-7-1911	20-7-1911	Romanzo di un fantino, Il

Fig. 5. Result of query 1: list of the screenings of the film

to rent it? We did a query for the Italian drama *Il Romanzo di un fantino* (The Romance of a Jockey, Ambrosio 1910). Figure 4 shows the title information from the database. We can see that it was bought from the Westdeutsche Filmbörse on 25 October 1910 for 45 cents per metre. The length on the bill was 277 metres, but according to Desmet it only measured 257 metres. We did a query to find out when and where the film was shown. In Figure 5 we see a list of all the exhibitions the film has had until halfway through 1911. From left to right we see the name of the exhibitor, the venue (cinema or travelling showman [kermis]), the city it was shown in, the first and last day the films were rented. In the database we find 14 exhibitions between 17 November 1910 and 14 July 1911. The film was rented to cinemas as well as to a travelling showman.

Search example 2

We used another title, *École de sauvetage en Australie* (Lifeguard school in Australia, Pathé

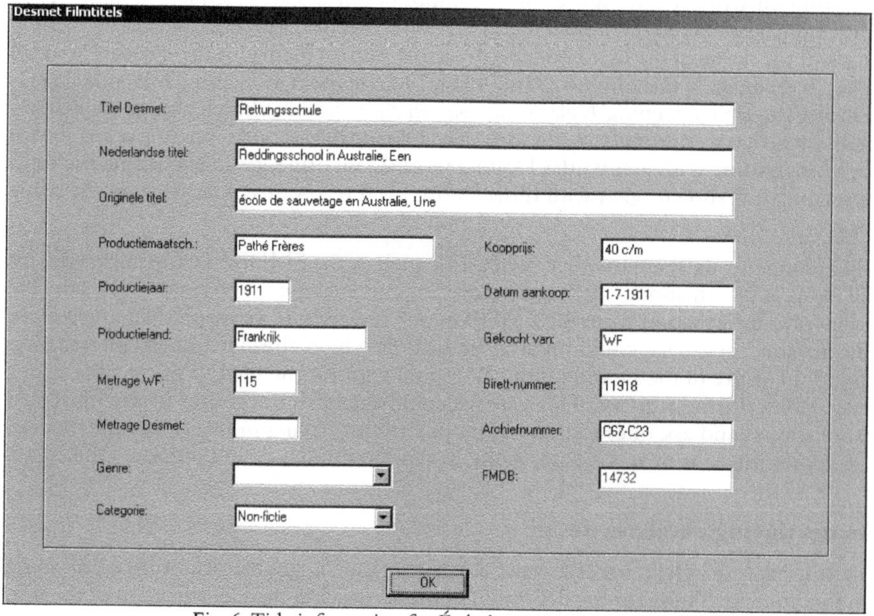
Desmet Filmtitels

Titel Desmet: Rettungsschule

Nederlandse titel: Reddingsschool in Australie, Een

Originele titel: école de sauvetage en Australie, Une

Productiemaatsch.: Pathé Frères

Koopprijs: 40 c/m

Productiejaar: 1911

Datum aankoop: 1-7-1911

Productieland: Frankrijk

Gekocht van: WF

Metrage WF: 115

Birett-nummer: 11918

Metrage Desmet:

Archiefnummer: C67-C23

Genre:

FMDB: 14732

Categorie: Non-fictie

OK

Fig. 6. Title information for *École de sauvetage en Australie*.

Orginele titel	nederlandse titel	Datum aankoop	begindatum	naam	locatie
Lonedale Operator, The	Moedige dochter van den stationschef, De	1-7-1911	28-7-1911	Silvius	Dordtsch bioscoop
école de sauvetage en Australi	Reddingsschool in Australie, Een	1-7-1911	28-7-1911	Silvius	Dordtsch bioscoop
Mitrailleuse, La	Echtelijke twist	1-7-1911	28-7-1911	Silvius	Dordtsch bioscoop
	Verdwenen baby, De	1-7-1911	28-7-1911	Silvius	Dordtsch bioscoop
Mensonge magnanime	Groothartige leugen, Een	1-7-1911	28-7-1911	Silvius	Dordtsch bioscoop
	Meibloemen	1-7-1911	28-7-1911	Silvius	Dordtsch bioscoop
Terrible aventure de Patouillard	Avontuur van Lemke, Een	1-7-1911	28-7-1911	Silvius	Dordtsch bioscoop
	Fritsje laat zich niet overbluffen	1-7-1911	28-7-1911	Silvius	Dordtsch bioscoop
	Kijk jij maar naar Fifi	1-7-1911	28-7-1911	Silvius	Dordtsch bioscoop
V dni Getmanov	Hoofdman Nicolajeff	1-7-1911	28-7-1911	Silvius	Dordtsch bioscoop
Raggio di salvezzi	Reddende licht, Het	1-7-1911	28-7-1911	Silvius	Dordtsch bioscoop
Watter-lilies	Waterlelies, De	1-7-1911	28-7-1911	Silvius	Dordtsch bioscoop
Pathe 4605	Van knop tot bloem	3-6-1911	28-7-1911	Silvius	Dordtsch bioscoop
Due innamorate di Cretinetti	Vereering van Gribouille, De	1-7-1911	28-7-1911	Silvius	Dordtsch bioscoop
Légende du vieux sonneur, La	Oude klokkenluider, De	26-4-1911	11-9-1911	Brasse, Fritz	Chicago bioscoop
	St. Lucien	10-6-1911	11-9-1911	Brasse, Fritz	Chicago bioscoop
Tontolini in Auto	Autotocht van Tontolini, Een	4-4-1911	11-9-1911	Brasse, Fritz	Chicago bioscoop
Rembrandt de la rue Lepic, Le	Ook een Rembrandt	22-4-1911	11-9-1911	Brasse, Fritz	Chicago bioscoop
Cretinette in soirée	Gribouille in gezelschap	22-4-1911	11-9-1911	Brasse, Fritz	Chicago bioscoop
	Manus moet duelleren	26-4-1911	11-9-1911	Brasse, Fritz	Chicago bioscoop
Verkehrte Berlin, Das	Verkeerde Berlijn, Het	29-5-1911	11-9-1911	Brasse, Fritz	Chicago bioscoop
école de sauvetage en Australi	Reddingsschool in Australie, Een	1-7-1911	11-9-1911	Brasse, Fritz	Chicago bioscoop
Léontine enfant terrible	Lotje is een Deugniet	29-7-1911	11-9-1911	Brasse, Fritz	Chicago bioscoop
Exode des Fées, L'	Wraak van de fee, De	22-4-1911	11-9-1911	Brasse, Fritz	Chicago bioscoop
	Verdwenen baby, De	1-7-1911	11-9-1911	Brasse, Fritz	Chicago bioscoop
	In het roode licht	17-1-1911	8-12-1911	Haan, J de	Cinema Parisien
école de sauvetage en Australi	Reddingsschool in Australie, Een	1-7-1911	8-12-1911	Haan, J de	Cinema Parisien
Mitrailleuse, La	Echtelijke twist	1-7-1911	8-12-1911	Haan, J de	Cinema Parisien
	Verdwenen baby, De	1-7-1911	8-12-1911	Haan, J de	Cinema Parisien
Due innamorate di Cretinetti	Vereering van Gribouille, De	1-7-1911	8-12-1911	Haan, J de	Cinema Parisien
Mensonge magnanime	Groothartige leugen, Een	1-7-1911	8-12-1911	Haan, J de	Cinema Parisien
Robinet studia una parte tragic	Nauke studeert een tragische rol	23-1-1911	8-12-1911	Haan, J de	Cinema Parisien
	Natuuropnamen Messina		8-12-1911	Haan, J de	Cinema Parisien
Lonedale Operator, The	Moedige dochter van den stationschef, De	1-7-1911	8-12-1911	Haan, J de	Cinema Parisien

Fig. 7. Result of query 2: programmes in which the film was shown.

Frères, 1911), to perform a query to find out in which programmes this particular film was shown. In Figure 6 we see the title information and we can see that Desmet received this film on 1 July 1911. Figure 7 is the output of our query. From left to right we see the original title, the Dutch title, the day Desmet received the film, the day a screening started, the name of the exhibitor and the name of the cinema. In the database we find three screenings of this film on 28 July 1911, 11 September 1911 and 8 December 1911. During the first screening *École de sauvetage en Australie* was shown almost exclusively with films that were bought on the same day. During the second screening it was shown in a programme with many titles Desmet received on other days. But during the third screening it is shown again with films Desmet had received as a package on the dame day.

By linking our database to other databases – such as the FMDB- we can enrich it with all kinds of information, which is not stored in our database. Then it should be possible to involve information from the FMDB in our research. If we would like to research, for instance, genre we could involve the FMDB which already contains information about the genre of the Desmet films. We could connect the FMDB genre table to our own tables during a query. This way we could establish the genres of the films that were shown and ask questions about them without having to insert the information on genres into our own database; again, to avoid redundancy and increase efficiency.

Issues during database design

During my research I came across two database related issues that are worth mentioning in this context. These are the definition of the *dataset*, and the identification of the film titles.

Definition of the dataset

What kind of information should a database dealing with local exhibition and distribution contain and what form should it have? The information specific to a distribution database is the connection of titles with exhibitors and dates, specified information about the exhibition and other information provided by the (archival) source. The question thereafter is if it should contain as much other information as possible, or just the information specific and unique to that database? We opted (as much as possible at this point) for the second option, that is to only insert information specific and unique to this database. The reason for this was that we could find additional information in other already existing databases, information about the films in the Filmmuseum database, and some in paper film catalogues. But these databases or catalogues all have their own ID-numbers, so sometimes I only added the original title, without referring further to the database or catalogue. For information about the Dutch exhibitors I referred to the Netherlands Cinema History Database.

The point is that by making a connection between the databases you can leave out the information that is not unique for the database you are building. I could also have inserted references to other sources (like the Internet Movie Database or Treasures from the Film Archives), but I did not because the number of differing references would have been confusing.

Identification (ID) Numbers

The other issue that arose from building the database, concerned the identification numbers, the *ID-numbers*. In every database (and catalogue) every item has its own ID-number. But those numbers for a unique title differ from database to database. In order to make references to other databases, we would have to include many different numbers that all refer to the same unique title. An ideal solution for this problem would be to agree on one universal standard identification number for each film title, for example for all films made before a certain date. This ID-number would then have the same function as the ISBN numbers for books. Of course there will be a lot of problems to solve before this can be implemented, organisational questions, such as: Who will organise this enterprise? Who will participate? How to accommodate different versions of one film? But the advantage of connecting databases with each other is that a database only has to contain the information specific to that database. Through the connection to other databases additional information will become available. And when the databases are connected to each other, researchers can access each other's information more easily. As digital information grows, and technology makes it more and more possible to link databases to each other, it would be very useful to consider a standard format for databases and a system of unique identification numbers to make the connection between them easier. Such a development would greatly enrich our studies into early cinema history.

Notes

1. I performed this project as a research internship at the Filmmuseum in 2003–4 and was supervised by Rommy Albers and Rob Zeeman at the Filmmuseum and by Ivo Blom at my former department of Comparative Arts Studies, Vrije Universiteit, Amsterdam. The project contributed to my BA-thesis, entitled *Distributie en programmering door Jean Desmet*.

2. Herbert Birett, *Das Filmangebot in Deutschland*, 1895–1911 (München: Winterberg 1991). Idem, *Verzeichnis in Deutschland gelaufener Filme. Entscheidungen der Filmzensur 1911–1920* (München: Saur, 1980).

3. *Netherlands Cinema History, Homepage.* http://www.xs4all.nl/~kd/

4. *Filmmuseum Amsterdam, Homepage.* www.filmmuseum.nl

Des fragments des premiers temps à l'esthétique de la ruine

André Habib
Université de Montréal, Canada

« Tous les hommes ont un secret attrait pour les ruines.
Ce sentiment tient à la fragilité de notre nature,
à une conformité secrète entre ces monuments détruits
et la rapidité de notre existence. »[1]
« Cinema is the art of destroying moving images. »[2]

Je voudrais proposer ici une esquisse de ce que Dominique Païni a appelé avant moi un « imaginaire de la ruine au cinéma »[3] et interroger certains recyclages contemporains de fragments des premiers temps du cinéma. J'insisterai particulièrement sur ces artistes qui exploitent et explorent les possibilités expressives de la pellicule abîmée ou morcelée. Je tenterai ensuite de suggérer une constellation discursive et médiatique à l'intérieur de laquelle il me semble fécond de penser ces films, l'esthétique qui les sous-tend, les modes de réception qu'elle induit et enfin, les questions qu'ils soulèvent.

Il ne devrait pas être indifférent aux thèmes et aux idées qui fédèrent les travaux réunis dans cette publication, de déplacer notre regard – ne fut-ce qu'à titre heuristique – et de le faire glisser de la forme et des modalités de la distribution des films des premiers temps, aux pratiques de re-diffusions et aux re-circulations de ces images dans les circuits d'art et d'essai, les programmations de films expérimentaux, d'en traquer les enjeux et d'analyser leurs modes de réapparition et de réexpostion. Il s'agit d'une façon, modeste, d'interroger le devenir du cinéma muet et des premiers temps, autrement dit, le « futur du passé », pour reprendre l'heureuse formule de Wanda Strauven.

L'imaginaire de la ruine : premières remarques

Les archives du cinéma doivent composer avec le fragmenté, le décomposé : films incomplets, bobines détériorées, pellicules décolorées, versions amputées. Pour une bonne part des archivistes, des restaurateurs et des historiens, on doit parvenir à combler ces manques au mieux des connaissances (classification, catalogage, datation, analyse des éléments, etc.), effacer les traces délitantes qui se sont déposées sur le matériau filmique, colmater l'incomplétude des éléments par des sources textuelles ou autres, quitte à sacrifier des pans entiers de collections où les bobines sont tantôt non identifiables, tantôt trop endommagées.

Il existe toutefois une utilisation plus proprement poétique du fragment et des ruines filmiques, appelée de leurs vœux par quelques rares archivistes et historiens du cinéma,[4] mais qui se trouve surtout chez des artistes et des cinéastes dits expérimentaux, chiffonniers-plasticiens, poètes-archéologues, collectionneurs-monteurs dont les œuvres sont apparues depuis les années 1980–90. Ces œuvres interrogent de diverses façons le travail du temps sur la matière-mémoire de la pellicule, participant ou réagissant, c'est selon, à un *zeitgeist* du cinéma, à l'époque de sa paradoxale mise au patrimoine, et surtout, à l'aube de sa soi-disant disparition, alors que nous nous enfonçons dans ce que Cherchi Usai a appelé le « *Digital Dark Age* ».

Malgré l'efflorescence et la diversité des travaux sur le cinéma des premiers temps, très peu, voire aucune, de ces recherches ne se sont penchées sur les « ré-emplois » de ce cinéma dans les productions expérimentales contemporaines, bien que ces films soient régulièrement vus dans des festivals, des festivals de « cinéma retrouvé », qu'ils apparaissent au programmes des cinémathèques, et qu'ils circulent relativement librement en VHS et en DVD.

Certes, divers chemins ont fait s'entrecroiser le cinéma expérimental et les recherches sur le cinéma des premiers temps depuis une vingtaine d'années. Elles ont par exemple donné lieu à un ouvrage passionnant de Bart Testa, publié en 1993, *Back and Forth : Avant-Garde and Early Cinema* qui tente de réfléchir aux histoires croisées de la nouvelle historiographie et du cinéma d'avant-garde depuis les années 60, et qui rappelait le mot de Tom Gunning, en 1979 :

> Comparing early films to recent films of the American Avant-Garde frees the early works from the ghetto of primitive babbling to which the progress-oriented model of film history has assigned them. Likewise it was undoubtedly my encounter with films by these and other avant-garde filmmakers (Frampton, Jacobs, Ernie Gehr) that allowed me to see early films with a fresh eye.[5]

De la même façon, je serai tenté de dire que ce corpus de films récents propose une autre façon « d'apprivoiser ces fantômes », selon la formule de Bazin,[6] de rendre à nouveau visible les images des premiers temps en en restituant une puissance de défamiliarisation, et en nous amenant à envisager une forme d'écriture de l'histoire plus sensible aux entrechoquements temporels, aux anachronismes, aux effets de sens induits par la matérialité du support que ces nouveaux types de montages-attractions font affleurer.

Je pense ici en particulier à l'éventail de films faits de films trouvés, *found footage* selon l'expression consacrée, qui usent, recyclent, détournent parfois des fragments des premiers temps du cinéma pour en faire des œuvres « originales ». Mais à la différence de certains de leurs prédécesseurs, les cinéastes expérimentaux américain du film « structurel » que citait Gunning (Ken Jacobs, Bruce Connor, Paul Sharits, Hollis Frampton, Malcolm Le Grice), les artistes qui m'intéressent (plus près, en cela, de la sensibilité d'un Joseph Cornell), mêlent au « goût de l'archive » une esthétique, souvent mélancolique, de la ruine et de la disparition. Ils soutirent de ces images dénichées des visions hallucinantes, de somptueuses compositions nées du hasard, des couplages fantasques, et parfois, des leçons d'histoire.

Apparus depuis une vingtaine d'années tout au plus, ces films explorent les voies de ce que j'appellerai une « archéologie poétique », à mi-chemin entre le film d'archives et le cinéma expérimental : c'est du moins ainsi que l'on peut caractériser les œuvres de Angela Ricci-Lucchi et Yervant Gianikian (*Dal polo all'equatore*, 1986, *Su tutte le vette e pace*, 1999), certains films de Peter Delpeut (*Lyrisch nitraat*, 1991, *Diva dolorosa*, 1999), de Gustav Deutsch (*Film ist 1–6*, 1998, *Film ist 7–12*, 2002), de Bill Morrisson (*Trinity*, 2000, *Decasia : The State of Decay*, 2001, *Light is Calling*, 2003), ou encore les travaux photographiques d'Éric Rondepierre (*Précis de décomposition*, 1993–1995, *Moires*, 1996–1998).

Ces œuvres tendent à arracher les images à leur récit particulier pour les introduire dans une autre dramaturgie, une autre tragédie, celle du temps, de l'ouvrage du temps qui dramatise de façon singulière l'histoire des films. Elles s'intéressent, plus précisément, à *ce qui se passe* au film (voire au photogramme individuel), aux puissances figurales de la décomposition du nitrate, aux effets de sens ou de récit qu'engendre l'accouplage de fragments hétérogènes, ou encore à l'inconscient visuel d'une époque que le ralentissement, le recadrage ou le montage permettent de révéler.

Ces artistes ont ceci en commun qu'ils trouvent leur matériau de base – et c'est souvent leur unique matériau – dans des archives (archives institutionnelles, publiques, corporatives), ou encore dans des stocks rachetés de films amateurs. Ces images, souvent fortement rongées par la moisissure et l'usure sont, selon le cas, transférées sur un support pellicule ou numérique, elles sont remontées, rephotographiées, retravaillées à la tireuse optique, et parfois (dans le cas de Ricci-Lucchi et Gianikian en particulier), recadrées, teintées, solarisées ou coloriées.[7] Pour ces artistes, la pellicule semble être un lieu, un site où se stocke *de l'histoire et de la mémoire*. Ces fragments des premiers temps sont devenus des traces, laissées par l'histoire, dont souvent plus personne ne se souvient : ils interpellent une mémoire impossible de la pellicule.

Dominique Païni, dans une de ses classifications chronologiques hâtives mais utiles dont il a le don, avançait l'idée suivante : au moment où se constituèrent les premières cinémathèques, au début des années 30, il s'agissait avant tout de sauver les films pour leur *valeur artistique*. Dans les années 60, ce fut pour leur valeur *documentaire*, leur puissance de témoignage. Enfin, depuis quelques années, toujours selon Païni, ce fut pour leur *valeur matérielle* : tout fragment de pellicule est désormais marqué du sceau d'une mémoire qu'il faut sauver à tout prix.[8] D'où, il me semble, les diverses élégies ou « célébrations du nitrate »[9] (pour reprendre le titre du pavé récemment publié par la FIAF), un certain engouement esthétique pour les films amateurs et de famille qui privilégie bien souvent moins le contenu des images, leur indicialité, que leurs propriétés plastiques et sensorielles qui viennent *signifier* le passé. Directement ou indirectement les films qui m'intéressent participent tous de cet horizon discursif.

Si tout film est matière *et* mémoire, il semble que, dans ces films, la matière est devenue mémoire, et se révèle telle avec d'autant plus d'éclat qu'elle se désagrège, se décompose, et se laisse apercevoir en disparaissant. Pour reprendre une expression de Bill Morrison, nous pourrions dire que ces films sont faits « d'images qui survivent aux films », d'images survivantes, pour user d'un terme à la mode, qui ont « partiellement survécu à la destruction, tout en demeurant immergé[es] dans l'absence. »[10] Leur mélancolie, pour reprendre une idée que Starobinski développe à propos des ruines, « réside dans le fait qu'elle[s] [sont] devenue [des] monument[s] de la signification perdue. »[11]

Je dirais également que ces images récupèrent une pleine valeur d'image en apparaissant comme fragments et ruines, précisément parce qu'elles se trouvent dépossédées de leur fonction initiale, narrative ou spectaculaire, voire même de leur utilité pour l'historien du cinéma. Les marques du temps produisent dans la matière de nouvelles figures que l'historien ne peut percevoir que comme un excédent a-signifiant : La matière abîmée *devient* image. Les rapports *naturels* que Cesare Brandi avait identifiés, dans sa *Théorie de la restauration*, entre le support matériel et l'image, se trouvent donc inversés.[12] Si nous considérons les marques lacunaires, les rayures explosives et les taches délitantes comme un surplus de sens et non comme son absence, ces images, tout d'un coup, peuvent donner lieu à des expériences esthétiques singulières, aussi complètes que complexes, et libérer une perception sensible du temps, à laquelle ne peut prétendre l'investigation historienne.

Ces œuvres valorisent donc les propriétés de la matière et les nouvelles mise en image que la ruine rend possible : luminosité instable, poudre écaillée des visages, explosions violente de couleurs, moiré incandescent de la grisaille, effet d'embrasement, dislocation du cadre, désaccords des plans. Par ailleurs, ces marques du temps rajoutent une valeur d'ancienneté[13] à la pellicule, singularisent chaque fragment, le chargeant d'une dose, forcément ambiguë, d'aura : ambiguë puisque l'on a bien souvent l'effet d'une « apparition unique d'un lointain », pour reprendre la terminologie benjaminienne, bien que, pour se rendre jusqu'à nous, cette pellicule soit nécessairement passée par des techniques de reproduction très sophistiquées (transferts pellicule à pellicule, pellicule à vidéo numérique, à pellicule, à DVD, à VHS NTSC, à PAL, etc.)

Les artisans de la ruine

Parmi les artistes qui explorent les voies de cette « imaginaire des ruines », je voudrais maintenant en nommer quelques-unes et dire quelques mots sur leurs œuvres.

On retrouve parmi eux le plasticien et photographe français Éric Rondepierre qui photographie des photogrammes de films décomposés, et qui s'intéresse à la façon dont la pellicule se défait et aux hasards heureux qu'elle occasionne, entre autre dans sa série *Moires, Masques, Trente étreintes* (1997–1999).[14]

Le new-yorkais Bill Morrison, a pour sa part réalisé tout au long des années 90 plusieurs *found footage* à partir d'images d'archives du début du siècle, en particulier pour des performances multimédia avec le Ridge Theater. Après avoir complété en 1997, *The Film of her* (1997), documentaire saupoudré de fiction sur la sauvegarde des *Paper prints* de la *Library of Congress*, il s'est mis à s'intéresser aux possibilités expressives de la décomposition de la pellicule. *Decasia*, son œuvre la plus connue, sortie en 2002, est une œuvre symphonique et visuelle composée, tout en grisaille, de fragments décomposés, portée par une réflexion sur le cycle, rendu visible par la ruine, de la création et de la destruction, sur la lutte entre le désir d'immortalité et l'embrasement, « la ruine poétique du monde », dirait Jean-Louis Schefer.

Angela Ricci-Luchi et Yervant Gianikian, travaillent de leur côté les traces de l'histoire conservées dans des fragments de films en lambeaux : ils explorent l'iconographie cinématographique du colonialisme, les campagnes alpines de la Première Guerre Mondiale, les expéditions exotiques, à la recherche de détails insignifiants dans lesquels se logent les symptômes de l'histoire, l'inconscient visuel d'une époque. Ils scrutent les films grâce à ce qu'ils appellent leur « caméra analytique », qui ralentit, recadre, solarise, afin, pour emprunter l'idée de Kracauer, de « rédimer » la réalité physique et historique.

Film ist de Gustav Deutsch expérimente un autre type d'analyse du fragment, qui passe par un examen des récurrences ou des survivances de gestes, d'usages, de codes visuels, de pratiques de montage, de clichés, etc. Atlas impressionniste du cinéma muet, classés en chapitres et en sous-section, *Film ist* est un vaste laboratoire-répertoire des tropes et des figures de ce cinéma, organisé sur un mode sériel (le meurtre, le rire, le voyage en train, l'escalade d'une échelle).

Peter Delpeut, enfin – dans *Lyrisch nitraat* tout particulièrement – propose des fragments du catalogue de Jean Desmet, remontant ces bouts de pellicule nitrate teintée, parfois endommagés, des années 1908–1915, et les regroupant en chapitres (« le regard », « le corps », « le voyage », « la mort », « l'oubli », etc.). Delpeut dresse un éventail élégiaque et émouvant des différents régimes visuels de l'époque, sur quelques grands airs de l'art lyrique.

Tous ces films fonctionnent sur un système de différence, de répétition et de ralentissement qui produisent du sens par la reprise de motifs ou d'images, ou la mise en valeur de détails qui resteraient autrement inaperçus. Les images qui les composent sont très rarement identifiées, et très difficilement identifiables : on y retrouve sans distinction des films de fiction, des films industriels, des films éducatifs, des bandes d'actualités. On traverse tous les genres, toutes les époques, toutes les géographies, sans qu'un contexte de production ni de réception ne soit fourni.

Tous ces films néanmoins documentent ou évoquent des regards du temps (une façon de regarder, une culture visuelle disparue). Ces nouveaux artistes-chiffonniers font affleurer un « air du temps », tout en insistant sur le *travail du temps*, les écarts de temps qui se sont inscrits sur le corps de ces films. Une singulière dialectique apparaît d'ailleurs entre la forme et le fond, entre l'instant de la captation, le regard qui s'y est posé, et le support matériel. Cette dialectique se matérialise précisément par les *accidents*, les *imperfections* de la matière. L'efficace de ces images a donc autant à voir avec le *filmé*, qu'avec le support dans lequel le film est *pris*.

Le champ discursif d'un imaginaire

L'intérêt de ces praticiens pour la matérialité de la pellicule et plus généralement pour les effets d'apparition/disparition que produisent la vue de certains fragments retrouvés des premiers temps du cinéma, est sans doute contemporain d'un questionnement sur « l'agonie » de la pellicule – qui survit tant bien que mal au raz-de-marée numérique – comme s'il s'agissait d'opposer la trace matérielle du film au flux immatériel de l'encodage numérique et au signal magnétique (et invisible) du ruban vidéo.

De la même façon qu'une poétique de la ruine émerge, au XVIIIe siècle dans la foulée de la Révolution française, en même temps que le développement des sciences historiques, de l'archéologie et d'une revalorisation, tant esthétique qu'historique, des œuvres du passé, on pourrait dire que l'imaginaire de la ruine au cinéma est contemporain – bien qu'elle en traverse toute l'histoire – de la sauvegarde des premiers films et, plus généralement, de la patrimonialisation du cinéma entendu comme dépositaire de la mémoire du siècle (on pense au monumental *Histoire(s) du cinéma* de Godard, et plus généralement, aux politiques de dépôt légal, aux lois pour la protection du patrimoine cinématographique et aux divers fonds alloués à certaines cinémathèques et archives du film depuis une vingtaine d'années). Il semble que l'investissement symbolique du cinéma soit directement proportionnel aux pertes qu'il a subies (on estime, c'est connu, que près de 80 pour cent de sa production des 30 premières années a aujourd'hui disparu). Il suffit de constater le regain d'intérêt pour le cinéma des origines dans les milieux académiques, la série de projets de « restaurations scientifiques » et d'initiatives de sauvegarde du cinéma (le « Plan Nitrate » en France) qui ont été mis sur pied, aux diverses célébrations entourant le centenaire du cinéma, ainsi qu'à la diffusion des films des premiers temps dans des éditions pédagogiques, souvent irréprochables, en VHS, en DVD et sur Internet. Dans ces mêmes années, Cherchi Usai prononce ses sentences sur la « mort du cinéma » et sur la disparition de la pellicule, et se développe une nouvelle cinéphilie résolument mélancolique.[15]

Les films qui m'intéressent sont donc apparus à la croisée de ces développements techniques, artistiques, médiatiques et discursifs. Mais il faut également les penser à l'aune de l'esthétique du cinéma moderne qui, depuis la Nouvelle Vague jusqu'aux pratiques contemporaines des vidéastes, en passant par le cinéma expérimental, ont mis en valeur, souvent de façon réflexive, le fragmenté, le haché, l'inachevé et les effets de palimpsestes temporels. Ce sont ces œuvres qui ont sans doute réalisé les conditions de visibilité pour ces films en ruines.

Ces constats, ces événements et ces pratiques disparates m'autorisent à penser qu'un « imaginaire des ruines » a investi notre rapport aux images cinématographiques. Les ruines, la destruction, semblent même pouvoir rendre compte allégoriquement de l'histoire du cinéma et, par extension, de l'histoire de la modernité et du XXe siècle.[16]

En tant qu'allégorie de l'histoire,[17] les ruines n'aspirent pas à restaurer la pleine présence d'un récit, l'intégrité ou l'intégralité du passé, ni de restituer l'ordonnancement placide des faits et des dates ; plutôt elles exposent un chantier foré d'oublis et d'énigmes, des blocs d'a-causalité où bruit le temps et d'où surgissent des formes, des visages, des espaces, des fantômes qui s'avancent vers nous, entre les lambeaux déchirés du temps. Ce serait des « allégories de la non-lisibilité », dirait Paul De Man, qui tentent moins de reproduire du familier – un discours historique qui pacifie le passé en élimant ses aspérités – que de re-présenter le passé dans son opacité, comme un site d'altérité qui ouvre le temps et l'image aux puissances signifiantes de sa dislocation, de sa décomposition. Peut-être que ces films en ruines, pour toutes les raisons que j'ai indiquées – et je tiens à le souligner – en disent au final beaucoup plus sur notre rapport aux images et aux images du passé, que sur les images et les films qu'ils ré-emploient et sur le passé qu'ils re-présentent.

Les cinéastes qui m'intéressent partagent un type de matériau et même des préoccupations communes, mais il faut être prudent quant aux effets d'homogénéisation. Chacun possède sa propre petite histoire, qui recoupe l'histoire de son art et une histoire, plus générale, des médias et des techniques. Je suis néanmoins de l'avis que ce corpus de films faits à partir de films faits forme actuellement un champ d'interrogation très fécond, et relativement peu étudié. Ils permettent de réfléchir sur ce que serait une esthétique de la ruine au cinéma (sur ce qu'elle réanime de l'ancienne poétique de la ruine telle que théorisée par Diderot, Chateaubriand, Simmel, Benjamin), et, surtout, par le biais de la ruine, d'amorcer un nouveau type de réflexion sur l'histoire et le temps du cinéma et ce, à partir des effets de sens induits par sa matérialité.

Enfin, je serais tenté de me demander si les ruines et ces films en ruines ne nous permettent pas de repenser le « temps vécu » du sujet-spectateur, qui serait autre chose qu'un « temps pour comprendre ». Ces films, je dirai, nous placent *devant le temps* : un temps, ni subsumé par le mouvement, ni ordonné par une narration, mais se jouant de ces effets de stratifications, de brouillage et d'opacité, appelant un sujet démultiplié à une expérience écartelée du temps. Ce que le cinéma et les films des premiers temps tout particulièrement évoquent – tout en demeurant impossible à restituer –, ce sont toutes les couches de temps vécus par les spectateurs au contact de ces captures de temps, de ces illusions de temps. C'est cette relation au temps qu'une archive du film conserve, et que ces films en ruines exposent et/ou problématisent. Ces palimpsestes des temps exposés, présents et trépassés, nous invitent peut-être à envisager une nouvelle mélancolie spectatorielle, une mélancolie des ruines, propre au cinéma, née du temps, de son archive et de son anachronique actualité.

Notes

1. De Chateaubriand, René, *Génie du christianisme*, tome 2, (Paris: Éditions Garnier-Flammarion, 1966 [1802]), 40.

2. Cherchi Usai, Paolo, *The Death of Cinema, History, Cultural Memory and the Digital Dark Age* (London: BFI Publishing, 2001), 7.

3. Païni, Dominique, « La résurgence du fragment », in *Le cinéma, un art moderne* (Paris : Cahiers du cinéma, 1997), 144.

4. Voir sur ce point De Kuyper, Éric, « Fragments de l'histoire du cinéma. Quelques remarques sur la problématique du fragment », *Hors cadre*, 10 (1992), 45. L'initiative menée par le *Filmmuseum* d'Amsterdam de monter et de présenter des fragments de films anonymes, souvent très courts, regroupés sous le titre *Bits and Pieces*, s'inscrit dans le même esprit.

5. Gunning, Tom, « An Unseen Energy Swallows Space : The Space in Early Film and its Relation to the American Avant Garde », in Fell, John L. (éd.), *Films before Griffith* (Berkeley : University of California Press, 1983), 355–356.

6. Bazin, André, « *Paris 1900* : À la recherche du temps perdu », *L'écran français*, 30 (septembre 1947), repris dans *Le cinéma français de la libération à la Nouvelle Vague (1945–1958)* (Paris: Cahiers du cinéma, coll. Essais, 1983), 168.

7. Sur les procédés employés par les deux cinéastes, voir Toffetti, Sergio (éd.), *Yervant Gianikian, Angela Ricci Lucchi* (Firenze, Hopefulmonster editore, Torino, Museo nazionale del cinema, coll. « Cinemazero », 1992).

8. Païni, Dominique, *Le temps exposé* (Paris: Cahiers du cinéma, coll. Essais, 2003), 25–26.

9. Voir Smither, Roger (éd.), *This Film is Dangerous. A Celebration of Nitrate Film* (Bruxelles : Fédération internationale des archives du film, 2002).

10. Starobinski, Jean, *L'invention de la liberté (1700–1789)* (Genève : Éditions d'art Albert Skira, 1964), 180.

11. Ibid.

12. Brandi, Cesare, *Théorie de la restauration* (Paris : Centre des monuments nationaux, Éditions du patrimoine, 1963).

13. Cette terminologie est bien entendue empruntée à Aloïs Riegl qui fut un des premiers à proposer une esthétique du culte moderne des monuments en fonction de leur valeur objective d'histoire et de leur valeur subjective d'ancienneté. Voir Riegl, Aloïs, *Le culte moderne des monuments. Son essence et sa genèse*, trad. Daniel Wieczorek (Paris : Éditions du Seuil, coll. Espacements, 1984 [1903]).

14. Sur l'œuvre d'Éric Rondepierre, voir notamment Lenain, Thierry, *Éric Rondepierre, Un art de la décomposition* (Bruxelles : La Lettre volée, coll. « Singuliers », 1999) et Arasse, Daniel, *et al.*, *Éric Rondepierre* (Paris : Éditions Léo Scheer, 2003).

15. J'ai développé ailleurs cet aspect de la mélancolie cinéphilique : André Habib, « Avant, après. De l'actualité et de l'inactualité de la cinéphilie », *Hors champ* (mars 2005), www.horschamp.qc.ca

16. Voir sur ces points Augé, Marc, *Le temps en ruines* (Paris : Éditions Galilée, coll. Lignes fictives, 2003), et Deshoulières, Valérie-Angélique, Vacher, Pascal (éds.), *La mémoire en ruines. Le modèle archéologique dans l'imaginaire moderne contemporain* (Clermont-Ferrand : Presses universitaires Blaise Pascal, 2000).

17. Sur les rapports entre allégorie, ruines et histoire, voir bien évidemment Benjamin, Walter, *Origine du drame baroque allemand*, trad. Sybille Muller (Paris, Editions Flammarion, coll. Champs, 1985 [1916–1925]), 187–203.

Distribuer les films ou distribuer les rôles ?

François Jost

Selon le lexique du cinéma français des origines à 1930, *distribuer* serait « répartir, placer les copies d'un film en vue de l'exploitation ». À la lumière de ce colloque, une définition aussi lapidaire semble bien insuffisante. Toute la question est en effet de savoir quelle est la visée et la fonction de cet acte de répartition. À sa manière chacun des articles regroupés dans ce volume s'efforce d'y apporter des réponses précises en l'envisageant dans toute sa complexité.

Est-ce que la distribution vise véritablement à rendre accessible un produit culturel, le film ? Auquel cas, le distributeur serait simplement une interface entre l'éditeur, le producteur, et le public, qui n'aurait aucune action sur le film et qui se contenterait de l'amener au public ? Ou agit-elle au contraire sur le film pour le rendre attirant par ce public ? ce qui impliquerait de renverser l'ordre chronologique de la communication cinématographique pour envisager les actions de la distribution sur l'étape apparemment première de la production. Pour reprendre l'idée de *missing link* avancée par Ivo Blom, on pourrait se demander si le chaînon distribution est bien à la place intermédiaire qu'on lui assigne et s'il n'est pas plutôt le premier, celui qui commande à tous les autres, ce qui accréditerait l'hypothèse, émise pendant ce colloque, que, dès le début du cinéma, le public agit comme une *idée régulatrice*, comme aurait Kant, sur la production elle-même. Phénomène qui se généralisera ensuite, au point qu'il est difficile aujourd'hui de produire un film sans l'apport financier du distributeur.

Kessler définissait, le premier jour, le but de ce colloque ainsi : « regarder le cinéma du point de vue de la distribution ». Les exposés nous ont montré qu'il existait une alternative à cette méthode, qui était de regarder la distribution de différents points de vue : notamment celui du producteur et celui du spectateur, qui éclairent fort différemment la fonction-distribution (Nicolas Dulac). Le point d'où se fait la vue de ce point de vue reste éminemment variable selon le type de regard : certains ont chaussé des lunettes grossissantes pour regarder dans le détail comment fonctionnait l'économie du cinéma à travers ses acteurs, comme Kleine, Gridson, Desmet ou Rolin, d'autres ont adopté un regard plus lointain (celui qu'on attribuerait à la théorie, au sens où la *théoria* est une contemplation), interrogeant parfois la raison des regards eux-mêmes (l'amour des ruines ? A. Habib) ou les divers modes de distribution des images (W. Strauwen).

Devant un tel enchevêtrement de points de vue et de regards, il y a *deux méthodes* :

- soit décider quel est le bon, et substituer à ces subjectivités, un regard prétendument objectif ;

• soit ajouter de la subjectivité à la subjectivité et proposer son propre regard.

Vous avez compris, j'imagine, que je vais opter pour la seconde solution.

Sous la distribution, une idée de la communication

Au terme de ce colloque, comment regarder la distribution *de mon propre point de vue?* Quel est mon point de vue, allez-vous dire?

Disons, pour aller vite, que c'est celui d'un chercheur qui travaille aujourd'hui dans une optique médiatique et communicationnelle.

La première question que je me poserai est celle-ci : sur quel schéma de la communication repose la distribution ? La définition minimale dont nous sommes partis – la distribution consisterait à répartir les copies de films en vue de l'exploitation – repose sur une idée de la communication structurale, popularisée par le linguiste Jakobson, selon laquelle communiquer un message, c'est simplement le faire transiter de l'émetteur au récepteur. Conception, si ce n'est naïve, du moins optimiste, que personne ici, je crois, n'a fait sienne.

Du point de vue pragmatique qui est le mien, la communication médiatique repose sur une promesse de sens effectuée par l'émetteur, que le récepteur peut prendre à la lettre (cela définit le groupe des *crédules*), peut mettre en cause (c'est le groupe des *sceptiques*) ou détourner (c'est la lecture *kitsch* ou *décadente*). Or ce qui est remarquable avec le cinéma, c'est que, dès ses débuts, il a fait sien ce schéma. Le cinéma est sans doute le seul art – c'est en tout cas le seul art que je connaisse – qui se soit fondé sur la communication pour asseoir son statut artistique. C'est bien ce que nous ont montré tous ceux qui ont étudié d'une façon ou d'une autre les catalogues ou les publicités pour film dans la presse. Car ce qui est frappant dans les différents exposés qui ont été faits à ce sujet, c'est que les catalogues, par exemple, décrivent moins les films, que les usages qu'il faut en faire. En d'autres termes, il ne s'agit pas, pour les distributeurs, de décrire le contenu, comme le ferait une étiquette indiquant la composition d'un produit, mais de prescrire des usages, comme le ferait une recette sur un emballage de pâtes. Il est remarquable à cet égard, combien le terme « effect » revient dans les catalogues, comme nous l'a montré Jonathan Auerbach. Ou encore les suggestions fortes d'usage comme «excellent opening pictures for a show about England », comme nous l'avons vu avec Ian Christie. Il me semble qu'il y a là une différence majeure avec les actuels dossiers de presse qui proposent plutôt des interprétations ou des lectures des films en vue de leur imposition au public par la presse.

Vue sous cet angle, la communication cinématographique pose toute une série de questions, qui touchent aussi bien ceux qui sont à l'origine du film (producteur, distributeur) que le public auquel il s'adresse ou le film lui-même. En voici quelques-unes:

1. *La question de l'identité du distributeur* : comment être identifié dans un contexte concurrentiel ? Comment être compris comme un partenaire qui autorise – au sens où le sceau royal autorisait la circulation des « actes » – des objets à circuler sous son nom ? Les logos dans le film, la lutte pour le *plus* (que représente la couleur, par exemple), l'invention de personnages récurrents, puis enfin des *serials* sont autant de façon de répondre à cette question.

2. *La question de l'identité du public.* Le problème de la fidélisation du public se pose presque dès l'origine du cinéma. Or ce problème est indissolublement lié aussi à une question d'identité, mais du public cette fois. En effet, le concept de fidélisation suppose que soient travaillées deux dimensions :

- La construction d'une communauté plus ou moins homogène;

- La reproduction à l'identique du produit proposé, puisque aussi bien, comme l'a bien montré U. Eco, le public, comme l'enfant, aime le retour du même, la répétition indéfinie de la même histoire. Ce qui a évidemment des implications sur la fabrication du film lui-même et, notamment, sur cette sérialisation, dont a parlé Nicolas Dulac.

Identité du public : de l'émotion au formatage

La première façon de faire une communauté, la plus universelle d'entre toutes, est de s'adresser à ce qui est le plus humain en nous, l'émotion, *l'affect*. C'est le rôle essentiel des genres de promettre des émotions au spectateur (une autre question est de savoir s'il y arrive ou non). R. Abel nous a montré des publicités qui parfois réduisaient à l'extrême le choix : « laughter or emotion ». Cette ambivalence est d'ailleurs au cœur de la majorité des programmes qui font alterner comédie et mélodrames.

Mais la communauté peut aussi se constituer autour de l'amour du cinéma. Il n'est pas sans intérêt de remarquer, de ce point de vue, que le mot « cinéphobie » est apparu avant celui de cinéphilie. D'où l'importance de la presse cinématographique, qui va être l'alliée objective des distributeurs en renvoyant au public des cinéphiles sa propre image et les raisons de leur amour pour le film : comme l'a bien montré Viva Paci, là encore « l'émotion forte » est au cœur des films impossibles qu'on imagine en rêve, et que l'on voudrait voir sur l'écran.

La seconde stratégie, qui a été bien mise en évidence, est le travail sur le local, qui ne serait pas loin, me semble-t-il, de caractériser la « fonction-distribution » (voir les exposés de Vanessa Toulmin, Renaud Chaplain). Les films en rapport avec la vie locale jouent de ce point de vue un double rôle. Soit ils construisent une communauté de citoyens qui se reconnaissent dans des rites identitaires (cf. Pierre-Emmanuel Jacques), soit ils jouent sur des ressorts beaucoup plus individuels, comme le montre Martin Loperdinger.

La stratégie de Marzen va plus loin, en effet, que la psychologie des émotions dont je viens de parler, puisqu'elle met à son service un phénomène plus obscur que ceux supposés par la psychologie, un mécanisme qui relève de la psychanalyse, le *narcissisme*. On se souvient que Marzen filmait des gens, dans l'espoir qu'ils viennent se voir sur l'écran. À voir ces images de mains qui s'agitent en direction de la caméra, on pourrait penser qu'il ne s'agit que de gestes provoqués par une sorte d'émerveillement devant la nouvelle technique et la « novelty ». Mais la persistance de ces saluts à l'ère de la télévision me laisse à penser qu'il s'agit plutôt d'une constante anthropologique : *l'attendrissement* que chacun éprouve devant sa propre image, et que prolonge d'ailleurs le film de famille, avec son repli sur une communauté où chacun est censé regarder l'autre avec indulgence.

La constitution de formats « amateur », comme le 17,5 mm – dont a parlé Martina Roepke ou le 28 mm dont a parlé Anke Mebold – est à lire comme une réaction non pas seulement contre le format du film institutionnel, mais plutôt contre le formatage communautaire imposé par les distributeurs. À la communauté de l'humain, trop humain, des spectateurs opposent d'autres communautés, plus restreintes, ou d'autres découpages de la communauté humaine, comme la famille ou le public curieux de sciences. Du format au formatage, il n'y a , en effet, qu'un pas. Et il suffit d'un autre encore pour déboucher sur un processus de colonisation, comme l'ont montré Pierre Véronneau pour le Québec et Panivong Norindr pour l'Indochine. La distribution est aussi le lieu qui permet de contrôler, voire d'impulser, la propagande en forgeant des valeurs nationales par opposition aux valeurs universelles de l'affect.

Tel est le paradoxe de la fabrication d'une communauté par les médias de masse : ils soudent cette communauté imaginaire qu'est le public en jouant sur des ressorts anthropologiques qui touchent au plus près, dans sa chair ou son inconscient – c'est parfois la même chose –, l'individu-spectateur.

La censure est évidemment l'autre versant de ces stratégies puisque l'acte de censure repose sur le fait qu'une communauté tout aussi imaginaire (nationale ou locale, variable en tout cas) se substitue à l'individu en décidant de ce qu'il peut voir ou de ce qui est bon ou mauvais pour lui. Parfois, ces deux conceptions, locale ou nationale, s'affrontent (cf. Yangirov).

À la recherche de l'aura perdue

Si donc la distribution consiste à optimiser quantitativement l'action d'un film (soit en touchant très vite le maximum de public, soit en pérennisant sa circulation dans diverses salles), il va de soi que, comme dans la dialectique du Maître et de l'esclave chez Hegel, où l'esclave finit par soumettre le maître parce qu'il garde seul la connaissance de la nature, le public finit par rendre esclave le distributeur. D'une part, celui-ci doit multiplier les produits, mais, d'autre part, il doit les valoriser, ce qui est en un sens contradictoire. On n'a pas insisté assez sur un problème essentiel du début du cinéma, qui est de le constituer en art pour lutter contre la perte de l'aura que subit tout produit à l'ère de la reproduction mécanique. À ce titre, la mise en place du cinéma d'exclusivité, explicitée ici par R. Chaplain pour la région lyonnaise, participe de cette revalorisation de l'objet lui-même en introduisant dans la communauté des spectateurs des ruptures brutales, entre ceux de la ville, qui sont au courant des nouveautés, et ceux des banlieues, qui prennent connaissance des nouveautés quand elles sont déjà anciennes. Cette lutte pour constituer une aura est aussi au centre de l'argumentaire de Pathé en Amérique du Nord, quand il fait valoir la beauté de la couleur de ses films (Charles O'Brien). Nouveau paradoxe : pour valoriser ce produit médiatique qu'est le film on recourt à des arguments qui vantent la transparence du cinéma et sa capacité, après la peinture et avant la télévision, a être une fenêtre sur le monde.

Un dernier continent de recherche, tout juste identifié, la programmation des salles. Si nous avons bien vu les promesses des distributeurs, voire leurs injonctions ou leurs consignes, il faudrait voir dans quelles mesures elles influaient véritablement sur les exploitants, et comment. Si, comme l'a montré Gaudreault, le distributeur est aussi celui qui propose une syntagmatisation du spectacle cinématographique, il serait temps de voir celui-ci autrement que comme un empilage aléatoire de numéros, à quoi on finit parfois à l'identifier, mais comme un ordre plus ou moins réglé de scènes. De ce point de vue, il faudra différencier les pratiques foraines, même si les sources nous manquent, les pratiques des vaudevilles, des salles de cinéma qui s'implantent au cœur des villes et de celles qui s'ouvrent en banlieue.

Beyond distribution: some thoughts on the future of archival films

Giovanna Fossati and Nanna Verhoeff

Nederlands Filmmuseum, Amsterdam, The Netherlands; and Department of Media and Culture Studies, Utrecht University, The Netherlands

In this essay we wish to reflect on the particular relevance to the topic of early cinema's distribution in the digital age. A decentralization of production – e.g. in terms of creative and discursive input – and the increase of cultural participation have fundamentally changed the traditional cultural and economical function of distribution. Now that we live, work, consume, and watch in a networked society, we can invent radically new systems of distribution – systems more attuned to the current demands for the circulation of cultural goods. In light of the new possibilities for (digital) distribution of today and tomorrow, the basic conception of distribution as the complex of *access*, *circulation*, and *exchange* as based on historical practices and market dynamics, needs rethinking.

Our main concern, here, is the impact of digitization on archival practices and how this may have its effects on contemporary distribution of archival films. At the end of this book we think it is useful to consider what happened, or what may happen, to the distribution of those films that were first distributed and exhibited a hundred years ago. The possibilities for restoration, storage, and exhibition, or "emanation", have changed radically as a result of digitization. This calls for a re-conceptualization not only of what distribution is, but also of what it can be.

In the past, both archivists and researchers have shown ambivalent and sometimes rather conservative attitudes towards the possibility for distribution of archival films. While on the one hand we register a more conventional protectiveness of cultural heritage, more recently, however, we also witness enthusiastic, if not fairly a-critical attitudes towards the possibilities for ubiquitous and permanent availability as a result of digitization. These contradictory attitudes shift between the traditional ideal of "making available" – a *push* model – and ideals of individual, immediate, and on-demand access – a *pull* model, if you will.

In the case of early cinema we are intrigued by the way in which archival films have made a transition from being part of a "living" film culture – a culture in which contemporary films are distributed for theatrical screening – to being part of an archival collection and being distributed digitally – in on-line catalogues, on DVDs, for theatrical screenings, or life performances. This transition is taken a step further, to a maybe more radically new "new life", when archival films become *content* – a content which is not distributed, but *grabbed* by the user. This material as well as functional transition may lead to what we can consider as an effacing of distribution.

Distribution of archival films

Simplifying things a bit, archival films are those films that have dropped out from active distribution. Once their commercial distribution has expired and they have ceased to circulate in the theaters, (some) film prints end up in the vaults of archives. It is at this point of "dead distribution" that it becomes relevant to make these films visible again. This new visibility – when old films are shown to new audiences – is obviously different from the initial distribution. Not only do the films circulate in a very different segment of exhibition venues, and are they shown to a new generation of spectators. Also, it is highly significant for this changed dynamics of distribution that the archive is often also the distributor *and* exhibitor – not to mention the fact that the circle of archive, distributor, exhibitor, and audience (in the case of early cinema so often the same crowd of people!) is a very intimate one.

However, even this form of archival distribution has changed over the years and is not a stable format for the "second run" for archival films anymore. Thanks to the countless digital scenarios that are envisioned daily, it could change even more radically in the near future. But before discussing this notion of (digital) archival distribution – what it looks like today, and what it may become tomorrow – it is useful to take a look at how it has evolved over the years.

Since the early years, archivists have seen themselves as collectors and guardians of forgotten films.[1] Their goal was to protect film heritage – a heritage whose value not everybody could immediately recognize and understand. This enterprise was fueled with the excitement of preserving the endangered species of cinema's history: the vanishing nitrate. Archivists have been aware of belonging to an elite – the happy few who can appreciate the importance, can recognize the beauty and, most importantly, who can be trusted with the fragility of these films. These are the fundaments of the protective attitude that in the past has made archives difficult to be accessed, even by scholars who have the same attitude towards the treasures that the archives harbor. This attitude has long been necessary, until the recognition of archives' institutional role in safeguarding cultural heritage in recent decennia.

The issue of copyrights has also played an important role in limiting the freedom of distribution of archival material, together with the fear for restrictions or financial consequences imposed by rights holders. With the exception of a relatively small number of films that were produced before a certain date – films that are within the *public domain* – all other films can be collected, stored and preserved in film archives but can not be shown without the rights holders' permission – let alone be enjoyed in a renewed, archival distribution.[2] This situation is still quite complex and far from being resolved, even though many new possibilities for distribution are emerging as a result of digital technology – possibilities that may benefit both rights holders and archives. The consequences of the rights' issue and new possibilities in this respect will be discussed below.

Although often necessary, the extreme protectiveness and the introvert nature that has characterized the attitude of most archives until recent years clearly prevented archival films from being seen and appreciated by a larger audience. Only since the late 1970s – and yet again, the FIAF Conference held in Brighton in 1978 cannot be ignored – archival films, especially silent films, have started to cross archive thresholds, since they are shown at specialized festivals such as Le Giornate del Cinema Muto, Il Cinema Ritrovato, The San Francisco Silent Film Festival and the Filmmuseum Biennale. At the same time, archives have started to make their programming activities better known to a larger audience and offer film programs for inter-archival distribution. Also, in recent decennia new means – both in terms of funding and technology – for film preservation have made it possible to restore and show films that were previously only available as unique and "unshowable" nitrate prints.

Despite the fact that commercial distribution had long been regarded as a dangerous territory, a new form of distribution started to develop as the natural bridge between the archive and new potential audiences. In the last decennium a wider form of archival distribution has been put into practice. With the growth of most film archives – such as the British Film Institute, the MoMA, the Nederlands Filmmuseum – and thanks to the strong network of FIAF archives, it has been possible to present film programs not only locally – in the archives' theaters – but also to have them tour other archives and art houses interested in finding audiences for these films.[3]

With a few years delay, when compared to commercial distribution, film archives also started new forms of distribution alongside traditional, theatrical distribution: video-tapes first and DVDs later. Since the late 1980s and early 1990s many archives indeed offer feature films or compilations of shorts in these forms. Although this kind of videos and DVDs have a quite limited distribution, it cannot be denied that their relative low cost and flexibility has made it possible for archival films to become visible to a wider public.

Both theatrical distribution, through the network of archives, and the more open video and DVD distribution can be defined as a *chaperone model* of distribution. The archival films in these cases are brought to the public with the archive as chaperone protecting the films, and showing the way. In this chaperone model, archives present film programs as *selections* made by the archive that holds the films, often with the use of explanatory titles or with an accompanying catalogue, which explain (and justify) the archive's choice and contextualize the films either historically or aesthetically. In the case of DVDs, the chaperone model is realized through the use of interfaces that offer this *interpretation key* to the viewer.[4]

This model can be partly explained by the fear of the "expert" that a contemporary audience needs help for understanding old films. This seems relevant if one thinks of the enormous differences between historically divergent cinematographic paradigms and visual cultures within which the films were once produced and now shown. On the other hand, the chaperone model also stands in the way of a direct and spontaneous appreciation of historical films by a contemporary audience, making the viewing experiences highly mediated with the interpretation key as provided by the archive.

In a media culture such as the one that is taking shape today, in which large and vaguely defined *audiences* are more and more being replaced by individual *users*, the chaperone model does not seem to be so suitable anymore. Although it can still be useful for educational purposes, alongside it, it should allow for a more open and direct model.

Although it is only a recent phenomenon, the growing demand for archival films – often referred to as *content*, in new-media terminology – by a larger segment of *users* seems to be insatiable already. The demand for archival films is not only coming from researchers, but also from students (from more disciplines than only film or media studies!), found-footage filmmakers and artists, and from anonymous users every-where on the Internet. Today's user-audiences demand a direct access to content. Users do not want their content to be brought to them within a traditional distribution (push) model: they want to grab it, tap directly from its source (pull model). New systems of content distribution are being invented to satisfy this demand.

A good example is the principle of the so-called *Long Tail*, as discussed in the homonymous article published in *Wired* in 2004.[5] The Long Tail model comprises a worldwide distribution system in which the relatively small number of mainstream hits – the head of the demand curve (the blockbusters, in film terms) – is substituted by a large number of niches – the tail (the art film, but also the archival film). Thanks to the new ways of on-line distribution this system is becoming economically viable. The need for a large number of people in one place (the film theater) to justify high production and distribution costs, is replaced by the need to satisfy the largest number of individual users spread world-wide with (cheaper) niche products.

Also, it seems to be possible to tackle the complex rights issue. With this respect the recently developed *Creative Commons* license offers a very interesting alternative to traditional copyright legislations.[6] Many archives look at Creative Commons because it facilitates distribution – especially on-line – keeping some of the original rights intact, but at the same time stimulating creative re-use of content. An ambitious example of an archival project that intends to use the Creative Common license (where possible) in making hundreds of thousands of hours of video, film and audio content available on-line, has been recently submitted for financing to the Dutch Ministry of Culture.[7]

Although the conflict mentioned in the introduction between protectionism and openness (maybe a renewed version of the old Lindgren-versus-Langlois dispute) is getting more and more visible, archives, often pushed by funding entities and by growing users' demand, are quickly adjusting to this new phenomenon.[8] Large-scale digitization projects of film collections have been intensively discussed in the last ten years by many archives. Different from broadcast archives, however, film archives still have to maintain film as a preservation medium, as digital alternatives today are not comparable yet with film in terms of life expectancy and quality. The consequence of this is that preservation costs cannot be reduced by film digitization. On the contrary: costs for digitization have to be added to the already existing costs for traditional preservation.[9] Nevertheless, many archives are looking for means for digitizing their collections.

But, once the content will be available in digital form, what kind of access will archives grant to their users? Will they move on from the chaperone model to a new form of opener distribution?

Archival distribution or archives online?

Today we can see more and more examples of archival distribution on a relatively large scale. Some of the more well-known silent titles have recently been re-restored using digital technologies at high resolution. An obvious example is the digital restoration of *Metropolis* realized in 2001 by the Friedrich-Wilhelm-Murnau-Stiftung and Bundesarchiv Filmarchiv. The use of digital technology for restoration provides the means to restore more in terms of image reconstruction, and it also provides a high quality master for all possible digital formats, scalable from HD to streaming formats. However, the kind of distribution that these films have experienced is quite similar to the already existing form of archival distribution used for traditionally restored films, only the potentials here are much bigger and it may provide a higher image quality in the future.[10] In theory, digitized films could be offered on-line to viewers/users, but this is still rarely the case. A few exceptions can be found on a limited number of film archives' web sites where samples of their collections can be viewed (but rarely can be downloaded) at low resolution.

One can wonder why archives (and we refer here principally to non-profit and publicly funded archives) maintain a monopoly on their content, even though this could be offered freely to users in a digitized form. Is it fear of copyrights' issues? Is it the idea we discussed earlier that these films need a chaperone to escort them to the users? Or

Fig. 1. *Beyond the Rocks* (1922). [Courtesy of the Nederlands Filmmuseum.]

is it fear of losing their *raison d'être*? We think that all these reasons partially apply, and that there are probably even more reasons to be taken into account, not in the last place the obstacle of know-how and experience with digital technology – still scarce within film archives – as well as the high added costs we mentioned earlier.

We wish to argue that archives can (and should) make their collections available through both systems without losing their *raison d'être*, combining the archival distribution of the films in a chaperone model, with free accessibility of their collections on-line.

Beyond the Rocks: an example of archival distribution

Beyond the Rocks (Sam Wood, 1922) is one of many mainstream films that have disappeared after having "lived" and circulated world-wide at the time of its production. The only film starring two of the biggest Hollywood stars of the Twenties, Gloria Swanson and Rudolph Valentino, *Beyond the Rocks* faded away after its commercial cycle, forgotten by the public and by the critics, who actually never considered it worth

Fig. 2. Interface of the 2006 DVD release of *Beyond the Rocks*. [Courtesy of Milestone Film & Video, design by Craig Cefola of Post Office.]

remembering. In the 1980s it was sadly established by film archivists and researchers (and by a disappointed Gloria Swanson, in her autobiography) that not a single print of this title was to be found. This is not an anomaly, however, since the majority of silent films have experienced the same fate. Between 2000 and 2004, a nitrate print of *Beyond the Rocks* miraculously resurfaced, reel by reel, from a private film collection that was donated to the Nederlands Filmmuseum by the family of a deceased Dutch collector. In 2005 *Beyond the Rocks* was restored by the Nederlands Filmmuseum and newly distributed.[11]

Besides restoring the film in its "original", silent version, the Nederlands Filmmuseum decided to produce a distribution version of *Beyond the Rocks* with a new soundtrack by Dutch composer Henny Vrienten. The production of this new version is in line with the Nederlands Filmmuseum's tradition of the last fifteen years to present films to the public in new and alternative ways. Note that this presentation practice does not replace the traditional restoration process, as each title presented by the Nederlands Film-museum with a new score is first preserved and restored to its original, silent form.

In addition, a High Definition tape was produced, which is to be used as a master for digital projection, for the production of a DVD, and for TV broadcasting. The new sound version was shown in May 2005 on thirteen Dutch screens with three 35mm film prints and ten digital projections.[12] The film was also presented at several festivals, including the festivals in Cannes, London and New York, and the Filmmuseum Biennale in Amsterdam. Milestone Film and Video released the film theatrically in the US where since October 2006 it has been shown in more than twenty cities. In May 2006 it was broadcasted on Turner Movie Classics and in the fall of 2006 it will be broadcasted on Dutch television. Milestone has recently released a DVD in the US, while the Nederlands Filmmuseum will soon release a DVD for distribution in the Benelux.

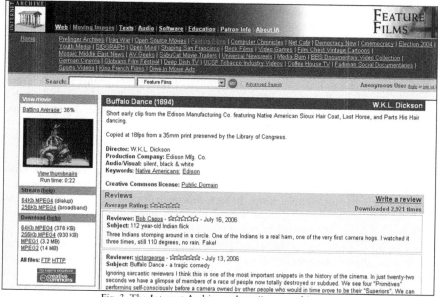

Fig. 3. The Internet Archive, at http://www.archive.org

This is a clear example of archival distribution (push model) where a film, found, restored, and stored by a film archive, is chaperoned outside the archive's threshold to the largest public such a film can possibly find. A project like this ensures that the *raison d'être* of film archives is substantiated. This is the case despite the fact that this one film title represents only the tip of an iceberg – one of the hundreds of less glamorous titles that are annually restored. Still, thanks to its large exposure, a project like this reinforces the social and cultural function of film archives.

The internet archive: an example of archives online

A quite different example is represented by The Internet Archive (http://www.archive.org), a non-profit organization founded in 1996 in San Francisco with the purpose of offering access to historical collections in digital format. The Internet Archive collaborates with institutions such as the Library of Congress and the Smithsonian and, today, its collection includes texts, audio, moving images, software and web pages. Although its main goal is to prevent *digitally born* material from disappearing, this on-line archive offers free access to a great quantity of *digitized* (film born) material as well.

With more than thirty thousand moving image items, The Internet Archive offers access to a wide collection of archival films, including many silent ones. Found footage, news reels, shorts as well as feature films, can be streamed or downloaded in various formats (e.g. mpeg1, 2, and 4, Cinepack and RealMedia). All kinds of material from new to early films can be found there – examples streching from Méliès' *Le voyage dans la lune* (1902) to Romero's *Night of the Living Dead* (1968). All content is offered under Creative Commons' licenses, and, depending on the status of the material they can be public domain or other licenses accepted by the rights holders. In the case of film-born content the image quality and the available information regarding the source material that has been used may vary greatly. When the Library of Congress makes a film available, for instance, it is possible to find out if the original material has been properly preserved and other sorts of information about the original film print are made available.[13] In many other cases, however, we do not have insight in the source of the content, and therefore we do not know where the original film is available and taken care of, or if it is available at all, for that matter.

The Internet Archive clearly shows us an example of content availability very different from what we have called archival distribution. In comparison, the archive is (relatively) open and the user is (relatively) free. On the other hand, in the case of digitized films, it often lacks a clear and crucial link to the original film.

Beyond distribution

New forms of distribution can thus be envisioned today. With the speed possible with digital technology and the virtually ubiquitous reach of the Internet, we can imagine a truly new new life for archival films. In fact, this open-source ideal is remarkably in the same vein as the ideal of film as "living" medium, when digitization breaks open the "code" of films for manipulation and performative editing.[14]

When we ask ourselves what the effect is of the digital turn in archives with respect to distribution, digital practices and possibilities challenge ideas and ideals about matters of accessibility, thus, about distribution in the larger sense of the word. Archives can become more flexible: from centralized, geographical house of storage, the archive can be the platform for a flexible delivery of content.

Both models described above are necessary and desirable for the future visibility of archival films. But it should not be a matter of choice between the two. In fact, they are two faces of the same coin. On the one hand, the chaperone model for archival distribution guarantees a secure and proper preservation of the films, without which on-line accessibility would not even be possible. On top of that, it provides today, still, the *raison d'être* of film archives, specifically to their (specialised) public and their funding entities. It is, however, the online archive that allows for a visibility to a larger, contemporary audience: today's users, who demand direct access to content. Both "distribution" models, if the term distribution still applies, thus feed one another when open, on-line access can create new, varied, and specialised audiences, as well as new practices based on the creative re-use of, or inspiration by archival material. In our view, at this moment it is the combination of these two models that will grant a true new life to archival films in the future.

Notes

1. For a comprehensive overview of the history of film archives see P. Houston, *The Keepers of the Frame. The Film Archives*, British Film Institute, London, 1994 and J. Ghislaine, *Film Archives in Europe* in Luisa Comencini and Matteo Pavesi (eds) *Restauro, conservazione e distruzione dei film/Restoration, Preservation and Destruction of Films* (Il Castoro, Milano, 2001).

2. The age by which artifacts pass on to the public domain is defined differently by each country of production. In the US, for example, it is films produced before 1923.

3. Examples of these touring programs are: *Dutch Silent Cinema* distributed by the Filmmuseum, *Biograph* distributed jointly by British Film Institute and the Filmmuseum, *American Beauties* by Library of Congress and *Unseen Cinema* by Anthology Film Archive.

4. Examples of archival DVDs are *Exotic Europe* and *Cinéma Perdu* (Filmmuseum), *Treasures From American Film Archives* (National Film Preservation Foundation), *Unseen Cinema – Early American Avant Garde Film 1894–1941* (Anthology Film Archive).

5. http://www.wired.com/wired/archive/12.10/tail.html See also: http://www.thelongtail.com

6. http://creativecommons.org

7. The project *Beelden voor de Toekomst* (Images for the Future), is the result of a collaboration between the following Dutch institutions: the Nederlands Filmmuseum, the Institute for Sound and Vision (NIBG), the Centrale Discotheek Rotterdam, the National Archive, the Association of Public Libraries and the foundation Kennisland. The text of the project can be found on http://www.kennisland.nl/nl/projecten/open-cultuur/Beelden-voor-de-Toekomst.html

8. While Henri Langlois, the legendary co-founder and first director of the Cinémathèque Française, is traditionally associated with a policy of 'showing' as many films as possible from the archive (whatever their physical condition was), Ernest Lindgren, first curator of the National Film and Television Archive, is remembered as the man who put film preservation before everything else, including exhibition. For more on this, see Houston's *Keepers of the Frame* (1994). A friction between showing and preservation seems to be an unavoidable aspect of archival practice and the new possibilities offered by digital technology are adding new challenging perspectives to this complex matter. See also D. Nissen, L. Richter Larsen, T.C. Christensen, and J. Stub Kohnsen (eds), *Preserve Then Show* (Danish Film Institute, Copenhagen, 2002).

9. For more on this matter see G. Fossati, "Digital Technology Entering Film Archives" in Mieke Lauwers and Bert Hogenkamp (eds.) *Audiovisueel. SAP jaarboek* no. 5, Stichting Archiefpublicaties, Koninklijke Vereniging van Archivarissen in Nederland (KVAN), 2006.

10. We refer here to the quality of the digital master that is used as the source for all digital by-products, from HD TV broadcast, to DVD to possibly on-line streaming.

11. For more information on the finding and restoration of *Beyond the Rocks* see: www.film-museum.nl/beyondtherocks

12. The digital distribution was carried out by CinemaNet Europe, a network of European art houses supported by the Media Plus Programme of the European Community. See: http://www.cine-maneteurope.com

13. We can for example read that the film *Buffalo Dance* (1894) was copied at 18 frames per second from a 35mm print preserved by the Library of Congress.

14. This it is not the same as found-footage films that are re-authored. We are talking here about user creativity.

The Authors

Richard Abel is Robert Altman Collegiate Professor of Film Studies and Interim Chair of the Department of Screen Arts & Cultures at the University of Michigan. His most recent books are *The Red Rooster Scare: Making Cinema American, 1900–1910* (California 1999) and *Americanizing the Movies and "Movie-Mad" Audiences, 1910–1914* (California 2006). He also has co-edited, with Rick Altman, *The Sounds of Early Cinema* (Indiana 2001) and served as general editor for the *Encyclopedia of Early Cinema* (Routledge 2005). [Chapter 10]

Luis Alonso García studied Communication Sciences at the Complutense University of Madrid, where he received his Ph.D. with a thesis on audiovisual enunciation in work of Andrei Tarkovski. He has worked as lecturer at several Spanish universities since 1992, and currently teaches at the University Rey Juan Carlos de Madrid. His research focusses on epistemology and historical methodology, semiotechnology of expressive forms and practices, and the construction of "cinema" in different discourses and practices. Among his publications, one can highlight *Once Miradas sobre la Crisis y el Cine Español* [*Onze regards sur la crise et le cinéma espagnol*] (Madrid, Aehc y Librería 8½, 2003), an analysis of the historiography of cinema in *El Extraño Caso de la Historia Universal del Cine* [*The Strange Case of the Universal History of Cinema*] (Valencia, Episteme, 2000), and an essay on the theory of cinematography : *La Oscura Naturaleza del Cinematógrafo* [*The obscure nature of cinematography*] (Valencia, la Mirada, 1996). [Chapter 8]

Jonathan Auerbach is a professor of English at the University of Maryland, College Park, who has recently completed a book entitled *Body Shots: Early Cinema's Incarnations* (University of California Press, 2007). He has also authored numerous publications on American literature and culture, including *The Romance of Failure* (1989) and *Male Call: Becoming Jack London* (1996). [Chapter 22]

Ansje van Beusekom teaches film history at Utrecht University. Her major publication is *Kunst en Amusement. Reacties op de komst van de film in Nederland, 1895–1940* (Haarlem: Arcadia 2001). Furthermore, she contributes publications on film and art history in encyclopaedia, magazines and conference proceedings. [Chapter 31]

Janelle Blankenship is Assistant Professor/Faculty Fellow in the Department of German, New York University. She received her Ph.D. in German Studies from Duke University. Her publications include an edited journal volume, *Media and Spatiality in Deleuze and Guattari*, and several articles on film theory and literary modernism. She is now completing a book on the early German film pioneers Max and Emil Skladanowsky. [Chapter 25]

Ivo Blom is lecturer in Film Studies at the Department of Comparative Arts Studies of the Vrije Universiteit, Amsterdam. Since the early 1990s, he has extensively written on early cinema, including early film distribution. In 2000, he defended his PhD. at the Universiteit van Amsterdam, which was published in 2003 as *Jean Desmet and the Early Dutch Film Trade*. [Chapter 16]

Marta Braun is professor and research chair at Ryerson University, Toronto. She is the author of *Picturing Time: The Work of Etienne Jules Marey 1830–1904* (University of Chicago Press). [Chapter 24]

Rudmer Canjels received his PhD from Utrecht University, the Netherlands, for his work *Beyond the Cliffhanger: Distributing Silent Serials. Local practices, Changing Forms, Cultural Transformation* (2005). He has published several articles on silent serials. Currently he is researching the sponsored documentaries of Royal Dutch Shell. [Chapter 20]

Renaud Chaplain is finishing a Ph.D. thesis, supervised by Sylvie Schweitzer, on the distribution of cinema in Lyon and its suburbs between 1895 and 1945. A part of this work was published in 2003 in the French review *XXème siècle*, no. 79. [Chapter 5]

Pierre Chemartin is currently enrolled as a PhD (co-thesis) student in Comparative Literature and Film Studies at Université de Montréal, and in Communication at Université Catholique de Louvain. He works at the Université de Montréal as a lecturer and as a research assistant for the GRAFICS (Groupe de recherche sur l'avènement et la formation des institutions cinématographiques et scéniques). His primary research interests include the rhetoric of media, intermediality and spectatorship. He mostly focuses upon theatre, cinema and comics at the turn of the 20th century. He has recently written academic studies about distribution, film editing, and gender stereotypes in early motion pictures. [Chapter 21]

Ian Christie is Professor of Film and Media History at Birkbeck College, University of London, and is involved in establishing the London Screen Archive as part of a continuing research project on early cinema in London. In addition to numerous publications on Russian and British cinema, he wrote and co-produced *The Last Machine*, a 1994 series on early cinema for BBC television; and is now working on a book and DVD about Robert Paul. He is a co-editor of the journal *Film Studies* and was Slade Professor of Fine Art at Cambridge University in 2005–06. [Chapter 23]

Nicolas Dulac is currently preparing a PhD dissertation about seriality in mass media, at both Université de Paris III and Université de Montréal. He taught classes in film history at the Département d'histoire de l'art et d'études cinématographiques at Université de Montréal and is a member of GRAFICS (Groupe de recherche sur l'avènement et la formation des institutions cinématographique et scénique). He has published in journals such as *1895*, *CiNéMAS* and *Invisible Culture*. [Chapter 19]

Tony Fletcher is a founder member of The Cinema Museum in London. His main area of research is the cinema history of London, prior to World War I. He has published on this theme in *Living Pictures: The Journal of the Popular and Projected Image before 1914*. Over the last six years he has contributed to the Nottingham British Silent Weekend Festival and has published articles based on his presentations. *Griffithiana* published an interview he did with the actress Joan Morgan. He is also presently researching the films of the Edwardian Period as well as the transition to Sound in Britain 1924–29 with particular emphasis on 'The Phonofilm'. [Chapter 26]

Giovanna Fossati is curator at the Nederlands Filmmuseum in Amsterdam. Fossati is also a member of the teaching staff of the MA Preservation & Presentation at the Universiteit van Amsterdam since its creation in 2003. Her recent publications include 'Digital technology entering film archives', in Mieke Lauwers and Bert Hogenkamp (eds.) *SAP jaarboek* no. 5, KVAN, 2006; *The Restoration of Beyond the Rocks*, in *Beyond the Rocks* (USA, 1922), DVD release, Milestone Film & Video, 2006. Fossati is currently working on a PhD dissertation at Utrecht University with the title: *From Grain to Pixel: Theorising Film Archival Practice in a Time of Transition from Analogue to Digital Technology*. [Chapter 37]

Wolfgang Fuhrmann is a film historian. He received his Ph.D. at Utrecht University with a study on German colonial cinematography. He teaches film studies at the University of Kassel, Mainz and Munich and is currently head of the film historical research project: Film and Ethnography in Germany 1900–1930. [Chapter 27]

Joseph Garncarz, Privatdozent in Theatre, Film and Television Studies at the University of Cologne and Research Associate at the University of Siegen in Germany, has published numerous articles on German film history in European and American journals and edited collections. He is the author of *Filmfassungen* and a forthcoming book on the emergence of cinema in Germany. [Chapter 28]

André Gaudreault is professor in the Département d'histoire de l'art et d'études cinéma-tographiques at Université de Montréal, where he is responsible for GRAFICS (Groupe de recherche sur l'avènement et la formation des institutions cinématographique et scénique). A visiting professor at several universities (São Paulo, Paris III – Sorbonne Nouvelle, Bologne, Paris I – Panthéon-Sorbonne, Buenos Aires et École Normale Supérieure – Paris), he has published on film narration and early cinema. Titles include *Du littéraire au filmique. Système du récit* (édition revue et augmentée, 1999), *Le Récit cinématographique* (1991 – avec F. Jost), *Pathé 1900. Fragments d'une filmographie analytique du cinéma des premiers temps* (1993), *Au pays* *des ennemis du cinéma* (1996 – avec G. Lacasse et J.-P. Sirois-Trahan) et *Cinema delle origini. O della « cinematografia-attrazione »* (2004). He is also editor of *CiNéMAS*. [Chapter 21]

André Habib is completing a Ph.D. in Comparative literature (cinema option) at Université de Montréal on the "the imaginary of ruins in cinema". He also teaches film at the Département d'histoire de l'art et d'études cinématographiques at Université de Montréal. He finished his Master's thesis in Film studies in 2001 at Concordia University, on Godard's *Histoire(s) du cinema*. He is a film critic and co-editor for the journal *Hors champ*, and also editorial coordinator for the journal *Intermédialités*. His articles have been published in *Substance, Senses of Cinema, Intermédialités, Offscreen, Discours social, CiNéMAS*. He is co-editing with Viva Paci a collective entitled *L'imprimerie du regard. Chris Marker et la technique*, which will be published in the collection "Esthétiques" at L'Harmattan in 2007. [Chapter 35]

Michael Hammond is a Senior Lecturer in Film and English at the University of Southampton. He is the author of *The Big Show: British Cinema Culture and The Great War* (Exeter University Press, 2006). He is also co-editor of two books, Contemporary US Cinema (Open University/McGraw-Hill, 2006) with Linda Ruth Williams, and *The Contemporary Television Series*, (Edinburgh University Press, 2005) with Lucy Mazdon. His current research is concerned with the impact of the Great War on the aesthetic practices of the Hollywood studios between 1919–1939. [Chapter 12]

Gunnar Iversen is Professor of Film Studies at the Department of Art and Media Studies at the Norwegian University of Science and Technology, Trondheim, Norway, where he teaches european and asian film history. He has co-authored and co-edited several books. Publications in English include essays in Film History and Scandinavica, in several anthologies, and the book "Nordic National Cinemas" (Routledge, 1998). [Chapter 15]

Pierre-Emmanuel Jaques is currently involved in the research project "Views and Perspectives: Studies on the History of Non-Fiction Film in Switzerland" (under the supervision of Prof. Margrit Tröhler and funded by the Swiss National Science Foundation) in the Film Studies Department at Universität Zürich. He is completing his PhD on the birth of film criticism in Geneva during the 1920s under the direction of F. Albera at Université de Lausanne. He has published *Le spectacle cinématographique en Suisse 1895–1945* (2003, with Gianni Haver) and articles on the history of cinema in Switzerland (for instance in: R. Pithon (ed.), *Cinéma suisse muet. Lumières et ombres*, 2002 and in: M. Tortajada, F. Albera (eds.), *Cinéma suisse: nouvelles approches*, 2000). [Chapter 6]

Rixt Jonkman is currently finishing the MA study "Preservation and Presentation of the Moving Image" at the Universiteit van Amsterdam. During this study she focusses on the one hand on (early) cinema and film history, and on the other hand on the preservation of the films. This interest also became apparent from the database project she presented at the DOMITOR conference in 2004. She made this database during her internship at the Filmmuseum Amsterdam on behalf of her bachelor study "Word and Image Studies" at the Vrije Universiteit, Amsterdam. Hereafter she wrote a bachelor thesis on the programming of films distributed by Jean Desmet, for which she made use of this database. [Chapter 34]

François Jost is Full Professor at the Sorbonne Nouvelle-Paris III University, where he is Director of the Centre d'Études sur l'image et le Son Médiatiques (CEISME), and teaches television analysis, narratology and semiology. He was also a visiting professor at numerous universities in Europe and in North and South America. He has authored numerous books and articles on cinema and television, including *L'Œil-caméra* (1987), *Le récit cinématographique* (with A. Gaudreault, 1990), *Un monde à notre image* (1993), *La Télévision du quotidien* (2001), *L'Empire du loft* (2002), *Realta/Finzione* (2003), *Comprendre la télévision* (2005). *Le Temps d'un regard* (1998) is especially focussed on Early Cinema. He has directed several films and published a novel (*Les Thermes de Stabies*, 1990). He belongs to the Domitor Board. [Conclusion]

Charlie Keil is Director of the Cinema Studies Program and Associate Professor in the Department of History at the University of Toronto. He is the author of *Early American Cinema in Transition: Story, Style and Filmmaking, 1907–1913*, and co-editor, with Shelley Stamp, of *American Cinema's Transitional Era: Audiences, Institutions, Practices*. [Chapter 24]

Frank Kessler is professor for media history at Utrecht University and currently the president of Domitor. Together with Sabine Lenk and Martin Loiperdinger he founded and edited *KINtop. Jahrbuch zur Erforschung des frühen Films*. As a guest editor he published an issue of the *Historical Journal of Film, Radio and Television*, "Visible Evidence, But of What? Reassessing Early Non-Fiction Cinema"(2002). [Introduction]

David Levy was born in Montréal, Canada, and educated at McGill University and Université de Montréal. His ground-breaking early cinema dissertation is entitled "Edwin S.Porter and the Origins of the American Narrative Film: 1894–1907". In addition to his work in film history, David has worked as a journalist, done media research and taught for a number of years in the film program at McGill. He has recently completed a book-length essay entitled, "The Ninety-Seven Pound Cold War" and is currently at work on a book about early cinema history, "Of Clocks, Dogs and Women". [Chapter 2]

Martin Loiperdinger, dr. phil., film historian and political scientist, is Professor of Media Studies at Trier University (Germany) since 1998. He was deputy director of the Deutsches Filminstitut – DIF, Frankfurt /M, from 1993 – 1997, and co-producer of documentaries on film history. Books on NS films (e.g. Leni Riefenstahl's Triumph of the Will, 1987) and on early cinema (Film & Schokolade, 1999, on Stollwerck's moving picture business). Co-editor of KINtop, the yearbook on early cinema history. Editor (with Uli Jung, 2005) of *Geschichte des dokumentarischen Films in Deutschland, Vol. 1: Kaiserreich 1895 – 1918*. [Chapter 14]

Anke Mebold is a film archivist at the Deutsches Filminstitut – DIF in Frankfurt, Germany. Her major projects include the restoration of the German feature film *Hamlet* (1920) with Asta Nielsen and a comprehensive DVD edition of silhouette animation films by Lotte Reiniger. She received her Bachelor degrees in Media Arts and Creative Writing from the University of Arizona, and a certificate in Film Preservation from the L. Jeffrey Selznick School at George Eastman House in Rochester, NY. This article is part of an ongoing investigation into the history and spread of the 28mm film gauge. On the subject she has previously co-authored "Resurrecting the Lost History of 28mm in North America", published in Film History 15.2 (2003).[Chapter 29]

Charles O'Brien teaches film studies at Carleton University in Ottawa, Canada. He is the author of *Cinema's Conversion to Sound* (Indiana U. Press, 2005), and has recently been appointed Ailsa Mellon Bruce Senior Fellow at the Center for Advanced Study in the Visual Arts in Washington DC. [Chapter 4]

Viva Paci is a PhD candidate at Université de Montréal, where she also teaches Film Studies and Contemporary Italian Literature. Her dissertation topic is "De l'attraction au cinema". She is a member of GRAFICS (Groupe de recherche sur l'avènement et la formation des institutions cinématographiques et scéniques) and CRI (Centre de recherche sur l'inter-médialité). Her recent research, at the Fondation Daniel Langlois pour l'art la science et la technologie, has dealt with comparing computer animation and the beginnings of cinema. She has published in journals such as *Cinéma & Cie*, *CiNéMAS*, *Comunicazioni sociali*, *Sociétés et Représentations*, *Médiamorphoses*, *Cahiers du GERSE* et *Intermédialités Web*. She is the author of *Il Cinema di Chris Marker* (2005) and co-editor with André Habib of *L'Imprimerie du regard. Chris Marker et la technique* (2007). [Chapter 33]

Martina Roepke is lecturer in film- and mediastudies at Utrecht University, The Netherlands. She is author of 'Privat-Vorstellung. Heimkino in Deutschland vor 1945' (2006). She is currently preparing a project on 'new' and 'old' media literacies. [Chapter 30]

Pelle Snickars, Head of Research at the Swedish National Archive of Recorded Sound and Moving Images. Snickars received his PhD at the department of Cinema Studies, Stockholm University in 2001 on a dissertation entitled, Swedish Film and Visual Mass Culture 1900. Snickars has published in various international journals on film and media historical issues. Research interest includes the history of media archives, mediated history and re-usage of audiovisual media in mediations of the past. Snickars recently co-edited the book, *1897. Mediahistories around the Stockholm exhibition.* [Chapter 13]

Begoña Soto is Professor at the Department of Communication Studies at University Rey Juan Carlos of Madrid where she teaches Film History, Film Theory and Spanish Cinema. She directed for seven years the Andalucian Film Archive and has written on Early Cinema in Spain and Portugal. [Chapter 1]

Paul C. Spehr is the retired former Assistant Chief of the Motion Picture, Broadcasting and Recorded Sound Division, Library of Congress, Washington, DC. He is an archival consultant and film historian who has written a number of articles on the beginning years of cinema. He is currently completing a book on the life and work of William Kennedy Laurie Dickson. [Chapter 17]

Wanda Strauven is Associate Professor in the Department of Media Studies at the Universiteit van Amsterdam, where she directs the Film Studies program. At the Amsterdam School for Cultural Analysis (ASCA), she co-directs, with Thomas Elsaesser, the research project "Imagined Futures". She is the author of *Marinetti e il cinema: tra attrazione e sperimentazione* (Udine: Campanotto, 2006). She has edited two anthologies: *Homo orthopedicus: le corps et ses prothèses à l'époque (post)moderniste* (with Nathalie Roelens) (Paris: L'Harmattan, 2001) and *The Cinema of Attractions Reloaded* (Amsterdam: Amsterdam University Press, 2006). [Chapter 32]

Nanna Verhoeff is assistant professor at the Department of Media and Culture Studies, Utrecht University. Her book on early American and European Westerns, *The West in Early Cinema: After the Beginning* was published by Amsterdam University Press in 2006. Her current research project about virtual travel and screen media is a historical comparison of emerging screen technologies and practices from both ends of the twentieth century, ranging from early cinema to digital games. [Afterthoughts]

Pierre Véronneau, a Ph.D. in history, is curator of Quebec and Canadian cinema at the Cinémathèque québécoise in Montréal. He is also professor of cinema at Concordia University and Université de Montréal. He has published on Canadian cinema, titles including *David Cronenberg: la beauté du chaos* (Cerf-Corlet, 2003), *Répertoire des séries, feuilletons et téléromans québécois de 1952 à 1992* (1993), *Résistance et affirmation : la production francophone à l'ONF – 1939–1964* (1987). He has curated several (real and virtual) exhibitions, such as *L'Aventure cinéma (v.o. québécoise)* (2006) and *De Nanouk à l'Oumigmag : le cinéma documentaire au Canada* (2001). His research focuses on early cinema of Québec. He is treasurer of Domitor. [Chapter 7]

Gregory A. Waller is chair of the Department of Communication and Culture at Indiana University (Bloomington, Indiana USA). He is the author of several studies of moviegoing and film exhibition in the United States, including Main Street Amusements: Film and Commercial Entertainment in a Southern City, 1896–1930. He is currently completing two projects: Movies on the Road, a history of itinerant film exhibition, particularly in the 1930s, and Japan-in-America, a study of the representation of Japan in American culture, 1890–1915. [Chapter 11]

Richard Ward earned his Ph.D. in Radio-Television-Film at the University of Texas at Austin. He is an Associate Professor in the Communication Department at the University of South Alabama. The author of several journal articles on American film and radio history, his book "A History of the Hal Roach Studios" was published by Southern Illinois University Press in 2005. [Chapter 18]

John P. Welle is Professor of Romance Languages and Literatures and Concurrent Professor of Film, Television and Theatre at the University of Notre Dame. He has recently published "The Last Days of Italian Silent Film: George Kleine's Correspondence with Henrietta Delforno and the Crisis of the 1920s", *Incontri con il cinema italiano* (Ed. Antonio Vitti. Caltanissetta: Sciascia Editore, 2003), pp. 45–68. [Chapter 3]

Rashit M. Yangirov Ph.D. is a historian specializing in various fields of the Russian artistic culture of the XXth century (film history, émigré literature et al.) and a leading researcher of the 'Russia Abroad' Historical and Scientific Foundation. He lives in Moscow (Russia). [Chapter 9]

Printed and bound by CPI Group (UK) Ltd, Croydon, CR0 4YY

13/04/2025

14656546-0002